**Profit planning
for real estate development**
The complete guide for builders,
lenders, and other investors

Profit planning for real estate development

The complete guide for builders, lenders, and other investors

Michael C. Halpin
Michael C. Halpin Consultants, Inc.
Santa Clara, California

Dow Jones-Irwin   Homewood, Illinois 60430

© Michael C. Halpin, 1977

All rights reserved. No part of this publication may be reproduced, stored in a retrieval system, or transmitted, in any form or by any means, electronic, mechanical, photocopying, recording, or otherwise, without the prior written permission of the copyright holder.

This publication is designed to provide accurate and authoritative information in regard to the subject matter covered. It is sold with the understanding that the publisher is not engaged in rendering legal, accounting, or other professional service. If legal advice or other expert assistance is required, the services of a competent professional person should be sought.

From a Declaration of Principles jointly adopted by a Committee of the American Bar Association and a Committee of Publishers.

First Printing, April 1977

ISBN 0-87094-132-1
Library of Congress Catalog Card No. 76-29387
Printed in the United States of America

To Bernadette, Denise, and Michele

Preface

This book is about how to increase profit margins in real estate development projects. In addition to helping builders and contractors make better use of their resources, it contains information of critical importance to those who finance new housing construction. It is essential to understand the builder and his business in order to develop high quality, low risk mortgage financing. This book is written with an emphasis on how a builder-developer should operate. It is intended as a procedural guide. It should be the primary guide when evaluating the feasibility of a proposed project.

The strategy required to increase profit margins is different than that required to merely increase gross profits. Gross profits can be increased by expanding volume, through increased sales, through acquisition, or through creative bookkeeping. Increasing profit margins requires a rethinking of the entire market planning and business process. It requires not just a tightening up of operations, a temporary speedup stimulus, or overhead reduction, but a better overall system of business planning and operation. Increasing profit margins requires an emphasis on the fundamentals and on common sense nuts-and-bolts business practices, as opposed to riding the crest of current fads and excesses which for the moment are "glamorous." This book addresses itself to a nuts-and-bolts common sense approach to enhancing real estate profit margins in a dynamic environment.

This book emphasizes the interdependence among all the parties involved in a real estate project: creditors, contractors, suppliers, craftsmen, and supervisors. It also stresses that there are opportunities to increase profits in planning and marketing activities as well as in the construction phase. Because real estate development is a business of people working together, there is much in here about how people can work together more effectively.

I have provided case studies to show how profit planning techniques, concepts, and strategies have been successfully implemented in actual situations. Detailed guides are included in the form of check lists, work sheets, standard forms, documents, and procedures.

I wish to express my gratitude to the National Association of Home Builders for their cooperation in permitting reproduction of source material. Acknowledgment is also due to GRALLA Publications, New York, New York, for permission to reproduce material and illustrations.

March 1977   MICHAEL C. HALPIN

Contents

List of illustrations .... **xxi**

List of exhibits .... **xxiii**

Introduction **1**

Chapter 1
Market planning for optimum results **5**

Management's need for a plan, 6
   The cyclical nature of business, 6
Creating new consumer satisfactions, 7
   Market planning as a companywide function, 8
Implementing the market-planning process, 8
Market planning recap, 9

Chapter 2
Establishing objectives and constraints **11**

Financial objectives, 12
   Yield, 12
   Risk, 13
Nonfinancial objectives, 13
Two basic strategies, 13
The developer's resources, capabilities, and constraints, 14
The key to success: A good fit between opportunity and capability, 15

Feasibility as related to developer objectives, 16
   More than "the numbers," 17
Operating ratios as yardsticks for preliminary feasibility requirements, 17

Chapter 3
Locational analysis and site evaluation **21**

When and where to purchase, 21
The land-value trend line, 22
Developing the criteria for purchase, 23
   Land purchase don'ts, 23
Finding the land, 24
Guidelines for selecting land, 24
   Regional analysis, 25
   Community analysis, 25
   Site identification, 26
Zoning and other regulatory influences, 27
Physical and environmental factors, 28
Opportunities and obstacles, 28
Case study I: Measuring degree of compatability between site, development concept and market opportunity, 29
Case study II: Overcoming obstacles and constraints by good planning, 30
Early recognition of opportunities and obstacles, 33

Chapter 4
Determining land value, optimum terms, and profitability ... 39

Land valuation: What price is justified? 39
  Time, 40
  Site evaluation, 40
  Location analysis, 40
  Off-site improvements, 40
  Zoning, legal, 41
Ranking the comparables, 41
Sensitivity analysis, 41
Leverage, 42
The profitability factors, 42
Negotiating optimum terms, 43
Negotiating strategies, 44
Computing profitability, 45
Enhancing the counteroffer, 46
Computing downside risk, 46

Chapter 5
Legal, political, and environmental constraints ... 53

Conflicting legislation, 53
Proliferation of planning agencies, 54
Federal guidelines and legislation, 54
  National Environmental Policy Act (1969), 55
  Clean Air Act (1970), 55
  Federal Water Pollution Control Act (1972), 55
  Flood Disaster Protection Act (1973), 55
  Coastal Zone Management Act (1972), 56
  Noise Pollution and Control Act (1972), 57
Land-use policies, 57
  Stepping stones to a national land-use policy, 57
  State land-use policies, 57
  Local and municipal land-use policies, 58
Energy legislation, 59
Keeping abreast of legislation, 60
Need for a public-private partnership, 60

Chapter 6
Competitive evaluation: How to obsolete the competition ... 63

Competitors' weaknesses: The key to opportunity, 63
  Maintaining a perspective to spot opportunities and limitations, 64
Guidelines for researching the competition, 64
Case study I: Researching the competition, 66
Researching as a means to leading the competition, 67
  How to research the leading developers, 68
  Innovation as a result of researching, 69
  Creating a monopoly on products or methods, 69
  Reevaluation of the developer's objectives, 70
  Formation of a preliminary concept, 70
Value relationship analysis: Setting the sales price range, 71
Procedure for value relationship analysis, 72

Chapter 7
Innovation: The key to profits ... 85

Success: The downfall of many a company, 85
Confusing luck with skill, 86
The element of risk in innovation, 86
Effects of company size, 87
  The advantages of being small, 87
  Opportunities for innovation in a segmented industry, 88
  The vulnerability of big, well-organized companies, 88
Innovation methods, 89
Social clues for innovations, 90
Opportunities for innovation, 91

Chapter 8
Market segmentation ... 95

How generalized data can be misleading, 95

Why it is important to understand market segmentation, 96
Identification of market segments, 97
    Where do they come from? 98
    Why do they buy? 98
    What do they buy? 98
    What are their buying capabilities? 99
Fitting market segments and product types to organizational objectives, 99

Chapter 9
Market cycles: Seeing beyond the horizon 101

Shaping the future, 102
National influences on local market conditions, 103
Why it is important to understand cycles, 103
    Guarding against static assumptions, 104
    The view beyond the horizon, 104
The new concept/market overkill cycle, 105
    Low-end condominiums, 105
    Swinger apartments, 106
    The fourplex boom, 106
The hot market/overkill cycle, 107
The business expansion/recession cycle, 108
The discardable commodity, energy waste/conservation cycle, 110
The urban sprawl/retreat cycle, 110
The mortgage money boom/bust cycle, 111
Legislative-induced cycles, 112
The institutional romance/fall-out cycle, 113
How to utilize an understanding of cycles, 113

Chapter 10
Base data and demographics: Knowing the market 117

Technical and economic needs, 117
Information sources, 119

Questions to be answered, 120
    Employment trends, 120
    Income trends, 121
    Population trends, 121
    Housing inventory, 122
    Housing occupancy, 122
    Retail activity, 123
    Industrial activity, 123
    Community facilities, 123
    Transportation, 124
    Developmental trends, 124

Chapter 11
Absorption forecasting: More than statistics 125

Absorption stratification by income distribution and market segmentation, 126
Absorption and competitive position, 126
Absorption and innovations, 127
    Absorption forecasting for innovations, 127
Preconstruction sales, 128
Effects of population characteristics on absorption, 129
Effects of income characteristics on absorption, 130
Effects of supply on absorption, 130
    Accumulated demand versus ongoing demand, 132
Effects of location on absorption, 133
Effects of value on absorption, 133
Current sales and rental rates as a measure of future absorption, 133
Sources of buyers and renters, 134
    Demand due to households moving within the market area, 134
    Demand due to population increase, 135
    Demand due to household formations, 135

Chapter 12
Utilizing market research to optimum advantage 137

Limitations of market research, 137

Management's need for market research, 139
  Decision making or rationalization, 139
  Management's fear of change, 139
  Case study I: The need for objective analysis, 140

Chapter 13
Value engineering: A management approach for increasing the profit middle ground between cost and value 143

Value engineering: What is it? 143
  More than a cost-saving device, 144
  A method of overseeing the interactions of specialists, 144
  A method of increasing productivity, 145
  A method of allocating capital dollars, 145
  A means of establishing a system of priorities, 145
  A means of minimizing waste, 146
  A means of creating investment leverage, 146
  A tool in investment planning and analysis, 147
How value engineering shapes planning decisions, 149
  Planning for cost reduction, 150
  Planning for merchandising, 153
  Planning for living, 153
  Planning individual buildings for profit: Back to back design, 153
How value engineering redirects expenses, 156
  Other tips for cost-conscious construction, 157
Case study I: Deviations from the profit concept, 158
Case study II: An eleventh-hour profit analysis, 160
Case study III: Identifying design and marketing risk factors, 163

Redesign of a two-bedroom unit, 164
Building structure and systems, 168
Case study IV: Value engineering with standard house plans, 173
Merchandising improvements, 173
$3,625 Cost-saving benefit from value engineering redesign, 174
The importance of a comprehensive overview, 175
  Offsetting value washes can erode profit, 175
  The need for proper assessment of primary investment considerations, 176
  Emphasis on the fundamentals, 177
Case study V: How primary investment values guide technical decisions, 177
Case study VI: Washing out self-advertising value of site, 178
Case study VII: Washing out value through poor planning, 179
Looking to the total profit picture, 180
  Reflecting value engineering in bidding and contract-letting processes, 180

Chapter 14
Product research: Taking the experimentations out of innovation 183

Structuring the activity, 183
  What to research, 184
  How to research, 184
Benefits of research, 185
Consumer research, 186
  Limitations, 186
  Benefits, 186
Technical research, 187
  Need for, 187
  Sources, 187
  Application, 188

Chapter 15
Establishing the development concept: Optimizing opportunities ... 189

Case study I: Internal economic needs versus market needs, 189
    Identifiable submarkets versus statistical generalizations, 190
    Achieving density without sacrificing marketability, 191
    Planning designed to meet the needs of specific submarkets, 192
Case study II: Meshing internal economic demands and market needs through sensitivity and innovation, 192
    Need for environmentally oriented housing to serve a discriminating market, 193
    How to meet the needs of the discriminating market and retain economic feasibility, 194
Case study III: Product and marketing innovation to achieve feasibility, 194
Common mistakes in matching concepts of market opportunities, 199

Chapter 16
Designing the product to optimize market potential ... 201

Case study I: Maximizing natural amenities and site potentials, 201
Case study II: The right product for the right market, 204
    Review of first phase, 204
    Marketing and feasibility studies, 206
    Strategy, 206
    End result, 210
Control of product development through formalized reviews, 210
    The need for both marketing and value engineering expertise, 211
Cost control, 211
    Caution: Lender oversteering, 212

Chapter 17
Amenities: Asset or liability? ... 215

Providing amenities the consumer is willing and able to pay for, 215
The importance of landscaping, 217
Increasing the amenity package through reductions elsewhere, 217
Income, absorption, and retention: Three keys to amenities economics, 219
Amenities must be functional as well as attractive, 220
Adding amenities as a way of reducing equity requirements, 220
Adding amenities profitably without increasing rents, 221
Amenities planning to encourage amenity/resident interaction, 221
Understanding the cost/benefit ratios of amenities, 222
Most common mistakes in planning amenities, 223

Chapter 18
Establishing feasibility ... 225

The feasibility process, 225
    The need for systematic simplification, 225
Identifying structuring the problem and objectives, 226
    A word of caution about standardized formats, 226
Components of feasibility, 226
The feasibility outline, 228

Chapter 19
Financial analysis: How to analyze and optimize return ... 233

Value classifications, 233
    Value of nonincome residential properties, 233

Value of income residential
  properties, 233
Price versus value, 234
Stabilized value, 234
Tangible and intangible
  benefits, 234
Analysis of the whole picture, 235
Present-value theory, 235
  Two methods for computing
    the time value of money,
    236
  Present-value analysis, 236
  Internal rate-of-return analysis,
    237
  Limitations of present-value
    indexing, 238
Market value, 239
  Three approaches to market
    value, 239
  Replacement or production-cost
    approach, 239
  Market approach, 240
  Gross income multiplier, 241
  Economic approach, 242
  Correlation, 243
Investment value, 243
  Leverage: Trading on the
    equity, 244
  Equity return: Measure of
    investment value, 244
Methods for measuring return, 245
  Components of return, 245
  Cash on cash return, 245
  Total return before tax
    savings, 246
  After-tax return for a single
    year, 246
  Percentage yield, 246
  Capitalization, overall rate, 247
  Average annual return, 248
  Land-residual method, 248
Risk analysis, 249
Sensitivity analysis, 249
Band of investment: How to
  determine the overall
  interest rate, 250
Significant ratios, 251
  Break-even point, 251
  Debt coverage ration, 251
Payback period, 251
Cash flow analysis, 252
  Cash flow analysis: An
    economic panorama, 253
  Cash flow projection: An
    evolutionary process, 253

Chapter 20
The management information system: Providing better information on which to act 255

Essential characteristics of a
  management information
  system, 256
General accounting, 257
Cost accounting, 257
Budgeting, 258
Setting up the budget, 259
  Establishing the level of detail
    desired, 259
Fixed and flexible budgets, 260
Cash budgets, 261
Effects of business capacity and
  activity on budget, 261
Control, 262
  How control facilitates
    delegation of authority,
    262
Automated versus manual
  systems, 264
Case study I: An automated
  accounting system for the
  real estate development and
  construction industries, 265
  Design objectives, 265
  Benefits of the system, 265
  The remote job entry environ-
    ment, 266
  General ledger–financial
    reporting subsystem, 267
  Project cost subsystem, 272
  Cash disbursements–accounts
    payable subsystem, 275

Chapter 21
Budgets, projections, controls, and analysis 279

Budget policy and procedures,
  279
  Purpose, 279
  Policy, 279
  Procedure, 280
  Budget relationship to the chart
    of accounts, 281

Chart of accounts, 282
Chart of accounts, policy and procedure for budgeting and accounting, 282
Balance sheet accounts, 283
Income and Expense Statement accounts, 287
Summary, budget plan: For-sale housing, 292
    Control—Information Flow Diagram, 292
    Planning—Information Flow Diagram, 293
    Schedule 1: Sales Plan, 293
    Schedule 2: Summary, Cost-of-Sales Plan, 294
    Schedule 3: Gross Profit Plan, 294
    Gross Profit Plan analysis, 295
    Schedule 4: Gross Profit Plan per Unit, 295
    Schedule 5: Summary, Operating Expense Plan, 295
    Profit Plan, 296
    Schedule 6: Profit Plan, 296
    Schedule 7: Cash Flow Statement, 297
    Balance Sheet Statement, 297
    Schedule 8: Balance Sheet Statement, 298
The Cost-of-Sales Plan: For-sale housing, 299
    Schedule 2-A: Summary, Cost Plan, 300
    Schedule 2-B: Land Cost Plan for Tracts, 301
    Schedule 2-C: Land Development Cost Plan, 301
    Schedule 2-D: Finished Lot Cost Plan, 302
    Schedule 2-E: Direct Construction Cost Plan, 303
    Schedule 2-F: Indirect Construction Cost Plan, 306
Operating Expense Plan: For-sale housing, 307
    Schedule 5-A: Financing Expense Plan, 308
    Schedule 5-B: Marketing Expense Plan, 308
    Schedule 5-C: General and Administrative Expense Plan, 311
Management reports: For-sale housing, 311
    Management Reports Summary, 312
    Sample Report A: Profit Plan Analysis Report, 313
    Sample Report B: Operating Expense Analysis Report, 314
Budget Plan: Rental housing, 315
    Schedule 1: Summary, Budget Plan, 315
    Schedule 1-A: Land Cost Plan, 316
    Schedule 1-B: Land Development Cost Plan: Off-site Development, 317
    Schedule 1-C: Summary, Direct Construction Cost Plan, 318
    Schedule 1-D: Direct Construction Cost Plan, 318
    Detail Backup to Direct Construction Cost Plan, 323
    Schedule 1-E: Detail Backup to Direct Construction Cost Plan, 325
    Schedule 1-F: Indirect Construction Cost Plan, 328
    Schedule 1-G: Financing Expense Plan, 330
    Schedule 1-H: Marketing and Management Expenses, 331
    Schedule 1-I: Management Reports Summary, 334
    Sample Report A: Indirect Construction Cost Analysis Report, 335
    Sample Report B: Direct Construction Cost Analysis Report, 336
    Sample Report C: Income and Expense and Annual Cash Flow Analysis Report, 337
    Sample Report D: Off-site Cost Analysis Report, 338
Rental housing cash flow, 338
Statement of Annual Net Income, 339

Significant Ratio and Economic Tests, 339
Construction Cash Flow, 1975, 340
Fill-up Cash Flow, 1976, 341
Backup schedules for rental housing cash flow, 342
Schedule A: Income and Expense Schedule and Annual Cash Flow, 342
Schedule B: Projected Rental Schedule, 343
Schedule C: Fill-up Projection, 343
Schedule D: Summary Budget, 343
Schedule E: Summary, Direct Construction Cost Budget, 344
Schedule F: Construction Loan Interest Projection, 344
Schedule G: Mortgage Computation, 345
Schedule H: Amortization Schedule, 345
Schedule I: Depreciation Schedule, 345
Schedule J: Basis Adjustments and Excess Depreciation, Tax preference item, 346
Schedule K: Hypothetical Sale after 7 Years Operation, 347

Chapter 22
Planning, organizing, and implementing a profit improvement program 349

A three-phase program, 349
    Appreciation, 349
    Education, 350
    Application, 350
Characteristics of the program, 350
Starting with a pilot program, 351
The pilot group, 352
    Pilot-group education, 352
    Pilot-group application, 353
The steering committee, 353
The program coordinator, 353
Project teams, 354
Management teams, 354
Reports and coordination, 355
Feedback, recognition, and reinforcement, 356
Examination of objectives, 356
    Basic formats of objectives, 356
    Objectives categorized by importance and specificity, 357
Programming of specific objectives, 357
Examination of policies and procedures, 358
    Purpose of policy, 358
    Developing policy and procedure, 358
    Emphasis on the most vital work, 359
Identification of leaks in cost control and profit erosion, 359
Developing a decision-making system, 360
    Decision making begins with problem definition, 360
    Information gathering, 361
    Identification of the real problem, 361
    Further information gathering and development of alternatives, 362
    Selecting the most appropriate alternatives, 362
    Implementing new objectives, policies, procedures, 363
Value engineering as applied to a formal profit improvement program, 363
    The underlying principle of value engineering, 364
    The value engineering process, 364
    Direction and support from the highest level, 365
Work simplification to control of administrative costs, 365
Cutting overhead by utilizing greater outside support, 366

Chapter 23
Loan submission 367

How and where to get the funds, 367
    Savings and loan associations, 367

Commercial banks, 368
Life insurance companies, 368
Mutual savings banks, 368
Private noninsured pension funds, 368
Real estate investment trusts, 368
Utilizing mortgage bankers and brokers, 369
Developing the loan package, 370

Chapter 24
Benefiting from standardization ... 371

Advantages and uses of standards, 371
   Provide restraint in change, 371
   Aid creativity and innovation, 372
   Allow wide design variations, 372
   Aid communication, 373
Standardizing floor plans and buildings, 373
Policy standardization, 374
Procedural standardization, 374
Standardized budgets, cost controls, 375
Standardized schedules, 375
Standardized documents, 375
Feedback to keep standards current, 376

Chapter 25
Management capability: The key to profit growth ... 379

Developing both people and technologies, 379
Management's role in innovation, 380
   Effects of size, 380
   Entrepreneurs and managers, 381
   Strategy and operating tactics, 382
   The value of expertness, 382
   Accountability of staff as well as line managers, 383
The environment of successful companies, 383
Leading an organization from prosperity to bust, 384
Increasing management productivity, 386
   Sowing initiative to harvest results, 386
   Increasing productivity by increasing expectations, 386
   Small advances add up to large gains, 387
   Conveying goals positively, 387
The management process, 389
   Planning, 389
   Organization, 389
   Staffing, 390
   Direction, 390
   Control, 390

Chapter 26
Production and field management ... 391

Why build so fast? 391
Organization for productivity and efficiency, 392
Need for an integrated accounting and control system, 393
The land and the architecture: Topography, design, working drawings, 394
Methods improvement to achieve cost benefits, 395
   Techniques of methods improvement, 396
Reducing field work through industrialization, 397
   The plant amortization problem, 397
Techniques for the field, 398
   Construction do's and don'ts, 400
The role of the superintendent, 400
Inspection and control of work, 401
   Inspection instructions, 402
   Guidelines for inspectors, 403

Chapter 27
Purchasing, contract letting, and progress payments ... 413

Keeping abreast of the market, 413

Locating subcontractors, 414
Contract negotiation, 415
Effective bidding, 416
Letting subcontracts, 417
   Matching subcontract accounts and budget accounts, 417
   Full documentation in contracts, 418
   Eliminating contingencies and reducing costs, 418
Materials management and purchasing, 419
   Providing controls through materials and construction schedules, 419
   Follow-up and delivery of materials, 420
Builder-subcontractor relations, 420
General conditions, 421
Subcontractor exhibits, 421

Chapter 28
Organizational development: Building the best team 475

Communication problems, 475
   Resistance to change, 476
   Appraising human resources, 476
Private and public corporations, 477
Small companies and large companies, 478
Development cycle of a private business, 479
   Initial organization and capitalization, 479
   Struggle-and-strife period, 480
   Survival-and-growth period, 480
   Success: The payoff period, 481
   Redirection: Continuity or obsolescence, 481
Entrepreneurial illusions, 482
   Illusion 1: My business is unique, 482
   Illusion 2: It's my money; I'll do what I want, 482
   Illusion 3: No one else can make my decisions because no one else has my experience, 483
Piercing illusions with management audit, 484

The organizational development process, 486
The organizational and control matrix, 487
   How the organizational and control matrix works, 487
   Correct sequential implementation: A prerequisite for success, 488
   Advantages of the matrix, 490

Chapter 29
Scheduling for profit improvement 501

Effectiveness of implementation determines the value of plans, 501
The overall project schedule, 502
The construction schedule, 503
   Developing and implementing the construction schedule, 503
Construction scheduling: A team effort, 505
A schedule is no better than its follow-through, 506
The schedule as a management tool, not a club, 507
   The builder not the subs, must run the job, 507
How construction specialization aids productivity, 508
The need to think ahead of schedule, 508
Project schedule work sheets, 509
Case study I: The project management network, 510
   Computer reports, 512
Construction schedules, manual method, 512

Chapter 30
Merchandising nonincome properties............................. 523

Merchandising: An extension of marketing, 523
Tapping emotions to develop project personality, 523
Zeroing in on the central theme, 524
Allocating advertising and promotion dollars, 524

Selectivity in a direct mail campaign, 525
Selling with the model complex, 526
Selling the community and establishing a theme, 527
Maintaining the mood, 527
Explaining the merchandising strategy, 527

Chapter 31
Merchandising income properties 529

Coordinating construction and marketing schedules, 529
Precompletion rents, 530
Setting and revising rental schedules, 530
Effects of amenities on rental schedules and absorption, 531
Attracting prospects through curb appeal and land planning, 532
Showing the apartments, 533
The rental office, 534
The opening, 534
Direct contact, 535
Generating traffic, 535

A quality rental staff equals quality residents, 536
Training the rental staff, 536
Evaluating the traffic to provide feedback, 536

Chapter 32
Applying profit planning and controls to commercial development: A case study approach 539

Garden office case study, 539
Learning from the competition, 540
Defining the market, 540
Accumulated versus ongoing demand, 541
Irrational versus rational behavior, 542
Effect of accumulated demand on absorption forecasting, 542
Location land cost, 542
Matching the concept and product to market need, 543
Financing the complex, 546
Marketing the complex, 546

Index **549**

List of illustrations

3-1   Land-value trend line, 22
3-2   Case study II: Configuration of property, 30
3-3   Case study II: Front development, 32
3-4   Case study II: Typical interior courtyard treatment, 33
13-1 Site plan for the use of primary and secondary courtyards, 151
13-2 Illustration of primary and secondary courtyards, 152
13-3 Illustration of back-to-back plans, 154
13-4 Building exteriors in a back-to-back building, 155
13-5 Case Study I: Site plan, 159
13-6 Case Study II: Floor plans before and after redesign, 161
13-7 Case Study II: Exterior after redesign, 164
13-8 Case Study III: Floor plans before and after redesign, 165
13-9 Case Study III: Building structure elevations, 169
13-10 Case Study IV: Floor plans before and after redesign, 173
15-1 Case Study II: Elevation and floor plan, 195
15-2 Case Study II: Housing designs, 196
15-3 Case Study II: Lakeside setting, 197
16-1 Case Study I: Site plan, 202
16-2 Case Study I: Project design, 203
16-3 Case Study II: First phase, 205
16-4 Case Study II: Product design, 207
16-5 Case Study II: Units added to first phase, 208
16-6 Case Study II: Landscaping concept, 209
17-1 Decked areas and layout of a small clubhouse, 216
17-2 Landscaping, planning, and detailing illustrated, 218
17-3 Illustration of units and landscaped pool area, 219
20-1 Case Study I: General ledger-financial reporting, 268

20-2 Case Study I: General ledger-financial reporting, 269
20-3 Case Study I: General ledger-financial reporting, 270
20-4 Case Study I: General ledger-financial reporting, 271
20-5 Case Study I: Project cost, 273
20-6 Case Study I: Project cost, 274
20-7 Case Study I: Cash disbursements and accounts payable, 276
20-8 Case Study I: Cash disbursements and accounts payable, 277
27-1 Detailed example of one type of masonry work, 416
27-2 A second example of masonry work, 416
29-1 Bar chart, 510
29-2 Simple network, 511
29-3 Definitive network chart, 511
29-4 Case Study I: Expected completion report, 512
29-5 Case Study II: Department report, 513
29-6 Case Study I: Critical path report, 514

List of exhibits

3-1	Site Selection Checklist, 33-38
4-1	Land Comparables Adjustment Sheet, 47
4-2	Land Comparables Ranking Sheet, 47
4-3	Land Comparables Relationship Chart, 48
4-4	Alternate A: Cash Flow Calculation and Internal Rate of Return, 49
4-5	Alternate B: Cash Flow Calculation and Internal Rate of Return, 50
4-6	Negotiation Checklist, 51
4-7	Title, Liens, Restrictions Checklist, 51
4-8	Existing Financing Checklist, 52
6-1	Summary of Comparable Developments Form, 74
6-2	Unit Mix of Comparable Developments Form, 75
6-3	Planned Developments Form, 76
6-4	Price Adjustments Format Sheets, 77
6-5	Lambert Gardens: Data Collection Sheet, 78
6-6	Lambert Gardens: Price Adjustment Sheet, 79
6-7	Green Acres: Data Collection Sheet, 80
6-8	Green Acres: Price Adjustment Sheet, 81
6-9	The Crossing: Data Collection Sheet, 82
6-10	The Crossing: Price Adjustment Sheet, 83
6-11	Development Comparables Relationship Chart, 84
11-1	Demand Estimates by Income Distribution Chart, 136
11-2	Demand Estimates by Population Increase Chart, 136
18-1	Feasibility Outline, 228-31
26-1	Job Inspection Checklist, 403-11
27-1	Subcontractor List, 422
27-2	Contractor's or Subcontractor's Statement of Qualifications, 423-24
27-3	Instructions to Subcontractors, 425-29

27-4   Subcontract Agreement Form, 429–31
27-5   Status of Bid Documents Form, 432
27-6   Application of Payment Form, 433
27-7   Conditions of Purchase Contract Sheet, 433–35
27-8   Request for Quotation Form, 435
27-9   Purchase Order Form, 436
27-10 Field Order Form, 437
27-11 Change Order Data Sheet, 437
27-12 Exhibit Sheet: List of Items on Change Order No. _____, 438
27-13 Change Order Authorization, 438
27-14 Affidavit of Release of Liens, 439
27-15 General Conditions, 440–73
28-1   Organizational and Control Matrix, 491–99
29-1   Project Schedule Work Sheets, 514–19
29-2   Hypothetical Project Plan, 519
29-3   Site-Work Schedule, 520
29-4   Rough-Work Schedule, 521
29-5   Finish-Work Schedule, 522

Introduction

In management literature there is a gap between pointing out what is wrong and placing in the hands of management the tools they can use to solve problems. Works published to aid in the solution of specific problems are directed to the specialized areas that deal with the immediate problems, but they often are not sufficiently helpful to the manager, whose responsibilities cover a much broader area. That is, the how-to literature is aimed at those practitioners or specialists who carry out particular functions and not at the manager, who is held responsible for both the successful performance of particular functions and profit-center performance. Profit-center responsibility requires the manager not only to solve specific problems as they arise but to anticipate changes and constantly shape and reshape the strategies and the organization in order to realize overall objectives in a dynamic environment.

It is a predicament of management that it can often identify problems and appreciate the need for solutions to them, but the manager, despite his specific skills and knowledge, may not understand the origin of the problems, their significance, or their interrelationships with other factors within the business as a whole. Thus the manager is unable to come up with effective solutions to the problems. There is a tendency to examine difficulties as individual problems, without a proper understanding of the interactions of the problem with the whole. A change in one element of the situation will produce change in others. For this reason, the solution to a specific problem may lie outside the perimeter of skills, or variables, normally associated with the problem.

A manager tends to evaluate a problem and assign priorities based on his particular background and area of expertise. Therefore, there is a tendency to analyze the problem from a narrow viewpoint (failure to properly identify the problem) and to propose solutions within narrow perimeters which may not cover the scope of the problem. A good analogy is the three blind men who were asked to describe an elephant. One felt the tail and said, "An elephant is like a rope." The second felt the legs and said, "An elephant is like a tree." The third felt the trunk and said "The elephant is like a snake." All were accurate in describing what they perceived in accordance with their limited experience. Their error was in attempting to perceive the total picture within that context. Though the perception of a part of the whole may be correct, the perception of the overall situation, based on isolated or incomplete experiences, can be very erroneous.

If problems are perceived and solutions are proposed on too narrow a basis, they will be ineffective and will cause disruption to other operations in the system. Specialization has tended to limit the view of many managers to an area that is too small. There are many examples of managers exerting intense effort, in the context of their specialization, to solve an immediate problem, only to find that their efforts have been defeated by events occurring in a larger context. Though the need for specialists is great, the need for generalists to conduct the interaction of these specialists toward acceptable ends is even greater.

This book is written for generalists, who have the profit responsibility for the work of specialists, and for real estate specialists who seek a broader view of the building and development system in order to increase their effectiveness within it. To meet the challenge, generalists must possess the expertise of specialists in numerous areas of the enterprise they are to oversee. By the term "generalist" we do not mean someone who has a general knowledge consisting of a smattering of insights into the diverse activities comprising the business. Rather, we mean a person who has specific knowledge, bordering on expert, in a number of the key operations which comprise it. When these diverse areas of specific expertise are combined in one individual, that individual can become a generalist with better insights into the overall business than those who possess a more limited scope of specialist expertise or a smattering of general knowledge. The effective generalist, then, does not have broad-brush capabilities but has developed as a generalist through gaining specific, in-depth, hands-on expertise in numerous key areas of the business.

To accomplish the challenging task of orchestrating areas of specialization, the generalist (or entrepreneur-manager) needs a system, a framework of reference, an ordered set of assumptions about the complex whole in which the various specialist functions must operate. To this end, a general model is required to interrelate the specialty areas in a manner appropriate to the problem at hand. Decision makers at every level consciously or unconsciously use mental models to structure policy in an understandable framework for decision making. The brain can keep track of only a limited number of simultaneous interactions, and a formalized structure or model of the entire network can make it possible to evaluate simultaneously how a change in one element will effect change in other elements comprising the whole.

These models are of necessity simple structures when compared to the operating environment in which they must function. The model the decision maker must work with is imperfect, oversimplified, and at all times unfinished. No matter how imperfect, however, it is indispensable to the decision-making process. The better the model, or data base, which forms the frame of reference, the better the decisions generally will be.

This book provides the framework of a working model for the entrepreneur-manager. While every decision maker already utilizes a model (though perhaps unconsciously), the definitive framework offered here is designed to extend the scope of current models.

Decisions are being made every day which will affect the very survival of building development businesses. These decisions cannot be put off until a perfect model is available to evaluate all the consequences, or an understanding of all the variables which may affect the outcome has been totally achieved. Models initially are bare-bones schemata, based on fundamentals, general perceptions, and past experiences and designed to interrelate diverse circumstances and make it possible to draw broad conclusions. The book attempts to cover a broad spectrum of the real estate development business, particularly the fundamentals. It is illustrated with numerous case studies, checklists, worksheets, and schedules.

In many areas of industry, the majority of decision makers seem to be actively pursuing goals that are inconsistent with what would commonly be called common sense. Common sense, however, is a misnomer, and it is not nearly as common as might at first be assumed. As popularly viewed, it represents what a reasonable man would do if he had knowledge and an overview of the facts and how they relate to a particular situation within the context of the whole (the system). The problem is that most decision makers do not possess adequate knowledge at the time the decisions are required. In hindsight, therefore, their decisions may be viewed as lacking an element of common sense. The rudimentary model this book provides for the decision maker is designed to improve understanding of the total business and to formalize and expand the mental models which all decision makers utilize to one extent or another. Thus it can help decision makers to employ more common sense in reaching their decisions.

Each chapter of the book provides detailed, nuts-and-bolts working knowledge, rather than the broad-brush type of treatment which yields sketches and glimpses of a field of expertise yet does not contain enough how-to and why information to be really useful. The fundamentals covered apply to both income properties and for-sale housing. Though the application of these fundamentals may vary somewhat, the principles remain fairly constant. Case studies are included, to give a clear understanding of how the fundamentals are applied differently to rental or for-sale housing. I have not tried to orient the book to either income properties or for-sale housing exclusively, feeling that this would give too narrow a view of the housing development industry. The overall purpose of the book, as I have suggested, is to expand the decision maker's horizons so that business decisions can be made in the context of the entire industry or the economic climate in which he must operate.

Though the chapters are diverse in their coverage, perhaps to the point of straining the capacity of one individual to consider them all in the decision-making process, they are in fact tied together by a central unifying theme or motive: profit enhancement. The executive with profit-center responsibility needs to simultaneously weigh the content and the interrelationships represented by all the chapters. In the aggregate, they form the whole of the activity—real estate development—which must be steered to the realization of acceptable objectives.

Each chapter represents an important building block within the system, and neglect or improper consideration of any of them could fatally weaken the potential opportunity. To use a different analogy, real estate programs, like automobiles, can suffer a substantial reduction in performance due to a malfunction in only one of their multiple components. Collectively, the chapters form a model by which the decision maker can fine tune the mechanism, so its parts operate in harmony and it does not break down in the journey from objectives to results.

If any of the chapters or segments of the development process, represents a blank spot to a profit-center manager, his ability to generate profits will be hindered, and the risk factor will be increased. When an area which was previously a blank is illuminated, the decision maker's perception of the problem and its possible solutions is enlightened.

To minimize redundancy, material more appropriate for one chapter is generally excluded from others, though it may have a bearing on them. As the whole is greater than the sum of its parts, so is each part incomplete outside its context within the whole. Therefore, while each chapter provides a concise coverage of its subject matter, essentially the format is designed to provide insights into the interrelationships of all the materials; that is, how materials in one chapter affect, or are affected by, materials in another chapter. To assist the reader in developing insights into the interrelationships between the various disciplines represented in the 32 chapters, we have provided numerous cross references in each chapter to direct the reader to related material in other chapters.

These insights should suggest new opportunities for creative application and innovation. Such insights, and the flashes of inspiration they can inspire, are capable of providing rewards that are not available through brute effort, diligent work, or cash infusion alone. The introduction of a better system or order can produce otherwise unobtainable results.

Profits rely primarily on quality of expertise, not on the magnitude of effort or expenditure. Expertise is measured by the ability to maximize value while minimizing expenditure within a dynamic environment. This process is generally called innovation. It is innovation in real estate development, its management and implementation, to which this book is directed.

1

Market planning for optimum results

A business enterprise launching a real estate development program hopes to achieve a result from the effort that is not only satisfactory but is the best or optimum result. Market planning is an organized method of developing the strategy, action plans, and controls which will produce the greatest yield, as compared to other alternatives.

Developing an optimum solution to arrive at an investment objective is a problematic undertaking; that is, the manager must work within an environment of uncertainty. Decisions are always required, even though critical information may be lacking. If a manager waited for an opportunity to be fully identified and "proven," it would have passed before he could act.

Statisticians distinguish between two types of error; errors of the first class and errors of the second class.

First-class errors—assuming false something that is true.
Second-class errors—assuming true something that is false.

We are trained from childhood to avoid errors of the second class: "Do not accept a statement as true unless there is overwhelming evidence to support it." Practical men often use an expression to describe themselves—"I'm from Missouri"—which means, "I'm hardheaded and you have to show me."

Leaders seldom make errors of the second class. However, the greater their skill in avoiding decisions without sufficient evidence, the more prone they are to errors of the first class. In market planning the manager must not presume to have knowledge that is not actually available, yet he must take into account all of the facts that are known and are pertinent to the endeavor.

If a man will begin with certainties, he shall end in doubts; but if he will be content to begin with doubts, he shall end in certainties.
Francis Bacon

MANAGEMENT'S NEED FOR A PLAN

To know where the company is going is the first priority of business. Everything an organization does in some way locks it into a future course of action, whether the company knows it or not. To ensure that the course of action corresponds with desirable objectives, the organization must have a plan. The plan should recognize the following factors:

1. The organization's competence in financing, production, marketing, research, merchandising, and sales, and the product areas into which this competence extends.
2. The organization's history; how and why it has gotten where it is at present, what its major weaknesses or strengths are, and whether the weaknesses be remedied.
3. How the organization ranks with its competition, what it is doing that the competition is not doing, and where it has an edge or potential edge on the competition.
4. What the customer's needs are and how they are changing; what the organization can do to encourage change favorable to organization objectives.

In addition, a systematic program of experimentation and innovation must be created and nurtured to implement plans resulting from marketing input. Marketing analysis without implementation of the results will do nothing to move the organization closer to desirable objectives.

To plan means to assess the future and make provisions for it. This starts with identification of major corporate or company objectives and continues with the allocation of resources. Comprehensive planning is geared to short- and long-term outcomes and is goal oriented. It not only considers the surface or variable elements of the situation, it also shapes policy and determines the objectives necessary to the attainment of desired values. Extensive feedback of results from existing operations also is necessary. Such planning can be contrasted to incremental decision processes, point-to-point planning, and fixed expectations about outcomes.

Successful business planning identifies and steers the company into new areas of profit potential. To know where the company and its markets are going is of paramount importance: If you don't know where you are going, any road will take you there. The chief executive must know at all times where his company is heading and develop the marketing strategies required to get it there. Then all policies and decisions, whether short or long term, can be put into perspective and fitted into the overall plan. Everything a company does fits it into some inflexible course of action. Every action or inaction inescapably leads to some future consequence, whether or not the company anticipates it.

The cyclical nature of business

In its broad applications, marketing recognizes market cycles (see Chapter 9) and deals with current issues related to the cyclical nature of the environment in which business must function. While it is not possible to predict the future accurately, what will happen in the future is often a foreseeable consequence of what one now does. Inability to predict the future is not an excuse for failure to anticipate the things that could happen. Indeed, what happens in the future should happen more or less because of what one does in the present. By recognizing business cycles, it is possible to anticipate the future, rather than relying on the whim of chance.

Man is not the creature of circumstances. Circumstances are the creatures of men.

Benjamin Disraeli

CREATING NEW CONSUMER SATISFACTIONS

Business is essentially buying customers, not producing "widgets." In order to buy customers, a company must create new value satisfactions. This need emphasizes the importance of innovation in marketing (see Chapter 7).

To survive, business must attract and hold customers. This is usually interpreted as selling, but salesmen generally are not esteemed in our society. Partly, this is because, once a customer has chosen and paid for a product, he or she always experiences some residual dissatisfaction or dissonance, wondering: "Could I have gotten more elsewhere, would service have been better elsewhere, could the quality have been better, did I really need what I bought, was I pressured into a needless or inappropriate purchase?" There is always going to be a residual feeling of dissatisfaction, needs not fully met, emotions unsatisfied.

This does not mean that the situation cannot be improved, however. A seller who looks deeply enough into buyer needs can focus on areas that will provide clear-cut buyer satisfaction and minimize those that may lead to dissatisfaction (see Chapters 6, 11, and 12). The process whereby this is done is called market planning. Marketing is different from selling in many ways. One of the primary differences is that marketing is customer oriented. Selling concentrates on the needs of the seller, marketing on the needs of the buyer.

Often organizations think they are implementing a marketing program when what they are really doing is selling. Analytical and research information is used to find out how to sell the company's product better rather than how to modify the product and implement its delivery to the customer so that it is more attractive than other products which are competing to fill the same need. This may sound like hair splitting, but it is not; marketing is attracting customers, and it is the customer who decides the fate of the business.

At the root of organizational objectives is the need to translate consumer need into opportunity for the company. A company recognizing need and opportunity can evaluate how its unique position, technology, and resources can best be directed and converted into sales. The marketplace is dynamic, and marketing is an ongoing, ever-changing process within the organization which requires discipline and planning.

Market planning as a companywide function

Marketing planning is a process engaged in by the entire organization and is not limited to the sales or marketing departments. The organization as a whole must be customer oriented, for it is the customer who provides the sales dollars which enable the organization to survive and grow.

Marketing is the total of all activities which go into delivering a product to meet users' needs. Market planning directs the company's uniqueness and resources to take advantage of opportunities created by consumer needs. Thus marketing is the process of planning and arranging all the company's resources.

IMPLEMENTING THE MARKET-PLANNING PROCESS

Market planning should be an orderly (see Chapter 2) process which begins with the identification of organizational objectives and continues through step-by-step development of strategies, action plans, budgets, and controls.

Implementing objectives calls for the formulation of a strategy or strategies of operation. These strategies, which outline the broad approach to be utilized in achieving objectives, provide the bridge between objectives and action plans and focus on the direction of effort required to achieve the goal. Strategies, like objectives, are somewhat fixed; thus they provide direction for subsequent actions and prevent the organization from engaging in scatter-shot, wasteful activities.

Action plans must be guided by objectives and strategies to the accomplishment of specific goals. Otherwise actions tend to become random and vague in meaningfulness, so that success rests on hopes that somehow a worthwhile result will occur as a windfall. It is only by chance that random actions will build a cumulative momentum and achieve purposeful results.

Without the direction laid down by comprehensive objectives and strategies, action plans may be ineffective, and with one plan working against another, the result may be loss of value. These are called value washouts. Value washouts can consume considerable resources without adding any value to the endeavor. Particularly in real estate development, there is vast room for savings of resources, without any commensurate loss of value or quality, through the elimination of value washouts. This will be explained more thoroughly in Chapter 13, on value engineering, and Chapters 14–17, on product development.

Genius—The ability to evade work by doing something right the first time it is done.

Action plans are drafted only after a comprehensive strategy has been worked out to arrive at a predetermined goal. The strategy not only sets direction but is quantitative, in that the type and amount of effort to be spent are stipulated. To engage in action outside the context of the strategy can be quite ineffective, because it will produce favorable results only by chance. When action plans are launched in the context of the overall strategy they are goal oriented, and the chances of wasted effort and resources are lessened.

Development programs must be carefully tuned so that all action plans work in a harmonious relationship with one another to achieve optimum performance. Development programs are like automobiles in that a small malfunction in one operative can have a dramatic effect on overall performance.

Action plans, are more flexible than objectives and strategies. If feedback gained through management controls indicates that a particular action is not generating the benefits anticipated, the action can be modified, replaced by a different action, or eliminated. A number of action plans can be implemented concurrently in the implementation of a specific strategy. Action plans are step-by-step procedures put into perspective by the strategy to reach a specific objective. These plans go into the specific details of how to, by whom, when, and with what resources.

Budget plans for individual action plans are important to establish their feasibility (see Chapter 18). Each action plan must compete with other opportunities available to the organization, on the basis of the anticipated return to be derived from the expenditure and how the benefits of the action relate to the long- and short-term objectives of the organization.

However, the formulation of action plans and budgets should be a two-step process. If action plans are dominated by purely cost and resource considerations, the decisions reached will tend to be based more on immediate resource considerations than on the attainment of long-term objectives. Expediency must not supersede the accomplishment of the fundamental objectives which guide the organization, or vitality will be sapped and profit opportunities lost; the organization will be paying for today by sacrificing all of the tomorrows. Budget and resource requirements, once approved, serve as a basis or source data for establishing control and review criteria (see Chapter 12).

MARKET PLANNING RECAP

A thorough review of the organization and its goals establishes the organization's objectives and constraints. The objectives and constraints of the organization provide the bounds within which all strategies and action plans must function.

Strategies are then formulated to provide general direction to the organization in accomplishing objectives within the bounds of the organization's constraints. Market analysis identifies the specific opportunities available to the organization in carrying out its strategies. An action plan or development concept is formulated to capitalize on the recognized opportunities. Concurrent with the development of an action plan or developmental concept, a feasibility analysis is carried out to determine how well the recognized opportunity enhances the organization's objectives and whether or not it can be accomplished within the bounds of the organization's constraints.

During these activities, a value engineering study is carried out, with the purpose of enhancing consumer satisfaction while reducing cost (see Chapter 13). The goal is to arrive at the optimum solution whereby the most consumer satisfactions are produced at the greatest profits to the organization. Appraisal then determines the market value the lender utilizes to determine the loan amount the program will justify.

2

Establishing objectives and constraints

Before entering into any development program, a clear identification of the developer's objectives is critical. Public corporations (those with stockholders) generally have a different set of objectives than privately owned companies (see Chapter 28), and within each there may be varying sets of objectives, depending on the project and the company's present internal needs. The developer may be already locked into an undesirable situation from which he cannot be readily extricated and may be looking for a solution that is no more than the better of two evils. Or the developer may have a site under control for a token fee, in order to evaluate the feasibility of developing it in relation to other available opportunities.

A developer's internal needs will at times have more influence on decision making than marketing considerations will. Long-term marketing or residual advantages may be subordinated to short-term operating considerations. For example, the developer may want to limit equity requirements and give this importance above all else, even though residual value and marketing strength may later suffer, or he may not be too concerned with the front-end equity load and place emphasis instead on buildup of equity or residual value. Pride of ownership or being a positive influence on the community may be objectives which the developer values enough to make sacrifices by accepting a lower return or increased risk.

The developer's objectives can be as varied and far-ranging as the internal needs of the organization or the individuals in authority within the development organization. They reflect developmental constraints which guide subsequent decision making from the outset. Objectives are not strategies or action plans but represent targets or goals to be achieved within a given period of time. Major objectives have three dimensions:

1. What is to be achieved—what type of result is expected?
2. How much is to be achieved (amount, quantity)?
3. When is the result to be achieved?

Objectives fall into two basic types or categories: going after new opportunities, or reducing or eliminating obstacles associated with the realization of current opportunities the organization is pursuing. The timetable for accomplishment is usually stated in terms of short-term and long-term goals. Long-term goals establish direction, and short-term goals are related to specific steps which make possible the accomplishment of subsequent steps leading to the realization of the long-term goal.

Stating both long-term and short-term goals determines the way capabilities and resources are to be utilized, what must be done to accomplish goals, and what resources must be allocated. Thus they provide a framework which establishes a perspective for subsequent decisions. (See "Examination of Objectives" in Chapter 22.)

FINANCIAL OBJECTIVES

Public companies make a greater effort to report profits in the form of immediate earnings rather than cash flow. For this reason, public companies typically want to report earnings from current operations as quickly as possible and to have minimum interest in depreciation benefits. On the other hand, private companies may be more interested in cash flow spread out over a longer period of time, the shelter aspects of depreciation, and prospects for substantial residual values and capital gains (see Chapter 28).

From the outset it is important to determine the form and amount of financial return and yield desired and the timing of the investment. This is generally the central motivating factor in real estate development. Once these objectives are determined they form criteria of conditions which, when satisfactorily met, establish feasibility for the sponsor.

Yield

The timing and method of yield are of critical concern to the developer. Public corporations favor shorter economic cycles and faster payout, to boost quarterly earnings. Private corporations favor the shelter aspects of real estate, are concerned more with cash flow than with earnings, and are often interested in developments which provide substantial residual values and capital gains, as opposed to rapid accumulation of immediate profits.

Public corporations, which once flocked to the rental markets, have since abandoned this market because changes by the Accounting Principles Board limited their ability to report immediate earnings from the sale of rental properties. Before abandoning the rental markets, however, they contributed largely to the overbuilding of rentals in many market areas. These corporations have changed their emphasis to the condominium markets and have done the same thing there. This fundamental change of emphasis and subsequent redistribution of supply and demand factors in the rental and condo markets can be traced back to yield, how it is reported, and the impact of the timing and method of profit recognition.

Risk The organization must determine the amount of risk and financial exposure it is willing and able to bear. A conservative program may reduce exposure, but it will also reduce potential profits. An aggressive, speculative program may allow for maximum potential profits but also increase exposure.

Risk can be reduced by buying land ready for use which does not require rezoning, and by buying land that can be built out in a short time frame. This reduces cyclical risk from economic downturns and potentially unfavorable events, such as sewer and power moratoriums, new taxes and fees, changes in ordinances and codes, unforeseen competition, materials and labor shortages, inflation, and ruinous mortgage and financial markets (see Chapter 9).

Attempts to reduce risk commonly reduce potential profits as well, requiring sharper operations to protect the smaller margins. The seasoned developer, however, utilizes techniques whereby, to some extent, he can reduce risk while increasing profit. Such techniques, which are an aspect of value engineering, will be presented throughout the book and illustrated with case studies.

Maintaining the proper balance between risk and profit calls for seasoned judgment and a comprehensive understanding of the entire developmental process. Ill-informed or seat-of-the-pants corner cutting usually increases risk while reducing profit potential.

NONFINANCIAL OBJECTIVES Every developer also has objectives which cannot be measured in financial terms. As mentioned above, the developer may place great importance on pride of ownership; utility of the development, which serves as a benefit to the developer; or establishment of a track record for company identity. The developer's organizational capacity and depth of personal and professional experience (or lack of experience) in specific developmental areas also serve as nonfinancial developmental constraints.

TWO BASIC STRATEGIES The developer has the choice of two basic strategies in development:

1. He can select a market and then research it to find a hole, and determine the development concepts that offer the best promise.
2. He can develop and polish a concept and then search for a market in which the concept will fill a need.

There are advantages and disadvantages to both approaches. In the first approach, the developer must have the capability, flexibility, and time to develop and implement new concepts to fill whatever hole may be found in a market. This can be difficult, because concepts are expensive to develop and require experience before they can be finely polished. Additionally, it may be difficult to staff an organization that is equally adept in producing all the varying concepts of the product line. An advantage to this approach, however, is being able to sustain a volume of business in a particular market area that would not be possible without a wide product mix. Diversity of product gives the developer potential for capturing a larger market share within a given market.

The second approach is widely used by the multimarket builders. This approach takes advantage of product standardization and can result in the development of a highly polished product, from both marketing and product efficiency standpoints. Disadvantages are that a multimarket operation puts a strain on management. The entrepreneurial capacity of the headquarters organization is diluted by geographics, and it is difficult to recruit executives who can run regional operations with the same efficiency as the home operation. Management must also be very sensitive to the adjustments and modifications required of their standardized product in new market areas.

THE DEVELOPER'S RESOURCES, CAPABILITIES, AND CONSTRAINTS

Availability of equity generally poses a major constraint for the developer, large or small. Leverage enables the developer to stretch the capacity of his resources, and this leverage principle will affect a great many developmental decisions, from outset to completion.

Leverage can be gained through a number of mechanisms, such as:

1. Taking in an equity partner.
2. Structuring development programs for rapid initial payout, which may require sacrifices in marketing strength and profit potential.
3. Building single-family, for-sale rather than rental housing, which requires more equity.
4. Structuring smaller project components to reduce the economic cycle to a series of steps, with each step funding subsequent steps.
5. Exercising tight internal management, controls, and keen market awareness to increase the productivity potential of the resources.

Overleveraging has its own set of problems. A developer who is overleveraging is exceeding the capacity of his resource and capability base. A builder is overleveraged when his business is running him rather than vice versa. An overleveraged developer may, for example, start marginal projects to generate cash flow as a temporary infusion to sustain previous marginal projects, which are bleeding the organization. Thus the overleveraged developer operates in an environment of constant crises, fire fighting to control yesterday's mistakes, and compromises of long-term objectives.

In developing strategies, there must be an objective realization of and respect for developer constraints. The temptation for overextension is very compelling: "Whenever money is available, builders will build." In his earlier years the developer tenaciously seeks out lenders and fights to win their confidence. After the developer has proved himself, and particularly when there is a strong inflow of savings, the tables will turn, and the lenders will seek out builders with good track records. The romance of this turnaround, from being the seeker to being the one sought after, is a compelling inducement to increase developmental volume. But as pride goeth before a fall, overleveraging of resources can lead to disaster. When lenders are flush with money they want to get it out in the worst way, and they generally do. Those who do resist the temptation of overleveraging operate on the philosophy that it's still a tough market, and it's going to get tougher any day.

THE KEY TO SUCCESS: A GOOD FIT BETWEEN OPPORTUNITY AND CAPABILITY

Because user needs are as broad and varied as they are, they provide numerous opportunities for profit. Some of these opportunities will be more suited to the uniqueness and resources of a particular company than others. Success in turning opportunity into profit depends on the extent and depth of the opportunity and the capabilities and resources of the organization which can be devoted to the opportunity.

An organization is limited in the number and types of opportunities it can pursue by its own capabilities and resources. The success rate will be highest where there is a good match between opportunity, capability, and resources. Opportunity must also be evaluated as it relates to the organization's long-range objectives. An opportunity within easy reach may not be as attractive as one on the fringes of the organization's capability if the latter works more harmoniously into its long-range objectives, and the former offers short-term benefits at the expense of long-term objectives.

Several opportunities may be similar in nature or have overlapping characteristics. There is a tendency to lump similar opportunities into a group and then plan to implement the group objective. This can be dangerous, because if the resulting plans are too general they will be ineffective. Implementation will be difficult because plans cannot be focused to the specific point-of-sale need of each opportunity in the group.

An example would be deciding to develop condominiums without a proper regard for the market segment or submarkets to be served. The family and empty-nester markets, for example, are two separate market segments which a condominium form of ownership can serve. They are, however, very different types of markets, requiring different concepts and strategies. A too-general approach leads to compromises which are designed to bridge markets but which fail to serve the needs of any of the sought-after market segments adequately. Some market segments are very compatible with one another from a marketing standpoint; others are not. The developer must be specific as to which markets he will serve and understand how they are compatible or incompatible (see Chapters 15 and 16).

The identification of appropriate opportunities and the establishment of objectives to capitalize on these opportunities must be carried out in a dynamic environment affected by internal and external influences. This requires an organized method for collecting, categorizing, and analyzing data to find out where a company and its markets are, how they got there, and where they are going. Analysis of trends—international, national, regional, and local—is required. This includes analysis of possible governmental legislation, which is often directed by the current attitudes of constituents.

If the interrelationship of the available opportunities with organizational capabilities and resources is not correctly evaluated, the organization's objectives may be unrealistic. When working toward unrealistic objectives, even the best laid action plans will be ineffective and wasteful of organizational resources (see Chapter 25).

The evaluation of an opportunity and decisions as to objectives must include an analysis of the organization's strengths and weaknesses, and its capacity and resources as they relate to the opportunity, the competition, and the socioeconomic environment. Objectivity is important in the evaluation process. The facts must be placed on the table early, to ensure that all known strengths and weaknesses can be considered within sufficient time so a firm foundation can be built for subsequent strategies and action plans. Objectives should be formulated to capitalize on the most promising of the opportunities, tempered by organizational limitations and external obstacles (see Chapter 18).

In counsel it is good to see dangers; but in execution, not to see them unless they be very great.

Francis Bacon

FEASIBILITY AS RELATED TO DEVELOPER OBJECTIVES

All plans must be in keeping with the organization's objectives and strategies. Plans that do not so mesh do not move the organization forward toward agreed-upon goals. Though a particular plan may show an attractive rate of return, it may nonetheless not meet feasibility requirements because it is not consistent with major organizational objectives. On the other hand, a plan may show a high rate of return, be consistent with objectives, and still not be feasible because of a lack of resources. Such a plan may require an overcommitment of resources in a particular area, like putting all your eggs in one basket.

Feasibility requires a correct mixture of external and internal circumstances; a plan that may be feasible for one organization could be fatal for another. Feasibility considerations for an action plan include the following questions:

1. What resources are required, and are they available?
2. Are there conflicting or prior commitments of these resources?
3. What is the desirability and value of the plan in achieving objectives, as compared to competing plans available to the organization?
4. In relation to other plans and objectives, does the plan represent duplication, conflict, or working at cross-purposes?

5. Can the plan be effectively administered through control devices, within the capabilities available to the organization?
6. Have the capabilities of the organization been objectively evaluated as related to the proposed plan?
7. Are the objectives realistic as related to the opportunities, and are they expressed in a comprehensive manner?
8. Has the market research been substantial, and are the premises based on facts and logical assumptions arrived at from objective analysis rather than preconceived ideas?
9. Does the plan take into account the dynamic, cyclical nature of the market and provide for alternate courses of action when actual conditions do not reflect projections?
10. Are the financial data realistic, consistent? Is this based on reliable information or piggyback figures?
11. Have the best opportunities been identified, expressing the highest and best use consistent with the organization's resources and the economic environment?
12. Have the problems and pitfalls been properly evaluated?

More than "the numbers"

There has been a recent tendency within institutions to overemphasize "the numbers" in real estate development, with the product being referred to as "eyewash." Feasibility has largely been determined by the numbers, which all too often have taken for granted the product, its market position in relation to the competition, market and economic cycles, and the operational capabilities of the organization.

The numbers are important, but they have their place. It is the product and the organization which must perform in the marketplace. The numbers are only a statistical representation of the capabilities of the product and the organization to perform in a given environment (see Chapter 19).

A particularly dangerous tendency has been to undertake a cosmetic redo of the numbers when the original numbers do not meet feasibility requirements. This reliance on numbers manipulation, rather than the underlying substance, underscores management's frequent inability to cope with the real-world issues which shape economic feasibility.

OPERATING RATIOS AS YARDSTICKS FOR PRELIMINARY FEASIBILITY REQUIREMENTS.

By establishing a chain of relationships among the key items or operations, it is possible to get a better understanding of how each item relates to the whole, and how a change in one item affects not only that item but the relationships of other items to the whole. For example, the approximate cost breakdown of an average single-family home, as computed by the National Association of Home Builders (NAHB) and the Federal Housing Administration (FHA), is as follows:

Item	NAHB	FHA
Direct cost of house to builder	56.7%	56.2%
Cost of developed lot	22.8%	21.5%
Total builder direct cost	79.5%	77.7%
Other costs		
Financing	6.5%	7.5%
Overhead and profit	12.7%	13.0%
Other expenditures	1.3%	1.8%
Total Other Costs	20.5%	22.3%
Total Cost of Units	100.0%	100.0%

Along the lines of this simplified example, it is a relatively simple matter for a company to determine its own operating ratios for a given period. These ratios can then be used to evaluate future projects by comparing the projected ratios against what the company has historically done in the past. The operating ratios will be of assistance not only in reaching marketing decisions, such as how much to pay for finished lot costs or hard construction, but also in monitoring operations.

By expanding the ratio categories to include the entire itemized costs by trade and function, each itemized job cost can be related to a ratio. Once the company has historical ratios to serve as a benchmark, future overruns on a particular cost category can be quickly isolated by comparison with historical averages. Additionally, the company can compare its own averages against the averages of the residential building community in general as computed by the NAHB in its *Construction Cost Data Components* publication, which is published on a semiannual basis and available through the NAHB in Washington, D.C.

There are some who maintain that the relationship of lot-cost and house-cost ratios, which add up to the total builder's direct cost, are very important in determining marketing success. The rule of thumb advanced is to minimize the lot-cost ratio and maximize the house-cost ratio. For example, when the house-cost ratio composes 55 to 60 percent of total cost, chances of marketing success are very good. When this ratio drops to 50 to 55 percent, marketing chances are reduced, and when the ratio drops below 50 percent, the marketing results are usually disastrous. As house cost as a percent of the total costs decreases, lot cost as a percent of total cost increases. The reasoning is as lot cost increases, available monies to spend on the house itself decrease, so that the developer must offer less actual house for the money.

This rule of thumb provides a good starting point for marketing and site analysis, but it is only that. The reasons for the ratios changing are more important than the mere fact that they do change. The ratio measures the change, but the more important information to be determined is what is responsible for the change and what marketing implications there are.

An increase in the lot-cost ratio can be either good or bad, depending on the reason for the change. If the developer paid more than he should have for the land or ran into unexpected finished lot improvement costs, this is bad. If the developer acquired buildable oceanfront property at a reasonable cost, but, as a result of the land cost, the lot-cost ratio increases, this could be good, because it reflects the premium value of the location and its excellent marketing position. It is not that uncommon for truly premium property to equal or exceed the cost of the improvement placed upon it. A lot-cost ratio of 37 percent could be excellent, even though it is substantially over the 22 percent which is an average lot-cost ratio, because it may have a retail value equal to a 65 percent lot-cost ratio. (See Chapters 19 and 21 for more on ratios.)

3

Locational analysis and site evaluation

WHEN AND WHERE TO PURCHASE

In land (as with stocks), the greatest appreciation will occur in those properties that are already experiencing robust growth in value. The buyer should not be dissuaded merely because a property is expensive compared to the cost of a property in a less active area. Nothing succeeds like success holds true for real estate properties.

There is a delayed reaction in property values reflecting property potential, particularly when events initially cause values to rise rapidly. For example, news of a new freeway or large employer may cause property to appreciate dramatically on the introduction of the news. But if the events contributing to the appreciation are significant and of an enduring nature, values will continue to rise even though the initial rises have been dramatic. Care must be exercised that the events justify the property potential reflected in the marketplace. Minor events of a less enduring nature can create speculative excesses, due to an unrealistic assessment of true potentials.

The land buyer should not be unduly deterred by price. It is the appreciation rate which determines the rate of return, regardless of the initial price paid. Properties in areas that are experiencing the greatest appreciation and can be expected to continue appreciating in the future, are best. Purchasing property in the hopes that it may soon experience robust appreciation is riskier than purchasing properties whose appreciation trend is already established.

The upside potential of land is measured by the economics of the end user. The land cannot reasonably appreciate beyond the economics of the end use; the price must allow for the end user to make a reasonable profit (see Chapter 19). When prices reach the plateau of what the end user can afford to pay, the land has reached its maturity phase. The land should continue to appreciate in the maturity phase but at a much slower rate, because it cannot realistically appreciate beyond the end user's ability to pay. When land owners do price close-in land irrespective of end-user economics, the land becomes bypassed as the end user seeks land farther out. This is one of the reasons for the suburban sprawl typical of so many cities. Otherwise-suitable land in the path of growth is leapfrogged over because of the excessive price demands for it.

Of course, end-user economics can be changed through rezoning or innovative multiuse planning. In this case value is added to the property over and above the normal appreciation due to location.

Quality property is preferable to bargain sites. The bargain price will often be more than compensated for by developmental constraints which increase risk beyond the benefits of the economy price. The nearer the property is to the point of final use in the appreciation curve, the less is the risk generally involved, assuming the property was bought right to begin with. Property nearer the point of final use provides greater leverage value because of the increased likelihood that the next sale will be a cash sale. If a buyer will sell a property on the same highly leveraged basis on which he seeks to buy it, he loses much of the leverage advantage of the initial purchase. The actual realization of the gain during the holding period is postponed, depending upon the amount of leverage the seller then has to give the new buyer. See the section on present-value theory in Chapter 19, on financial analysis.

THE LAND-VALUE TREND LINE

Property appreciation cannot readily be measured by an average annual rate of growth because the growth rate will vary dramatically, depending on the relationship of the land to its use cycle. Land receives value in

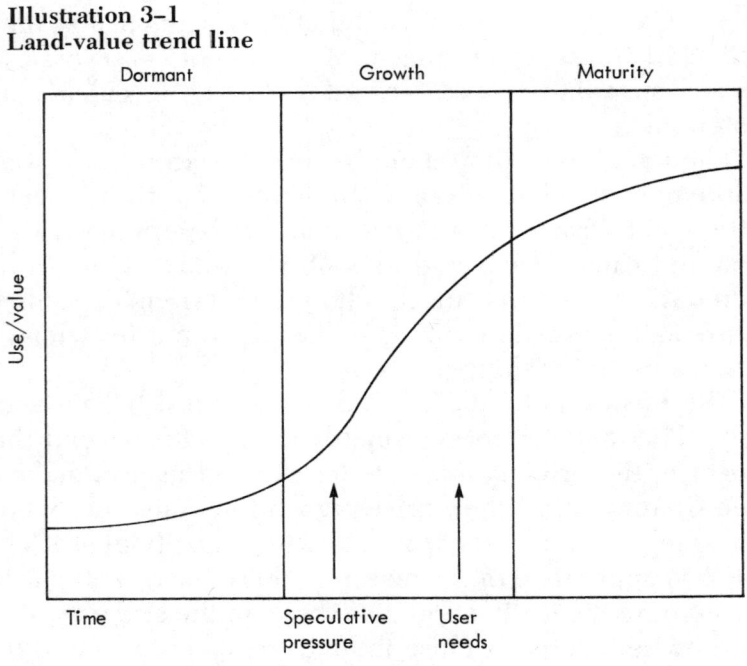

Illustration 3-1
Land-value trend line

relation to its potential use. There are three stages in land use: the dormant stage, the growth stage, and the maturity stage (see Illustration 3–1).

Buying land in the dormant stage poses risks because the land may appreciate very little while in the dormant stage. As growth pressures approach the property, speculative buyers bid up land prices in anticipation of near-term user needs. As user needs are met, land approaches the price that can be supported by the economics of the end user. Since land value cannot realistically exceed the economic capability of the end user, the land enters the maturity stage (see Chapter 10).

During the maturity stage land continues to appreciate, but at a much lower pace than it did during the growth stage. In that land needs to appreciate at approximately 20 percent compounded annually to be attractive as an investment, land in the maturity stage of use is generally no longer suitable as an investment in itself.

DEVELOPING THE CRITERIA FOR PURCHASE

Before evaluating a property purchase it is helpful, perhaps necessary, to have a definite end purpose in mind for it. The suitability of the property for fulfilling the end purpose can then be determined and the opportunities and obstacles evaluated at an early date. The intended end purpose of the property may be quite different from that envisioned by the current owner and may require a rezoning or some alteration of the physical characteristics of the property.

Land purchase don'ts

1. Don't purchase far-out land not ready for immediate development.
   a. Too many imponderables.
      (1) Environmentalism.
      (2) Utilities.
      (3) Changing growth pattern.
      (4) No growth.
      (5) Unfavorable legislation.
   b. Buy where the action is, to reduce risk.
      (1) Pay more.
      (2) Build superior product.
      (3) Maximize marketing and merchandizing.
      (4) Create value.
2. Don't purchase land prematurely. An economic downturn or changes in local outlook may cripple plans.
3. Don't improve land too early. Improvements which accelerate carrying costs lessen holding flexibility.
4. When taking control of several parcels in a market area, do not concentrate purchases in same economic level. Diversify holdings to achieve a mix of property suitable for development in several income ranges. If one parcel turns slow, because of softness in the market segment being served, the other parcels provide balance and entry into other market and income segments.

FINDING THE LAND

Local brokers who know the area well are a good source of available land. This source, properly utilized, can provide valuable data and information on trends, and brokers can do some of the buyer's leg work.

Builders who have misjudged their inventory requirements are another good source of land. Their land is generally ready to go. Public builders who are required to report quarterly earnings can be a good source of land in the event that they need to dispose of a currently nonearning asset in order to boost a quarterly earnings figure.

Professionals who are aware of development and sales activity are also a good source of information on land. These include mortgage bankers, real estate investment trusts, (REITs), banks, savings and loans, real estate and tax attorneys, accountants, civil engineers, soil engineers, architects, and appraisers.

Municipal officials also have knowledge of land activity and availability. So do utility companies, planning agencies, and traffic departments. City planning department proposals can be studied for major thoroughfares, freeways, and transit routes. Accessibility generates volume and creates value. The chamber of commerce is also a good source of information.

Newspaper and other media advertising can serve as source for available properties. A buyer may also generate land proposals from land owners and others by advertising a desire to acquire a specific type of property.

Driving through the territory in which one is interested will provide information on activity in the area. Signs on the property indicate the availability of property, and in the case of property handled by brokers, the signs will also indicate the most active brokers in the area. Builder activity should be watched, since development tends to occur in "hot spots." Early identification of these areas can put a developer into a desirable location.

GUIDELINES FOR SELECTING LAND

Regional growth is encouraged by overall economic vitality. This can be measured by signs of new industry, commercial activity, recreational facilities, environmental communities, improvements in the transportation network, a political environment conducive to new development, housing quality, and the availability of residential shelter for all economic levels. A combination of these factors can provide a catalyst for regional growth.

However, this growth does not occur homogeneously within the region but tends to be concentrated in growth corridors or pockets. In selecting land for purchase, the qualification and quantification of the overall growth potential is the first step. Identifying the corridors or pockets into which growth pressures are concentrated is the second step. Selecting sites within the growth areas is the third step.

This land selection process requires research at each of the three steps. For simplicity the steps will be referenced geographically as regional analysis, community analysis, and site identification.

Regional analysis

The area should be researched to determine which communities within the overall area promise the greatest value appreciation potential. Considerations include the following:

1. Those areas most suited geographically for development. Mountains or rivers may funnel growth in a particular direction. Soil condition, water tables, or climatic considerations may encourage growth in one direction rather than another.
2. Historic developmental patterns. Growth corridors or pocket growth areas can be identified by research, and future land needs to accommodate projected growth can be calculated. The buyer can then identify the direction of growth and timing of land inventory needs.
3. Income distribution by census tract. This will give the buyer information on the purchasing power of the population within a particular area. In this manner end-user economic capabilities can be measured and used as a yardstick in projecting appreciation potential.
4. High-pressure areas for development. These include the following areas:
    a. Those near municipal boundaries. Development will occur in county areas just outside the city, where the benefits of the city can be enjoyed without the high tax rates that accompany being within the city boundary.
    b. Those with waterways, lakes, rivers, streams, or ocean or bay frontage.
    c. Those adjacent to undeveloped natural areas, foothills, preserves, parks, or locales with particularly attractive views.
    d. Those along major highways.
    e. Those close in to and within urbanized areas.
5. Identification of growth trends. This requires a knowledge of the constraints which can channel or contain growth. Constraints to growth include:
    a. Municipal boundaries.
    b. Ecologically sensitive areas.
    c. Swamps and flood-prone areas.
    d. Difficult terrain, soil problems.
    e. Difficulty and cost of providing utilities.
    f. Political and social resistance to growth.
    g. Inadequate community facilities or resistance of the community to supplying increased facilities, such as police and fire protection, schools, and surface transportation.
    h. Pollution.

Community analysis

Once the most suitable areas of growth pressure have been identified, the site selection research can be narrowed down to the community or communities offering the greatest appreciation potential. It is possible to get a good grasp of overall trends in a metropolitan area but more difficult to gain a good understanding of every community within the area. For this reason the search is best confined to a chosen community or two, and the research should be concentrated there. The quality of the purchase will depend to a good extent on knowledge of the community.

Competition should be taken into consideration in site selection. This includes existing competition; competition that is in the pipeline, as reflected by permits issued; and potential future competition, as measured by the available land inventory in the vicinity. The developer must be cautious in his assumptions that his proposed development can take a certain percentage of the market away from existing competitors. Even when there is justification for assuming he can outperform the competition by creating a monopoly and thereby obsoleting competitors' products, he must use constraint in calculating how much of a market share can be wrenched from competitors. Though the product may truly be unique and skillfully matched to market needs, the potential customers who will perceive this uniqueness may be fewer than anticipated. Of course, their perception can be broadened through skillful merchandizing (see Chapters 30 and 31).

This is not to say that competition is always a constraint to absorption, or complete sale or occupancy of a project. Up to a point competition can be an advantage. The competitors' merchandizing will create traffic in the vicinity, and once there, the potential buyer will tend to visit more projects serving his specific housing needs. To a point, the presence of competition can create greater traffic of potential buyers or renters than an individual project could draw on its own merit.

Absorption rate is a most reliable measure of development outlook. The land buyer must equate price with absorption rate. The developer seeking to make a killing on the land may buy cheap, far-out, or poorly located land. However, if the absorption rate is low, the developer can pay dearly in carrying and merchandizing costs before absorption is achieved. This can more than wipe out the benefit of initial cheap land cost (see Chapter 11).

Not only will the buyer need to know comparable land costs in the area, but he should also research historical prices; what appreciation has been in the past and what it is likely to be in the future. This requires a knowledge of current and probable changes in the area that will influence the value of the property.

Site identification

Visibility has a great influence on rentals or sales, and the self-advertising virtues of a site will have a marked effect on absorption costs. The self-advertising benefits of a site are also an important consideration in establishing the planning concept. It is not uncommon for a developer to pass over a self-advertising site for another because of a relatively small cost differential and then have to pay significantly more to achieve absorption. Or the developer may pay the price for a self-advertising site but plan the development so it does not take advantage of the self-advertising aspects, and thus lose much of the benefit.

Traffic count is an important consideration for residential income property. To a degree traffic count is a measure of the self-advertising value associated with site visibility. Being near a freeway is an advantage to the extent that a high degree of visibility can be achieved, and the freeway extends the geographic market area.

Accessibility can be important to consumer satisfaction, because easy accessibility adds to convenience. Also, the easier it is for a consumer to buy or rent a specific property, the more likely he is to do so. The environmental attractiveness of the immediate access route is a strong determinant in establishing the all-important first impression. The environmental quality or lack of it in the immediate access and entry areas will set the emotional tone for potential buyers or renters before they even consider the merits of the product offered.

In selecting specific sites within target regions, a good plan is to work closely with regional realtors. They are well paid for their services and can provide valuable research data on prospective buyers relative to developmental patterns, prices and price trends, local improvement plans, the political environment, acceptable terms, and so on.

Exhibit 3–1, the site selection checklist, provides for consideration of all the varied details to be taken into account in evaluating a specific site.

ZONING AND OTHER REGULATORY INFLUENCES

Zoning represents a definite constraint on the use of property. Property which is already zoned may have zoning constraints in addition to those specified in the zoning code. Some communities, before issuing a permit for development of a zoned piece of property, may require a dedication for street widening, parks, utility right-of-ways, flood control, or any number of other purposes. The amount and nature of fees imposed (park fee, sewer-tap fee, water fee, flood district fee, bedroom tax, and so on) may affect planning and developmental feasibility. Communities also may utilize building code restrictions to discourage the development of certain type of structures.

Unzoned properties or properties that require rezoning can represent hazards, and a comprehensive understanding of the zoning process and the environment in which this process must take place is required. A developer who seeks a change in straight zoning or to planned unit development (PUD) zoning should investigate zoning matters thoroughly, including:

1. The area planning department's informal position on the proposed rezoning.
2. The relationship of the property to the regional plan.
3. Requirements for an environmental impact report (EIR).
4. Political considerations.

5. Availability of community facilities to support the proposed new use under the rezoning.
6. Community support or lack of it.

Even projects which are good self-contained planning solutions and are recognized as such by planning boards are sometimes turned down because the officials are concerned both with the fiscal impact and the impact upon the character and lifestyle in the community. The desirability of growth itself is in question, even well-planned growth (see Chapter 5).

PHYSICAL AND ENVIRONMENTAL FACTORS

In addition to the on-site and off-site physical factors noted above, the size and shape of the property itself, aside from its location, is probably the most significant factor in site selection. As a property's size increases, so does the potential for planning a self-contained environment independent of off-site physical factors. Additionally, the larger the site, the more the need of diversity of product to achieve absorption. Soil conditions, terrain, tree cover, water-table level, and availability and capacity of utilities provide constraints to the use of the property. Environmental assets inherent in a particular property also may require a substantially different type of land utilization and developmental strategy than would otherwise be appropriate for the same location.

OPPORTUNITIES AND OBSTACLES

Site and proximity evaluation narrows the options available to the builder. In evaluating a site its limitations will become apparent, as well as its potential for the highest and best use. The developer cannot afford to overlook either obstacles or opportunities; these considerations should guide site study from the outset. Not only will they provide limitations for the developer and thus focus the marketing and feasibility analysis to follow more sharply; they may also necessitate a reevaluation of the developer's initial plans. This should be done at an early date so that all work is channeled to the accomplishment of a desirable action plan.

At times, plans will have to be modified to reflect local conditions, and the earlier the better. For example, the developer's initial plan may have been to produce middle-income housing, but an independent evaluation of the site may indicate that it is better suited to a higher income market because it has desirable inherent features and location. The density required for the middle-income housing may destroy the most desirable features of the site. With a different planning and marketing solution, the site could prove to be a very compelling sales feature in the luxury range and could justify handsome lot premiums not possible in the middle-income range.

Potentials and constraints of a property may result from on-site circumstances, off-site circumstances, or a combination of both. These circumstances may be physical, legal, economic, political, or all of these. An analysis of the site should answer such questions as: What major problems are there which act as constraints on the property? What have they been in the past? What are they likely to be in the future?

The next step is to find answers to these questions: What opportunities are available for overcoming these problems? What can be done to transform the liabilities into assets? Then answers are sought for: What assets does the site possess? How can it be utilized to create the greatest opportunity? What effects do the potentials have on the competitive marketing position?

From these kinds of questions it is possible to identify the opportunities and the major obstacles to be overcome. This will ensure that opportunities and obstacles are considered within sufficient time to receive the attention they require. Then a chief planning concern will be to maximize the value of the potentials and minimize the limitations imposed by the constraints. At times, through innovative planning, a constraint can be transformed into a potential.

The following case studies illustrate the importance of early identification of opportunities and obstacles.

CASE STUDY I: MEASURING DEGREE OF COMPATABILITY BETWEEN SITE, DEVELOPMENT CONCEPT AND MARKET OPPORTUNITY

A developer had purchased a site on a heavily traveled and noisy main street in a good neighborhood for the purpose of constructing luxury condominiums for "empty nesters." He had paid a premium for the site because of the location on the main thoroughfare, which was a good commercial location though zoned multifamily residential.

As consultants, we were brought in to do a marketing–value engineering report after the developer had completed his preliminary drawings based on the multifamily zoning. After examining the site to determine potentials and constraints, we found several constraints to be readily apparent. The proposed units which faced onto the thoroughfare had a view of the traffic and were exposed to street noises. The units facing the sides had views of older properties ranging from less desirable to unattractive. Small side yards cut down on available light.

The property was not of sufficient size to allow a controlled environmental planning solution which related inward, and feasibility required a minimum of four stories over parking. Comparable development in the area generally had better off-site orientation and a lower land cost per unit because it was not located on the main thoroughfare. As a result, the subject units would be at a disadvantage in competing with comparable property, or comparables, in the immediate market.

In essence, the developer had paid a premium for a site that had severe constraints as related to the proposed development concept. A redesign based on marketing findings minimized the negative effects of the constraints, and the concept was adjusted to better reflect the potentialities of the site. The site potential was somewhat less than the luxury market the developer had intended to serve, and he found that he had overpaid for the site. Additionally, the marketing study indicated that the luxury market had been thinned out by significant recent activity.

Had the developer objectively assessed the site's opportunities and constraints from the beginning he could have saved much time and expense. Once they were pointed out to the developer, the constraints were so obvious he wondered how he could have missed them. The site was generally a good one, on an excellent street in a good neighborhood, and the developer was willing to pay for quality. The problem arose when he did not, at an early date, look into the specifics of the site as it related to the intended development concept and target market. The restructured concept presented a viable development opportunity but at less profit than anticipated at the time the property was acquired. It was, in effect, the lesser of two evils.

CASE STUDY II: OVERCOMING OBSTACLES AND CONSTRAINTS BY GOOD PLANNING

Another developer had purchased a large site zoned for in excess of 700 units, with only 760 lineal feet of street frontage, for the purpose of developing multifamily rental units. Because of the narrow property configuration and limited frontage, the developer was able to purchase the

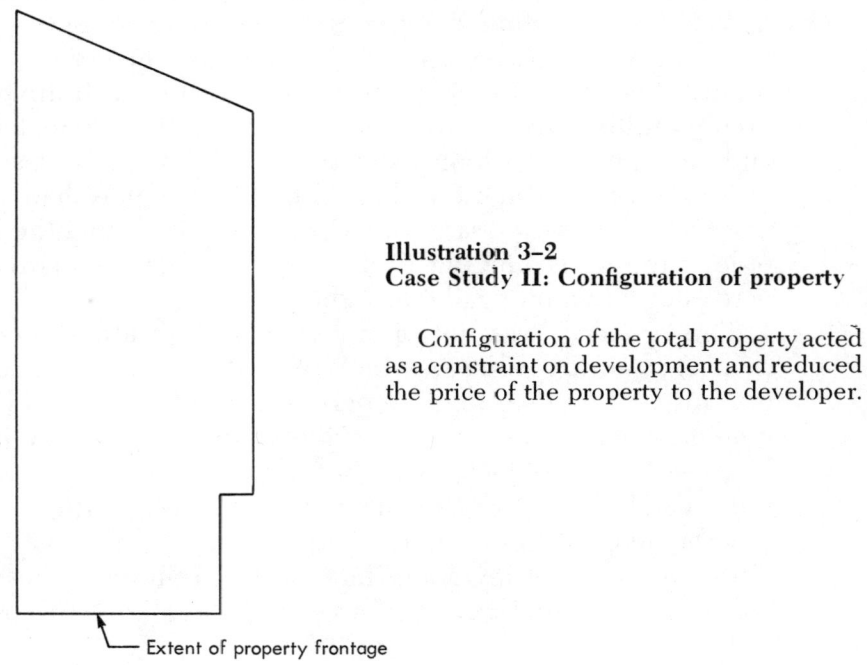

**Illustration 3–2
Case Study II: Configuration of property**

Configuration of the total property acted as a constraint on development and reduced the price of the property to the developer.

land for an attractive price. In other words, the price reflected the constraints imposed by the property (see Illustration 3–2).

Because of the size of the property, it was not feasible to develop it in one stage. Additionally, flexibility required that the development stages be designed as separate entities to facilitate financing and ultimate sale. With the very narrow frontage, the developer was having great difficulty in land planning the property for two or more developments, while at the same time providing a self-advertising window for each of the developments in the limited frontage. He had asked several consultants to attempt to develop a workable land plan. Most of these plans consisted of varying approaches for dividing the property lengthwise, front to rear, with each portion fronting (though narrowly) on the frontage street. The resultant internal layouts were environmentally unattractive and created severe internal traffic and fire department access problems.

The solution ultimately utilized was to divide the property into two parcels, front and rear, with the front parcel claiming most of the street frontage (see Illustration 3–3). This approach provided for a better internal planning solution, with a controlled interior environment (see Illustration 3–4), which the long, thin development strips did not. The rear parcel was given a window onto the front street by an impressive divided private street, with dramatic landscaping and heroic-size trellises and fountains at the entry. The dramatic entry gave promise of the rich environment within.

The merchandizing and land-planning concepts were developed together. The front development, with four lakes, was planned to merchandize lakeside living. The rear development, with the existing large trees and natural stream at the rear of the property, would emphasize a woods and creek environment. With the front part of the development aimed for the adult market, the rear phase of the development could go either adult or family, depending on current market conditions at the time.

Because of the dramatic entry on the frontage street, the gracefully curving, landscaped private road entrance, and the large trees and brook, the rear development does not take a back-seat position to the front development. It has its own exclusive, unique appeal and an entry that provides a dramatic and exclusive self-advertising bonus.

The solution was enthusiastically received because it was successful both in circumventing a severe constraint imposed by the property and in maximizing the inherent potentials of the site. By neutralizing the constraint imposed by the shape of the property, the planning solution increased property values for the developer. Had the seller offered the planning solution to the developer he would not have had to discount the property because of the constraints imposed by its shape. Most importantly, the planning solutions allowed for a quality development. The previous unacceptable plans would have resulted in a marginal development with a restricted market. For such a development, even the discounted land price would have been high.

Illustration 3-3
Case Study II: Front development

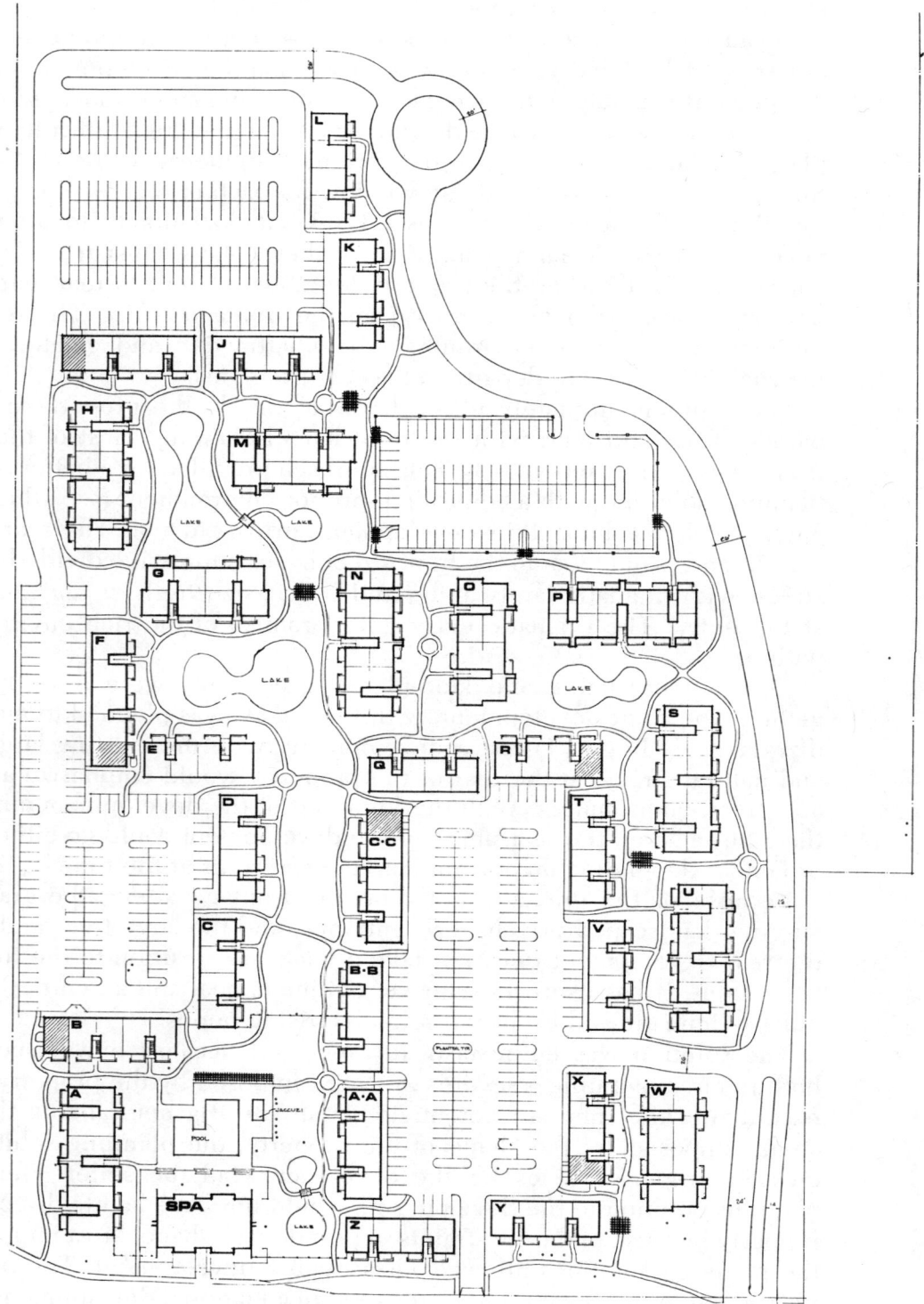

Main frontage road

How first phase of 358-unit project utilizes property frontage, while allowing for a private entry road to service an additional development behind. Curb identity for the second project is developed by dramatic treatment of entry road at public street, including trellises, fountains, mounding, boulder treatment, and signs.

Illustration 3–4
Case Study II: Typical interior courtyard treatment

Parking areas have been screened from primary court areas, and parking is hidden in secondary parking courts.

EARLY RECOGNITION OF OPPORTUNITIES AND OBSTACLES

The case studies presented above illustrate the importance of recognizing site opportunities and obstacles at an early date. In the first study, had the developer recognized the constraints early he would not have purchased the site at the price he did. In the second case, had the seller recognized the opportunities for solving constraints due to the shape of the property, he would not have sold the property for the price he did.

Exhibit 3–1
Site Selection Checklist

Date _____

Owner's name _____
Address _____ Phone _____
Property location (major crossroads) _____
_____
City _____ County _____
Broker's firm name _____ Address _____
Phone _____
Current use of property _____
Is any income produced? _____
If land is   , what are terms? _____
Property currently zoned _____ Master plan calls for zoning to be _____

3 / Locational analysis and site evaluation   33

Exhibit 3–1 (*continued*)

PHYSICAL ANALYSIS

Size of property _____ net; _____ gross
Frontage feet _____ Other frontage _____
Planning problems due to:
  Site configuration _____
  Access _____
  Topography _____
  Easements _____
  Water courses and storm drainage _____
  Objectional off-site features: Noise, unsightly development which would require special planning solutions _____
_____

Planning opportunities due to:
  Lake, river, stream, pond _____
  Attractive, mature trees _____
  Attractive views _____
  Attractive neighboring uses _____
Is site self-advertising? _____
Topography _____
Type of soil _____ Soil report available? _____ Summary of report _____
_____

Will much earth movement, fill, or compaction be required? _____ Cost _____
Will excessive foundation costs result from soil and topographical conditions?
_____

How much land may be lost due to:
  Vertical slopes _____
  Flood areas _____
  Unusual site configurations _____
  Setbacks and easements _____
Physical improvements _____ Approximate value _____ Condition _____
Can improvements be utilized? _____ Is demolition necessary? _____ Cost _____
Does site possess any outstanding attributes? _____ What potentials do these attributes contribute? _____
_____

Are there major constraints identified with property? _____
_____

Does property have any of the following constraints:

	Yes, No	*Explanation*
Floods	_____	_____
Earthquake faults	_____	_____

Exhibit 3-1 (*continued*)

	Yes, No	*Explanation*
Objectional traffic	_____	_____
Poor drainage	_____	_____
Objectional air traffic	_____	_____
Unsightly views	_____	_____
Unsightly neighbors	_____	_____
Noise	_____	_____
In-flight pattern	_____	_____
Fire hazards	_____	_____
Slide danger	_____	_____

ACCESSIBILITY

	Driving time	*Miles*
Distance to commercial hub	_____	_____
Distance to employment center(s)	_____	_____
Distance to airport	_____	_____
Distance to entertainment	_____	_____
Distance to freeway(s)	_____	_____

Type of construction and condition of frontage road _____

Ingress/egress restrictions _____
Will frontage road accommodate proposed traffic? _____
Private road _____ State highway _____ County road _____
U.S. Highway _____ Other _____
Any costs to acquire or improve access? _____
If private road, is there legally guaranteed right-of-ingress/egress to property? _____

Any proposed highway and freeway plans that would affect property? _____

Bus service: Good _____ Fair _____ Poor _____
Other rapid transit available _____ Distance _____
How frequent is service? _____ Cost _____
Tolls: Bridges _____ Freeways _____

UTILITIES

Gas at site: Yes _____ No _____ Distance from site _____
Size _____ Cost to extend _____ Any problems with use? _____ Service fee _____

Electricity at site: Yes _____ No _____ Distance from site _____
Must relocate? _____ Go underground off site? _____ Cost _____
Any problems with use? _____ Service fee _____

Water at site: Yes _____ No _____ Distance from site _____
Size, pressure _____ Cost to extend _____ Any problem with use? _____ Water furnished by _____ Are costs refunded to

Exhibit 3–1 (*continued*)

developer? _____ Formula _____ Service fee _____
Water wells _____ Depth _____ Capacity _____
Any problems with use? _____ Depth of ground water _____
Sewer at site: Yes _____ No _____ Distance from site _____
Size _____ Depth _____ Cost to extend _____
Service fee _____ Will pumping station be required? _____ Cost _____

POLITICAL, SOCIAL, AND ENVIRONMENTAL FACTORS

Is community discouraging growth through:
  Moratoriums _____
  Excessive processing time, indecision _____
  Excessive fees _____
  Environmental impact restrictions _____
  Refusing services _____
Will there be vocal antigrowth citizens' groups to contend with? _____
Is there danger of zoning rollbacks? _____
Are there conflicting policy guides and jurisdictions which make it difficult to ascertain requirements and to secure approvals? _____

Are elections forthcoming which would place heavy political influence on governmental and municipal policies? _____ Would these influences be positive or negative? _____

Are there planning policies or studies in the works which would affect the master plan and create an interim vacuum of indecision or no decision? _____

Are there any new taxes or tax hikes on the horizon which would have a material effect on feasibility? _____

Are there building code restrictions which would economically discourage certain types of construction? _____

Are there fire department restrictions which would economically discourage certain types of construction and planning? _____

Are there traffic department policies which would economically discourage development? _____ or reject development plans? _____

Are there polution policies which would discourage or halt development plans? _____

Is environmental impact report required? _____
Are there rent controls? _____ Possibility of controls in near future _____
FHA outlook:
Area _____
Site _____
Sales or rental range _____
How many commitments will they give? _____
Do they have recent studies available? _____

Exhibit 3-1 (*continued*)

VA outlook:
Area _____
Site _____
Sales or rental range _____
How many commitments will they make? _____
Do they have recent studies available? _____
Local bank advice _____
Local savings and loan advice _____
Local builder's association advice _____
Local title company advice _____
Local engineer's advice _____
Local mortgage banker–broker advice _____
Building department discussion _____
_____

Planning department discussion _____
_____

Availability of subcontractors, suppliers, and workmen _____
_____

Local appraiser's evaluation of market _____
Realtor's advice _____

COMPARATIVE EVALUATION

How does property compare with other comparable properties in area? _____
_____

Is property higher or lower in price than comparables? _____ Why? _____

Is there a particular potential for adding value to this property though creative financing, planning, subdivision, or rezoning that others may have overlooked?
_____

Is there a current or emerging new development pattern, trend, fad, or cycle which will change the potential of the property from what others have recognized it to be in the past? _____
_____

What development is land suitable for at this moment? _____
_____ In 2 to 3 years? _____ In 5 years? _____
Would the land be an attractive investment, from inflation and speculative interests alone, if no value were added through planning, packaging, or rezoning? _____
_____

What was cost of comparable land 1 year ago? _____ 2 years ago? _____
4 years ago? _____
Where is the price in relation to the ultimate end user price? _____
_____

Exhibit 3–1 (*concluded*)

At what time will the property justify the ultimate end user price? _____
_____

If property is currently at the end user price, what can realistically be anticipated for inflationary-appreciation gain per year? _____

Considering terms and price, how long can the organization afford to hold the land before developing or selling it? _____

Tax advantages associated with property:
    Interest deduction _____
    Property tax deduction _____
    Tree removal _____
    Depreciation of trees _____
    Depreciation of equipment _____
    Depreciation of buildings _____
Major constraints associated with property _____
_____

Major opportunities associated with property _____
_____

How does investment in property compare with other opportunities available to the organization? _____
_____

4

Determining land value, optimum terms, and profitability

Residential non-income-producing land is measured by two basic values; owner value (subjective) and market value. Residential income-producing property is measured by three basic values: owner value, market value, and investment value.

In this chapter on site valuation, only market value will be covered (so as not to duplicate the material in other chapters). See the section on the land-residual method in Chapter 19, Financial Analysis, for how to determine highest and best use and value at highest and best use. See the same chapter for value concepts, components, and additional material on market value analysis.

Though the emphasis in this book, is on real estate development rather than land investment, the fact is that many real estate developers warehouse land in order to add a land profit to developmental or builder profit. For this reason, in this section land will be considered as an investment as well as a necessary element in the development and building process.

It is important to exercise care not to overpay for property, and analytical tools should be used to determine a justified price, but it is also necessary to recognize that value appreciation is more important to profitability than price. Obtaining an attractive appreciation factor requires skill and patience in selection of the property. Once the opportunity has been identified through skillful search and selection, the buyer will want to determine what price is justified by the site.

LAND VALUATION: WHAT PRICE IS JUSTIFIED? The first step in the land valuation of a specific parcel is to assemble a representative sampling of land comparables. The land comparables may vary in location, size, zoning, price, quality of on-site features, and cost of off-site improvements required for development. Though it is desirable to assemble comparables which are very similar to the subject site to be evaluated, this is not always possible. Analysis will then be required to adjust the price of the comparables to reflect the variances listed above.

The Land Comparables Adjustment Sheet (Exhibit 4–1) can be utilized to adjust the price of the land comparables. The various price adjustment factors are explained below.

Time   The price of the comparables must be adjusted to reflect the appreciation which has occurred from the time of sale to the present. For example, if land in the area is typically appreciating at a 12 percent yearly rate, and two years has elapsed from the time of sale of a comparable, add 24 percent to the price to adjust the historical price to the current market price.

Site evaluation   Some sites are inherently better or worse than others, irrespective of location. The quality will be reflected in the sales price. Sites with poor soils will not command the same price as otherwise equal sites with good soils. Poor drainage, grading problems which render a portion of the site unbuildable, poor ingress and egress also affect price. An unusual site configuration may hamper planning and reduce potential utilization. On the other hand, attractive trees and views, and compatible neighbors will enhance the value of the property. The prices of the comparables should be adjusted to reflect variances between the comparable sites and the subject site.

Location analysis   The price of the comparables should also be adjusted to reflect variances in price due to location. The object is to adjust the price of the comparables so that the adjusted price reflects a location value similar to that of the subject property. If a comparable is in a better location than the subject property, then the price of the comparable should be adjusted down to reflect what its price would be if it were in a similar location to that of the subject property.

Off-site improvements   The cost of required off-site improvements affects land pricing. For example, most buyers will evaluate off-site improvement costs as a part of the price of the land. If a buyer must pay $15,000 to extend water and sewer lines to a $100,000 piece of property, he will generally consider his property cost to be $115,000. If the subject property has all necessary services to the property line and a comparable property does not, the price of the comparable should be adjusted upward to reflect the cost of the necessary off-site improvements. That is, the comparable property should be made similar to the subject property as far as off-site improvements are concerned.

Zoning, legal

The value of a property is constrained by easements, encumbrances, and restrictions. For example, a portion of the property may be unbuildable because of an easement, or a title may be clouded by complex restrictions requiring expensive legal work to clarify the title. Property which is zoned multifamily has more value than property which is potentially multifamily but requires rezoning. If the subject property is zoned multifamily and a comparable is potential multifamily but not yet so zoned, then the value of the comparable should be adjusted upward to reflect its zoned value. This would then make it similar, from a zoning standpoint, to the subject property.

The actual price adjustment can be accomplished by using either a percentage or a fixed-cost adjustment factor. A percentage adjustment factor has been utilized on the Land Comparables Adjustment Sheet included as Exhibit 4–1.

RANKING THE COMPARABLES

It is helpful to rank the comparables according to their relative similarity to the subject site. In the Land Comparables Ranking Sheet (Exhibit 4–2), each site is ranked for each of the price adjustment factors. In the off-site improvements column, Site 3 is comparable to the subject site and requires no adjustment to establish comparability. Sites 1 and 5 require more off-site improvement costs than the subject property, so their price needs to be adjusted upward to reflect the added costs. Sites 2, 6, 4, and 7 require fewer off-site improvement costs than the subject site, so their prices need to be adjusted downward by the difference between what is required to improve the subject property and each of the comparables. The cost unit being utilized is cost per net acre.

Once the adjusted price per net acre has been determined for each of the land comparables, each comparable is plotted on the Land Comparables Relationship Chart (Exhibit 4–3). The relationship chart establishes the relationship between property size and cost per net acre. The vertical axis represents acres and the horizontal axis represents price. When all of the comparables have been plotted, a trend line is drawn which represents the market price trend for the subject property. If the subject property is 22 acres, its market value will be approximately $17,000 per net acre, according to the Land Comparables Relationship Chart.

Once the market value is determined for the property (opportunity), the negotiator can use this as a starting basis for negotiation. Through skillful negotiation, the profitability of the opportunity can be further enhanced.

SENSITIVITY ANALYSIS

In calculating the desirability of a land investment there is a problem in developing the criteria required for analysis. It is not known for certain how much the property will appreciate in value over the holding period or how long the holding period will be. Additionally, both the buy and sell prices and terms must be known in order to calculate profitability. In that these conditions cannot be predetermined with accuracy, it is prudent to calculate profitability within a range of conditions varying from pessimistic to optimistic. Also it is beneficial to know which specific conditions produce the greatest variance in profitability calculations as they vary from pessimistic to optimistic.

Giving consideration to variances in conditions and the sensitivity of the individual conditions in affecting profitability, is termed sensitivity analysis. Sensitivity analysis is required for the negotiation of optimum terms and measurement of the risk associated with the profitability. See Chapter 19 for more on sensitivity analysis.

LEVERAGE

Land can be purchased with no leverage (all cash), leverage (equity and borrowed funds), or ultimate leverage (all borrowed funds—no purchaser equity). Ultimate leverage requires an unsecured line of credit based on net worth, or additional security in addition to the land.

Leverage enables the investor to control land values far in excess of the equity contribution and to benefit from the total value increase on the land. Leverage also works in reverse, however, thus increasing risk. To benefit from leverage one must buy property on a highly leveraged basis and sell it on a low-leverage or no-leverage basis. If the land is sold on the same high-leverage basis on which it is purchased, much of the value of leverage is lost. A highly leveraged sale will not generate a significant cash gain to the investor-seller, even though the property may have appreciated handsomely. The present value of future payments to be received is diminished the further the payments extend into the future (see Chapter 19).

To preclude the loss of leverage on the sale, land can be purchased in the intermediate to latter stages of the growth stage and resold to the ultimate end user. Because the end user will desire to develop the property, he will generally clear the title immediately, or in the very near future. This will provide a no-leverage or relatively fast payout to the investor who sells to the end user.

In times of high interest rates, investors will sometimes purchase land with minimal or no leverage. This reduces risk and can produce an acceptable investment by eliminating costly financing carrying costs.

THE PROFITABILITY FACTORS

Before-tax land profitability is affected by six basic factors:

1. The buy terms.
2. The sell terms.
3. Natural and inherent appreciation during the holding period.
4. Value added during holding period, leasing, rezoning, and subdivision.

5. Expenses paid out during the holding period.
6. Duration of both the holding and cash-out periods.

These six factors include variables or terms which express the substance of the factors. For simplicity, only the principal elements comprising these six profitability factors will be considered. The buy and sell terms include contract duration, interest rate, percentage down payment, allocation of fees, and miscellaneous expenses. The natural and inherent appreciation during the holding period includes natural appreciation in the region and community and any unforseen, one-time or ongoing developments which affect the value of the site. Value added during the holding period includes leasing income and value appreciation due to rezoning or subdivision efforts. Expenses paid out during the holding period include taxes, improvements, costs associated with rezoning or subdivision, and maintenance. Duration of both the holding and cash-out periods include length of time between buy and sell, length of contract and length of time to cash out of buy contract, length of contract, and length of time to cash out of sell contract.

NEGOTIATING OPTIMUM TERMS

Negotiation for optimum terms requires sensitivity analysis to determine which terms and relationships have the greatest profit sensitivity. The object is to trade off terms with low profit sensitivity to gain terms with favorable, high profit sensitivity. The profit sensitivity of the terms will be dependent on the opportunity value of capital. The opportunity value of capital is defined as that rate of return which the investor could reasonably expect to receive on other competing investments which are available to him.

The negotiator needs to know the answer to such questions as:

1. How much of an increase in price is justified by a given reduction in down payment?
2. How much of a reduction in down payment is justified by a given increase in interest rate?
3. What adjustments can be made concerning contract period versus price, price versus interest rate, and interest versus contract period, while maintaining the same profitability?

Basic options available to the negotiator include:

1. Interest rate versus price.
2. Interest rate versus down payment.
3. Interest rate versus contract period.
4. Contract period versus down payment.
5. Price versus down payment.
6. Price versus contract period.

Though there are many other subtleties in land negotiation — nonfinancial terms, rights and responsibilities which affect risks and rewards, release and subordination provisions, and miscellaneous costs and fees—the options listed above are the basic trading or negotiation options in land transactions. The sensitivity of these six options to the profitability must be known if the negotiator is to be effective. Knowing the profit sensitivity of the options with exactness requires a computer capability or the utilization of charts based on computer output.

NEGOTIATING STRATEGIES

The optimum strategy will show the optimum profitability available within the confines of the negotiator's objectives, financial capabilities, and constraints. That is, certain terms may possess more subjective value to the negotiator than others, regardless of the effect on profitability of the subject negotiation. For example, if immediate liquidity is a problem, the negotiator will want to reduce the down payment requirement for subjective reasons (lack of liquidity) and sacrifice some profitability, if necessary, to negotiate within the liquidity constraint. Or conversely, if liquidity is no problem, the negotiator may want to offer a larger down payment in return for lower price, a longer contract period, or lower interest.

An example of the negotiating options available in presenting a counter-offer to a property investment proposal will provide an insight into the profit enhancement potential of optimum-terms negotiation. Assume that a property in which a purchaser is interested is offered under the following terms:

Alternate A: The offer
  $100,000 price
  30% down payment
  7% interest
  Balance due on a 10-year contract

Assume further that the opportunity value of capital for the potential purchaser is 15 percent.

Given the above terms and opportunity value of capital, the sensitivity of the six basic negotiation options listed in the preceding section can be investigated. The actual calculations, however, are beyond the scope of this book, since (as noted above) they require computer capability or reliance upon graphs developed from computer output. The exercise is merely to show the profitability consequences of the possible negotiating options and the importance of understanding these consequences in the negotiating process. The six basic negotiating options are listed below, along with the consequences (sensitivity) of variations in the terms.

1. Interest rate versus price.
    a. Increasing the interest rate to $8\frac{1}{2}$ would justify a price reduction of 4 percent.
    b. Reducing interest rate to $5\frac{1}{2}$ percent would justify a price increase of $4\frac{1}{3}$ percent.

  c. Observation: In this instance, changes in the interest rate justify small changes in the price.
2. Interest rate versus down payment.
  a. Increasing the interest rate to 8½ percent would justify a reduction in down payment from 30 to 16 percent.
  b. Reducing the interest rate to 5½ percent would justify an increase in down payment from 30 to 41 percent.
  c. Observation: In this instance, the amount of down payment justified is sensitive to changes in the interest rate.
3. Interest rate versus contract period.
  a. Reducing the interest rate to 5½ percent will justify a reduction in the contract period from ten to eight years.
  b. Increasing the interest rate to 8½ percent will justify an increase in the contract period from 10 years to 13¾ years.
  c. Observation: The contract period is not that sensitive to changes in the interest rate.
4. Contract period versus down payment.
  a. Increasing the contract period to 20 years from 10 years justifies an increase in the down payment from 30 to 48 percent.
  b. Reducing the contract period to seven and a half from ten years justifies a reduction in down payment from 30 to 15 percent.
  c. Observation: In this instance, the amount of down payment justified is sensitive to changes in the contract period.
5. Price versus down payment.
  a. Reducing down payment to 15 percent justifies a price increase of 5½ percent.
6. Price versus contract period.
  a. Increasing contract period to 20 years justifies an increase in price of 13 percent.
  b. Reducing contract period to seven and a half years justifies a decrease in price of 4½ percent.

Upon reviewing the sensitivity of variances in the six basic negotiation options, the negotiator can prepare a counteroffer to enhance his subjective position and profitability. Assuming that the negotiator's subjective position is one of limited liquidity, he can enhance his position by achieving a lower down payment. He then can make the following counteroffer:

Alternate B: The counteroffer
 $110,000 price
 15% down payment
 8% interest
 20-year contract

COMPUTING PROFITABILITY To determine the profitability to the negotiator of the offer (Alternate A) versus the counteroffer (Alternate B), a holding term of seven years, an annual appreciation of 20 percent, and a cash sale at the end of the holding period is assumed for both alternates. A simplified, pretax cash flow position is then projected for both alternates (see Exhibits 4–4 and 4–5), and the internal rate of return is calculated for each of the cash flows. Alternate A shows a 21 percent internal rate of return and Alternate B shows a 24 percent internal rate of return to the negotiator. Should the negotiator be successful in purchasing the property with his counteroffer terms, he will have greatly enhanced his subjective position (limited liquidity) and increased his internal rate of return in so doing.

ENHANCING THE COUNTEROFFER

To enhance his counteroffer to the seller, the negotiator could additionally offer several alternatives:

1. He could offer to pay 4 percent rather than 8 percent interest to the seller and add the difference between 4 and 8 percent to land cost, to make the seller's profit a capital gain rather than an ordinary gain. This would also enhance the negotiator's subjective position (limited liquidity).

2. In setting up rolling options, he could leave the most desirable land, from the standpoint of highest and best use, until last, to provide the seller with good security.

3. As an incentive to the seller, when tying up land with a contract of sale, the negotiator can offer to the seller the market and engineering studies that may have been completed in seeking rezoning, in the event the rezoning is unsuccessful.

4. The negotiator could offer tax-fee municipal bonds for deposit money. These bonds can often be bought at a discount of as much as 50 percent of the face value. In this manner, the negotiator gets credit for a $10,000 deposit payment that may only represent $5,000 to $7,000 in out-of-pocket cost.

5. The negotiator can attempt to purchase the mortgage rather than the property, with an option to purchase the property during the life of the mortgage. This plan has the seller paying the negotiator to control his land. The mortgage, which is tax free to the seller, can be used by the seller to pay off current debts or an existing mortgage about to expire. The seller (current land owner) continues to pay property taxes in addition to interest on the new mortgage.

The buyer can now spin the mortgage off to his bank. The negotiator can charge the seller the placement fee and the legal fees to close the deal. It is important that the option be superior to the mortgage. In the event the mortgage is paid off, the option will still live.

After making mortgage payments for a time, the owner may reanalyze the deal and want out. At this point he may be willing to sell at a discount from the price stated in the option.

COMPUTING DOWNSIDE RISK

Having determined that the counteroffer, if accepted, will produce a 24 percent internal rate of return if the land appreciates at 20 percent per year, the negotiator should recalculate to determine downside risk in the event that the 20 percent appreciation rate does not materialize. The negotiator should calculate the land appreciation rate which will allow a 15 percent internal rate of return, since 15 percent has been established by the negotiator as his opportunity value of capital. A land-appreciation rate which will produce an internal rate of return less than 15 percent will result in an unsatisfactory investment.

Exhibit 4–1
Land Comparables Adjustment Sheet

Site No.	Date	Area		Net price (per acre)	Zoning		Price adjustment factors				Adjusted price, net (per acre)
		Gross (acres)	Net (acres)		Present	Future	Site evaluation	Location analysis	Off-Site improvements	Zoning, legal	
1	Sale 1 yr. ago	8.0	8.0	$16,000	Agriculture	Multi-family	+15%	+8%	+10%	0%	+45% $23,200
2	Current sale	12.0	11.5	$24,000	Agriculture	Multi-family	−10%	0%	−5%	0%	−15% $20,400
3	Current sale	15.0	14.7	$22,000	Multi-family	Multi-family	0%	+12%	0%	−15%	−3% $21,340
4	Sale 1 yr. ago	20.0	19.3	$19,000	Agriculture	Multi-family	0%	−10%	−8%	0%	−6% $17,860
5	Sale 2 yrs. ago	26.5	25.0	$12,000	Multi-family	Multi-family	+10%	0%	+4%	−15%	+23% $14,760
6	Sale 2 yrs. ago	34.0	32.0	$11,000	Multi-family	Multi-family	+15%	+8%	−5%	−15%	+27% $13,970
7	Current sale	37.0	36.0	$19,000	Multi-family	Multi-family	+10%	−10%	−10%	−20%	−30% $13,300

Exhibit 4–2
Land Comparables Ranking Sheet

Rank	Time	Location analysis	Off-site improvements	Zoning, legal	Site analysis
Inferior to subject	Sites 5, 6	Site 3	Site 1		Sites 1, 6
	Sites 1, 4	Sites 1, 6	Site 5		Sites 5, 7
Comparable to subject	Sites 2, 3, 7	Sites 2, 5	Site 3	Sites 1, 2, 4	Sites 3, 4
Superior to subject		Sites 4, 7	Sites 2, 6	Sites 3, 5, 6	Site 2
			Site 4	Site 7	
			Site 7		

Exhibit 4-3
Land Comparables Relationship Chart

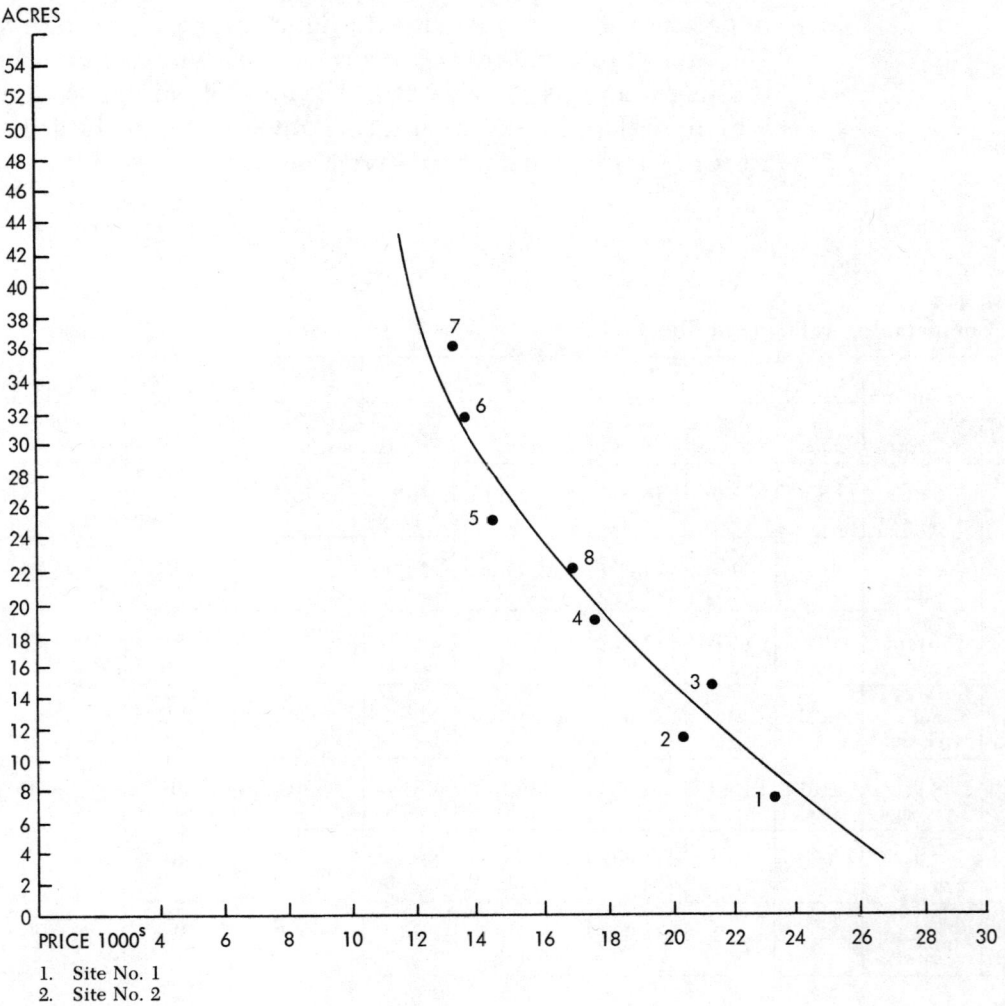

1. Site No. 1
2. Site No. 2
3. Site No. 3
4. Site No. 4
5. Site No. 5
6. Site No. 6
7. Site No. 7
8. Subject property

Exhibit 4–4
Alternate A: Cash Flow Calculation and Internal Rate of Return

	Period							
	0	1	2	3	4	5	6	7
Cash Outflow								
1. Down payment	$300							
2. Contract payments		$ 98.3	$ 98.3	$ 98.3	$ 98.3	$ 98.3	$ 98.3	$ 98.3
3. Balloon payments								
4. Cash-out payment								262.5
5. Improvements								
6. Maintenance								
7. Property tax		25	25	25	25	25	25	25
8. Buy costs								
9. Sell costs								394.0
10. Fees, services								
11. Income tax								
12. Subtotal—Outflow	($300)	($123.3)	($123.3)	($123.3)	($123.3)	($123.3)	($123.3)	($ 779.8)
Cash Inflow								
13. Down payment								
14. Contract payments								
15. Balloon payments								
16. Cash-Out payment								$3,583
17. Rental income								
18. Tax benefit								
19. Subtotal—Inflow								($3,583)
Net Cash Flow								
20. Net outflow	$300	$123.3	$123.3	$123.3	$123.3	$123.3	$123.3	
21. Net inflow								$2,804.2

Internal Rate of Return

Period	21% discount factor	Present-worth outlay	Present-worth inflow
0		$300	
1	.8950	110.3	
2	.7268	89.6	
3	.5902	72.8	
4	.4793	59.1	
5	.3892	49.0	
6	.3160	39.0	
7	.2566	200.1	$919.4
		$918.9	$919.4

Exhibit 4–5
Alternate B: Cash Flow Calculation and Internal Rate of Return

	Period							
	0	1	2	3	4	5	6	7
Cash Outflow								
1. Down payment	$165							
2. Contract payments		$ 94.2	$ 94.2	$ 94.2	$ 94.2	$ 94.2	$ 94.2	$ 94.2
3. Balloon payments								
4. Cash-out payment								756.4
5. Improvements								
6. Maintenance								
7. Property tax		27.5	27.5	27.5	27.5	27.5	27.5	27.5
8. Buy costs								
9. Sell costs								433.5
10. Fees, services								
11. Income tax								
12. Subtotal—Outflow	($165)	($121.7)	($121.7)	($121.7)	($121.7)	($121.7)	($121.7)	($1,311.6)
Cash Inflow								
13. Down payment								
14. Contract payments								
15. Balloon payments								
16. Cash-out payment								$3,941.3
17. Rental income								
18. Tax benefit								
19. Subtotal—Inflow								($3,941.3)
Net Cash Flow								
20. Net Outflow	$165	$121.7	$121.7	$121.7	$121.7	$121.7	$121.7	
21. Net Inflow								$2,629.7

Internal Rate of Return

Period	24% discount factor	Present-worth outlay	Present-worth Inflow
0		$165	
1	.8813	107.2	
2	.6949	84.6	
3	.5479	66.7	
4	.4320	52.6	
5	.3406	41.4	
6	.2686	32.7	
7	.2118	277.8	$834.8
		$828	$834.8

Exhibit 4-6
Negotiation Checklist

Does seller really want to sell? _____
What are seller's financial objectives? _____
Does owner have good understanding of real estate? _____ Finance? _____
Will broker cooperate on commission? _____ Can commission be deferred? _____ What is commission? _____
Asking price: _____, per gross acre _____, net per acre _____, per unit _____
Down payment asked _____ Mortgage interest percentage _____ Is seller firm on price and terms? _____
Will seller subordinate? _____
How will land be secured? _____
How and when will land be transferred? _____
Releases _____
Time to closing _____ Extensions _____
Amount of purchase money mortgage _____
Payments: Monthly _____ Quarterly _____
Semiannually _____ Annually _____
Amount of installment payment(s) _____ Terms _____

Exhibit 4-7
Title, Liens, Restrictions Checklist

Mechanics liens _____ Tax liens _____
Judgment liens _____ Will liens be cleared prior to closing? _____
Assessments _____ Will assessments be paid by buyer or seller? _____
Public utility easements _____ Other easements _____
Required Dedications _____
Who has mineral rights? _____
Can harmful easements, rights be cleared prior to closing? _____
Is condemnation being considered? _____
Park _____ School _____ Freeway _____
Open Space _____ Watershed _____ Other _____
Is current title report available? _____
Is plot shown? _____ Is title as represented? _____
Anything detrimental that cannot be cleared prior to closing? _____

Title insurance at expense of seller or buyer? _____
Type of title insurance _____ Title Company _____
Other proof _____

Exhibit 4-8
Existing Financing Checklist

FIRST LIEN: Principal to be paid _____ Payable to _____
Monthly _____ Quarterly _____
Semiannually _____ Annually _____
Other _____
Interest _____ Balloon payments _____
Can lien be assumed? _____
Prepayment penalty _____
Releases _____ On what basis _____
SECOND LIEN: Principal to be paid _____ Payable to _____
Monthly _____ Quarterly _____
Semiannually _____ Annually _____
Other _____
Interest _____ Balloon payments _____
Can lien be assumed? _____
Prepayment penalty _____
Releases _____ On what basis _____
Balloon payments _____
Can mortgage be assumed? _____
Any prepayment penalty? _____
Who is trustee? _____
Duration of escrow? _____ Escrow agent _____
Escrow to be split, _____ % seller, _____ % buyer.
Whose contract documents? _____
Who pays legal fees? _____ % seller _____ % buyer.
Conditions to buyer's obligations: Availability of utilities _____
Buyer's approval of soil report _____ Minimum soil condition _____
Free and clear title _____ Approval by buyer of engineering cost study
_____ Costs not to exceed _____ Approval of zone change from
_____ to _____ Approval of annexation _____ Approval of PUD permit
_____ Use permit _____ Building permit _____ Financing _____
Other _____

5

Legal, political, and environmental constraints

The recent proliferation of land-use policy regulations at the national level has been piecemeal and uncoordinated, often lacking either economic justification or practical guidelines or tools for implementation. In general, national policies slow the growth rate of the construction industry, increase the cost of construction, and redirect growth. With national policies in effect, housing growth is guided more by political and social considerations than by economic factors. Thus the valuable constraints and checks and balances controlling the private sector, which are necessary if profit is to be realized, are lacking.

CONFLICTING LEGISLATION

Much of the legislation at the federal level creates a conflict between environmental and social goals and economic objectives. This general failure to mesh social-environmental and economic goals into a workable plan creates continued conflict and uncertainty, as reflected in legal action. Though the legislation is well intentioned and designed to promote admirable economic and social goals, nonetheless federal legislation has created a no-growth rather than a growth housing policy. It matters little whether the no-growth policy has been developed by conscious intent or by accident, as a result of uncoordinated efforts to promulgate regulations without a comprehensive understanding of their implications.

The zealous attempts of the environmentalists to put into effect strict environmental standards, which are in effect no-growth policies, have created a backlash which has been emphasized by the realistic demands of the energy crisis. Failure to establish workable procedures and set reasonable targets has created a rash of lawsuits involving the private sector. As a result, federal agencies, state governments, and municipalities are now exercising more discretion in the use of environmental controls. The larger metropolitan areas, which were the first to introduce tough standards, have pulled back and relaxed standards, in recognition of the economic and social costs that have resulted. On the other hand, the smaller communities, which have not yet adopted strict controls, are continuing to introduce increasingly rigid environmental and land-use policies. That is, the larger municipalities are becoming somewhat more lenient and the smaller municipalities are gradually becoming more stringent in their formulation and application land-use and environmental policies.

PROLIFERATION OF PLANNING AGENCIES

There has been a proliferation of agencies to work on piecemeal solutions to solve specific problems as they occur, with no overview of the entire system. This tendency for agencies to focus on close-up shots rather than the entire panorama has resulted in legislation which in the aggregate serves to defeat the achievement of the very goals the individual programs were designed to achieve. Lack of coordinated effort has resulted in overlapping jurisdictions and confusion as to requirements and regulations. This has resulted in long delays in processing housing plans and requirements for a bewildering variety of permits, approvals, and fees.

Housing agencies and planning departments which have not properly planned for growth and have mismanaged municipal programs to support it have reacted to the nevertheless inevitable growth by the imposition of moratoriums. Sewer, water hookup, and gas or electric moratoriums often are imposed with little or no advance notice. Adding to the hardship for builders and developers, they often are imposed for indeterminate periods. Such moratoriums and the lack of clear and consistent guidelines regarding them have greatly increased the risk and reduced the yield in real estate development.

FEDERAL GUIDELINES AND LEGISLATION

Land-use regulations have altered the climate of land use and changed dramatically the land development industry. These regulations are largely a result of changes in the public attitude on land use.

The problem of pollution of all sorts has led to concern over land-use practices and the recognition that land is a resource of environmental value. Additionally, homeowners are coming to regard further development as an infringement of their property rights and not to their best interests. Communities have come to see land development as spoiling the environment, creating increased property taxes, and raising the costs of local government. Development is often viewed as a prime breeder of congestion and a despoiler of a way of life.

Whatever the community perceives to be its problems, it seeks to remedy them through legal action. Communities and legislators have thus created legislation to regulate the development and use of land, to reflect the general public's perception of its problems. Some of the key legislation is reviewed below.

National Environmental Policy Act (1969)

The National Environment Policy Act created the Council on Environmental Quality, and the President then created the Environmental Protection Agency (EPA) to serve as the administrator of the Council. This Agency guards the quality of water and air resources and protects against noise pollution. It is the agency with the greatest impact on land use.

Clean Air Act (1970)

The goals established by the Clean Air Act are to maintain air quality standards and to prevent deterioration in the quality of the air where it is superior to national standards. The act requires the states to review projects in their preconstruction stages to determine the probable impact of new developments on air pollution, and it provides the authority to prevent construction of developments which would have a negative effect. Thus it provides the power to control land use and requires that land-use control be developed and utilized to achieve and maintain air-quality standards.

Not only must existing pollutants in the air be reduced or eliminated, but new sources from developments must be controlled to keep the air quality within prescribed guidelines. This includes both direct and indirect sources of pollution; an indirect source would be the pollution due to auto traffic created by a proposed development.

Federal Water Pollution Control Act (1972)

All federal agencies and state and local governments, are called on by the Federal Water Pollution Control Act to develop comprehensive programs to prevent, reduce, or eliminate the pollution of water. States are required to develop plans for areawide waste treatment management; the governor of each state must create an agency for developing and administering a waste treatment management plan. These agencies have comprehensive authority for land-use planning and usually take the form of a local council or regional planning agency.

In this act, Congress intended to provide regulation of land use as a method of controlling pollution of waters. Areawide waste treatment management plans determine the location and size of new sewerage plans funded by the EPA.

Flood Disaster Protection Act (1973)

The Flood Disaster Protection Act requires communities to enact and enforce ordinances restricting construction of new buildings in areas of flood hazard. The act also clears the way for a reduction in grants and loans under the Federal Disaster Relief Program by requiring present property owners to purchase flood insurance for structures in flood-prone areas. In requiring this insurance, however, the act provides a subsidized program for residents whose homes and businesses are currently located in these areas.

The act requires the cooperation of local authorities in controlling development in floodplains, as a means of reducing future disaster losses.

Local governments are required to control construction in areas of flood hazard by amending their building permit and subdivision regulations.

The Flood Disaster Protection Act is a new approach to regulating the use of land subject to flooding and paying for flood damage. Making the highly subsidized flood insurance available to property owners areas with potential flood damage is an attempt to reduce federal expenditures for disaster relief by encouraging potential victims of flood damage to contribute to their own protection. The act requires property owners to enroll in the Federal Flood Insurance Program if they are to receive real estate loans in flood-hazard areas.

Specific flood hazards for an area are published in the form of a map showing 100-year flood elevation data for the community. The 100-year flood elevation is the floodwater level that is estimated to have a 1 percent chance of occurring each year in a given location. The rate map shows the true actuarial rate to be charged for insurance on buildings constructed after the map is published. The rate is based on the actual risk depending on the location of the building and the elevation of the basement floor.

Once the rate map has been published, purchase of insurance is mandatory if a real estate loan is to be made, increased, extended, or renewed by a lender. Communities must enact a 100-year flood elevation ordinance to get into the insurance program. However, there is no language currently in the law which prohibits issuing building permits for construction below this elevation. The constraints to building within the 100-year elevation are the cost of the actuarial rate of the insurance. Rates are extremely high, $10 per $100 of coverage is common on buildings constructed well below the 100-year flood elevation.

Coastal Zone Management Act (1972)

The Coastal Zone Management Act authorizes the Secretary of Commerce to make grants for the purpose of developing a program of management for the land and water resources in coastal zones which defines permissible land and water uses there. The plan provides for enforcement procedures to see that compatible land uses are undertaken.

Essentially, the act has two purposes. One is to assist and encourage local governments in developing management programs for the use of costal resources, giving consideration to cultural, ecological, historical, and aesthetic values as well as economic considerations. The second is to preserve and protect the costal resources of the nation, in recognition of the importance of the costal zone as an environmental and recreational resource.

At the federal level the act is administered by the National Oceanic and Atmospheric Administration of the Department of Commerce. To qualify for grants for management plans, a state must submit a costal management plan acceptable to the agency. The legislation provides for a federal review of (1) procedures for designating areas that need restoration or preservation, (2) provisions for implementing the overall program,

(3) procedure to assure that the plans meet requirements that are more local in nature and concur with national goals, and (4) procedures which assure that the local regulations do not unreasonably restrict land and water uses of regional benefit.

Noise Pollution and Control Act (1972)

The Noise Pollution and Control Act requires federal agencies and state and local governments to comply with established provisions and to set noise limits for construction equipment, transportation equipment, electrical equipment, motors and engines, and other related equipment. The act, which recognizes noise as a major pollutant of the environment, indirectly affects land use by determining that the environment around residences should be free of noise. The Department of Housing and Urban Development (HUD) regulations regarding noise allow no federal assistance for residential areas subject to high noise impact, such as zones near airports, highways, or railroads.

LAND-USE POLICIES

Stepping stones to a national land-use policy

The acts described above are stepping stones toward a national land-use policy. Though they are currently piecemeal approaches, they represent the response of Congress to the deterioration of specific aspects of the environment of the nation. Their enactment does not ensure coordination of state and local implementation, however. Much work is needed to tie the legislation together into a coordinated, vital national housing growth policy. The acts serve as guides for the development of state and local land-use policies.

State land-use policies

The federal environmental protection laws require states to implement directly or designate substate entities to plan and regulate certain land uses. The state has been a weak link in the past between federal and local government in implementing land-use policy. Now, regulations require the states to be in a strong position of coordination, for the implementation of statewide land-use strategies and plans. States are beginning to take back control powers and land-use planning powers traditionally delegated to localities and municipalities. Local controls and planning have failed to produce land-use patterns sufficient to serve larger metropolitan and regional requirements and assure environmental quality. Some states already have enacted comprehensive statewide environmental laws establishing land-use policies.

It is the states that will have to implement the federal environmental laws and establish priorities in a rational, coordinated manner. Such state laws and policies will help guide planning and zoning at the local level and will have an effect on the evaluation of any major real estate development proposal. The move for states to take back some of the land-use regulatory powers formerly awarded to local governments and municipalities is a trend developing throughout the country. State agencies then will assist local governments in implementing and administering state land-use management plans and will require permits as a method of control in implementing standards.

Thus developers will be working with both the local government and with the state agencies. As state agencies establish statewide planning goals and guidelines for local governments, they will require local governments to set up local regulations reflecting state requirements. If the local jurisdiction does not regulate its areas properly and establish sufficient controls, then the state will apply its own regulations.

State agencies will review comprehensive plans prepared by local governments to check conformance with state policies and will grant permits for activities having statewide significance. States will be taking greater initiative in encouraging and demanding the initiation and administration of comprehensive land-use policies by local governments, as well as subdivision ordinances which reflect comprehensive plans and zoning maps and take into consideration timing along with land use.

Local and municipal land-use policies

Local governments, in an attempt to control growth and maintain the environment, are adopting policies and creating regulations which not only implement federal and state plans but reflect the social and political desires of local constituents. Much of the legislation at the local level has the effect of a no-growth policy.

Attempts are often made to justify such no-growth legislation by citing the inequitable costs development places on residents already living in a community. Though there is much emphasis on the cost of development, a lot of this is merely a disguise for the underlying social reasons behind no growth: the desire of those in the community to foster segregation and retain environmental amenities exclusively for the use of residents currently in the community. Apparently, each homeowner wants to be the last person to move into the community and wants all further households excluded, in order to retain its exclusiveness and the quality of the environment.

This tendency is reinforced and nurtured by the political reality that current residents within a community are voters, whereas potential residents who desire to live in a community are not. Politicians often see growth as a threat to their existing political constituency; new growth might disturb the current political balance which keeps them in office. If a developer who wishes to develop land in such a climate is to be effective in working within the system, he must understand both the indicated and the underlying reasons for legislation.

Local governments have sought to control growth (or, more correctly, to foster nongrowth) by a variety of measures, such as:

1. Excessive permit fees.
2. Mandatory dedications.

3. Minimum floor area standards for structures.
4. Minimum lot area requirements.
5. Restrictive covenants.
6. Putting limits on the total number of dwelling units or households within a community.
7. Zoning rollbacks.
8. Refusing to support bond issues for new schools.
9. Placing limits on the number of dwelling units per year for which permits will be granted.
10. Disallowing multifamily zoning.
11. Establishing costly hearing and review processes which require extensive up-front costs to the developer before approvals will be given.

Such policies by local governments have resulted in a great deal of litigation regarding land-owner compensation. Much of the legislation regarding land-use policies of local agencies has resulted in suits by developers which have challenged the actions of local agencies as a taking of property. There has been little consensus or consistency in court rulings on such cases.

Local governments are learning, through experience in land-use litigation, to maximize their chances of winning in court. The courts have established certain guidelines which, if followed to the letter, would greatly enhance the local government's position. These guidelines are roughly as follows:

1. Policies must not be no-growth policies but must show some kind of positive commitment to growth.
2. There must be a capital management plan to support growth, and the plan must be budgeted.
3. The plan must incorporate a timing schedule to serve as a guide for when specific properties can be developed.
4. The plan must take into account the regional impact; that is, if every community chose to limit growth within a region, the region would experience a severe housing shortage. The plan of the community must be compatible with the regional pattern.
5. The plan must include a procedural mechanism and must have the necessary legal basis.

ENERGY LEGISLATION

There has been a rash of legislation at both the federal and state levels with the goal of conserving energy. The National Energy Program Project Independence has particularly targeted transportation as a sector of the economy where energy consumption must be reduced. This will have a significant impact on land-use planning. The Office of Economic Opportunity has established programs to improve home insulation and cut down fuel bills, and HUD has imposed stricter insulation standards for new construction. A Federal Energy Administration has been created, and building codes have been revised to reduce the allowable amount of glass which can be used in residences, among other things. The Commission on Housing and Community Development, at the state level, is implementing energy conservation policies for housing construction.

There is a change taking place in the accounting systems and decision models utilized in allocating tax dollars for transportation purposes. The highway trust fund has been opened up to permit urban public-transit systems to create a single urban transportation fund for operating expenses as well as capital outlays. In the past highway systems were compared on a dollar-for-dollar basis with rapid transit systems without proper regard for the hidden costs, follow-up costs, or the environmental energy implications associated with the systems.

Governments typically are slow in reacting, managing, and planning in the area of resource and environmental management. When the government does recognize a growing problem, it too often reacts quickly, without a real analytical basis for identifying the problem and its magnitude, or the actual impact of the legislation as opposed to the intended impact. The 1973 oil embargo by the Organization of Petroleum Exporting Countries (OPEC) probably did more to aid in environmental and research management than the bulk of the U.S. legislation passed in recent years.

KEEPING ABREAST OF LEGISLATION

The onslaught of legislation has created a bewildering situation resulting in confusion, jurisdictional overlaps, unclear review processes, and uncertainty as to the magnitude and scope of information needed to fulfill requirements. Legislation governing land development and building has created a huge burden for the real estate and development entrepreneur. Most organizations lack both the finances and in-house intellect to deal with problems of such magnitude. However, trade associations are gearing up to meet the critical needs of members by keeping them abreast of the legislation, interpreting it for them, and lessening its implication for them where possible. Such associations as the National Association of Home Builders and the Mortgage Bankers Association are playing key roles in assisting their members to work within the new environment.

The associations also are working at the federal, state, and local levels to see that the interests of their members are taken into account in framing the legislation. The associations are helpful in providing legal counsel and spearheading the litigation of key issues involving members. Many of the associations are adding key technical personnel to their staffs to assist their members in understanding, controlling, and adopting the new legislative policies.

NEED FOR A PUBLIC-PRIVATE PARTNERSHIP

With greater emphasis by the government at the federal, state, and local levels, the land development process has recently become much more public than it was in the past. Where formerly the course of development was determined by the private sector through supply and demand and market pressures, in the future it will be set more by legislation. This produces a situation in which the role of the private sector is in effect an implementer of development.

Though these roles have been emerging for some time, the full consequences of this dual relationship are now much more visible and obvious, and they will become more so in the future. The private sector needs the environmental and resource management planning of the public sector, and the public sector needs the entrepreneurial abilities and marketing, financial, and economic skills of the private sector. Those in the private sector whose livelihood is associated with land use and development can work with the public sector individually or through participation in their trade associations. For many, a more active membership role in associations will provide the most productive benefits in shaping land-use policy. When both the public and private sectors see themselves in the dual role of partners in land-use development, hostility can be minimized in the review process, where the two groups tend to view one another as enemies working at cross-purposes.

The developer, if he is to be the implementer of land-use plans, must take an active role in shaping the legislation which guides land use. It is important for the developer not only to have his views expressed in land-use legislation but also to understand the view of the public sector and local governmental bodies. In this manner the developer can not only understand the needs and desires of his local community, he can assist it to implement its growth plans.

The developer who is in a position of selling the community what it desires will be in a much better position than the one who does not understand the community's plan and its indicated and underlying desires. This provision for the public and private sectors to work together rather than at cross-purposes is no panacea, however; when the public sector does not have clearly defined plans, goals, or policies, it is difficult for the developer to work within its guidelines.

Because the developer cannot assist the public sector in implementing its goals when the latter does not clearly know what they are, the developer must be ready to assist the public sector in establishing goals and making sure land-use plans and zoning maps reflect goals and policy. The developer can reduce his risk by improving his understanding of these goals, both stated and unstated, so he can propose developments which are consistent with them. The developer can then exercise greater care in site selection and land planning to reflect public goals. He should be sure that his proposed development will not have an adverse impact on the environment, that the capital improvements are sufficient to support the proposed development, and that the market is ready to support it.

Legislation and attitudes which result in legal, political, and environmental constraints are in a constant state of flux, and require continual monitoring. The reader should be careful to appraise himself of current legislation and public attitudes which may affect his developmental activities. The legislation outlined in this chapter may not be current, due to inevitable change, and it is not all-inclusive but merely constitutes a general introduction to legal, political, and environmental constraints on land development.

6

Competitive evaluation: How to obsolete the competition

In looking for opportunities in a market area, the competition may provide the best clues. The competitive marketing strength of a product is largely determined by two factors: how well it supplies the needs of the consumer, and its competitive position relative to that of others offering to supply the same need. Careful research will identify both competitors' strengths, which can be incorporated into the product to advantage, and competitors' weaknesses and vulnerability.

Discovering the vulnerability of competitors may well provide the edge necessary to outperform them. To merely match competitors in their areas of strength is to meet them head on, and since they are already established, they carry the advantage. If, however, a developer correctly identifies his competitors' weaknesses and builds strength in his own product and strategies in the very areas where they are weak, he can then meet them advantageously in a marketing situation. He will have significant strength in their weak areas; all else being equal, strength should prevail.

Sometimes we may learn more from a man's errors than from his virtues.
Henry Wadsworth Longfellow

COMPETITORS' WEAKNESSES: THE KEY TO OPPORTUNITY

Market leadership can be gained by making a breakthrough in the state of the art of land development within the market area. In looking for the competition's weaknesses, it is common to find that in a specific market area the majority of the competitors will have many of the same weaknesses in common. This can be attributed to two considerations:

1. The competition is typically not doing adequate market and product research independently. Consequently competitors are playing follow the leader after one another, copying each other's weaknesses as well as strengths.
2. The competition is constrained by the state of the art of developmental expertise within their particular market area.

This is more the case with local single-market developers, but even multimarket developers often fall into the same follow-the-leader rut. Consultants within a specific market area will also generally be no better than the developers they serve, because the consultants are constrained by the same state of the art as are the developers.

Great opportunities come to all, but many do not know they have met them.

A. E. Dunning

Maintaining a perspective to spot opportunities and limitations

Having identified competitors' weaknesses in a specific market area, it may be necessary to go outside of that area for expertise to lend the strength necessary to correct the deficiencies. Indeed, it may be necessary to go outside the market area, in any event, for expertise to identify competitors' weaknesses. The competitors, even in their areas of weakness, may be doing an adequate job, considering the current state of the art in the market area.

It is sometimes difficult to spot a weakness in a specific situation unless it can be compared to a comparable situation which is substantially better by comparison. To be able to identify weaknesses, then, calls for a knowledge of better quality comparables and exposure to a higher state of the art than is prevalent in the immediate market area (see Chapter 7).

Knowledge is of two kinds. We know a subject ourselves, or we know where we can find information upon it.

Samuel Johnson

Research of the competition will suggest early certain limitations and opportunities available to the developer. A grasp of these limitations and opportunities should be gained as soon as possible because it may require a modification in the developer's strategies. The most common modification in strategies occurs when the competition is found to be particularly weak in the delivery of a concept or simply to be missing a marketing opportunity. In such instances the researcher may point out strong areas of opportunity of which the developer was not aware, and the discovery may require a modification in the developer's initial strategies. On the other hand, the researcher may also find the competition to be in such a strong position, as compared to limitations with which the developer may be faced, that it is unwise to continue with his initial strategies.

GUIDELINES FOR RESEARCHING THE COMPETITION

In researching the competition, answers should be sought to the following general questions (see Chapter 14):

1. How do the competitors' projects differ from the proposed development as outlined in the developer's objectives?
2. Has the competition made mistakes that can be avoided or capitalized

upon? Has the competition left an opening so that the proposed concept can obsolete his product (in floor plans, mix, amenities, land plan, merchandizing, landscaping, interior decor, size, location, management, maintenance)?

3. Has the competition utilized a particularly appealing concept which can be adapted or improved to advantage?
4. What have the leaders done to make them leaders in the market? How vulnerable are they? Where?
5. Has absorption been satisfactory? If not, are there any specific clues to why not?
6. What type of consumers (market segments) have been buying and renting? Why? Which type have not been interested? Why?
7. Is management making costly concessions to move the product? Are they paying down the loan, throwing in extras in the sale, or, in the case of rental properties, giving free rent or omitting leases or cleaning deposits?
8. Are there any foreclosures or chronically ill projects in the market? What were the chief problems?

The developer should also look for specific mistakes made by the competition which, when remedied, will provide a competitive edge. The following are typical:

1. Poor location. A project which would be comparable in other respects may be compromised by a poor location. A better located project could provide a strong competitive edge, in that location is a strong moderating factor in choosing housing.
2. Poor curb appeal. A project may have a good location, but, due to planning mistakes, may not put up a good front, so there is a resultant loss of prestige. It is common to see the self-advertising value of a site destroyed because of poor design and planning considerations.
3. Following the leader. Competitors often play follow the leader, seeking safety in numbers rather than blazing a new trail. This results in a glut of similar-type projects with similar mixes going after similar markets. Researching these competitors might suggest there is a soft market, but the softness could be concentrated in a specific market. A different mix, size, or price range could stimulate strong consumer demand.
4. Environmental problems. Do the competitors tend to think in terms of building housing rather than environments? Buying or renting is an emotional process which requires that emotional needs be satisfied. If competitors think in terms of bricks and mortar rather than environment, they have left a large competitive opening. Superior planning, design, decoration, color, landscaping and amenities offer strong competitive advantages, regardless of market segment or price.
5. Management and maintenance sins. How are competitors managing and maintaining their projects, amenities, landscaping, leasing or

sales offices, models, parking lots, and so on? In either rentals or homeowners' associations, management and maintenance reflect image and environment and rank high in resident satisfaction.

CASE STUDY I: RESEARCHING THE COMPETITION

This case study illustrates some of the points covered above regarding researching the competition. We were brought into a market area on the East Coast by a builder who wanted an innovative product on a large parcel and gave us carte blanche as to what should be done with the property.

In researching the market it was found to be a currently healthy, robust market, yet there were signs of near-term softening because of current high-level building activity in the area. Numerous multimarket builders had recognized the opportunities in the market and had already rushed in to exploit it.

The market had traditionally been a townhouse market, with the bulk of rental units two- and three-bedroom townhouses. Why this was so is a matter of conjecture: Was it because of consumer preferences? Or did the product take its shape more because of zoning, code, and economic pressures within the area? After researching the pertinent data it was felt that the product had developed as a result of zoning, code, and economic pressures, more than consumer preferences.

Zoning allowed for relatively light densities as compared to many other market areas around the country—16 to 22 units per acre under straight zoning, with the preponderance in the 16-unit-per-acre category. In contrast, 25 to 35 garden apartment units per acre is not uncommon in California and many other market areas. It appears that in an effort to obtain maximum net rentable square footage for the property, developers in the market area had been constructing large two- and three-bedroom townhouse units.

Fire prevention requirements in the market were among the strictest in the nation, particularly regarding ingress and egress requirements. For second-floor units, two separate stairways were required for emergency exit from each, and each unit was required to have two exit doors with reasonable separation. The townhouse design gets around the requirements for two stairways and two exit doors on the second floor because the townhouse exit is only on the first floor, with vertical circulation handled by a single interior stairway in each unit.

It was evident that the zoning and fire code requirements were having a far greater impact on product development than consumer preferences because although consumers were demanding one-bedroom units, relatively few were being produced. This had occurred because it was generally believed a one-bedroom townhouse is tough to make work economically, and a one-bedroom stacked apartment is expensive to construct because of the fire safety requirements. The one-bedroom unit also reduces net rentable square footage per acre.

Though most of the projects visited in the area had two- and three-bedroom townhouses available for immediate occupancy, few had one-bedroom apartments for immediate occupancy, some had none whatsoever, and a number had waiting lists for the one-bedroom units. In addition, site planning and amenities generally lacked consumer and environmental appeal. Though there were some standouts, most projects were utilitarian.

There was clearly a strong demand in this market for more environmental and consumer orientation, for adult-only communities, planned activities, and more one-bedroom units. Yet there was the obstacle of low density: One-bedroom units would provide much less net rentable square footage per acre than two- or three-bedroom units. And there was the obstacle of increased costs due to fire prevention requirements: With one-bedroom units, these costs per unit would have to be distributed over less square footage. Also, added amenities are difficult to work into the budget if where to cut the costs is not known.

Other out-of-town builders in the market area had generally followed the traditional pattern set by the local developers, and for the most part they were producing two- and three-bedroom townhouses. In effect, they were following the market, and as a result they were hastening the process of softening the market in two- and three-bedroom townhouses. Yet the one-bedroom market was robust and showed no signs of softening.

Sound strategy often consists not in doing a better job of what the competition is doing but in doing what they are not doing. Once a hole in the market was found, a consumer-oriented product was delivered which took advantage of the weakness of the competition. The proposal was for no three-bedroom units and a large number of one-bedroom units, junior one-bedrooms, and studios with about one half of the units two bedrooms. Though with this plan it was not possible to put as much net rentable square footage on an acre as the competition, it was possible to provide better bottom-line figures because of the ability to achieve higher rents per net rentable square foot. This was achieved by careful attention to amenities, site planning, and interior decor. Though not as many dollars were coming in per unit, neither were there as many going out. Trying to maximize total dollars coming in is not too meaningful in itself because income is only half of the profit formula: Income − Expenses = Profit.

Fire safety expenses were diminished while at the same time the safety features to fulfill the intent of the codes were maintained. For example, code requirements were fulfilled with only one exit stairway available to a second-floor apartment, where the competition typically was providing two.

RESEARCHING AS A MEANS TO LEADING THE COMPETITION

Carefully shopping the competition does not necessarily provide the answers needed to outperform them. By researching the competition, one can gain information to follow them closely, but how does one find out how to get in front of them? What should be done that they are not doing?

By conventional market analysis, a developer can learn to closely follow the competition. To create marketing monopolies to lead the competition, however, requires somewhat different marketing strategies than those conventionally practiced.

It is not always necessary to be out in front in a market area which has attracted national leaders. A good market strategy is to closely research the leaders on a regular basis and to keep a file on each company researched. By mentally charting changes in product, design and materials, and price and marketing strategies, a developer can gain considerable knowledge about how the national leaders are adjusting to the changes in the marketplace and developing strategies for continued change. After having researched a number of trend-setting leaders, he can then chart a course with excellent current feedback and historical perspective (see Chapter 14).

Some persons do first, think afterward, and then repent forever.
Secker

If there are no national leaders in a certain market area but the developer wants to emulate the national leaders to become better than the local competition, then he must go outside of the immediate market area for expertise. Local consultants generally will not be any better than the local competition. It is necessary to go outside to bring in fresh ideas.

We gain nothing by being with such as ourselves: we encourage each other in mediocrity. I am always longing to be with men more excellent than myself.
Charles Lamb

How to research the leading developers

In researching national leaders, their product should be thoroughly documented with photographs. Their brochures will provide price and floor plans, and square footage can be determined whether given in the brochure or not. From this information it is possible to calculate price per square foot. By utilizing average operating ratios, hard costs, land costs, and profits can be approximated.

Talking to the salespeople can provide information on which plans are selling best and why and which plans are not moving and why. What would they do differently if they were to start over again? Salespeople may also indicate the socioeconomic profiles of the buyers and why they are buying, and who is not buying and why. They will generally give absorption rates, financing terms, and typical down payments made by the buyers, and they may indicate what submarkets the product was intended to serve and what submarkets are actually buying. The point-of-sale marketing program and its effectiveness can be observed. Armed with this information, the developer can then make an evaluation of the leader's product and its success.

Researching, or shopping, a leading developer on a one-time basis is helpful, but the evaluation can be even more meaningful if the same developer is shopped on a periodic basis. By evaluating what the same developer is doing today compared to one year ago, two years ago, or three years ago, it is possible to spot trends, relate the trends to cycles, and deduce the marketing strategies employed by the leading developers.

Innovation as a result of researching

A developer who has researched leading developers outside of the immediate market area and has assembled all of the input discussed above may go back to his own market area and begin to see holes. Through this type of market research he can see how to obsolete competitors' products by following the successful patterns of leading developers in another market area. He has the benefit of hindsight; not only has he seen completed products he is considering innovating with, he has information as to who is buying the product and who is not elsewhere, how fast it is selling, and so on.

In this manner the developer can introduce proven innovations from the more advanced market areas where they were shopped. Comparing the more advanced market area to his own, he will find opportunities for innovation in his market area. This is a benefit of the perspective gained by going outside for fresh ideas.

Discovering weaknesses and transforming areas of weakness into marketing opportunity is an innovative process. The end result of successful innovation is to obsolete a competitor's product for the specific market area in which he is challenged. This creates a temporary monopoly for the innovative developer and his product.

Since an innovation is by definition the introduction of something new, there may be few or no comparables to guide evaluation of it in the immediate market area. Since there are few or no comparables, researching the market area might suggest that there is no market for a particular innovation because there has been no activity in such a price range, unit size, or concept in the past. Or perhaps there has been no activity in housing aimed at a particular market segment. This does not suggest that there is no demand, only that there has not been a supply. Too often demand is measured by past activity in the marketplace, but this approach is not effective in finding holes in the market or evaluating the absorption rate of market innovations (see Chapter 11).

Creating a monopoly on products or methods

If an area of strong demand can be identified which is not being met with an adequate supply, an opening has been found in the market which can support new supply. If the disparity between a specific demand and a specific supply is particularly strong, the market has a hole in it. It is this hole, or relatively unfulfilled demand, which provides the key to profits. Profits, not prophets, foretell the future.

The sensitive researcher or developer will be able to spot latent needs that are not yet recognized by the competition. Since these needs have not been recognized, and the attendant opportunities have not been sought after with an innovative product, they do not as yet show up as demand in statistical form. When a product which successfully fills the need has been introduced, the need is no longer latent, and it takes the form of demand as the market absorbs the new product offered. When this happens, the developer has not merely responded to demand but has created his market.

Reevaluation of the developer's objectives

Once the site has been reviewed and the competition in the area researched, enough information will be available to begin to form an intuitive "feel" for the opportunities and obstacles that may exist in reaching the developer's objectives. This is a good time to check direction and possibly reevaluate or refine the strategies employed by the developer to reach his objectives.

Should research at this point have identified obstacles that were unforeseen or of greater magnitude than anticipated by the developer, the point of a go or no-go decision has been reached, or a reevaluation of strategies is in order. It must be kept in mind that decisions based on the information thus far are best efforts, based on the information available and subject to change on the basis of subsequent input. These checkpoints for evaluating direction are necessary throughout development of the program.

Formation of a preliminary concept

Though the formal market research and consumer research portions of the planning study have not been produced at this point, the exposure to the market in researching the competition and discussing growth trends gives the researcher or developer a strong feel for the market and the consumer and enables him to more clearly focus his marketing energies.

In order for demographics to be generally understood, they do not have to be qualified and quantified in the form of statistics. Indeed, demographics can be seen in driving around the market area and observing the industry existing and under development, hospitals, shopping centers, highway networks, and housing developments. These are the realities which statistical data represent. It is not necessary to have the statistical data in hand in order to determine developmental trends, opportunities, and obstacles. The statistical data, however, certainly do better qualify the opportunities and obstacles that exist and at times they may provide unexpected surprises.

Once a concept has taken shape as a result of the initial review, there is a point of reference or context into which subsequent information fits or does not fit. When the opportunities and obstacles have been generally identified from review of the site and the competition, further research serves to qualify and quantify the opportunities and obstacles that have been recognized. The demographics themselves do not so much identify specific developmental opportunity as they measure the opportunity and flesh-in additional data useful in further plan formulation and programming.

VALUE RELATIONSHIP ANALYSIS: SETTING THE SALES PRICE RANGE

Value relationship analysis is a method of determining the comparative relationship of various values within a market area. It is a means of arriving at prices, sizes, and features which will be competitive among a number of other competing values within the marketplace.

Value relationship analysis requires input from sensitivity analysis. Sensitivity analysis is used to identify those features of a home that have the most pronounced effect on value and to identify the dollar's worth of the individual features. The features and space for inserting their respective values are listed on Price Adjustment Format Sheets. In Exhibit 6–4, representative amounts have been inserted.

Square footage is one of the best indicators of price, and price is often quoted as a price per square foot. To increase the reliability of this price indicator, those features that will have the most pronounced effect on price per square foot are subtracted from the standard price of a house in order to reduce price to a base price or stripped price. The base price per square foot of competing properties in the market can then be compared on an objective basis once all the homes have been reduced to their base price. To arrive back at the standard price, the price of the features is added back on to the base price.

The purpose of reducing standard prices to base prices is to analyze the relationship between the base price of various properties in the market area and determine how the subject property can best fit competitively into the price structure. By reducing properties to their base elements, apples can be compared to apples.

Value relationship analysis begins with gathering a cross-section of comparable projects and their prices (Exhibit 6–1). If enough recent comparables are not available dated sales may be used, but they must be adjusted to reflect the cost differential due to the time spread. For purposes here, prices or sales will be assumed to be recent, so that no time adjustment is required. The properties selected are not limited to those close in size or price to the proposed product for the subject property to be analyzed.

The selected properties are reduced from their standard prices (base price plus price of standard feature package) to their base prices by subtracting the prices of the listed features included in each property. The features referred to are listed on Price Adjustment Format Sheets.

Once the base prices per square foot are determined for the individual homes within the comparable projects selected, they are plotted on the Development Comparables Relationship Chart (Exhibit 6–11). The vertical axis of the chart represents the price per square foot, and the horizontal axis represents the square footage. When each house is located on the chart according to its base price per square foot and square footage, a trend line is drawn to graphically illustrate the average relationship between the square footage and the price per square foot. The most probable base price per square foot for the square foot range of the houses is thus indicated by the trend line.

When the proposed square footage and price per square foot of the subject property are placed on the chart, its relative price position can be seen at a glance. If the proposed base price per square foot is high in relation to the market, it will be shown at a point above the trend line; if it is low, it will be shown below the line. The most probable selling price of the subject property is indicated at the point where the trend line crosses the point on the graph representing the square footage of the subject home(s).

A higher base price than that indicated by the trend line may be justified by the location or superior design appeal of the subject project. If this is not the case, it may be necessary to adjust the base price of the subject property down to the trend line, to remain competitive. Trends, however, are averages, with some projects occurring below the trend line and others above. The deviation from the trend line by the various projects which, in the aggregate, create the trend provides a measure of the magnitude of deviation allowable on either side of the trend line. Highly competitive markets will generally allow less deviation, while less competitive markets allow greater deviation from the trend line.

After the relationship has been determined between the base price per square foot and the trend line, allowances can be made for deviations from the trend line by introducing subjective or intangible considerations, such as evaluation of the overall project, appearance, location, and amenities offered. If the base price deviation from the trend line cannot be justified by such subjective considerations, then it may be necessary to adjust the base price of the proposed project to bring it more in line with the trend line indication of most probable selling price.

Once the base or stripped price is established, standard feature costs are added to the base price to establish the standard price (price including a standard feature package). Care has to be exercised so as not to over-improve for the market, because markets reach a point of diminishing price increases related to additional features. That is, the improvement advances beyond the market's ability to pay.

A standard price relationship trend line is developed in the same manner as the base price relationship trend line, indicating the most probable standard selling price. A greater deviation is allowable from the standard selling price trend line than from the base price trend line, due to large variations in the scope of standard features for the individual projects and unadjusted variations in location or design and planning.

PROCEDURE FOR VALUE RELATIONSHIP ANALYSIS

1. Utilize the Data Collection Sheet for information gathering. Use one sheet for each project. Exhibit 6-5, 6-7, and 6-9 give examples of Data Collection Sheets for the three projects ranked in Exhibit 6-11.
2. Utilize Price Adjustments Format Sheets and Price Adjustment Sheets to adjust prices to stripped prices. Price Adjustments Sheets for the three projects in the Data Collection Sheets are given as Exhibits 6-6, 6-8, and 6-10.
3. Record adjusted prices on the top Data Collection Sheet.

4. Plot adjusted prices on Development Comparables Relationship Chart.
5. Plot standard package prices on the same chart.
6. Record product recommendations for the subject project, including standard optional items on the subject project Data Collection Sheet.
7. The ranking chart will give market price ranges for both adjusted price and standard package price.
8. Set the adjusted price of the subject project within the market price range as indicated by the ranking chart.
9. Check the standard package of the subject development against the adjusted price sheet to determine the standard package price.
10. Check the standard package price against the standard price trend line.
11. Check the adjusted and standard prices for the subject project and modify product recommendations as required to adjust price to price trend lines indicated on chart.
12. Check both adjusted prices and standard package prices against preliminary budgets and profit projections.

Exhibit 6-1
Summary of Comparable Developments Form

Development and developer	Sales started	Units planned	Total sold	Price range	Sq. ft. range	Price Sq. ft. range	Lot size density	Weekly sales

Exhibit 6-2
Unit Mix of Comparable Developments Form

Development and developer	1-bedroom		2-bedroom		3-bedroom		4-bedroom		Other		Totals
	No.	%	No.	%	No.	%	No.	%	No.	%	
Totals											

Exhibit 6-3
Planned Developments Form

Development and developer	Location map key	Status	Size	Type	Price range	Mix	Density lot size

Exhibit 6-4
Price Adjustments Format Sheets

Parking
   Parking space .... Standard
   One-car carport $500
   Two-car carport $700
   Two-car garage $2,000
   Three-car garage $2,600

Driveway
   Asphalt .... Standard
   Concrete $125

Fencing
   No fence .... Standard
   Wood, 5,000 sq. ft. $500
   Wood, 7,000 sq. ft. $600
   Wood, 9,000 sq. ft. $700
   Block, add over wood 20%

Patios, atriums
   None .... Standard
   Fenced $400
   Paved $500
   Covered $700
   Interior $800

Landscaping
   None .... Standard
   Complete $350
   Front or rear only $150

Fireplace
   None .... Standard
   One $850
   Two $1,700

Carpeting
   None .... Standard
   Partial $400
   Complete $600

Wet bar
   None .... Standard
   One $500

Oven
   Single .... Standard
   Double $225
   Self-cleaning $275

Dishwasher
   None .... Standard
   One $250

Trash compactor
   None .... Standard
   One $200

Sprinklers
   None .... Standard
   Front or rear only $300
   Complete $600

Volume ceiling
   None .... Standard
   ¼ House $1,000
   ½ House $2,000

Luminous ceiling
   None .... Standard
   Bath $200
   Kitchen $300

Roofing
   Asphaltic .... Standard
   Shake, shingle, ½ $500
   Shake, shingle, Entire $1,000
   Tile, ½ $700
   Tile, entire $1,400

Air conditioning
   None .... Standard
   Evaporative cooler $350
   Thru the wall $350
   Central, 1,000 sq. ft. $1,200
   Central, 1,500 sq. ft. $1,500
   Central, 2,000 sq. ft. $1,800

Balconies, decks
   None .... Standard
   20 sq. ft. $200
   40 sq. ft. $400
   80 sq. ft. $800
   120 sq. ft. $1,000

Tile
   None .... Standard
   Kitchen counter $100
   Entry $50
   Bath $50

Bonus room
   None .... Standard
   Unfinished $2,200

Drapes
   None .... Standard
   Partial $250
   Complete $500

Lot size
   Std. 6000 sq. ft. .... Standard
   For each sq. ft. over or under, add
     or subtract .... —°

Baths
   1 Bath .... Standard
   1½ Bath $700
   2 Bath $1,400
   2½ Bath $2,100
   3 Bath $2,900

° Use a cost figure representative of the square foot land value for each project surveyed.
Note: The price adjustments must be developed to reflect the pricing structure of each subject market area.

Exhibit 6–5
Lambert Gardens: Data Collection Sheet

Development	Lambert Gardens	Type	Detached
Developer	Alert Develop. Inc.	Date	6/29/75
Location	Shaw & Capital Express	Map key	C

Plan No.	1	2	3	4	5
Bedrooms	2	3	3	4	5
Sq. footage	1,100	1,480	1,640	1,860	2,250
Price	$34,320	$44,104	$46,740	$51,708	$58,725
Price/Sq. ft.	$31.20	$29.80	$28.50	$27.80	$26.10
Adjusted price	$27,770	$36,854	$37,890	$42,358	$48,075
Adjusted price/Sq. ft.	$25.24	$24.90	$23.10	$22.77	$21.36
No. units	21	30	43	28	32
No. unsold	6	3	14	9	10
Baths	1½	2	2½	2½	3

FEATURES

Parking	2-Car garage	Oven type	Double	Balconies	40–3, 4, 5
Driveway	Concrete	Dishwasher	One	Tile	Entry
Fencing	7,000	Trash Compactor	–	Bonus room	–
Patios	Paved	Sprinklers	–	Drapes	–
Landscape	Front	Volume ceiling	¼–4, 5	Lot size	Standard
Fireplace	1, 2–4 & 5	Luminous ceiling	–		
Carpeting	Complete	Roofing	Shake		
Wet bar	3 & 5	Air conditioning	–		

SUBJECTIVE EVALUATION

Floor plans		Merchandizing		Very good
Density	4.0/Acres	Site		Good
Land plan	Good	Location		Average
Building design	Good	Amenities		Average

SALES

Sales start	12/15/74	Unsold; in construction	15
For sale to date	154	Presales	7
Completed and unsold	5	Sold to date	112
Development size	154	Weekly sales	3.6

FINANCING

Financing	%	8½	Down	10%
	%	9¾	Down	20%

Exhibit 6-6
Lambert Gardens: Price Adjustment Sheet

Plan No.	1	2	3	4	5
Standard price	$34,320	$44,104	$46,740	$51,708	$58,725
Parking	$2,000	$2,000	$2,000	$2,000	$2,000
Driveway	125	125	125	125	125
Fencing	600	600	600	600	600
Patios, atriums	500	500	500	500	500
Landscaping	150	150	150	150	150
Fireplace	850	850	850	1700	1700
Carpeting	600	600	600	600	600
Wet bar	—	—	500	—	500
Oven	225	225	225	225	225
Dishwasher	250	250	250	250	250
Trash compactor	—	—	—	—	—
Sprinklers	—	—	—	—	—
Volume ceiling	—	—	—	1,000	1,000
Luminous ceiling	—	—	—	—	—
Roofing	500	500	500	500	500
Air conditioning	—	—	—	—	—
Balconies, decks	—	—	400	400	400
Tile	50	50	50	50	50
Bonus room	—	—	—	—	—
Drapes	—	—	—	—	—
Lot size	—	—	—	—	—
Baths	700	1,400	2,100	2,100	2,900
Subtotal	$6,550	$7,250	$8,850	$9,350	$10,650
Adjusted price	$27,770	$36,854	$37,890	$42,358	$48,075

Exhibit 6-7
Green Acres: Data Collection Sheet

Development	Green Acres	Type	Detached
Developer	Hill Bros. Inc.	Date	6/29/75
Location	Jackson & Dupont	Map Key	

Plan No.	1	2	3	4
Bedrooms	3	3	4	4
Sq. footage	1,375	1,410	1,480	1,600
Price	$42,625	$42,582	$44,178	$45,760
Price/Sq. ft.	$31.00	$30.20	$29.85	$28.60
Adjusted price	$34,405	$34,362	$35,358	$36,940
Adjusted price/sq. ft.	$25.02	$24.37	$23.89	$23.08
No. units	23	18	34	18
No. unsold	14	6	20	5
Baths	2	2	2½	2½

FEATURES

Parking	2-car garage	Oven type	Double	Balconies	34–40
Driveway	Concrete	Dishwasher	One	Tile	Entry, Bath
Fencing	Wood, 5,000	Trash Compactor	–	Bonus room	–
Patios	Covered	Sprinklers	–	Drapes	–
Landscape	Front	Volume ceiling	¼-All	Lot size	62,000
Fireplace	One	Luminous ceiling	Kitchen		
Carpeting	–	Roofing	Asphalt		
Wet bar	1.2	Air conditioning	–		

SUBJECTIVE EVALUATION

Floor plans		Merchandising		Average
Density	3.6/acre	Site		Good (view)
Land plan	Good	Location		Good
Building Design	Good +	Amenities		Average

SALES

Sales start	2/15/75	Unsold, in construction	10
For sale to date	70	Presales	4
Completed and unsold	9	Sold to date	48
Development size	93	Weekly sales	2.5

FINANCING

Financing	%	8¾	Down	20%
	%	9	Down	10%

Exhibit 6–8
Green Acres: Price Adjustment Sheet

Plan No.	1	2	3	4
Standard price	$42,625	$42,582	$44,178	$45,760
Parking	$ 2,000	$ 2,000	$ 2,000	$ 2,000
Driveway	125	125	125	125
Fencing	500	500	500	500
Patios, atriums	700	700	700	700
Landscaping	150	150	150	150
Fireplace	850	850	850	850
Carpeting	—	—	—	—
Wet bar	500	500	—	—
Oven	225	225	225	225
Dishwasher	250	250	250	250
Trash compactor	—	—	—	—
Sprinklers	—	—	—	—
Volume ceiling	1,000	1,000	1,000	1,000
Luminous ceiling	300	300	300	300
Roofing	—	—	—	—
Air conditioning	—	—	—	—
Balconies, decks	—	—	400	400
Tile	100	100	100	100
Bonus room	—	—	—	—
Drapes	—	—	—	—
Lot size	120	120	120	120
Baths	1,400	1,400	2,100	2,100
Subtotal	8,220	8,220	8,820	8,820
Adjusted price	$34,405	$34,362	$35,358	$36,940

Exhibit 6-9
The Crossing: Data Collection Sheet

Development	The Crossing		Type	Detached
Developer	Far Horizon Development		Date	6/28/75
Location	Turner at Webner		Map key	A

Plan No.	1	2	3	4	
Bedrooms	2	3	3	4	
Sq. footage	1,200	1,450	1,500	1,640	
Price	$35,400	$40,600	$41,100	$43,132	
Price/Sq. ft.	$29.50	$28.00	$27.40	$26.30	
Adjusted price	$30,650	$35,150	$34,450	$35,282	
Adjusted price/sq. ft.	$25.54	$24.24	$22.96	$21.51	
No. units	10	12	18	10	
No. unsold	3	5	12	6	
Baths	$1\frac{1}{2}$	2	2	$2\frac{1}{2}$	

FEATURES

Parking	2-car garage	Oven type	Single	Balconies	20, 3-4
Driveway	Asphalt	Dishwasher	One	Tile	Entry
Fencing	—	Trash compactor	—	Bonus room	—
Patios	1, paved	Sprinklers	—	Drapes	—
Landscape	—	Volume ceiling	$\frac{1}{4}$ P., 3-4	Lot size	Standard
Fireplace	One	Luminous ceiling	—		
Carpeting	Partial	Roofing	Asphalt		
Wet bar	4 only	Air conditioning	—		

SUBJECTIVE EVALUATION ± $/UNIT _____

Floor plans		Merchandizing	Fair
Density	4.2 per acre	Site	Good
Land plan	Fair	Location	Fair
Building Design	Good	Amenities	Fair

SALES

Sales start	3/24/75	Unsold, in construction	8
For sale to date	50	Presales	0
Completed and unsold	7	Sold to date	24
Development size	50	Weekly sales	2.0

FINANCING

Financing	%	$8\frac{3}{4}$	Down	20%
	%	9.0	Down	10%

Exhibit 6–10
The Crossing: Price Adjustment Sheet

Plan No.	1	2	3	4
Standard price	$35,400	$40,600	$41,100	$43,132
Parking	$ 2,000	$ 2,000	$ 2,000	$ 2,000
Driveway	—	—	—	—
Fencing	—	—	—	—
Patios, Atriums	500	500	500	500
Landscaping	—	—	—	—
Fireplace	850	850	850	850
Carpeting	400	400	400	400
Wet bar	—	—	—	500
Oven	—	—	—	—
Dishwasher	250	250	250	250
Trash compactor	—	—	—	—
Sprinklers	—	—	—	—
Volume ceiling	—	—	1,000	1,000
Luminous ceiling	—	—	—	—
Roofing	—	—	—	—
Air conditioning	—	—	—	—
Balconies, decks	—	—	200	200
Tile	50	50	50	50
Bonus room	—	—	—	—
Drapes	—	—	—	—
Lot size	—	—	—	—
Baths	700	1,400	1,400	2,100
Subtotal	$ 4,750	$ 5,450	$ 6,650	$ 7,850
Adjusted price	$30,650	$35,150	$34,450	$35,282

Exhibit 6-11
Development Comparables Relationship Chart

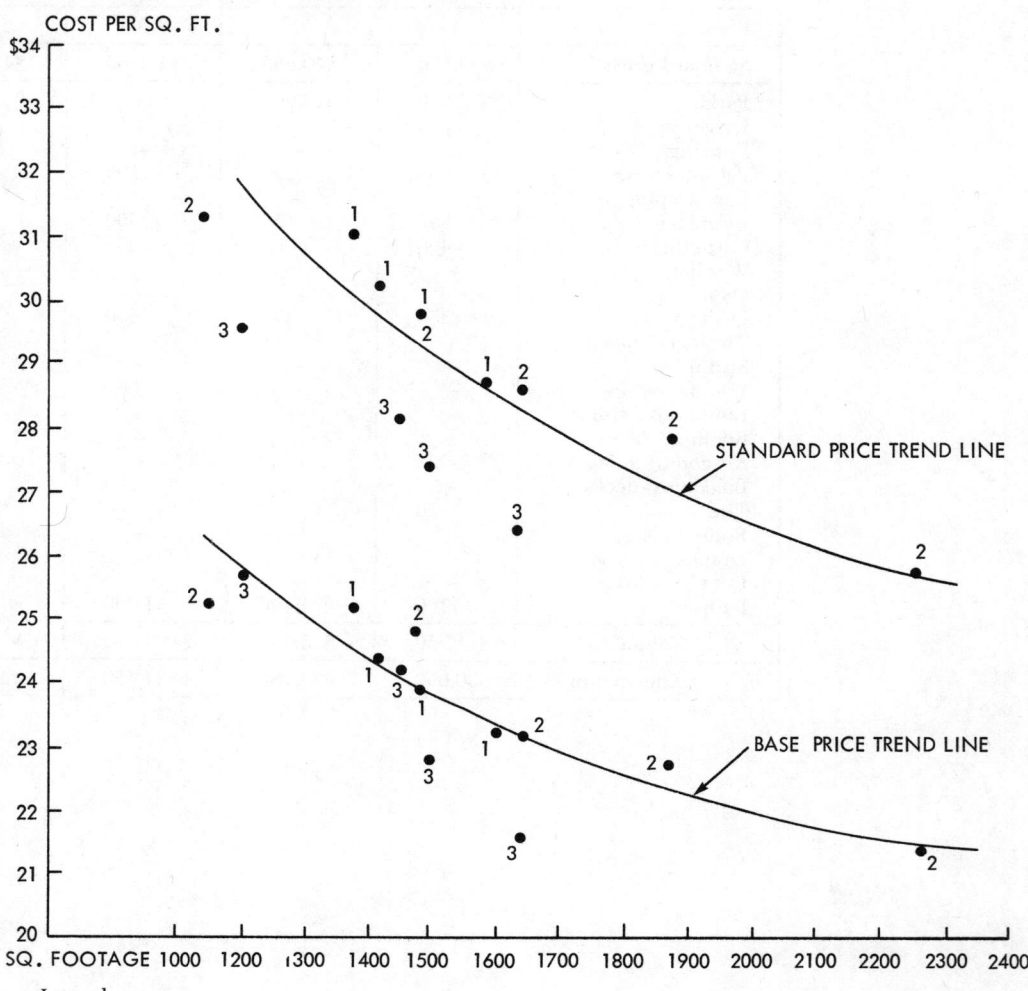

Legend
1. Green Acres
2. Lambert Gardens
3. The Crossing

7

Innovation: The key to profits

The key to ongoing profit is to achieve consistently some sort of monopoly on products or methods, however temporary that may be. By following a success formula in a market area, a real estate developer can generally achieve average profits. If the organization is particularly well managed, he may be able to produce average profits for a time. However, if he wants to produce above-average profits consistently and to control his risks, he must innovate.

The combination of identifying an unfilled demand and filling that demand with a product which emphasizes the weakness of the competition enhances the chances of success. Shrinking margins and intensified competition, however, are gradually changing the fabric of the building industry and may ultimately mean rather ordinary profits, plus more competition for the companies that do a really good job today and near disaster for those that continue to drift along with management and business practices that are not geared for today's intense competition. The executive directing a business with average prospects will find it increasingly difficult to earn above-average profits, even if he is very capable.

SUCCESS: THE DOWNFALL OF MANY A COMPANY

It is fair to state that a company that is rather ordinary in most respects can earn extraordinary profits if it plans and manages skillfully. The very success of these companies, however, guarantees a change in the competitive environment.

If thinking is an intelligent response to a problem, then the absence of a problem leads to the absence of thinking. In an automatically expanding market, one does not give much thought to how to expand it or develop new products. However, there is no guarantee against cyclical downturns and product obsolescence. If a company's own research does not make its product obsolete, another's will. If a company itself does not overbuild the market, its competition probably will.

I'll say this for adversity: People seem to be able to stand it, and that's more than I can say for prosperity.

Kin Hubbard

Too often developers fail to investigate properly consumer's wants and how they are being affected by social and economic change. They only investigate his preferences among the variety of products they have already decided to offer.

A growth company which has an apparently assured expansion of demand tends to underevaluate the importance of marketing and innovation. Too often, when a developer has found his niche and has produced a reasonable profit, he assumes he is doing things right. In the long run this could be a fatal assumption, because quite possibly his assumption is valid only for part of his operation.

CONFUSING LUCK WITH SKILL

While steady profits are coming in, the developer may be unaware of the offsetting deficiencies in his programs. What was assumed to be skill may later prove to be merely luck. This tunnel vision blocks out the perspective needed to identify the unfilled needs or holes in the market or to recognize new technology that may not be required for success. The usual result of this narrow preoccupation with so-called concrete matters is that instead of growing, the company dies (see Chapter 28).

All too often the company is so preoccupied with the success of its own operation that it does not see how it is being made obsolete. It is too easy to become dominated by the economics of standardization and production and develop a dangerously lopsided product orientation.

THE ELEMENT OF RISK IN INNOVATION

Especially in times of overbuilding, the developer must do something the competition is not doing to maximize profits and bring the development in at or below the market rate. By being innovative, he can outperform the competition and ease the financing job. However, testing out innovative concepts by building them can be a time-consuming and risky process.

Markets are becoming somewhat homogenized through such forces as television, mass media publications, national franchise organizations, and the geographical diversity of major corporations. National development corporations are adding to the homogeneity of markets every day. By knowing what has been successful in many market areas, it is possible to predict more accurately what will work in a specific market.

An individual canvas of the local market to look for a hole in the market, or marketing gaps, can be a time-consuming, nonproductive job. In a sense, one is looking for something which is not there; that is, it generally cannot be identified or proved by statistics. It is quite difficult to identify what innovations a market area is lacking and to know whether these would reliably produce profits if introduced. The job requires broad industry exposure and creative expertise (see Chapter 14).

To minimize risk, a developer can innovate for a specific market area only, adopting and modifying a tested and proven innovation in other similar but advanced markets. The developer can additionally reduce his risk by bringing in the services of a multimarket consultant with a good track record of innovation in other similar market areas. In this manner he can reduce risk by introducing proven products rather than total innovations.

> *Originality is nothing but judicious imitation. The most original writers borrowed one from another. The instruction we find in books is like fire. We fetch it from our neighbor's, kindle it at home, communicate it to others, and it becomes the property of all.*
>
> Voltaire

EFFECTS OF COMPANY SIZE

The advantages of being small

Smaller company size can be of advantage. Name or company visibility is becoming a liability in the sense that the most visible companies are the first targets of consumer protests and class-action suits. The wave of social and consumer dissatisfaction hits the largest, most visible companies first. Smaller companies can observe and correct their course, independent of the pressures which are brought to bear on larger competitors. This works with zoning as well as with product and management concerns. The well-managed smaller companies, by tapping outside expertise, can actually put themselves in a better position to respond quickly to changing markets than can their larger, more institutional competitors.

The new rules on Accounting for Profit Recognition on Sales of Real Estate, created on July 1, 1973 by the Committee on Accounting for Real Estate Transactions of the American Institute of Certified Public Accountants, give private companies an edge over public companies. Privately held companies, which are not concerned with reporting quarterly earnings, have much greater flexibility under the new rules in structuring their real estate deals and can thus be more competitive and innovative in the marketplace. Privately held companies, interested in producing economic income, are not as concerned with accounting income as are the public companies.

The new guidelines have a dramatic effect in reducing the immediate accounting income on the sales of income-producing properties and land sales from the way they had popularly been structured by public companies prior to the new guidelines. Privately held companies can continue to structure deals with incentives to the buyer which are not now practically available to public companies. As long as the private companies are chiefly concerned with generating economic as opposed to accounting income, they enjoy substantially more room for innovative structuring than their larger competitors.

Opportunities for innovation in a segmented industry

Almost all innovation seems to come from small companies outside of the mainstream of activity in the industry in which they are innovating. Many of the innovations that have been developed were accidental and unplanned. Housing is such a segmented industry that it has an advantage over many others; it can repeat innovations by going to new geographic areas and reaping the same benefits as though the innovation were totally new. Since the innovation has already been proven under a given set of circumstances, its application entails less risk than total innovation.

In a business environment where total innovations are so difficult to come by, borrowed innovations offer a distinct opportunity to the executive who is sensitive to trends outside his immediate area which have the facility of being transportable. The innovations need not come from the homebuilding industry but may be identified and utilized to advantage from other remote sources. The executive must have sensitivity and awareness to recognize the possibilities.

The vulnerability of big, well organized companies

Innovation requires entrepreneurial audacity, willingness to take risks, and the ability to be wrong. Experimentation and speculative activity are called for, but most people in a position to make an impact tend to be tough-minded, day-to-day doers who emphasize immediate results. The line manager wants practical ideas which closely conform to the current way of doing things and create the least disruption. It is really too much to expect the line manager to be otherwise, because he is judged and rewarded on the basis of meeting short-term performance goals. Line managers continually need to make a good showing of their present setup and to justify the decisions which have brought them to the present point.

New ideas are abstract and cannot be proven until tried. New ideas are worth pursuing, however, because the more novel an idea, the harder it is to implement, the more important it is—the greater the profit to the organization which can make it work. Most business failures occur not because of new ideas but because of a lack of them. Developments fail because someone did not stop to analyze how things had changed in the marketplace. Changes of any substance in the marketplace require different strategies from those that were previously in use. Too often, managers would rather maintain past judgments than be audacious and pursue an untried course.

There are two basic types of error: error of commission and error of omission. Errors of commission are generally readily detectable because they have launched some specific action which has not worked out according to the objectives. Errors of ommission generally do not show up immediately because no specific action has been launched. Because opportunities missed through omission may not be detected until a much later date, they are often regarded as safer to the individual. However, an organization is more vulnerable to the unseen errors of omission than to the more visual errors of commission.

Predominant opinions are generally the opinions of the generation that is vanishing.

Disraeli

INNOVATION METHODS

The success formula for organizations require them to be more knowledgeable about how to attract customers than the competition is. An essential starting point is to assess change and how it will affect the organization's business environment one, three, or five years from now. Few organizations do this because it is so difficult to project into the future, but the leading organizations in the future will be those that have anticipated and planned for it.

The people put in charge of charting the future are often high-level executives who have gotten to the top through their tough-minded, nononsense handling of day-to-day business and their reliable judgments. Their usual lack of sensitivity to abstracts or intangibles and their practical mindedness can stifle the venturesome audacity required to project into the future. The line executive will continue to think in terms of the concepts and actions to which he attributes his success and will downplay new ideas. To expect him to deviate from his preference for practicality and immediacy of results in order to speculate on future maybes, with no proof of payoff, may be expecting too much.

The executive also has to think of himself. His peers are more apt to look up to him for the soundness of his judgment and lack of mistakes than for coming up with many new ideas. This in effect puts a lid on imagination and innovation.

To make the leap from the routine to the new and untried, from cautious skepticism to the entertainment of radical notions and theories, requires a different type of background than the line executive usually possesses. Innovators must be selected who are known for their imaginativeness and audacity, without regard to position in the hierarchy. Since the permissiveness necessary to provide for such people generally does not exist within the organization, implementation may require outside consultants.

Eyes will not see when the heart wishes them to be blind. Desire conceals truth, as darkness does the earth.

Seneca

Innovations and projections of how external forces are likely to affect the company should be reported directly to top management, preferably the president. Lower-level managers are likely to review such reports with fear and hostility, because they are generally more interested in perpetuating the present order, which they were instrumental in bringing about, than in planning to obsolete it. Managers who are expected to be practical doers are not the best judge of the undefined future and the innovations that future may require.

The top executive is that judge, or should be. The major facet of his job is charting the future and positioning his organization to benefit from the inevitable change. To do this, he must unlearn to an extent the day-to-day, judicious practicality that got him to his top spot. He must leave this to his subordinates and concentrate his energies on seeing that they are going in the right direction (see Chapter 25).

SOCIAL CLUES FOR INNOVATIONS

Social developments which stress environmental quality and physical fitness are changing the patterns of what people expect or will tolerate in their housing. Only a decade or so ago, for example, large shopping centers requiring long walks from car to counter were considered chancy investments. Since then the success of malls has created a whole new generation of promenade shoppers. If rewarded by a more attractive, environment, Americans will carry their bundles a good distance.

Along with the concern for environmental quality is the basic human need for social involvement. People are naturally attracted to community focal points which provide a natural setting for mingling, impromptu chatting, and people watching. On a small scale, the community pool or recreation facility serves this purpose. On a larger scale, the enclosed mall-type, environmentally oriented shopping centers with planned events are becoming community focal points.

The shopping center has become a destination in itself as a social outlet —a pleasant way to spend an afternoon. These centers are being built in the midst of prime housing areas, in marked contrast to the recent past, when status was roughly proportional to one's distance away from commercial activity. When these areas are carefully designed, with social and environmental needs guiding design policy, people will enthusiastically accept a radical mix of shops, offices, apartments, and homes. The resultant environment acts as a magnet to create a community focal point. Residents buying or renting in such planned communities are buying not just shelter but a social support system, an environmental and social way of living.

In the past, developers have typically utilized a site for only one type of activity such as shops, offices, or housing, thereby contributing to the segregation of activities. This has precluded a cumulative buildup of activity or "excitement" and has produced cities and suburbs that are monotonous and dull.

A new phenomenon is the mixed-use developer who can put together all the basic elements of a focal point, with the conscious aim of a whole that exceeds the sum of its parts and produces excellent bottom-line results. In some instances the focal point, or social/environmental result, has been a result, rather than a cause, of mixed-use development. That is, the developers did not consciously set out to create a community focal point but rather sought to diversify their product mix within a market area.

OPPORTUNITIES FOR INNOVATION

As the law of contrary opinion in the stock market indicates, one way to create opportunities is by going against the prevailing trend. For example, in a high-technology, new-product-oriented, materialistic society, nostalgia, antiques, and memorabilia have a strong appeal. Opportunities can be found hiding in the opposite shadow of a strong prevailing trend.

Most everything in life occurs in the context of a cyclical pattern. Some cycles are longer and more enduring than others, but nonetheless the pattern is there. Understanding the cycles can be as rewarding in the marketing of real estate as it can be in the buying and selling of stocks or commodities (see Chapter 9).

Markets can be created by delivering product innovations into a market area. People can be won over by innovations and experiences they are unfamiliar with. A consumer questionnaire of the marketplace will not generally identify a need for the innovation because people cannot objectively comment on what they have not experienced. A person who has never eaten pizza cannot say how he likes it, though he can objectively comment after he has tasted it, and it might take more than one test to be objective. The same with real estate innovations: They can only be objectively evaluated by the public after they have been shown. If the public is positively responsive, the showing of the innovation has created a demand out of a latent need. If there is a single or limited supply in the market, a monopoly has been created (see Chapter 12).

The goal of innovation is to create a monopoly in a market area where there is a need. The monopoly may be in better merchandizing, interior design and landscaping of models, the best price, the best location to serve a particular submarket, making only studio or junior one-bedroom apartments available, exceptional recreational facilities, or planning superior to any in the market. Researching the competition to find their most glaring weaknesses is a good way to uncover needs.

By educating the public or making a "showing" in the market, a company can itself create change in the marketplace. The organization should examine the implications of every change to determine:

1. How will this change affect the organization negatively?
2. How will this change affect the organization positively?
3. In the light of the first two questions, what can the organization itself do to affect change, to the organization's betterment?

With every adversity there is the seed of an equivalent benefit. The benefits to be derived out of current adversity external and internal to the organization should be sought.

Changes of the recent past and how organizations have successfully responded also should be observed. This will provide strategy for charting today's course, and projections can throw light on tomorrow's.

What changes are occurring in taste, and why? What started the change, where is it leading, what is its significance to housing, to the company?

How should it affect merchandising, image, product mix, product type?

What changes are occurring in leisure? As leisure increases, spirits become lighter, and the emphasis is increasingly on fun. People want to steal away from work and play more. How should leisure trends affect product, strategies, merchandising?

Are there going to be tougher times ahead? How will customer wants be affected by anxiety and economic uncertainty? How will the organization and its products be affected? Is there a way the product or organization can reassure the customer that he is doing the right thing?

The customer's preferences for simplicity and convenience provide opportunities for innovation. Simplicity and convenience will create a more desirable product, and in merchandizing they will make it easier for the customer to buy.

The product and its merchandising also can be designed to reflect the growing social independence of people. Independence is creating smaller household sizes and releasing women from household concerns. One's friends are not necessarily one's neighbors because of the liberating influence of easy transportation and communications.

People's emotional needs also affect the success of innovations. When the right emotional appeal is found, people can be stimulated to do things they might otherwise consider unusual. Buying habits are composed of emotional and irrational stimulants, not sound logic.

Any possible course of action should be considered, no matter how much it may depart from the present order. The more novel and daring the innovation, the greater is its capacity to create change in consumer habits. The greater the capacity to create change, the greater the chance of success. Television and the airplane are prime examples of this effect of innovation.

Submarkets which are not being served provide opportunities for innovation. Even in markets clarified as overbuilt, there are opportunities within specific market segments to which others are not giving proper attention (see Chapter 8).

Sensitivity to market cycles also provides opportunities; profits can be increased with appropriate timing. One can also create one's own market cycles. Transferring a hot product mix, concept, or merchandising technique out of a market where it is peaking to one which has not been exposed to the innovation can create a sharply ascending profit cycle for the developer.

Smaller or static market areas often have a large percentage of older dwellings as compared to new construction, accompanied by low rental schedules or low average selling prices. Many of the builders in such a market may be mom-and-pop organizations who do not charge the company for their own time and other related expenses. They may therefore have an unrealistic view of their profits; they may think they are doing well, but by acceptable professional feasibility and measurement-of-return standards, that may not be the case.

In such a market, meeting the competition head-on may not prove to be feasible because prevailing rental or sales figures do not justify new construction. Often the only way to enter such a market is through a total innovation for the area which will create a monopoly situation and provide for commensurate premiums. In this instance innovation is an absolute necessity for feasibility. On the other hand, it is necessary to exercise some caution in bringing innovations into new market areas, because if it is a concept totally new to the area or one against which the area has a prejudice, the market may not accept it even though it is remarkably well done. The time required for the market to accept the concept could cause project failure (see Chapter 11).

Outstanding achievements have all been individualistic. Indeed, any original achievement implies separation from the majority. Though the majority may admire outstanding achievement, they can never produce it. What the many see is called a fact, what only one sees is called a dream.

Not armies, not nations, have advanced the race; but here and there, in the course of ages, an individual has stood up and cast his shadow over the world.

E. H. Chapin

8

Market segmentation

A geographic market is the aggregate of numerous submarkets or market segments. In considering a market in general, certain markets may be identified as overbuilt or soft. This observation may be true of the aggregate market, but it does not indicate much about the activity in the submarkets which comprise the aggregate market. Perhaps the condominium market in general is very overbuilt but, on the other hand there may be opportunities in the luxury, single-family, detached market.

Generalizations can be misleading when looking for specific opportunities. There will always be some builders in a market doing quite well, while the bulk of their competitors may be suffering. The difference is made by marketing sensitivity, an understanding of market segments and cycles, good management, and the courage to act.

It never troubles the wolf how many the sheep may be.
Virgil

HOW GENERALIZED DATA CAN BE MISLEADING

A housing concept must be aimed at a marketing opportunity with enough depth to support it. The larger competitors tend to go for the larger market segments in order to provide sufficient depth for their volume. Smaller market segments are attractive to smaller, specialty builders. However, when a market segment has been overlooked, large or small, it can provide rich opportunity for those deveopers who are in it early. A problem develops when a few developers do very well in a particular market segment and their competition, seeing their success, attempts to get in for the "easy money."

The initial success of the few and the subsequent increase in competitor interest change the market by filling the need, and thus the opportunity is eliminated. This does not, however, stop newcomers from entering the market, often in droves, because they are basing their analysis on past performance rather than the present reality and its implications for the future.

The multitude is always in the wrong.
                                    Roscommon

As an example, high vacancy rates in an apartment market do not necessarily suggest lack of opportunity. There may be geographic pockets with low vacancy rates that are in need of added supply. Additionally, vacancy rates do not affect apartment types uniformly. For example, there may be a strong demand for efficiency or junior one-bedroom apartments in an area with a high vacancy rate. The introduction of a supply that better fits the need could meet with immediate acceptance and rapid absorption (see Chapter 11).

WHY IT IS IMPORTANT TO UNDERSTAND MARKET SEGMENTATION

To hit the sales target, the product must be aimed at specific identifiable submarkets, not statistical generalizations. Aiming at the "broad market" without a proper regard for the submarkets which make it up is aiming at a phantom. One can't hit what isn't there. The broad market is made up of submarkets, is a statistical representation of what all of the combined submarkets represent, and is not a definable market itself which can be used as a target. To take aim on a statistical category almost assures a hit in between the submarkets which, in the aggregate, constitute the market statistics.

Condominium projects across the country have experienced difficulty because the developers and their lenders often did not understand the markets that the condo projects were developed to serve. Though these are numerous submarkets which condominiums can serve, they can be divided into two basic groupings as related to condominium marketing: concept and economic necessity.

The concept market is composed of those who choose condo living because they feel that they can thereby achieve a lifestyle which is generally not available in single-family, detached housing. They may be attracted to the condo's social and recreational aspects, maintenance-free living, security, or environmental features not available in comparable detached homes. Those interested in concept in the condo market generally do not have children; most families with children who have the alternative and the economic capability to do so will choose single-family, detached housing.

Those who are buying condos because of economic necessity are much more likely to have children, because they generally do not have equal opportunities to purchase a single-family home in their market area. The economic-necessity group, then, is composed of families with children who cannot find comparably priced single-family housing in the area and those who want ownership for financial advantages but can only afford moderately priced shelter. This can include less affluent singles, widows, and empty nesters.

An attractive, well-planned condo project in the suburbs will more than likely be attractive to those who are interested in concept; they will be empty nesters, widows, and young couples planning to put off development of a "family." The very same project located close in to a dense urban area could attract those motivated by economic necessity, because comparably priced single-family housing may be scarce or prohibitive in price close in to the city. The very same project may appeal to concept or economic necessity, depending on its location. It is important for the developer to know which grouping he is in—building for concept or for economic necessity. To land in the middle could be fatal. It could mean being too expensive to serve the economic-necessity market yet lacking the amenities or overall environmental attractiveness to serve the concept market.

It is into this middle ground that a number of competing projects throughout the country seem to have fallen. Because of the pricing structure, they were directly and unsuccessfully competing with the single-family detached market, and because of their density and lack of sophistication in planning and design, they were not attractive to the concept market.

In going for a purely concept market, it is important to recognize that a strong design concept is very important to marketing success. The difference between a routine design solution and an exciting, thematic one can be the difference between success and failure. Dilution of the concept, in order to reduce costs and thus attract a broader base of households which can qualify for the purchase, can have the opposite effect from that intended. The market the product is designed to attract is upper end. Dilution of the product in order to reach a broader income segment of the market could result in the product being less attractive and marketable to the specific market at which it is directed, yet too expensive for the broad-base market.

IDENTIFICATION OF MARKET SEGMENTS

Even those within an identifiable market segment buy for varying reasons, come from various sources, and may be attracted by various products. The principal market segments are the following:
1. Single unmarried.
2. Single divorced or widowed—may have children.
3. Young married.
4. Small family, one or two children.
5. Large family, three or more children.
6. Empty nester—older couple whose children have left home.
7. Active retired—working part time or active in civic and community affairs. Still active and often away from home.
8. Retired—activities limited to immediate community, spends most of time around home.

In addition to knowing how the market breaks down into segments, it is beneficial to know (1) where buyers are from, (2) why they buy, (3) what they buy, and (4) what their buying capabilities are.

Where do they come from?
1. Out of town — relocation, transfer; generally have an immediate need, want to buy from inventory.
2. Move up within community — need to accommodate larger family size; want better environment, better life-style, more prestige.
3. Move down within community — children have left home; separated; adverse economic conditions; old place requires too much time and maintenance; changed, less active interests require less space.
4. Renter turned buyer — interested in appreciation, tax shelter, pride of ownership, more space, better environment, roots.
5. New household formation — children leaving home, divorce, marriage.

Why do they buy?
1. Enticed by a concept — interested in better planning, environment, amenities, recreational aspects, maintenance-free living, security, better design of floor plans, interiors to reflect lifestyle preferences.
2. Out of economic necessity — want most house possible for the money in terms of space; budget constraints limit frills; little flexibility in ability to pay; may be turned on by extras and environmental way of living concepts but cannot readily afford them. Have little in the way of discretionary dollars, so purchases are influenced greatly by price, and preferences are limited to what is affordable with a limited, fixed monthly payment. Economic necessity does not necessarily mean low or moderate income; it is relative to the immediate community and the economic structure.
3. Want second or third homes in addition to primary home — for recreational and vacation purposes, for business purposes; could be from within metropolitan area or out of town.
4. Attracted by investment aspects — look upon home as a way of saving and building an estate; interested in tax-saving aspects, appreciation.
5. Strictly speculation — not so much interested in living in a home or the tax shelter or savings aspects as in turnover at a profit. Speculators will buy from a builder, never occupy the home, and sell within a relatively short holding period. Others will rent in the interim or establish a temporary residence for themselves. Some developments in Florida have sold as much as 30 percent of inventory to speculators. The speculator is eventually in competition with the builder in larger projects.
6. Want a particular location — present neighborhood may be deteriorating; want to live in a better school district, better neighborhood; job change may require relocation within the community; cost of fuel and traffic congestion may prompt a family to look for a home closer in to existing work, shopping, entertainment.

What do they buy?
1. Single family detached — scattered lot, subdivision, planned unit development.
2. Cluster housing — single-family housing with common open space.

3. Zero-lot-line housing—small-lot, single-family housing, with the home generally built on one of the side lot lines. When lots are too small, less than a 50-foot zero lot line can take on multifamily housing characteristics.
4. Townhouses—attached housing generally sold as condominiums.
5. Patio homes—townhouses with wider lots and private patios.
6. Attached single family—a single-family house on such a small lot that the homes are attached. Similar to zero-lot-line and patio homes.
7. Apartments—high-rise, medium-rise, garden.
8. Fourplex
9. Duplex.

What are their buying capabilities?

1. Luxury—largest discretionary income; price not as important as concept, location. Environmental way of living aspects very important. Flexibility in pricing, willing and able to pay more for prestige, pride of ownership. More conscious of environment and quality than price.
2. Middle-class comfort—much influenced by concept and environment. Will pay premiums for the features and location of their choice; however, more constrained by price considerations. These buyers have arrived at their potentials and have reached a plateau in their economic and social achievements.
3. Starter home—want concept and environment that are presently out of reach, and are willing to settle for less than they desire in order to live within what their pocketbook will presently allow. See themselves as being upwardly mobile and investing in a starter home to build up equity so they can afford middle-class comfort.
4. Economic necessity—decision made more by pocketbook than environmental preferences. Does not necessarily mean low or moderate income but is relative to the community, vicinity.

FITTING MARKET SEGMENTS AND PRODUCT TYPES TO ORGANIZATIONAL OBJECTIVES

Though opportunities may be identified within specific market segments, they nonetheless may not qualify as opportunities to the organization. For example, the organization may not have the resources or capabilities to capitalize on a particular opportunity, or the opportunity may not fall within the scope of the organization's long-term objectives. A strong opportunity may exist for a high-rise development, but the organization may have no experience in the market. The market may have a need for low-cost housing, but the organization's expertise and objectives are oriented to upper-income housing. An opportunity may exist for a rental development, but the organization may not have the financial muscle to handle it or the property management expertise required to make it work.

If a development program is to be viable, it must fill a definite market need, contribute to the organization's long-term objectives, and be within reach of the organization's capabilities and resources (see Chapter 2).

9

Market cycles: Seeing beyond the horizon

There is a tendency to assume that a recognized trend will continue on its trend line indefinitely. The tendency becomes impulsive after the trend has continued long enough to be obvious to nearly everyone. However, when trends are obvious to even the office boy, they are generally at their peak and preparing for a slide down the back side of a cycle.

Managers must be aware that events occur not in unbroken trends but in cycles. The long-term trend may be an upward trend, a downward trend, or a horizontal trend, but its near-term progress will be reflected by cyclical changes. Even though a manager may be intellectually aware that his industry is cyclical, however, he may become emotionally committed to continued nonstop growth. Visualizing the rewards to be had if present favorable trends can be maintained until his firm has exhausted the opportunities they present, the manager may allow his emotions to overrule his intellect. Then it is likely the boom and bust cycle will be reinforced.

For age and want save while you may: No morning sun lasts a whole day.
Proverb

At the time of the two-tier stock market, fund managers sought safety in the "one-decision stock." Even these astute, seasoned professionals were taken in by the promise of an ever-ascending trend line, in the belief that some situations are so good, so unique, that they will react differently to pressures affecting the rest of the nation and the market in general. The strongest belief in the certainty of the two-tier market came just before its fall.

No great thing is created suddenly, any more than a bunch of grapes or a fig. If you tell me that you desire a fig, I answer you that there must be time. Let it first blossom, then bear fruit, then ripen.
Epicetus

Trends always come in cycles. Cycles create change, and change provides opportunity for those sensitive enough to comprehend their meaning and decisive enough to act. However, change also produces obstacles for those who lack sensitivity to their environment and who work with the tunnel-vision view of their narrow preoccupation with day-to-day "fire fighting." Those who are too satisfied with current success and abide by the criteria of today also resist change.

The increasingly shorter duration of market cycles and the greater spread between their valleys and peaks is thinning out competitors who cannot chart a course through such a stormy sea and providing opportunities for the skilled professional who can do so. Such rapid change is reminiscent of the old Chinese curse, "May you be condemned to live in interesting times."

Happy those who knowing they are subject to uncertain changes, are prepared and armed for either fortune; a rare principle, and with much labor learned in wisdom's school.

Philip Massinger

A decision maker who does not know how profits will be affected by cyclical change, both short- and long-term, works at a disadvantage, particularly if the competition is more knowledgeable than he is.

SHAPING THE FUTURE

While it is not possible to accurately predict the future, what will happen then is often a foreseeable consequence of what is done now. Inability to predict the future is not an excuse for failure to anticipate. Whatever happens in the future should be more or less due to deliberate actions, and not strictly by chance.

National issues are having an increasing impact on local markets (see Chapter 5). Such outside factors, over which the developer has little control, have a major effect on the developer's business. However, the developer has quite a bit of latitude as to how he will anticipate and plan a strategy to cope with these factors.

Success in anticipating the future needs and responses of consumers, and therefore success in helping to shape their needs and wants, requires two things. The first is an understanding of the direction in which the society or market area is moving; how forces being generated within the market are affecting direction, even though they may not have surfaced as yet; and how forces outside the market area are shaping market conditions.

The second requirement for success is an understanding of the cyclical and long-term nature of the market, along with knowledge of where a market is in its cycle and where the cycles are heading. Knowing where a market is and in which directions its tastes and preferences seem to be going provides an important basis for judging not only the appropriateness of a plan but its feasibility as well. Most importantly, knowing these things puts the developer in a position to consider how to create new markets by discovering to what suggestions the consumer is open and what he can be taught to want. That done, all else is easier. Possession of such knowledge provides some initial assurance that the company, instead of being (as most are) an imitator, will be an innovator.

The greater the difficulty, the more glory in surmounting it. Skillful pilots gain their reputation from storms and tempests.

Epicurus

NATIONAL INFLUENCES ON LOCAL MARKET CONDITIONS

Marketing and feasibility research should evaluate the effect of national political and social trends as related to the developer's objectives, as well as local trends. In the past developers have had only a passing interest in the national economic outlook in evaluating the marketing feasibility of land development projects. However, since so many developers have recently experienced setbacks in their local market areas as a direct result of issues at the national level, they are attaching more importance to the national outlook in evaluating local feasibility of projects. Additionally, developers are becoming more aware of the radical shifts occurring in competitive position.

The peaks and valleys in homebuilding will increasingly be the result of conditions outside the immediate market area. Inflation and insufficient mortgages funds are not themselves a cause of homebuilders' problems; rather, they are an effect of national and international economic events. Feasibility studies require more than a rudimentary understanding of the international and national economic environment.

One does not have to be an economist able to sort out the implications of economic events to benefit from such knowledge, since the opinions of economists who make it their lifework to interpret economic events are readily available. Numerous homebuilders' trade and technical publications, newsletter services, the *Wall Street Journal,* and NAHB economists all contribute to this knowledge. Knowing the economic environment in which one must operate is an important first step in any planning, for the economic environment may well have more of an impact on the outcome of a business than the planning itself. A mediocre organization may fare much better in an expansive business environment than an excellent organization in a restrictive or declining environment.

Though economists can project national trends and prognosticate what the short- or long-term implications of these trends are, it is up to the developer to be sensitive to the opportunities or obstacles these trends place in the path of his objectives.

WHY IT IS IMPORTANT TO UNDERSTAND CYCLES

The obvious reason why an understanding of market cycles is essential is that the developer does not want to commit himself to a development program aimed at a market which is peaking and about to decline. Another reason, equally important, is that by understanding cycles and their nature it is possible to positively affect market cycles, instead of merely reacting to them. Stated another way, one can create one's own cycles and ride them from bottom to top, and let the others go after the crumbs.

Innovation makes it possible to open up a latent market which has had no activity or to create a product monopoly which captures a good share of an existing market. To innovate it is not always necessary to create a new concept from scratch; a successful concept in one market area can be modified and relocated in another which has not been exposed to the concept. In this way the developer becomes a creator of cycles rather than a follower (see Chapters 7 and 15).

Guarding against static assumptions

If he is to successfully innovate and start up his own cycles, the developer must guard against static assumptions. He has to think in terms of how the market can be changed by the introduction of something new, and how that change in the market can reap profits for those who are timely enough to fill the needs of a new demand situation. As has been noted, the demand is created by the introduction of something new; until that introduction is made, the potential demand remains latent.

When an executive limits his organization by static assumptions he can only see the market as it has been or currently is, and he tends to follow the market rather than affecting its direction to his benefit. There was no demand for radios, television, frost-free refrigerators, or airplanes until they had been introduced on the market. The introduction of these products changed the market, in a very significant manner.

The view beyond the horizon

Real estate development is so dependent on overall conditions that numerous cycles—national and local, political and economic, social and environmental—have a bearing on land development feasibility. In addition, new issues or cycles which affect the business environment are constantly emerging. For example, the drain of assets to the OPEC countries to pay for energy sources eliminates dollars that ordinarily would have gone into home purchases. Thus shortages and increased costs of fuel alter development patterns, as well as building codes and construction costs.

The developer can be mislead by relying on a consensus of opinion, demographics, or statistics. Opportunities are often created for going opposite directions at the same time. Tearing down the old to replace it with new products and technologies provides a growing market for nostalgia and memorabilia. Boredom with frozen dinners and packaged prepared foods of all types has provided support for an opposite market: "food like mama used to make."

Though the local, national, and international influences which have a bearing on the land development industry are numerless, the review of some of the more important cycles in the following sections should help increase awareness of the impact of cycles on feasibility.

> *Surely in vain the net is spread in the sight of any bird.*
> Proverbs 1:17

THE NEW CONCEPT/ MARKET OVERKILL CYCLE

Low-end condominiums

A good example of the new concept/market overkill cycle is in the market for low-end condominiums. When monthly payments are about equal to good-quality apartments in the area and below those of single-family detached housing, the market has been good. Developers who act first can draw a large number of apartment dwellers into their condominiums and do quite well. This has been successful in various markets around the country. However, let's look at how the particular submarket is affected by the new development.

Certain groups of apartment renters will be very much taken up with a condo sales presentation, and the initial absorption from the apartment market will be fairly large. After the first big chunk is taken, the next four or five competitors will get less and less, however. The concept initially sounds good to the people in apartments; the condominium appears as nice as or maybe even nicer than the apartment. The apartment resident says to himself, "I enjoy my apartment because I have nice neighbors: a lawyer living across the courtyard from me, a young intern here, an accountant next door. So why shouldn't I move into the condominium? It's pretty close to what I am living in now."

The resident sometimes finds, however, that people who will live in apartments such as he is living in generally will not buy into the condominium he is thinking about. The lawyer, accountant, or doctor does not want ownership at this time, preferring the flexibility of renting. So, though the buyer into a condo project often assumes he is buying into a socioeconomic environment similar to that of his apartment, he finds that this is not so. Where before he was living next to the doctor, lawyer, and accountant, he is now living next to the milk truck driver, butcher at the Safeway, and shoe store clerk. In apartments there can be a broad range of social and economic interests. In low-end condos this range is narrower, and the appeal is to a different socioeconomic group.

As new developers rush in to exploit the "proven" development opportunity, the market thins out and the potential buyers remaining have become very educated to the pitfalls. At this point the market becomes saturated and sales slide into a decline, which is attributable to either a drop in aggregate sales or too many developers chasing the buyers.

Though the development concept has peaked in a given market, a developer can transport it to a new market where it has not yet been introduced. There he can start his own money machine, while the competitors in the overbuilt market are left behind.

Swinger apartments

A good example of how innovation can create its own booming cycle is the swinger apartment. When swinger apartments were first introduced they offered a new concept in living to singles and were very popular, the "in-place" to live. Their popularity and initial exclusiveness merited premium rents.

At first the influence leaders and trend setters were attracted because they knew a good thing when they saw it. When it became common knowledge that the swinging apartments were a good place to get in the swim and "body snatch," they were frequented by others. As the type of residents gradually changed, a negative image became associated with living in a swinger apartment complex. As quality of residents deteriorated, management problems increased, and waiting lists for occupancy disappeared. The negative image became so pervasive that some managements changed the names of their developments and initiated new policies.

This does not mean that the original concept of swinger apartments was lacking; far from it. It does suggest, however, that management was not timely enough in adapting the concept to changing market conditions. An important point is that a concept can peak out, not only because of changes in the supply and demand forces in the marketplace but because the concept itself changes the market. The length of time it takes for a concept to change the nature of the market is a measure of its upside potential. This is a separate and possibly more fundamental consideration than depth of market, for changes in the nature of the market affect its depth.

As noted above, a concept that has peaked because of changes in nature and depth of market in one locality can be transferred to another locality and can succeed as an entirely new innovation. The second and third time around management also gets a better feel for adapting to changes in the nature of the market which it creates.

The fourplex boom

A similar example of how innovation can produce a strong profit cycle for the forward-thinking developer is the fourplex boom. A developer who had been made nationally prominent through his success in merchandizing fourplex communities exported his formula from one market area to the next, enjoying repeat success wherever he went. When he had changed the demand and character of one market he would move into the next. However, he experienced problems by not adopting his concept in a timely manner to meet the changing character of the market. Though he was the prime instigator in changing the character of the market, he did not adequately understand the implication of the change, or if he did he failed to act upon it in a timely manner.

The individual fourplex units were an economic-necessity form of housing, offering price to a market which had had few buying alternatives in the past. Problems developed when the competition came in with product and concept improvements that often provided a better environment. Satisfied with his current success, the innovator failed to introduce product improvements soon enough, and he began to develop a reputation for poor quality planning and a ticky-tacky product.

So prominent was the developer's growth record that he became known nationally for his developments. Not all of the reputation was good, however. Though highly regarded by the development community for his success, he was becoming infamous to planning boards and community groups in areas to which he sought to transfer his concept. Zoning became difficult and sales lagged. With his national prominence, he had educated a national market and produced changes in the nature of the market nationally. This prominence, in conjunction with his failure to modify the concept to reflect preferences of the market, diminished his ability to transfer the concept to a new market. The new market was not only already educated, but at times it contained competitors who had already introduced the fourplex with a better concept.

THE HOT MARKET/OVERKILL CYCLE

When more and more large corporations were diversifying into housing as a vogue industry, they reshaped industry patterns and economics. Particularly evident was the trend toward large multimarket producers who were ever-eager to expand into new areas. Expansion-minded managers systematically researched regional statistics throughout the country and were quick to attach a growth label when the statistics match up with management's guidelines as to what constitutes a growth area. Unfortunately, many of the best yardsticks of growth tend first to be self-fulfilling and then self-destroying. The forecast reveals an opportunity; developers rush in to exploit it, and in the competitive overkill that follows, the profit opportunity vanishes.

The single-market or hometown developer can be particularly vulnerable to overkill, because he has no other markets to provide him with balance and flexibility while his market is being attacked by multimarket competitors. With the ever-present threat of overkill adding uncertainty to the economics of any market area, there is little room for the marginal or unprofessional developer. Whatever market the developer is seeking to capture—luxury, moderate income, low income, subsidy—he must have the most competitive product and most flexible real estate investment package within his market. He needs this as insurance against unforeseen competition and rampant change.

The migration of big business into housing has been a chief factor contributing to overkill, but there is an equally important pattern emerging which produces overkill as a side effect. The pattern is itself a result of big-business, long-range corporate planning. Big business initiates and evaluates major policy directives to conform to and fulfill the organization's long-range plans (such as a five-year plan). In turn, day-to-day operating decisions are influenced and guided by the major policy directives.

As an example of how this works, say that management finds it necessary to open a new market area in order to fulfill the earnings projections in the long-range plan. The new market area is assigned the task of contributing X amount of dollars in earnings as its contribution to total earnings. Therefore, when a multimarket builder enters a new area, it is generally with the proviso that the new area will add X amount of units per year (say 500) to total volume. It is now necessary for local managemeant to gear day-to-day operations for the production of X number of units per year, in order to conform with the major policy decision of management, which itself was initiated to fulfill the objectives of the long-range plan.

Areas identified with a growth label receive new inventories of thousands of units, not because of demand for thousands of units of housing in the area, but because of corporate planning. Granted that some corporations are more flexible in revising long-range plans than others, nonetheless the pattern exists.

Part of the problem is that developers mistakenly identify the type of opportunity or do not want to recognize that the opportunity primarily exists because of accumulated demand, which is not the same thing as ongoing demand. Once accumulated demand has been worked off, only ongoing demand remains, which in itself may not even come close to supporting the current building start rate. The start rate, however, may continue to swell after accumulated demand has been worked off. This leads to a market bust (see Chapter 11).

Another version of the market bust occurs when strong ongoing demand is curbed through restrictive legislation. Those who have already arrived in a community want to insulate themselves from continued growth and its environmental consequences. They do this through restrictive legislation of wide-ranging implications, and failure to vote in bond issues required for the expansion of municipal and support facilities. This type of bust can be particularly damaging to the developer because it is not market oriented but politically and socially motivated, and the extent and severity of the legislation may be completely unanticipated in the market-planning process. This may leave the developer fatally vulnerable, for he cannot successfully execute long-range planning and protect his commitments in an environment of hostility where major forces are working against his economic interests (see Chapter 5).

THE BUSINESS EXPANSION/ RECESSION CYCLE

There is no fixed relationship between the number of families or family formations and the number of housing units that will be sold or rented to these families. The relationship is a dynamic one which is sensitive to the economic ability of the families to pay for housing.

During difficult times, when there is substantial unemployment and economic uncertainty, many families cannot support an individual housing unit and therefore contrive to share housing. When economic ability to pay dwindles, inventory cannot be readily removed from the market, since buildings are relatively permanent. All of the housing which exists must compete for the housing dollar at a level where families can afford to again become consumers. This may produce sharp breaks in the price and rental structure.

In an economic recession ability to pay shrinks rather than ceases; the vital functions must continue. During the adjustment period people will continue to eat, wear clothes, and utilize housing, furniture, and related household goods. The rate of consumption may vary quite widely for some goods, but for others the rate of consumption and depreciation will be largely the same. In a recession it is the rate of replacement which changes more dramatically than the rate of consumption.

Families that have been able to maintain their incomes at previous levels cut spending, not because of inability to pay but because of economic uncertainty. These families postpone replacement of goods, thus exhausting inventories and allowing greater depreciation to occur than was previously acceptable in more optimistic times. At some point these consumers are no longer willing to postpone replacement and are enticed into the market by the price structure, which typically has been driven lower. At this point, presumably, prices cease to fall and trend upward, creating a buy-now momentum based on the fear of missing the opportunity to purchase at bargain prices.

The recent recession is different from those of the past in that it has been accompanied by inflation rather than deflation. This makes it more difficult to turn the economy around; the bargains are not in evidence to entice the consumer back into the market in strength. In addition to lacking motivation, the consumer also lacks economic ability to pay when there is inflation in the midst of recession. When the consumer does return to the market, as a result of acute need and less uncertainty, he will not generally be able to pay for the standard of living enjoyed before the recession. He will of necessity settle more for the basics and forego the extras or luxuries. This will be a middle-class phenomenon.

The more affluent and those with disposable dollars will tend to indulge themselves in the niceties of life, reasoning that it is better to spend their money before it is eroded by inflation. This two-tier condition has been identified by some as the doom boom. Whatever its label, it is eroding the lifestyle of the middle class, and it will continue to be reflected in, changed consumer spending patterns.

To determine consumer buying power, the developer should ask three prime questions:

1. What is the consumer's attitude regarding spending versus saving?
2. How many consumers have the economic ability to transfer need into market action?
3. What is the trend in unemployment and earnings?

THE DISCARDABLE COMMODITY, ENERGY WASTE/ CONSERVATION CYCLE

The energy crisis and reappraisals of energy consumption patterns will continue to have a strong effect on land development patterns. The second-home and recreational land sales industries were particular casualties of the 1973 "energy shortage." Feasibility will be more and more dependent on national issues which have increasing importance as influences on the fabric of life of all Americans. Though some local markets may vary sharply from the national pattern, they all become caught up in national trends to one degree or another.

Materials shortages also affect the way housing is built. Housing with more permanence is called for in a materials-scarce economy, which cannot afford to build discardable housing. Longer life cycles in housing will result, as well as more emphasis on rehabilitation and remodeling. Longer depreciation life can lead to longer mortgage terms, thus reducing monthly constant payments and enabling more families to qualify for housing purchases.

Buyers, who formerly were unwilling to pay for superior insulation and other energy-saving home features, are now demanding them. The increased cost and potential shortages of gasoline are changing consumer preferences in where they want to live; long drives from suburbs to work are not accepted as readily. This encourages urban renewal and closer-in, higher density housing. Mixed-use developments can be expected to come into their own as an energy-saving consideration. The benefits of living, shopping, and possibly working in the same area will gain in appeal as energy conservation is given economic significance.

A related cycle is exclusionary zoning in communities. At the present time, zoning which excludes builders appears to be backfiring. For instance, a West Coast community which did not allow developers to come in lost its tax base and also created a housing shortage. As a result of the housing shortage, prices of existing housing skyrocketed. Tax bills on homes in the area one year had a 50 percent increase over previous bills because of increases in resale comparables in the area.

People with fixed incomes can be forced out of their homes if they cannot meet skyrocketing tax bills, and communities can experience high unemployment rates because of their no-growth policies. Whereas growth has been presumed to sap community resources, people in certain areas are finding that no growth also has adverse economic effects. Perhaps this finding is a signal that exclusionary zoning will peak out in its cycle for a particular community, it might be the right time to submit new development plans. Following such local cycles provides a clue to trends with which cycles in similar market areas can be compared.

THE URBAN SPRAWL/ RETREAT CYCLE

As a result of the new energy consciousness, more development can be expected to occur in close-in, formerly bypassed properties, and builders will need to be more careful in developing surburban sites remote from employment centers.

The move to close-in development patterns will cause some marketing aberrations and create new yardsticks for feasibility evaluation. For example, close-in communities that have been designed for predominately blue-collar residents will shift in many instances to white-collar and professional residents. This trend will be accentuated in the immediate vicinity of commercial retail hubs, because of the convenient location for shopping as well as convenience to employment centers.

The higher-quality development in formerly blue-collar areas will produce changes in the socioeconomic mix of these communities. As the energy crisis, which has become an emotional as well as financial concern to families, creates a rise in land values in close-in communities, the entry of many new blue-collar families will be economically excluded.

It is interesting that white-collar and professionals residents who can afford the prices now being demanded for close-in locations will buy in to these communities and not be dissuaded by the lower economic base. The increased valuation of these close-in sites will generally preclude the development of single-family residences, and these properties will primarily be developed in a multifamily manner. The new multifamily developments will be attractive to families with children, because of economic necessity; multifamily construction may be the only alternative for those desiring to live in the community. In many of these communities, there will not be competition from existing condominium developments because previous construction has been predominately small-lot, single-family homes. This will not necessarily be a general pattern, but it will occur in certain close-in areas with focal points sufficient to create a regional hub outside of the central employment center.

Not only will these close-in communities be revitalized by the reentry of higher income families, but economic and functional obsolescence of the older existing housing inventories will be stemmed by greater emphasis on rehabilitation and remodeling. The increased tax base as a result of this socioeconomic shift in the community will provide for better community services, to further enhance desirability and stem obsolescence.

THE MORTGAGE MONEY BOOM/BUST CYCLE

It has been noted that when lenders are flush with money they try to get it out in the worst way, and they usually do. When lenders search out builders to put out funds, the temptation for the builder to try to utilize all of the funds he can get his hands on is enormous. The developer then wants to expand in the worst way, and he usually does.

Money, its price and buying power, is as important to the level of real estate activity and price as the supply and demand forces in the local marketplace. However, real estate for use such as homes, industrial properties, and farmland is not affected in the same way as income real estate. Whereas inflation, and the consequent increased interest and operating costs, may reduce the net income and market value of income properties, it has dramatically increased the value of properties for uses such as homebuilding. Replacement cost is a more relevant measure of value in properties for use than it is in income properties, which earn their value based on their ability to produce income. Though there are differences in the effects of money on use properties and income properties, both are nonetheless affected by fluxuations in the money market (see Chapter 19).

In properties for use, a high lending rate tends to curtail activity more than values; in income properties, a high lending rate depresses both activity and value proportionate to the increase in rate. In times when money is scarce, regardless of rate, income properties of some size may fare better, activitywise, than use properties, because the developer may have financial options open to him. For example, when funds initially dried up in Florida the builders of for-sale housing were brought to a halt because they depended heavily on local savings and loans and banks. However, developers of sizable income properties could shop nationally for funds. National lenders were still attracted to income properties of merit but could not be bothered with the administrative expense which would result in placing a loan on a project of individual dwelling units for sale.

LEGISLATIVE-INDUCED CYCLES

Legislative-induced cycles can result from stringent building department requirements being placed on a type of construction. For example, requiring fire sprinklers on all apartment buildings three stories and over is, on the surface, a fire safety requirement. However, its effect is one of creating a moratorium on three-story apartment construction, with the purpose of reducing allowable densities without going through the formality of a change in zoning or zoning laws. Construction is economically discouraged through park fees, mandatory dedication bedroom taxes, disportionate utility fees levied on new construction, and so on.

These types of legislative-induced conditions can have a dramatic impact on development trends and can create cycles which are difficult to predict because the events are often unexpected and cannot be charted by supply/demand projections or logical analysis. Real estate is one of the most controlled industries in the country, and the inability to forecast legislative-induced change makes it one of the highest risk industries (see Chapter 5).

Environmental reporting requirements, conservation, and no-growth extremes make it particularly difficult to project land economics and risk. Builders are tending to counter the risk by paying more for land that is already zoned, rather than incurring the risk involved in rezoning. Even zoned land cannot be bought too far in advance of its actual use. The uncertainty of use which is due to unfavorable legislation is in proportion to the length of the holding period. These developments have tended to split land development into two groups of operations: (1) land packaging, preparation, and development, and (2) building and construction.

Accounting standards board rulings are having a major effect on publicly held real estate development and land sales companies and will also affect all companies, whether or not they are publicly held. Because of the impact board rulings are having on the way public companies report profits on the sale of rental housing and land, many of the large national housing producers have cut back on rental housing or suspended rental development entirely. Though a company's reportable earnings may not be directly affected by the board rulings, and though a company is not public or in rental housing, its market area and business climate will be affected nonetheless.

What the multimarket giants did to the local multifamily rental market, they have repeated in the condominium market. There has been a significant movement of the giants into the for-sale market, particularly condominiums. As the majors are downplaying the multifamily for-rent market, this will mean more competition for developers in the for-sale market.

To the nonpublic, small- to medium-sized for-sale builder, this is going to mean reduced competition and new opportunities in the rental markets. The sweeping change that is reshaping the for-sale market is providing a back door via new opportunities in the rental market.

THE INSTITUTIONAL ROMANCE/ FALL-OUT CYCLE

There are also cycles in the national scene. Capital-intensive companies are leaving the housing marketplace, and many of the large public companies are getting out of housing because of dismal experiences there. Most notably, they are getting out of rental housing because of rulings by the Committee on Accounting for Real Estate Transactions (see Chapter 7) and other changes that affect the way earnings are reported. The big builders (the public companies) who are getting out of housing are not going to be coming back, because it does not make sense to them.

HOW TO UTILIZE AN UNDERSTANDING OF CYCLES

The cycles discussed in this chapter are only a small portion of the cycles affecting the business environment in which developers must operate. The developer must be constantly on the alert to identify new cycles and their implications. An awareness of cycles will enable the executive to see the business environment as the dynamic arena it is. It will blunt his natural tendencies to project trends indefinitely or to form static assumptions based on conditions as they presently exist.

Success in development (as in the stock market) requires a sensitivity to the law of contrary opinion: What appears to be obviously right is generally wrong. Excellence can only be achieved by the few who take a path contrary to that of the multitude. To remain with the many is to be mediocre at best; excellence and mediocrity are self-exclusive. The multitude may admire excellence but can never achieve it. A sensitivity to business cycles and the courage to venture from consensus opinion will give the executive the all-important knowledge of time and place and enable him to keep his head while others are losing theirs.

Cowards do not count in battle; they are there, but not in it.
                                                           Euripides

The obvious should be regarded with caution; when vacancies are at very low levels, that is not necessarily the time to build apartments. Too many other developers get the same signal and launch construction, so that the market is soon glutted. When occupancy is at an all-time high, it is reasonable to expect that it will top out, and possibly a bust will follow. A better strategy might be to gear up for construction when vacancy rates are improving and the competition has been discouraged by poor projects to that point.

The same thinking can also be applied to hot market areas. Growth markets constitute a compelling stimulus for developers to increase their volume by opening up new regions. The problem again is that too many get the same idea at the same time, and the market is glutted. Markets in Denver, Memphis, many of those in Florida are examples of many which have experienced such cycles.

In interpreting and reacting to cycles, it is well to remember that things are seldom as bad or as good as they seem at present. Prudence in interpreting cycles and in policy formulation calls for moderation. The majority moves like a pendulum, from one extreme to the other and with wide swings from the central balance point. In development as in the stock market, sometimes it pays to be a bear, other times a bull; but moderation, a cool head, and sense of balance and place should prevail. In a cyclical industry such as homebuilding, management needs to be evaluated by two yardsticks, much as mutual fund managers are, with different standards for performance rating in bull markets and in bear markets.

Decision of character will often give to an inferior mind command over a superior.
                                                           W. Wirt

Adversity has the effect of eliciting talents which in prosperous circumstances would have lain dormant.
                                                           Horace

A manager is not fully tested until he has shown capability in capital preservation as well as capital gain. Capital gain puts the emphasis on audacity, flexibility, venturesomeness, diversification, and leverage capital, whereas preservation emphasizes tightness, controls, consolidation, and liquidity. Different economic environments require differing management styles. Industrial managers in the growth school thought that through careful planning they could internally diversify sufficiently through acquisition of both cyclical and countercyclical industries, to produce compounded earnings gains through both up and down markets. The advocates of uninterrupted growth through diversification found that the diversification itself created an inflexible situation of sorts which compromised the organization's ability to adjust rapidly to sharp market fluxuations. That is, the problem of running many companies absorbed management's capabilities and resources to such an extent that it could not devote the energies required to manage the individual companies to turn on a dime, along with a sharply divergent economic environment.

Though the premise of diversification is basically sound, it is not the whole answer, as some have supposed. To survive violent cyclical change it is necessary to alter the management concept as well as the product line; that is, management must, when conditions require, change emphasis from growth to capital preservation. This can be difficult a feat because management styles tend to become personalized as part of the total personality, and as such they can be more difficult to change than product line. In some instances a radical change in the economic environment may require radical change in management style. It may be necessary to change management.

10

Base data and demographics: Knowing the market

In evaluating real estate, it is necessary to look beyond the real estate itself to the consumer, for it is the consumer—his availability, motivations, and ability to pay—which gives value to real estate. Real estate values often are directly related to the density of people per square mile of area, trend of growth, and the people's buying power. An apartment tower, for example, would have no value in the middle of Arizona's desert, minimal value in a Midwest farm town, but potentially great value on Wilshire Boulevard in Beverly Hills. Value, then, is determined more by the appropriateness of the development concept in filling the market need than by replacement cost, quality of product, or excellence of property management.

TECHNICAL AND ECONOMIC NEEDS

Housing needs of the market can be classed as technical and economic. A technical demand exists when the needs for housing in an area are greater than the supply. A technical need, however, may not represent economic demand, in that those in need may not be able to pay the required rate.

Rarely does a market contain an oversupply of housing to fill technical need; housing oversupplies are most always economic. That is, though the community technically needs a greater supply of housing, the housing available may exceed the consumer's purchasing power, and the result is an economic market glut.

Housing scarcity or oversupply, then, is related more to the correlation of supply with the levels of buying power and preference than to the correlation of number of dwelling units to number of families. An understanding of this point clarifies how demand can be stimulated by correctly matching concept and product with the needs and economic capabilities of consumers. This match can create a greater impact on specific demand than an across-the-board increase in consumers per se. Thus comprehensive market planning is essential in anticipating and meeting consumer demand.

The development analyst should be careful not to look upon demographics as frozen statistics, as has been noted. The marketplace is in a constant state of change. Demographics can indicate current status and direction of the trends, but duration of trends cannot generally be forecast. It is important, therefore, that demographics be looked to for trends rather than current status. Occupancy, demand, and market growth are never stationary; they always trend either up or down. Knowing which way the trend is going and how fast is the type of information required for effective market planning.

Occupancy shows the relationship between supply and demand according to current prices. The prices themselves indicate the current economic strength of the market and the level of current demand. It is not possible to reduce the number of existing housing units offered to the public the way producers in the oil or auto industries, for example, can cut supply to reflect reduced demand in an attempt to stabilize prices. Regardless of conditions in the economy as a whole, real estate, being fixed in location, will always react to the supply and demand factors of the local marketplace. Real estate cannot be readily removed from the market to balance supply and demand and meet the changing conditions of the business expansion recession cycle.

Many owners of income properties have found, to their misfortune, that rents cannot be raised to reflect inflationary cost increases as long as there is a greater supply of income property in a market than can be accommodated by current demand. When new supply is curtailed and existing supply is consumed by ongoing demand, there will be a change in the economic strength of the market. Vacancies will disappear, and households will experience difficulty in finding suitable housing. As vacancies disappear, rents increase.

There are two basic types of rental increases; economic and nuisance. Economic increases result from market pressure, and nuisance increases represent consumers' willingness to accept higher rents because they do not want the nuisance associated with moving.

When supply and demand pressures justify economic rent increases, they can generally be passed on even though there is no concurrent increase in consumers' family income. The percentage of its income a family pays for rent is not a static figure but constantly varies according to supply and demand pressures in the rental market. There is an upper limit which a family cannot generally go beyond, however, and at this point it must accept lower housing standards. To some measure, rental levels are more dependent on local supply and demand factors than family income and inflation in the economy as a whole. The strength of the income real estate market is therefore established by the level of occupancy, and the level of occupancy is the basis upon which rental rates are determined, within wide perimeters.

The demand for housing is tied to the number of jobs and the employment trends in the locality, but the ratio of jobs to housing is not fixed. With recent increases in economic capability and life expectancy, more families in the senior citizen category are demanding housing after departure from the labor market. Because these families and individuals tend to relocate after retirement in warmer climates, states such as Arizona, California, and Florida are experiencing job/housing ratios lower than those in northern states. This type of consideration must be included in conclusions reached from evaluation of employment/housing trends.

Building activity does not create real estate prosperity but itself is an effect of a favorable economic environment. While it is true that building activity reinforces the economy by feeding back jobs and income to improve the business climate, nonetheless it is an effect of a positive supply/demand relationship, and not a cause. Building activity is, however, an indication of the potential and practical value of undeveloped land, up to a point. When building activity becomes excessive, that is, exceeds consumer demand, the supply/demand relationship is impaired. This will lead to a downward trend in activity and prices.

In a like manner, real estate sales reflect real estate prosperity rather than creating it. A high rate of sales suggests confidence in real estate, and this provides for a relatively high liquidity or absorption rate at a particular point in time. The absorption rate is an effect of the supply/demand relationship and not a cause. In evaluating sales activity, the analyst should be aware that a high rate of sales activity may alter the supply/demand relationship which was its cause, and thus increased sales activity could provide the basis of a downward trend (see Chapter 11).

Analysis and interpretation of findings of housing supply and demand in a local market must be conducted in the context of national and regional outlooks, since local conditions are heavily influenced by national and regional conditions (see Chapter 9).

INFORMATION SOURCES

Information and base data on market conditions are available from many sources. In communities with well-established planning departments, a great deal of economic information from varying sources is compiled in the preparation of overall development plans. These data are generally updated on a fairly regular basis, and copies are made available to the public for a nominal fee. In preparing the general plan, the planning department also makes its own independent forecast of community growth.

Nearly every chamber of commerce or industrial development agency in a community also provides published information on a wide range of economic indicators. Banks, particularly those that are heavily involved in construction lending, are often good sources of economic information. Some banks publish, on a regular basis, economic reports, which are generally available upon request.

Regional publications are another source of information. *Florida Trend*, for example, provides very good coverage of selected market areas within the state. An inquiry to the publisher or a review of back copies can provide good information on activities within a particular metropolitan area and how it relates to and is influenced by the state economy.

National publications also provide good source data on local market areas. *Editor and Publisher* estimates population and income data for all parts of the country; *Sales Management's* survey of buying power is another source of comparable data.

In smaller communities the information available through planning department or chamber of commerce sources may be sketchy. Additional information may be available through reports on larger geographic regions prepared by banks or other institutions. Information which may be applicable to the smaller community in question or the county in which the community is located can be extracted from the regional report. Colleges and universities also often prepare population projections for specific areas.

QUESTIONS TO BE ANSWERED

Having reviewed some sources of data which can provide answers in real estate evaluation, we will review some of the questions that need answering.

Employment trends

Growth in new jobs is an excellent indicator of community vitality. A chart of employment trends not only provides a basis for assessing the capabilities of the community to support population growth but is a good benchmark by which to check population growth projectors. Population cannot grow economically at a faster rate than employment unless there is an increase in household size (minors not in the job market), in unemployment, or in retired households.

Growth. Local offices of state employment services compile and publish information on the estimated number of employed and unemployed workers, the distribution of jobs by industry category, and employment trends as related to the industry categories. Some perspective into shifts in the job market is also provided.

Unemployment. The level of unemployment in the community will be affected by national as well as local considerations. Whether the primary cause be local or national, a high rate of unemployment bodes poorly for the housing market. High unemployment creates uncertainty, which has a dampening effect on sales and rentals. It may also mean that immigration has occurred at a more rapid rate than can be supported by opportunities available in the community, or that job opportunities are leaving the community. A high level of employment suggests that the community can readily support new growth.

Distribution. Distribution of jobs by industrial categories gives an indication as to housing needs. Particularly relevant are shifts in distribution. For example, if job distribution is shifting from manufacturing to office or professional, this could indicate a trend toward more educated residents and a shift in housing preference from meeting shelter needs to an awareness of the quality of the housing and environmental factors.

Income trends

Income is an important indicator of the local economy, for it represents the ability of the residents to purchase goods and services. Having lower incomes than the national or state average is not a negative factor in itself, because quite often the lowest paying industries are the largest and fastest growing employers.

Income trends are particularly useful in identifying the size of the market for the various income groups. Census information breaks down family income distribution by income groups, total number of families in each group, and the percentage of total households represented by each group. Knowing the number of households in each income group is a useful tool in determining housing demand in relation to ability to pay.

Population trends

Population trends are a useful tool for projecting absorption rates. A strong influx of population not only is an indication of developmental opportunity but also serves as a hedge against moderate amounts of product oversupply.

Increases in population and employment can translate into demand for housing units only insofar as the income levels will permit. In some areas there will be great need but little opportunity because there is not sufficient income to turn the need into demand to support market action (see Chapter 11).

Population growth and household formation. The absorption rate of housing depends on population growth, net outcome of births and deaths, growth as a result of migration, and household formations. There is a national trend toward smaller households as a result of several factors: fewer children per family, more divorces, grown children moving away from parents' homes earlier, more senior citizens living in their own homes, later marriages, and single living as a way of life. These socio-economic changes produce household formations which translate into housing demand, even though the aggregate growth of the population may be static. For this reason, household formations have to be considered, as well as population growth, in measuring demand.

Demographics of population. Population demographics of age mix provide a tool for projecting household formations. An unusually large number of persons in the 20–25 age bracket, for example, would indicate that household formations would be on the increase; many young adults would be leaving their parents' homes to form new residences, either as singles or young marrieds. Data on age distribution, sex distribution, and household size are available from U.S. Bureau of the Census reports. In addition to giving an insight into overall housing demand, such information provides clues as to which market segments may be regressing or emerging.

Housing inventory

Employment, income, population growth, and household formations, and quantity and quality of existing housing are indicators of aggregate demand. However, the net demand, after subtracting current and proposed housing supply, is the measure of potential opportunity in the market area.

Housing obsolescence. Demand will be affected by obsolescence in the housing inventory. The number of housing units removed from the market is not necessarily an indication of how many new units it will take to replace them. Old units may have been unoccupied before their removal, be in an undesireable location, or possess other characteristics which make it unnecessary for them to be replaced. As a rule of thumb, however, more than half the units removed will have an economic justification for replacement. Housing units are removed from the inventory because of considerations of health and safety, urban renewal, and new transportation systems. Other currently sound housing is demolished to allow construction of a higher and better use.

Construction of new units. The number of new homes and apartments started is best measured by building permits. The community's building department or local chamber of commerce in the area can provide these figures. The planning department can also provide information on housing in the planning stages.

Existing inventory. Though there is an ongoing demand for timely information on housing inventories, little has been done to meet this demand. Direct observation in the field is a time-consuming method of calculating inventory. Private reports are available in some areas. The Federal Housing Administration (FHA) and Veterans Administration (VA) often issue such reports, as do homebuilding associations, construction lending departments of banks, and some mortgage bankers. The National Association of Home Builders (NAHB) has recently come out with a publication entitled *Inventory of Unsold New Homes* which provides housing data for 99 standard metropolitan statistical areas (SMSAs) in the United States.

Reports usually reinforce statistically what can be seen from a personal inspection of the market area. The personal inspection is very beneficial in that it can show what not to do.

Housing occupancy

Housing occupancy rates are an important indication of market health in both the for-sale and rental markets. It is important to obtain occupancy information by unit type and market segment. For example, there may be a large unsold inventory of medium-priced condominiums which has an adverse effect on the occupancy rates for the overall market, yet there may be a strong demand with little inventory to serve the luxury condo market.

In apartments, there may be a low overall occupancy rate of 87 percent, though within certain rental ranges and unit types there may be a 98 percent occupancy within the same market. This suggests a marketing opportunity for specific units. Specifics are needed to analyze and develop strategies and action plans (see Chapter 8).

General occupancy rates are available from the same sources that provide information on inventory, and utilities companies also can be a very helpful source of this type of information. Very specific information on occupancy by market segment or unit type requires some legwork and personal observation.

Households have the ability to change housing needs quite sharply, and thus they affect occupancy rates. Household size can be quite elastic to social and economic conditions. For example, young people may leave home for the independence of their own apartments, but should they become unemployed they may move back home, thus removing one household from the occupancy figures. Married households may move in with other families or with parents or move to smaller quarters.

Retail activity

Developmental patterns of retail outlets, particularly large shopping centers, provide meaningful information for projecting local and regional growth trends. The quality of overall development and individual retailers provides insight into local buying habits and tastes.

The construction of a regional center is based on anticipation of a particular type of growth in the area. The introduction of the center changes the markets, and to an extent, the anticipation of growth becomes a self-fulfilling prophecy. Quality restaurants and entertainment and recreational facilities not only indicate tastes and preferences but serve as a catalyst to future growth.

Industrial activity

As with retail activity, the anticipation of industrial expansion can stimulate growth of the housing market. The location of planned industrial parks and the type of industry attracted indicate employment trends. Particular attention should be paid to changes in the makeup of industry. A shift from low-skilled, blue-collar workers to skilled and professional personnel is an advance indication of a shift in housing and environmental preferences. Those who do not realize the significance of the shift may be building to yesterday's market and overlooking the emerging one.

Community facilities

The desirability of a location will be influenced to some degree by the availability of community facilities. Depending on household needs, the attitude of consumers as to the importance of community facilities in the buying or rental decision will range from indifference to regarding them as an absolute necessity. Analysis of community facilities should include the location of parks and recreational facilities and of churches and the location and type of medical and educational facilities.

Transportation The transportation system plays a major role in determining the shape and direction of urban development. The relative adequacy of the transportation system can influence the rate and size of urban growth. The patterns of the transportation network are intertwined with the land development pattern in that their influences are mutual.

Analysis of transportation should include: (1) Existing and proposed highway networks, (2) existing and proposed rapid transit systems, (3) travel time from a development to employment and retail centers via highway and rapid transit systems, and (4) distance and travel time to airports.

Developmental trends An understanding of local history is helpful in interpreting demographic data. Knowledge should be sought on how the community got started, what factors have contributed to its growth, how it got to its present point, and probable implications for the future. An analysis of developmental trends should identify (1) extent of existing development, (2) areas of growth pressure, (3) land most suitable for development, and (4) land-use projections.

11

Absorption forecasting: More than statistics

Even where employment is shrinking and a market is stagnant or decreasing in size, there is a demand for housing. In a shrinking or no-growth market, demand may be created in the form of households moving from present dwellings to others that better suit their desires and needs. Households are enticed out of existing dwellings by new products, which change the market by increasing the rate of obsolescence of the existing inventory.

In other instances, the introduction of an innovation can be a catalyst to new growth in a market, thus creating a demand that previously did not exist. An example would be the introduction of retirement or recreational housing into a community that previously had had no activity in these markets because there was no inventory of such housing. Retirement and recreational housing do not require an increase in the job market to support demand. The existence and proper marketing of the inventory are sufficient to create demand, given that the community is suitable and desirable for such purposes.

Innovation can also spark demand by obsolescence of the existing product. In the case of rental housing, an innovation may create market action by increasing vacancy rates in existing older inventory. For example, in a market where occupancy is 96 percent, the number of potential residents of new developments from the existing inventory if the occupancy rate in that inventory were reduced to, say, 92 percent could be computed. A strong marketing innovation introduced into an area could skim off a portion of the 4 percent from existing inventory without creating chaos in the market. A percentage of this 4 percent potential market could be used to calculate absorption, assuming others are not doing the same.

When households have the ability to buy or rent housing which they need or desire, there is a market demand. At times households will live in housing unsuited to their needs or preferences because limited alternatives are available to them in the market. A developer spotting this latent or accumulated demand can turn it into active demand by introducing a product which compels a household to move from housing that does not adequately fill present needs to housing that does.

ABSORPTION STRATIFICATION BY INCOME DISTRIBUTION AND MARKET SEGMENTATION

Demand by price range will be related to the distribution of family income. Income distribution is available from census data. A family is usually willing to pay 20 to 30 percent of gross monthly pay for housing, but this is only a rule-of-thumb figure. Low-income families typically pay a higher percentage of gross income for housing than middle-income families, and affluent families allot it a smaller percentage of gross annual income.

Not only is demand stratified by income distribution; it is also broken into increments as related to market segments. Though demographics provide general trends, estimates of demand broken down by market segments require a good measure of seasoned judgment. Opportunity occurs when demand within a market segment is not being sufficiently met with competitive supply.

ABSORPTION AND COMPETITIVE POSITION

How many homes a developer can reasonably expect to sell in an established local market will usually be dependent on the following factors:

1. How many new homes of all kinds are sold in that area in a typical year.
2. How many homes are in the price range in which the developer expects to operate.
3. How many sales his most successful competitor completed in the past 12 months, and how many were completed by his No. 2 and No. 3 competitor.
4. In the light of the developer's competitive position, how many sales can be expected in the next 12 months.

Marketing position is a very important consideration in projecting product absorption. Absorption will depend on whether the developer is following the competition or leading it. Following the competition, or repeating a competitor's successful pattern is an attempt to take away part of the competitor's market. Following competitors implies that the competition is doing an adequate or good job as a leader in the market area, and the leader must be head on in his area of greatest strength. Success in taking market share away from such a competitor depends on how well the developer compares to the competitor in production and marketing capabilities. To take a sizable market share from the leading competitors, he must be better in competitive position (see Chapters 7 and 15).

God gives every bird its food, but he does not throw it into the nest.
J. G. Holland

Often market leaders have skimmed the cream off the top. Then following the leader means competing for a smaller and smaller market share. The market share will depend on where the particular submarket in question is in relation to its cycle. Is the cycle just beginning, or is it peaking? (See Chapter 9.)

ABSORPTION AND INNOVATIONS

By going into a market with an innovation, a developer can start up a new cycle and skim the cream. By going for a submarket that his competitors are not zeroing in on, he may be in the position of having the only appropriate supply to fill a demand unrecognized by the competition.

When submarkets are overlooked, this does not mean that the existing competitors are not serving the overlooked market in some manner. For example, if there is both a need for high-quality environmental planning and open space and a latent submarket demand for such a development concept, that demand may be partially being met by the existing competition, by default. Though the competition does not have the type of product a particular submarket really desires, the developer may get absorption from the submarket because of a lack of alternative choices to buyers there.

By offering a housing supply tailored to the specific requirements of the demand, it is possible to obsolete the competitors' supply, which was reaching a portion of the demand by default. However, what often happens when an innovation is introduced into a market area is that the supply itself will create a demand. An example is the low-priced condos designed to lure buyers from the apartment rental market with monthly payments comparable to rental payments. If prior to this innovation there were no for-sale housing on the market offering the same monthly payments, a market study of sales in the area would indicate that there was no market activity in this price range. However, the introduction of the innovation changes the market and creates the market activity.

Absorption forecasting for innovations

Thus marketing innovations can obsolete the competition's product in a submarket and also can create market action that previously did not exist. Seeking project absorption for market innovations requires a somewhat different approach than when following the competition. By utilizing innovations proven in other geographic market areas, one can chart the pattern established in the other market areas and evaluate how it relates to the subject market area. Projecting absorption for innovations is not as dependent on historical performance of the local market as are absorption projections for supply which is merely following the market.

Innovation creates its own markets which do not show up in statistical data. This is so because the introduction of an innovation changes the market from what it has been in the past. Builders who operate in static markets often have a better understanding of this than those in the high-growth markets. Residents can be pulled from their previous dwellings because of a better concept, location, amenities, environment, merchandising, or unit mix, or for any number of other reasons that grab the prospect by his emotional hook.

Of course, the best way to determine how a concept will perform in a market area is to build it and watch what happens. But this is the old way, fraught with risk which marketing analysis has promised to reduce. A better was is to analyze how similar projects have done in the market area and how they are currently prospering. However, this also has its limitations in that innovative concepts cannot readily be tested in this manner. An innovation is the introduction of something new. This means there will be few to no comparables in the subject market to study (see Chapter 12).

What may be innovative for one market area may be a tested and proven concept in another market area. By analyzing projects in similar market areas one can determine, in much the same way as one would research a local project, how well the project can expect to be absorbed. Better yet, when one has an expert knowledge of how a similar project does in numerous similar market areas, one can readily project the outcome in the subject market area. Allowances will need to be made for differences that may exist between market areas, but even when researching local projects such allowances must be made (see Chapter 14).

PRECONSTRUCTION SALES

Preconstruction sales are dependent on economic climate, the desirability of the product and merchandising programs, and the source of buyers. For example, in a booming economy presales will be attractive to speculative and investment-minded purchasers who may be more interested in obtaining the deed than taking occupancy. In less optimistic times the speculative market, on margin, may be a seller's rather than a buyer's market. A product that is particularly desirable because of scarcity, location, or unique environmental features, coupled with expert merchandising, has a better chance of preselling than a run-of-the-mill project. If the source of buyers is largely transferees or relocation buyers from out of town, presales will be soft. These type of buyers generally need immediate occupancy and will buy from existing inventory.

A presales program has the best chance of success when the economy is ripe for speculation and the product has a compelling, unique quality. Some of the best sources of buyers for a presale campaign are second-home buyers, families moving up or down on the economic scale, those switching from rental to ownership, empty-nesters and retirees. An allowance must be made for buyer dropouts in the presales program. The farther ahead the sale is made, the greater the percentage of buyer dropout. A 50 percent buyer dropout is not uncommon. This means that presales units may have to be sold on the average of two times before the sale is finally closed.

Presales are difficult to estimate. They are largely dependent on the merits of the individual situation, the quality of the product, and the merchandising and sales follow-up required to hold on to initial sales (see Chapter 30).

EFFECTS OF POPULATION CHARACTERISTICS ON ABSORPTION

Shifts in the age distribution of the population will have an effect on absorption. For example, an increasing percentage of persons entering the 20–25 age category bodes well for rental absorption rates. Those in this category will be forming new households which will be attracted primarily to the rental market, with some being attracted to low-cost owner housing.

As this percentage bulge moves into the 25–30 age group, prospects for swelling moderate-priced owner housing improve. In this age group families will be forming and will generally desire to own their own homes. Many of these new family formations will benefit the for-sale market at the expense of the rental market, in that new families often desire to own the homes in which they raise their children.

A national trend toward smaller household size has developed. Some of the influences which have encouraged this trend are the increasing social acceptance of divorce and singles living arrangements, the propensity of young adults to leave home earlier, a tendency to marry later in life, and widening use of birth control measures. When household size is in a downward trend, there is an increase in the number of households desiring shelter even though the absolute number of people remains constant. This creates housing demand. However, this demand can be very transitory; a contraction in economic growth and an increase in unemployment can slow or reverse the trend toward smaller households. Couples who might be divorced may remain together out of economic necessity, young adults may move back home, relatives may share the same domicile. Those who had been living alone get roommates; and couples share a single home or apartment.

A contraction or reduction in rate of household formations has a more negative effect on rental markets than on for-sale markets. The rental market is composed of numerous heads of households, many of whom are single, whereas the ownership market is composed largely of heads of married households. It is easier for a single person to double up with another single person in an apartment than it is for two married households to double up in a home. For this reason much of the impact of reduced household formations is absorbed by the rental markets. A rental vacancy is created when two single individuals, each with a one-bedroom apartment, decide to share only one apartment.

Though the construction of rental apartments dropped off dramatically between 1972 and 1975, the absorption rate of new units was slow in many markets because of the reduction in household formations and the increase in household size within the rental segment of the housing market. This, along with other factors, contributed to a two-tier condition in the housing market whereby the housing recovery following the recession was primarily in single-family construction. Without participation by the rental markets, the recovery was much weaker than anticipated.

Population characteristics shape both the magnitude and the nature of housing demand. For example, smaller households create demand for smaller dwelling units. The increase in the percentage of elderly people in the population creates demand of a specialized nature; housing designed to meet the specific needs of the elderly and infirm. The increase in the number of single households creates a demand for studio or junior one-bedroom apartments.

EFFECTS OF INCOME CHARACTERISTICS ON ABSORPTION

Economic capability is required to transform housing need into housing demand. The income characteristics of the population will provide an insight into housing demand at various price or rental levels. The U.S. Bureau of the Census provides data on family income distribution. Within a specific measurement area, both the number and percent of households are given for each income level, ranging from less than $1,000 to more than $50,000.

The number of households within an income level can be used to project housing demand at that level. By determining the percentage of income which people in each economic level typically pay for housing, the buying capability can be translated into demand for a given price range of homes or apartments.

The percentage demand for either for-sale or rental housing within an earnings range can be determined by utilizing the current percentage mix between rental and for-sale housing in the market area and making adjustments for the earnings range in question. That is, in the higher earnings ranges there is a smaller percentage of renters than in the lower earnings ranges, which typically are also composed of a younger housing consumers.

Demand in an earnings range will not necessarily indicate a development opportunity, in that there may currently be adequate or excess supply intended to serve the demand. It is the net amount by which demand exceeds supply which produces the development opportunity (see Chapter 10).

EFFECTS OF SUPPLY ON ABSORPTION

Supply consists of housing in various stages of the housing life cycle, ranging from planned housing to obsolescent housing. It includes housing in various stages of development and decline, as follows:

1. Housing in the planning stage.
2. Unconstructed housing on which permits have been issued.
3. Housing in construction.

4. Unsold inventory.
5. Existing occupied housing.
6. Vacant housing.
7. Housing in transition.
8. Housing approaching obsolescence.

The first two of these categories represent potential rather than actual housing supply, but by the time a proposed development which is the subject of an absorption study comes onto the market, the first two categories may have progressed to the construction state, in which case they would represent actual supply. Conversely, the last two categories represent development potential, in that they are either in transition down to a lower buyer earnings level or moving out of the housing inventory entirely. These two categories provide absorption potential because many of the owners of this property will desire to move up in housing quality, so a buyer move-up market is provided. Only a portion of this market, however, will move up into new housing; much of the move-up market will move into existing housing.

Of the total number of households within an economic level, there will be a percentage who are currently living in housing below their economic means and who desire to move up to more suitable housing. This percentage of households will depend on the quality and age of the existing inventory and the economic growth of the area. If a market area is experiencing economic growth which results in higher household incomes, due to a transition in the makeup of the work force, the move-up market will be more pronounced. The move-up market can provide opportunities within an income range even though there may be no increase in absolute numbers of households in that range. This type of a market is sometimes classified as a market in transition.

The three charts in Chapter 6, Competitive Evaluation—Exhibit 6–1, Summary of Comparable Developments Charts; Exhibit 6–2, Unit Mix of Comparable Developments Form, and Exhibit 6–3, and Planned Developments Form—for a listing of the competitive supply offered or proposed to be offered in the market. This new supply, along with the existing supply, can be matched up with demand figures by price and rental category to determine supply and demand relationships for the various categories.

New supply is also required to replace obsolescent supply within the marketplace. As supply becomes obsolescent in the market, its value diminishes, and it moves down the scale in sales value or rental price categories until the supply becomes totally obsolescent and is either abandoned or condemned. As the obsolescent supply moves downward through value categories, it becomes obsolescent to the higher value category and represents supply to the lower category, until it finally is eliminated from the market altogether. The point is that the obsoleting supply does not have to be removed from the aggregate housing supply before it can be termed obsolete.

When a product no longer serves the needs of a value category, it is obsolete as far as that specific value category is concerned, and residual demand for that category or market segment is increased. Obsolescence of supply can produce an accumulated demand within specific value categories if it is not regularly replaced with new supply. Without such a regular introduction of new supply, many families in the market area may be living below their current economic means and below their personal environmental and lifestyle preferences.

Accumulated demand versus ongoing demand

Accumulated demand, in addition to ongoing demand, occurs in situations where a static market area is in transition, a growing market area has not received sufficient supply to keep abreast of demand, or consumer confidence to justify new construction is lacking in a temporarily economically depressed market area. An accumulated demand, is a one-time demand as opposed to an ongoing demand. Once filled, the accumulated demand ceases to provide land development opportunities.

At times, accumulated demand is mistakenly assumed by builders to be ongoing demand. Some may experience very rapid absorption rates for a particular product due to a combination of accumulated and ongoing demand. A number of their competitors, encouraged by their absorption rates, may enter the same market with a similar product in order to participate in the "proven" bonanza, only to find that the market has vanished. They may have failed to realize that most of the absorption success of the initial builders was attributable to accumulated demand. Once the initial projects were sold, they could already have absorbed a substantial portion of the accumulated demand. Additionally, the new builders attempting to capitalize on the bonanza may be surprised to find how many other builders have also had the same idea. The ongoing demand may only support a fraction of the supply now on the market, because the later builders reacted to a false signal.

The market then becomes characterized as soft and the product concept is questioned. Builders caught holding products which they cannot successfully market lay the blame on the product or on an abrupt change in consumer housing preferences. Closer to the truth is that neither the ongoing demand nor consumer preferences have changed materially, but the market has been overbuilt as a result of the failure of the builders to distinguish accumulated demand from ongoing demand.

Spotting an accumulated demand is often referred to as finding a hole in the market. The hole may be represented by accumulated demand for housing within a particular price range, design type, way-of-living concept, or unit mix or size. It may even consist of merchandising methodology, or achieving a high absorption rate by substantially outmerchandising the competition. Once the competition rises to the newly established level of merchandising, the hole closes and another must be found.

See Chapter 10, Base Data and Demographics, for the effects of the overall health and vitality of the community and the economy on absorption, and Chapter 9, Market Cycles, for the effect of market cycles on absorption.

EFFECTS OF LOCATION ON ABSORPTION

Though the absorption rates for various income levels within a geographic region, such as a municipality or a county, may be known, the absorption rates of varying products serving the same income level will not be homogeneous throughout the area. The location of the product within a region will affect the absorption rate. There are marked differences in the growth rates of communities or localities within larger demographic measurement areas.

Growth tends to concentrate within growth corridors or hot spots within a geographic area. A builder will generally experience greater absorption within a growth corridor or hot spot than he will if he is in a slower growth location in the area. The better the location, the greater the share of absorption that can be anticipated by the builder. Refer to Chapter 3, Locational Analysis and Site Evaluation, for more on the relationship of location to absorption.

EFFECTS OF VALUE ON ABSORPTION

Within a given market area, those developments that offer the best value to the housing consumer will generally be absorbed at a more rapid rate than those that offer less value. The developer who provides the best match between product and the needs of a specific market segment will generally provide the best value for that segment. Value can be further enhanced through planning and design expertise and sensitivity to the environment. Value engineering, by cutting dollars out of a project where they are least valued and designing them back in where they are most valued, adds to value and absorption potential. See Chapter 13, Value Engineering; Chapter 15, Establishing the Development Concept, and Chapter 16, Designing the Product to Optimize Market Potential.

CURRENT SALES AND RENTAL RATES AS A MEASURE OF FUTURE ABSORPTION

Sales and rental rates are not a cause but an effect of demand. Absorption rates in themselves do not create demand; they merely reflect market action at a particular point. Additionally, absorption rates may only measure the activity of products already on the market which are primarily serving the ongoing demand needs of particular market segments. If there is an accumulated demand which is not currently being served by products on the market, a measurement of current absorption rates will not indicate potential absorption rates which result from serving a previously unrecognized accumulated demand.

On the other hand, absorption rates may reflect a developer's successful identification and filling of an accumulated demand. The absorption figures may be misleading if they are used as a basis for future projections, because the ongoing demand, once the accumulated demand has been satisfied, may support a much reduced absorption rate than that enjoyed while the developer was satisfying both ongoing and accumulated demand.

Thus it can be seen that it is necessary to know not only the magnitude of absorption but the market conditions accompanying the absorption rates. Without an understanding of general and specific market conditions, the absorption rates in themselves may be misleading in their indication of market potentials and thus may provide false signals. Market need, buying potential, and consumer confidence, taken together, are more reliable indicators of absorption potential than current sales rates alone. Nonetheless, a knowledge of current sales rates is valuable in measuring market health and in projecting future absorption when there is an understanding of the underlying reasons for the sales and an understanding of the contribution due to accumulated demand and ongoing demand (see Exhibit 6-1, Summary of Comparable Developments, in Chapter 6). The final column, Weekly Sales, will provide absorption rates of comparable developments in the market area. These figures can be utilized for reference in arriving at an absorption rate for the development being studied.

SOURCES OF BUYERS AND RENTERS

There are three primary sources of buyers and renters for housing projects: (1) households moving within the market area, (2) increases in number of households entering the market area because of population growth, and (3) newly formed households within the market. The three sources of buyers and renters are listed in their order of importance. Households moving within the market area are generally the largest source of buyers and renters in housing projects in most market areas. A fourth source of buyers is the speculative investor, but this buyer is not actually an end user of owner-occupied housing. Unless the speculative investor can find an end user in one of the three buyer categories, the house may revert back to the developer, who will then have to resell it (see Chapter 8).

Demand due to households moving within the market area

By applying a price/income ratio to income distribution statistics such as those produced by the U.S. Bureau of the Census, the housing demand of a population can be stratified by housing price range (see Exhibit 11-1, Demand Estimates by Income Distribution Chart). By utilizing a rent/income ratio, housing demand can also be stratified by housing rent range. The portion of households within an income distribution range that will select for-sale as opposed to rental housing will depend upon the characteristics of the market in question and the specific income distribution ranges of interest. Typically, there is a lower percentage of homebuyers in the lower income ranges than in the higher income ranges.

The Number column of the chart indicates the number of eligible households with the economic capability to buy housing within the price range indicated in the Housing Price Range column. These households, however, will already be housed within the market area. The significance of the chart is that it shows the number of households within each price range who are potential buyers in the buying category of households moving within the market area, which is the largest of the three basic buyer categories. The reason for a move within the market area may be a desire to move up (larger family, more prestige), move closer to work, satisfy the family, make recreation available, or adopt a new lifestyle.

The propensity of families to move within an area can be measured by mobility studies which indicate the percentages of households that move each year. There is, however, a greater mobility in rental housing than in owner-occupied housing. Rental mobility can be measured by the yearly apartment turnover rate in the market area, and mobility in owner-occupied housing can be roughly measured by new-home sales divided by qualified households.

Demand due to population increase

Exhibit 11-2, the Demand Estimates by Population Increase Chart, shows how to translate an annual compound increase in population into number of households within an income distribution range. This information can then be translated into potential buyers or renters within a housing price or rental range. The chart utilized assumes that while the population increases, the percentage within each income distribution range remains constant with Bureau of Census findings. However, if the market area is in transition, to higher income households, for example, the percentage distributions should be adjusted to reflect the transition.

Demand due to new household formations

Market demand resulting from new household formations will depend on population age characteristics, economic climate, consumer confidence, and family stability within the market area.

Recently household formations have occurred primarily within two age groups; household heads under 25 years of age and those over 65 years of age. Due to the fact that households in these age ranges are largely headed by primary individuals (nonfamily), household size is diminishing. The rate of increase in primary individuals has been more than three times that of primary families since 1960. Thus the share of total households represented by primary individuals has been increased from 1 in 7 in 1960 to 1 in 5 in 1974.

Exhibit 11-1
Demand Estimates by Income Distribution Chart

Income distribution	Number	Percent	Price/income ratio	Housing price range
Less than $1,000	3,522	2.7%		
$ 1,000– 1,999	5,313	4.1		
$ 2,000– 2,999	7,190	5.6		
$ 3,000– 3,999	8,043	6.3		
$ 4,000– 4,999	8,376	6.5		
$ 5,000– 5,999	9,655	7.5		
$ 6,000– 6,999	10,185	8.0	3.0–2.9	$18,000–$20,300
$ 7,000– 7,999	10,173	7.9	2.9–2.8	$20,300– 22,400
$ 8,000– 8,999	9,850	7.7	2.8–2.7	$22,400– 24,300
$ 9,000– 9,999	8,740	6.8	2.7–2.6	$24,300– 26,000
$10,000– 11,999	14,793	11.7	2.6–2.5	$25,000– 30,000
$12,000– 14,999	14,368	11.2	2.5–2.3	$30,000– 34,500
$15,000– 24,999	13,814	10.8	2.3–1.7	$34,500– 42,500
$25,000– 49,999	3,371	2.6	1.7–1.5	$42,500– 75,000
$50,000–or more	708	.6	1.4–down	$75,000–up
	128,101	100%		

Exhibit 11-2
Demand Estimates by Population Increase Chart

Income distribution	Percentage	Number°
Less than $1,000	2.7%	93
$ 1,000– 1,999	4.1	142
$ 2,000– 2,999	5.6	194
$ 3,000– 3,999	6.3	218
$ 4,000– 4,999	6.5	224
$ 5,000– 5,999	7.5	259
$ 6,000– 6,999	8.0	277
$ 7,000– 7,999	7.9	273
$ 8,000– 8,999	7.7	266
$ 9,000– 9,999	6.8	235
$10,000–11,793	11.7	404
$12,000–14,999	11.2	387
$15,000–24,999	10.8	373
$25,000–49,999	2.6	90
$50,000–or more	.6	21
	100%	3,456

Annual compound increase in population = 2.7%
Population base = 358,682
Average household size = 2.8
Households represented = 128,101
Increase in households @ a 2.7% growth rate = 3,458
° Numbers rounded off.

12

Utilizing market research to optimum advantage

The importance of market research and planning has been established in the preceding chapters. It is especially important to know how to use the available research to the best advantage. The research alone will not improve the competitive advantage or the profit potential of the firm.

LIMITATIONS OF MARKET RESEARCH

There are numerous limitations to the market research which is ordinarily available. For one thing, imaginative audacity may be lacking. Researchers are often irresponsible about their findings in that they do not adequately interpret what the findings mean and what the company should do to improve its position relative to the findings.

Many reports contain mediocrities because researchers do not want to present what they cannot readily verify with statistics. When enough statistics are available to make a position ironclad, that position will assuredly be mediocre because it is readily apparent. More often than not, a follow-the-leader course down a well-worn path is suggested.

Research often unintentionally covers up more than it uncovers. Large amounts of data make it difficult to separate the relevant from the irrelevant and can disguise a budding opportunity so it cannot be recognized under the mass of statistical data. Emphasis is turned down the path that is most readily documented and away from the opportunity that has not yet had a path worn to its door.

Managers who want to be safe also base their judgments on verifiable facts. The plans that win in this self-defense method of decision are not necessarily the right ones, but those most easily verified statistically. Methods which rely on full and complete documentation can be the organization's worst enemy when it comes to attaining market leadership. When data are so clear that everyone can get the point, it is too late for them to be of use.

Expert analysts must not confine their recommendations to what the statistics can confirm. Used creatively, data can act as a stimulus to the imagination. Technicians do not have the sensitivity for this probing; it takes the imaginative audacity of experts to see what the hard data alone do not indicate. Flair, courage, and enthusiasm are necessary to get the ideas across to others, because they are not apparent to all. Their believability often rests on the expert and his conviction about them, and not on analytical data. If the expert merely says what the figures say, there is no need for an expert—a technician can do the same thing.

Too often, managers order research studies merely to take refuge in statistics. Rather than put their own personal status on the line, they seek reassurance by reporting what others are doing. They can then follow the same worn path others have trod and point to the distinguished company they are in when the path is found to be a dead end.

A manager's flight from risk to conformity is actually a retreat from accountability; he feels he cannot be held responsible or to blame if he is merely part of the herd. It is important for management to take risks. For management to demand a blueprint of what to do is to abdicate its responsibility. While research can reduce uncertainty and risk, this capacity should not be relied on. Overreliance on statistics diminishes the intuition, hunch, and insight which come from the powerful subconscious portion of the mind to inspire innovation.

The highest form of achievement is art, not science. Management is an art. Managers who attempt to replace the art with a more predictable, workable science neglect their functions and diminish their stature.

Forecasts are often projections of what has happened in the past. It is difficult for the researcher to predict when a trend will break or when a cycle will top or bottom out. It is difficult for a researcher to forecast how long an opportunity will remain. Demand may drop sharply due to unforeseen economic events or the entry of unanticipated intense competition. Since local forecasts are dependent on regional, statewide, national, and international events, any major shifts in events can have a profound impact on the local market.

Projections can help plan only for the likely events, but it is the unlikely ones that often dominate. It is presumptuous to believe that one can make meaningful long-term forecasts of anything. The psychology in the marketplace takes strange turns. For example, investors sold Disney stock because attendance was down in their parks as a result of the recession and the energy shortage. However, after Disney had been sold down, and while the recession was deepening, attendance figures jumped at the parks. Though there are far fewer discretionary dollars, people are splurging on recreation. The unanticipated reversal in projection, which has been called the doom boom was as unforeseen as the Watergate affair before it burst into the news.

There is a tendency to evaluate market need by evaluating the market response accorded the product the developer has chosen to offer in the past. This approach does not identify unfulfilled needs, or holes in the market; it only concerns itself with what has already been offered in the market in the past and is not sensitive to new needs and product innovations with which the developer has not had experience.

Organizations tend to look for marketing opportunities to satisfy their pressing internal needs to move existing product, rather than looking for the needs of the consumer or customer. Looking for markets to satisfy internal needs to move product is selling. Researching markets to determine consumer needs and the type of product required to fill those needs is marketing.

Too often, market researchers lack the line manager's sense of responsibility for the meaning of their findings. Either there will not be sufficient point-by-point recommendations management can use to implement product development and policy planning to capture the market, or the recommendations given, though they may reflect true needs in the market area, will not survive the crucible of economic feasibility.

Every advantage has its disadvantage.
Latin Proverbs

MANAGEMENT'S NEED FOR MARKET RESEARCH

The effectiveness of the marketing activity rests primarily on the quality, experience, judgment, broad market exposure, audacity, and courage of the executive performing the service. All other considerations are secondary. Highly capable marketing people are not easy to come by and can be difficult to hold on to.

The pros and cons of utilizing in-house or outside consultants can be argued persuasively on either side of the question. The best situation for many companies will be to utilize a limited in-house market function and go outside for special studies, fresh insights, and a detached objective view. An outside consultant can be particularly helpful in introducing and implementing innovations (see Chapter 7).

Decision making or rationalization

At times the organization's decision making becomes little more than a rationalizing process. When decisions develop as rationalizations of previous events, they do not reflect overall objectives. The process occurs so unconsciously that those participating in it are unaware of what is happening. They need insight, someone to point out the obvious and redirect the group to a course which will lead to fulfillment of agreed-upon objectives.

We like a man who comes right out and says what he thinks, when he agrees with us.

Management's fear of change

Most managers want to ensure the survival of the present system and seek to systematize and standardize current operations. Operating tactics are concerned with near-term implementation and immediate effects on current production. Marketing innovation, however, produces changes and obsoletes current operations. If the same people who are responsible for optimizing current operations are also responsible for innovation or the creative destruction of current patterns or operations, the possibilities for innovation are dim. To have the same people pursue both short-term tactics and long-term strategy is to ensure the dominance of tactics to the discredit of strategy. The pressing day-to-day need will always have more sway with line management than overall, comprehensive strategy.

Often line management would rather be wrong than to go through the disruption to current production scheduling or operations that change entails. Of course, not all changes can justify disruption of operations, but the decision is not one which should be left solely with production management.

If one company is not enterpreneurial, another will be. If line management of one company does not want to disturb the present order through "constructive obsolescence" of the product or organization, a competitor will do it for them. An outside consultant can provide the perspective needed to weigh marketing advantages against production advantages.

Developing strategy in an environment of rapid change can be compared to investing in the stock market. We have noted that in trading stocks, there is the law of contrary opinion, which states that what appears to be obviously right is generally wrong. The law of contrary opinion applies to business expansion and real estate development decisions as well. Though there are very capable line executives within the organization, they may be too close to the situation; they cannot see the forest for the trees. As one philosopher said, "I don't know who discovered water, but I'm certain it wasn't a fish."

Marketing skills provided by an outside consultant can often give management the perspective needed to see trends and opportunities that are not evident inside the organization because of the tunnel vision that is inevitable in any organization (see Chapter 28).

The shell must break before the bird can fly.
Alfred Tennyson

CASE STUDY I: THE NEED FOR OBJECTIVE ANALYSIS

As consultants, we were brought in to review a proposed rental development in one of the southern states. The project had advanced to the stage of completed working drawings. The following information came to light:

1. It was observed that the buildings, designed for the luxury range, were three-story walk-ups. When questioned why elevators had not been included, management said that feasibility would not allow for the costs elevators would entail.

2. The buildings consisted of back-to-back units without a central hallway. To eliminate the need for exterior walkways on the outside of the building and the resulting loss of privacy, stairways were provided for every two units per floor. That is, a floor with 12 units required six stairways. Little wonder the project could not afford elevators. Even if it was decided to provide elevators, the layout would require an elevator at every stairway location.

3. The third-floor apartments were the most elaborate in the development, containing such amenities as beamed volume ceilings, fireplaces, split-level plans, and large balconies. The units were larger in size than those on the first and second floors due to a cantilever condition at the third floor. When asked why the least desirable location (three-story walk-ups) were designed as the top-of-the-line units, management explained that this was necessary as an incentive for people to walk up three stories. There were no plans to charge a premium rent for the third-floor units; the expense put into the units was to "solve" the marketing problem introduced by the three-story walk-up condition.

4. The buildings were not provided with garbage chutes, for the same reason that the elevators were omitted. Too many would have been required, and the budget could not have withstood the expense. The elaborate third-floor unit designs were also intended to take potential tenants' minds off of the missing garbage chutes.

Observation Management lost its perspective when it was discovered that there was a marketing problem due to lack of elevators. Rather than curing the marketing problem, it was rationalized by an expensive design treatment for the third-floor units. To design in an extra margin of safety, the third-floor units were increased in size. A further step was to utilize semi-private entrance stairs serving only two units per floor. To save on the cost of elevators, management had introduced design features that were substantially more expensive than the elevators they sought to eliminate. Now, even with cost savings from eliminating elevators, the management found itself faced with a serious cost overrun and did not know where to turn. In spite of all the added expenses, they still had a three-story walk-up marketing problem, and had their most elaborate units were in the least desirable location.

This is a good example of tunnel vision: Management had built a complex box for itself that grew from a series of rationalizations. The management was so intimately involved with the development of the concept it felt that each decision was a logical move to solve problems as they were recognized. However, in reality they were fire fighting, not planning. Management was so involved in the rationalization process they could no longer see the problem objectively. Their intimate involvement blinded them to the obvious.

Solutions   Because as consultants we did not have an intimate involvement in the rationalization process, we could see the obvious: The planning concept did not fit the marketing need.

By introducing a central corridor, it was possible to omit four stairways per building. The corridors need not be fully enclosed; the plan can allow for them to be partially open to the exterior. Stairways could be further reduced by providing bridges between buildings. Instead of a stairway at each end of the bridge, one would suffice, thus reducing stairways to one and one half per building. One garbage chute in the vicinity of the bridge intersection will serve two buildings. The bridges, properly designed, serve as design amenities. The elaborately designed third-floor units, if retained, could justify a premium rental, with the third-story walk-up stigma eliminated. Or the units could be designed down to further reduce costs.

There were other planning solutions that would have solved the marketing problem while at the same time reducing costs, but this example is more concerned with the method of dealing with tunnel vision than a study of planning solutions.

Conclusions   When management gets too close to its problems and begins to rationalize, it loses sight of its objectives and the real problems that confront the organization in achieving them. Management then needs the perspective of an outsider to point out the obvious and get strategies and action plans back on course towards agreed-upon objectives.

13

Value engineering: A management approach for increasing the profit middle ground between cost and value

When profit margins get thinner and the future is less sure, management gets tougher and develops better tools. One of the newer tools of management is value engineering, which is simply a highly organized effort to achieve more for less.

Outstanding management can make significant percentage improvements to profits when margins are thin. By utilizing value engineering techniques, organizations can outpace the competition faster when there are narrow margins than they can when margins allow almost anyone to make a sure profit.

VALUE ENGINEERING: WHAT IS IT? Value engineering consists of the entrepreneurial thought process and tough management analysis necessary to create value. But what is value, and what values are being engineered? Value is relative worth, utility, or importance. Its degree of excellence is measured by the return it produces in equivalent goods, services, money, or gratification. Value is largely measured by emotions and subjective attitudes, and it is dependent on cyclical monetary conditions, fashion, and general industrial health. There is no one value or key value that is sought in value engineering, but a multitude of values that are interdependent in the creation of a high-quality investment.

The component values which comprise a total real estate investment value must be analyzed both separately and as they relate to one another. The important question is: As the component values interrelate, do they reinforce each other to create a sum greater than the total of the parts, or do they tend to wash each other out so that the sum is less than that total?

In engineering for value, it is important to recognize that not only are there numerous component values which comprise the total value, but these values are ever changing. The increasing velocity of value change confront the organization not merely with the question of what consumers, investors, lenders, and so on will value in the next two, three, or four years, but also with the more pressing question of what the organization's or its management's objectives will be then. The latter question arises every day as management goes about its business of making the decisions it will have to live with when current yardsticks are no longer applicable. Thus flexibility is a key value affecting the total real estate investment.

More than a cost-saving device

Costs are only half of the profit formula; value is the other half, and profit is the difference between the two. Value engineering is a tool which affects value enhancement as well as cost reduction, recognizing that both are equally important in the profit formula (Value − Cost = Profit). There is a mistaken notion that value engineering is primarily a cost-cutting tool. Cost reduction does not necessarily imply profit increase, in that many cost reductions can produce a more than commensurate decrease in value, netting a profit reduction. Neither cost nor value can be considered separately, because both must be known to determine the profit middle ground. Value engineering is a systematic business approach to expanding the profit middle ground.

Cost cutting for its own merit is a simplistic approach to increasing profitability. Total cost considered separately or total value considered separately is rather meaningless, for it is the profit middle ground between the two that is the essence of the business. The tough management work is maximizing the spread between cost and value.

A method of overseeing the interactions of specialists

What is the right way to approach a problem that has many facets? The answer is: By recognizing that it has many facets, by working on all of them, and by understanding that they must be worked on in relation to one another (see Chapter 22).

Synthesizing complex issues to arrive at an understanding requires input from others. Nothing that is approached from a narrow viewpoint can be given intelligent consideration. The pieces must be put together in a somewhat reasonably consistent whole, and this implies group effort. This challenging task is the province of generalists, who are able to direct the interactions of specialists to arrive at overall objectives.

In its broadest scope, value engineering implies planning on a high level, including the study of trends and future possibilities. Because of the scope and breadth of the value engineering referred to here, its function must be carried out at a very high level in the organization. Generally the only person having the overview of the entire investment and development operation is the top executive of the organization. Thus value engineering, in its broad context, is a complement or extenuation of one of this executive's primary functions; comprehensive planning for immediate and long-term profit potential.

In larger organizations, top executives often lack the time required for all the value engineering efforts throughout the organization. Subordinate executives tend to become too departmentalized in their interests, more often than not, they are unequipped for a value engineering overview, or they lack the authority to cut through departmentalization. In smaller organizations, the top executive may have a broader overview of all operations and the authority to deal with them, but he will generally lack the in-depth, specialized skills required to maximize the output of the various operations. In large organizations or small, it is difficult to find executives who can go beyond maintaining the status quo (whatever compounded growth rate that may be) to produce significant innovations which result in overall improvement in *profit margins*.

Assistance from an outside value engineer can provide the innovative spark necessary and compensate for some of the tunnel vision that is inevitable in any organization. The overall strategy, planning, and implementation of profit improvement is a specialty of the broad-gauge value engineer.

A method of increasing productivity

Value engineering, by overseeing the interactions of the various specialists, not only assures profit improvement on a project-by-product basis. It also creates an environment wherein line executives can function much more productively, and thus the overall development or production capabilities of the organization are increased.

A method of allocating capital dollars

Value engineering is not a method of accounting for investment dollars. Rather, it is a means of maximizing the return on the investment dollars and as such requires an entrepreneurial bent. At the highest level, value engineering deals with investment fundamentals which constitute the framework for incremental, point-to-point specialist considerations. Each specialist decision is in a broad sense a money decision affecting the allocation of capital dollars. By establishing priorities, a framework can be set up to guide specialist considerations (see Chapter 16).

A means of establishing a system of priorities

Every developer is faced with budgets and must continuously make value decisions as to the best allocation of each construction dollar in the budget. Once the overall budget is established, the question is how and where a limited amount of dollars can be spent to best advantage.

A system must be in every economy, or the best single expedients are of no avail.

Ralph Waldo Emerson

The value engineering approach in real estate does not try to maintain a homogeneous quality of improvements throughout a project because blanket spending of this nature does not create benefits commensurate with costs. There is no question that quality and excellence are desirable throughout the project; what is at question is the priority of expenditures to achieve them. Improvement costs must be reduced in areas of low priority and a portion of the savings redirected into high-yield environmental features which produce a significant impact on the marketability of the project.

Dollars need to be pulled out in the initial value engineering planning. These are called discretionary dollars because, at the developer's discretion, they can be either pocketed by the developer or partially reinvested into the product, where they will increase marketability and produce maximum return. These plowed-back discretionary dollars are the highest yielding dollars the developer has. The competition, which does not have the benefit of discretionary dollars allocated to highlight their projects in the same way, will probably suffer in comparison.

Value engineering in land development includes analysis of those features of the site, land plan, design, or marketing plan which could have an adverse effect on the marketability or feasibility of the product.

A means of minimizing waste

Vast amounts of resources can be wasted in the process of planning value on an incremental basis through the creation of offsetting value washes, which are in effect, incongruities in the product or investment planning. An investment decision that can be made on its own merits is almost nonexistent; these decisions either reinforce one another or wash out one another. When they wash one another out, a value wash is said to have occurred. Value engineering, by eliminating incongruities, can have a marked effect on profit.

A means of creating investment leverage

Value engineering is not an added project cost. Rather, it represents a net savings to the project; not just a life-cycle savings or a total in-place cost savings, but a savings in the front-end equity or venture capital. As such, it is a means of creating investment leverage.

To take an example: It is not uncommon to deliver a $100,000 project cost saving through value engineering while at the same time maintaining, or more generally increasing, overall values. If value is not diminished in the value engineering process, neither is the loan amount, even though there may be a marked reduction in project cost. Say the value engineering study costs the owner $10,000. Subtracting the value engineering cost from the total project cost saving, the owner has a net saving of $90,000. In that there is no commensurate reduction in the loan amount, this represents a $90,000 reduction in equity or venture capital requirement on the front end. Thus, value engineering in this example represents not a $10,000 front-end cost but a $90,000 front-end saving. It can mean the difference between having to bring in another equity partner or arranging for secondary financing.

Production costs are increasing dramatically, while rents, which are remaining relatively constant, are holding down the value of the buildings and eroding the developer's ability to finance the costs. The developer must come up with more equity to obtain less profit. Consequently, these changes in the development industry necessitate a high degree of sophistication in product development to put together a real estate development package.

A tool in investment planning and analysis

A typical investment-planning and product development analysis is as follows. The analysis is to determine the profitability of a typical one-bedroom apartment unit and the effect of construction cost on profitability.

The inputs to the problems are four. (The dollar figures utilized are not intended to be representative of a particular market area or economic cycle.)

1. $180 per month rental.
2. 700 square foot net rentable area.
3. $14 per net rentable square foot (total cost, exclusive of land).
4. $1,500 per unit land cost.

The questions are three:

1. What is the profit if investment parameters are met?
2. What is the percentage spread between cost and capitalized value?
3. What happens to profit as development cost per square foot varies?

There are five steps in the solution of the problem.

1. The first step is to determine capitalized value, loan amount, and equity value, exclusive of secondary financing or equity money cost. Twelve months' rent at $180 per month provides a yearly gross of $2,160. From the gross are subtracted the expenses and vacancy factor, which represent 40 percent of the gross, or $864. This leaves $1,296.00 net after expenses. At a capitalization rate of 10, the net justifies a loan or capitalized value of $12,960. Using a 75 percent loan/value ratio yields a loan amount of $9,720. The debt service on $9,720, using a 10 percent loan constant, is $972. Adding the debt service to the expenses provides a total of $1,836 for expenses and debt service. Subtracting expenses and debt service from the $2,160 gross gives a cash flow, exclusive of secondary debt service, of $324 annually. At a capitalization rate of 10, the cash flow represents a $3,240.00 equity value.

2. The second step is to determine cost; 700 net rentable square feet times $14 total development cost per net rentable square foot, exclusive of land, equals $9,800 development cost. Adding $1,500 per unit land cost to the development cost gives $11,300 as the total land and development cost per unit.

3. The third step is to determine amount and cost of secondary financing, or equity cash. The $9,720 loan amount is subtracted from $11,300 total land and development cost, netting a $1,580 equity or secondary financing requirement over and above the first deed of trust. Assuming a 12 percent cost of equity or secondary financing, debt service on secondary financing comes to $190 per unit.

4. The fourth step is to determine the equity value after including debt service on secondary financing. The $190 secondary debt service is subtracted from the $324 cash flow, exclusive of secondary debt service, for a net cash flow of $134 per unit. At a capitalization rate of 10, the $134 cash flow represents a $1,340 equity value per unit.

5. The fifth step is to determine equity value as a percentage of cost. The $1,340 equity value divided by $11,300 total cost equals an 11.8 percent spread between cost and capitalized value.

Assume now that the developer cannot deliver the project at $14 per square foot and must revise his budget up to $15 per square foot total cost, exclusive of land. By plugging the $15 per square foot construction cost into the formula, the equity value per unit is reduced from $1,340 to $510, or from an 11.8 percent markup from cost to a 4.2 percent markup from cost. To the developer, this means a 64.5 percent reduction in profit, and an infeasible project.

To go the other way, if the developer established a $15 per square foot budget and later cut the budget to $14 per square foot, a 120 percent increase in profit would result. What is the ingredient that has the potential of increasing a developer's profit by 120 percent, where can one get it, and how much does it cost?

The ingredient is comprehensive value engineering and product development. It can be a developer's in-house project or purchased from outside consultants. Our experience has shown that value engineering and product development cost approximately 20 cents per net rentable square foot. A *20-cent per square foot expenditure that has the potential of increasing profits by 120 percent* is, needless to say, the highest priority expenditure in the entire project.

A well-placed 20-cent per square foot investment in value engineering and analytical analysis has the potential of throwing off an added $830 per unit, whereas, in the example above, a $15 per square foot investment threw off only $510 per unit. Staggering as the comparison may be—a 20-cent per square foot expenditure can throw off more income than a $15 per square foot expenditure—it is nonetheless valid. Those who do not recognize its significance will find they have less and less profit margin in which to operate.

It is a socialist idea that making profits is a vice. I consider the real vice is making losses.

Winston Churchill

HOW VALUE ENGINEERING SHAPES PLANNING DECISIONS

For an income-producing housing project, a feasibility study and a site analysis and selection procedure precede a value engineering analysis of various development programs. First, various unit mixes are explored to determine the economics of each. Construction costs per square foot for each unit type can be projected to determine the development costs for a particular unit mix. Next, the income for each unit mix is projected. From the projected gross income of the mix, the capitalized value and loan value are determined. Loan value is subtracted from the development cost and land basis to establish the equity requirement. At this point, the chief planning concern is generally to maximize yield through reduction of the equity requirement. The equity requirement and yield for each unit type are calculated to determine the relative contribution on a per unit basis. Once the economic attractiveness of each unit type has been determined, the overall yield of the project can be adjusted by appropriate shifts in the unit mix.

Providing a greater concentration of high-yield units while minimizing low-yield units can generally reduce the equity requirement. This adjustment, however, must be accomplished within the market constraints of the specific area. The development cannot be flooded with units which show a high return on paper but which are not supportable by the existing economic conditions, lender guidelines, and habitation preferences of the area (see Chapter 14).

In an area which will support higher rents, the inclusion of a selective amenities package can often enhance the rentability and income of the project while actually reducing the equity requirement. Amenities must be selected which will justify increasing the gross income, thereby increasing the loan value. To obtain the desired results, however, the cost of adding the amenities must naturally be lower than the resultant increase in loan value.

The value engineering process should be carried out for every planning decision. A typical planning decision is how to handle the parking requirement—should the covered parking by on grade under carports, on grade but tucked under the apartment buildings, subterranean under the buildings, in a separate parking structure? This type of decision is more an economic decision than a land-planning and architectural design decision, and it must be analyzed on that basis.

An enlightened decision as to how to handle the covered parking requirement requires the implementation of the value engineering process. Typical questions that must be answered are: What is the cost per parking stall of the various alternatives? What effect do the alternatives have on the overall density or the aesthetics of the project? What effects are there on the income and absorption schedule, the capitalized value of the project, loan value, equity requirements, lender guidelines? What effect is there on the overall investment objectives?

An enlightened decision cannot be made until the answers to all these questions have been resolved. The developer who proceeds without obtaining the answers is not properly controlling the investment.

Planning for cost reduction

In site planning/multifamily rental buildings, for example, it is advantageous to distinguish between primary and secondary courtyards. Primary courtyards are essential to establishing the way of living concept, and generous provision should be made for environmental impact effects. Secondary courtyards are arears where costs can be trimmed. No attempt should be made to maintain a homogeneous quality of improvements throughout the project, because blanket spending of this nature does not yield income commensurate with costs.

Parking courts should be thought of as secondary courtyards which residents are exposed to for only about six minutes a day: three minutes when leaving for work in the morning and three minutes when returning at the end of the day. These secondary court areas can be hidden within the project by screen buildings. (See the site plan in Illustration 13-1.) Screen buildings have living and dining areas oriented to a garden courtyard, the bedrooms are oriented to the rear and a secondary parking area. The elevations facing the garden courtyard are primary, so they receive special design emphasis. The elevations facing the secondary courts, though attractive, are stripped of the more expensive environmental amenities.

While there is no doubt that handsome, detailed building elevations are desirable, even those related to parking areas, there is a question as to the priority of expenditures. All development decisions must occur within budget constraints. The manager must continuously make value decisions as to the best allocation of each construction dollar comprising the total budget. The budget being established, the question is how and where a limited amount of dollars can be spent to the best advantage.

All improvement costs in secondary courts can be kept to a minimum so that a portion of the savings can be redirected into high-yield environmental features in primary courtyards (see Illustration 13-2). Carport costs can be reduced in secondary courts to $1.30 per square foot. Where carports are seen from the street or are visual from resident living and activity areas, they generally require a $3 plus cost per square foot. Lighting costs can be reduced in secondary areas through floodlights mounted on buildings. This reduces the cost of trenching and underground wiring to landscape pole lights required in primary court areas, for a saving of $75 per fixture installation.

Landscaping and landscape sprinkler costs also can be reduced in secondary court areas. Concrete curbs can be replaced with asphaltic curbs or redwood headers at paving perimeters, and a substantial amount of concrete flatwork can also be eliminated in the design process.

On-site distribution of all underground work should be designed for economy of piping runs and trenching and should be coordinated so as

Illustration 13–1

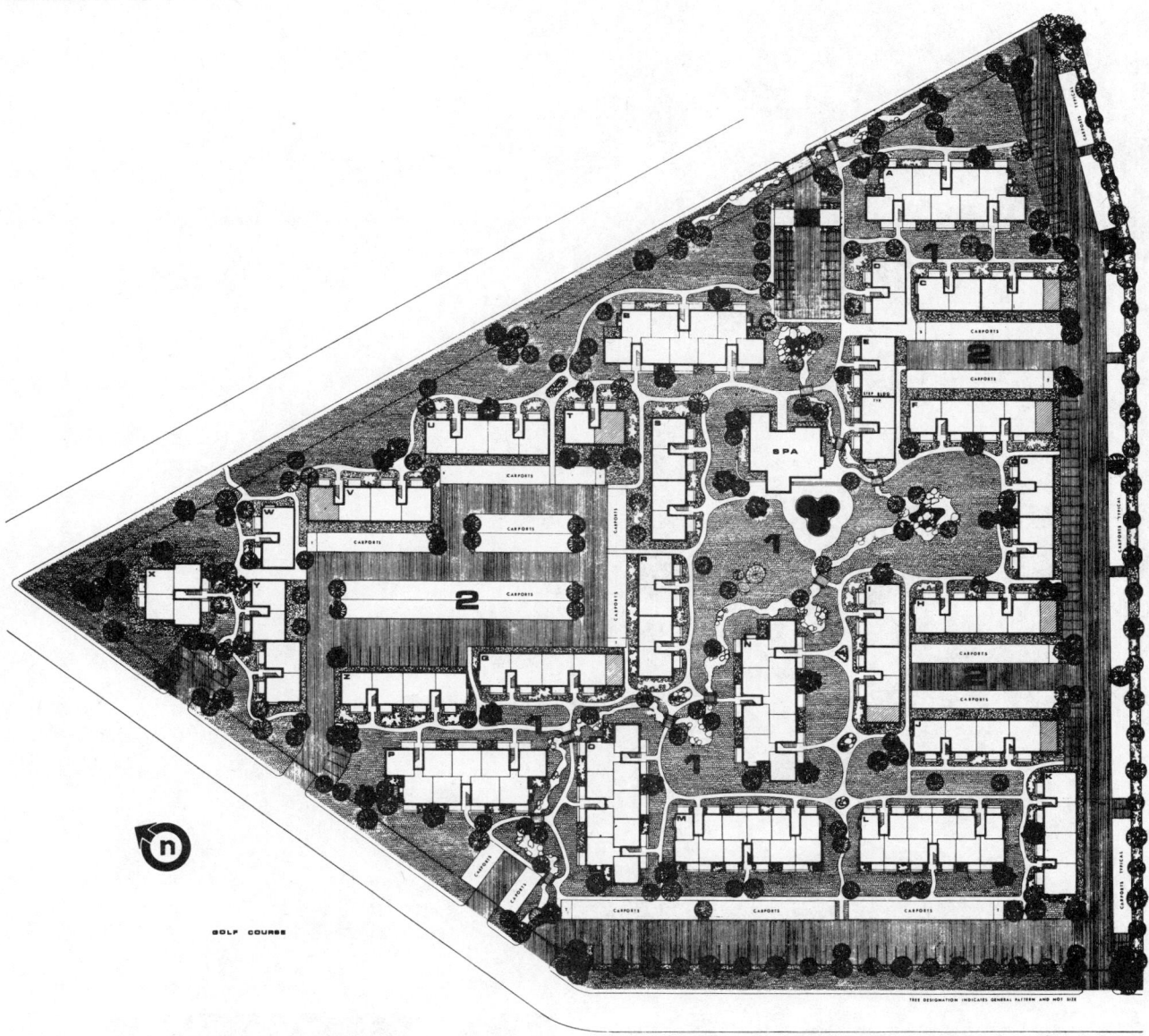

Site plan illustrating the use of primary and secondary courtyards. Courtyards labeled 1 are typically primary courtyards with environmental amenities; courtyards labeled 2 are typical secondary courtyards for parking. The latter are designed for cost reduction purposes; the dollars saved can be more profitably spent in the primary courtyards.

not to interfere with or slow up the work of others. Transformers should be located close to building meter centers. Primary electrical runs from off-site locations to transformers is much cheaper than runs from the transformer to meters and disconnect service at the building. More importantly, the power company generally pays for or provides cost rebates on runs from off-site to on-site transformers.

Illustration 13-2

Dollars saved in the secondary courtyards are redirected to primary courtyards, shown in these illustrations. Such high-yield environmental features highlight the project and create the environment which merits rental premiums. If dollars were spent homogeneously throughout the project, there would not be enough left in the budget to create the lush landscaped environment and way-of-life concept shown, while keeping rents within the target market range.

Planning for merchandising

Curb appeal of developments is a must. Most tenants are generated from two sources: traffic passing by the property, and word-of-mouth recommendations from tenants currently living in the project. In order to capture the traffic (potential residents), it is first necessary to stop them and to get them across the curb into the project. This is accomplished through special design emphasis (as a promise of the delights awaiting within) given to improvements fronting onto trafficked areas.

Once the potential resident is inside the project, he must be immediately reinforced with positive first impressions and a sense of intimacy and belonging. The relationships of the rental office, amenity package, model units, and landscape planning are very important in forming a positive first impression. The proper setting should presell the resident before he or she even sees the unit (see Chapters 30 and 31).

Planning for living

Visual separation between parking areas and landscaped garden court areas is mandatory in establishing the way-of-living concept. Pedestrian circulation within a project should take advantage of garden courts and minimize resident's use of the less environmentally desirable parking areas.

Recreational facilities should be planned for easy and pleasant access by all tenants. Additionally, the trip from the resident's car to his unit should be a pleasant experience, reflecting prestige and pride of ownership.

Garden court areas of the project should be self-contained, highly controlled environments. Undesirable service functions, parking areas, and neighboring eyesores should be effectively screened out. The maximum number of units should overlook the prime amenity features; these units can justify premium rents. Recreational features should be designed with a specific predetermined use in mind, to reflect the social and recreational needs of the residents. If an activities program is visualized, amenities design should be closely coordinated with the activities program at time of design. Amenities provided are often not utilized because no thought was given to their actual utilization. An amenity which is provided as a marketing gimmick to achieve absorption but which does not work in practice does not retain residents (see Chapter 17).

When a cost expenditure delivers only half results, there is a commensurate loss in value. This lost value, which is referred to as a value washout, can assume large proportions; it must be eliminated and the dollars redirected into more profitable areas.

Planning individual buildings for profit: Back-to-back design

One of the many cost-saving techniques which can be utilized is back-to-back building design. Such design reduces foundation and framing costs, reduces heat loss and air conditioning load, and cuts down on mechanical and electrical distribution costs. Most importantly, none of these cost savings are noticeable to the resident, even though they can be substantial.

Back-to-back placement of kitchens and bathrooms is critical to economy in mechanical and electrical distribution. It is surprising, however, that often the back-to-back unit designs of architects do not allow for doubling up on plumbing stacks, and thus much of the savings in back-to-back design is missed. Not only must fixtures be doubled or tripled up on stacks, but design must minimize horizontal run from stacks to main plumbing runs through the building. Central location of the electrical service area to building load areas reduces distributed costs within the building. Apartment switchboxes located close to load areas in the kitchen reduce distribution costs within the apartment unit. Illustration 13–3 shows a back-to-back plan.

In back-to-back designs, particularly, otherwise monotonous roof lines should be broken with architectural features that give enjoyment to the eye. Often the first impression one gets of a garden-type multifamily project

Illustration 13–3

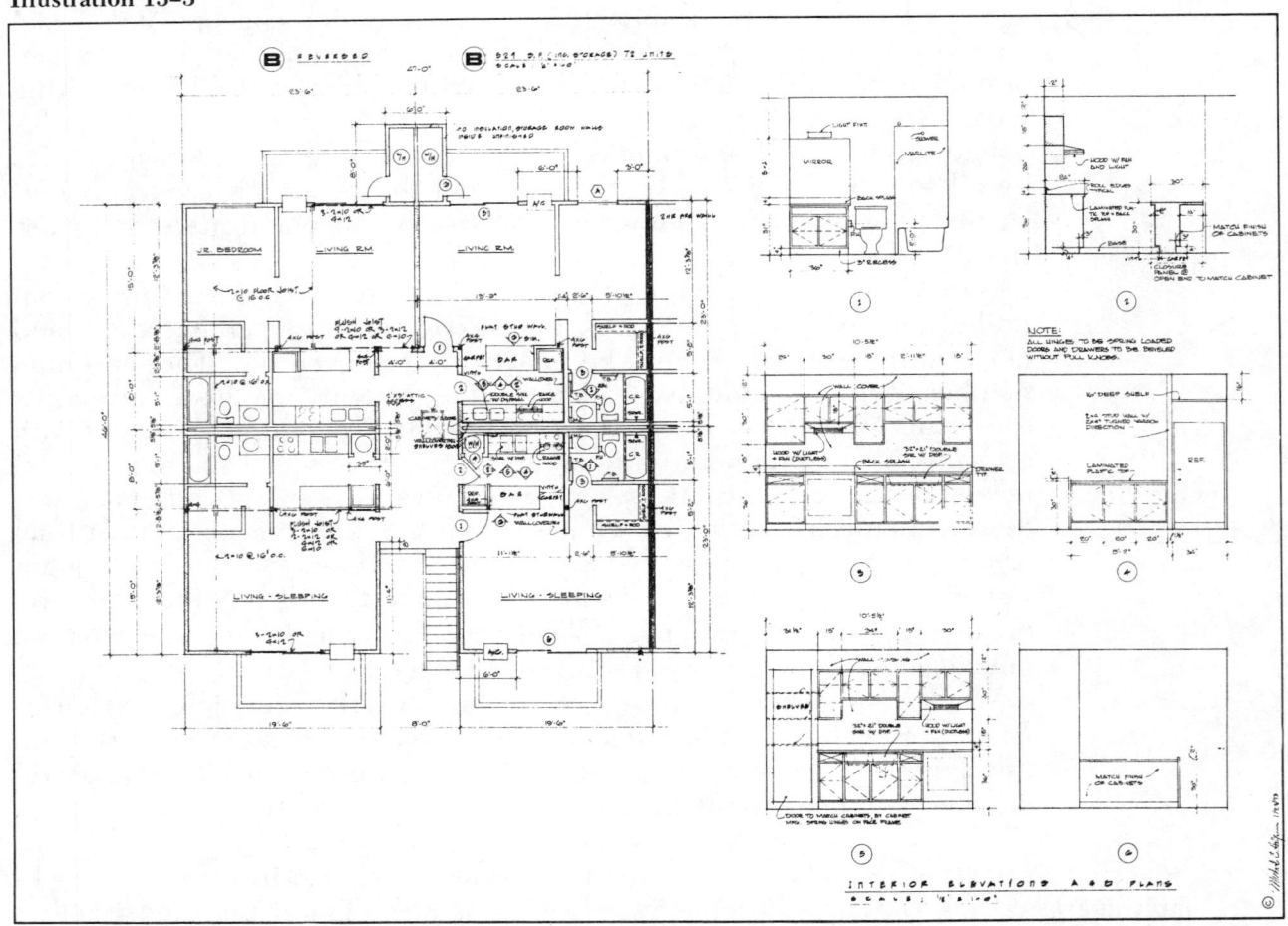

The back-to-back plans shown are very economical from the standpoint of structural framing and utilities distribution. All plumbing fixtures and most electrical appliances are located along one common wall running the length of the building, and most utility distribution takes place in this wall. This permits doubling up on plumbing stacks and elimination of horizontal runs from primary distribution to outlet locations for both plumbing and electrical facilities, except for convenience outlets and switches.

is a sea of roofs. Breaking roof lines adds greatly to curb appeal and first impression (see Illustration 13–4). Visual relief, however, should be in the nature of architectural appendages such as towers or chimneys (large enough to really stop the eye), rather than integral structural breaks and setbacks, which require extensive framing, structural detailing, flashing, and weather protection. Structurally complex breaks in exterior walls and roofs should be minimized to reduce costs and speed construction time.

In back-to-back planning, as many apartment entries on an exit enclosure should be grouped as are allowed under local codes, to reduce vertical circulation costs to the second floor. Grouping of entries also simplifies landscape and sprinkler design and reduces exterior sidewalk costs. As many as eight apartments (four on the second floor) can be grouped to a single notched-in entryway with one stair.

Illustration 13–4

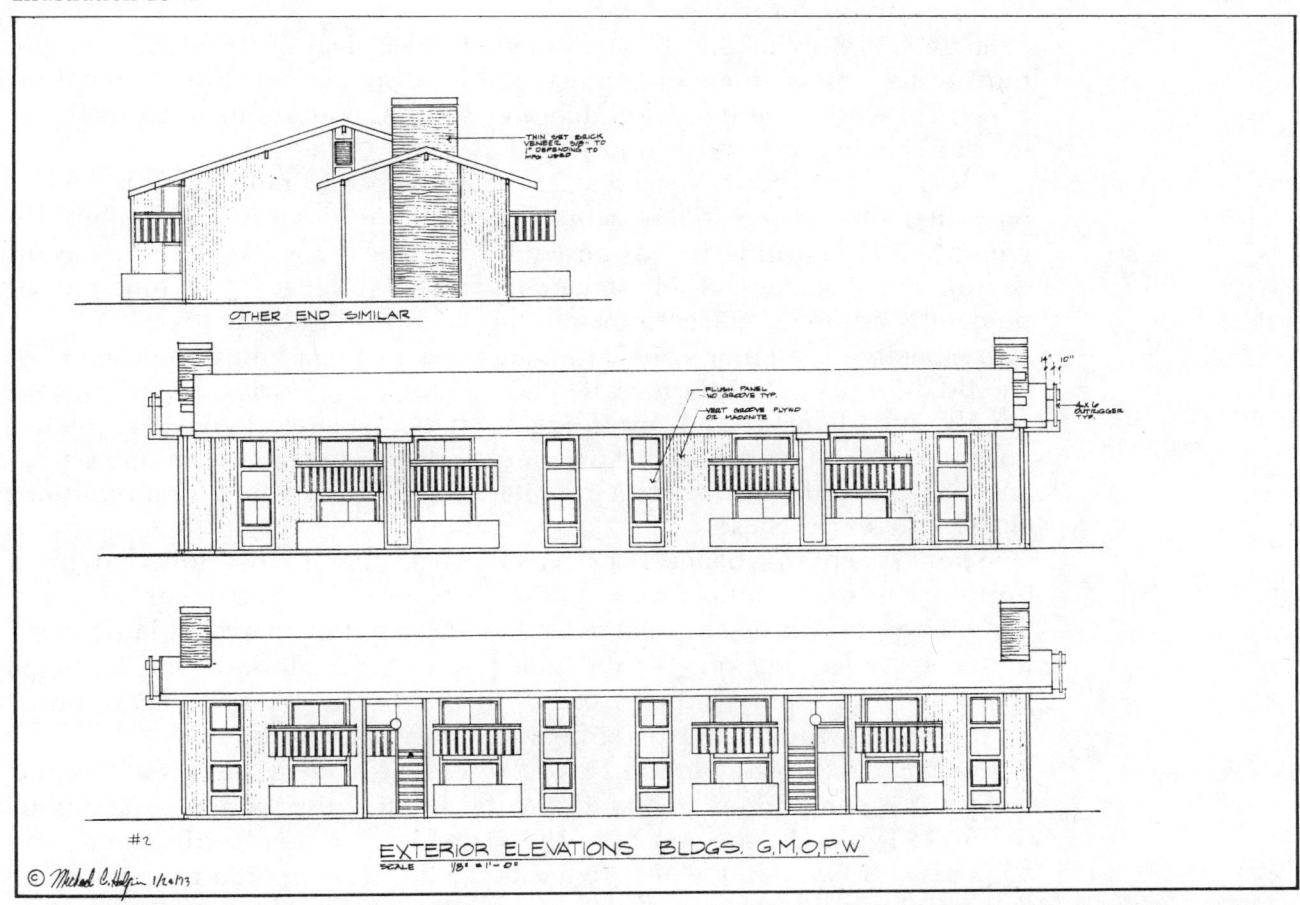

In a back-to-back building, the building exteriors are designed for construction simplicity, with minimal roof or wall breaks to add to framing expense. Openings are modular for economy in material cutting and spacing of joists. Roof lines are broken with false chimney stacks, which are cheaper and less complex than more complicated roof breaks. There are 8 units on the second floor served by only 2 stairs.

Design character is tasteful and unobtrusive. The building is used as a backdrop for the landscaping which completes the design effect. Architects sometimes mistakenly attempt to provide the entire design solution with the elevations, leaving little in the budget for the landscaping. In this event the total environment suffers.

HOW VALUE ENGINEERING REDIRECTS EXPENSES

A good rule of thumb for making value decisions is to omit less frequently utilized conveniences and amenities the resident does not have continuing awareness of in favor of those that are used more often and are highly visual. For example, infrequently used hallway lights and switches between living rooms and bedroom areas can be eliminated or reduced in number by better planning, at a cost saving of $22 for each light, switch, and wiring. Some of the savings can be pocketed, and the remaining portion allotted to a better quality lighting fixture over the dining table.

By efficient plumbing design and grouping of fixtures, the number of plumbing riser stacks can be reduced, as well as horizontal distribution costs throughout the building. Efficient planning can also reduce air conditioning and heating costs by allowing less heat gain or loss and reducing ducting and duct for-in costs by planning which permits air to be thrown across the room rather than ducted. The savings can be put into a better quality refrigerator or a wet bar.

Savings are obtainable through efficient electrical distribution, locating transformers close to meter centers, and locating outlets close to switches. Electrical work should parallel floor joists rather than running across them, to avoid having to bore each joist.

When possible, joists spaced at 24 inches on center rather than 16 inches on center should be used, to achieve a saving in board feet of lumber. By going to 2 × 12s at 24 inches on center in lieu of 2 × 10s at 16 inches on center, board footage of joist materials can be reduced by as much as 20 percent. With fewer joists to install, the labor factor also is less.

In specifying lumber sizes, alternate sizes that can be used on the plan should be specified, because the board-foot price varies depending on supply and demand and according to size of material. Because of the volitility of the lumber market, the price advantage shifts from one size to another. It is difficult to foresee which sizes will be going for a premium at the time of purchase.

When specifying beam sizes, an alternate should be provided for a built-up beam or solid beam, particularly for East Coast construction. Sometimes a solid beam, such as an 8 × 12, is not even available in a particular materials market. Rather than import the material from the West Coast or other remote supply source, the subcontractor can elect to build up the beam with 2 × whatever beam depth is required.

Interior panel boxes located close to electrical load areas such as the kitchen, air conditioner, and water heater reduce distribution costs within the unit. Typically, the run from the switchbox to the electric range runs $5 per foot. In deciding where to locate the box it is important to remember that a six-foot difference in distance from the range to the box can increase costs by $30 per unit. A portion of the electrical savings can be put into decorative exterior architectural lighting in courtyards, accent lighting of buildings at curb front, and lighting of reflecting pools.

Color is a very good design tool for achieving low-cost architectural interest. Exterior colors can make or break a project. Four colors on a building exterior are not unusual, the roof color and door color, if included, make six colors. In low-end projects in particular, where structural relief must be minimized due to budget constraints, color relief has great importance. It is a good idea to withhold final appraisal of a color selection until a representative portion of the building has been painted. Colors often look altogether different on the building than they do on the color chart. Color on the building should be fine tuned until the exact effect looked for has been achieved.

By modular placement of doors and windows in exterior walls, cutting and wasting of plywood materials can be minimized, as well as requirements for extra studs in exterior walls. For nonbearing stud walls, 2 × 4s at 16 inches on center can be made 24 inches on center, and 2 × 4s can even be replaced with 2 × 3s. The second sill plate at the second floor above lightweight concrete can be eliminated. Through efficient design, lineal feet of interior partitioning and number of doors can be reduced, with a portion of the savings going into handsome trellises and decorative screening fences in courtyards, and decorative pole-timber landscape groupings.

Waste space can often be designed out of units without reducing room sizes, with the savings put into larger rooms, recreation building space, or decorative wall coverings. Of course these savings can also be pocketed, at the discretion of the builder. These front-end dollar savings, or discretionary dollars, are the most important funds in the project. The average resident will not notice where the costs have been cut, but he or she will notice, through frequent use and visual impact, where extras have been "thoughtfully" provided by redirection of the discretionary dollars.

Other tips for cost-conscious construction

1. Omit wing walls at sliding or bifold closet doors; omit headers over sliding or bifold closet doors, use full ceiling-height doors.
2. Omit the light switch in walk-in closets and use a pull-chain light.
3. Use dropped ceiling headers when compatible with design, to eliminate joist hangers and the need to cut joists to exact size.
4. At non-load-bearing partitions, cut out the sill plate at door and use for the door head.
5. Use cripples under windows at 24 inches on center, even though the studs in an adjacent bearing wall need to be at 16 inches on center.
6. Omit floor-joist bracing for the second floor where the local building department allows. Test studies indicate the ceiling of first-floor space provides adequate lateral restraint for joists.
7. Whenever possible, design footings so they can be poured in the trench, thus eliminating the need for foundation forming.
8. Design foundations according to soils conditions as determined by an engineer, rather than using standard accepted building department details, which are generally overdesigned.
9. Use one-coat paint application on interiors over taped and textured gypboard.

10. Use glass with factory sash. Glass without factory sash installed on the job site into wood stops is more costly.

CASE STUDY I: DEVIATIONS FROM THE PROFIT CONCEPT

On the surface, this is an attractive project. Numerous costly amenities and design features were incorporated to establish and emphasize the luxury concept. However, planning of the overall development went contrary to most of the profit concepts we have suggested, and reverses soon followed.

The ways this project deviated from the profit concepts are discussed below. Had these concepts been generally adhered to, the project would undoubtedly have been a more successful investment vehicle.

As Illustration 13–5 shows, there is no distinction between primary and secondary courts. Parking areas are not secondary and cannot be played down because the front entries of the units are off the parking areas. Improvements in parking areas must be first quality and prestige oriented; they are necessarily costly, with little leeway to cut costs on either the building elevations facing them or the parking court area. When spending is spread over such a broad area, there is little money remaining to build up impact where it is really needed.

The extensive use of lakes throughout the project also is costly. Had the lakes been in one or two primary areas only, a handsome premium could have justifiably been charged on units facing them. However, all the units cannot go for a premium, as suggested by the plan, because the market cannot absorb all cream. Absorption requires bread and butter units as well.

Additionally, the very extensive use of the lake amenity is tiring. In this instance, too much of a good thing reduced the premium value. Some of the money spent on the lakes could have been better spent elsewhere.

The economics of the project pushed the rental rates into a very thin market. This was partially due to the size of the units. The rates per square foot were not out of line at all, but the total rental per unit was high. It is very difficult to offer both extensive amenities and large units. The economics will generally push the rents beyond the bounds of most market areas. The developer has to be very selective as to what he can and cannot afford to offer. For example, a cash expenditure that does not create more than commensurate income is washed out; that is, if there is no related income stream to be capitalized, the cash investment cannot be retrieved. Needless to say, there is no profit. A cash investment that does not produce a related income stream does nothing to increase value and limits the developer's ability to finance the cost.

The project is poorly laid out from a pedestrian circulation standpoint. Entryways and walkways to entrys are related almost exclusively to the parking lot areas or to narrowly restricted courts paved with concrete. People relate, by association and repetitious exposure, to what they are close to. Most foot traffic is directed through the parking lots, so that the

Illustration 13-5
Case Study I: Site plan

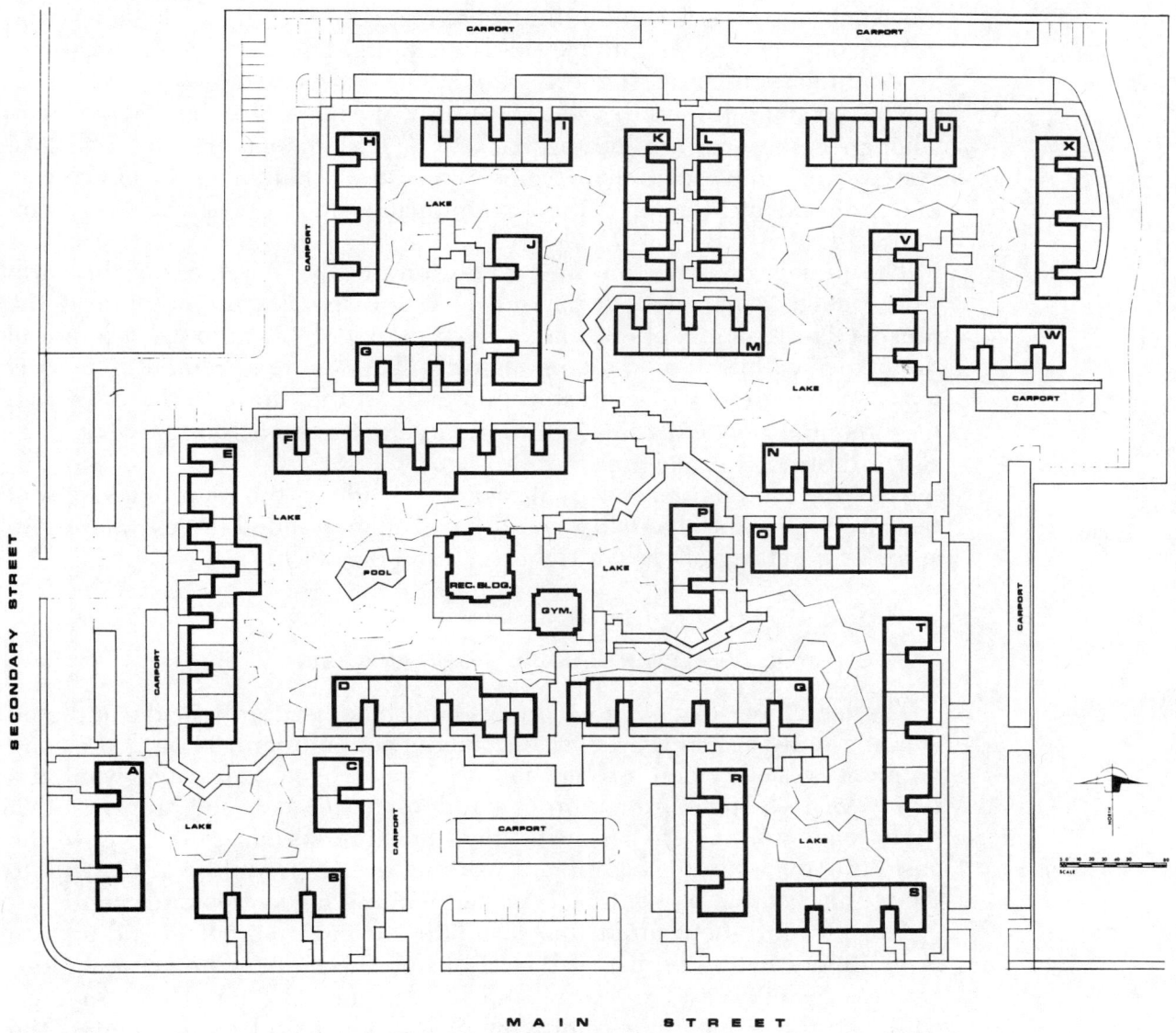

residents feel identity with the parking lot rather than the luxurious landscaped courts. Even when well handled, a parking lot is still a parking lot. This constant overexposure to the parking area and underexposure to courtyards washes out part of the value of the expensive amenities in the landscaped courts. For example, follow the path of a resident in building M in walking to and from his car. Could this route suggest prestige living conditions to the resident and guests he wishes to impress?

The recreation complex does not reflect the community and social needs of the residents. Though centrally located in the project, access to the recreation complex is difficult. A resident in the lower end of building E, directly facing the recreation facility, has to travel through two parking areas and between several buildings to reach it. Easy mingling is not suggested, nor is a sense of intimacy and belonging. The absence of pedestrian access to garden courts suggests "Look, but don't touch."

The economy of back-to-back building design is lacking in the plan. Though bathrooms are located back to back, kitchens are not. The lake system must have presented some interesting challenges in circulating underground utilities, and their maintenance may prove even more interesting.

The project does not put up a good front. Fully 50 percent of the curbside footage is devoted to parking lots, and the first impression of the prospective tenant is of entering a large parking lot. There is little hint of the luxury within to the passing motorist. The first requirement in renting to the passing motorist is to stop him and getting him into the project. If the potential resident cannot be pulled across the curb to see what is inside, all else is for naught.

Had a value engineering analysis been made in the planning stages of this project, undue hardship could have been avoided. (See Chapter 15 and 16 for getting off on the right foot from the start.)

CASE STUDY II: AN ELEVENTH-HOUR PROFIT ANALYSIS

The developer of a 160-unit project contacted us after he had completed working drawings and received his takeout commitment. Though the commitment was a favorable one, he had not yet accepted it and wanted a review of his project from a profit standpoint. He made the provision that if any changes were to be made, they must be accomplished within the basic framework of his completed working drawings and be acceptable to the lender, so that he could accept the pending takeout commitment.

This eleventh-hour profit analysis under the constraint of a pending loan commitment naturally placed limitations on the profit improvement alternatives. Nonetheless, we were able to deliver substantial cost savings, while at the same time improving the product and strengthening the developer's marketing position. We were able to pull out approximately $80,000, or $500 a unit, from the project without jeopardizing the existing loan commitment. The floor plans, exterior elevations, foundation and framing plans, and the livability of the project were all enhanced.

For brevity, discussion of the redesign of the one-bedroom plan will illustrate a number of the value engineering techniques utilized to deliver a $500 profit increase per unit (see Illustration 13–6).

The kitchen in Plan 1 had no windows or view to the outside. The sink was moved to the common living room wall and a hole was cut in the wall, creating a wet bar effect. The wall, bar, door, and shutters between the kitchen and dining area were removed to provide more openness in the

Illustration 13-6
Case Study II: Floor plans before and after redesign

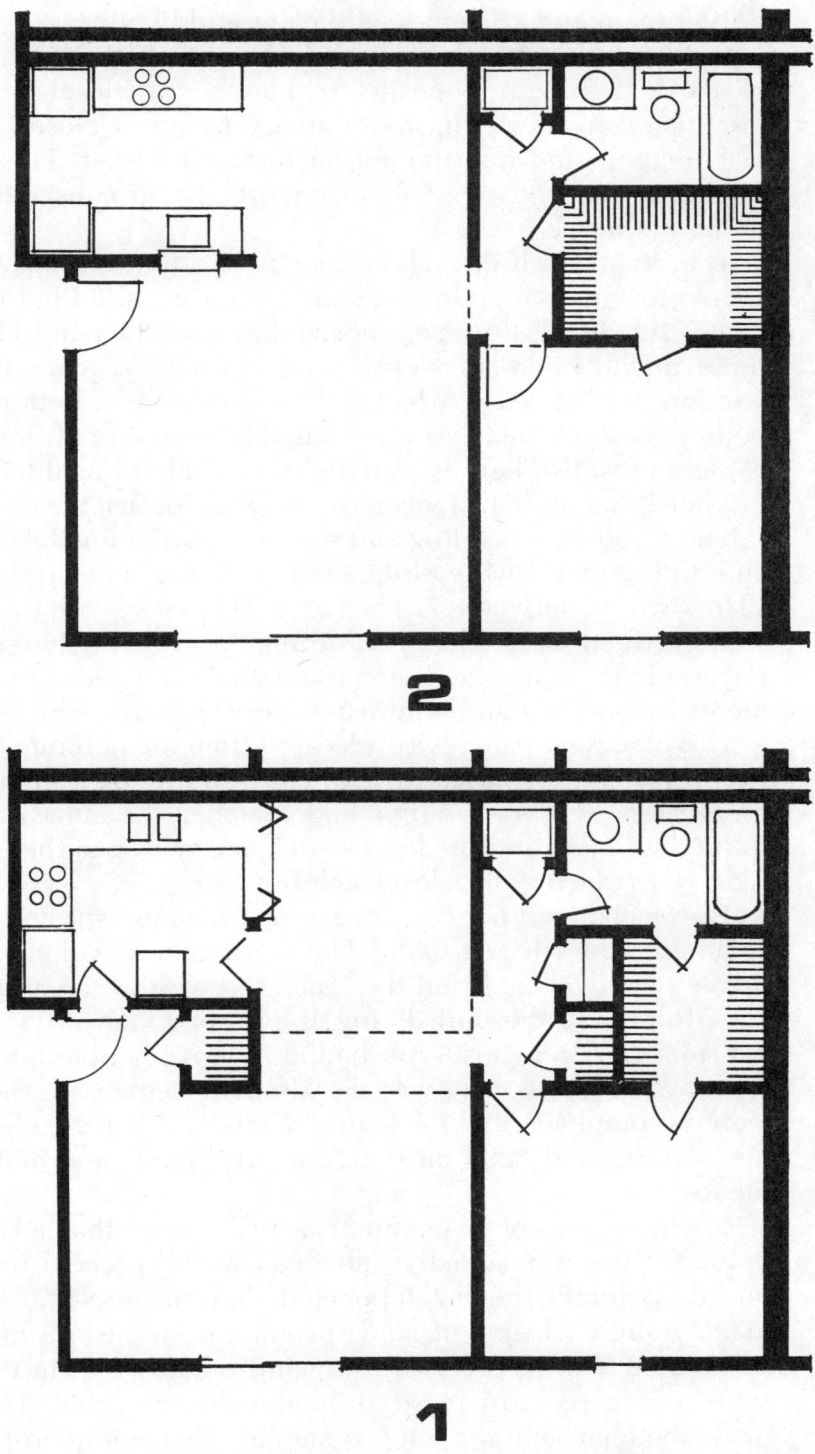

Plan 1 is the floor plan before value engineering redesign. Plan 2 is the floor plan after value engineering, showing how $500 per unit could be saved.

plan. The unnecessary door between the kitchen and living room was eliminated. A wall covering was introduced along the back wall of the dining room and kitchen to add color and liveliness.

In Plan 1, the front door opened directly into the too-small foyer, with the closet door directly opposite. In Plan 2, the closet has been completely eliminated in the living room area. The guest closet, being off the hall, was incorporated into the master bedroom closet. This gave a more open feeling at the entry, but more importantly, it substantially increased the living room size by $3\frac{1}{2}$ feet.

The six-foot, sliding glass door in the living room was the only light source for the living, dining, and kitchen areas in Plan 1, and it was inadequate. In Plan 2, the opening size has been increased to 8 feet. The windows in the bedroom were changed from a 2-foot-wide, floor-to-ceiling window to one 4 by 5 feet, which serves as a better light source. The bedroom closet area was redesigned in Plan 2 to eliminate two doors and $8\frac{1}{2}$ feet of wall. There is actually more usable lineal feet of hanging space in Plan 2 than in Plan 1, even though the closet at the entry was eliminated.

The firred-down ceiling and the air conditioning duct between the living and dining rooms were eliminated in Plan 2. The air conditioning duct in Plan 1 was to serve the kitchen area. However, with the elimination of the wall between the kitchen and dining area, the kitchen can be served by a register in the opposite dining room wall. This reduced duct work requirements by one half and eliminated the expensive firred-down ceiling.

The electrical panel was relocated from the hall into the kitchen, nearer to the primary electrical loads. The exterior patio light and switch were eliminated, as were the light and switch at the entry foyer, a ceiling light in the bedroom, and the light switch and wiring in the closet. A pull-chain light is satisfactory for closet lighting.

These changes netted a more open, more spacious plan and a substantially larger living room. The wet bar and wall coverings are a strong marketing advantage, and the increased window areas add brightness and cheerfulness to the unit. Being able to look out of doors through the wet bar from the kitchen is a substantial improvement to the windowless workroom which previously was the kitchen. Best of all, these improvements were accomplished while saving $500: $130 on the electrical, $75 on the mechanical, and $295 on the carpentry, hardware, and painting requirements.

A $500 savings of this nature is actually more than a $500 profit increase, in that value was actually enhanced in the process rather than compromised. Assuming the developer could have made a $1,000 per unit development profit, exclusive of land speculation profits, on his plans before the value engineering process, the value engineering in this instance represents a 50 percent increase in the developer's profit. The lender who had made the loan commitment prior to the value engineering process accepted all of the changes, recognizing that value had been substantially enhanced.

The developer was able to close on the loan amount previously set, even though we pulled $80,000 of cost out in the value engineering process.

Development projects cannot be evaluated as generalities. Each must be analyzed in very specific terms to determine risk for the lender and feasibility for the sponsor. In the value engineering study of the one-bedroom plan, a cursory review might indicate that the two plans are for typical one-bedroom units, somewhat standard for the market area. Our more detailed analysis indicates that this is not so; one plan is substantially more attractive from a marketing, risk, and development feasibility standpoint. The difference between a project that receives this type of analysis throughout and one that does not can be major, for both the lender and the developer.

CASE STUDY III: IDENTIFYING DESIGN AND MARKETING RISK FACTORS

A large rental apartment complex located on one of the western states had progressed to the point of a building permit, was out to bid, and had received a loan commitment. From the early bid figures, the developer realized the project was going to materially exceed the preliminary cost estimates, and cost analysis was required to bring the project within feasibility guidelines. He did not fully realize at this time, however, that there were fundamental design and marketing considerations which needlessly increased the investment risk. All changes had to occur within the limitation of the existing building permit, as well as within a number of other overriding considerations.

In analyzing this project, certain design and marketing risk factors were identified which were as serious an impediment to project success as the cost overrun. Through the value engineering process, costs were brought into line, and a number of design and marketing risk factors were eliminated. Though not all of the risk factors could be eliminated, a number were appreciably reduced, the design was enhanced, and $1,200 per unit was pulled out in the process.

Through the value engineering process, floor plans and elevators were improved, and overall livability of the project was enhanced. A thorough project analysis is a tedious task, so for brevity, the redesign of a typical two-bedroom unit will be analyzed to illustrate some of the value engineering techniques utilized to provide a $450 per unit savings within the confines of the unit itself. Then a building within the project will be analyzed to illustrate some of the value engineering techniques utilized to provide a $750 per unit savings within the building structure and its systems (independent of the savings credited to the unit itself), and the elevations of a typical building within the project will be reviewed.

In that the project planning was fixed, allowing only minor revision to the site plan, the value engineering analysis was limited to unit and building design and did not consider site-planning considerations.

Illustration 13–7
Case Study II: Exterior after redesign

The completely redesigned buildings which resulted from the value engineering analysis in Case Study II.

Redesign of a two-bedroom unit

The architect was innovative and already utilizing back-to-back building design techniques. However, within the individual apartment units themselves, there were opportunities for many design economies. Plan 1 is the plan on which the original building permit was based, and Plan 2 is the plan as revised through value engineering (see Illustration 13–8).

The kitchen in Plan 1 had no windows or view to the outside and was enclosed on three sides and substantially enclosed on the fourth with a counter and overhead cabinets. In Plan 2, the counter and cabinets on the fourth side were removed to provide a feeling of openness. The closet hanging space opening onto the living room and projecting into the kitchen was relocated into the hall and bedroom areas, freeing up the kitchen space and removing an objectionable closet door from the living room. The sink was then relocated from the back wall to the common wall between the kitchen and living room, and reduced in size from a double to a single sink; a double sink is not required when a dishwasher is provided. An opening was then cut in the wall over the sink, permitting a view to the outside from the kitchen. The opening over the sink creates a wet bar effect and is trimmed out with wood trim paneling below and a wine rack shelf above.

The two straight runs greatly simplified the cabinet design and reduced

Illustration 13–8
Case Study III: Floor plans before and after redesign

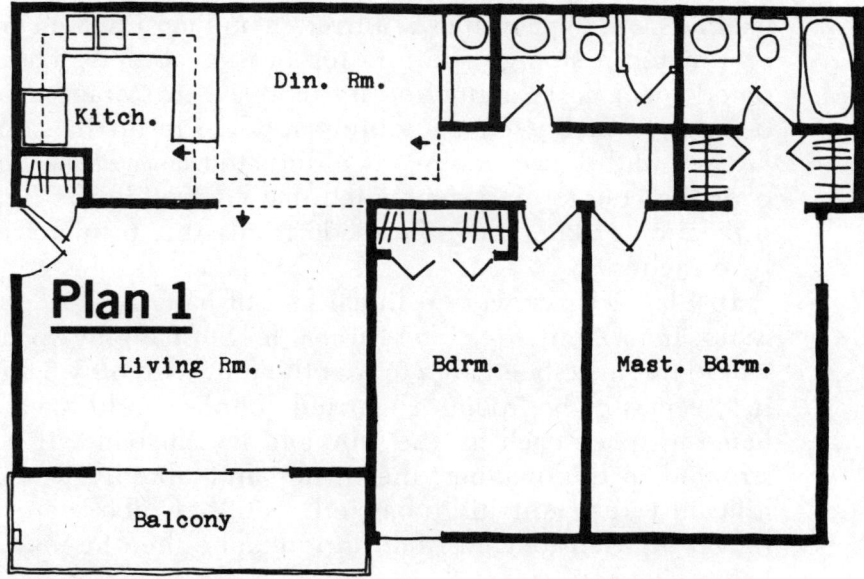

Potential loss to builder was averted when he realized that the original plans for his apartment building were going to exceed estimates. Typical two-bedroom apartment shown above had hidden cost risk factors which could have resulted in marketing and equity problems.

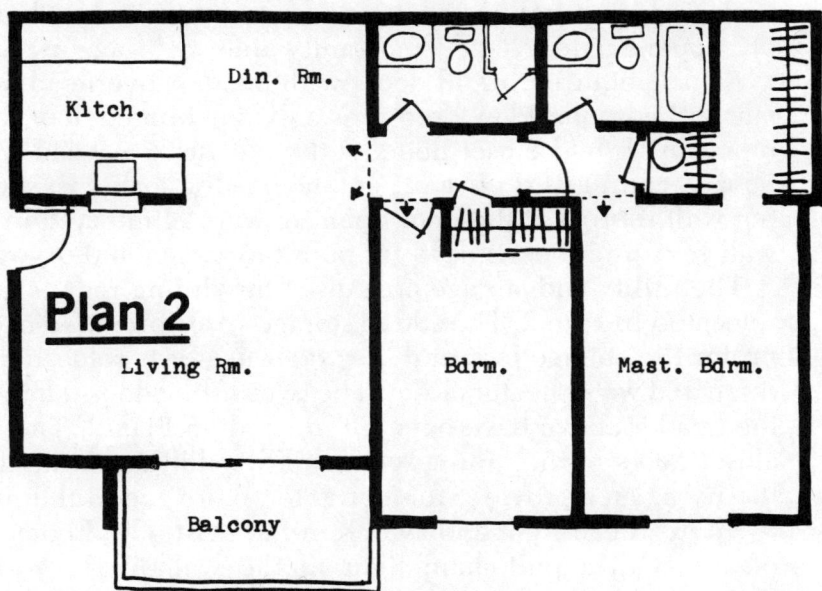

Improved layout in every room was achieved through extensive value engineering to arrive at the revised design above, which represented a saving of $450 within each unit.

both cost and wasted cabinet space in the corners. The new design achieves more usable storage space at less cost. The space between the top of the cabinets and the ceiling was furred in on Plan 1, which created expense and eliminated a storage shelf on top of the cabinets. The furring was eliminated for a cost saving and an increase in storage area. The need for a decorative facing on the dining room side of the counter between the kitchen and dining room was eliminated, as well as three pendant lights over the counter and the switch that controlled the lights. More efficient utilization of kitchen space made it possible to increase living room size by 8 inches.

In Plan 1 there were 6 lineal feet of hanging space in the master bedroom; Plan 2 provides for 14 lineal feet of hanging space. Many prospects would not have been able to rent the unit with only 6 feet of hanging space in the master bedroom; a married couple would have had only 3 feet of hanging space each for the wife and the husband. If the units were constructed in this manner, the owner undoubtedly would have had to significantly discount his projected rentals, which were in the semiluxury range, in order to achieve absorption, and then he may have put his holdback in jeopardy.

An improved bedroom suite arrangement resulted from the closet change. Plan 2 has the very desirable feature of a walk-in closet, whereas in Plan 1 it was necessary to pass through the narrow closet area, which becomes a point of congestion, to get to the bath. The bath itself is much more pleasant. In Plan 1 the door opened directly onto the toilet (very undesirable visually) and stacked against the tub, whereas in Plan 2 the door opens onto a handsome vanity and stacks against the wall.

Plan 1 required bifold doors with headers overhead for the closet in the master bedroom; Plan 2 requires only one hinged door. In the second bedroom, the bifold closet doors with a header overhead were replaced with floor-to-ceiling sliding doors and no header, for a cost saving. Additionally, the wall returns at the door opening were eliminated in Plan 2. The small wall returns are expensive for both the framer and drywall subcontractors.

The utility and storage area off of the dining room shown in Plan 1 was relocated in Plan 2. The added storage space provided in the kitchen makes up for the storage lost, and the water heater is relocated in a combination linen and water heater closet. The two sliding doors off the dining room and the header above have been eliminated on Plan 2. The elimination of the closet doors in the dining room and the shifting of the dining area toward the living area provides for a brighter, more cheerful dining area in Plan 2.

An overhead light and switch in the master bedroom closet area was replaced with a pull-chain light in the walk-in closet, for a cost saving. Pendant light fixtures in both bedrooms of Plan 1 were eliminated. Lighting in Plan 2 will be provided by tenants' own lamps, to be activated by a hot-and-cold plug with a switch at the door. The doorbell was eliminated, as it is unnecessary for a small apartment and not expected as a rental feature by most tenants. Additionally, Plan 1 had a patio light and a waterproof electric outlet on the balcony, both of which were eliminated. These conveniences are very seldom utilized and are rarely missed; sliding glass doors spill enough light onto the balcony from inside to serve most purposes.

Plan 1 had a switch at the front door activating two hot-and-cold electric outlets in the living room. Both of the switches were at the opposite side of the living room from the switch at the door. The switch control was eliminated from one of the outlets, as one outlet serves the purpose of initially lighting the living area when entering the door. The remaining hot-and-cold switch was placed on the same wall as the switch, to eliminate both length of wiring run and the necessity of boring the floor joists to run the wiring across the room.

Bedroom windows have been relocated to the center of bedrooms, rather than in the corner, to provide better light distribution within the room and allow for the use of bifold drapes. Corner windows require single-stacking drapes, which are unattractive and give a harsh effect to window. Entry into the master bedroom from the door is very drab without a window on the end wall or anywhere near it.

The balcony in Plan 1 was 4 feet wide and only marginally useful. In Plan 2 the balcony has been shortened in length but increased to 6 feet in depth to render it more useful. (Window and balcony cost savings are discussed below as aspects of the value engineering of the exterior elevations.)

Plan 1 had a heating and air conditioning system which distributes air into every room through ceiling diffusers. In Plan 2, the ceiling diffusers have been replaced by wall diffusers. Ceiling diffusers are unattractive in the middle of the ceiling, where they were shown; additionally, grime is often deposited on the ceiling around the diffusers, particularly when there are cooking oils in the air from the kitchen. Plan 2 shows the location for the wall diffusers.

In Plan 2, the kitchen area is served by a diffuser in the dining room wall which throws air into the kitchen, making it no longer necessary to have a ceiling diffuser in the kitchen. This makes it possible to eliminate the unattractive firred-down ceiling between the dining room and the living room. The firring was required to enclose the air conditioning duct in Plan 1, which ran under the joists to the kitchen from the firred-down hall area. In Plan 2 the unattractive ceiling registers and ceiling were eliminated, as well as 72 lineal feet of duct work. The design modification netted both anaesthetic improvement and mechanical and framing cost savings.

These design modifications netted a brighter kitchen with more storage space and a view to the outside. A wet bar was incorporated as a marketing feature, and the living room was made 8 inches wider. The dining room is more cheerful without the closet door and located in closer proximity to the living area and an outside view.

The walk-in closet, dramatic increase of hanging space in the master bedroom, better bathroom layout, better light distribution, and curtain arrangement make the bedroom suite area far more competitive in the projected rental range. Increasing the balcony width from 4 to 6 feet introduces usable outside space for relaxation. Elimination of the ceiling diffusers and firred-down ductwork in the living area nets a more desirable, uncluttered living area. Best of all, these improvements were accomplishable while saving $450 net within the unit itself: $210 on carpentry, cabinet work, doors, hardware, and so on; $110 on mechanical systems (hot water system not included); and $130 on electrical work. These savings do not include savings for the building structure itself or for the exterior elevations.

Building structure and systems

The building structure is illustrated in Illustration 3–9; Plan 1 shows structure elevation as it was initially designed, and Plan 2 shows redesign input. The concrete parking garage base on which the building rests projects out 12 feet from the side of the building, and at its high point it is a 14-foot-high blank, exposed concrete facade facing the apartment units across a narrow court. The openings in the concrete are for light and ventilation into the enclosed parking garage. To soften the design, the formed, reinforced concrete was replaced with slump block and terra-cotta tiles, with the voids providing light and ventilation and a better screening effect for the garage. Replacing formed reinforced concrete with block and terra-cotta tiles produced a cost saving of $23,200 around the perimeter of the building. Also, the terra-cotta screening effect greatly expanded ventilation into the garage and changed the garage classification from an enclosed to unenclosed classification (according to the code), thus eliminating the requirement for mechanical ventilation to the garage.

Surface treatments in Plan 1 were somewhat harsh, lacking softness of residential detailing and scale. Brick veneer areas have been reduced in Plan 2, and a more residential scale has been incorporated into the elevation. The brick veneer was also reduced from 4 inch-thick to $3/4$-inch-thick veneer. Reducing square footage and thickness of veneer resulted in less structured support being required in the garage superstructure and lateral shear wall costs, for a masonry and structural saving for the building of $24,600.

Balconies in Plan 1 were 4 feet wide and had limited utility. Also, the metal-rail and stucco soffit treatment were rather harsh. In Plan 2, the balcony is shortened in length but increased to 6 feet in depth, to give better utility. Sides of the balcony return all the way to the back of the notch-in, rather than terminating in the side walls. This gives a more interesting three-dimensional feel and visual interest. The balcony is then supported by a heavy timber beam spanning the two side walls, all of which adds richer detail to the balcony treatment. The underside of the balcony of Plan 2 is exposed timber construction, stained in a rich earth color, rather than the plaster soffit called for in Plan 1, thus an exposed beam effect replaces the plaster soffit, which all too often becomes water stained because of poor flashing or waterproofing treatments on the deck above.

Illustration 13–9
Case Study III: Building structure elevations

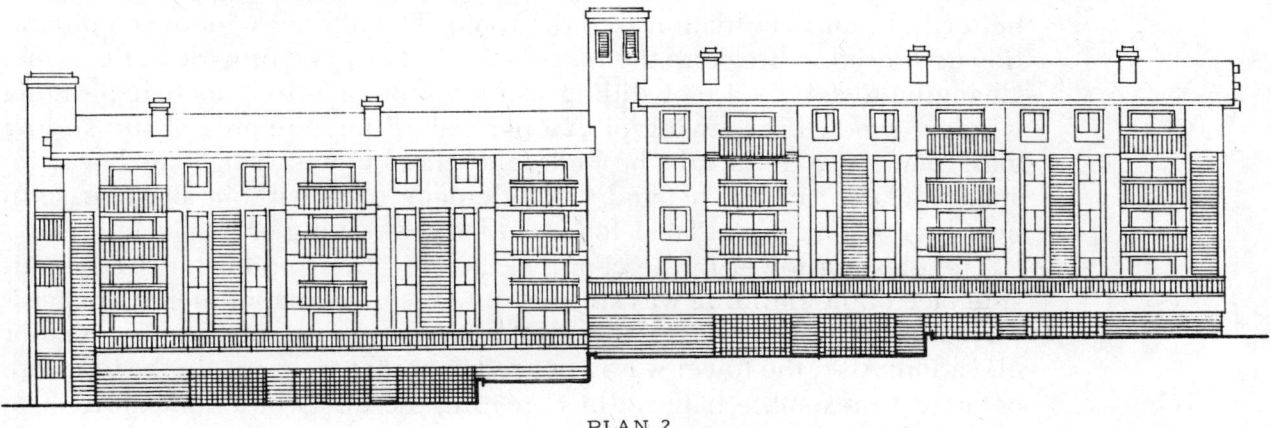

PLAN 2

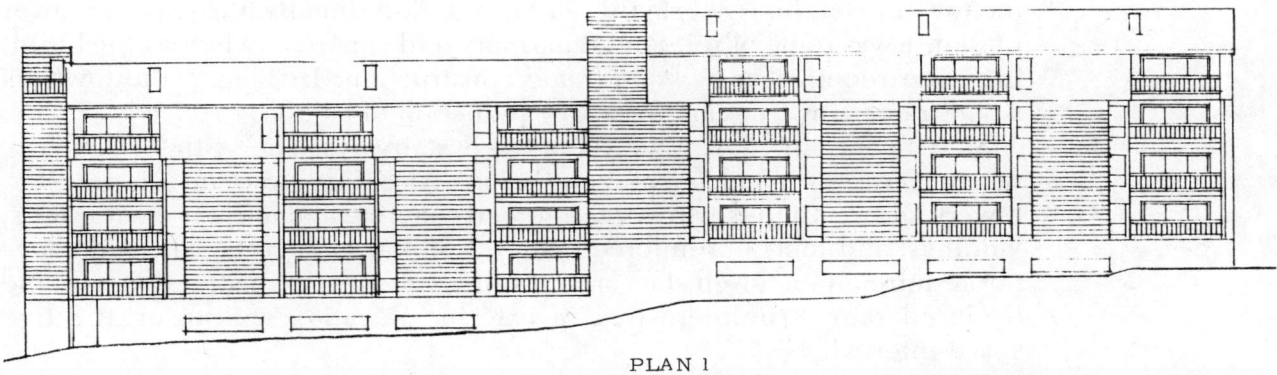

PLAN 1

Plan 1 shows building elevation before value engineering. Plan 2 shows building elevation after value engineering, which saved $750 per unit in the building structure and $450 a unit within each unit plan, for a total savings of $1,200 per unit.

The metal handrail treatment in Plan 1 is replaced by a wooden handrail treatment to provide more natural textures and warmth of detail. Replacing metal with wood railing; eliminating the plastic soffit, the cantilever of balcony joists, and side flashing and waterproofing requirements; and simplification of deck construction resulted in a balcony cost savings of $87 per unit.

The 12-foot-wide, three-leaf insulated sliding glass doors in Plan 1 are an asset but not a requirement for the rental range the project was aiming for. In this instance, it was felt that the overall profit picture would be enhanced by reduction of cost in this area. The three-leaf 12-foot slider and three-leaf 9-foot slider were replaced by a two-leaf 8-foot slider, for a door and header cost reduction of $105 per unit average.

The 3- by 6-foot single-hung bedroom windows in Plan 1 were changed to 4- by 4-foot sliding glass windows in Plan 2. The window was also relocated from the corner of the bedroom to the center, thus providing for better light and ventilation into the room. The altered window configuration and location break up the harshness of Plan 1 and provide better scale. Changing to a 4- by 4-foot sliding window from a 3- by 6-foot single-hung window produced a saving of $29 per unit. Since the area of the sliding glass doors was reduced, the bedroom window, which in Plan 1 was insulated glass, can be changed to single-pane glass without an increase in heat loss or gain over Plan 1 for an added cost saving of $9 per unit.

The elevator tower in the center of the elevation and flush with the outside face of the building was set back into the building, reducing unnecessary interior hallway space and producing design interest on the exterior elevation. Also, the tower was increased in height and vents in the top were detailed to resemble baffles, thus creating the effect of a companile. The roof of the elevator enclosure was changed from concrete to wood. Though an added cost was incurred in raising the height of the tower, 320 square feet of interior corridor space were eliminated on four floors as a result of the tower inset, for a net savings of $2,300. Additionally, the elevator tower in Plan 1 was to be of reinforced masonry and concrete, whereas the building code requires only wood-frame construction. In Plan 2, the tower is wood-frame construction, for a cost reduction of $1,800.

Stair towers in Plan 1 were enclosed stairways, one with a vestibule, which requires mechanical ventilation. Also, construction of the stair towers and vestibules were of reinforced concrete and masonry, with stairs, landings, and roofs of reinforced poured-in-place concrete. The code does not require an enclosed stair or vestibule or masonry construction, and the enclosed stair is uninteresting in exterior elevation and an unattractive space internally.

To improve aesthetics and reduce cost, an unenclosed exterior stair is utilized in Plan 2. The vestibule was entirely eliminated at each floor, as well as the vestibule door and the mechanical ventilation. The reinforced masonry and concrete construction was replaced with simple wood-frame construction. The poured-in-place, formed, reinforced concrete stairs and landings were replaced by prefabricated units with metal tubular supports and individual concrete treads. In that two end walls of the stair tower are eliminated, to achieve the unenclosed classification, there is an additional savings in exterior wall costs. The net effect of these changes is a cost savings of $7,000 for the building.

A handrail is provided in Plan 2 at the perimeter of the parking garage roof on which the building rests. The rail is required for health and safety reasons and is one of many features picked up in the value engineering process that otherwise may not have emerged until the building construction phase. At that time it is a change order and much more costly than if it had been provided for before the contracts were let. Value engineering reduces initial contract costs and total contract costs by minimizing change orders in the field and eliminating troublesome oversights and irregularities which slow construction and increase overhead. Numerous opportunities existed for cost savings and product improvement within the building itself which are not directly related to unit plan design or exterior elevation treatment.

Sound insulation methods between floors were costly in relation to the benefits provided. Original design called for 1-inch mastacal over a $5/8$-inch subfloor, insulation bats between joists, and resilient clips separating gypboard ceiling from floor joists, attached with self-tapping screws. From both a lender and resident standpoint, sound-deadening material over $5/8$-inch subfloor provides adequate sound control between floors. As added insurance to protect against impact noise, a denser carpet, denser pad, and sound-deadening resilient flooring with backing in the kitchen and bath areas will fill the bill. In addition, the resident can immediately recognize underfoot the extra expense put into quality floor coverings. The modifications resulted in a $16,500 cost saving, while at the same time giving a more expensive feel, both visually and underfoot.

While no expense was spared in providing sound control between floors in the original drawings, there were sound leaks designed in between units on the same floor. Back-to-back plumbing walls were utilized in the design which consisted of two 2×4 stud walls side by side with gypboard sheathing on the outside, and with no chase space between the studs. Having no chase to run plumbing in, the plumbing stacks and runs must be cut into the 2×4 stud areas. However, the sound insulation was also to go between the 2×4 studs, so that wherever the plumbing stacks and runs passed through, the insulation would be displaced.

To alleviate this problem, the studs were spread apart 5 inches to provide for a plumbing chase and alleviate the problem areas where the insulation would be displaced. If this design incongruity were not alleviated, there could have been serious sound control problems, in spite of all the money that was earmarked for through-the-floor sound control. It is particularly aggravating to have sound control problems after an owner has paid heavily in attempting to avoid them.

Providing the plumbing chase in the back-to-back plumbing walls also had a marked effect on plumbing economy. With no chase the floor-joist blocking and plates at each floor level must be cut to enable the stacks to pass through. In most instances the cutouts must then be strapped and patched to provide structural continuity. Also, the studs in the walls must be notched to let the plumbing runs through. This again requires strapping and patching to provide structural continuity, particularly when the wall is load bearing or restraining lateral forces. Providing for the chase greatly facilitates plumbing distribution, allows the plumber to move at a much more rapid pace, and cuts days out of the construction schedule. Though a handsome saving and better sound control are anticipated by providing for a chase area, the savings is not put into dollar figures and included in the cost savings, because it is difficult to estimate with accuracy.

The original working drawings had 3,600 lineal feet of 2×6 stud wall in the building shown in Plan 1. The 2 × 6 studs were provided to take increased loads from the floors above. However, there are disadvantages in utilizing 2 × 6 studs for the particular design solution. The 2 × 6 stud walls took up 600 square feet more floor area than 4-inch stud walls do. For this reason, the 2 × 6 studs were replaced by 3 × 4 studs, netting a 13 square foot increase in net usable floor area per apartment unit.

At the lower floors, where shear wall requirements are greatest, the closeness of the edge nailing on the plywood shear wall panels would have split the 2 × 6 stud, whereas the 3 × 4 stud can take the nailing.

Cross bridging between joists at midspan was eliminated. The Uniform Building Code (UBC) — the governing code in the area — no longer requires cross bridging at midspan of joists, since tests have shown that bridging in this area is not required for structural integrity.

Plan 1 showed fireplaces in every one- and two-bedroom apartment unit. Fireplaces are generally considered a luxury and can justify a premium, but, placing them in all of the units reduces the premium value. Not everyone wants a fireplace or is willing to pay a premium for one. To place fireplaces in every unit is to suggest that every unit should go for a premium. If management is only going to rent to people who are willing to pay a premium, management is taking risks in achieving absorption.

On the other hand, management could offer the fireplaces but not get a premium for them; but this is not good business either. In smaller units, such as the two-bedroom unit shown with a 12- by 16-foot living room, the addition of a fireplace greatly limits the amount of furniture that can be placed in the room. There will be a number of prospects who cannot rent the unit with a fireplace because their living room furniture will not fit.

The fireplaces were removed from one third of the units without affecting the projected rental schedule, because the fireplaces remaining could justify a premium without adversely affecting overall absorption.

Though the amount of detail in Case Study III may appear to be cumbersome, it nonetheless cannot be ignored. Value engineering requires this type of attention to detail. To generalize, to spend the bulk of the time with the dollars and let the pennies take care of themselves, or to go for the jugular and let the details fall as they will, is not value engineering.

The competitive forces at work in the marketplace demand strict attention to detail. If the competition is taking this approach and a developer has not because he does not want to get involved in this type of detail, he may not be able to afford to stay in business. As more organizations take the value engineering approach, the competitive forces will assume even larger proportions.

The detail may appear to be of agonizing proportions, but the industry must adjust its attitudes and become even more detail conscious, with a comprehensive cost/benefit overview. Successful management will permeate its organization with this type of thinking at all levels (see Chapters 18, 22, and 25).

CASE STUDY IV: VALUE ENGINEERING WITH STANDARD HOUSE PLANS

We were contacted to do a value engineering analysis of a group of house plans for a developer in the Midwest who was reusing the standard plans for various developments in his market area. This case study illustrates how costs were reduced and merchandising value increased as a result of the value engineering analysis. To simplify, only one of the house plans will be presented, and elevation redesigns will not be included. The single-family Plan 1 is one of the house plans before the value engineering analysis, and Plan 2 is the revised plan after the analysis (see Illustration 13–10).

Merchandising improvements

The merchandising improvements made possible by value engineering in this case include the following:

1. The living room has been made 35 percent larger through elimination of a needless hall space.

Illustration 13–10
Case Study IV: Floor plans before and after redesign

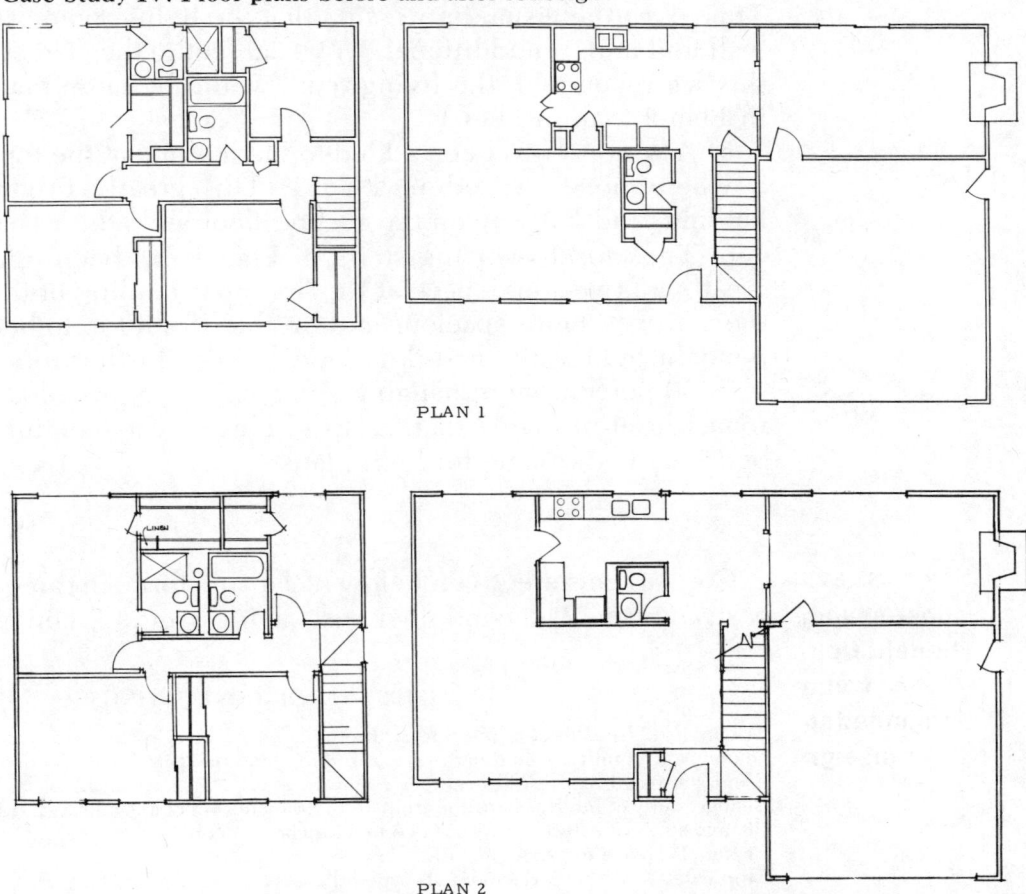

Plan 1 is the floor plan before the value engineering review. Plan 2 is the plan after the review, which projected a $3,625 cost saving for the plan.

2. The entry has been made much more interesting and brighter. The front door opens onto a raised entry foyer in Plan 2, whereas in Plan 1 the entry was into a dark hallway with a view of a narrow hall and closet door. In Plan 1 there is a view from the entry door through the house and into the back yard through a large window in the breakfast area. Additionally, there is a large floor to ceiling window in the entrance foyer at the foot of the stair. On entry, the house appears much brighter and larger in Plan 1 than in Plan 2, adding to sales appeal.

3. The living room has been made brighter in Plan 2 through addition of the window in the foyer and elimination of the wing walls between the living and dining room. The living room now borrows light from the breakfast room window, and eliminating the wing walls adds to spaciousness in that the living and dining room can "borrow" space from one another. This makes the living area appear even more than 35 percent larger in Plan 2 than in Plan 1.

4. The elimination of the hallway at the entry disposes of a congested unattractive space on the first floor of Plan 2. With the elimination of the hallway, the stairway to the second floor is now located in the living room. This gives the visual impression that the living room extends to the garage wall and adds an additional 3½ visual feet to the size of the living room. If this were counted, the living room would be more than 50 percent larger in Plan 2 than in Plan 1.

5. A window has been added to the landing at the top of the stair in Plan 2 where none existed in Plan 1. This greatly brightens the stairway, landing, and hallway on the second floor and adds visual interest as well.

6. The closet over the stairs in Plan 1 has been eliminated in Plan 2, creating a two-story space at the first floor landing of the stair. This makes the stairway more spacious and brighter from top to bottom. An attractive pendant light at the first-floor landing adds further interest.

7. 50 percent more hanging space has been provided in the master bedroom closet in Plan 2 than exists in Plan 1. The hanging space in the other bedroom is the same for both plans.

$3,625 cost-saving benefit from value engineering redesign

Cost savings are given below in capsule form, in three parts: (1) first-floor cost savings, (2) second-floor cost savings, and (3) general cost savings.

FIRST-FLOOR COST SAVINGS

Eliminate 42 lineal feet of interior partition	$ 230
Doors, pantry, mill-finished hardware, carpentry, and painting—two less doors	90
Eliminate wood base, 170 lineal feet	60
Change studs of interior partition from 16 to 24 inches on center	40
Change studs of exterior wall from 16 to 24 inches on center	75
Change fireplace to prefab metal	100
Eliminate ½-inch underlayment at carpeted areas	94
Eliminate four electrical outlets	80
Change family room to slab on grade	250
Total first-floor cost savings	$1,119

SECOND-FLOOR COST SAVINGS

Doors, finish hardware, and paint—eliminate two hinged doors and add one sliding door	$ 60
Eliminate 28 lineal feet of interior partition	204
Redesign baths so they are back to back and stacked over first-floor plumbing (significant savings in labor and modest saving in materials)	150
Eliminate wood base, 240 lineal feet	84
Eliminate ½-inch carpet underlayment	140
Eliminate two electrical outlets	40
Add bath exhaust fan	(50)
Change studs of interior partitions from 16 inches to 24 inches on center	75
Change studs of exterior walls from 16 inches to 24 inches on center	62
Eliminate 4 × 12 header at doors in nonbearing partitions	25
	$ 790

GENERAL COST SAVINGS

Eliminate soffit framing at overhang	$ 218
Eliminate brick at rear and side elevations and substitute stucco or other finish (per local preference)	1,000
Change roof sheathing from ½ to ⅜ inches with ply clips	128
Eliminate blocking and bridging at joists	50
Change double-hung windows with six lights to sliding aluminum sash	780
	$2,176

RECAP

First-floor plan	$1,119
Second-floor plan	760
General	2,176
	$4,055
Costs incurred in Plan 2 not incurred in Plan 1	−430
Net savings as a result of value engineering	$3,625

THE IMPORTANCE OF A COMPREHENSIVE OVERVIEW

To enhance a specific project value, a comprehensive overview must be achieved so as not to engineer one value at the expense of another. Though developers often make decisions on an incremental point-to-point basis, the effects of the decision are nonetheless comprehensive in nature. Vast amounts of resources can be wasted out in the process of planning value on an incremental basis through the creation of offsetting value washes, which are, in effect, incongruities in the product of investment planning. Piecemeal planning approaches are too often used to make situations which are inherently bad more efficiently bad.

Offsetting value washes can erode profit

Most decisions that will be made regarding a real estate investment are interrelated. A decision that can be made on its own merit, independent of others, is almost nonexistent. Therefore, investment decisions either reinforce one another or wash one another out.

If decisions reinforce one another, it is reasonable to expect a project worth more than the sum of its parts. If they wash one another out, a developer should not be too surprised to find he has a project whose total is worth less than the sum of its parts.

To narrow down investment decisions to their essential elements, it is helpful to think in terms of specific investment objectives. For example, cooling an apartment unit is not an investment objective, but creating financing acceptability, absorption and retention of tenants, and increased capitalized value is. Therefore, in making a value decision on air conditioning—to use or not to use, and what type system—the developer must think in terms of the air conditioning's effect on financing, absorption and retention of tenants, and capitalized value, because these are investment objectives. Cooling an apartment unit is not an investment objective but a specialized engineering consideration whose importance is directly related to its impact on the investment objectives.

A developer must be careful not to confuse his role in the marketplace. The developer and the tenant are on different sides of the bargaining table, both trying to maximize the return on their money. However, the tenant is striving for the greatest environmental return on the rental dollar, whereas the developer is seeking the greatest cash return on the investment dollar.

If a developer spends heavily for environmental amenities but cannot obtain commensurate rents, he is fulfilling the tenant's objectives—but not his own. From an inventor's standpoint, the money spent on environmental conveniences or amenities which will not draw commensurate income has washed itself out. The saying, "A design award is the kiss of death for a project," did not develop without some basis in fact.

The need for proper assessment of primary investment considerations

It is imperative that the developer have the proper value approach toward investment decisions and be able to make a proper assessment of the values that must be achieved. Primary investment considerations are as follows:

1. Financing acceptability. Very basically, this is a measure of how acceptable the project is to lenders. In developing the project, lender preferences must be kept in mind. The project cannot be built if it cannot be favorably financed.
2. Optimized loan value. One of the key objectives of product development is creating the greatest loan value at the least cost by maximizing capitalized value and minimizing cost. As loan amount approaches cost, equity dollars are squeezed out of the project.
3. Optimized absorption rate. The real test of the product is the marketplace. Consumer acceptance of the product over the competition's product establishes the absorption rate.
4. Ability to retain. The ability of the product to retain the initially absorbed tenants and remain competitive in the face of aggressive rental programs and new inventory is a primary consideration.
5. Self-advertising value. Most all projects have self-advertising value to one degree or another. Curb appeal, site location, and exposure to trafficked areas creates self-advertising value.
6. Saleability, transferability. Financial structure, tax planning, cash

flow, and overall business flexibility largely determine saleability and transferability.
7. Risk reduction. A good real estate investment exists when all the component values are maximized, with a minimum of value washouts. For income properties, Low cost/Sq. Ft. + High rent/Sq. Ft. = Competitive leverage and risk reduction.

Emphasis on the fundamentals

Both fundamentals and incremental cost controls are important, but the emphasis is on the fundamentals. Even the most extensive point-to-point cost cutting cannot remedy a fundamentally unsound project or investment structure. It is the fundamentals that determine outcome; incidental decisions affect the inevitable outcome only by degree.

The developer must provide only that value which the consumer is willing to pay for. Value that does not create income is washed out; that is, the cash investment cannot be capitalized. On hindsight, it should never have been classified as value in the first place (at least so far as an investor is concerned).

On the other hand, cost cutting for its own merit is a simplistic approach to increasing profitability. Cost cutting that also cuts value does nothing to increase the profit spread between cost and value. The reverse is also true; spending increases in many areas of the project budget do not necessarily increase value and can actually have the reverse effect. An enlightened cutting and filling process must take place. Value engineering of this sort requires tough analysis and a thorough understanding of the product and its design, construction, financing, and marketing.

CASE STUDY V: HOW PRIMARY INVESTMENT VALUES GUIDE TECHNICAL DECISIONS

To examine how investment values narrow down product decisions to their net effect on the total investment, consider the following field-trip to inspect a new apartment complex along one of the freeways in the San Francisco bay area. In approaching the project from the freeway, it was first observed what great self-advertising value the site possessed, but the next observation was the unsightly air conditioner expansion units mounted on the roofs without benefit of decorative enclosures. The curb appeal was immediately affected by the low prestige occasioned by the air conditioning treatment.

Most developers will pay a premium for self-advertising exposure. Say the self-advertising value of the location deserves a premium of $250 per unit in land cost. However, the exposed air conditioner units on the roof so damaged the environmental aspects of the project as seen from the freeway as to wash out half the value.

Though often optional in California climates from an investment standpoint, the air conditioning is beneficial in obtaining lender acceptability, absorption and retention of tenants, and increased capitalized value. (Notice air conditioning is not considered in the context of cooling apartments, a practical but secondary engineering concern, but is considered as it relates to the basic investment objectives.) In temperate California climates, through-the-wall air conditioners meet with good acceptance by tenants and most lenders. Through-the-wall units can be located behind patio and balcony fences so they are not to be visible from the exterior and do not have negative environmental effects on absorption and retention. Yet they can support air conditioned rents, and they can be installed for $450 less per unit than roof-mounted systems.

Thus the roof-mounted air conditioning condensers and forced air system cost $450 more in installation, than through-the-wall units, yet they substantially washed out the self-advertising value of the site. Due to poor design considerations, they also had an undetermined negative effect on absorption and retention of tenants.

This example is not provided to encourage the use of wall air conditioners, but to make a point. The cost in providing the roof-mounted system exceeded the through-the-wall system by $450 in direct cost and $100 in indirect cost, did not provide justification for increased rents to capitalize the added $550 expenditure, and actually produced negative side effects to diminish the very values the system was intended to enhance. In this particular example, $550 per unit of the developer's investment was washed out from an investment standpoint and possibly detracted from overall value. The really big project savings and large competitive gains are available through elimination of these types of washes and redirection of the dollars into high-yield design features.

Peak performance can only be achieved when all the investment values are maximized and incongruities and conflicts have been eliminated. Those that can control their investment in this manner can set a blistering pace for their less enlightened rivals.

CASE STUDY VI: WASHING OUT SELF ADVERTISING VALUE OF SITE

As another example of a value washout, it is not uncommon to see housing projects built alongside freeways or toll roads with the most undesirable portion of the project facing onto the highway. The parking is often used as a buffer between the buildings and the highway and the bland, stripped rear elevations of the buildings also face the road.

This solution no doubt has some advantages in creating a buffer between the freeway and the housing, but it completely ignores the self-advertising advantages the sight enjoys by being in close proximity to the highway, and it washes out much of the inherent self-advertising value of the property. If properly utilized, this self-advertising feature can be a real asset to the sales program and can even contribute to the project's prestige by putting its best foot forward where it can be seen.

If the land planner is not properly marketing oriented, he can wash out the strong self-advertising marketing advantages that the site possesses. In a situation where the project is immediately adjacent to a highway, the parking can be buried in the middle of the project and screened with buildings rather than being placed on the highway perimeter. At these perimeters the land can be contoured to create landscaped mounds as a buffer, and amenities such as fountains or trellises can be placed at points of high-volume exposure to create identity. The exposure of rear building elevations to high-volume traffic areas should also be minimized—again to put the best foot forward at the point of greatest exposure to the community. In this manner an adequate buffer can be achieved without washing out the self-advertising value inherent in the property.

CASE STUDY VII: WASHING OUT VALUE THROUGH POOR PLANNING

As another example of value wash, we were brought into a project in the Midwest to do the second stage at a time when the first-stage apartments were just being brought onto the market. Condominiums were planned for the second stage.

The market study and feasibility analysis made several things clear very quickly. The first phase had been designed without due consideration to an overall master plan of how the entire property should be developed. The property remaining was cut up by the first phase in such a manner as to preclude an orderly contiguous second phase. Any second-phase development was dependent upon ingress or egress through the first-phase apartment parking areas.

Because access to future condos in the second phase would be through the first-phase apartment section, it was determined that the second phase would make a marginal condo development. Further investigation indicated that the reason for going to condos in the second phase was that only five units of the apartments had been rented in six weeks, in a market that had a vacancy rate of 4 percent.

The site was not self-advertising, and in checking with the lease personnel, it was found that the traffic through the models was approximately 25 cars per month, or less than one per day! The only marketing being done was through a small, uninspired ad in the newspaper.

It was observed that though the first phase had some negative factors, the primary problem was in not marketing the project enough to create traffic through the models. Without traffic, absorption cannot be achieved, regardless of the qualifications of the product.

Without proper marketing, the condos would experience the same fate as the rentals. We suggested that the premise for going to condos was not a proper one, and that the decision as to use of the second phase should be delayed until the first phase could be given a proper chance by upgraded marketing. Larger, more imaginative newspaper ads were suggested, as well as billboard advertising on a nearby highly trafficked street, and radio spots. Within a short time after introducing a beefed-up marketing program, the traffic and absorption picked up markedly in the first-phase apartments.

Having demonstrated that with proper marketing apartments can do well in the area, the decision was made to continue with apartments in the second phase. Condos would have presented much more difficult marketing problems, because of the limited access created by the first-phase development. However, the first phase had cut up the property in such a way that even with extending the apartment use, the second phase could not be developed in a contiguous manner.

This is a good example of how poor land and market planning washed out inherent value in the property and led into other value washes that could have so deteriorated investment potential as to create investment failure.

LOOKING TO THE TOTAL PROFIT PICTURE

When steady profits are coming in, who needs comprehensive profit planning? The self-satisfied businessman tends to perpetuate, standardize, or even automate the status quo. Improvement becomes a forgotten Cinderella in a business whose maturation consists simply of acquiring more firmly established ways of doing things. In an ever-renewing society, however, what matters is a system or framework within which continuous innovation, renewal, and rebirth can occur (see Chapter 22).

Cost saving cannot be considered a gain in productivity or profitability on an incremental basis. There is too much interdependence of all operational functions. A saving in one function may create a substantial cost gain in other functions, netting a cost overrun rather than a saving.

A developer must increasingly look beyond the immediate cost to determine the net effect on the total profit picture. Management of value, productivity, and profits in a business development enterprise is today becoming so large and complex that a knowledge of the individual parts is not enough. In management, as in engineering, the interactions between the components of the system or production operation may often prove to be more significant than the separate components themselves.

A total package must be planned. The emphasis is on shaping the component values which comprise the total investment and is not limited to the incremental brick and mortar considerations. The tough management work is maximizing the spread between cost and value and bridging the gap between the investment concept and profit-making reality.

Reflecting value engineering in bidding and contract-letting processes

In building, as elsewhere, the aim is always to shave costs where they are not seen by the consumer, so that there is no commensurate reduction in the value of the project. The builder, however, should be aware that these hidden savings are also hard to detect by the subcontractors who establish the costs for the various segments of the work. Subcontractors are often prone to bid work based on very broad unit-cost techniques. For example, a framer will often bid a job based on a given cost per square foot of construction because he finds that he can make a reasonable profit, on the average, when his contracts come in at that price.

This type of bidding procedure does not recognize the cost savings that may have been designed into the project through value engineering processes. A cost savings that is not realized by the builder in the bidding and contract-letting processes is not really a cost saving to the builder at all. It may look good on paper, but the effect of the value engineering may never reach the bottom profit line unless there is a follow-through all the way to completion of construction (see Chapter 27).

The developer must take the time to review drawings with the subcontractors and point out the cost-saving techniques that have been incorporated into the job. Particular care should be taken to point out techniques which may be new to subcontractors in order to get the full benefit of the cost savings. Additionally, the developer should work closely with subcontractors to ascertain how they propose to reduce costs on the project.

It is typical for a builder to reuse the same subcontractors over and over again. In this case, the subcontractor will base his unit-price bidding on previous experiences he has had with that builder. For this reason, it is important to the builder, in working with the subcontractor, to hold down the subcontractor's costs as well as his own (see Chapter 26).

Cost-saving features incorporated into drawings should be pointed out throughout the construction process, so that the advantages will not be lost to the subcontractor. Helping the subcontractor save money, once the contract is let, does not particularly benefit the builder on the immediate project, but it will put him in a better light with the subs on subsequent projects, because they will find they can make a profit with a builder who is value conscious.

14

Product research: Taking the experimentation out of innovation

The success or failure of a project is assured by the time it reaches the marketplace. Further marketing is essential, but this only affects the inevitable outcome by degree. Projects are structured as successes or failures before reaching the marketplace.

As we have noted, the process of discovering weaknesses and transforming them into strengths is called innovation. The goal of successful innovation is to obsolete the competitor's product for a specific market area, and in so doing to create a temporary monopoly for the new product. Product innovation requires product research representing the highest current state of the art to be found. If such a product does not exist within the target market area, it will be necessary to go to those market areas where it does exist to do the research required for successful innovation. Attempts to innovate without research follow a haphazard course, and the outcome of such efforts is dependent on chance (see Chapter 7).

A dwarf standing on the shoulders of a giant may see farther than a giant himself.

Robert Burton

STRUCTURING THE ACTIVITY

Research required for innovation should be carried out on a systematic, thorough basis. There are lessons to be learned from unsuccessful projects as well as from successful ones. In studying an unsuccessful project, however, the goal is only to learn from its mistakes. For this reason, unsuccessful projects take much less time to research than successful projects. Successful projects need thorough, detailed documentation to serve as a guideline for the successful infusion of the winning concepts and details into a product development program. While we recognize that much can be learned from unsuccessful projects, we will consider only the comprehensive research of successful projects.

What to research

Once the market segments to be served by a development program have been identified, the product types that have been generally utilized to attract those segments should be researched. It is important that the research cover the most successful types of product currently being produced, whether it be in a developer's immediate market area or one far away.

The researcher can keep aware of successful developments through word-of-mouth suggestions; award presentations; notices and advertising in national publications, newspapers, and home buyers' magazines; inquiring of other developers and their salespeople, and keeping abreast of what the leading or more innovative developers, planners, and decorators are currently doing.

Research requires legwork. The researcher may visit many more uninspired developments than developments that possess obvious merit. However, there is generally something to be learned from most every development. Even an uninspired development can possess an outstanding feature or two that may be very relevant. Additionally, it is important to research other's mistakes to benefit from them so that one does not repeat the same mistake.

The research should not be limited to a particular type of housing or to the housing market, for that matter. Many good condominium ideas can be found in single-family detached housing. Commercial development may provide many graphics, landscaping, and thematic ideas. Apartments, as a result of their very competitive nature, can offer many ideas to the for-sale market on landscaping, recreation facilities, graphics, and design. Cemeteries, industrial parks, and country clubs may yield good ideas for entry treatments and landscaping to enhance curb appeal and screen parking.

How to research

Once which housing developments are to be researched has been determined, the next step is to decide on the research methodology. The research format suggested here will unearth rewarding marketing and product information.

1. Introduce yourself to the salesman in the office as a researcher with an interest in the project. Ask permission to photograph the models (permission is generally given).
2. If the project is a particularly successful one, photograph it extensively. (If it is a good distance from home base, you may never get the opportunity to take additional pictures.) For best results, use a wide-angle lens. Inside the models, photograph areas to document space relationships; the cabinet work for design, finishes, and detail; stair, wet-bar, planter, window, and entry details; and the interior decorating, for solutions which soften problem areas and create strong emotional appeal. Outside the models, photograph the elevations,

landscape treatments, graphics, and the "sales trap." The objective is to fully document all elements of the planning and design solution so that the details are readily available after the memory has faded.

3. Evaluate each of the models, and write the evaluation on the appropriate model plan in the brochure collected while in the sales office.
4. Return to the sales office and ask the salesman which plans have sold best, and why, and which plans have had the poorest acceptance, and why. If they were to start over again, what would they do differently?
5. Ask who has been buying, in order to get a socioeconomic profile of the type of buyer attracted to the development. Also ask who specifically is not buying, and why. In this manner it is possible to identify which submarkets are attracted to the development, which are not, and why.
6. Ask what the absorption rate has been, and how it compares to projections. Have there been presales? If so, how many? What percentage of presales have been lost?
7. Get as much information as the salesman will give on marketing and sales program, and how effective or ineffective they have been.

For the most part, obtaining the information in steps 1 through 7 is not as difficult as it may appear. Other developers realize that marketing research is a necessity for the orderly management of business affairs. They themselves know that they must do it, and so must their competitors, and a determined competitor will get the information he seeks with or without cooperation. Most developers are more open than is generally believed by those who do not get into the field to ask searching questions.

Though developers are generally open regarding routine performance yardsticks, their salespeople are even more open. Salespeople are like any others who take pride in their work and are seeking to better themselves: They are flattered to know that their opinions are important, and they take pride in their knowledge of their industry. Most salespeople welcome the opportunity to demonstrate the knowledge they have. Probably also they would like to make a good impression on a prospective future employer (see Chapter 6).

BENEFITS OF RESEARCH

Having researched the best product representing some of the most advanced state of the art in the industry, and having documented the market responses to the product in terms of which submarkets are buying or not buying and why, the developer can get a good perspective on the subject market in which he wishes to compete. By comparing the proposed product to the competitor's product in the area, he can ascertain the potential competitive advantage to be gained if a similar type product were to be produced in the subject market area.

Additionally, the developer has the knowledge of which submarkets are attracted to the researched product and the type of merchandizing programs utilized. Armed with this information, it is possible to identify submarkets which are not being adequately served in ones own market area. The combination of introducing a superior product into a market, aimed at a submarket which is not being adequately served by the competition, is the stuff that monopolies are made of.

> *If a man look sharply and attentively, he shall see Fortune; for though she is blind, she is not invisible.*
>
> Francis Bacon

CONSUMER RESEARCH

Limitations

When filling holes in a market through innovation, consumer research, or depth studies into consumer attitudes in the specific market area, are not too reliable. Asking a consumer his feelings about likes or dislikes for a new product that he has not had experience with is like asking a person who has never tasted spinach how he likes it, or how he thinks he would like spinach if he had the opportunity to taste it.

A while back supermarkets introduced delicatessen foods in separate sections in an attempt to bolster profit margins. Up to that time delicatessen items had been sold exclusively in delicatessens. Once delicatessen items were shown in the supermarkets, the market for them was greatly expanded. People who never would have gone to a delicatessen were purchasing delicatessen items because they were presented to them where they shopped. Prior to introduction into supermarkets, the volume of delicatessen items sold would not suggest they would generate much sales volume. The showing of the items where the people shopped created a market which did not exist previously. The size of the preintroduction market alone would not have justified the decision to place delicatessen items on the shelf. In a like manner, housing innovations, once introduced, create their own market.

A more reliable way to evaluate the feasibility of an innovation in a market area is to go to similar but more advanced market areas where the innovation has already been introduced and research how that market responded to the innovation. It is even better if this can be done with a number of test market areas. Successful concepts in these several test market areas can be relocated and modified for the subject market area. The test market concept is much the same concept as utilized in the consumer goods market, the difference being that the test need not be staged at the expense of the researcher; it merely needs to be observed.

Benefits

Consumer research in the target market area related to the introduction of an innovation can also be beneficial in identifying consumer prejudices. The consumer often does not know what he wants, but generally he has a better feeling for what he does *not* want. By identifying strong consumer prejudices the areas of resistance to be encountered can be identified, and development concepts can be structured accordingly. Consumer prejudice is also identified by researching projects that have failed. As previously mentioned, there is much to learn from unsuccessful projects.

TECHNICAL RESEARCH

Need for

Value-conscious design requires a vigilance and awareness of innovations in technical aspects of development and construction. Thinner profit margins demand close attention to the technical aspects of the business. Even small gains cannot be overlooked, for in the end it is the aggregate of many small gains that makes the profit difference. No one gain may have much effect on the overall investments, but added collectively or omitted collectively these small gains or losses, as they may be, will have a profound effect on the profit margin (see Chapter 13).

Sources

One of the best sources of technical information is the developer's own operations. The company's purchasing agent is an excellent source of technical data of a cost/benefit nature. It is of utmost importance that this information be communicated to those who design and specify the product. The bidding and contract-letting personnel, if not the same as the purchasing agent, are important sources of data for product decision making and should have regular communication with those who do make product decisions (see Chapter 27).

Similarly, the construction field organization has to work out those problems created by design which do not reflect subcontractor practices and field techniques. It is particularly important that good communications between the field and the design staff be maintained in order that mistakes, omissions, and impractical applications can be remedied. There is a great amount of wasted effort and cost in most organizations, because the construction and design people do not get together to benefit from one another's experience.

Much can be learned from those who do the construction scheduling. All else being equal, a simple application can be constructed much faster than a complex application. Design, product, and phasing decisions can have a profound effect on construction speed. Communication between those responsible for scheduling and the designers can produce cost-saving construction efficiencies (see Chapter 29, scheduling).

Subcontractors are an excellent source of grass-roots construction expertise; they are the ones who must finally do the work and establish the hard costs. Information from subcontractors has to be carefully evaluated, however, because a subcontractor is often prone to make recommendations which make his portion of the work easier at the expense of another, or at the expense of overall quality. Nonetheless, the subcontractor can be an excellent source of practical expertise.

Competitors, particularly those who are pioneering new technical applications and the use of work-saving equipment and procedures, should also be researched. Only so much cost can be taken out in the design of the product. Additional savings require innovation in construction procedures such as panelization, use of prefinished materials and applications, relocatable job shops, prefabrication, and so on.

Various institutes, associations, and organizations sponsor and publish housing industry research. The National Association of Home Builders, The Urban Land Institute, The Institute of Real Estate Management, The Department of Housing and Urban Development, The International Conference of Building Officials, American Plywood Association, National Lumber Manufacturers Association, are a few. Additionally, trade publications and technical books published on a wide variety of subjects by independent publishers are a rich source of technical data which should be included in the company's library.

Application   Technical research, to be of value, must be applied. There must be a conscious and organized effort to introduce the benefits of technical research into operations. Giving lip service to the appropriateness and desirability of keeping technically current, without follow-through, is self-deceptive and dangerous.

Though technical advancement produces attractive benefits, it does have a cost. Too often management desires results but expresses little willingness to support a positive program. Subordinates and consultants, aware that management is hesitant to fund technical advancement with either funds or recognition, view the situation as being problem oriented rather than opportunity oriented and leave it for others to deal with. In the absence of leadership, application languishes, and only lip service remains.

15

Establishing the development concept: Optimizing opportunities

The challenge in establishing the concept of a real estate development is to match the correct development concept or product to the marketing need. Guidelines for arriving at a decision as regards product type are given at the end of the next chapter. The three case studies in this chapter provide insights into matching up the correct product with the marketing need. The better the match of the product with market need, and with organizational capabilities and objectives, the better the chance of success.

Objectives must be properly structured from the outset because a better order is equivalent to vast amounts of effort or capital. Profit does not come from labor or intensification of capital but lies in a better order and timeliness in meeting the right opportunity with the right concept, resources, and capabilities. The real estate analyst who recommends jumping into the hot market areas or producing a particular concept in a market area because that is what the leaders in that market are doing should be regarded with caution. He may be recommending taking a commodity to where it abounds rather than to where it is scarce (see Chapter 12).

CASE STUDY I: INTERNAL ECONOMIC NEEDS VERSUS MARKET NEEDS

We were retained by a developer on the East Coast to do a marketing–value-engineering review for a large scale-regional planned unit development (PUD). The PUD has already been planned and approved but had not progressed into the detailed design development or construction phases.

Part of the development was planned for single-family housing and a substantial portion was designed for multifamily use, with 10 to 13 units per acre density. The extensive multifamily density was planned by the developer to achieve enough units to establish feasibility. So much land was utilized for a golf course and a wilderness area, the remaining buildable portion required a fairly high density.

When the developer realized that his land-use plan reflected his internal economic requirements more than external marketing demands, the question arose: How do you design multifamily housing at 10 to 13 units per acre while maintaining construction economies and enough open-space planning to be attractive to the market? The broad market, as identified by the developer, was families with children in the middle- and upper-income range. To achieve acceptable absorption, he felt he would have to pull families to his project out of single-family housing or have new homeowners choose multifamily housing as a way of living over single-family detached homes.

To achieve the open feeling that he knew he must have, the developer was contemplating reducing his density by as much as 40 to 50 percent in the multifamily areas, going to zero-lot-line housing, and charging a substantial enough premium on the zero-lot-line sites to maintain the gross income projected before the reduction in density. It was at this time that we were brought into the team to provide a marketing–value engineering analysis.

Identifiable submarkets versus statistical generalizations

Our study of the market area indicated that there was a large inventory of garden-type condominium housing on the market that was not moving well. Though not entirely new to the area, condominium housing was still in the early stages. Some of the developers, it appeared, had attempted to aim their condo projects at the broad middle-income family market, which the demographics indicated represented the largest market segment.

One of the projects, located on a lake, had sold out all its lakefront units (a small percent of the total) at a hefty premium to concept buyers, but it had run into a sales problem on the rest of the units. They were not attractive to the condo concept market and could not compete pricewise with the single-family detached market for the economic-necessity buyer (see Chapter 8).

There were a very few examples, however, of successful condo projects in the market, which served to establish that there was a market for a well-planned and imaginatively marketed condominium project.

There was a need in the market area for more specific identification of submarkets and a closer tie between the needs of submarkets and the product designed to serve them. Competitors were shotgunning, while what was needed was a rifle approach to submarkets with products developed to serve their specific needs. In large projects, it is a mistake to try to serve the market with a single product. Absorption generally requires sales to a combination of submarkets. By being precise in aiming for submarkets, it is possible to obsolete the competitors' shotgun approach to a particular submarket (see Chapter 11).

Achieving density without sacrificing marketability

One of the problems with the large multifamily-zoned area in the property being studied was that families with children do not generally prefer multifamily living. Yet in order to reach acceptable absorption, a portion of the sales in this area had to come from families with children.

The principal problem was how to achieve density required for feasibility, while meeting market needs. Zero-lot-line housing was introduced in the planning because it can be attractive to families with children and also can allow increased density over single-family detached housing. However, when zero-lot-line homes are designed too close together, they take on many of the aspects of multifamily housing, and this makes them less attractive to families. In order to leave sufficient space for families with children, zero-lot-line housing should not generally be designed on less than 45- to 50-foot lots. Though the zero-lot-line home is an answer to the problem of attracting families with children, it does not adequately solve the density problem. In this case it provided more density than single-family detached homes but much less than required by the economics of the project.

Having utilized approximately 50 percent of the multifamily zoning, with zero-lot-line housing it was necessary to put density not utilized in the zero lot line area in the remaining multifamily area, requiring an averaging of densities. Because of economics, densities could not be increased by resorting entirely to underground parking garages. However, a portion of the market could bear this expense if there were sufficient offsetting environmental advantages to be gained. The affluent empty-nester, young family, and widow market is willing to pay a premium for attractive units with direct views to a golf course or an open, landscaped park area. By going to a three-story building over underground parking, densities of 25 units per acre are achievable. By keeping clusters small, in the 80-unit range, virtually all of the units orient outwardly from the cluster, onto the golf course and landscaped, open space. With all units oriented onto a golf course or open space, the cluster does not appear overly dense; on the contrary, it provides a welcome change of pace from the zero-lot-line planning into which the clusters are introduced.

In going for a purely concept market, it is important to recognize that a strong design concept is very important to marketing success. The difference between a routine design and an exciting, thematic solution can be the difference between success and failure. Those willing to pay the premium required will not be motivated by routine solutions.

Many of the singles, young families, and less affluent empty-nesters in the market would not be able to afford housing over parking garages because of the construction cost increases this necessitates. They also have different preferences in lifestyle. In order to keep the parking solution inexpensive in the remaining multifamily zoning and provide an alternative lifestyle, the marketing–value engineering analysis indicated going to townhouse construction at ten units to the acre. To achieve this density without losing environmental character and openness, it was determined that the townhouses should be designed into clusters not to exceed 30 to 40 units in a cluster. The clusters were designed in proximity to the existing golf course and wilderness areas. In this manner, substantially all of the dwellings could be outwardly related to open space bordering the cluster, thus achieving density without sacrifice of marketability or increase in parking costs. The clusters also provide an interesting change of pace in the overall project planning.

Planning designed to meet the needs of specific submarkets

A homogeneous development of 10 to 13 units per acre, as initially planned, would have risked marketing failure because product weaknesses would have resulted in lack of focus on submarkets. By replanning the multifamily area to meet the needs of specific submarkets — with zero-lot-line houses, townhouses, and security apartments over garages — it was possible to maintain density without sacrificing marketability. The original multifamily plan was redesigned to attract specific submarkets — families with children, singles, young marrieds without children, widows, and empty-nesters of various economic means and lifestyle preferences. The plan reflects the economic needs of the developer for feasibility, as well as the needs of the submarkets which the project was to serve.

The concept of high-density clusters within a medium-density, zero-lot-line, multifamily community required a redesign of the traffic network to reflect the new land usage. The mixed-use aspect of the plan adds diversity and interest to what would have otherwise been a dense, homogeneous sprawl of housing, lacking in sufficient appeal to be a strong competitor in either the economic-necessity or concept condominium market.

CASE STUDY II: MESHING INTERNAL ECONOMIC DEMANDS AND MARKET NEEDS THROUGH SENSITIVITY AND INNOVATION

Another study was designed to determine, for a preselected site of 33 acres containing two lakes and zoned for 4.8 units per acre, what type of housing should be utilized and toward what market it should be directed. The developer was assuming that he would offer some type of condominium housing.

The first step in approaching this problem was to review the map to get a familiarity with the geographic and transportation layout. The developer then led a tour to review the competition in the market area, while discussing general development trends, economic growth, social and political overtones, and future growth. By comparing this input to similar market areas, we were able to develop a feel for certain patterns and opportunities which we saw developing. Then by talking to numerous professionals, salesmen, other developers, the planning department, and chamber of commerce representatives, we developed documentation to support or refute the feeling we had obtained by driving around and researching the product and the competition.

Throughout the process, three primary indicators were being analyzed: (1) submarkets which had not yet been recognized by competitors, (2) market cycles, and (3) weaknesses of competitors, or areas where they are leaving themselves vulnerable. The formula for achieving a temporary monopoly in the market area is: Find a market being overlooked, evaluate it against the perspective of market cycles, and fill the vacancy with a product which meets market needs and takes advantage of competitors' weaknesses.

Need for environmentally oriented housing to serve a discriminating market

There was much emphasis on multifamily development in the market, but single-family homes had not experienced the same type of increases in supply. There was a need for particularly high-quality, single-family housing and environmental planning; 1,349 single-family homes had been constructed in the same period as 3,023 apartments. The supply and demand factors were seen in the vacancy rates: a 2.9 percent vacancy rate in single-family housing and a 7.5 percent vacancy rate in multifamily housing. The work force and income potential of the area were changing from those characteristic of agricultural and manufacturing pursuits to professional and service-oriented activities. The presence of a leading university, new medical facilities, and industrial park expansion was partially responsible for a more sophisticated, better paid worker entering the consumer ranks.

Heretofore the retirement market had not been strong in the area; this market had preferred the nearby beach communities. However, with rising land costs and congestion in these communities, more of the retirement market was tending to go toward the subject market area. The accelerating growth of a retirement market generates new housing requirements. For that portion of the retirement market desiring and able to pay for a superior way-of-living concept, little was available in the market area.

Also, limited lake property was available. Because of the desirability of lake frontage, this type of land had been developed early. However, a good portion of the early development was composed of aging and unattractive housing, and it was not in competition with the property being developed. High-quality water-related housing was scarce and at a premium.

Housing quality and environmental design, therefore, were not keeping pace with changing consumer preferences in the area. The more affluent buyer was often living in housing below his financial means and below the aesthetic standards he would choose if the alternative were available.

When the farmer's peaches are taken from under the tree, and carried into town, they have a new look, and a hundredfold value over the fruit which grew on the same bough, and lies fulsomely on the ground. The craft of the merchant is this bringing a thing from where it abounds, to where it is costly.
Ralph Waldo Emerson

Observations indicated that there was greater demand than supply in the marketplace for quality, environmentally oriented housing. A superior environmentally oriented community in the market area aimed at the more affluent, discriminating market would, in effect, create a product monopoly. Competitors who were reaching a portion of this market by default would find their product obsoleted by a more refined type, such as has been developed in the leading housing markets to serve the more discriminating upper-middle-income and affluent tastes.

How to meet the needs of the discriminating market and retain economic feasibility

The principal problem in Case Study II was how to achieve the density required for economic feasibility while meeting the needs of the discriminating market. In this particular instance we designed zero-lot-line housing (see Illustrations 15–1 and 15–2) because it can be attractive to families with children, and it also allowed increased density over single-family, detached-type housing.

By going to zero-lot-line housing, it is possible to achieve the benefits of both condominiums and single-family detached living, while minimizing some of the limitations in either of these housing lifestyles. Zero-lot-line plans allow for an increased density over single-family detached homes. Through the increased density, a larger base of homeowners is established to carry the cost of an amenity package including lakes, clubhouse, pools, landscaped common areas, hike and bike trails, tennis courts, playground, and picnic facilities (see Illustration 15–3). If the same amenities were provided with a standard single-family subdivision lot size, the market size would diminish because of increased costs. If these amenities were provided with a condominium development, the market size would likewise shrink, because families with children are not easily attracted to condominium living, and the price could not have been brought in at a level to be attractive to those in the economic-necessity category. Zero-lot-line planning made it feasible to offer an attractive amenity package, while at the same time continuing to attract families with children from the single-family market, empty-nesters, and childless householders who would ordinarily gravitate toward the condo market.

CASE STUDY III: PRODUCT AND MARKETING INNOVATION TO ACHIEVE FEASIBILITY

In a small agricultural and military-service community of approximately 40,000 population, a need was found for a singles-oriented (not synonymous with swingers) rental project stressing environmental appeal and social and recreational facilities. One of the reasons for the need was that the bulk of the competition offered housing which provided basic shelter but little in the way of environment and amenities. Additionally,

Illustration 15–1
Case Study II: Elevation and floor plan

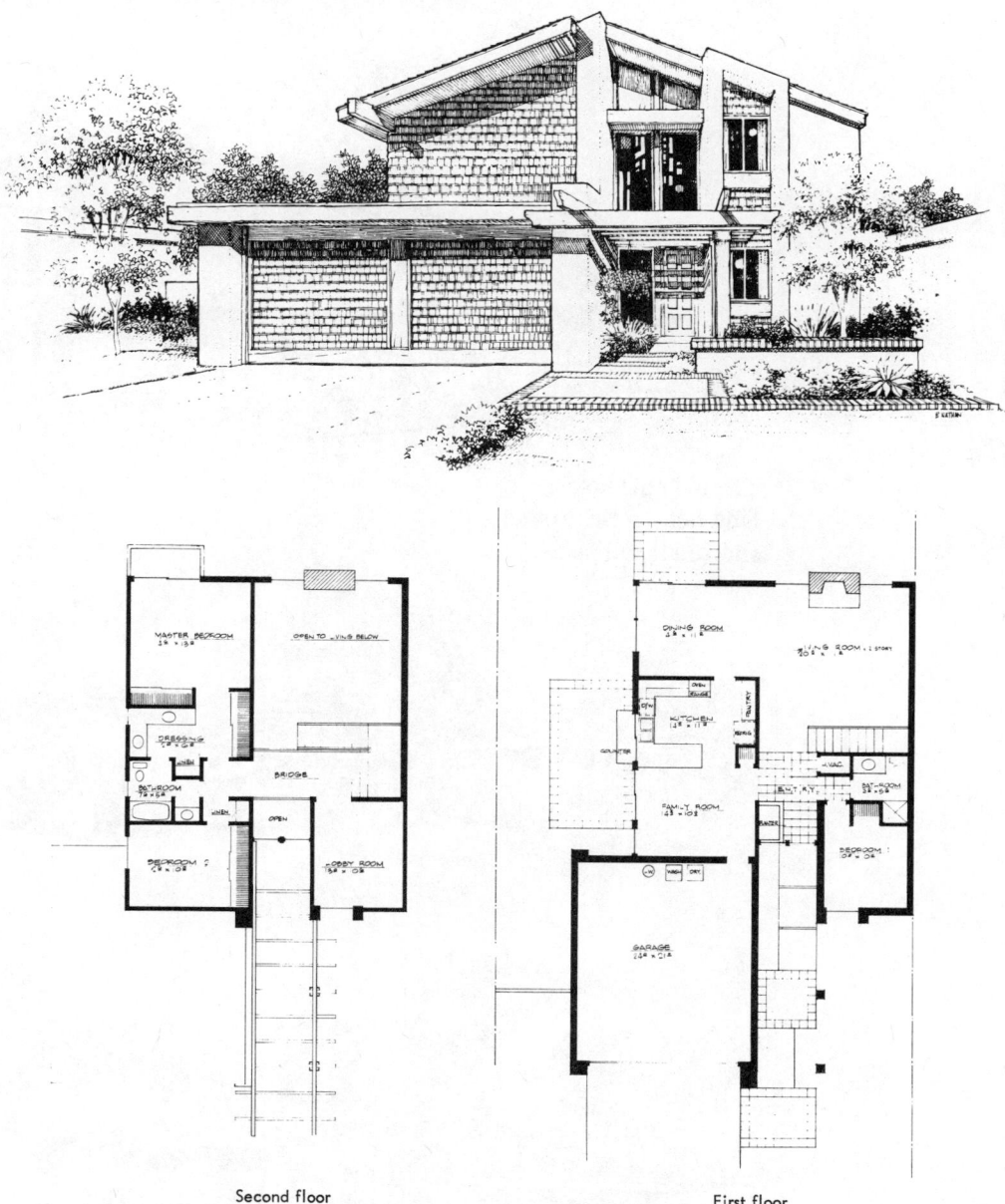

Example of zero-lot-line housing utilized in Case Study II.

the bulk of the competition's product was older construction and commanded very moderate rents.

An analysis of the income in the market area indicated that there was an ability to support higher rent structures than were prevalent. A representative portion of those who could afford higher rents were military personnel and single.

Illustration 15-2
Case Study II: Housing designs

**The old rule holds:
Find hole in the market
and you'll sell fast**

Zero-lot-line housing designs utilized in Case Study II.

Illustration 15–3
Case Study II: Lakeside setting

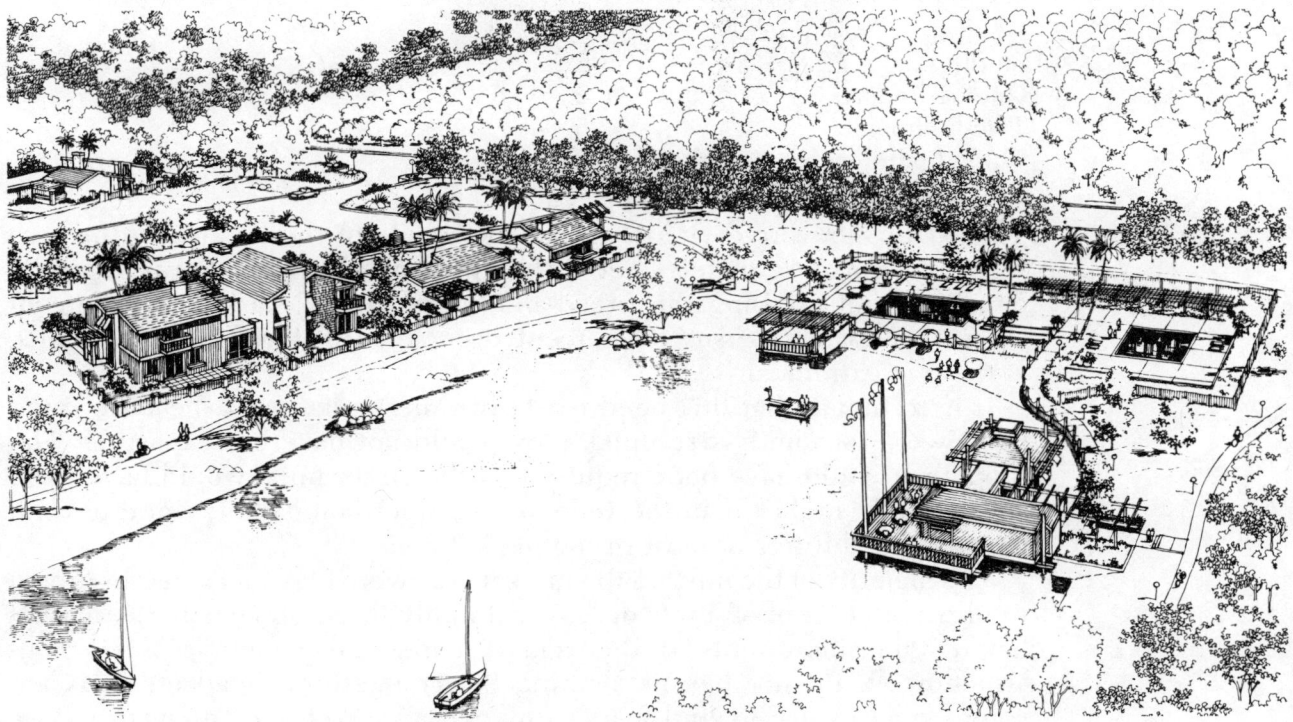

Birds-eye view of a lake portion of the community in Case Study II.

Within the market area there was no focal point for social or recreational gatherings. There were no singles bars, so popular in the larger metropolitan areas. There also was no recreational-oriented multifamily housing project in the area. There was no congregation point for lonely singles (or married couples, for that matter) to meet neighbors and make acquaintances.

As is common in smaller towns, a good percentage of those who had not married soon after graduation moved on to larger metropolitan areas. However, there were a growing number of divorced persons and widows who had remained in the area.

Thus a definite need took shape for social-recreational, environmentally oriented housing within the community. Such housing would be attractive to young singles, divorced singles, and widows and widowers, as well as outgoing, socially oriented marrieds. They could be interested in an atmosphere in which residents could comfortably mingle and meet neighbors. In such an atmosphere, there could be enough activities to provide social outlet without dominating lives, creating social pressures, or providing a negative image.

A survey of the area indicated that there was a 94.5 percent apartment occupancy level, broken down as follows:

Studio	100%
One-bedroom	96.2
Two-bedroom	93.5
Three-bedroom	80.0

The occupancy survey verified that the needs of the singles in the area was not being adequately met with supply, whereas there was an abundance of units serving the bread-and-butter family market (100 percent studio occupancy versus 80 percent occupancy of three-bedroom units, at the two extremes).

It is fortunate that this need existed in the market area, because if the need were for family-size units, they would not have been feasible. The rents that would have been required on the larger units would have been substantially higher than the rents of the older comparables, and beyond the income abilities of most in the market area.

The majority of the units in the market area were two- and three-bedroom in older projects of 35 units or less, with only three projects in the market having 90 or more units. In such a market area, the economics of new construction would not permit meeting the competition head on. It is absolutely necessary to find a hole in such a market and innovate with a product which will obsolete the competitors' product seeking to fill the same need. Thus a marketing monopoly can be created which will justify premium rents.

The proposed development consisted of 114 units: 20 studios of 449 square feet, 20 junior one-bedrooms of 530 square feet, 30 one-bedrooms of 611 square feet, 36 two-bedrooms of 818 square feet, and 8 two-bedrooms of 869 square feet. A recreational building of 1,232 square feet included a sauna, wet bar, billiards, fireplace, and a dance area. Outdoor recreation facilities included a swimming pool and Jacuzzi. Private patios and extensive landscaping, with a fountain and trellises, were part of the development package.

By planning a mix stressing smaller units in comparison to the competition, the units could be offered for rents equal to or somewhat higher than the competition's, yet offering substantially better environment and amenities. Though the aggregate rent of a studio is comparable to the aggregate rent of a competitor's one-bedroom unit, the rent per square foot is substantially higher—32 cents per square foot versus 19 cents per square foot. This may seem an unreasonable spread, but the fact remains that the resident can get a substantially better environment for the same number of dollars. For many of them this is a compelling consideration, and it is the makings of a marketing monopoly. If it were not for a marketing monopoly which justifies the rental spread, construction in this town would not be feasible from an economic standpoint.

COMMON MISTAKES IN MATCHING CONCEPTS TO MARKET OPPORTUNITIES

Builders sometimes confuse need with demand. There may be a tremendous need in a market for a product, but the consumer must also have the economic ability to translate his need into market action. If the economic ability to pay does not also exist, apartments will not rent even though the need on the part of the consumer may be desperate. Absorption in such a market would require reduction in rents until they come in line with the economic ability of the consumer. Of course, the project would then operate at a loss (see Chapter 10).

It is not unusual for developers to zero in on a particular concept of design, planning on amenities which they feel will give them competitive strength but forgetting about the cost. In setting out to build a better "mousetrap," it is easy to add refinements here and there, disregarding their added costs. The developer ends up with a beautiful product which gives him a warm glow, and he is reassured by pride of ownership. Too often what the developer has done, however, is to put a product on the market which the market cannot afford. Then the developer must make up the difference out of his own pocket. Pride of ownership can be expensive.

The flexibility the developer may have been looking for in down markets generally is not there, either. While his competition may be able to offer rental concessions and elaborate planned activities or other amenities that the market may require, the developer who has overspent initially has no reserves to fall back on. Rental concessions more than likely will mean negative cash flows.

The skill required in real estate development is to deliver design and amenity packages without commensurate cost increases. An increased environmental impact at a proportionately increased cost does not necessarily benefit, and it can destroy the development's feasibility if rental requirements are not competitive with the target market.

The developer should not strain to take in too many market segments with a particular concept. The intent, of course, is to increase absorption by going for a larger potential market, but the result is generally the opposite. Ill-suited compromises reduce potential market share.

An example is a condominium project located in the suburbs. Because of its price in relation to single-family homes in the area and its quality of design, it was suited to the concept market, which does not include families with children. However, the developer had apparently decided to go for the family market with one of his four model units, a four-bedroom plan with one of the bedrooms designed as a retreat and another as a nursery.

A check on sales performance indicated that the four-bedroom model was experiencing negligible sales compared to the other three models. The problem was not one of design or decoration, but rather that the traffic was not interested in larger units because it consisted of empty-nesters, young marrieds, retired couples, or compact families. Those who were looking for four or more bedrooms were not attracted to the development concept being offered. The fourth model, in effect, did not offer a buying alternative to the traffic through the models.

Thus the developer had offered a model that prospective buyers interested in four-bedroom homes would never see, because they could not be attracted to the overall concept. For the traffic that was generated, only three buying alternatives existed. The developer in effect reduced his product mix to his real market by 25 percent by introducing a product to serve a market which, for his development, was extremely thin to nonexistent.

16

Designing the product to optimize market potential

Marketing does not just happen when the producer is ready to put a product on the market; rather, it is a fundamental factor in shaping all product decisions. This is particularly true for decisions regarding income-producing properties. Most decisions are marketing decisions as well as money decisions. Product development should maximize marketing strengths and minimize those conditions that adversely affect marketability.

CASE STUDY I: MAXIMIZING NATURAL AMENITIES AND SITE POTENTIALS

By designing at 10 units to the acre instead of the 14 units to the acre possible under existing zoning, we showed the developer of a lake-oriented project in Florida how to create open space and provide lake views to approximately 80 percent of the units. (See the site plan, Illustration 16–1.) The alternative of going to a higher density with two-story construction would have resulted in very tight site plan and fewer units with lake views. The alternative of going to three-story construction, with a flat on the ground floor and a townhouse above, would have achieved the open-view effect but would have increased construction cost and produced a less desirable unit.

Maximizing the developer's position does not necessarily mean maximizing the density. Had the developer sought maximum density with a slightly less desirable unit, the profit projections per unit would have been lower. In other words, it was possible to project approximately the same profits to the developer at 10 to the acre as at 14 to the acre. Of course, land and site development costs play an important part in any such projection. In this case study, the land and site development costs were such that they were not a major decisive factor. The costs were very attractive at a density of ten to the acre.

From the market study, conservative projections were made for a $4,000 premium for units with a direct lake view. Had three-story construction

Illustration 16–1
Case Study I: Site plan

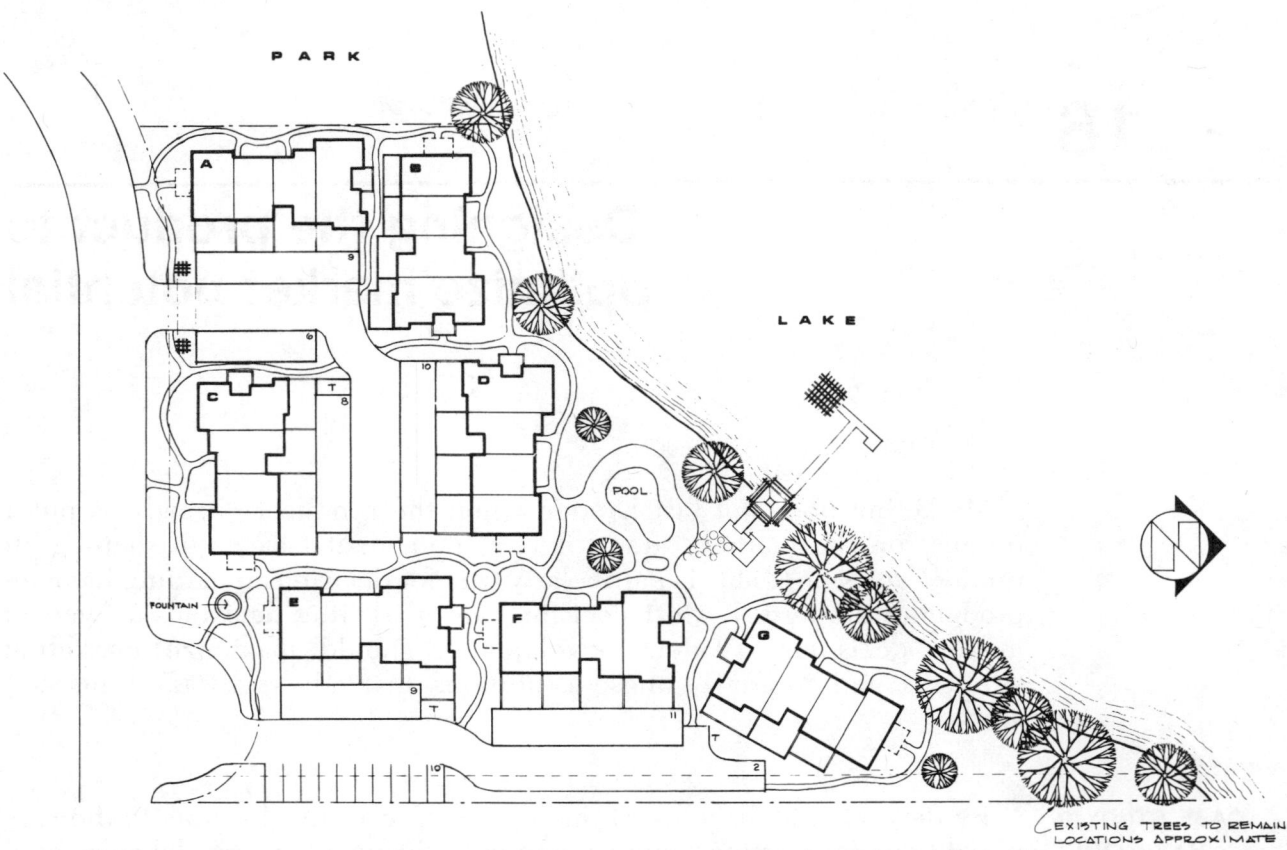

First phase of a larger development program to be carried out on noncontiguous land parcels. Models in the first phase were to be utilized for preselling housing on other noncontiguous parcels. Planning maximizes the potential of existing lake and park amenities.

been utilized, allowing 14 units per acre, it would have been possible to maintain the same 80 percent of the units with a direct lake view, but the units would have been less desirable and more costly to construct. The eroded desirability and increased construction costs would have had the effect of reducing the profit potential of the $4,000 premium for lake view. The three-story construction also would not have been as compatible to the immediate neighborhood as the two-story construction (see Illustration 16–2). The evaluation was that the three-story construction would have required greater risk and outlay of capital for the developer, while showing potential overall profits only slightly in excess of those that could be reasonably expected from the two-story construction at less density.

In one of the comparable projects researched, only 15 percent of the units had a direct lake view. The developer was demanding a $5,000 premium for these units and had sold all of them in the construction stage prior to the formal sales opening and before any advertising had been done.

Illustration 16–2
Case Study I: Project design

Product design utilizes landscaping as an integral part of the total environmental package.

The really meaningful data, however, was that although all of the lakefront homes had been sold prior to opening ceremonies and advertising, not one of the homes with an off-lake or nonlake view had sold at the time of the consultant's study. Not only were the lakeside homes going for a hefty premium, they were also the strongest contribution to sales. Thus risk was reduced while at the same time return was maximized.

The marketing input showed how to increase return substantially by maximizing the lake orientation, without necessitating an offsetting increase in developmental costs. Slightly greater profits could have been projected with higher density and three-story construction, but the increased profits would have been accompanied by more than commensurate risks. Potential gains always have to be weighed against the risks incurred in attempting to achieve them.

When capitalizing on an already existing amenity, everything possible should be squeezed out of the existing amenity because heavy reliance and utilization of an existing amenity feature does not necessarily increase cost. In such an instance, significant added value can be attributed to the project by superior planning which maximizes the potential of the amenity without offsetting costs. Though the income in a particular market may not allow the amenities planning to be fully reflected in the sales price, its effect will be felt in the sales rate and the risk benefit analysis of the development program (see Chapter 15).

CASE STUDY II: THE RIGHT PRODUCT FOR THE RIGHT MARKET

An example of how the right product for the right market can produce substantial rewards is a project in the Florida market. The developer had built a 120-unit apartment complex and had spent more than the competition in order to achieve an outstanding product. However, he had not spent money in the right areas to achieve the expected end result. He was only able to obtain rents equal to the average prevailing rent structure in the marketplace, and this allowed him no rental premium for the additional construction expenditure. The result in financial terms was that the project, when stabilized, was only worth the loan. The developer, however, had invested the principal portion of his assets into the project. The dilemma was that he could not continue to develop because his assets were tied up. He could not sell the property to free his assets, because the equity would have been lost. The property was only worth the loan.

However, the developer did have land adjacent to his property that could accommodate 130 additional units, according to the zoning. The problem was to deliver a development package with enough added value that the property could be developed substantially within the loan amount, and, in the process, to improve the performance of the first-phase 120 units so that the developer could pull equity out on a refinance.

This was an ambitious assignment in a tough market area characterized as being overbuilt. It was a market area which historically absorbed 4,500 rental units a year and was facing 20,000 units in the pipeline.

Review of first phase

In reviewing the developer's existing 120-unit first phase (see Illustration 16–3), it was found that there was no segregation between parking areas and garden court living areas. From an environmental standpoint, the resident lived in a parking lot, fully exposed to on-site parking and off-site surroundings which are not subject to control. There was no prime court area and no justification for premium rental units. There were no pleasant, confined areas to sit, relax, and enjoy in, or exciting areas to prompt activity, mingling, and exchanges between residents.

The recreational amenity area was divorced from the project in general and was not used. The amenity had a minimal effect on retention of residents and a doubtful effect on absorption, in that the rental office was at the extreme other end of the project.

There were also unjustifiable expenses in the building design. Building configurations were overly elaborate, creating structural complexity in exterior wall construction and roof framing. Exit and breezeway arrangements in the buildings were elaborate and costly, and the breezeway trapped noise and reduced the privacy level (see Chapter 13).

In the first phase of the project, individual units throughout were of generous size, but the rooms themselves were average to small in size and did not have a good inside-outside relationship due to poor interior planning. The developer paid for a large space but did not achieve spaciousness. Rental income was limited because of room size and layout. The

Illustration 16–3
Case Study II: First phase

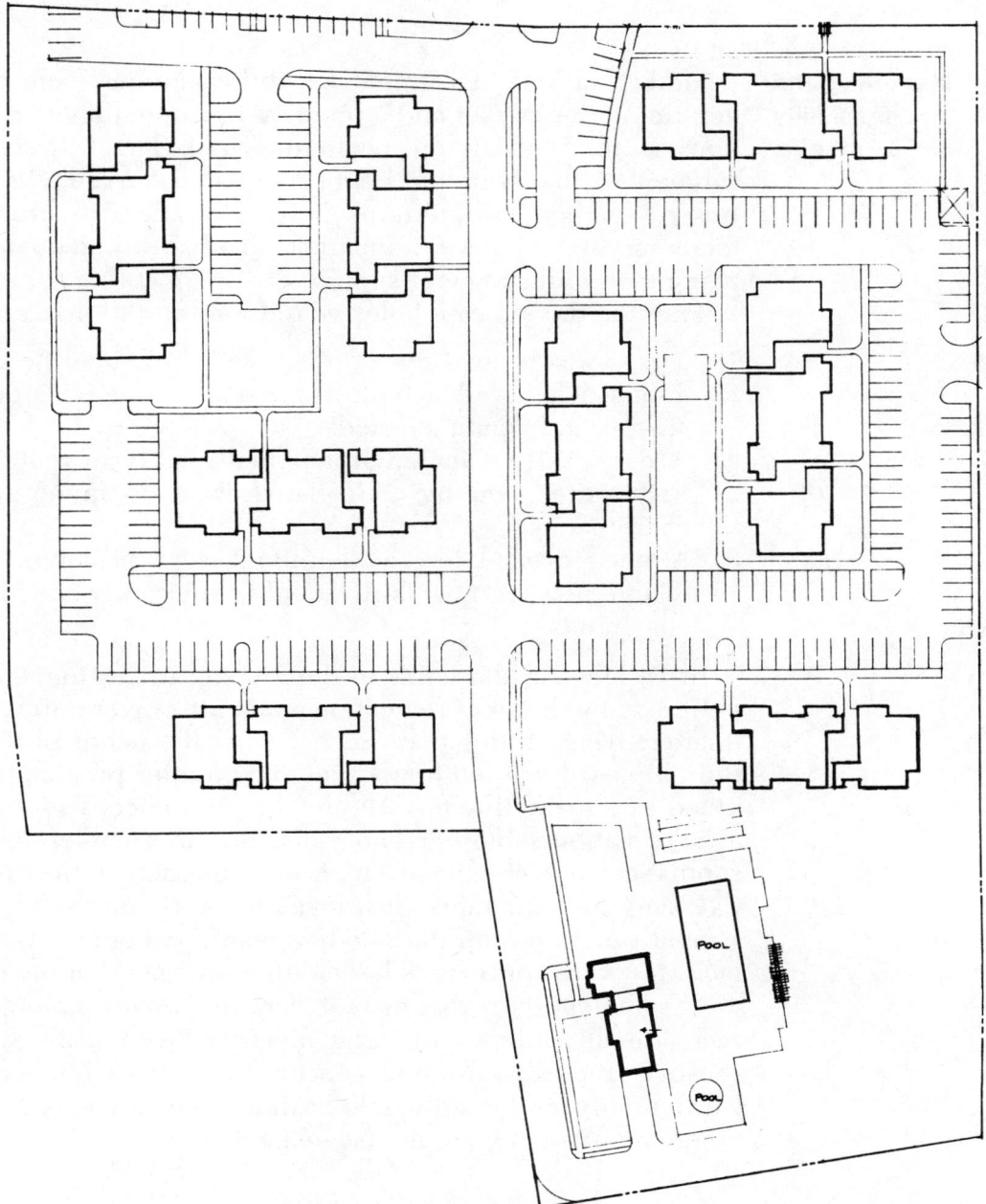

Site plan shows the 120-unit first phase of the apartment community.

cost of constructing square footage which does not contribute to room size or a feeling of spaciousness is substantially washed out.

Marketing and feasibility studies

Marketing and investment feasibility studies were first carried out to determine the market and a program for capitalizing on the market conditions, with emphasis on maximum yield. The first step was to look for submarkets that were not being adequately served. Next, the competition was researched to determine how to obsolete its products and create a temporary monopoly in submarkets that had strong demand which was not being met with sufficient supply.

Through this process holes were found in the market, as follows:

1. There was a need for a project with high-quality recreation facilities and a scheduled activities program designed around the needs of singles and young marrieds.
2. A need existed for environmental quality in rental housing through better site planning, unit planning, landscaping, graphics, and color coordination.
3. A need existed for smaller units, such as junior one-bedrooms, to enable prospects to afford a quality environment within their economic constraints.

In looking for the holes in the market, it was found that the few competitors who did offer recreational amenities were providing poor quality, unattractive facilities that did not meet the needs of the residents. They did not coordinate with any type of activities program and had been provided as a marketing feature but were not effective in practice. However, a large national builder had come into the market area with very large sophisticated recreational facilities combined with a professional, effective activities program. This developer was successful in achieving a $30 a month premium on the one-bedroom apartments. As far as recreational facilities were concerned, he had the only game in town.

A hole found in the market was to provide comparable to superior recreational facilities, but at a much reduced scale. In this manner the prestige and way-of-living concept was affordable for a $10 premium, substantially undercutting the national developer yet offering what the other competitors were not (see Chapter 17).

Strategy

The strategy was to deliver a quality environment at competitive rents to obsolete the competition. Costs were held down through value engineering. One means utilized to make the environment affordable within the economic constraints was to reduce unit size and utilize a unit mix favoring smaller units, including junior one-bedrooms. In this manner high rents per square foot could be achieved, while holding the line on the aggregate monthly rental figure.

For example, the one-bedroom unit in the second phase was substantially smaller than the one-bedroom unit in the first phase. Yet the aggregate rental on the second phase was slightly higher, netting a rental increase per net rentable square foot of 33 percent, with construction costs per square foot comparable to those of the first phase.

A planning priority was to create controlled garden court environments to foster a feeling of intimacy and belonging within the project (see Figure 16–4). In Development Area 1 (Illustration 16–5), a courtyard was formed between buildings E, F, and one of the existing buildings in the first phase. This common courtyard solution was not possible with the second grouping of buildings in Area 1 because a common garden court between the new and existing buildings would have included the existing parking lot. Instead, a courtyard was created between the new buildings, which were effectively screened off from both the existing and the new parking courts.

Once the courtyard was effectively screened from undesirable influences, an environment was created within. Illustration 16–6 shows a development plan for the courtyard which includes a pond and fountains in a natural setting including a dry creek (utilized instead of a stream for economy purposes), decorative bridges where the walkway crosses over the creek, landscape mounding with decorative boulder arrangements, a kiosk, trellises, patios with enclosure fences, creeping ground cover and

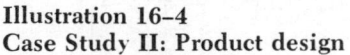

Illustration 16–4
Case Study II: Product design

In this product design, the landscaping was designed along with the site plan and elevations as an integral part of the market-oriented environmental package.

16 / Designing the product to optimize market potential   207

Illustration 16-5
Case Study II: Units added to first phase

Plan shows the units which were added to the first-phase development shown in Illustration 16-4. Note that the density of the first phase was increased by the addition of buildings L, M, and I.

shrub arrangement against buildings, and handsome landscape and architectural lighting. These features, planned with finesse, contribute greatly to the absorption and retention of residents.

The outdoor recreation area adjacent to the recreation building was surrounded by buildings to incorporate the recreation area better into the living area of the project and to create a screening effect for environmental control. The courtyard was then developed as in Illustration 16-6. There are now units overlooking the primary amenities which can justify prime rents.

The amenity complex was enlarged and designed to be utilized in conjunction with a scheduled activities program. Added facilities include

Illustration 16–6
Case Study II: Landscaping concept

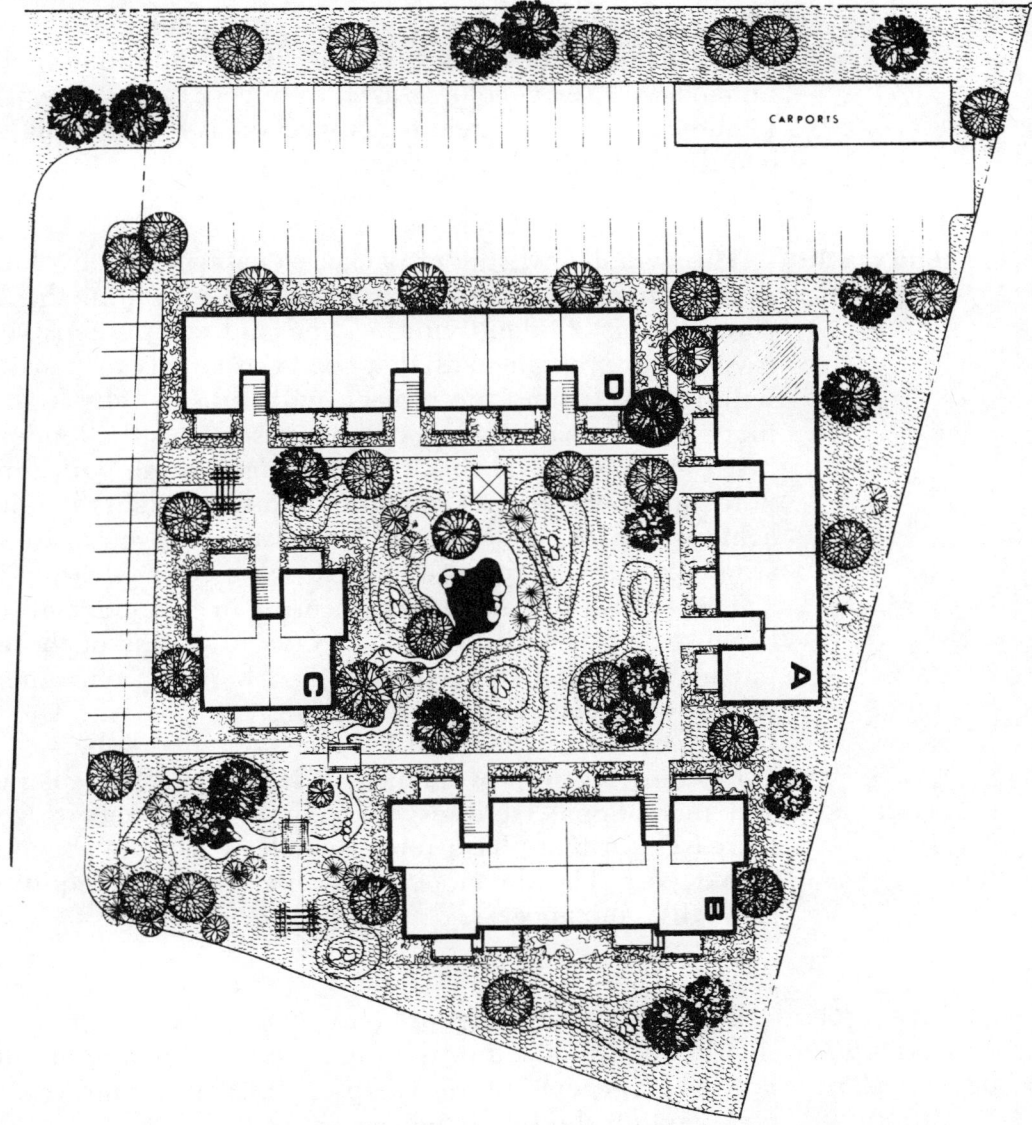

This plan, an enlargement of development Area 1 in Illustration 16–5, indicates the general landscaping concept accompanying the building design. The creek between the two ponds is a dry creek lined with boulders, river rock, and sand. The land has been contoured to create interest and provide a break from flatness typical in the area.

tennis, shuffleboard, volleyball, health gym, sauna, ping pong, billiards, and bar. Long, narrow buildings with sleeping rooms oriented to the rear were used to screen parking and unsightly off-site areas from the garden court areas.

The majority of the new units are of a back-to-back building design (see buildings B and C in Illustration 16–6). Great care was given to maintain structural simplicity, with the emphasis provided by treatment of trim, panels, decorative tower, and color treatments.

The inside floor plans were simplified and indoor-outdoor relationships enhanced. Lively color was introduced through wall coverings in the kitchen and dining area. A comprehensive decorating scheme used fully coordinated colors and patterns.

End result The overall investment package enabled the developer to produce the project, including land cost, substantially within the loan amount. The combination of identifying a need and comprehensively structuring the investment program to fill that need was largely responsible for the lender's willingness to fund the project, with substantially higher rent per square foot possible than in the existing phase. Thus the lender who financed the first phase agreed to finance the second phase with rental projections 33 percent greater per net rentable square foot than the rents that were being achieved in the first phase. This was achieved with second-phase construction costs comparable to first-phase costs per square foot.

The lender did not make an error in judgment on the second phase, because it was fully rented at rents in excess of those projected in the prospectus, and it has continued to benefit from rental increases while maintaining occupancy approaching 100 percent. And this has occurred in a rental market that is still characterized as soft.

Further, the improvements made and the land planning, landscaping, and recreational facilities enabled the developer to achieve substantial increases on first-phase rents, which he had not been able to do in the recent past. The developer was able to free up equity in the first phase through a refinance.

CONTROL OF PRODUCT DEVELOPMENT THROUGH FORMALIZED REVIEWS

Before a real estate product is actually developed, product criteria should be formalized in writing in the form of a preliminary criteria specification. (See exhibits in Chapter 6). At this time the criteria should be reviewed for the following:

1. Conformance to developer objectives.
2. Relationship to opportunities and obstacles identified.
3. How they fit identified marketing needs.
4. How they optimize opportunity created by competitors' weakness or neglect.

The budget as well as sales price or rental range should also be included in the criteria spec.

When the site plan, floor plans, and preliminary sections have been developed, a second product review should be conducted to compare the preliminary product as it relates to the criteria spec. Where deviations from the criteria have resulted they should be discussed and, if appropriate, the reasons should be recorded and the criteria revised. Preliminary cost estimates should be developed at this point. If there are cost overruns, refinements can be introduced before working drawings are fully developed.

At the time the drawings are completed, and prior to construction, a final review should reevaluate the criteria in light of existing market conditions. This is necessary to see if the criteria developed at the time of the initial market study and at the beginning of the product development stage are the same as those now required for success. The market may change so much as to invalidate the marketing position held at the time of the initial feasibility.

Formalizing the criteria and review activities helps to assure that the initial criteria is not lost sight of. By recording the product development activities it is possible to go back over the project when it gets in trouble to see where things went wrong. More importantly, the written record provides a more lucid record of the decision-making process and brings ideas into sharper focus for scrutiny. This provides some protection from purely subjective impulses and rationalizations by more clearly showing them for what they are.

THE NEED FOR BOTH MARKETING AND VALUE ENGINEERING EXPERTISE

A successful profit formula requires both identifying a hole in the market and being able to deliver the real estate package to plug that hole. Knowing the need is beneficial, but being able to fill it successfully is where the profit is.

One of the key elements in product development, once the hole in the market has been identified, is how to produce a significantly better product than the competition, within the budget guidelines dictated by the economics of the project. The response desired from the consumer is: "How can they offer such quality at the price they are asking?"

The solution requires both marketing and technical expertise. Marketing wise, it is important to know what the consumer values and what he does not value. Technically, the value engineering expertise must be available to show how to cut dollars out of a project where they are least valued. This is important to all market considerations, because when dollars are utilized inefficiently there is less remaining to build up marketing impact where it really counts. Marketing superiority requires no less than a tightening up of all development operation to ensure that the building dollar is spent where it is most needed.

Without frugality none can be rich, and with it very few would be poor.

COST CONTROL

In order to retain price flexibility, the decisions as to which features will be standard or optional must be held in abeyance until base hard costs are in. Only then is adequate information available to determine if the fireplace should be offered as a standard optional feature. The same holds true for mirrored closet doors, trellises, choice of roofing materials, and so on. By varying the quality and finishes required, cost adjustments can be made in order to fine tune the relationship of cost to price.

When it is impossible to predict accurately what a product is going to cost six months from now, a margin of flexibility needs to be designed in. In the high end of the market there is more price flexibility, because if the consumer really likes the product, he would just as soon pay another $5,000, and most importantly he can still qualify. Particularly when the builder does not have a day-to-day input of construction cost movements and very current comparables, he should proceed with the initial bid set of working drawings, with materials, appliances, fixtures, finishes, and design amenities conservative or comparable to the competition in the area. The initial bid set, then, would reflect hard costs based on the standards of other builders in the area. Once the hard costs are established, the developer can selectively upgrade to the desired quality. Upgrading is more effective in cost control than downgrading.

In the entry, for example, the builder would not put in quarry tile but would use vinyl asbestos. For windows and doors, he would not use anodized aluminum but its plain counterpart. On kitchen counter tops, he would not use tile but formica. And so on, right down the line. He would go to bid with a conservative package to establish base hard costs, and then upgrade from there. Then he could go to the subcontractors and ask how much it costs for quarry tile rather than vinyl asbestos counter tops, how much more anodized aluminum costs than plain aluminum? This approach gives the developer optimum flexibility to fine tune cost and price.

If the initial bid set called for too-high quality materials and finishes throughout and resulted in a cost overrun, the developer would not receive 100 percent on the dollar for the deletions from the drawings. It is widely known that the subs who initially figure the hard costs will not give full credit for deductions when the builder attempts to downgrade.

The best policy, therefore, is to go lean on the bid set and then upgrade with an itemized cost for each upgrade item. The itemized costs on the upgrade serve as excellent input for deciding on whether the upgrade shall be accepted or rejected, and whether it shall be a standard item written in the base price or an optional feature. This fine tuning, guided by value engineering analysis, can result in cost variations of $4 per square foot or more of net area on better quality housing.

Caution: Lender oversteering

At times the developer must fight off lenders' attempts to alter development programs, particularly in tight money markets. If income development programs have been properly structured at the outset, modifications by lenders often serve to weaken them as investment vehicles. The lender may require expensive features which increase (in the leader's opinion) the collateral value of the project in the event of foreclosure but often do not add to the project's return on investment in current markets.

The developer must exercise care not to give in to the lender's self-protection instincts by, in effect, reducing his own chances through a decrease in the project cash flow. A narrow margin to the developer reduces his rental rate flexibility and narrows the vacancy factor allowable before reaching the break-even point.

17

Amenities: Asset or liability?

Is it important to have recreation facilities? How extensive should they be in size and cost? What should they include? How should they be designed? What is their marketing function? Where should they be located?

Too often developers look at recreation facility decisions as a go–no go type of decision when really the decision is related to degree of magnitude. It is not a whether-or-not type of decision but a how-much type of decision. Developers may look at the decision as involving a question such as "Should I spend $100,000 on recreation facilities or not have them?" rather than asking themselves, "How much should I spend?" The latter approach narrows the problem down to a reasonable figure that should be spent, while the former questions the advisability of pursuing one of two arbitrary courses of action — whether to spend $100,000, or nothing.

PROVIDING AMENITIES THE CONSUMER IS WILLING AND ABLE TO PAY FOR

In approaching the recreation-amenity decision, developers often lose sight of the fact that price is as important as environment or amenities. Environment is great, but it must be offered at the right price to achieve absorption. In one market area a national competitor had provided a large recreation facility, the only one in the market area. It was experiencing some success through absorption, but it could have done better. Another developer did everything the national firm did, but on a much smaller scale, undercutting the competitor's rents with substantially reduced construction costs for amenities. This developer was able to achieve an absorption rate in excess of one unit per day, at rentals per square foot 33 percent higher than the average competition but at aggregate rents only slightly higher. The right combination of environment, amenities, unit size, and price for that particular market area had been found (see Chapter 16).

When too large a recreation facility is provided, so that the rental is strained, it is common to find potential residents of that project seeking an apartment in the vicinity of the high-rent, recreation-oriented project. In this manner the resident enjoys lower rent and is conveniently located to the high-rent, plush-amenity project. Some high-end rental projects find that their facilities are being utilized by those who do not rent within the project, especially in projects which emphasize singles living.

Amenities should not be provided uniformly throughout the project; rather, Impact should be built up in key areas, where premium rentals can be charged. Premiums are available in bread-and-butter projects as well as in their premium rental counterparts. Only a certain percentage of those in the rental market will pay a premium. The developer should provide premium locations for this percentage only, and leave the bread-and-butter areas for those who are interested in lower rentals.

A developer going into a market area where he has the only recreation building in the market needs only a modest recreation building. With no comparables, any facility will set the project apart, and anything larger may put rents through the top of the market (see Illustration 17–1). A 114-unit apartment complex might call for a 1,200-square-foot building which incorporates a social-recreation area with fireplace, two billiard tables, bar, vending area, men's and women's saunas, showers, and toilet facilities. Outside

Illustration 17–1

This clubhouse contains less than 800 square feet of enclosed area yet serves the needs of the residents while providing a dramatic focal point. The club appears much larger because of the space-stretching decks and trellises. The decked areas and the layout make the small clubhouse suitable for large gatherings as well as small ones.

might be a swimming pool, Jacuzzi pool, and a night-lighted reflecting pool. Landscape mounding, raised planters, decorative trellises, and patio fencing could add to environmental impact.

The importance of landscaping

Landscaping is critical to low-cost as well as upper-end apartments (see Illustration 17–2). On a very tight budget, the limited dollars spent on architectural niceties do not go too far, whereas the same dollars spent on landscaping continue to grow.

To stretch landscaping dollars, a large percentage of the dollars available should go for trees. Trees provide better privacy than do shrubs, ground covers, and seasonal color, and they also are a better screen against building monotony. After the project has stabilized itself, additional seasonal color and shrubs can be added.

Over the long term, one will get more for the dollar in small trees than in large ones. If the budget is limited, the best long-term decision is to reduce initial size of trees rather than number; with luck, small trees grow into large ones. However, some larger trees should be provided in the front of the project, regardless of rental range, to create curb appeal.

INCREASING THE AMENITY PACKAGE THROUGH REDUCTIONS ELSEWHERE

In order to afford the amenities previously not available in a market area, unit sizes are often scaled down. This is necessary because the developer cannot bring substantially more amenities than the competition into a market area, maintain the unit sizes of the competition, and keep rents within tolerable limits, all at the same time. A definite ceiling exists on rents; that is, they must be within the capabilities of prospective residents. If the developer cannot offer both quantity and quality of space for a fixed dollar, the choice in a particular market area is usually to emphasize quality while reducing unit size.

The net effect of increasing amenities while reducing unit size is a dramatic increase in income per net rentable square foot of rental properties over what the average competition is able to achieve. In one project in California, an average of 26 cents per square foot was projected where the competition was achieving 19 cents per square foot. In Florida, a 26-cent per net rentable square foot rental was projected where the competition was achieving rentals of 20 cents per square foot. These are rental projections 34 percent higher than those of the average competition. In Florida, the project has been completed and rents stabilized. The bulk of the units rented up at $5 to $10 per month over the projected rents, at a rate in excess of one per day in a softening market with give-aways. It is important to point out that in both the California and Florida projects mentioned, the aggregate rents were close to the averages in the area, though the rents per square foot were substantially higher.

Illustration 17-2

Landscaping, planning, and detailing are among the most desirable and appreciated amenities a developer can offer. Unlike buildings, landscaping does not depreciate but appreciates with the years.

INCOME, ABSORPTION, AND RETENTION: THREE KEYS TO AMENITIES ECONOMICS

There are three primary reasons for providing recreational facilities: (1) to maximize income and return, (2) to absorb residents, and (3) to retain residents. All decisions regarding recreation facilities should be related to these three primary considerations—income, absorption, and retention.

To achieve maximum absorption, it is often beneficial to locate recreation facilities so they can be seen off site. This creates self-advertising value. A large percentage of residents attracted to projects is comprised of people driving by who are drawn in by the curb appeal. An attractive recreation facility should be placed where it will draw people into the project (see Chapters 30 and 31).

The relationships of the recreation building, pool area, leasing office, model units, and parking are important marketing factors. Since renting an apartment is an emotional involvement, it is necessary to establish and sustain impact. Driving by the property, a prospective resident is attracted by curb appeal which gives future promise of what awaits within. Upon entering the recreation building, the propsective resident should be immediately reinforced by the lively interior appointments. If the rear wall opposite the front door of the recreation building is in glass, upon opening the door the prospective resident will see at once both the plush interior of the recreation building and the outside recreation features immediately behind the building. Once inside the recreation building, the potential resident can be immediately confronted with the leasing-manage-

Illustration 17–3

The units facing onto this landscaped pool area receive a 10 percent rental premium over units with less desirable locations. Creating rental premiums is a vital planning and design function.

17 / Amenities: Asset or liability? 219

ment office. This office should be inside the recreation building for two purposes: The facility provides an excellent backdrop for the leasing function, and the presence of the office within the recreation complex serves a security function in the area where it is most needed.

When planning allows, a vista of trellises, lakes or reflecting pools, and landscape mounding should be part of the recreation core area, to add visual impact. The outside recreation (amenities) area and adjacent vistas form the central core area of the project, a highly controlled environment. To maintain environmental control, parking and other undesirable environmental features should be effectively screened out. The model units are then located facing onto the core area to maintain emotional influence on the leasing process.

Maintaining the continuity of emotional impact is a strong sales tool not only for achieving absorption but for maximizing per-square-foot rental income. The highly favorable impression results in increased rental incomes for the project as a whole. In addition, those units directly facing onto the core area can generally justify at least a 5 percent–10 percent per month rental premium (see Illustration 17–3). These units are often the first to be rented, even with the premium.

AMENITIES MUST BE FUNCTIONAL AS WELL AS ATTRACTIVE

In order to retain residents, the recreation facilities should be designed with a specific predetermined use in mind which reflects the social and recreational needs of the residents. If an activities program is visualized, amenities design should be closely coordinated with the program at the time of design. All too often, amenities provided are not utilized because no thought was given to their use. An amenity that is provided as a marketing gimmick to achieve absorption but which does not work in practice does not retain residents. When a cost expenditure delivers only half results, there is a commensurate loss in value.

ADDING AMENITIES AS A WAY OF REDUCING EQUITY REQUIREMENTS

The inclusion of a selective amenities package can often enhance the rentability and income of the project, while actually reducing the equity requirement. Amenities must be selected which will justify increasing the gross income, thereby increasing the loan amount. To obtain the desired results, however, the cost of adding the amenities must naturally be lower than the resultant increase in loan amount.

A good rule of thumb for making value decisions is to omit less frequently used amenities, or amenities that can be used practically by only a few residents at a time, in favor of those that are more frequently utilized or can be utilized by groups.

An example of an investment planning and product development analysis to determine the profitability of a recreation building on a 114-unit apartment complex is as follows. The marketing study suggests that a well-appointed, functional recreational facility can justify an across-the-board average rental premium of $7 per month per apartment. The question then is twofold; How much can be spent on the amenity features without increasing the equity requirement? Can the equity requirement actually be lowered by the inclusion of the amenities package?

An increase of $7 per month represents a yearly rental increase on 114 units of $9,576. At 6.7 times the gross rental increase of $9,576, the recreation facilities represent a value increase of $64,149. Assuming a 75 percent loan/value ratio, $48,111 can be borrowed against the added income attributable to the recreation building.

Marketing and design studies indicate that the necessary amenities to achieve the $7 rental increase can be incorporated within a 1,200-square-foot structure. Assuming a construction cost per square foot of $25 for a well-appointed building, this is a total construction cost of $30,000. If an allowance for furniture and accessories of $8,000 is added, the total cost comes to $38,000, which is $26,000 less than the market value and $10,000 less than the loan value. The result is a $10,000 reduction in the equity requirement and a $26,000 added gain upon sale (see Chapter 13).

ADDING AMENITIES PROFITABLY WITHOUT INCREASING RENTS

As insurance in soft markets, it may not be desirable for rents to reflect a $7 premium over the competition, even though it might not have comparable recreation facilities. In this case, the solution suggested above—decreasing the unit size in order to bring aggregate rents in line with the competition—is in order to avoid the high end of the market.

When unit size is reduced quality should be upgraded where possible over that offered by the competition, though the inclusion of wall coverings, better quality lighting fixtures over dining tables, color-coordinated finishes, pass-through wet bars, and efficient planning. The net effect will be a cost reduction which makes lower rents possible, to meet or undercut the competition on the aggregate. This provides a two-edged marketing advantage in that both price and superior environment can be offered, at the expense of square footage.

In some instances where unit size is reduced it is possible to increase density. In one instance, it was possible to increase density by 17 percent over what the developer had previously planned, because of smaller unit sizes. This provided 17 percent more household incomes to support the amenity package. Marketing input and judgment should be used to establish the proper relationship between quality, quantity (unit size and mix), and cost (monthly rentals).

AMENITIES PLANNING TO ENCOURAGE AMENITY/ RESIDENT INTERACTION

In planning recreation facilities, compatible recreation facilities should be placed in close proximity to one another so that there is a cumulative buildup of activity. For example, the billiards area should be in close proximity to the bar, socializing and dancing areas, to provide for a break-the-ice buildup of activity. Early arrivals to a planned party can busy themselves in the billiards area and strike up conversations. Parties can be difficult to start because the early arrivals keep leaving.

In the same way, TV consoles should be located in the main social activity area rather than in a separate room. Though the separate room offers less disturbance to viewers, it also creates an uncomfortable situation whereby people coming into the room feel they are imposing on others' privacy. In large projects where TVs are located both in a separate viewing room and in a larger social recreation room, it has been observed that viewing is more popular in the larger multiuse area than in the intimate TV room. If people wanted intimacy, they would probably view the TV in their apartment. Those watching it in the recreation building apparently use it as a social outlet and are seeking a sense of involvement with others.

Outdoors, the pool should be close to the recreation building, and the volleyball, shuffleboard, and table tennis areas close to the pool area. Active participation activities draw people from the more passive poolside lounging areas. The participation events thus help act as ice-breakers.

If the facilities offered do not serve the purpose of bringing people together in a comfortable, casual manner, they most probably will not be utilized. Likewise, if they are unattractive or poorly located, they also will not be utilized.

UNDERSTANDING THE COST/BENEFIT RATIOS OF AMENITIES

In smaller rental projects of 130 units and less, tennis courts often are not recommended because of the space they take up. If not properly buffered with landscaping, they can be unattractive for units facing them directly. Because of their cost and because their utility is limited to individual use and not suited to groups, in small projects with limited budgets amenities which afford broad utilization by all residents are substituted. Volleyball is favored over tennis because of lower cost, less space required, and utilization by anywhere from 2 to 16 people at a time. In addition to high utility value, volleyball has proved very popular as a meet-your-neighbor type of activity.

Jacuzzi pools have proved popular on a 24-hour basis, in some projects as popular as the swimming pool. Though requiring much less space than a swimming pool (8×12 feet is a comfortable size) they are nearly as expensive to operate and maintain because the water temperature must be maintained and the rapidly evaporating chemicals replaced. In market areas where the competition provides both an indoor and outdoor pool, an indoor-outdoor Jacuzzi can be an acceptable substitute for an indoor pool. Of course, housing an 8×12 pool is much less expensive than housing one of 20×40 feet. If the competition does not have a Jacuzzi, the indoor-outdoor Jacuzzi, plus an outdoor pool, may count more to the prospective resident than two conventional pools (inside and outside).

If gym facilities are provided, only one gym in projects up to 400 units in size is usually called for. Rather than duplicating the facility to produce both men's and women's gyms, it may be preferable to spend the money on adding another amenity, to increase the number offered. However, separate men's and women's saunas, rather than one to be used alternately by both sexes are usually provided.

Recreation facilities should stress quality rather than quantity. It is the feel rather than the extent of the facilities which creates the emotional appeal and the pride of the resident (or owner) which generate premium rents. Finishes in activities areas might have wall coverings as opposed to paint, and meticulous attention could be given to colors, textures, trim, and architectural detailing.

Often activities buildings are provided only because the developer feels he needs an activities building to keep up with the competition. Little or no thought is given to the location, utilization, or decor of the facility. Such a facility provides little resident satisfaction and is therefore a liability to the project. Its cost necessitates rental increases without offsetting benefits.

MOST COMMON MISTAKES IN PLANNING AMENITIES

1. The facility is poorly designed from an artistic standpoint and is decorated like storage room, and with as little emotional appeal.
2. Facilities are poorly located within the project. Often they are located in the parking lot area or in some other part of the project which was left over because apartments could not be squeezed into it. In this instance, facilities contribute neither to a core area which justifies premium rents or to self-advertising value and curbside appeal.
3. No thought is given to actual utilization and activities within the facility. The facility will not be effective in retaining residents because it cannot be practically utilized.
4. Recreation facilities do not produce the desired absorption and retention of residents because too much money was spent on them. Though the facilities may be attractive aesthetically, they are not attractive economically; the positive effects of the aesthetics and social benefits are offset by the rental increases they demand.
5. Builders try to protect themselves from future soft markets by providing an abundance of recreational and social features. However, the excessive cost reduces rental rate flexibility and raises the occupancy figures required to meet the break-even point. The builder is then in an inflexible position because he has already utilized his reserves. If the competition has sufficient flexibility to reduce rents and offer added competitive services currently in demand in the market area, it may be in a superior position to attract residents. A builder can lose a project from having too many recreational facilities as well as from too few.
6. Facilities are not properly maintained, in which case the impression is of poor management and shoddy eye appeal.
7. Landscaping is left out of the amenities budget. Extensive clubhouse and outdoor recreational facilities may be placed in arid surroundings devoid of greenery or landscape detailing.

18

Establishing feasibility

The purpose of a feasibility analysis is to determine the chances of success for a specific project or development concept, or a specific site to be developed by a specific study sponsor. Feasibility is distinguished from appraisal in that appraisal concerns itself with value to the market in general, whereas feasibility is concerned with value to a specific sponsor.

Feasibility also differs from appraisal in that appraisal theory presumes rational behavior in the marketplace, whereas optimization through feasibility analysis attempts to maximize value (return) by encouraging irrational or emotional behavior in the marketplace through skillful marketing. The appraisal concept of fair market value or market value is objective in nature and dependent on average conditions. Feasibility analysis includes subjective considerations which add to or subtract from fair market value (determined through appraisal), to arrive at investment value as related to a specific opportunity.

THE FEASIBILITY PROCESS

Feasibility is concerned with properly identifying the investment problem, structuring or evaluating the objectives, and formulating or evaluating an action plan to accomplish these objectives. The process consists of maximizing the opportunities and neutralizing and minimizing the obstacles, in order to achieve the optimum solution to the investment problem.

The components of feasibility are not generally analyzed in a single report produced by a single individual. The total feasibility represents a consolidation of efforts by numerous specialists. The feasibility report may utilize work and reports by others as backup to the final consolidated report.

The need for systematic simplification

The feasibility analysis must be limited to the elements that have the most bearing on increasing or decreasing the success of the program. A common danger in analysis is to assume information which one does not actually possess. The analyst must exercise discretion not to presume information which he does not have, and not to utilize information that is not critical to the outcome. Irrelevant detail increases opportunity for error and exaggerates credibility. The findings can be no more specific than the credibility and suitability of the information on which the findings are based.

Oversimplification of a problem is a discovery process, designed to identify the priorities and concentrate energies on them in order to make the problem manageable.

Steady, patient, persevering thinking will generally surmount every obstacle in the search after truth.

Emmons

IDENTIFYING STRUCTURING THE PROBLEM AND OBJECTIVES

Feasibility analysis will depend on the characteristics of the property and the objectives. The sponsor or developer determines the purpose of the analysis (e.g., to establish value as a basis for a loan), and the analyst defines the objectives of the analysis. The feasibility analyst's first function is to identify the problem and then formulate an objective in light of the problem recognized. In formulating his initial purpose which prompted value analysis, the sponsor may not have taken into account or been aware of the actual problems that have a direct bearing on the purpose.

A word of caution about standardized formats

Because problems in land development can be as diverse as the circumstances associated with any individual property, problem identification and structuring of objectives require resourcefulness and creative thought. For these reasons it is not always feasible for the analyst to work from standardized models for the detail analysis.

Standardized models or formats are a great tool in reducing costs of analysis and stabilizing output. However, models can only be used as general guides; if the analyst attempts to use a model as a detailed guide for a wide class of problems and objectives, he will shape them to the format rather than developing a format to handle specific objectives related to specific problems. The best a model can do is to show how a specific problem can be generally approached, and the objectives and procedures generally formulated.

COMPONENTS OF FEASIBILITY

Feasibility analysis is more than a numbers analysis. Its components include economic feasibility, legal and political feasibility, performance feasibility, and compatability with the sponsor's objectives.

Economic feasibility questions the suitability of the investment as related to the following questions:

1. Does the investment represent the highest and best uses of the resources to be committed?
2. Does the indicated return meet or exceed the minimum investment standards of the sponsor?
3. Are the equity requirements within the means of the sponsor to contribute or to generate from other sources?
4. Does the investment proposal fill a true need in the marketplace?
5. Does the investment proposal fill the market need with a product equal or superior to the competitive product?
6. Are the absorption income and expense projections reliable and consistent with industry standards? Do they allow margin for error or unforeseen circumstances?
7. Is the proposed investment package as attractive to lenders as competing investment packages, or more attractive? Are there sufficient mortgage and construction funds available in the marketplace to create a favorable environment for project financing?
8. How will the proposed investment be affected by market trends and cycles?

Legal and political feasibility considers the suitability of the investment as related to the following questions:

1. Is the property properly zoned for the proposed use? If not, is the rezoning legally and politically feasible?
2. Are there legal environmental, political, or social considerations which would jeopardize the use of the property as zoned or proposed?
3. Are there legislative or environmental and social trends which would jeopardize or hinder the ongoing operation of the proposed investment?
4. Does the proposed investment conform to existing codes, ordinances, deed restrictions, and state and federal laws?
5. Is title to the property clear of restrictions which would impede the development as proposed?
6. Is the development entity properly structured from a legal and tax standpoint?
7. Have all tax considerations been properly analyzed and structured?

Performance feasibility and compatability with sponsor objectives considers the stability of the investment as related to the following questions:

1. Is the proposed investment a sound strategy and action plan for implementing sponsor objectives?
2. Is the proposed investment feasible within the limitations imposed by sponsor constraints? Does the sponsor possess the management team and consultants required to implement the investment program?
4. Are the required separate contractors, subcontractors workmen, and material suppliers available and capable of performing according to the performance schedules?

5. Are the performance schedules complementary and in the proper sequential order so as not to create conflicts or bottlenecks in implementation?

THE FEASIBILITY OUTLINE

The Feasibility Outline presented as Exhibit 18-1 is a comprehensive guide for a total feasibility analysis which will require editing and deletions to conform to the scope of a given problem. The scope is constrained by budget, timing, and the size and sensitivity of the problem. To provide more than is required for the satisfactory solution of the problem is to waste resources; to do more than the budget allows or the problem justifies is a misuse of resources.

The Feasibility Outline closely corresponds with the outline of this book. The chapters and subchapters correspond with the Feasibility Outline and should be referred to for direction in implementing the comprehensive feasibility analysis. In this respect the book represents a comprehensive guideline for market planning and project feasibility analysis.

The Feasibility Outline also provides a guide for the development of a comprehensive loan package. All loan packages do not require the comprehensive treatment suggested by the feasibility outline, however. The comprehensiveness of the loan package will be dependent on developer objectives, project requirements, relationship of developer to the financing sources, and current familiarity of the financing sources with the subject market area. See Chapter 23, Loan Submission, for more on loan submission requirements.

Exhibit 18-1

Feasibility Outline

    I. Letter of Transmittal
   II. Scope, Limiting Conditions
  III. Summary
       A. Loan request
       B. Demographic
       C. Target market
       D. Concept
       E. Product
       F. Development team
       G. Construction
       H. Merchandising
       I. Absorption
       J. Profit
  IV. Developer Objectives, Constraints (Chapter 2)
       A. Financial objectives
          1. Leverage, liquidity
          2. Yield
          3. Risk

Exhibit 18–1 (*continued*)

      B. Nonfinancial objectives
      C. Resources, capabilities, constraints
      D. Development, strategy preferences
      E. Attachments, exhibits
         1. Corporate financial statement
         2. Personal statement(s), guarantor(s) and spouses.

V. Locational Analysis and Site Evaluation (Chapters 3 and 4)
      A. Regional analysis
      B. Community analysis
      C. Site evaluation
         1. Physical analysis
         2. Accessibility
         3. Self-advertising aspects
         4. Utilities availability
         5. Comparative evaluation
      D. Zoning and regulatory influences
      E. Opportunities and obstacles
      F. Compatability with development concept and market opportunity
      G. Comparability with developer objectives
      H. Attachments and exhibits
         1. Locational maps
            a. Region
            b. Vicinity
         2. Transportation
            a. Major arterial plan
            b. Mass transit plan
         3. Graphic illustration of trends
         4. Aerial photos
         5. Site photos
         6. Survey
         7. Topographical map
         8. Zoning map
         9. Verification of utilities availability
        10. Verification of zoning
        11. Preliminary title report
        12. Deed, land contract, or option agreement

VI. Legal, Political, and Environmental Constraints (Chapter 5)
      A. Legal feasibility
      B. Political feasibility
      C. Environmental feasibility

VII. Competitive Evaluation (Chapters 6 and 14)
      A. Opportunities due to competitor's weakness
      B. Opportunities due to competitor's mix
      C. Opportunities due to competitor's lack of product suitability for specific submarkets.
      D. Opportunities due to competitors' price structure
      E. Comparables
      F. Value relationship analysis

Exhibit 18–1 (*continued*)

- G. Attachments and exhibits
  1. Competitors' brochures
  2. Photos of competitors' product
  3. Locational map of competitors
  4. Work sheets

VIII. Market Segmentation (Chapter 8)
- A. Identification of submarkets which correspond with developer's objectives.
  1. Submarkets not being adequately served
  2. Submarkets being over supplied
  3. Where they come from
  4. Why they buy/rent
  5. What they buy/rent
- B. Opportunities and obstacles associated with submarkets

IX. Market Cycles (Chapter 9)
- A. Opportunities and obstacles resulting from cycles outside the immediate market area.
- B. Opportunities and obstacles resulting from cycles within the immediate market area.

X. Base Data and Demographics (Chapters 10, 11, and 12)
- A. Employment trends
  1. Growth
  2. Unemployment
  3. Distribution
- B. Income trends
- C. Population trends
  1. Population growth and household formation
  2. Age distribution of population
  3. Ethnic distribution of population
- D. Housing inventory
  1. Housing obsolescence
  2. Construction of new units
  3. Existing inventory
- E. Housing occupancy
- F. Retail activity
- G. Industrial activity
- H. Community facilities
- I. Transportation
- J. Development trends

XI. Developmental Strategy
- A. Opportunities for innovation, market monopoly (Chapter 7)
- B. Value engineering contribution (Chapter 13)
- C. Matching the concept to the market segment (Chapter 15)
- D. Amenities (Chapter 17)

XII. Product Concept (Chapters 14, 15, and 16)
- A. Product type
- B. Amenities
- C. Price rental range, premiums

Exhibit 18–1 (*concluded*)

    D. Attachments, exhibits
      1. Work sheet for product mix and features
      2. Price/rental schedule
      3. Architectural drawings and renderings
XIII. Absorption, Phasing (Chapter 11)
    A. Presales, rents
    B. Sales/rental period
    C. Demand, supply characteristics
    D. Justification for absorption projection
    E. Phasing
    F. Attachments, exhibits
      1. Comparable sales/rents
XIV. Development Team (Chapter 28)
    A. Developer
    B. Marketing, feasibility, appraisal
    C. Planning, architecture, engineering
    D. Construction
      1. Bonding capability
      2. Construction contracts, agreements
    E. Sales
    F. Attachments, exhibits
      1. Resumé of experience of team members
      2. Brochures of companies
      3. Accomplishments, outstanding achievements
      4. Resumé of key personnel
XV. Management recommendations
    A. Control of product development (Chapters 13 and 16)
    B. Standardization (Chapter 24)
    C. Management capability (Chapter 25)
    D. Production management (Chapters 26 and 27)
    E. Organization (Chapters 22 and 28)
    F. Scheduling (Chapter 29)
    G. Budgets, projections, and controls (Chapters 20 and 21)
XVI. Merchandising Strategy (Chapters 30 and 31)
    A. Model complex
    B. Sales, rental office
    C. Unifying theme
    D. Sales/rental strategy
    E. Advertising and promotion
XVII. Financial Analysis (Chapter 19, 20, and 21)
    A. Cash flow analysis
    B. Back up schedules
    C. Sensitivity analysis
    D. Ratio analysis

19

Financial analysis: How to analyze and optimize return

VALUE CLASSIFICATIONS

In the scope of this book, value is considered under two property classifications: residential nonincome property and residential income property. Residential nonincome property has two kinds of value: owner value and market value. Income property has three kinds of value: owner value, market value, and investment value.

Value of nonincome residential properties

The owner value and market value of a residence often net out to the same value. In instances where the owner prefers the location to all others —because of proximity to relations, nostalgia, particularly suitable design characteristics, or overimprovement in relation to the neighborhood—the owner value may be more than market value. Where the owner is uninformed as to value or must sell in distress, the owner value may be less than market value. Market value of residential user properties is determined by two approaches: replacement cost, and a comparative sales or market approach.

Value of income residential properties

With income properties, owner value is much the same as with nonincome residential properties. An income property may have a special utility for one owner that it does not for another, such as pride of ownership. The property may also be a key property in a large overall development which the owner may want to keep control of to protect the overall investment. The other two kinds of value, market value and investment value, are generally close to owner value. A skilled entrepreneur, however, can often add increased investment value by trading on the equity through enlightened financing, structuring, and management to increase his investment value over the market value.

In boom times, speculators buy properties assuming that they will rapidly increase in value, or in the hope that they can be resold at a profit to an uninformed investor. In such times speculative market pressures may drive market value ahead of investment value. When this occurs, investors generally withdraw from the real estate market, as in the stock market. Speculation cannot support itself without the backing of the investor, and soon market value drops until it reaches or descends below investment value (see Chapters 3 and 4).

Price versus value Price differs from value or cost. Price is the amount asked or paid for property and may be more or less than value. Value is the amount which a purchaser is "justified" in paying for a property. Under this definition, justified price is the same as value. Justified price is the sum of the mortgages and the value of the equity investment.

$$\text{Total mortgage(s)} + \text{Value of equity} = \text{Justified price.}$$

Stabilized value Stabilized value is the same as loan value. When property values are in a state of flux, due to speculation or unusual supply/demand pressures in the market, the current market price may not be indicative of the market value in the near future, when the market stabilizes. To protect themselves from market excesses, lenders have established a value for loan purposes called loan value, or stabilized value, which may be different from current market or investment value. This stabilized value is intended to reflect the long-term market value in which prices are stabilized. The concept of stabilized value serves to wring out temporary excesses in current prices to stabilize lender risk.

Tangible and intangible benefits Just as investors may have two basic sets of investment criteria—financial and nonfinancial—returns or benefits are both tangible and intangible. A tangible benefit is generative in nature, whereas an intangible benefit is sustaining. The terms "tangible" and "generative" and the terms "intangible" and "sustaining" are interchangeable; that is, a tangible benefit is a generative benefit.

Generative benefits are those that can be valued in dollars and are subject to quantitative analysis. They produce a measurable enhancement to the business and investment return. Sustaining benefits are those that cannot be readily measured in a quantitative manner but are necessary to sustain the business or investment objective.

Since sustaining (or intangible) benefits cannot be measured quantitatively, they are beyond the scope of return on investment (ROI) analysis to rank them in order of preference. Judgment and experience are the best measures of sustaining benefits. This points up the limitations of ROI analysis—it is not an effective measure of intangible benefits. Recognition of the sustaining and generative benefits is necessary from the outset so that both can be measured by the most appropriate approach. A total reliance on ROI analysis in the decision-making process when the alternative investment opportunities contain sustaining as well as generative considerations may suggest a faulty picture.

ANALYSIS OF THE WHOLE PICTURE

In analyzing an investment decision, analysis must be based on the whole picture, not a close-up shot of a portion of it. For example, the framing contractor may inform the job superintendent that he can save $5,000 by modifying the structural system, with no difference in visual effects, and may ask for approval to do so. If the superintendent does not fully analyze the proposal as to its effect on all other trades, codes, and schedules, he may arrive at an erroneous conclusion because of incomplete information. The change could produce increased costs for the concrete, mechanical, and electrical subcontractors, or it could disrupt the construction schedule and thus produce aggregate costs in excess of the savings on framing. Investment alternatives behave in the same manner and must be fully analyzed as part of the whole picture.

The creative real estate analyst will not limit the analysis to three alternative actions which may be offered for consideration but will legitimately question if there is not a fourth alternate, as yet unpresented, which would yield the most desirable benefits. His inquiry should be extended to include the optimum alternative to achieve the firm's objectives, rather than being limited to the already presented alternatives, which may not include an optimal solution.

Investment analysis aids are not a substitute for judgment; rather, they serve as guides for its application. If a numerical measurement of value were solely relied on for decision making, a child could select and rank investments in order of desirability by selecting the numbers that correspond to a predetermined guideline. Qualitative as well as quantitative analysis is required to formulate the decision criteria to fit the investment objectives.

PRESENT-VALUE THEORY

The essence of present-value theory is that a dollar received today is more valuable than a dollar received at a future date. The difference in value between a dollar today and a dollar received at a future date is the amount that can be earned in interest or investment return on that dollar between today and the date the future dollar is received. Also, adjustments must be made for the effects of inflation.

It is important, therefore, in measuring investment return on a sum to measure not only the amount of the return but the points in time when the amount is received. For example, if the dollar received today can be invested at 10 percent, it will be worth $1.10 one year from now. Barring inflation, if the same dollar were received one year from today, it would be worth only $1, or 10 cents less than the dollar received today.

Present-value theory likens the investment return to a mortgage; that is, income streams over a period of time will return the original amount of the investment plus a return. However, the return will not always be the same for every year and will consist of spendable dollars and a deferred return available at the time of recovery through sale or refinance. The various returns are adjusted or discounted by the yield rate utilized to express the flows as a single present-value worth. The various inflows are equated to a single inflow having an average return over the investment period. By reducing alternate opportunities to their equivalent average return over the life of the investment, these equivalent average returns can be indexed, compared, and ranked in order of magnitude or desirability.

Two methods for computing the time value of money

There are two methods for computing the time value of money: present-value analysis, and internal rate-of-return analysis. Present-value analysis begins with a presumed rate of return based on the cost of capital or on minimum earnings, or cut-off rate, established for the company. This method computes the present worth of future income streams as a present-dollar amount. Present-value analysis does not compute a rate of return.

Unlike present-value analysis, the internal rate of return computes a percentage rate of return which can be used to rank investments in their order of desirability. Present-value theory is useful in decision making for two basic types of decisions:

1. Given an opportunity or course of action requiring the outlay of money, should the company accept it?
2. Given several opportunities or courses of action requiring the outlay of money, which is the more attractive?

Present-value analysis

Present value is measured by equating two factors: amount of net benefits to be derived, and degree of certainty or probability in achieving the benefits as projected. Present value is the present worth of future net benefits, calculated at a percentage rate which corresponds to the time value of money and risk involved. An increase in benefits increases present value; a decrease in probability reduces present value. Present value establishes the maximum amount of investment which is justified by the earning capacity of the property. Property is economically sound when earnings are sufficient to pay an adequate yield and repay the original investment during the economic life of the property.

The principle of present value is that on a particular valuation date the present value is equivalent to a series of future net returns; that is, the owner or sponsor is as well off possessing the right to the future net returns as having the present values of these net returns as cash in hand.

There are three basic steps in estimating present value:

1. Projection of the future net returns.
2. Estimating the accuracy, probability, or risk of the projections.
3. Calculating the present worth of the future net returns, in light of the risk.

The risk associated with the future net returns is a determinant factor in selecting the yield or rate to be utilized in the present-worth calculation. The probability of achieving the projected returns, which are only estimates, is largely determined by the judgment of the analyst after examining the yield rates realized on comparable investments.

Internal rate-of-return analysis

From a discount table, an analyst can select a rate that will discount cash flows to a present worth which is equal to the initial equity investment. The rate which discounts the cash flows to the original investment is called the yield or internal rate of return (IRR), and their rate provides a quantitative index for ranking investment alternatives. As an example, three investment alternatives can be ranked in their order of desirability by determining the IRR for each investment alternative, as listed below:

	Alternative A		Alternative B		Alternative C	
Year	Outlay	Inflow	Outlay	Inflow	Outlay	Inflow
0	$3,000	0	$4,000	0	$5,000	0
1	0	$1,000	0	$2,000	0	0
2	0	1,000	0	2,000	0	0
3	0	1,000	0	2,000	0	$2,000
4	0	1,000	0	0	0	2,000
5	0	1,000	0	0	0	4,000
	$3,000	$5,000	$4,000	$6,000	$5,000	$8,000

ALTERNATIVE A

Year	20% discount factor	Present-worth outlay	Present-worth inflow
0	0	$3,000	0
1	.833		$ 833
2	.694		694
3	.579		579
4	.482		482
5	.402		402
		$3,000	$2,990

The internal rate of return for Alternative A is 20 percent.

ALTERNATIVE B

Year	25% discount factor	Present-worth outlay	Present-worth inflow
0	0	$4,000	0
1	.800		$1,600
2	.640		1,280
3	.512		1,042
4	.410		0
5	.328		0
		$4,000	$3,922

Present worth of inflow for Alternative B, using a 20 percent discount factor, is $4,217. The internal rate of return is thus approximately 24 percent.

ALTERNATIVE C

Year	12.5% discount factor	Present-worth outlay	Present-worth inflow
0	0	$5,000	0
1	.889		0
2	.790		0
3	.702		$1,404
4	.624		1,248
5	.555		2,220
		$5,000	$4,872

Present worth of the inflow for Alternative C, using a 10 percent discount factor, is $5,352. The internal rate of return is thus approximately 12 percent.

The investment alternatives, ranked according to their internal rate of return, rate as follows:

Investment B: 24%
Investment A: 20%
Investment C: 12%

When measuring alternative investment opportunities of similar risk which possess different patterns of payment over time, it is assumed that the income during the life of the investment can be reinvested at a rate equivalent to the computed internal rate of return. Only when income can be reinvested at a rate equivalent to the computed IRR can the alternatives be compared by IRR analysis. For example, if two investments produced equal internal rates of return, but one of them received most of the income in the early stages of the investment life and the other received most of the income in the latter stages, the two alternatives would not yield equal dollar amounts before discounting. If, however, the dollars can be reinvested at the computed IRR as received, the total dollar accumulation at the end of the investment life will be equal for both alternatives.

Limitations of present-value indexing

Problem solving and risk analysis involve both quantitative and qualitative considerations, and the solutions require both objective and subjective analysis. Present-value theory is essentially a quantitative approach to problem solving which does not evaluate the qualitative or subjective aspects of the problem. If problem solving and analysis were merely quantitative, involving only numbers, weighty business decisions could be made by clerks. However, the quality and relevance of the data and the suitability of the measures of performance are as important to the decision outcome as the present-worth values and methodology. The judgmental portions of the problem solving cannot be overlooked or minimized. Quantitative analysis is not a substitute for judgment; it is an analytical process to reinforce and aid judgment in optimizing the use of resources.

All investment proposals cannot be evaluated in quantitative terms, because in some of them intangible return may be more relevant than tangible return as a measure of performance. Investments must first be classified as to which measure of performance is appropriate: tangible, intangible, or, as in most investment decisions, a combination of tangible and intangible benefits.

MARKET VALUE Market value is determined by the most probable price that will result in a transaction between a willing buyer and seller within a reasonable period of time. Market value is based on the assumption that, if comparable properties have sold at a certain price or within a certain range, then the subject property will sell at a comparable price or within a comparable range, assuming the continuation of current trends and supply/demand relationships.

The market value at any one time is based on conditions at the moment—money market conditions, supply and demand pressures, the degree of knowledge possessed by potential purchasers, consumer confidence, and the impact of existing or pending legislation which can have a positive or negative effect on income. Legislative effects can include tax consequences, rent controls, and court decisions having to do with landlord/tenant relationships and the environmental and social responsibilities of landlords (see Chapter 5).

Three approaches to market value There are three traditional ways to determine market value: (1) the replacement or production-cost approach, (2) the comparative sales or market approach, and (3) the economic or income approach. Of the three approaches to determining value, the income approach is the one most relied upon in establishing market value for income-producing properties, because it provides the best measure of the value of a specific property. In theory, the income approach sets the lower limit of value, and the replacement cost sets the upper limit of value. Correlation of the various measures for determining value is required to arrive at the market value within the value range established by the various measures.

Replacement or production-cost approach The replacement cost of a new property can be determined by figuring the lesser of two costs: for duplication, or for substitution. If a property can be readily substituted in the market (market approach), the market price can serve as replacement cost. However, if the actual cost to duplicate the property is less than the substitution cost, the duplication cost will serve as replacement cost. Should duplication cost exceed substitution cost, then substitution cost serves as replacement cost.

In setting the upper limit on value, production cost serves as a check on fictitious investment valuation. "Blue sky" is the term attributed to investment values which are substantially and unrealistically projected above production cost. Production cost serves as a check for the lender against blue-sky excesses.

The cost approach to value is represented in the following formula:

Land valuation + Improvement valuation = Production cost.

The section on land valuation in Chapter 4 discusses the market approach to land valuation. The improvement valuation is developed by estimating the cost of the improvements based on published cost data and the developer's cost data, when available.

Market approach

The premise of market value is that a buyer will not pay more for a property than for an acceptable substitute. Great weight is given to supply and demand factors in determining the market approach for determining market value. Market value is based on comparison of past sales with current market trends and asking prices. The forms in Chapter 6, Competitive Evaluation, provide a standardized format for collecting information for both marketing analysis and determining market value by the market approach.

The market approach to value is well suited for the valuation of non-income-producing residential properties. The economic approach is the most suitable for income-producing properties such as rental apartments.

When the appropriate data have been gathered and recorded on the forms included as exhibits in Chapter 6, they generally provide the value range for the subject development. However, when an innovation is offered which creates a temporary monopoly in the market area, a market value above the upper limit of the comparables may be justified by the unique supply and demand situation (a market monopoly) created by the innovation (see Chapters 7 and 11).

In comparing comparables and their respective prices, the real estate analyst must take into account value components which add to or detract from market value. Value components may include location, design, construction quality, amenity features existing on site or added as an improvement, trends, size, and numerous other components which add to or detract from value. Identifying value components is a marketing function requiring skill and sensitivity. Time of the sale and age of the property are other value components to be considered in equating costs, particularly in times of rapid price movements.

The price for which a comparable property is sold varies with the aggregate of the component values. Though the buyer of a property may not weigh component values separately to arrive at a judgment of price, he does weigh the component values in the aggregate to arrive at a judgment of whether or not the price is fair. Separate component values are often weighed by the buyer on a subconscious level; that is, the component values create an emotional response which triggers the buying motivation.

The real estate analyst must attempt to weigh the value components in the same way the buyer does. He can do this intuitively relying on his judgment, based on his experience and track record, but he can present the best case if he can base his findings on both detailed analysis and judgment. Then he can forecast with greater confidence and accuracy and demonstrate, with data, how he arrived at his findings. This process is not a substitution of analysis for judgment but a reinforcement of judgment with analysis.

The two market approaches to determining market value are value relationship analysis, and the gross income multiplier. The value relationship analysis is a method of value ranking for residential non-income-producing properties (see the section on value relationship analysis in Chapter 6). The gross income multiplier is a method of estimating value of income residential properties, as described below.

Gross income multiplier

The gross income multiplier is a tool to be used in conjunction with the market approach to determining value and a popular method for converting monthly or yearly gross income into value. It is a rule of thumb for early feasibility analysis and not to be relied upon for an exacting measure of value. The multiplier is based on average multiples of comparable properties and is computed by dividing the price by the gross annual income of the property:

$$\frac{\text{Price}}{\text{Gross annual income}} = \text{Gross income multiplier}.$$

	Comparables			
	1	2	3	4
Price (adjusted)	$700,000	$550,000	$900,000	$800,000
Gross income	$100,000	$ 84,615	$126,760	$117,647
Gross multiplier	7	6.5	7.1	6.8

Gross multiplier (average all sales): 6.85

To obtain the price for a subject property with a gross income of $85,000, the gross income is multiplied by the gross income multiplier derived from market comparables:

Gross income	$ 85,000
Gross income multiplier	× 6.25
Value	$582,250

The gross income multiplier is not a capitalization or income approach to value. A capitalization approach converts net income into a present value. The gross income multiplier does not consider net income, depreciation, deferred income, or any other components of return.

Multiples vary depending on type of property and location. The multiplier itself is determined by dividing the sales price by the gross income. When this is done on a representative sampling of comparable transactions in the market area, it is possible to arrive at an average gross multiplier figure.

The gross income multiplier should be used as a check only and in conjunction with capitalization and income approaches to value. It is possible that the property value, as determined by the gross multiplier, may allow no net income or even may result in negative income. However, when used with caution the gross income multiplier provides a quick initial feasibility check.

Economic approach

Using the economic approach, the market value is the present worth of the future net benefits from the property. The economic approach sets the lower limit to value.

The amount that can be borrowed on income-producing properties is based on the return of the property, and return is measured by the income approach to value. Lenders utilize a variety of concepts within the income approach to value to arrive at the market or economic value of a property. Loan amounts are then based on a loan/value ratio. A 75 percent loan/value ratio is typical on income-producing residential property.

The economic approach to market value assumes the most probable financing, both terms and amount, which the typical buyer is likely to achieve. The available amount, rate, and terms of financing have a significant influence on the amount a purchaser is justified in paying for the property. The financial assumptions, however, must be based on the availability and cost of funds to the typical investor.

To assume that the typical investor can structure and negotiate the "optimum" financing is to interject subjective criteria into the capitalization process. Market value is based on criteria applicable to the typical investor and must not be confused with investment value. Investment value is based on the criteria applicable to a specific investor, as opposed to the typical investor, and may reflect the specific investor's expertise in "trading on the equity." That is, a property may have significantly greater (investment) value to a specific individual than (market) value to the typical investor in the marketplace. Though a property may be sold at its investment value, the loan amount will generally be based on the market value.

The timing of resale of income-producing real estate will have a significant influence upon the overall yield projected. Income-producing properties are generally held for less than ten years, and use of a projection term within a five- to ten-year period is a true representation of market action. Use of a shorter projection period than the economic life of the property relies more on current data and increases the accuracy over projections for the economic life of the property. The total economic valuation is enhanced by the shorter projection period, due to the residual value of the equity position on reversion.

The economic approach to market value produces the indicated yield that the typical investor (usually assumed to be in the 50 percent tax bracket) can expect to receive. The yield is expressed as a before-tax and after-tax yield. The present worth of the yield enables the investor to compare the investment opportunity with other available opportunities.

Correlation

Analysts compute market value through a process of correlation whereby the three methods of determining market value (reproduction cost, market approach, and income approach) are evaluated as to their appropriateness to the specific value analysis. The analyst will give more weight to the most appropriate approach for the specific value analysis.

Correlation helps the analyst discover errors that might not come to light if a single evaluation technique were used. Correlation also adds support to the final opinion of value. It sets the value range from which the analyst will choose the most probable value, replacement cost setting the upper limit and income analysis setting the lower limit on the value range.

INVESTMENT VALUE

The market value approach, based on income capitalization, establishes value to the market in general. The investment value approach, based on mortgage equity methods of capitalization, establishes the price an individual investor is justified in paying. When market value has been established, based on typical market and financial considerations, the price that the investor is justified in paying—the investment value—can be determined. This will generally result in an addition to or subtraction from market value. Such attributes as pride of ownership, exceptional management, financial terms, encumberances, utility to the owner, and trends which have a bearing on the benefits to be derived by the owner are taken into consideration in establishing the investment value of the property for a specific owner.

It is not appropriate to consider how such attributes of the property affect a specific owner when establishing the economic market value. To do so would inject price-influencing personal considerations into the capitalization process and undermine objectivity in determining value in relation to the market as a whole.

It is important, in any measurement of value, to distinguish between market value and investment value. Market value is a single value derived by utilizing information and experiences typical to the market area. Investment value of a property is not a single value but a value which will vary according to the wide differences in buyers and their subjective position relative to the investment.

Market value, then, can be termed "objective" value, and investment value can be termed "subjective." The objective value is adjusted by the subjective value differentials applicable to the individual investor, to establish the justified price. The subjective value adjusts for the entrepreneurial skill of the investor in trading on the equity. Subjective value also adjusts for the management expertise of the investor and the effects of trends including inflation or deflation.

The sophisticated buyer does not constantly shop for underpriced properties or uninformed sellers but creates his own bargains by adding subjective value to property. The bargain can be created through creative structuring and trading on the equity, or by seeking out properties with a low subjective value to the seller but a high subjective value to the buyer. A creative buyer with marketing and merchandising expertise can often transform obstacles into opportunities or envision new, more productive uses for the property that were not envisioned by the seller.

Leverage: Trading on the equity

It is advisable to borrow funds when the use to which the funds are to be applied shows a higher return than the cost of borrowing. Trading on the equity increases not the earning capacity of the property but the percentage compensation, on equity, to the investor by reducing the investor's equity position. Reducing equity, which increases mortgage indebtedness, also increases risk by raising the break-even point and reducing the loan coverage ratio. (This is not to be confused with the loan/value ratio.)

Trading on the equity is particularly rewarding when there is a generous spread between return on investment (gross assets) and the cost of funds (percentage return). As the cost of funds approaches the return on investment, the advantages of leverage diminish. This does not necessarily mean that the investment is no longer feasible. It may not suit the investor with limited equity, but for an investor who can put up all cash—generally an institutional investor such as a pension fund—it may be feasible.

Equity return: Measure of investment value

When sufficient margin exists between return on assets and the cost of mortgage funds, trading on the equity can increase the value of the equity position. A simplified example, using three investment alternatives, is as follows:

	Alternative A	Alternative B	Alternative C
Market value	$200,000	$200,000	$200,000
Net income	20,000	20,000	20,000
Overall rate percentage	10%	10%	10%
Mortgage loan	130,000	150,000	170,000
Interest cost at 8%	10,400	12,000	13,600
Cash flow	9,600	8,000	6,400
Equity required	70,000	50,000	30,000
Equity yield percentage	13.7%	16.0%	21.3%

Though the market value of the property remains constant, the investment value varies with the capability of the investor to trade on the equity. In the example above, the yield on the equity was increased from 13.7 to 21.3 percent by varying the loan/value ratio or by leveraging the investment. If the interest rate can also be lowered, because of the risk reduction resulting from stability of the investor, the subjective or investment value is increased further.

METHODS FOR MEASURING RETURN

Various methods may be utilized to measure return. Some of the methods frequently utilized in the industry measure various aspects of return and thus present only a partial picture of return. That is, they may measure one or more of the components of return (cash flow, tax shelter of cash flow, excess tax shelter, equity buildup, and appreciation) without considering all of the components of return and the timing or present value of the return. These incomplete methods can be useful for rule-of-thumb decision making in the preliminary stages of analysis, but they can also be misleading in the hands of investors who do not fully understand their limitations.

Present-value theory, the most meaningful measure of investment return, is expressed as a present worth of future net incomes, or as the internal rate of return of the future income streams. These measurements of return take into account the time value of money and all the other components of return. Other popularly utilized measures of return provide a less complete picture of the investment and are not suitable for ranking competing investments in their order of desirability. However, they are nonetheless widely used measures of return and should be understood in terms of their general usefulness and limitations.

Components of return

The benefits of real estate investment are both financial and nonfinancial. All of the benefits cannot be reduced to financial terms, but for the purpose of determining investment value only the financial components of return will be included here. These include benefits in:

1. Cash flow.
2. Tax shelter of cash flow plus excess tax shelter.
3. Equity buildup—the value which results from amortization of the mortgage.
4. Appreciation—the margin of appreciation over actual depreciation of the property over time.

Cash on cash return

Cash on cash return, sometimes called percentage cash flow return, includes (1) cash on cash return, one-year basis, and (2) cash on cash average return. These methods compute return before taxes and are not an overall indication of return, in that they do not take into consideration the other components of return: tax savings, mortgage reduction, and appreciation. Because the measurement does not consider taxes, the cash flow is not certain in that a portion may not be spendable due to tax obligations. The percentage cash flow method does not consider timing of the cash income, which can have a marked effect on the present value of the income stream.

$$\frac{\text{Cash flow}}{\text{Cash equity}} = \text{Cash on cash return}$$

Total return before tax savings

The method for ranking investments most often used by syndicators and brokers is on the basis of total return before tax savings. It is utilized in marketing properties to investors because it will normally lead to conclusions which overstate the present value of the cash flow. The procedure for computing total return before tax savings is as follows:

$$\frac{\text{Average cash flow} + \text{Average equity buildup} + \text{Average appreciation}}{\text{Equity investment}}$$
$$= \text{Total return before tax savings}$$

This method does not take into consideration the tax aspects of return or the timing of the return. It cannot rank alternative investment opportunities because it does not reduce the income to a present value. Taxes will be due on sale at both the capital gain and ordinary income rate which are not accounted for. The equity buildup and appreciation is a deferred yield and not spendable as accrued. Because the equity buildup increases in the later stages of the holding period but is figured as an average annual amount, the total return method leads to erroneous conclusions as to present worth. This is also true for appreciation because it cannot be realized until converted into cash through refinance or sale.

After-tax return for a single year

$$\frac{\text{Cash flow} + \text{Tax savings}}{\text{Cash investment}} = \text{After-tax return}$$

The tax savings in the formula above represent the net benefit to the investor of the tax losses. Tax losses are not uniformly valued because the value is dependent upon the tax bracket of the investor and his need for excess-tax shelter. The tax savings in the formula are the sum of the net interest expense benefits and net depreciation benefits to the individual investor. After-tax return does not consider the other components of return — mortgage reduction and appreciation. It also does not consider the timing of the cash income.

Percentage yield

Percentage yield is the measure of cash flow plus principal payments as a percentage return on investment. Percentage yield is a rule-of-thumb measurement in that the principal payment is not available or spendable until the property is sold or refinanced. As such, the principal payments are a deferred yield available at such time as there is a recession through sale or refinance.

$$\frac{\text{Cash flow + Principal payments}}{\text{Cash investment}} = \text{Percentage yield}$$

Capitalization, overall rate

The overall rate is the ratio which represents the relationship between the capitalized value of a property (land and buildings) and the annual net income of the property. The overall rate is generally greater than the land rate and less than the building rate of capitalization. Higher quality properties with dependable incomes have lower capitalization rates, and the lower the quality of a property and its income, the higher the capitalization rate.

To determine the overall capitalization rate, the annual net income for both land and buildings is divided by the price; thus, $9,000/$100,000 = 9 percent. When both land and building income are converted directly into value through an overall capitalization rate, the method is called direct capitalization. The direct capitalization method is a shortcut and not recommended when more information is available, because it assumes that the subject property is identical in characteristics, age, and land/building ratios as the comparables used to compute the ratios. This is seldom the case.

Conventional capitalization, which deals with annual income as a return on total property values over the life of the property improvement, is often used to determine the economic market value of a property. Another way to utilize the capitalization process to determine value is to capitalize the equity to arrive at an equity value. When equity value is added to mortgage amount(s), the overall value is determined. This is called equity capitalization; it is used to determine investment value rather than market value.

Investment value, based on the equity capitalization technique, is dependent on return on equity, not return on investment (the total property). More information is required for equity capitalization than for conventional capitalization. For equity capitalization the analyst must know the following:

1. Duration of the holding period.
2. The anticipated yield.
3. Financing terms, including loan/value ratio, interest, and length of mortgage.
4. Projected appreciation or depreciation over the holding period.
5. The tax consequence.

Then, given the net income, the resulting value will provide for the anticipated yield, utilizing the other inputs.

Average annual return

Average annual return considers all of the components of return—including cash flow, tax shelter, equity buildup and appreciation—but does not consider the timing of the returns so as to develop a present-value worth of the income streams. Because of this deficiency, average annual return is limited in its ability to rank alternative investments in their order of desirability.

Computation of average annual accounting return involves the following procedure:

1. Total all net benefits and subtract the initial investment from the total. The remainder is profit.
2. Divide profit by the number of years to arrive at average annual profit.
3. Divide average annual profit by the initial investment to arrive at the average annual return.

To illustrate how return is figured, the average annual return is computed for three investment alternatives as shown:

Year	Alternative A inflow	Alternative B inflow	Alternative C inflow
1	$2,000	0	$1,000
2	2,000	0	3,000
3	1,000	$1,000	1,000
4	1,000	3,000	1,000
5	0	2,000	1,000
Total	$6,000	$6,000	$7,000
Investment	4,000	4,000	4,000
Profit	$2,000	$2,000	$3,000
÷ Years held	5	5	5
Average annual profit	$ 400/yr.	$ 400/yr.	$ 600/yr.
÷ Investment	$4,000	$4,000	$4,000
Average annual rate of return	10%/yr.	10%/yr.	15%/yr.

Land-residual method

The land-residual method separates income property into two economic parts: the land, and the investment exclusive of land. Investment exclusive of land includes cost of improvements and services. When investment exclusive of land is deducted from the total investment value, the remainder is land value, referred to as the residual land value.

The residual land value technique is useful in determining the highest and best use of the land. When studies are made for various potential uses of the land, the one that produces the highest residual land value is the highest and best use. The amount which will amortize the investment, exclusive of land, at an appropriate rate is deducted from the total projected return. The remainder of the total projected return is capitalized to give land value. When land is not developed to its highest and best use, the residual land value method measures the extent to which value losses are attributable to the physical improvements. This is a measure of functional or economic obsolescence.

The residual method is an income check on value as established by the market approach. Because of speculative and other pressures in the marketplace, the market approach may indicate a value in excess of that justified by the income approach.

Land is residual in character from an economic standpoint. That is, the physical improvements constructed upon the land must be compensated first, or they will cease to function. The balance remaining after compensation for the physical improvements is the residual to compensate for the land. The residual income based on highest and best use provides the basis for land value.

The land-residual technique is utilized when buildings are new or their values are known with reasonable accuracy. The technique is then used to determine land value. By adding land and improvement value together, the value of the property as a whole is known. The technique is also utilized when land is vacant and available for development under its highest and best use. The land-residual method can be used to determine which land uses, over a period of years, will produce the highest residual land income and consequently the highest present value of the land.

RISK ANALYSIS

There are two basic types of risk involved in an investment proposal: business risk, and financial risk. Business risk is concerned with the capability of the business to meet the equity requirements at any given time, to provide for the continuance of the endeavor. Financial risk is concerned with the ability of the investment to generate income sufficient to meet the expense obligations of the enterprise.

Risk analysis is both quantitative and qualitative. Cash flow and sensitivity analyses provide a measure of the quantitative return, or risk. Measuring the qualitative risk, however, requires judgment and experience, since quality of input cannot be readily judged through a quantitative or numbers approach. ROI analysis as a numbers approach is limited to quantitative analysis.

SENSITIVITY ANALYSIS

Feasibility must also be concerned with the quantitative risk consequences of variations in input; it not be limited to projecting a single average or optimum investment return. One method of representing risk is to present the range of financial consequences that could foreseeably occur due to variations in the backup budgets, schedule projections, and financing (see Chapter 21). This method of valuation and risk is commonly called sensitivity analysis.

Sensitivity analysis is most generally utilized, with equity capitalization techniques, to project equity value, since investment expectations vary from assumed conditions. There are seven variables which affect the equity capitalization:

1. Mortgage interest.
2. Loan/value ratio.
3. Projected appreciation.
4. Projected depreciation.
5. Holding period of investment.
6. Length of mortgage.
7. New annual income.

In sensitivity analysis, the variables are changed within wide parameters to show how value changes with changes in the variables. Each variable is changed from the assumed position, without changing any of the other variables, to indicate the magnitude of variance in value created by the variable being tested.

Through sensitivity analysis, the investor can determine which of the variables have the greatest impact on value as they vary. In this manner the investor becomes sensitive, in the negotiation or structuring process, to those variables or bargaining positions he can relinquish because they have minimal effect on equity value, and those that he cannot relinquish because they have optimum effect on equity value. The informed investor can trade off positions which have a low subjective value to himself for those that have a high subjective value. He is thus in a better position to trade on the equity (see Chapter 4).

In that sensitivity analysis provides a range of conditions resulting from variations in the input, the calculations are much more extensive than those required when only a single set of assumptions is analyzed. Sensitivity analysis requires a computer capability, but, since packaged, nontechnical computer programs are available, specialized computer technology is not necessary. Computers can be relatively simple to use. Packaged or standard investment models make further programming or calculations unnecessary. The analyst merely enters his input data on source cards or enters them directly into a terminal unit.

As an alternative, preprinted charts, graphs, and tables developed by computer can provide the same information as is available through direct use of a computer facility. These preprinted materials provide the analyst with tools so he can easily test out multiple assumptions within the variables, with a minimal amount of time and effort.

BAND OF INVESTMENT: HOW TO DETERMINE THE OVERALL INTEREST RATE

The band-of-investment method is a procedure for determining the overall interest on a property with a combination of mortgages and equity participations. When the analyst or developer is structuring an investment from a preliminary feasibility standpoint and the details are not yet known, a typical transaction can be structured as discussed below.

First, the typical loan/value ratio (assume 65 percent of value) and interest rate (assume 8 percent) required by lenders on similar properties is determined. Then the amount of equity investment (assume 20 percent) and the rate of return (assume 14 percent) required by the investor are determined. If the difference between the first mortgage amount and the cost required for the venture is more than the sponsor can supply in equity, a second mortgage (in this case 15 percent of value) may be required to fill the gap (assume 10 percent interest). The overall interest rate for the first mortgage, equity investment, and second mortgage would be calculated as follows:

	Percent of value	Interest
First mortgage	65%	8%
Second mortgage	15	10
Equity	20	14

The overall rate of interest for capitalization purposes can then be computed as follows:

$$8\% \text{ first mortgage} \times 65\% \text{ of value} = 5.2\%$$
$$10\% \text{ second mortgage} \times 15\% \text{ of value} = 1.5$$
$$14\% \text{ equity} \times 20\% \text{ of value} = \underline{2.8}$$
$$\text{Overall interest rate} = 9.5\%$$

SIGNIFICANT RATIOS

Break-even point

The break-even point, like the debt coverage ratio, is a measure of the cushion available to meet debt obligations. Thus it is a measure of the probability that debt obligations will be met in good times and bad.

$$\frac{\text{Vacancy} + \text{Operating expenses} + \text{Debt service}}{\text{Indicated gross income}} = \text{Break-even point}$$

A typical percentage distribution of the components appears below:

Vacancy	5%
Operating expenses	40
Debt service	45
Cash flow	10
Indicated gross income	100%

Debt coverage ratio

The annual debt service should be covered by the income, with a sufficient margin that the likelihood of default will be minimal. The concept is that there should be sufficient funds in the project so that the developer will not be bankrupt by negative cash flows in bad markets or lose interest by getting most of the profit out in the initial financing.

$$\frac{\text{Net income}}{\text{Debt service}} = \text{Debt coverage ratio}$$

PAYBACK PERIOD

The payback period is a measure of the time it takes to pay back the original investment out of the cash flow. This is the reciprocal of percentage return on investment. Developers generally look for a payback period of less than five years, whereas passive investors seek a payback period of ten years or more. The payback period measurement is most meaningful to developers who plan to plow back the investment into continued development operations.

The cash flow to be used in figuring the payback period can be figured on a before-tax or after-tax basis. The after-tax basis, which considers spendable tax savings, presents the most realistic picture for investments which are heavily tax oriented. Cash flows for the three investment alternatives considered above are as follows:

	Alternative A		Alternative B		Alternative C	
Year	Outlay	Inflow	Outlay	Inflow	Outlay	Inflow
0	$1,000	0	$4,000	0	$2,000	0
1	1,000	$2,000	0	0	1,000	$1,000
2	500	2,000	0	0	1,000	3,000
3	500	1,000	0	$1,000	0	1,000
4	500	1,000	0	3,000	0	1,000
5	500	0	0	2,000	0	1,000
	$4,000	$6,000	$4,000	$6,000	$4,000	$7,000

In the investment decision example, the payback periods for the three alternatives are as follows:

Alternative A: Two years
Alternative B: Four years
Alternative C: Three years

The payback analysis ranks the alternatives in order of preference according to payback as follows:

First order of preference: A
Second order of preference: C
Third order of preference: B

While the payback analysis tells the investor when he should receive his money back, it does not indicate the profitability of the alternatives and their return. (See Chapter 21 for more on significant ratios.)

CASH FLOW ANALYSIS

The cash flow analysis is the backbone of economic analysis. The two key measurements of cash flow analysis are return on investment and return on equity. The return on investment is a key indication of feasibility. Once it is determined that there is a suitable return on investment, the manager can analyze methods to increase return through leverage and structuring to produce the optimum return on equity. If the return on investment is inadequate, leveraging will tend to increase risk disproportionately to the incremental investment returns to be gained from leverage. By adding cash flow returns through depreciation write-offs, the investment return can be further enhanced. It must be remembered, however, that depreciation is often real, and a postponement of tax obligation rather than an elimination of obligation. The return on investment, as previously stated, sets the magnitude of return and is a good measure of preliminary feasibility.

Cash flow analysis: An economic panorama

The cash flow analysis is a summation of all the backup analysis which goes into the preparation of the feasibility analysis. It relies on the correctness of the backup income and expense projections, the market analysis, financing assumptions, and overall project scheduling and phasing. Orderliness in the sequential presentation is important, in order to present an economic panorama of the cash flow consequences.

Mortgage interest and principal payments are deducted from the net operating income to yield before-tax cash flow. Depreciation, as calculated in the depreciation schedule, plus interest payments are subtracted from the cash flow. The resulting taxable income (loss) is processed according to the investor tax bracket, to indicate the tax obligation to be deducted from the cash flow or the tax savings to be added to cash flow.

The resulting after-tax income stream is then indicated in dollar amounts per year. The present value of the after-tax cash flow stream is given as an internal rate of return, so that the investment opportunity being studied can be ranked with other alternate investment opportunities. (See the cash flow exhibits in Chapter 21.)

Cash flow projection: An evolutionary process

Cash flow projections represent a development's timetable and income and expense projections over a period of time. Because conditions inevitably change over time, these changes must be reflected, as time progresses, to reflect changes which have occurred over the time that will affect future projections.

That is, a cash flow projection is not a static, cast-in-stone game plan but a projection based on current, incomplete information which must be revised as more complete and more timely information is received. For this reason cash flow projections require periodic review and updating to reflect current conditions, rather than the conditions that existed at the time the cash flow analysis was originally cast.

20

The management information system: Providing better information on which to act

There is a tendency for systems and programs specialists to resist change in their programs once they have been established. Change in the information and control system thus does not keep pace with changes in the operating organization and its objectives. In this respect, this system may not relate well to the real world. There is a tendency to force the problem to conform with the system, rather than changing the system to suit the problem.

Management information systems (MIS) exert pressures because they are management's most vital tool in measuring performance. Managers will commit resources to produce whatever the MIS will report as good results. If the MIS does not properly reflect the current operation and objectives, the "results" reported can be misleading because they are not a measure of attainment of current critical objectives. Management will also tend to deemphasize some critical results because measurement is difficult. In this manner the system puts pressure on noncritical objectives at the expense of those that are critical but more difficult to measure. This creates an imbalance, the archenemy of economy.

First-level management is where the results are achieved in an organization; at this level the product is produced and sold, most of the revenue is spent, and most of the employees are managed. All other levels of management exist to support first-level management and make it as effective as possible. A misconception in higher levels of management is that first-level management should be adaptable to the control policies and procedures of upper management, so that upper-level management can perform as efficiently as possible. In such a case the tail tends to wag the dog, and management's roles become reversed. It is the upper levels management that must conform to the needs of first-level management, not vice versa. When policy procedures and controls are geared to upper management's needs, without regard for those of first-level management, upper-level management drags down first-level management performance.

Management information systems often are deficient in providing data that fit first-level management problems. This is a common reason why computer programs frequently produce disappointing results or run into excessively high costs. Upper-level management must continuously receive feedback on first-level management problems as they currently exist (not one, five, or ten years ago) if the MIS is to be practical. Decisions, policies, procedures, and controls should be directed to first-level needs. If upper management is not fully aware of first-level needs, then management does not really understand the business it is to manage.

Computerized management information systems have provided a large breakthrough in management control. The computer makes possible fast, exacting, and flexible control of work in process, thus allowing management to identify and correct variances and deficiencies sooner and to forecast final results better.

ESSENTIAL CHARACTERISTICS OF A MANAGEMENT INFORMATION SYSTEM

An effective management information system should raise the right questions with the right persons at the right time. Characteristics which are essential to an MIS include the following:

1. Integrated reporting. Each level in the reporting system is tied to the level above and the level below, so management can trace an activity from a top-level report to a lower-level one, with no intervening gaps. The lower-level report should be summarized as one line or figure in the next-higher-level report. Any deviations can then be traced in the reporting system level by level, to the lowest operational or cost level.
2. Zero-base reporting. Information is captured at its origin or source. Unless information is gathered at the lowest meaningful level, lower-level management will not be able to provide meaningful reports or to answer questions critical to higher levels of management. If information is not captured at its origin, it will not be available for future reporting and analysis.
3. Reporting by responsibility or function. Reporting must reflect responsibility and accountability to enable management to measure performance against projected goals. All costs should be assigned to an individual, whenever possible.
4. Reporting by exception. A reporting system should bring to the attention of management exceptions in procedures and results about which it should be concerned. Exceptions concentrate the attention of management on deviations from goals which require immediate attention.
5. Reporting against a standard. A standard of comparison must exist to make reported information meaningful. Two meaningful standards are the budget and the previous year's performance. (See budget exhibits in Chapter 21.)

6. Reporting performance ratios. Reporting performance information in the form of key ratios provides valuable information to management for tracking trends, identifying emerging problems, and analyzing performance.
7. Reporting external economic data and marketing data. This is as necessary as the reporting of internal data. The company must be kept well advised at all times of its relation to the economy, the market, and cycles to keep market planning, objectives, and strategies current.

GENERAL ACCOUNTING

General accounting or financial accounting is primarily concerned with record keeping and the preparation of monthly and annual financial statements to keep management, owners, creditors, and the public informed. Cost accounting is that phase of general accounting which informs management of the unit cost of goods produced and sold.

COST ACCOUNTING

Cost accounting is a management tool to compare actual costs and expenese with predetermined budgets and standards. It also enables management to compare the economic consequences of alternate choices. Cost accounting provides systematic, comparative cost records to assist management in the following functions:

1. Establishing profit goals.
2. Setting strategies and action plans to accomplish goals.
3. Measuring and controlling progress.
4. Analyzing and evaluating alternate courses of action and remedial actions required when activity strays from objectives.

The accounting operation provides action reports to various levels of management for communication and control. Reports are directed to three levels: top management, middle management, and first-level management. The information provided must be appropriate to the management level and function of the individual to which it is directed. The accountant's method of classifying costs, called the chart of accounts, must be closely associated with the organizational structure and individual functions. (See chart of accounts in Chapter 21.)

Costs must be associated with the existing jurisdictional areas within the organization and tied to projects, subcontracts, functions, and programs in such a manner as to align them with those individuals responsible for their execution. Cost accounting brings to the attention of management any results that require correction. Thus cost accounting is a method for executive control.

There are three basic functions in cost accounting: (1) cost determination, (2) cost control, and (3) cost analysis. To serve these three cost accounting functions, costs must be classified and grouped so that:

1. The significant unit costs can be determined.
2. Trends and velocity in cost movement can be observed and controlled.
3. Analysis can be based on cost movements to remedy or improve operations.

The construction of a cost accounting system requires a thorough understanding of the organizational structure of the company, the manufacturing or construction process, and the type and detail of cost information desired by management. The cost system and the operating accounts must correspond with the organizational chain of authority so that specific individuals can be held responsible for specific costs. The cost presentation should be designed to flag deviations from projections, in order to promote "management by exception."

BUDGETING

Budgeting is a means of planning, coordinating, and controlling the total resources of an organization into an action plan based upon historical performance, current opportunities and obstacles, and an enlightened judgment of the probable influence of unknown future conditions. The objective of budgeting is to substitute astute, sensitive deliberation, analysis, and planning for haphazard success or failure in a business enterprise. Budgeting compels discipline in identifying problems and reaching decisions and serves as a policy statement which guides incremental decisions and forecasts.

Budgeting is a planning tool in that it provides management with a projection of revenues and expenses in sufficient time for corrective action to be taken before it is too late. Budgeting is a coordinating tool in that it provides management information with which to fine tune the relationships between revenues and expenses (sales and capacity). Various operations or divisions within an organization will function at optimum performance to meet corporate objectives when their activities are coordinated by a budget which establishes policy and priorities. Budgeting does not itself establish control, but it is necessary before a disciplined control can be established. Controls are the procedures necessary to ensure the organization's adherence to the budget once established; they act as flags which signal the need for corrective action.

The budget enables planned results to be expressed in quantitative terms. Results stated in quantitative terms are easier to measure and monitor than results stated in qualitative or subjective terms. Budgets provide a point against which activities may be measured and controlled. When all phases of a business have been incorporated into a budget program, the budget becomes a written quantitative expression of the management plan. The budget coordinates all strategies and action plans into a homogeneous unit and helps promote internal harmony and unanimity of purpose.

SETTING UP THE BUDGET

Since effective budgets represent a commitment by the people who must carry them out, these people must have a large role in developing the budget if their commitment is to be meaningful. Budgets prepared solely by operating personnel or by top management and staff budgeting personnel are generally less successful than budgets prepared both from the top down and the bottom up. Knowledge and measurement of cost and profit should be pushed to the lowest meaningful level of the organization, in order to optimize profit, yet the effort should be directed, coordinated, and controlled from the top down.

The two basic frameworks for setting up a budget are the company's organization chart and the chart of accounts (see Chapter 21). The chart of accounts should reflect organizational structure, so that the accounts can be tied directly to the operations or activities which justify a budget. Small organizations may have a single individual directing the development of the budget, and larger ones may use a budget committee composed of executives responsible for major functions in the business.

In the development of budgets, executives and specialists perform the following functions:

1. Sales or marketing executives are requested to estimate sales and sales budgets.
2. Production executives are requested to estimate costs of running their organizations and producing the inventory justified by sales projections.
3. The budget director supplies executives with information regarding historical costs and projections for trends.
4. Estimated budgets are received from various executives, reviewed, and included in the master budget.
5. The various budgets are coordinated and revised to optimize resources and serve as a statement of policy.
6. Executives are informed of revisions made in their estimated budgets as a result of coordination of all budgets and the setting of policy and priorities.
7. Executives are informed of their performance on a periodic basis by comparing actual results with budgeted results.

Establishing the level of detail desired

Budgets must contain the detail required by management for operations control. Budget formats should closely follow operational procedures and formats to simplify the task of interfacing budgets and controls with operations. As management tools, budgets depend on the quality of the source material received from operations.

Budgets and schedules are recapitulated into their simplest summary forms for use in the investment analysis. Budgets may be consolidated into major headings, and schedules may be summarized in monthly or annual terms.

Particularly in times of unstable costs, a detailed cost recovery system is necessary to provide historical data for future budget projections. Costs should be broken down into as many components as is practical. Future budgets should be estimated by component cost groups which match the component cost groups of completed and in-stream projects. In budgeting, projected costs are then based on current or recent costs, with adjustments to reflect cost increase or decrease.

There can be dramatic fluctuations within the component costs which comprise the total cost of a project, with some costs going down and others exploding upward. For this reason, component costs should be considered and adjusted separately. An adjustment of aggregate costs, which in effect bypasses an analysis of component costs, is chancy at best and can be very misleading.

When working with component costs, each cost component can be evaluated against historical costs and material and labor cost trends. For example, asphalt may be up 20 percent from historical costs and climbing at a 20 percent annualized rate, whereas plywood may be down 15 percent from historical costs and have a level price trend.

There are numerous sources for gathering information on costs and current prices and trends:

1. A company's own purchasing experience.
2. Newsletters from trade associations.
3. Suppliers and manufacturers.
4. Subcontractor estimates.
5. Government reports.
6. Private reports available to subscribers and published, updated cost-estimating manuals.

FIXED AND FLEXIBLE BUDGETS

When the activities of a company can be estimated within close limits, a fixed budget is satisfactory. The word "fixed" is somewhat misleading because it merely means that the budget is not adjusted to actual results. The budget represents figures, fixed in advance, with which actual results are compared.

Budgets are based on definite assumptions regarding volume or velocity and costs of materials and labor. If business conditions take a radical change from fixed projections, the projections cannot be expected to be reliable or effective. Because outcomes are affected by fluctuations in volume and prices which are not subject to management control, flexible budgets are used. For any given volume of business or pricing structure, there should be a norm for expenditures, and that norm should be known beforehand to provide a reference point for actual expenditures.

Variation in absorption rates and rates of change in costs for financing, materials, and labor require a series of budgets to determine economic consequences due to changes in the assumptions on which the budget is based. This incorporates sensitivity analysis into the budget process. Projects with a long payout over a period of years are more benefited by sensitivity analysis than those with a short payout, since those with a short cycle offer less risk therefore justify less analysis.

CASH BUDGETS

Cash budgets include budgets for a period, and budgets for a project or activity. The cash budget estimates cash receipts and disbursements for the budget period. This is an extremely useful management tool for planning cash requirements and coordinating cash inflow and outflow to synchronize cash resources and needs. The cash budget points up the need for additional debt or equity funds, and as such it can affect the timing or structure of the proposed budgeted activity.

Cash budgets are prepared to extend over a budget period, which will vary depending on the company and its cash position. Smaller companies, which generally have fewer assets and greater volatility in operations, need shorter budget periods than do larger companies with more working capital. Smaller companies may require a weekly budget period, and larger ones may utilize a monthly or quarterly period.

EFFECTS OF BUSINESS CAPACITY AND ACTIVITY ON BUDGET

The objectives of a budget are to provide management with an organized procedure for planning; a method for coordinating the activities of various activities, departments, or divisions of a business; and a base for cost control. To accomplish these objectives, an acceptable projection of costs under varying conditions should be available.

Capacity is the amount of resources in land, subcontractors, financing, personnel, consultants, expertise, and so on, which an organization has available to conduct its business. Activity is related to capacity by the fact that activity attempts to make the best use of existing capacity. Sales determines activity up to the point that capacity acts as a constraint on increasing activity. The budget assists by bringing harmony between sales volume or activity and capacity. There are three levels of capacity: theoretical, practical, and normal.

1. Theoretical capacity assumes that an organization can perform at full speed, full time, without interruption. This is referred to as 100 percent capacity.
2. Practical capacity makes allowances for unavoidable interruptions, failures, labor shortages, strikes, and so on. The practical capacity may range from 70 to 85 percent of theoretical capacity. This capacity is the result of internal influences and does not consider the chief external cause for reduced capacity—lack of sales.
3. Normal capacity requires a modification downward from practical capacity to reflect actual capacity over a period of time long enough to level out the peaks and valleys which come with seasonal and cyclical

variations. The normal capacity may be only 50 percent or more of the theoretical capacity. Finding the optimum or best obtainable balance between capacity and sales volume constitutes one of the greatest challenges to management.

When normal capacity has been determined and "normal" operating expenses determined, operating expense rates can be determined. Subtracting operating expense rates from the gross profit will result in all overhead for the period being absorbed, provided normal capacity and expenses prevail during the period.

The difficulty with budgeting in a highly inflationary environment is that standard costs become unreliable, to the point of standards being almost nonexistent. When a market is whipsawed with a combination of inflation and scarcity, costs can rise as much as 100 percent or more in a month's time, when movements are stated on an annualized basis. In such an environment standard costs are unreliable, to say the least, and costs can only be determined with reliability by going out to bid. This increases risk because profit and risk cannot readily be determined on the basis of cost estimates but must await actual bid costs. In times of inflation and scarcity, profit margins are generally reduced, compounding the risk to the developer in packaging a real estate development.

CONTROL

Control is the process whereby management monitors results by measuring actual results against a plan or standard. Companies are structured into staff and line functions. The line function does the directing, guiding, and restraining, and the staff function prepares and analyzes data on the basis of which recommendations are made to line personnel for controlling.

Small companies tend to have staff and line functions performed by the same individuals. The owner or manager of a small organization can often maintain adequate control without a highly developed management information system, because of his intimate knowledge of the business. In larger companies the controller supervises general accounting, cost accounting, budgeting, statistics and analysis, and systems procedures. The treasurer relies on information prepared by the controller for financial administration, forecasting, and the provision of cash requirements.

How control facilitates delegation of authority

The manager can delegate only to the extent that he can be assured that the work is being accomplished within prescribed limits. The better the controls, the greater the potential for delegation. Controls are necessary to both the manager and his subordinates. For the subordinate, they provide a specific standard to be measured against and feedback on performance, which is essential to the employee's security, confidence, and satisfaction with the work being accomplished. When the subordinate is aware of his responsibility and accountability, he or she is a more enthusiastic worker.

There are four activities in the control process:

1. Development of performance standards—the plan.
2. Measurement of performance against the standards.
3. Evaluation, analysis, and interpretation of results.
4. Correction and improvement.

In control, managers often do not perceive the distinction between technical and management activities, so they get involved in techniques as opposed to results. In such an instance the manager controls the technique of how a function is to be performed. When techniques must conform to the manager's personal standards, initiative and innovation are discouraged.

The management function is planning, setting the standard, and measuring the performance against the standard. The "how to," or the technique, should be delegated to a subordinate. This frees the manager from excessive detail and provides a challenge and an opportunity for independent action for the subordinate. Thus the manager can devote more time to planning, to eliminate the ill effects of variance before they occur (see Chapter 25).

To maximize the accountability of subordinates, reports should enable them to identify and correct variances from the program before they are called to account for them by the manager. Self-direction and independence of action on the part of subordinates are the essence of management by exception. Work checked by others leaves a residue of resentment, but when employees have the information to correct their own work, they find much more satisfaction in it and are enthusiastic about it. For self-direction to be effective, however, the employee should be directly involved in formulating the standards, policies, and procedures by which he must operate.

Control can be most economically administered at the immediate point of action. The person actually doing the work should have the most information about the work being done and should be the first to receive report results. When subordinates utilize self-direction in correcting their own work, there is more economy in coordination and greater speed in instituting corrective action.

The better the plan and standards, the better the reporting will be because it is easier to report variances and exceptions on well-defined plans and standards than on those that are general or vague. Highlighting variances and exceptions promotes management by exception. A variance is a deficiency which occurs within the limits of predetermined tolerances; variances should be corrected by the accountable manager and, with effective self-direction, should not require an inquiry by the next-level manager. An exception in a deficiency which occurs outside the limits of predetermined tolerances; exceptions require immediate inquiry by someone other than the accountable manager. Exceptions therefore should be reported to staff and to higher level management for corrective action. Frequently they involve a broader area of accountability than that held by the manager in charge.

Lack of inquiry into variances by upper-level management does not imply that the accountable manager can continue to produce variances. It merely means that this manager is given the opportunity to correct the variance himself, without intervention from others. When variances go uncorrected, the tolerance becomes in effect the standard.

There are two types of corrective action for deficiencies: management action and operating action. Operating actions generally correct symptoms rather than causes, and as such they have short-term patch-up capabilities. Management actions go to the root causes of deficiencies and are often long-term in nature; this requires improving the plan or modifying the standards, policies, procedures, or organization. If operating action is not supported by management action, a deficiency can become a recurrent problem.

AUTOMATED VERSUS MANUAL SYSTEMS

An automated management information system can reduce costs for many companies, compared to a manual system. More effective, more accurate, and more timely data can also be generated with an automated system. Management can obtain reports for sensitivity analysis, to spot trends, isolate trouble spots, and make forecasts which would not be feasible with a manual system.

There are comparatively low-cost packaged computer programs on the market which can spare a company the expense of developing its own program from scratch, such as by hiring a software company to develop a custom program. Some of the packaged programs possess a good deal of flexibility in meeting the differing needs of various companies. One such program was developed by Kenneth Leventhal and Company for the real estate development and construction industry. A description of this program is presented as Case Study I below.

In the budget, projections, controls, and analysis chapters, budget and control formats are illustrated to inform the reader of type, scope, and level of detail of accounting information generally required by management. These schedules do not include the entire accounting function but are presented to show the general scope of information required and the format used.

The general format of these plans follows closely that established in the *Accounting System for All Builders*, formulated by the National Association of Home builders, Washington, D.C., in order to maintain the standardization which the NAHB encourages. Though the Standardized Policy for Budgeting presented in this book generally reflects the major accounts established in the NAHB format, there are some marked departures in the manner in which costs are accounted for within the major cost categories.

CASE STUDY I: AN AUTOMATED ACCOUNTING SYSTEM FOR THE REAL ESTATE DEVELOPMENT AND CONSTRUCTION INDUSTRIES

The system described in this case study, developed by Kenneth Leventhal and Company, is included to show the types of packaged information systems which are available to developers and contractors. This particular system was chosen to illustrate packaged systems because its development was commissioned by the National Association of Home Builders, one of whose purposes is to promote accounting standardization in the industry.

Design objective

The system was designed to be used by companies involved in real estate construction, development, and management. This includes builders of for-sale housing, apartments, and commercial properties. It can also be used by subcontractors or general contractors.

The system is highly adaptable to both the large firm with many processing requirements and to the smaller firm just implementing a mechanized system. This is accomplished by the system design concept of a fully integrated system in the Remote Batch Entry mode.

The system is comprised of independent, yet fully integrated, modules or subsystems. This enables the user to implement the system in various phases as his processing needs expand, without the burden of costly reprogramming or conversion effort. For example, the check writing, project cost, and general ledger modules may be implemented to start; then other modules can be added as desired.

The Remote Job Entry concept (explained more fully below) enables the user to incur only the processing costs that he needs, without heavy or expensive fixed monthly commitments.

Benefits of the system

1. Adaptability to various accounting principles. Each user may select those accounting principles most applicable to his particular business. For example, the user may choose to have accounts payable processed on a memo basis only, rather than being fully accrued.
2. User oriented. All documents are kept in house, and the data is entered and corrected by the users. Reports are easy to read and understand.
3. Flexibility of scheduling. The design of the system allows any module to be run independently of the others, thus saving time and processing charges. Any of the reports can be selected for printing, and data entry can be accomplished in accordance with the user's normal processing cycle. The system can even print daily checks if desired. In addition, the system can accommodate the different types of users and divisions in different businesses within the operational framework.
4. Low entry point. The system has been designed so that it can be used by a small builder with a minimal clerical staff. The user can control his processing charges by selecting the processing schedule that suits

him best. For example, checks may be produced monthly, weekly, daily, or on request.
5. Solves the Multiregion problem. The necessity for transmitting documents by mail is eliminated, thus significantly reducing the lag between document creation and report generation. The system also makes practical a policy of centralized cash control.
6. Growth oriented. An increase in transactions volume or a diversification into other locations or operations does not necessitate a change in procedures or equipment. In addition, the additional transactions volume can be accomplished with a less than proportionate increase in processing cost.
7. Dynamic processing. A single change is automatically carried forward to all affected modules. Data can be entered, a preliminary report produced, adjustments made, and a new report scheduled, all within a one- to two-hour time period. The user has the ability to print only selected reports on a low-cost, in-house terminal and to retrieve specific information when desired.

The remote job entry environment

1. Problems to be solved. The following problems are typical of data processing using a local service bureau or in-house computing equipment:

    1. Slow processing turnaround due to scheduling conflicts.
    2. Documents must be sent out of the office.
    3. User dealing with third parties and *their* priorities.
    4. User must rely on keypunchers to interpret data.
    5. User must wait for multiregion transmittal.
    6. User must bear high monthly cost of in-house equipment.

    These problems are eliminated under the Remote Job Entry approach.

2. Explanation of solution. Under the Remote Job Entry concept, computer time is purchased similar to any other utility resource. Common programs are set up at a central computer facility. The computer owner's communication network is utilized to eliminate toll charges. A typewriter-type terminal located in the user's office is used for data entry and report retrieval, thus making the system easy to use by current personnel.

3. Advantages. The basic advantages to Remote Job Entry are the exact opposite of the problem with other methods, namely:

    1. Fast response.
    2. In-house terminal for data entry by *user's* employees and report printing at *user's* command.
    3. Immediate transmission of data to and from remote divisions.
    4. Low monthly equipment cost.

4. Proven concept. Remote Job Entry is a proven data processing concept. It is currently in use by developers and has been used extensively in other industries for many years.

General ledger–financial reporting subsystem

System features

1. Contains all year-to-date detailed transactions by general ledger account for all nonsubledger accounts.
2. At year end, there is an automatic year-end balance forwarding and closing of the profit and loss accounts to retained earnings.
3. Ability to carry multiple companies or divisions with different fiscal year ends is offered.
4. Monthly and quarterly balance sheets and profit and loss statements compare actual results to budgeted prospects.
5. Consolidation of all or some companies into combined balance sheet and profit and loss statements is provided (e.g., joint ventures can be excluded).
6. All project-oriented accounts (e.g., inventory or sales) are summarized by project within general ledger account.

Reports generated

1. *Profit and Loss Statement.* The Profit and Loss Statement Report gives overall operating performance by division on both a current month and year-to-date basis (see Illustration 20–1). Monthly and year-to-date operating budgets are also presented for comparison to actual performance. Variances from budgets are calculated and reported for each income and expense item.

If quarterly operating data are desired, both divisional and consolidated statements can be prepared on a quarterly basis, presenting financial results for the current quarter and for the year to date (see Illustration 20–2).

2. *Balance Sheet.* The Balance Sheet Report gives the overall financial position of each division at the end of each monthly reporting period (see Illustration 20–3). Year-to-date budgets are also presented, and variances from actual figures are calculated and reported for each item (Illustration 20–4).

Included in the balance sheet is the ability to group general ledger accounts in any manner desired. This means that balance sheet presentation can be varied to fit the needs of a variety of users.

3. *Overhead Budget Variance.* The Overhead Budget Variance Report gives data on the performance of each division in the area of overhead expense, on both a current-month and year-to-date basis. Monthly and year-to-date overhead budgets are also presented for comparison to actual expenditures. Variances from budgets are calculated and reported for each overhead item. This report indicates to management whether or not pro-

Illustration 20-1
Case Study I: General ledger–financial reporting

```
GL110B   DIV 100 COMPANY X CALIFORNIA        PROFIT AND LOSS STATEMENT                    P/F 1/31/74 PAGE  1
                                                                                           RUN 2/07/74
```

	---- CURRENT MONTH ----			----- YEAR TO DATE -----			----------- ANNUAL -----------		
	BUDGET	ACTUAL	VARIANCE	BUDGET	ACTUAL	VARIANCE	BUDGET	FORECAST	VARIANCE
SALES:									
RESIDENTIAL		213,620	213,620		213,620	213,620			
OPTIONS		13,320	13,320		13,320	13,320			
RENTAL PROPERTIES									
LAND									
JOINT VENTURES									
TOTAL SALES		226,940	226,940		226,940	226,940			
COST OF SALES:									
RESIDENTIAL									
OPTIONS									
RENTAL PROPERTIES									
LAND									
JOINT VENTURES									
TOTAL COST OF SALES									
CONTRACTORS FEE									
GROSS PROFIT		226,940	226,940		226,940	226,940			
GENERAL AND ADMIN	15,690	26,749	11,059	178,394	26,749	(151,645)	178,394	178,394	
CORP O/H ALLOCATION									
INTEREST EXPENSE									
OTHER (INCOME) EXPENSE									
CONSULTANT FEES									
INTEREST INCOME									
MISCELLANEOUS									
TOTAL OTHER(INC)EXP									
INCOME BEFORE TAXES	(15,690)	200,191	215,881	(178,394)	200,191	378,585	(178,394)	(178,394)	
INCOME TAXES (CREDIT)									
OTHER UNCLASSIFIED		196,289	196,289		196,289	196,289			
NET INCOME (LOSS)	(15,690)	3,902	19,592	(178,394)	3,902	182,296	(178,394)	(178,394)	

jected levels of overhead expenditures are being maintained. This is essential information, since current income is normally being charged with a pro rata portion of the overhead budget.

Budget comparison information can be presented either by departments within each division or by overhead expense category (e.g., salaries, office expense) for the division as a whole. Thus, a variance by either department or expense category can be computed, allowing the most meaningful comparison possible, based on the format of management forecasts.

4. *Trial Balance.* The Trial Balance Report is a monthly report of all general ledger account balances. It presents the previous month's balance, current month's activity, and the current month's ending balance. The trial balance can also indicate the current accounts payable by account.

An important feature of the trial balance is that balances for those general ledger accounts associated with current construction (e.g., inventory,

Illustration 20-2
Case Study I: General ledger–financial reporting

```
GL1208    1000        CONSOLIDATED   PROFIT   AND   LOSS   STATEMENT              P/E 1/31/74 PAGE  1
                                                                                  RUN 2/07/74
                      ---- CURRENT MONTH ----  ----- YEAR TO DATE -----   ------------ ANNUAL ------------
                      BUDGET    ACTUAL   VARIANCE   BUDGET    ACTUAL   VARIANCE    BUDGET    FORECAST   VARIANCE

SALES:
   RESIDENTIAL                  213,620   213,620            213,620   213,620
   OPTIONS                       13,320    13,320             13,320    13,320
   RENTAL PROPERTIES
   LAND
   JOINT VENTURES

      TOTAL SALES               226,940   226,940            226,940   226,940

COST OF SALES:
   RESIDENTIAL
   OPTIONS
   RENTAL PROPERTIES
   LAND
   JOINT VENTURES

   TOTAL COST OF SALES

CONTRACTORS FEE

      GROSS PROFIT              226,940   226,940            226,940   226,940

GENERAL AND ADMIN     15,690     26,749   11,059   178,394    26,749  (151,645)   178,394    178,394

CORP O/H ALLOCATION

INTEREST EXPENSE

OTHER (INCOME) EXPENSE
   CONSULTANT FEES
   INTEREST INCOME
   MISCELLANEOUS

   TOTAL OTHER(INC)EXP

INCOME BEFORE TAXES  (15,690)   200,191  215,881  (178,394)  200,191   378,585  (178,394)  (178,394)

INCOME TAXES (CREDIT)

OTHER UNCLASSIFIED              196,289  196,289             196,289   196,289

   NET INCOME (LOSS) (15,690)     3,902   19,592  (178,394)    3,902   182,296  (178,394)  (178,394)
```

sales, cost of sales) are *presented by project*. Thus, all current balances for projects in progress are readily identifiable.

5. *General Ledger.* The General Ledger Report is a detailed listing, prepared monthly, of all transactions posted to each general ledger account during the current fiscal year. Thus, all cash disbursements, cash receipts, and journal entries are listed by general ledger account, together with a year-to-date total which ties into the trial balance. Monthly control totals are shown for those accounts supported by subsidiary ledgers (e.g., job cost).

At the end of each fiscal year, all of the transactions listed in detail for that year are summarized automatically, and ending balances are brought forward for the next fiscal period.

6. *Month-End Check Register.* The Month-End Check Register Report is a detailed listing of all checks drawn during the current month. A sep-

Illustration 20-3
Case Study I: General ledger–financial reporting

```
GL110A   DIV 100 COMPANY X CALIFORNIA           BALANCE SHEET                              P/E 1/31/74 PAGE    1
                                                                                           RUN 2/07/74
```

	---- CURRENT MONTH ----			----- YEAR TO DATE -----			----------- ANNUAL -----------		
	BUDGET	ACTUAL	VARIANCE	BUDGET	ACTUAL	VARIANCE	BUDGET	FORECAST	VARIANCE
CASH		(59,849)	(59,849)		(59,849)	(59,849)			
COMMERCIAL PAPER									
RECEIVABLES									
CLOSING PROCEEDS									
NOTES									
MORTGAGE		174,267	174,267		174,267	174,267			
OTHER		(64)	(64)		(64)	(64)			
TOTAL RECEIVABLES		174,203	174,203		174,203	174,203			
REAL ESTATE INVENTORY									
RESIDENTIAL DWELLING									
UNITS IN PRODUCTION		208,824	208,824		208,824	208,824			
LAND NON-PRODUCTION									
LAND PURCHASE OPTION									
TOTAL R/E INVENTORY		208,824	208,824		208,824	208,824			
INVESTMENTS & ADVANCES									
PARTNERSHIPS/VENTURE		98,312	98,312		98,312	98,312			
INTER-CO RECEIVABLES									
OTHER									
TOTAL INV. & ADV.		98,312	98,312		98,312	98,312			
NON-CURRENT RECEIVABLE									
OTHER ASSETS									
EQUIP FURN FIXTURES		600	600		600	600			
ACCUM DEPRECIATION									
NET		600	600		600	600			
DEFERRED CHARGES &									
OTHER ASSETS									
TOTAL OTHER ASSETS		600	600		600	600			
OTHER UNCLASSIFIED		2,297,858	2,297,858		2,297,858	2,297,858			
TOTAL ASSETS		2,719,948	2,719,948		2,719,948	2,719,948			

arate register is prepared for each bank account, with the checks listed in numerical sequence. Cumulative monthly check totals are presented for each bank account, each division, and for the entire system as a whole.

If the machine check feature has been selected, checks printed on the user's terminal are automatically entered on the monthly check register. If the machine check feature is not being used, or if some hand checks are drawn in addition to those prepared on the terminal, check data are entered on the register through normal transaction input channels.

Although the primary purpose of this report is to facilitate monthly bank reconciliations, it also serves as a cash disbursements journal and provides necessary audit traceability.

7. *Cash Deposits.* The Monthly Cash Deposits Report is a detailed listing of all deposits made during the month, grouped by bank account within each division and listed in chronological order by transaction date

Illustration 20-4
Case Study I: General ledger-financial reporting

```
GL120A    1000              CONSOLIDATED  BALANCE  SHEET                      P/E 1/31/74 PAGE  1
                                                                               RUN 2/07/74
```

	CURRENT MONTH			YEAR TO DATE			ANNUAL		
	BUDGET	ACTUAL	VARIANCE	BUDGET	ACTUAL	VARIANCE	BUDGET	FORECAST	VARIANCE
CASH		(59,849)	(59,849)		(59,849)	(59,849)			
COMMERCIAL PAPER									
RECEIVABLES									
CLOSING PROCEEDS									
NOTES									
MORTGAGE		174,267	174,267		174,267	174,267			
OTHER		(64)	(64)		(64)	(64)			
TOTAL RECEIVABLES		174,203	174,203		174,203	174,203			
REAL ESTATE INVENTORY									
RESIDENTIAL DWELLING									
UNITS IN PRODUCTION		208,824	208,824		208,824	208,824			
LAND NON-PRODUCTION									
LAND PURCHASE OPTION									
TOTAL R/E INVENTORY		208,824	208,824		208,824	208,824			
INVESTMENTS & ADVANCES									
PARTNERSHIPS/VENTURE		98,312	98,312		98,312	98,312			
INTER-CO RECEIVABLES									
OTHER									
TOTAL INV. & ADV.		98,312	98,312		98,312	98,312			
NON-CURRENT RECEIVABLE									
OTHER ASSETS									
EQUIP FURN FIXTURES		600	600		600	600			
ACCUM DEPRECIATION									
NET		600	600		600	600			
DEFERRED CHARGES &									
OTHER ASSETS									
TOTAL OTHER ASSETS		600	600		600	600			
OTHER UNCLASSIFIED		2,297,858	2,297,858		2,297,858	2,297,858			
TOTAL ASSETS		2,719,948	2,719,948		2,719,948	2,719,948			

within each bank account. Cumulative monthly deposit totals are presented for each bank account, each division, and for the entire system as a whole.

Although the primary purpose of this report is to facilitate monthly bank reconciliations, it also serves as a cash receipts journal and provides necessary audit traceability.

8. *Distribution.* The Weekly Distribution Report is a detailed listing, prepared weekly, of all transactions posted to each general ledger account for the current month. Each cash disbursement, cash receipt, and journal entry is listed by general ledger account affected and referenced to the appropriate source journal. Essentially, this report is a month-to-date transactions register useful for reviewing account activity on a weekly basis and for correcting miscoded transactions prior to the monthly update of the general ledger.

9. *Administrative Overhead Budget Register Report.* This report presents a detailed breakdown of the overhead budget used to calculate variances between actual and budgeted overhead expenses on the Overhead Budget Variance Report. Thus it serves as both a tool for analysis of indicated variances and as a work sheet for updating overhead budgets. Budget changes entered on this register are automatically summarized and carried forward to update the Overhead Budget Variance Report.

Project cost subsystem

System features

1. The subledger contains all detailed transactions from the inception of the project to date, to provide complete records by cost account.
2. The ability to enter and modify a wide range of construction-oriented items is provided (e.g., retention percentages, completion percentages, estimated volumes or quantities, budgets or estimates, contracts, change orders and purchase orders, voucher loan accounts and balances, feasibility estimates).
3. Produces key report of project cost analysis.
4. Also produces key report of plan monitor that controls direct construction costs by model type or plan.
5. Fully integrated with rest of system.
6. Automatic closing or balance forwarding of individual jobs when desired.

Reports generated

1. *Job Cost Summary.* This is the summary management report on construction projects in progress. It enables project managers to monitor estimate and contract revisions, payments to date, and estimates to complete, in order to determine whether or not the project will meet established goals.

The report presented in Illustration 20–5 is a sample. Project costs are so interrelated with each division's philosophy of operation that the project cost analysis is uniquely tailored to the needs of each client.

2. *Plan Monitor.* The Plan Monitor Report gives direct construction costs by plan type within each project currently under construction. It presents the original and revised estimates for each plan, and the original and revised commitment. In addition, it compares the current total contract to the original estimate and displays the variance. It is, therefore, an effective tool for identifying changes in direct construction cost at the plan level, and it serves as a key determinate of both initial sales price and of price increases necessitated by rising costs.

3. *Project Cost Detail.* This subsidiary ledger is a detailed listing of all transactions affecting job costs for each project currently under construction (see Illustration 20–6). All transactions from the inception of the project are shown. The transactions are listed and summarized by cost ac-

Illustration 20-5
Case Study I: Project cost

COST ACCT	DESCRIPTION	LAST EST REVISION	BUDGET	VARIANCE	CURRENT FORECAST	ORIGINAL CTR/PO	CTR/PO CHANGES	REVISED CTR/PO	PAID NON-CTR	TOTAL	VARIANCE (UNDER)	TOTAL PAID
4120	SECURITY GUARD S	6/19/73	4,000	225	4,225	4,225		4,225		4,225		3,875
4130	SALARIES AND WAG	9/18/73	6,000	837	6,837	6,837		6,837		6,837		6,322
4140	PAYROLL TAXES	9/18/73	2,100	318	2,418	2,418		2,418		2,418		1,988
4210	EQUIPMENT REPAIR	7/31/73	800	(394)	406	416		416		416	10	278
4220	CONCRETE BLOCK U	12/04/73	3,200	683	3,883	3,883		3,883		3,883		3,883
4230	DEPRECIATION	6/19/73	1,900	225	2,125	2,125		2,125		2,125		1,625
4310	EXPENDABLE TOOLS	9/12/73	500	164	664	664		664		664		96
4320	SUPPLIES	5/03/73	200		200	200		200		200		170
4330	EQUIPMENT RENTAL	6/03/73	2,100	(211)	1,889	1,889		1,889		1,889		1,640
4410	ARCHITECT AND EN	1/22/74	26,400	3,319	29,719	25,000	3,129	28,129		28,129	(1,590)	28,129
4420	PERMITS AND INSP	5/03/73	800		800	800		800		800		800
4510	THEFT AND VANDAL	11/19/73	1,000	259	1,259	1,259		1,259		1,259		984
4520	SHORTAGES AND OT	5/03/73	700		700	700		700		700		
4610	CONSTRUCTION OFF	6/12/73	1,800	300	2,100	2,100		2,100		2,100		2,100
4620	CONSTRUCTION OFF	5/03/73	100		100	100		100		100		665
4630	CONSTRUCTION OFF	5/03/73	300		300	300		300		300		280
4710	TEMPORARY UTILIT	11/25/73	2,500	277	2,777	2,777		2,777		2,777		2,011
4712												2,319
4720	TRASH REMOVAL	5/03/73	400		400	400		400	80	480	80	340
	COST MAJOR TOTAL		66,800	5,032	71,832	67,123	3,129	70,252	80	70,332	(1,500)	62,199
5010	LANDSCAPING	1/23/74	17,800	2,700	20,500	19,000	1,500	20,500		20,500		17,570
5020	SIDEWALKS	5/03/73	12,400		12,400	12,000		12,000		12,000	(400)	11,210
5030	POOLS	7/19/73	4,000	500	4,500	4,500		4,500		4,500		2,005
5040	SPRINKLERS	1/08/74	6,000	1,150	7,150	6,680	470	7,150		7,150		5,440
5050	LIGHTS	5/03/73	3,100		3,100	3,000		3,000		3,000	(100)	3,220
	COST MAJOR TOTAL		43,300	4,350	47,650	45,180	1,970	47,150		47,150	(500)	39,445
6110	CONSTRUCTION LOA	5/19/73	20,000		20,000	20,000		20,000		20,000		60,000
6120	CONSTRUCTION LOA	9/12/73	50,000	6,000	56,000	56,000		56,000	18,780	74,780	18,780	58,280
6130	TAKE-OUT LOAN FE	9/12/73	20,000	4,000	24,000	24,000		24,000		24,000		15,473
6310	PROPERTY TAXES	12/09/73	18,000	1,472	19,472	19,472		19,472		19,472		20,104
6410	CLOSING COSTS	5/19/73	4,000		4,000	4,000		4,000		4,000		2,800
	COST MAJOR TOTAL		112,000	11,472	123,472	123,472		123,472	18,780	142,252	18,780	156,657
7120	MAGAZINE AND NEW	10/12/73	4,000	875	4,875	4,875		4,875		4,875		3,162
7130	BROCHURES AND ST	5/19/73	2,000		2,000	2,000		2,000		2,000		1,659
7210	INSULATION, BUIL	5/19/73	60,000		60,000	60,000		60,000		60,000		
7410	SALES OFFICE	12/19/73	5,000	3,000	8,000	8,000		8,000		8,000		6,745
7510	ROOFING, BUILT-U	5/19/73	3,000		3,000	3,000		3,000		3,000		2,250
	COST MAJOR TOTAL		74,000	3,875	77,875	77,875		77,875		77,875		13,816
8010	SUITE ENTRANCE D	12/31/73				4,628		4,628		4,628	4,628	5,107
8020	PATIO	12/31/73				3,895		3,895	874	4,769	4,769	4,769
8030	CARPET UPGRADE	12/31/73				6,840		6,840	522	7,362	7,362	7,362
8040	DISHWASHER	12/31/73				2,580		2,580	163	2,743	2,743	163

count, thus facilitating a detailed comparison with current budgets and commitments, both of which are also presented on the report. In addition, key contract information, such as the retention percentage and contract quantities is also shown.

This report serves two basic functions. From a project control standpoint, it enables project managers to compare budgets and commitments on a cost account basis, to compare the cumulative contract disbursements to field reports of percentage completion for individual contracts, and to evaluate at a glance all significant information in relation to construction progress. From an accounting standpoint, it enables the supporting detail for the construction-in-progress inventory account to be kept out of the trial balance and general ledger reports, while at the same time alerting accounting personnel to contracts that may require amendments or additional purchase orders and to estimates that may require reevaluation.

Illustration 20-6
Case Study I: Project cost

```
JC100A DIV 100 COMPANY X CALIFORNIA        P R O J E C T   C O S T   D E T A I L              P/F  1/31/74 PAGE   5
20,000 PROJECT PINETREE MEADOWS           20 UNITS                                              RUN  2/07/74

  COST ORDER       DESCRIPTION         CMPL     C/F EFF     TRANS                           E S T I M A T E D      D I S B U R S E D
  ACCT LOT T VENDOR   VENDOR       INV DATE INV DESCR DATE P.O. CHECK     DATE    LN        BUDGET    CONTRACT     NON-CONTR  CONTR/PO
  ---- ---- - ------ -------------- -------- ---------- ----- ---- ------ -------- ---     ------------------     ----------------------
                                                                 COST MAJOR TOTAL              42,620                            42,305.00
                                                          A/P                                  42,620       .00
  ==== ==== = ====== ============== ======== ========== ===== ==== ====== ======== ===     ==================     ======================

  3110 RETAINING WALLS
                    B & G CONST                            H010010  4/28/73  ORIG     1,700    1,700
       C 10015      BEGINNING BALANCE 01/01/74    1/74     J01-001 1/12/74                                                        1,700.00
                    ---- ---- - ------ -------------- -------- ---------- ----- ---- ------ -------- ---
                    RETENTION    .0%                       A/P                    COST TOTAL     1,700    1,700                   1,700.00

  3120 FOUNDATIONS
                    A-1 CONCRETE                           H010010  4/28/73  ORIG    27,800   27,300
                    OVER SUPPLY                            H010010  5/13/73  ADJ       500-
       2584         SETTLING                               H010010  1/19/74  ADJ       850      850
       C 10035      BEGINNING BALANCE 01/01/74    1/74     J01-001 1/12/74                                                       26,900.00
         10035      A-1 CONCRETE  1/19/74 M952    1/74 2584   01005 1/31/74                                                         850.00
         10035      A-1 CONCRETE  1/19/74 M952    1/74         01005 1/31/74                                                        400.00
                    RETENTION    .0%                       A/P                    COST TOTAL    28,150   28,150                  28,150.00

  3130 UTILITY SERVICE
                    DWP                                    H010010  4/28/73  ORIG     4,000    4,000
       C 10039      BEGINNING BALANCE 01/01/74    1/74     J01-001 1/12/74                                                        3,600.00
         10039      DWP           1/12/74 GCN4392 1/74         01006 1/31/74                                                        400.00
                    RETENTION    .0%                       A/P                    COST TOTAL     4,000    4,000                   4,000.00

  3210 ROUGH LUMBER
                    A1 CONCRETE                            H010010  4/28/73  ORIG    15,700   15,550
       2604         PRICE ADJ                              H010010  1/06/74  ADJ     5,060    6,860
       C 10043      BEGINNING BALANCE 01/01/74    1/74     J01-001 1/12/74                                                       76,400.00
         10043      CARTR LUMBER  1/06/74 CP9964  1/74 2604  01007 1/31/74                                                        6,860.00
         10043      CARTR LUMBER  1/06/74 CP9964  1/74        01007 1/31/74                                                       1,600.00
                    RETENTION    .0%                       A/P                    COST TOTAL    20,760   22,410                  84,860.00

  3220 FINISH LUMBER
                    CARTR LUMBER                           H010010  4/28/73  ORIG    14,200   13,300
       8295         PRICE ADJ                              H010010  1/28/74  ADJ       920    1,820
       C 10043      BEGINNING BALANCE 01/01/74    1/74     J01-001 1/12/74                                                        9,870.00
         10043      CARTR LUMBER  1/28/74 CP0019  1/74        01007 1/31/74                                                       2,590.00
                    RETENTION    .0%                       A/P                    COST TOTAL    15,120   15,120                  12,460.00
```

Additional control functions are also available. For example, accounts payable and retentions payable can be accrued on a memo basis, indicating potential liabilities and cost problems on a current invoice basis.

4. *Customer Options/Deposits.* This subsidiary ledger provides a detailed listing, by lot, of the transactions affecting each option ordered by the customer. Customer deposits and the cost of each option are shown in detail by option type. Additionally, standard revenue and cost by option type are provided to facilitate the calculation of gross profit and to account for cost overruns.

From an accounting standpoint, the customer-option subsidiary ledger enables accounting personnel to verify that deposits have been received before options are ordered, and it provides audit traceability to individual transactions while at the same time keeping supporting detail for customer deposits out of the trial balance and general ledger reports.

Cash disbursements–accounts payable subsystem

System features

1. Produces machine-written checks and remittances at the terminal.
2. Offers ability to produce machine checks from multiple bank accounts, all in the same processing cycle.
3. Offers dynamic capability to switch bank accounts for checks prior to processing.
4. Can cut checks from one central bank account and make automatic intercompany bank transfer entries.
5. User can either enter items to be paid through the normal accounts payable route to produce regular open-item entries by vendor or can use the check-writing function, which cuts check immediately.

Reports generated

1. *Machine Checks and Remittance Advices.* This module enables the user to have checks and remittance advices printed on the in-house terminal. These machine-printed checks are automatically listed on the check register. In addition, this capability enables the client to select the use of either divisional bank accounts or a single corporate bank account for cash disbursements.

2. *Check Register.* The Check Register Report is a detailed listing of all checks drawn during the current check cycle (Illustration 20–7). This report is useful both for an immediate review of current cash disbursements and as a quick reference for questions concerning recent checks.

3. *Accounts Payable, Division–Vendor.* The Accounts Payable, Division–Vendor Report (Illustration 20–8) is a detailed listing of all open invoices grouped by division and within the division by vendor. Based on a payment date assigned when each invoice is recorded, this report presents a forward aging of accounts payable, indicating total prescheduled payments for each vendor and for the division as a whole. This report is used both for a prepayment review of accounts payable by vendor and as an aid in forecasting short-term cash requirements.

An important feature of the Accounts Payable Module is that once a payment date is assigned to an invoice, that invoice will automatically be paid during the check cycle encompassing that date. Of course, if a prepayment review indicates that a particular invoice should not be paid, the automatic check feature can be overridden.

Also available is an Accounts Payable Report which presents open invoices grouped by division, general ledger account, and job, to facilitate a possible accrual of accounts payable.

4. *Retentions Payable.* The Retentions Payable Report presents a detailed listing of retentions grouped by division and vendor. This report enables the project manager to analyze retentions held for each vendor and to compare those retentions with contract payments. Retentions are held by the system until scheduled for payment. This report provides detailed support for the retentions payable general ledger account.

Illustration 20-7
Case Study I: Cash disbursements and accounts payable

```
 CD1009  BANK 110                         CHECK  REGISTER                         P/E  1/31/74 PAGE   2
                                                                                  RUN  2/07/74

 DIV   G/L      JOB    COST  LOT  TYP LN VENDOR           TRAN  INV DATE  INV DESCR  P.O.   DATE    DFT AMOUNT    AMOUNT  CHECK
 ---  -------  ------  ----- ---  --- -- --------------   ----- --------  ----------  ----  -------  ----------  --------- -----

 100  121.010  20.00   04210           10071 S&S RENTALS  000053 1/19/74 017429            1/31/74      43.00
 100  121.010  20.00   04610           10071 S&S RENTALS  000058 1/27/74 019184            1/31/74     300.00
                                                                                                              $343.00 01014

 100  121.010  20.00   03510     C     10075 BUILDERS EMP 000028 1/24/74 1246              1/31/74     365.00
 100  121.010  20.00   04310           10075 BUILDERS EMP 000054 1/10/74 11347             1/31/74      96.00
 100  121.010  20.00   04320           10075 BUILDERS EMP 000055 1/10/74 11347             1/31/74      27.00
                                                                                                              $488.00 01015

 100  121.010  20.00   04630           10079 PACIFIC TEL  000040 1/15/74 887-4392          1/31/74      31.00
 100  800.330                          10079 PACIFIC TEL  000064 1/16/74 687-0932          1/31/74     284.25
                                                                                                              $315.25 01016

 100  121.010  20.00   04720     1     10083 OLSEN TRASH         1/31/73 LOTS 18,19        1/31/74             $80.00 01017

 100  121.010  20.00   04710           10087 SO CAL EDISN 000043 1/19/74 S-9124768         1/31/74           $1,218.00 01018

 100  121.010  20.00   05010           10091 GREEN THUMB  000044 1/23/74 097436            1/31/74    2,790.00
 100  121.010  20.00   02220           10091 GREEN THUMB  000045 1/23/74 097436      BKCG  1/31/74     115.00-
                                                                                                            $2,675.00 01019

 100  121.010  20.00   05030           10095 ANTHONY POOL 000047 1/19/74 A-7549            1/31/74             $730.00 01020

 100  121.010  20.00   07120     C     10103 L A TIMES    000030 1/04/74 ADV-DEC           1/31/74             $472.00 01021

 100  121.010  20.00   07130     C     10107 PIP          000032 1/18/74 PIP4392           1/31/74     119.00
 100  800.320                          10107 PIP          000063 1/23/74 PIP4421           1/31/74     118.72
                                                                                                              $237.72 01022

 100  121.010  20.00   03410     C     10111 SANDOVAL MAS 000024 1/19/74 SANDO-JAN         1/31/74           $1,945.00 01023

 100  121.010  20.00   08010     A   0 10111 SANDOVAL MAS               OT 16        9721 1/31/74             $479.00 01024

 100  121.010  20.00   03620     C     10115 CLASSIC DRAP 000029 1/24/74 CL-175            1/31/74    2,250.00
 100  121.010  20.00   08030   6 1     10115 CLASSIC DRAP 000034 1/19/74 CL-194      9395 1/31/74      522.00
                                                                                                            $2,772.00 01025

 100  800.220                          10175 SO CALIF GAS 000060 1/12/74 1974362           1/31/74              $56.19 01026

 100  800.310                          10179 OFF SUP UNL  000062 1/19/74 401956            1/31/74             $359.60 01027

 100  800.420                          10183 UNION OIL CO 000065 1/06/74 U5943J6           1/31/74              $50.06 01028

 100  800.420                          10187 STANS UNION         1/31/74 STANS             1/31/74              $47.43 01029

 100  800.710                          10191 LEVENTHAL    000066 1/22/74 KL&CO-JAN         1/31/74             $630.00 01030

 100  800.710                          10195 FURST&FURST  000067 1/19/74 F&F-JAN           1/31/74             $925.00 01031

                                             HAND                        31 MACHINE  $55,569.25   DIV    $55,569.25
```

Page 39

Illustration 20–8
Case Study I: Cash disbursements and accounts payable

```
AP110A DIV 100 COMPANY X CALIFORNIA   A C C O U N T S   P A Y A B L E   D I V / V E N D O R        P/E  1/31/74 PAGE   3
                                                                                                    RUN  2/07/74

                              TRAN    INV-DATE  INV-DESCR   P.O.    PAY-DATE            THIS WEEK    2ND WEEK   3RD WEEK   4TH & OVER
-------- --------- ---- ---- -----   ---------  ---------         ---------            ----------   --------   --------   ----------
                                        RET                        TOTAL      343.00 *      343.00
-----------------------------------------------------------------------------------------------------------------------------------

   10075   BUILDERS EMPORIUM
                              000028  1/24/74   1246                PAY   H P V           365.00
                              000054  1/10/74   11347               PAY   H P V            96.00
                              000055  1/10/74   11347               PAY   H P V            27.00
                                        RET                        TOTAL      488.00 *      488.00
-----------------------------------------------------------------------------------------------------------------------------------

   10079   PACIFIC TELEPHONE
                              000040  1/15/74   887-4392            PAY   H P V            31.00
                              000064  1/16/74   687-0932            PAY   H P V           284.25
                                        RET                        TOTAL      315.25 *      315.25
-----------------------------------------------------------------------------------------------------------------------------------

   10087   SO CALIF. EDISON
                              000043  1/19/74   S-9124768           PAY   H P V         1,218.00
                                        RET                        TOTAL    1,218.00 *    1,218.00
-----------------------------------------------------------------------------------------------------------------------------------

   10091   GREEN THUMB INTERNATIONAL
                              000044  1/23/74   097436              PAY   H P V         2,790.00
                              000045  1/23/74   097436    BKCG      PAY   H P V           115.00-
                                        RET                        TOTAL    2,675.00 *    2,675.00
-----------------------------------------------------------------------------------------------------------------------------------

   10095   ANTHONY POOLS, INC.
                              000047  1/19/74   A-7549              PAY   H P V           730.00
                                        RET                        TOTAL      730.00 *      730.00
-----------------------------------------------------------------------------------------------------------------------------------

   10103   LOS ANGELES TIMES
                              000030  1/04/74   ADV-DEC             PAY   H P V           472.00
                                        RET                        TOTAL      472.00 *      472.00
-----------------------------------------------------------------------------------------------------------------------------------

   10107   POSTAL INSTANT PRESS
                              000032  1/18/74   PIP4392             PAY   H P V           119.00
                              000063  1/23/74   PIP4421             PAY   H P V           118.72
                                        RET                        TOTAL      237.72 *      237.72
-----------------------------------------------------------------------------------------------------------------------------------

   10111   SANDOVAL MASONRY
```

21

Budgets, projections, controls, and analysis

BUDGET POLICY AND PROCEDURES

Purpose

The purpose of setting budget policy and procedures is to standardize the organization's budgeting policies and procedures. Standardized policy enables the organization to retrieve the residual benefits of its activities over a period of time by recording the experience gained during them. This recording of experience and on-the-job performance provides operating information and policy to generating personnel so they will not be mired down with already-solved problems. When personnel are freed from reworking the 80 percent of the work which is repetitious from project to project, they can devote themselves to the 20 percent of the work which is creative in solving the specific problems unique to a particular development (see Chapter 24).

The Standardized Policy for Budgeting is a format for retrieving and recording feedback from operations, through information systems and communications, in order to improve operations consistently. This results in a policy which keeps personnel informed of management's desires, objectives, and intentions, thus providing a basis for predictable decision making and action.

While policy standardization sets standards for decision making and planning, procedural standardization provides guidelines for implementing policy in a specific situation. Standardized budget and control policies and procedures simplify the management process and greatly aid the preparation of current budgets. Standardized formats enable management to compare all projects within a development type on the same basis. The historical record of activities and results which standardized policies, procedures, and formats provide assists in projections for current projects and forward planning (see Chapter 20).

Policy

There are four distinct types of budgets required for each project:

1. A preliminary or feasibility estimate.
2. A precontract estimate.

3. A firm contract or construction budget.
4. Construction-in-progress current forecasts.

The budget evolves from the less specific to the more specific as information is received.

Procedure Once an estimated budget is drafted, dated, and approved, the document is fixed and is not subject to further change, except for the construction-in-progress current forecast. The second budget then evolves from the first budget and is compared for variance; the third budget evolves from the second, and so on. The previous budget is always referred to in formulating the revised one. By not updating a previous budget but rather reflecting changes in a new, updated budget, a historical record is created. Thus management can, at a later date, analyze the project development to see where results went astray from objectives. The process also gives management the ability to see where plans are diverging from objectives in time to react with remedial measures. (See Chapter 27 for how budgets coordinate with purchasing, contract letting, and progress payments.)

The preliminary cost estimate. The preliminary cost estimate is often made prior to the development of plans. Where plans of a standard nature are being utilized, this does not present a problem; budgets from previous utilizations of the standard plans will provide an excellent starting point for the new budget.

In projecting new costs from the historical costs, various unit measurements of cost should be cross-checked for consistency or variances, in order to spot inappropriate comparisons of historical costs to projected cost and to spot planning and design features which heavily impact costs. Both costs per unit and costs per square foot should be compared. The cost per square foot is not as sensitive to changes in unit mix as it is to unit size. That is, as unit size per square foot decreases, construction costs per square foot generally increase.

The same cost plan formats should be utilized in the preliminary estimate as will be used in the precontract estimate. The preliminary estimate, however, may not employ as much detail cost data as the later estimates do. For example, only the major headings under direct construction costs may be estimated, without working up the detail cost estimates under the major headings. The sitework–on site account for rental housing would be estimated without the detail cost estimates for site clearing and grubbing, demolition, on-site staking and layout, and so on.

If there are any unusual site work conditions which depart from conditions in the historical cost comparisons, the detail cost estimates should be developed even in the feasibility stage. And if there has been unusual volatility in materials and labor pricing, more detailed cost estimates are required in the feasibility stage. For example, if concrete or asphaltic materials have gone up in price 30 percent in the past 12 months, this wide variation must be reflected in a more detailed preliminary cost analysis.

At such time as the preliminary estimate is finalized, it should be dated and approved. From the approval date forward the preliminary estimate does not change. All further changes are incorporated into the postcontract estimate, until such time as the postcontract estimate is dated and approved.

The precontract budget. The precontract estimate should be completed and approved before the construction contracts are let, but after the bids are received. The estimate should be based on as many firm estimates from subcontractors and suppliers as is practical.

The firm contract budget. The firm contract budget is an update of the precontract budget. The firm contract budget should be completed and approved at the beginning of construction and should contain as many firm contracts and purchase orders as is practical, consistent with good pricing considerations and industry conditions. The firm contract budget is the budget against which all construction-in-process forecasts are measured for variance.

Construction-in-process forecasts. Construction-in-process forecasts are presented in the formats shown in the sample management reports for rental housing: Off-Site Cost Analysis Report (D), Direct Construction Cost Analysis Report (B), and Indirect Construction Cost Analysis Report (A). In preparing these reports it is necessary to monitor the percentage of construction completion as compared to the percentage of construction cost billed. All additional purchase orders, change orders, and changes in forecast because of knowledge of possible cost changes in any of the accounts must also be taken into account.

Developing information through monitoring costs and schedule completions and field inspections make it possible to anticipate problems before they are actually reflected in purchase orders and change orders. This forethought makes time available for remedial action to be taken to redirect potential variances back to the course indicated by the budget plan. Anticipating variances before they get out of hand is critical to the management function; merely reporting variances after they have happened is a clerical function (see Chapter 29).

Budget relationship to the chart of accounts

All the budgets, estimates, and forecasts are coded to the Chart of Accounts. Each budget item, at least each major category item, relates directly to the Chart of Accounts and is identified with its Chart of Accounts code number (account number). The chart of accounts and budget format in the book follows the same major account headings as does the chart of accounts and budget formats in the *Accounting System for All Builders*, copyrighted in 1971 and published by the NAHB in Washington, D.C. The same major account headings are utilized in the book to promote consistency in the industry, a goal of the NAHB. There are, however, some major changes within the material covered under the major account headings to reflect differing business approaches.

CHART OF ACCOUNTS

The Chart of Accounts, Policy and Procedure for Budgeting and Accounting Report contains policy and procedures for budgeting and accounting for all cost and expense accounts within the chart of accounts. This report should be referred to for all budgeting and accounting activities, to ensure consistency in decision making and conformity to established accounting procedures. The policy portion of the report is particularly useful for decision making when events do not correspond to established procedures. In this manner personnel can make on-the-spot decisions which are consistent within the framework of management policy. The Chart of Accounts, Policy and Procedures Report is not included as an exhibit.

The information contained in this chapter is provided to illustrate the general scope of budget information required by management, so it can plan and control in a professional manner. The exact amount and exact format of the information which may be appropriate for a particular organization's planning and control needs will vary from organization to organization. We are not providing accounting or legal consultation or advice in this chapter, nor is the information presented intended to replace or augment accounting or legal consultation.

The reader should consult an accountant or attorney before proceeding with activities requiring accounting or legal advice. The percentages and amounts shown in the rental housing cash flow at the end of the chapter are hypothetical and for illustration purposes only; the reader should utilize amounts based on his own consultation and experience. There is a great deal of uncertainty as to tax legislation, and great caution is required in this regard. Legal and accounting advisers should be consulted to ascertain the current status of income tax regulations.

The balance of this chapter consists largely of exhibits of forms or schedules showing how the budgetary and control accounting system is achieved. Following the Chart of Accounts, the exhibits are divided into two main categories: those for for-sale housing and those for rental housing. Text is introduced between the forms where needed to explain them.

CHART OF ACCOUNTS, POLICY AND PROCEDURE FOR BUDGETING AND ACCOUNTING

The accounting format for classifying transactions so that similar transactions can be reported together is called the Chart of Accounts. The Chart of Accounts is a vehicle for budgetary and control accounting and is divided into two broad categories:

1. Balance sheet accounts for assets, liabilities, and capital (net worth).
2. Income statement accounts for sales, cost of sales, and expenses.

Costs are broken down into units, or unit costs, to facilitate classification and control of costs. In the selection of unit costs, care must be taken that neither too large nor too small a unit is selected. When the cost unit chosen is too large, cost trends may not be detected, due to the averaging of costs associated with large cost units. When the cost unit is too small, clerical work may be too costly and unjustified by the potential savings due to tighter control. The Chart of Accounts included in this chapter is a long form Chart of Accounts. This is presented to illustrate the broad number of accounts on income and expense units which must be controlled. However, the income and expense units do not necessarily have to be broken down into the units to the degree shown in the long form Chart of Accounts. This form is flexible in that the income and expense units can be consolidated into a short form Chart of Accounts by dropping a level of detail from the Chart of Accounts: that is, consolidating to the point where the account is appropriate for any particular organization's planning and control needs. The schedules and forms may also be consolidated to reflect the desired degree of planning and control (see Chapter 20).

The Chart of Accounts is as follows.

BALANCE SHEET ACCOUNTS

10000 SERIES—ASSETS
- 10000 Cash
    - 10100 Cash on hand
    - 10200 Cash on deposit—general
    - 10300 Cash on deposit—payroll
    - 10400 Cash on deposit—held in trust
    - 10500 Cash on deposit—escrow or pledged accounts
- 11000 Short-term Investments
    - 11100 Stocks
    - 11200 Bonds
    - 11300 Savings deposits
- 12000 Receivables
    - 12100 Accounts receivable—trade
    - 12200 Accounts receivable—other
    - 12300 Notes receivable—trade
    - 12400 Notes receivable—other
    - 12500 Mortgages receivable
    - 12600 Due on construction and development loans
    - 12700 Contracts receivable
    - 12800 Accrued interest receivable
    - 12900 Allowance for doubtful accounts
- 13000 Construction Materials Inventory and Raw Land Inventory
    - 13100 Construction materials inventory
    - 13200 Land cost
        - 13210 Purchase price
        - 13215 Legal fees
        - 13220 Property taxes
        - 13225 Planning fees
        - 13230 Engineering fees

    13235 Interest—seller
    13240 Interest—institutional
    13245 Interest—unsecured
    13250 Land escrow and title fees
    13255 Market research fees
    13260 Insurance
    13290 Other

14000 Work-in-Process Inventory
  14100 Development cost of land
    14110 Land cost
    14120 Direct Construction cost
    14130 Indirect construction cost
    14140 Financing and interest
    14150 Professional services
    14190 Other

  14200 Finished lots
    14210 Development cost of land
    14220 Financing and interest
    14230 Realty taxes
    14240 Purchase price of finished lots
    14250 Other

  14300 Direct construction cost
    14310 Site work
    14315 Concrete work
    14320 Masonry work
    14325 Metal work
    14330 Rough carpentry
    14335 Finished carpentry
    14340 Miscellaneous carpentry
    14345 Moisture protection
    14350 Doors, windows, glass, and mirrors
    14355 Finishes
    14360 Specialties
    14365 Appliances
    14370 Plumbing
    14375 Electrical
    14380 Heating, ventilating, and air conditioning
    14385 Amenities' budget—common area
    14390 Furnishings, equipment
    14395 Contingencies

  14400 Indirect construction costs
    14410 Salaries, wages, and fees
    14420 Equipment expense
    14430 Utilities expense
    14440 Field office, warehouse and storage shed expense
    14450 Bonding of construction
    14460 Warranty expense
    14470 Miscellaneous expense

    14480 Professional Services—Land Development and Construction
      14481 Architectural, engineering services
      14482 Reproduction and prints
      14483 Arts and graphics
    14490 Permits, bonds, fees, taxes, insurance
15000 Finished Houses Inventory
  15100 Finished houses
  15200 Trade-ins
  15300 Repossessions
  15400 Models
16000 Other Current Assets
  16100 Refundable deposits
  16200 Prepayments
    16210 Prepaid insurance
    16220 Prepaid rent
    16230 Prepaid commitment fees
    16240 Prepaid interest
    16250 Prepaid taxes
  16300 Salary advances
  16400 Payroll transfer
  16500 Due from affiliates, short term
  16600 Other
17000 Investments and Other Assets
  17100 Investments—long term
    17110 Subsidiaries' capital stock
    17120 Income property
    17130 Depreciation—income property
    17140 Land, long-term investment
  17200 Cash surrender value of officers' life insurance
  17300 Due from public agencies
  17400 Due from affiliates, long term
  17500 Due from officers
  17600 Organization expense
18000 Property, Plant, and Equipment
  18100 Land for offices, warehouses, etc.
  18200 Buildings, for use in operations
  18300 Furniture and equipment
  18400 Motor vehicles
  18500 Construction equipment
  18600 Model home furnishings
  18700 Other
19000 Accumulated Depreciation
  19200 Buildings
  19300 Furniture and equipment
  19400 Motor vehicles
  19500 Construction equipment
  19600 Model home furnishings
  19700 Other

20000 SERIES — LIABILITIES AND NET WORTH
  21000 Current Liabilities
    21100 Deposits by customers
      21110 Deposits on purchases, potentially refundable
      21120 Customers' prepayment of taxes and insurance
      21130 Tenants' security deposits
    21200 Accounts payable
      21210 Trade accounts payable
      21290 Other accounts payable
    21300 Notes payable
      21310 Trade notes payable
      21390 Other notes payable
    21400 Deferred income
    21500 Accrued taxes payable
      21510 Employee payroll taxes
        .01 Federal witholding
        .02 State witholding
        .03 FICA Tax
      21515 Employer taxes and insurance
        .01 FICA Tax
        .02 Workmen's compensation fund
        .03 Federal unemployment
        .04 State unemployment
      21520 Sales and use tax
      21525 Realty tax
      21530 Personal property tax
      21535 Inventory tax
      21540 Federal income tax
      21545 State income tax
      21550 Other
    21600 Construction and development loans payable
    21700 Customers' payments on contracts
    21800 Accrued interest payable
    21900 Other current liabilities
      .01 Accrued salaries and wages
      .02 Accrued commissions
      .03 Due to affiliates
  22000 Noncurrent Liabilities
    22100 Long-term notes payable
    22200 Mortgages payable
  25000 Net Worth
    25100 Preferred stock
    25200 Common stock
    25300 Paid-in capital
    25400 Retained earnings
    25500 Profit and loss — year to date
    25600 Capital accounts
      .01 Partnership
      .02 Proprietorship

  25700 Drawing accounts
     .01 Partnership
     .02 Proprietorship
  25900 Other

INCOME AND EXPENSE STATEMENT ACCOUNTS

30000 SERIES—SALES AND OTHER REVENUE
  31000 Sales
    31100 Sale of raw land
    31200 Sales of finished lots
    31300 House sales
      31310 Basic sales
      31320 Extra sales on customer orders
    31400 Trade-in sales
    31500 Other sales
  32000 Other Revenue
    32100 Rental income from investment property
    32200 Investment income other than rentals
    32300 Brokerage and commission income
    32400 Warehouse income
    32500 Miscellaneous job income
    32600 Other services sold
    32700 Other revenues

40000 SERIES—COST OF SALES
  41000 Cost of Sales
    41100 Cost of raw acreage sold
    41200 Cost of finished lots sold
    41300 Cost of houses sold
      41310 Cost of basic house sales
      41320 Cost of extra sales
      41330 Cost of trade-in sales
  42000 Cost Related to Other Revenue
    42300 Direct costs related to brokerage and commission income
    42400 Costs related to warehouse
    42500 Direct costs related to miscellaneous job income
    42600 Direct cost related to other services sold
    42700 Other costs

50000 SERIES—FINANCING EXPENSE
  51000 Land Development Loans
    51100 Title insurance
    51200 Service charges
    51300 Inspection fees
    51400 Points
    51500 Interest on land development loan
    51600 Escrow recording fees
    51700 Other

52000 Construction Loan Expense
    51100 Title insurance
    51200 Service charges
    51300 Inspection fees
    51400 Points
    51500 Interest
    51600 Escrow recording fees
    51700 Other

53000 Permanent Mortgage — Points and Fees
    53100 Points
    53200 Standby fees

54000 Fees and Appraisals
    54100 Brokerage fees
    54200 Legal fees
    54300 Appraisal fees
    54400 Other
    55000 Closing Costs Paid for Customers
    56000 Interest on Notes
    57000 Interest on Completed Houses
    59000 Other

60000 SERIES — MARKETING EXPENSE

61000 Start-up Budget
    61100 Models' expense
    61200 Models' compound expense
    61300 Sales or rental office expense
    61400 Advertising and public relations
    61500 Miscellaneous expense

62000 Ongoing Site Budget
    62100 Personnel, salaries/fees
    62200 Supplies
    62300 Advertising and public relations
    62400 Carrying costs
    62500 Utilities, services

63000 Closing-Cost Budget
    63100 Commission to outside brokers
    63200 Multiple listing fees
    63300 Commissions to salesmen
    63500 Warranty expense

64000 Sales-Training Expense
    64100 Courses — external
    64200 Courses — internal
    64300 Travel and transportation

65000 Market Research and Consultation

66000 Other Marketing Department Expense
    66100 Travel and entertainment
66200 Auto expense

70000 SERIES — OPERATING AND MANAGEMENT EXPENSES
- 71000 Renting Expenses
  - 71100 Advertising and public relations
  - 71200 Commissions
  - 71300 Credit reports
  - 71400 Rental personnel salaries
  - 71500 Other
- 72000 Administrative Expenses
  - 72100 Administrative salaries
  - 72200 Property management fees
  - 72300 Office expenses
  - 72400 Telephone and telegraph
  - 72500 Bad debts
  - 72600 Collection costs
  - 72700 Data processing
  - 72800 Other
- 73000 Professional Services
  - 73100 Legal
  - 73200 Accounting
  - 73300 Market research
  - 73400 Other
- 74000 Operating Expenses
  - 74100 Utilities
    - 74110 Gas
    - 74120 Electricity
    - 74130 Fuel
    - 74140 Water and sewer
    - 74150 Other
  - 74200 Engineering
  - 74300 Janitorial
    - 74310 Janitorial payroll
    - 74320 Janitorial services
    - 74330 Janitorial supplies
  - 74400 Trash removal service
  - 74500 Exterminating
  - 74600 Snow removal
  - 74700 Other contractual services
  - 74800 Vehicle and equipment expenses
  - 74900 Other
- 75000 Maintenance and Repair Expenses
  - 75100 Redecorating
  - 75200 Maintenance payroll
  - 75300 Maintenance and repair contracts
  - 75400 Ground maintenance and repairs
  - 75500 Vehicle and equipment maintenance, repairs
  - 75600 Recreational facility payroll
  - 75700 Recreational facility services
  - 75800 Recreational facility supplies
  - 75900 Other

76000 Taxes and Insurance
    76100 Real property taxes
    76200 Personal property taxes
    76300 Franchise taxes
    76400 License fees
    76500 Payroll taxes and insurance
        76510 FICA taxes
        76520 Workmen's compensation
        76530 Unemployment insurance
        76590 Other
    76600 Property damage and liability insurance
    76700 Multiple peril and hazard insurance
    76900 Other

77000 Financial Expense
    77100 Interest on mortgage payable
    77200 Interest on long-term notes payable
    77300 Other interest
    77400 Mortgage insurance
    77900 Other

78000 Depreciation Expense
    78100 Buildings and components
    78200 Maintenance equipment
    78300 Motor vehicles
    78400 Furniture and fixtures
    78500 Recreational facilities
    78600 Other

79000 Other Management and Operating Expenses

80000 SERIES — GENERAL AND ADMINISTRATIVE EXPENSE

81000 Salaries
    81100 Owners
    81200 Officers
    81300 Management
    81400 Other salaries
    81500 Payroll taxes and employee benefits
        81510 Health and accident insurance
        81520 Retirement and pension plan
        81530 FICA taxes
        81540 Workmen's compensation
        81550 State unemployment compensation
        81560 Federal unemployment compensation

82000 Office Expense
    82010 Rent
    82020 Supplies
    82030 Postage
    82040 Repairs and maintenance
    82050 Interest
    82060 Office machines and equipment expense
    82070 Heat, light, and power

		82080	Telephone and telegraph
		82090	Contract office services
		82190	Miscellaneous office expense
	83000	Depreciation and Amortization	
		83010	Buildings
		83020	Furniture and equipment
		83030	Motor vehicles
		83040	Amortization of leasehold improvements
		83050	Amortization of organization expense
		83090	Other
	84000	Taxes	
		84010	Sales and use taxes
		84020	Realty taxes
		84030	Personal property inventory taxes
		84040	License fees
		84090	Other
	85000	Insurance	
		85010	Hazard
		85020	Property damage and liability on vehicles
		85030	General liability
		85090	Other
	86000	Professional Fees	
		86010	Accounting
		86020	Legal
		86030	Market research
		86040	Public relations, advertising
		86090	Other
	87000	Travel and Entertainment	
		87010	Automobile expense
		87020	Transportation expense
		87030	Meetings
		87040	Business entertainment
		87090	Other
	88000	Contributions	
	89000	Other	
		89010	Bonding expense
		89020	Corporate expense
		89030	Contribution to profit-sharing plan
		89040	Directors' fees
		89050	Dues and subscriptions
		89090	Miscellaneous
90000	SERIES—OTHER INCOME AND EXPENSE		
	91000	Other Income	
		91010	Discounts
		91020	Rebates or refunds
		91030	Income from other investments
		91040	Brokerage and commission income
		91050	Gain or sale of assets

	91060	Recovery of bad debts
	91070	Other services sold
	91090	Other
92000		Other Expense
	92010	Bad-debt expense
	92020	Loss on sale of assets
93000		Provision for Income Taxes
	93010	Federal income taxes
	93020	State income taxes

SUMMARY, BUDGET PLAN: FOR-SALE HOUSING

The summary of the Budget Plan for for-sale housing consists of the following diagrams:

1. Control—Information Flow Diagram.
2. Planning—Information Flow Diagram.

The Budget Plan also includes the following schedules or forms:

Schedule 1: Sales Plan
Schedule 2: Summary, Cost-of-Sales Plan
Schedule 3: Gross Profit Plan

Control—Information Flow Diagram (for-sale housing)

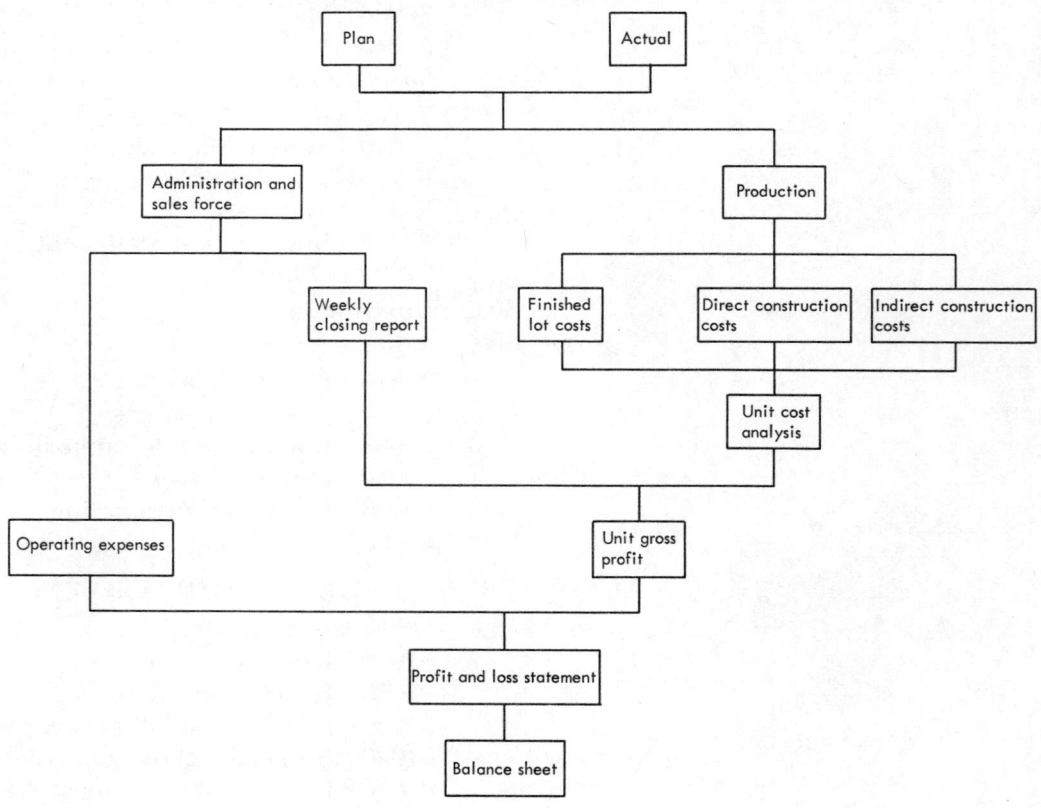

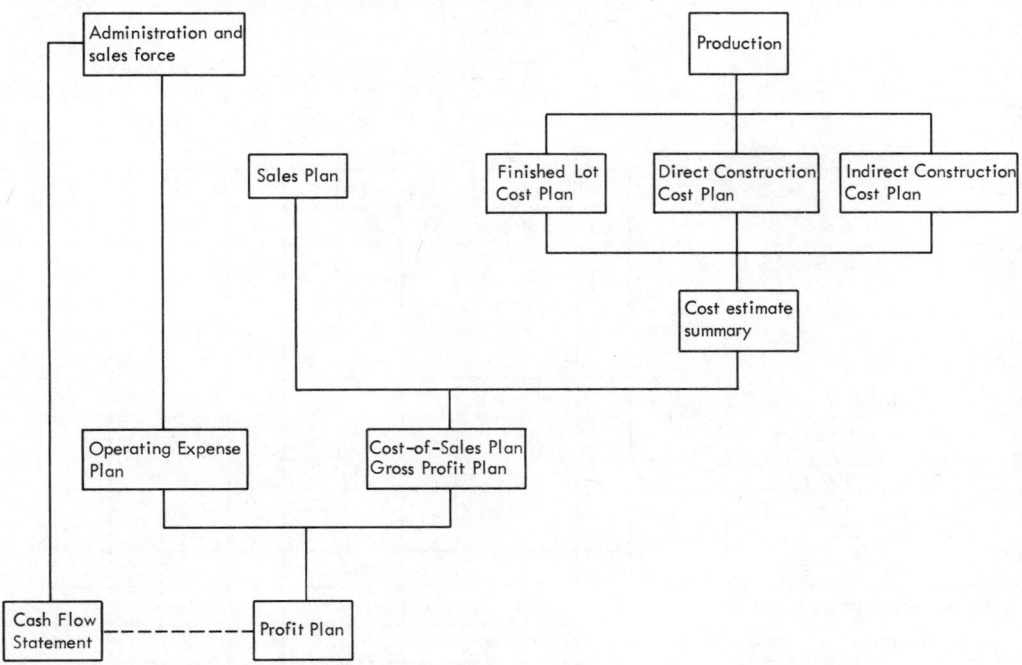

Planning—Information Flow Diagram (for-sale housing)

Schedule 1: Sales Plan (for-sale housing)

Approved by: _____
Date: _____

Schedule 1
Job No. _____
Date:
By:

Sales	January		February		March		April		Year total	
	No.	Amount	No.	Amount	No.	Amount	No.	Amount	No.	Amount
31200 Lot sales										
Tract _____ $ _____										
Tract _____ $ _____										
Tract _____ $ _____										
Tract _____ $ _____										
Subtotal										
31300 House sales										
Plan _____ Tract _____ $ _____										
Plan _____ Tract _____ $ _____										
Plan _____ Tract _____ $ _____										
Plan _____ Tract _____ $ _____										
Subtotal										
31400 Trade-in sales										
Subtotal										
Total Cost of Sales										

21 / Budgets, projections, controls, and analysis   293

Schedule 2: Summary, Cost-of-Sales Plan (for-sale housing)

Approved by: _____   Schedule 2
Date: _____   Job No. _____
                      Date:
                      By:

	January		*February*		*March*		*April*		*Year total*	
Costs	No.	Amount	No.	Amount	No.	Amount	No.	Amount	No.	Amount

41200 Cost, finished lots sold
   Tract ____ $ ____
   Tract ____ $ ____
   Tract ____ $ ____
   Tract ____ $ ____
   Subtotal										

41300 Cost, houses sold
   Plan ____ Tract ____ $ ____
   Plan ____ Tract ____ $ ____
   Plan ____ Tract ____ $ ____
   Plan ____ Tract ____ $ ____
   Subtotal										

41330 Cost of trade-ins sold Subtotal										
Total Cost of Sales										

Schedule 3: Gross Profit Plan (for-sale housing)

Approved by: _____   Schedule 3
Date: _____   Job No. _____
                      Date:
                      By:

	January	*February*	*March*	*April*	*Total year*

Lots:
  31200 Sales
  41200 Cost of sales					

Gross profit					

Houses:
  31300 Sales
  41300 Cost of sales					

Gross profit					

Trade-ins:
  31400 Sales
  41330 Cost of sales					

Gross profit					
Total Gross Profit					

Schedule 4: Gross Profit Plan per Unit
Schedule 5: Summary, Operating Expense Plan
Schedule 6: Profit Plan
Schedule 7: Cash Flow Statement
Schedule 8: Balance Sheet Statement

Gross Profit Plan analysis

The Gross Profit Plan is the responsibility of the sales and production departments. The sales department must explain the changes in prices and sales-mix shifts, and the production department must account for cost

Schedule 4: Gross Profit Plan per Unit (for-sale housing)

Approved by: _____ Schedule 4
Date: _____ Job No. _____
 Date:
 By:

		Unit _____	Unit _____	Unit _____	Unit _____	Total
31300	House sales					
41300	Cost of sales					
14200	Finished lots					
14300	Direct construction costs					
14400	Indirect construction costs					
	Total Cost of Sales					
	Gross Profit					

Schedule 5: Summary, Operating Expense Plan (for-sale housing)

Approved by: _____ Schedule 5
Date: _____ Job No. _____
 Date:
 By:

Operating expenses		January	February	March	April	Year total
50000	FINANCING EXPENSE					
60000	MARKETING EXPENSE					
80000	GENERAL AND ADMINISTRATIVE EXPENSE					
	Total Operating Expenses					

variations. Changes in the gross profit are due to any one or a combination of the following causes:

1. Changes in the selling price.
2. Changes in the volume of units sold.
3. Changes in the cost.

The second cause listed above has two distinct characteristics: changes in the number of units sold, and changes in the mix of the units sold.

The Gross Profit Plan is an indicator of the profitability, as opposed to the volume, of sales activities. It indicates how much the organization can afford for selling and administrative expenses if the net profit goal is to be achieved.

Profit Plan

The projected Profit Plan contains summaries of the sales and cost of sales and operating expenses. Its purpose is to project the net income. No new estimates are actually made; the statement is a summary of figures taken from various backup budgets. The sales budget provides projected sales revenue, and the cost-of-sales budget provides costs of land, land development, and housing. When cost of sales is subtracted from projected

Schedule 6: Profit Plan (for-sale housing)

Approved by: _____   Schedule 6
Date: _____   Job No. _____
   Date:
   By:

		January	February	March	April	Year total
30000	SALES					
40000	COST OF SALES					
	Gross Profit					
Operating Expenses						
50000	FINANCING					
60000	MARKETING					
80000	GENERAL AND ADMINISTRATIVE					
	Total Operating Expenses					
	Net Operating Profit (Loss)					
91000	Other Income					
92000	Other Expenses					
	Net Income (Loss) before Tax					

Schedule 7: Cash Flow Statement (for-sale housing)

Approved by: _____
Date: _____

Schedule 7
Job No. _____
Date:
By:

	January	February	March	April	May	Year
Cash balance—first of month						
Receipts						
Cash sales						
Collection on receivables						
Collection of notes receivable						
Deposits by customers						
Construction loan						
Other income						
Total Receipts						
Disbursements						
Cost of sales						
Financing						
Marketing						
General and administrative						
Other expenses						
Total Expenses						
Cash excess (shortage)						
Borrowed funds required						
Borrowed funds repaid						
Cash balance—end of month						

sales, the estimated gross profit results. Operating expenses are then subtracted from gross profits to arrive at net operating income. Other income and expense items are added or subtracted to arrive at a net income.

Balance Sheet Statement

The Balance Sheet Statement for the forecast budget period uses as a starting point the balance sheet from the preceding budget period. There are numerous advantages to be gained from preparation of a forecast balance sheet. The balance sheet may disclose unfavorable ratios which management may wish to change in the upcoming budget period, and it serves as a check on the accuracy of budgets. The balance sheet makes possible the computation of a return-on-investment ratio by relating net income to capital. An inadequate return would flag the need for budget changes.

Schedule 8: Balance Sheet Statement (for-sale housing)

                                                        Approved by: _____ Schedule 8
                                                                Date: _____ Job No. _____
                                                                                     Date:
                                                                                     By:

ASSETS

Current Assets:
    Cash .... $_____
    Short-term investments .... $_____
    Accounts and notes receivable .... $_____
        Less: Allowance for doubtful accounts .... $_____ $_____

    Inventories:
        Construction materials and raw land .... $_____
        Work in process .... $_____
        Finished housing .... $_____ $_____
    Refundable deposits, prepayments .... $_____
        Total Current Assets .... $_____

Fixed Assets:
    Property, plant and equipment:
        Land .... $_____
        Buildings .... $_____
        Furniture and equipment .... $_____
        Motor vehicles .... $_____
        Construction equipment .... $_____
        Other .... $_____
            Less: Accumulated depreciation .... $_____ $_____
        Total Fixed Assets .... $_____

Other Assets:
    Capital of affiliated companies .... $_____
    Long-term land investment .... $_____
    Developed income property .... $_____
    Organization expense .... $_____
    Deferred charges .... $_____
    Cash surrender value, life insurance .... $_____
    Other .... $_____ $_____
        Total Assets .... $_____

Schedule 8 (*continued*)

LIABILITIES AND STOCKHOLDERS' EQUITY

Current Liabilities:
- Refundable deposits .... $_____
- Accounts payable... $_____
- Notes payable .... $_____
- Accrued taxes payable.. $_____
- Construction loans payable.. $_____
- Accrued interest payable .... $_____
- Current portion of long term debt.............................. $_____
- Other current liabilities.. $_____
- Total Current Liabilities... $_____

Long-Term Debts (less current portion)............................. $_____

Stockholders' Equity:
- Capital stock .... $_____
- Retained earnings.. $_____ $_____

Total Liabilities and Stockholders' Investment ..... $_____

THE COST-OF-SALES PLAN: FOR-SALE HOUSING

The Cost-of-Sales Plan (see the summary in Schedule 2) consists of the following cost plans or backup schedules:

Schedule 2–A: Summary, Cost Plan
Schedule 2–B: Land Cost Plan
Schedule 2–C: Land Development Cost Plan
Schedule 2–D: Finished-Lot Cost Plan
Schedule 2–E: Direct Construction Cost Plan
Schedule 2–F: Indirect Construction Cost Plan

Schedule 2–A: Summary, Cost Plan (for-sale housing)

Approved by: _____
Date: _____

Schedule 2–A
Job No. _____
Date:
By:

		Plan ____	Plan ____	Plan ____	Plan ____	Plan ____	Total
14200	Finished lots						
14300	Direct construction costs						
14310	Site work						
14315	Concrete work						
14320	Masonry work						
14325	Metal work						
14330	Rough carpentry						
14335	Finished carpentry						
14340	Miscellaneous carpentry						
14345	Moisture protection						
14350	Doors, windows, glass, and mirrors						
14355	Finishes						
14360	Specialties						
14365	Appliances						
14370	Plumbing						
14375	Electrical						
14380	Heating, ventilating, and air conditioning						
14385	Amenities budget, common areas						
14400	Indirect construction costs						
	Total Cost of Sales						

Schedule 2–B: Land Cost Plan for Tracts _____ (for-sale housing)

Approved by: _____
Date: _____

Schedule 2–B
Job No. _____
Date: _____
By:

- 13200 Land cost
  - 13210 Purchase price
    - 13211 Tract _____ $_____
    - 13212 Tract _____ $_____
    - 13213 Tract _____ $_____
    - 13214 Tract _____ $_____
  - 13215 Legal fees $_____
  - 13220 Property taxes $_____
  - 13225 Planning fees $_____
  - 13230 Engineering fees $_____
  - 13235 Interest – seller $_____
  - 13240 Interest – institutional $_____
  - 13245 Interest – unsecured $_____
  - 13250 Land escrow and title fees $_____
  - 13255 Marketing research fees $_____
  - 13260 Insurance $_____
  - 13290 _____ $_____

  Total Land Budget for Tracts _____ $_____
  No. of lots _____
  Land budget/lot $_____

Schedule 2–C: Land Development Cost Plan (for-sale housing)

Approved by: _____
Date: _____

Schedule 2–C
Job No. _____
Date:
By:

- 14100 Cost of land development
  - 14110 Cost of land $_____
  - 14120 Construction – land improvement
    - .01 Site clearing and grubbing $_____
    - .02 Demolition $_____
    - .03 Site staking and layout $_____
    - .04 Grading, earthwork $_____
    - .05 Soil input $_____
    - .06 Soil export $_____
    - .07 Retaining walls $_____
    - .08 Storm drainage $_____
    - .09 Flood control $_____
    - .10 Water systems $_____
    - .11 Telephone $_____
    - .12 Gas $_____
    - .13 Electrical $_____
    - .14 Fire hydrants $_____
    - .15 Perimeter wall, fencing $_____
    - .16 Relocations $_____
    - .17 Sanitary sewer $_____
    - .18 Street improvements $_____
    - .19 Sidewalk, curb, and gutter $_____
    - .20 Street lighting $_____
    - .21 TV installation $_____
    - .22 Landscaping $_____
    - .23 Landscape sprinklers $_____
    - .24 Street signs $_____

Schedule 2–C (continued)

```
            .25  Entry treatments                              $_____
            .26  _____               $_____
            .27  _____               $_____
            .28  _____               $_____
            .29  _____               $_____
            .30  _____               $_____    $_____
        Refunds
            .31  _____               $_____
            .31  _____               $_____
            .33  _____               $_____    $_____
  14130  Indirect construction cost
         Refer to the land development column of Schedule 2–F,
         Indirect Construction Cost Plan, for those costs
         allocated to land development                                    $_____
  14140  Financing and interest
         14141  Land development loan
                    .01  Title insurance                       $_____
                    .02  Service charges                       $_____
                    .03  Inspection fees                       $_____
                    .04  Points                                $_____
                    .05  Interest on loan                      $_____
                    .06  Escrow recording fees                 $_____    $_____
         14142  Interest on notes                                         $_____
         14143  Other                                                     $_____
  14150  Professional services
         Obtain professional services cost information from
         Indirect Construction Cost Plan, Schedule 2–F
         (Account 14480).

            Total Land Development Cost for Tract             $_____    $_____
            Number of lots _____
            Land development cost/lot                         $_____    $_____
```

Schedule 2–D: Finished Lot Cost Plan (for-sale housing)

Approved by: _____
Date: _____

Schedule 2–D
Job No. _____
Date:
By:

```
14200  Finished-lot costs
       14210  Development cost of land                        $_____
       14220  Financing and interest                          $_____
       14230  Realty taxes                                    $_____
       14240  Purchase price                                  $_____
       14250  Other                                           $_____    $_____
              Number of lots _____
              Cost/lot                                                   $_____
```

Schedule 2-E: Direct Construction Cost Plan (for-sale housing)

Approved by: _____
Date: _____

Schedule 2-E
Job No. _____
Date:
By:

Tract _____
Plan _____

- 14300 Direct construction costs
    - 14310 Site work
        - .01 On-site stalking and layout $_____
        - .02 Grading $_____
        - .03 Asphalt paving and base course driveway $_____
        - .04 Landscaping $_____
        - .05 Irrigation sprinkler system $_____
        - .06 Wood fencing $_____
        - .07 Masonry walls $_____
        - .08 Storm drainage $_____
        - .09 _____ $_____
        - .10 _____ $_____ $_____
    - 14315 Concrete work
        - .01 Structural $_____
        - .02 Floor slab $_____
        - .03 Garage $_____
        - .04 Driveway $_____
        - .05 Patios $_____
        - .06 Walks $_____
        - .07 Steps $_____
        - .08 _____ $_____
        - .09 _____ $_____ $_____
    - 14320 Masonry work
        - .01 Fireplace $_____
        - .02 Veneer $_____
        - .03 Walls $_____
        - .04 _____ $_____
        - .05 _____ $_____ $_____
    - 14325 Metal work
        - .01 Miscellaneous structural metal work $_____
        - .02 Ornamental metal work $_____
        - .03 _____ $_____
        - .04 _____ $_____ $_____
    - 14330 Rough carpentry
        - .01 Subcontract $_____
        - .02 _____ $_____
        - .03 _____ $_____ $_____
    - 14335 Finished carpentry
        - .01 Subcontract $_____
        - .02 _____ $_____
        - .03 _____ $_____ $_____
    - 14340 Miscellaneous carpentry
        - .01 Carpentry materials $_____
        - .02 Wood stairs $_____
        - .03 Cabinet work $_____
        - .04 Shower and tub wainscot $_____
        - .05 Insulation $_____
        - .06 Gypsum wallboard $_____
        - .07 Interior millwork materials $_____
        - .08 Laminated structural members $_____
        - .09 Trusses $_____
        - .10 _____ $_____
        - .11 _____ $_____ $_
        - .12 _____ $_____ $_____

Schedule 2–E (*continued*)

14345 Moisture protection
    .01 Roofing: Asphaltic $_____
    .02 Roofing: Built up $_____
    .03 Roofing: Wood $_____
    .04 Roofing: Tile $_____
    .05 Sheet metal $_____
    .06 Damp and waterproofing $_____
    .07 Weatherstripping $_____
    .08 _____ $_____
    .09 _____ $_____
    .10 _____ $_____ $_____

14350 Doors, windows, glass, and mirrors
    .01 Garage door(s) $_____
    .02 Wood doors and frames $_____
    .03 Shower doors $_____
    .04 Glass doors and windows $_____
    .05 Mirrors $_____
    .06 Wardrobe sliding or bifold doors $_____
    .07 _____ $_____
    .08 _____ $_____ $_____

14355 Finishes
    .01 Painting, staining, bleaching $_____
    .02 Wall covering $_____
    .03 Stucco $_____
    .04 Tile work $_____
    .05 Resilient flooring, top-set base $_____
    .06 Carpet, labor, material, underlayment $_____
    .07 _____ $_____
    .08 _____ $_____ $_____

14360 Specialties
    .01 Carports $_____
    .02 Clean up work $_____
    .03 Draperies $_____
    .04 Finish hardware $_____
    .05 Counter tops $_____
    .06 Luminous ceilings $_____
    .07 Garage door openers
    .08 _____ $_____
    .09 _____ $_____
    .10 _____ $_____
    .12 _____ $_____ $_____

14365 Appliances
    .01 Refrigerator $_____
    .02 Dishwasher $_____
    .03 Disposal $_____
    .04 Trash compactor $_____
    .05 Range hood $_____
    .06 Range $_____
    .07 _____ $_____
    .08 _____ $_____
    .09 _____ $_____ $_____

14370 Plumbing
    .01 Plumbing subcontract $_____
    .02 Plumbing and miscellaneous equipment supplied by builder $_____
    .03 _____ $_____
    .04 _____ $_____
    .05 _____ $_____ $_____

14375 Electrical
    .01 Electrical subcontract $_____
    .02 Master TV antenna system $_____

Schedule 2–E (*concluded*)

	.03	Electrical fixtures and miscellaneous equipment supplied by builder	$_____
	.04	_____	$_____
	.05	_____	$_____ $_____
14380	Heating, ventilating, and air conditioning		$_____
	.01	Subcontract	$_____
	.02	Equipment and materials supplied by builder	$_____
	.03	_____	$_____
	.04	_____	$_____
	.05	_____	$_____ $_____
	Subtotal Direct Construction Budget For Unit_____		$_____ $_____
14385	Amenities budget, common areas		
	.01	Buildings	
	.02	Building furniture and assessories	$_____
	.03	Trellises, Kiosks, benches	$_____
	.04	Fencing and walls	$_____
	.05	Retaining walls	$_____
	.06	Lakes, ponds, streams	$_____
	.07	Indoor equipment and games	$_____
	.08	Appliances	$_____
	.09	Outdoor furniture	$_____
	.10	Pool and jacuzzi	$_____
	.11	Pool decking	$_____
	.12	Pool fencing	$_____
	.13	Landscaping	$_____
	.14	Landscape maintenance during construction	$_____
	.15	Landscape sprinklers	$_____
	.16	Tennis courts	$_____
	.17	Lighting	$_____
	.18	Concrete decks, walks	$_____
	.19	Asphaltic walks	$_____
	.20	Outdoor play equipment	$_____
	.21	Design fees	$_____
	.22	_____	$_____
	.23	_____	$_____
	.24	_____	$_____ $_____
	Total Amenities, Budget		$_____ $_____
	Amenities budget/unit		$_____ $_____
	Subtotal Direct Construction Budget for Unit_____		$_____ $_____
	Amenities budget/unit		$_____ $_____
	Total Direct Construction Costs for Unit		$_____ $_____

Schedule 2–F: Indirect Construction Cost Plan (for-sale housing)

Approved by: _____
Date: _____

Schedule 2–F
Job. No. _____
Date:
By:

			Housing	Land development
14400	Indirect construction costs			
	14410	Salaries, wages, and fees		
		14411 Superintendents	$_____	$_____
		14412 Assistants, helpers, laborers	$_____	$_____
		14413 Purchasing	$_____	$_____
		14414 Watchman, security patrol	$_____	$_____
		14415 Trash cleanup	$_____	$_____
		14416 Trash hauling	$_____	$_____
		14417 Snow and water removal	$_____	$_____
			$_____	$_____
	14420	Equipment expense		
		14421 Temporary toilets	$_____	$_____
		14422 Material hoisting	$_____	$_____
		14423 Scaffolding	$_____	$_____
		14424 Temporary fence	$_____	$_____
		14425 Miscellaneous tools and equipment	$_____	$_____
		14426 Automobile and truck expenses	$_____	$_____
		14427 Taxes and insurance on equipment	$_____	$_____
		14428 Depreciation on equipment and tools	$_____	$_____
		14429 Other	$_____	$_____
			$_____	$_____
	14430	Utilities expense		
		14431 Temporary electricity, lighting	$_____	$_____
		14432 Water, hookup, and related utilities	$_____	$_____
		14433 Temporary heat	$_____	$_____
	14440	Field office, warehouse, and storage shed expense		
		14441 Cost attributed to structures	$_____	$_____
		14442 Set up of office and shed(s)	$_____	$_____
		14443 Move office and shed(s)	$_____	$_____
		14444 Telephone	$_____	$_____
		14445 Miscellaneous office expense	$_____	$_____
		14446 Warehouse expense	$_____	$_____
		14447 Depreciation	$_____	$_____
		14448 Other	$_____	$_____
			$_____	$_____
	14450	Bonding of construction	$_____	$_____
	14460	Warranty expense	$_____	$_____
	14470	Miscellaneous expense		
		14471 Job signs	$_____	$_____
		14472 Access roadwork	$_____	$_____
		14473 Vandalism and theft	$_____	$_____
		14474 Maintenance and repairs	$_____	$_____
		14475 Other	$_____	$_____
			$_____	$_____
	14480	Professional services—land development and construction		
		14481 Architectural and engineering services	$_____	$_____
		.01 Planning and architecture	$_____	$_____
		.02 Landscape architecture	$_____	$_____
		.03 Engineering—civil	$_____	$_____
		.04 Engineering—soil	$_____	$_____
		.05 Engineering—hydraulics	$_____	$_____
		.06 Engineering—structural	$_____	$_____

Schedule 2–F (*continued*)

			Housing	Land development
	.07	Engineering—mechanical	$_____	$_____
	.08	Engineering—electrical	$_____	$_____
	.09	Environmental impact report	$_____	$_____
	.10	Construction scheduling	$_____	$_____
	.11	Computer service	$_____	$_____
	.12	Construction management service	$_____	$_____
	.13	Architectural construction Supervision	$_____	$_____
	.14	Other	$_____	$_____
			$_____	$_____
14482		Reproduction and prints	$_____	$_____
14483		Arts and graphics	$_____	$_____
14490		Permits, bonds, fees, taxes, insurance		
	.01	Bonding of construction	$_____	$_____
	.02	Offsite improvements bond	$_____	$_____
	.03	Variance fee	$_____	$_____
	.04	Zoning fee	$_____	$_____
	.05	Tentative parcel map fee	$_____	$_____
	.06	Subdivision map fee	$_____	$_____
	.07	Annexation fee	$_____	$_____
	.08	P.D. permit fee	$_____	$_____
	.09	Building permit fee	$_____	$_____
	.10	Off-site improvement inspection fee	$_____	$_____
	.11	Plan check fee	$_____	$_____
	.12	Area and hook-up fee—storm	$_____	$_____
	.13	Area and hook-up fee—sanitary	$_____	$_____
	.14	Architectural and site control fee	$_____	$_____
	.15	Utility service fee—water	$_____	$_____
	.16	Utility service fee—telephone	$_____	$_____
	.17	Utility service fee—sewer	$_____	$_____
	.18	Utility service fee—electrical	$_____	$_____
	.19	Utility service fee—gas	$_____	$_____
	.20	Real property taxes	$_____	$_____
	.21	Workmen's compensation	$_____	$_____
	.22	Insurance—builders' all-risk	$_____	$_____
	.23	Insurance—earthquake	$_____	$_____
		Total Indirect Construction Cost	$_____	$_____
			$_____	$_____

Allocation of Indirect Construction Cost
A. Total Direct Construction Cost $_____
B. Total Indirect Construction Cost $_____
   Percent of Indirect to direct (B ÷ A)   _____%
Note: The percentage shall be applied against the direct construction cost for each house built, to allocate indirect construction cost per house.

OPERATING EXPENSE PLAN: FOR-SALE HOUSING

The Operating Expense Plan (see the summary in Schedule 5) consists of the following expense plans or backup schedules:

Schedule 5–A: Financing Expense Plan
Schedule 5–B: Marketing Expense Plan
Schedule 5–C: General and Administrative Expense Plan

Schedule 5–A: Financing Expense Plan (for-sale housing)

Approved by: _____
Date: _____

Schedule 5–A
Job No. _____
Date:
By:

- 50000 FINANCING EXPENSE
  - 51000 Land development loans
    - 51100 Title insurance — $_____
    - 51200 Service charges — $_____
    - 51300 Inspection fees — $_____
    - 51400 Points — $_____
    - 51500 Interest in land development loan — $_____
    - 51600 Escrow recording fees — $_____
    - 51900 Other — $_____ $_____
  - 52000 Construction loan expense
    - 52100 Title insurance — $_____
    - 52200 Service charges — $_____
    - 52300 Inspection fees — $_____
    - 52400 Points — $_____
    - 52500 Interest on construction loan — $_____
    - 52600 Escrow recording fees — $_____
    - 52700 Other — $_____ $_____
  - 53000 Permanent mortgage—Points and fees
    - 53100 Points — $_____
    - 53200 Standby fees — $_____ $_____
  - 54000 Fees and appraisals
    - 54100 Brokerage fees — $_____
    - 54200 Legal fees — $_____
    - 54300 Appraisal fees — $_____
    - 54400 Other — $_____ $_____
  - 55000 Closing cost paid for customers — $_____
  - 56000 Interest on notes — $_____
  - 57000 Interest on completed houses — $_____
  - 59000 Other — $_____

    Total Financing Expense — $_____

Schedule 5–B: Marketing Expense Plan (for-sale housing)

Approved by: _____
Date: _____

Schedule 5–B
Job No. _____
Date:
By:

- 60000 MARKETING EXPENSE
  - 61000 Start-up budget
    - 61100 Model home expense
      - 61110 Landscaping not in sales price — $_____
      - 61115 Built-ins — $_____
      - 61120 Wallpaper labor — $_____
      - 61125 Extra paint — $_____
      - 61130 Carpets and draperies — $_____
      - 61135 Excess construction expense — $_____
      - 61140 Air conditioning — $_____
      - 61145 Furnishings — $_____
      - 61150 Accessories — $_____
      - 61155 Interior plants — $_____
      - 61160 _____ — $_____

Schedule 5–B (*continued*)

```
        61165  _____   $_____
        61170  Recoverable costs                 $(_____)  $_____

  61200 Models' compound expense
        61210  Landscape of compound             $_____
        61215  Fencing of compound               $_____
        61220  Music and alarm system            $_____
        61225  Parking lot                       $_____
        61230  _____   $_____
        61235  _____   $_____
        61240  Recoverable costs                 $(_____)  $_____

  61300 Sales office expense
        61310  Trailer rental                    $_____
        61315  Excess construction expense       $_____
        61320  Structure remodel                 $_____
        61325  Furnishings                       $_____
        61330  Accessories                       $_____
        61335  Carpet and drapes                 $_____
        61340  Air conditioning                  $_____
        61345  Interior plants                   $_____
        61350  Wallpaper, labor                  $_____
        61355  Sales displays                    $_____
        61360  Special artwork                   $_____
        61365  _____   $_____
        61370  _____   $_____
        61375  Recoverable costs                 $(_____)  $_____

  61400 Advertising and public relations
        61410  Initial brochures and stationery  $_____
        61415  Newspaper                         $_____
        61420  Direct mail                       $_____
        61425  Magazine                          $_____
        61430  Radio                             $_____
        61435  Television                        $_____
        61440  Signs prior to opening            $_____
        61445  Billboards prior to opening       $_____
        61450  Public relations                  $_____
        61455  Agency commissions                $_____
        61460  _____   $_____
        61465  _____   $_____
        61470  Recoverable advertising allowances $(_____) $_____

  61500 Miscellaneous
        61510  Extra clean-up costs              $_____
        61515  VIP party                         $_____
        61520  _____   $_____
        61525  _____   $_____
        61530  _____   $_____      $_____

        Total Start-up Budget                                  $_____
        Start-up budget/unit                                   $_____

62000 Monthly Site Budget
  62100 Personnel, salaries/fees
        62110  Inside cleaning                   $_____
        62115  Landscape maintenance             $_____
        62120  Pool maintenance                  $_____
        62125  General maintenance               $_____
        62130  Security guard                    $_____
        62135  Sales managers' salary            $_____
        62140  Salesmen's salaries               $_____
        62145  Miscellaneous sales office salaries $_____
        62150  _____   $_____
        62155  _____   $_____     $_____
```

Schedule 5–B (*continued*)

```
62200   Supplies
        62210   Cleaning                                    $_____
        62215   Landscape                                   $_____
        62220   Pool                                        $_____
        62225   Sales office                                $_____
        62230   Replacement of exterior plant cover         $_____
        62235   _____            $_____
        62240   _____            $_____     $_____

62300   Advertising and public relations
        62310   Billboard rent                              $_____
        62315   Billboard repaint                           $_____
        62320   Special signs and flags                     $_____
        62325   Bootleg signs                               $_____
        62330   Brochures and stationery                    $_____
        62335   Newspaper                                   $_____
        62340   Direct mail                                 $_____
        62345   Radio                                       $_____
        62350   Magazine                                    $_____
        62355   Television                                  $_____
        62360   Public relations                            $_____
        62365   Advertising agency fees                     $_____
        62370   Advertising production costs                $_____
        62375   Special events                              $_____
        62380   _____            $_____
        62385   _____            $_____
        62390   Receivable advertising allowances           $(_____)    $_____

62400   Carrying costs
        62410   Interest on models                          $_____
        62415   Amoritization of sales office               $_____
        62420   Furniture and fixture replacement           $_____
        62425   Community association dues                  $_____
        62430   _____            $_____
        62435   _____            $_____     $_____

62500   Utilities, services
        62510   Telephone                                   $_____
        62515   Electric                                    $_____
        62520   Gas and water                               $_____
        62525   Music system                                $_____
        62530   Burglar alarm                               $_____
        62535   Interior plant maintenance                  $_____
        62540   _____            $_____
        62545   _____            $_____     $_____

                Total Monthly Site Budget $_____ × _____ Mo.            $_____
                Total Monthly Site Budget/Unit                            $_____

63000   Closing-Cost Budget                                 PLAN _____
        63100   Commission to outside brokers               $_____
        63200   Multiple listing fees                       $_____
        63300   Commissions to salesmen                     $_____
        63400   Sales escrow charges                        $_____
        63500   Warranty expense                            $_____
        63600   _____            $_____
        63700   _____            $_____

                Total Closing Costs for Plan _____         $_____     $_____

64000   Sales-Training Expense
        64100   Courses — external                          $_____
        64200   Courses — internal                          $_____
        64300   Travel and transportation                   $_____     $_____

65000   Market Research and Consultation                                  $_____
```

Schedule 5–B (*concluded*)

66000	Other Marketing Department Expense		
	66100 Travel and entertainment	$_____	
	66200 Auto expense	$_____	$_____
	Total Closing, Training, and Consultation cost		$_____
	Cost per Plan _____		$_____
	Total Marketing Expense		$_____

Schedule 5-C: General and Administrative Expense Plan (for-sale housing)

Approved by: _____ Schedule 5–C
Date: _____ Project No. _____
                Date:
                By:

80000	GENERAL AND ADMINISTRATIVE EXPENSE		
	81000 Salaries	$_____	
	82000 Office Expense	$_____	
	83000 Depreciation and Amortization	$_____	
	84000 Taxes	$_____	
	85000 Insurance	$_____	
	86000 Professional Fees	$_____	
	87000 Travel and Entertainment	$_____	
	88000 Contributions	$_____	
	89000 Other	$_____	$_____

MANAGEMENT REPORTS: FOR-SALE HOUSING

The need for and effectiveness of management reports to upper levels of management and first-line management should be reviewed on a regular basis. Reports are necessary to inform, maintain control, analyze, and forecast. The fewer the number of reports that can accomplish these objectives, the better. Reports which are not effective in contributing to the objectives should be redesigned, redirected, or discarded.

The provision and distribution of management reports should be coordinated throughout the organization. Chapter 28, Organizational Development, establishes information needs and reporting requirements through an organizational and control matrix.

The Management Reports Summary schedule which follows is not intended to be all-inclusive. We include it to indicate that reports should be summarized on a reports schedule so that it is possible to see at a glance the type of reports generated, the frequency with which they are issued, to whom they are directed, the information they convey, and their purpose. Included with the report summary are two sample reports: (A) the Profit Plan Analysis Report and (B) the Operating Expense Analysis Report.

Management Reports Summary (for-sale housing)

Report	Frequency	Directed to	Information conveyed	Purpose
Preconstruction Phase				
Market Analysis				
Feasibility Analysis				
Updated Market Analysis				
Updated Feasibility Analysis				
Preliminary Budget				
Preconstruction Budget				
Project Progress Report				
Summary Budget Comparison				
Construction and Sales Phase				
Updated Market Analysis				
Project Progress Report				
Detailed Construction Progress Report				
In-Process Construction Budget Analysis				
Operating Expense Analysis				
Unit Cost Analysis				
Unit Gross Profit Analysis				
Closing Report and Forecast				
Profit and Loss Statement				
Detailed Profit and Loss Statement				
Cash Flow Statement				
General Ledger/Financial Reporting				
Profit and Loss Statement				
Balance Sheet				
Trial Balance				
General Ledger				
Month-End Check Register				
Cash Receipts				
Distribution				
Administrative Overhead Budget				

Sample Report A: Profit Plan Analysis Report (for-sale housing)

REPORT
JOB NO.
DATE:
BY:

Approved by: ___
Date: ___

	Current month			Year to date			Annual		
	Budget	*Variance*	*Actual*	*Budget*	*Variance*	*Actual*	*Budget*	*Variance*	*Forecast*
30000 SALES									
40000 COST OF SALES									
Gross Profit									
Operating Expenses									
50000 FINANCING									
60000 MARKETING									
80000 GENERAL AND ADMINISTRATIVE									
Total Operating Expense									
Net Operating Profit (Loss)									
91000 Other Income									
92000 Other Expense									
Net Income (Loss) before Tax									

Sample Report B: Operating Expense Analysis Report (for-sale housing)

Operating expenses	Current month			Year to date			Annual		
	Budget	Variance	Actual	Budget	Variance	Actual	Budget	Variance	Forecast
50000 FINANCIAL EXPENSE									
51000 Land Development Loans									
52000 Construction Loan Expense									
53000 Permanent Mortgages-Points and Fees									
54000 Fees and Appraisals									
55000 Closing Costs Paid for Customers									
56000 Interest on Notes									
57000 Interest on Completed Houses									
59000 Other financing costs									
50000 Total									
60000 MARKETING EXPENSE									
61000 Start-up Budget									
61100 Model home expense									
61200 Model compound									
61300 Sales office									
61400 Advertising and public relations									
61500 Miscellaneous									
Subtotal									
62000 Monthly Site Budget									
62100 Personnel, salaries fees									
62200 Supplies									
62300 Advertising and public relations									
62400 Carrying costs									
62500 Utilities, services									
Subtotal									
63000 Closing Cost Budget									
64000 Sales-Training Expense									
65000 Market Research and Consultation									
66000 Other									
60000 Total									
80000 GENERAL AND ADMINISTRATIVE EXPENSE									
81000 Salaries									
82000 Office Expense									
83000 Depreciation and Amortization									
84000 Taxes									
85000 Insurance									
86000 Professional Fees									
87000 Travel and Entertainment									
88000 Contributions									
89000 Other									
80000 Total									
Total Operating Expenses									

BUDGET PLAN: RENTAL HOUSING

The Budget Plan for rental housing consists of the Summary Budget Plan and the following backup schedules or forms:

Schedule 1:	Summary, Budget Plan
Schedule 1-A:	Land Cost Plan
Schedule 1-B:	Land Development Cost Plan: Off-Site Development
Schedule 1-C:	Summary, Direct Construction Cost Plan
Schedule 1-D:	Direct Construction Cost Plan
Schedule 1-E:	Detail Backup to Direct Construction Cost Plan
Schedule 1-F:	Indirect Construction Cost Plan
Schedule 1-G:	Financing Expense Plan
Schedule 1-H:	Marketing and Management Expenses Plan
Schedule 1-I:	Management Reports Summary
	Sample management reports

    A. Indirect Construction Cost Analysis Report
    B. Direct Construction Cost Analysis Report
    C. Income and Expense and Annual Cash Flow Analysis Report
    D. Off-Site Cost Analysis Report

Schedule 1: Summary, Budget Plan (rental housing)

Schedule 1
Job No. _____
Date:
By:

	Cost	Per unit	Total
13200	Land cost		
14100	Land development cost		
14300	Direct construction costs		
14400	Indirect construction costs		
50000	FINANCING EXPENSE		
60000	MARKETING EXPENSE		
80000	GENERAL AND ADMINISTRATIVE		
	Total Costs		

Approved By: _____
Date: _____

Schedule 1–A: Land Cost Plan (rental housing)

Schedule 1–A
Job No. _____
Date:
By:

13200 Land cost
- 13210 Purchase price
  - 13211 Release section_____ $_____
  - 13212 Release section_____ $_____
  - 13213 Release section_____ $_____
  - 13214 Release section_____ $_____
- 13215 Legal fees $_____
- 13220 Property taxes $_____
- 13225 Planning fees $_____
- 13230 Engineering fees $_____
- 13235 Interest—seller $_____
- 13240 Interest—institutional $_____
- 13245 Interest—unsecured $_____
- 13250 Land escrow and title fees $_____
- 13255 Market research fees $_____
- 13260 Insurance $_____
- 13290 Other $_____

Total Land Budget $_____
No. of units _____
Land budget/unit $_____

Approved by: _____
Date: _____

Schedule 1–B: Land Development Cost Plan: Off-site Development (rental housing)

Schedule 1–B
Job No. _____
Date:
By:

14100 Development cost of land (off-site development)
    14120 Direct construction costs (off-site construction)
        .01 Grading $_____
        .02 Retaining walls $_____
        .03 Import, export soil $_____
        .04 Street lighting $_____
        .05 Street improvement $_____
        .06 Sidewalk, curb, and gutter $_____
        .07 Landscaping $_____
        .08 Storm drains and catch basins $_____
        .09 Flood control structures $_____
        .10 Water systems $_____
        .11 Telephone $_____
        .12 Gas $_____
        .13 Electrical $_____
        .14 Fire hydrants $_____
        .15 Perimeter wall, fencing $_____
        .16 Relocations $_____
        .17 Sewer $_____
        .18 Contingency $_____
        .19 _____ $_____
        .20 _____ $_____
        .21 _____ $_____
        .22 _____ $_____
        .23 _____ $_____ $_____
        .24 Less refunds $_____
        .25 _____ $_____
        .26 _____ $_____
        .27 _____ $_____ $_____
        Total after Deduction of Refunds $_____
    14130 Indirect construction cost $_____

Refer to the off-site column of Schedule 1–F, Indirect Construction Cost Plan (below) for those costs allocated to land development.

    14140 Financing and interest

Financing and interest are not generally changed to off-site work but added on to the entire project as an operating expense in Account 50000 (Financing expense). $_____

    14150 Professional services

Obtain professional services cost information from the Indirect Construction Cost Plan, Schedule 1–F (Account 14480). $_____

        Total Land Development Cost
        (Off-Site Cost) $_____
        Number of units _____
        Total Land Development Cost/
        Unit (Off-Site Cost/Unit) $_____

Approved by: _____
Date: _____

Schedule 1–C: Summary, Direct Construction Cost Plan (rental housing)

Schedule 1–C
Job No. _____
Date:
By:

Cost item		Total	Per unit
14300	Direct construction costs		
14310	Site work		
14315	Concrete work		
14320	Masonry work		
14325	Metal work		
14330	Rough carpentry		
14335	Finished carpentry		
14340	Miscellaneous carpentry		
14345	Moisture protection		
14350	Doors, windows, glass, mirrors		
14355	Finishes		
14360	Specialties		
14365	Appliances		
14370	Plumbing		
14375	Electrical		
14380	Heating, ventilating, air conditioning		
14385	Recreational specialties		
14390	Furnishings, equipment		
14395	Contingencies		
Total Direct Construction Cost Approved by: _____ Date: _____			

Schedule 1–D: Direct Construction Cost Plan (rental housing)

Schedule 1–D
Job No. _____
Date:
By:

14300 Direct Construction Costs   *Total*   *Per unit*

    14310 Site work—on site
- .01 Site clearing and grubbing $_____ $_____
- .02 Demolition $_____ $_____
- .03 On-site staking and layout $_____ $_____
- .04 Earthwork $_____ $_____
- .05 Soil export $_____ $_____
- .06 Soil import $_____ $_____
- .07 Storm drainage $_____ $_____
- .08 Concrete for exterior flatwork $_____ $_____
- .09 Asphalt paving and base course $_____ $_____
- .10 Parking and traffic controls $_____ $_____
- .11 Irrigation sprinkler system $_____ $_____
- .12 Landscaping $_____ $_____
- .13 Wood fencing $_____ $_____
- .14 _____ $_____ $_____
- .15 _____ $_____ $_____
- .16 _____ $_____ $_____
- .17 _____ $_____ $_____

        Sub total $_____ $_____

Schedule 1–D (*continued*)

			Total	Per unit
14315		Concrete work		
	.01	Concrete	$____	$____
	.02	Lightweight concrete	$____	$____
	.03	Medium-weight concrete	$____	$____
	.04	_____	$____	$____
	.05	_____	$____	$____
	.06	_____	$____	$____
		Subtotal	$____	$____
14320		Masonry		
	.01	Subcontract	$____	$____
	.02	_____	$____	$____
	.03	_____	$____	$____
	.04	_____	$____	$____
	.05	_____	$____	$____
	.06	_____	$____	$____
		Subtotal	$____	$____
14325		Metal work		
	.01	Structural steel and miscellaneous metal	$____	$____
	.02	Ornamental metal work	$____	$____
	.03	_____	$____	$____
	.04	_____	$____	$____
	.05	_____	$____	$____
	.06	_____	$____	$____
		Subtotal	$____	$____
14330		Rough carpentry		
	.01	Subcontract	$____	$____
	.02	_____	$____	$____
	.03	_____	$____	$____
		Subtotal	$____	$____
14335		Finished carpentry		
	.01	Sub Contract	$____	$____
	.02	_____	$____	$____
	.03	_____	$____	$____
	.04	_____	$____	$____
	.05	_____	$____	$____
	.06	_____	$____	$____
	.07	_____	$____	$____
	.08	_____	$____	$____
	.09	_____	$____	$____
		Subtotal	$____	$____
14340		Miscellaneous carpentry		
	.01	Carpentry Materials	$____	$____
	.02	Sauna	$____	$____
	.03	Wood stairs	$____	$____
	.04	Cabinet work	$____	$____
	.05	Marlite	$____	$____
	.06	Insulation	$____	$____
	.07	Gypsum wallboard	$____	$____
	.08	Interior millwork materials	$____	$____
	.09	Laminated structural members	$____	$____
	.10	Trusses	$____	$____
	.11	_____	$____	$____
	.12	_____	$____	$____
	.13	_____	$____	$____
	.14	_____	$____	$____
		Subtotal	$____	$____

Schedule 1–D (*continued*)

			Total	Per unit
14345		Moisture protection		
	.01	Roofing	$____	$____
	.02	Sheet metal	$____	$____
	.03	Damp and waterproofing	$____	$____
	.04	Weatherstripping	$____	$____
	.05	_____	$____	$____
	.06	_____	$____	$____
	.07	_____	$____	$____
	.08	_____	$____	$____
	.09	_____	$____	$____
	.10	_____	$____	$____
	.11	_____	$____	$____
	.12	_____	$____	$____
		Subtotal	$____	$____
14350		Doors, windows, glass, mirrors		
	.01	Wood doors and frames	$____	$____
	.02	Shower doors	$____	$____
	.03	Metal doors and frames	$____	$____
	.04	Glass doors and windows	$____	$____
	.05	Mirrors	$____	$____
	.06	Wardrobe sliding doors	$____	$____
	.07	_____	$____	$____
	.08	_____	$____	$____
	.09	_____	$____	$____
		Subtotal	$____	$____
14355		Finishes		
	.01	Painting, staining, bleaching, decorating, wall covering.	$____	$____
	.02	Stucco	$____	$____
	.03	Tile work	$____	$____
	.04	Resilient flooring, top-set base	$____	$____
	.05	Carpet, labor, material, underlayment	$____	$____
	.06	_____	$____	$____
	.07	_____	$____	$____
	.08	_____	$____	$____
	.09	_____	$____	$____
	.10	_____	$____	$____
	.11	_____	$____	$____
	.12	_____	$____	$____
	.13	_____	$____	$____
	.14	_____	$____	$____
	.15	_____	$____	$____
		Subtotal	$____	$____
14360		Specialties		
	.01	Carports	$____	$____
	.02	Toilet compartments	$____	$____
	.03	Clean-up work	$____	$____
	.04	Fire extinguishers	$____	$____
	.05	Draperies	$____	$____
	.06	Finish hardware	$____	$____
	.07	Countertops	$____	$____
	.08	Elevators	$____	$____
	.09	Waste removal	$____	$____
	.10	_____	$____	$____
	.11	_____	$____	$____
	.12	_____	$____	$____
	.13	_____	$____	$____
	.14	_____	$____	$____
	.16	_____	$____	$____
	.17	_____	$____	$____
		Subtotal	$____	$____

Schedule 1-D (continued)

			Total	Per unit
14365	Appliances			
	.01	Refrigerator	$_____	$_____
	.02	Dishwasher	$_____	$_____
	.03	Disposal	$_____	$_____
	.04	Trash compactor	$_____	$_____
	.05	Range	$_____	$_____
	.06	Range hood	$_____	$_____
	.07	Beer dispenser	$_____	$_____
	.08	Icemaker	$_____	$_____
	.09	_____	$_____	$_____
	.10	_____	$_____	$_____
	.11	_____	$_____	$_____
	.12	_____	$_____	$_____
		Subtotal	$_____	$_____
14370	Plumbing			
	.01	Subcontract	$_____	$_____
	.02	Reflecting pool pumps and equipment	$_____	$_____
	.03	Plumbing and miscellaneous equipment supplied by builder	$_____	$_____
	.04	Fire protection system	$_____	$_____
	.05	_____	$_____	$_____
	.06	_____	$_____	$_____
	.07	_____	$_____	$_____
	.08	_____	$_____	$_____
	.09	_____	$_____	$_____
		Subtotal	$_____	$_____
14375	Electrical			
	.01	Electrical subcontract	$_____	$_____
	.02	Master TV antenna system	$_____	$_____
	.03	Electrical fixtures and miscellaneous equipment supplied by builder	$_____	$_____
	.04	_____	$_____	$_____
	.05	_____	$_____	$_____
	.06	_____	$_____	$_____
	.07	_____	$_____	$_____
	.08	_____	$_____	$_____
	.09	_____	$_____	$_____
	.10	_____	$_____	$_____
	.11	_____	$_____	$_____
	.12	_____	$_____	$_____
	.13	_____	$_____	$_____
	.14	_____	$_____	$_____
		Subtotal	$_____	$_____
14380	Heating, ventilating, and air conditioning			
	.01	Subcontract	$_____	$_____
	.02	Equipment and materials supplied by builder and not covered in another section	$_____	$_____
	.03	_____	$_____	$_____
	.04	_____	$_____	$_____
		Subtotal	$_____	$_____
14385	Amenities budget, common area			
	.01	Pool tables and equipment	$_____	$_____
	.02	Ping pong tables	$_____	$_____
	.03	Stero, hi-fi	$_____	$_____
	.04	Sound system	$_____	$_____
	.05	Television	$_____	$_____
	.06	Outdoor equipment	$_____	$_____
	.07	Gym equipment	$_____	$_____
	.08	Dance floor	$_____	$_____
	.09	Pool	$_____	$_____

Schedule 1-D (*continued*)

			Total	Per unit
	.10	Pool decking	$_____	$_____
	.11	_____	$_____	$_____
	.12	_____	$_____	$_____
		Subtotal	$_____	$_____
14390		Furnishings, equipment		
	.01	Furniture — models	$_____	$_____
	.02	Furniture — outdoor	$_____	$_____
	.03	Furniture — recreation building	$_____	$_____
	.04	Furniture — office	$_____	$_____
	.05	Furniture — rental	$_____	$_____
	.06	Furniture — miscellaneous	$_____	$_____
	.07	Accessories — models	$_____	$_____
	.08	Accessories — recreation building and office	$_____	$_____
	.09	Laundry room machines, equipment	$_____	$_____
	.10	Vending machines	$_____	$_____
	.11	_____	$_____	$_____
		Subtotal	$_____	$_____
14395		Contingencies	$_____	$_____
		Total Direct Construction Cost	$_____	$_____

Approved by: _____
Date: _____

ESTIMATE SHEET

Job No. _____

Account No. _____   Description _____

By: Date:
By: Date:
By: Date:

	Estimate			Cost Per:			
Est. No.	Date	Unit	Price	Amount	Unit	Sq.Ft.	Acre

Schedule 1-D (*concluded*)

CONTRACT/PURCHASE ORDER

No.	Date	Amount	Contractor	Description

Detail Backup to Direct Construction Cost Plan

The Detail Backup to the Direct Construction Cost Plan (Schedule 1-E) lists in detail all costs included in each cost account of the Direct Construction Cost Plan. The backup also lists items as "excluded" which may mistakenly be included in a cost account. For example, the cost account 14310, Sitework—on site, .08, concrete for exterior flatwork, is a single-cost account but represents an accumulation of various costs related to concrete for exterior flatwork.

Most accounting or budget systems do not carry the budgeting format any further than in the above example. This provides some uncertainty for the purchasing, construction, and accounting departments as to what costs to include or exclude in specific cost accounts. The result is a cost allocation problem whereby different departments or individuals may allocate differently, in the absence of a more definitive description of the cost account.

When budgets are terminated at a particular detail level, there is the assumption that the technology exists within the organization to accumulate and allocate all detail costs below that detail and to allocate these costs properly to the correct cost accounts. This assumption is generally an incorrect one, and this is one of the chief reasons why many budgets do not promote or facilitate the desired control.

The detail backup schedule lists all work and materials included in each cost account, so that all departments and personnel have exact information on this. Assuming that the budget, as a tool of control, reflects the firm's operations and procedures, the Detail Backup to the Direct Construction Cost Plan is utilized as the outline for the architectural specification. In this manner the work specified is broken into subcontract and purchase order accounts the same way the budget is.

The construction department then bids, subcontracts, and purchases work in the same manner in which it is budgeted and specified. This greatly reduces problems associated with cost allocation, simplifies the work function in each department, and eliminates many areas of potential coordination difficulties. This concept of carrying the budget plan all the way to the source of the cost is referred to as zero-base budgeting.

When the construction department lets the subcontract for 14310.08 concrete for exterior flatwork, for example, it includes the specifications in the contract to establish the scope of the work, quality standards, tolerances, and so on. The specification clearly and in detail specifies what is and is not included in the cost account. The construction department enters the subcontract amount into the budget cost account (see Chapter 27).

This zero-base standardization of the budget, specification, and contract-letting documents does not necessarily introduce rigidity into the architectural and contract-letting functions. For example, a subcontractor may select the cost accounts on which he wishes to bid; he may wish to bid only one or a combination of cost accounts. When a subcontractor bids a combination of cost accounts, he is requested to provide a separate bid amount for each account. If this is not practical and the preferred subcontractor refuses or is not able to break costs out for each cost account, the aggregate amount is entered into the cost account most representative of the overall work of that subcontractor. The other cost accounts represented in the aggregate amount, then, are not allocated a cost in the budget, but it is noted that this amount has been included in the cost account credited with the aggregate amount of the subcontract.

As subcontracting practices vary in different parts of the country, and even within states, the makeup of the cost accounts may differ, so that each cost account represents how work is actually subcontracted or purchased within a particular vicinity. Even within the same vicinity, subcontracting procedures vary over time. Unions are in constant struggle with one another, each seeking to claim a larger share of the work to be performed. When one subcontractor is successful in taking work from another and claiming the work for his own trade, this produces a change in the work included in specific cost accounts within the budget. Therefore the Detail Backup to the Direct Construction Cost Plan must be reviewed periodically to see that it remains in conformance to the way work is actually subcontracted and purchased.

This sounds more difficult than it actually is. When the purchasing agent finds that work must be subcontracted differently than it has been specified, he amends the specification by making the change in the contract document. He also notes the change in the detail backup retrieval file, into which all charges are collected and stored awaiting the periodic review. On a regular basis, perhaps annually, all changes in subcontracting and purchasing procedures are reviewed. At this time the changes can be incorporated into the Detail Backup to the Direct Construction Cost Plan so that the detail backup (which is also the detail outline for the architectural specification) continues to reflect accurately how work is actually subcontracted and purchased. Changes in the detail backup generally do not require changes in the chart of accounts. That is, the cost account headings retain the same titles as before, though the scope of the work under the heading may have changed somewhat because of changes in subcontracting and purchasing operations.

We utilize standard specifications which follow the scope of the work outline in the Detail Backup to the Direct Construction Cost Plan. The standard specifications are reviewed periodically to assure that they continue to reflect current and optimum procedures and practices, materials, and systems utilization. Feedback is retained in a file which is reviewed periodically to decide whether to discard feedback material as irrelevant or modify the detail backup specifications to take advantage of the new information and ideas for profit improvement (see Chapter 24).

It is important that changes in the standardization are tackled on a periodic rather than a day-to-day basis as new information is received. Time and economy do not generally allow for standards to be reviewed and adjusted on a day-to-day basis. Keeping standards current will be more successful if the job is performed semiannually or annually.

In addition to the detail backup and the standard specification, a policy standard is established for each cost account to guide decision making by first-line management and staff. Even with a high degree of standardization, many decisions must be made by first-line management and staff that can be made better if there is a policy to relate the account in question to the organization's objectives. The policy also indicates management's objectives which should guide in the choice between quality, durability, speed, and so on, versus price. It provides decision making parameters to first-line management and staff when procedures and events are not adequately reflected by the standards, and it informs first-line management of the emphasis and importance of objectives and policies relative to a particular cost account. The standard specification and cost account policy standards have not been included in this book.

Only the first account in the Direct Construction Cost Plan (14310, Site work—on site) is shown in Schedule 1-E, which follows. Details for Accounts 14315, concrete work, through 14390, furnishings and equipment, are not given. The site-work account illustrates how the backup to the Direct Construction Cost Plan is developed, which is also the detail outline for the architectural specification not included herein. See Chapter 27 for how Schedule 1-E is used in conjunction with the architectural specification in purchasing and contract letting.

Schedule 1-E: Detail Backup to Direct Construction Cost Plan (rental housing)

14310 Site work—on site

    .01 Site clearing and grubbing
        Included:
          1. Removal of shrubbery and vegetation, and trees.
          2. Removal of existing miscellaneous construction and debris as may occur.
          3. Removal of existing sidewalks where indicated on drawings.
          4. Removal of existing ground-floor slabs and foundations as may occur.
        Excluded:
          1. Building demolition above ground-floor slab.
          2. Existing features shown to remain: trees, fences, etc.

Schedule 1–E

.02 Demolition
Included:
1. Removing all structures down to ground-floor slab foundation or ground line.
2. Hauling surplus and demolished materials from premises.
3. Disconnecting all utilities; notifying all private and/or public agencies concerned; plugging all open sewers, septic tanks, and drains. Capping all water lines, checking with builder on how to plug or cover septic tanks and well openings. Leaving site in a clean and safe condition.
4. Providing safety barriers and lights as required. Taking all required precautions to protect workmen and public at all times.

Excluded:
1. Clearing and grubbing.
2. Removal of ground slab and/or foundations and sidewalks.
3. All subsurface work.
4. Existing features marked to remain: trees, fences, structures, etc.

.03 On-site staking and layout
Included:
1. Staking and layout of rough grades.
2. Staking and layout of finish grades.
3. Staking and layout for paving, sidewalks, walkways, drives, final grades.
4. Staking and layout of excavations, slopes lines, low points, high points, and levels as required by drawings.
5. Staking and layout of building corners and grades, stake for swimming pool, top corners, each building, and reflecting pool.
6. Establishing two (2) reference points on the premises. (Locations shall be given by the builder.)

.04 Earthwork
Included:
1. All excavating, grading, filling, and compaction work.
2. Preparing building pads to subgrade, three feet (3'0") beyond building line.
3. Bank forming, sloping, backfilling and compaction.
4. Scarifying, filling, and compaction for building pads, raised areas, driveways, sidewalks, and all other paved areas.
5. Removal and stockpiling of topsoil as directed by builder.
6. Spreading of stockpiled topsoil as directed by builder.
7. Intermediate staking and layout.

Excluded:
1. Control staking and layout (done by engineers).
2. Excavation and backfill for utility trenches.
3. Excavation and backfill for concrete footings.
4. Clearing and grubbing.
5. Excavation for swimming pool.

.05 Soil export
Included:
1. All costs to export soil.

.06 Soil import
Included
1. All costs to import soil.

.07 Storm drainage
Included:
1. Required incidental work, such as staking of bed elevations, slopes for trenches, checking elevations for catch basins.
2. Excavating and backfilling.
3. Culverts, thrustblocks, sandbagging, spillways, wing walls, etc.
4. Connection to sewer service.
5. Pipe for culverts and storm drains.
6. Drainage structures, catch basins, area drains, clean-outs, manholes, only if required.

Excluded:
1. Area fees and assessments paid by owner.

Schedule 1–E (*continued*)

.08 Concrete for exterior flatwork
   Included:
   1. Concrete sidewalks and driveways on site. (No reinforcing unless called for on drawings.)
   2. Concrete walkways. (No reinforcing unless called for on drawings.)
   3. Concrete patios. (No reinforcing unless called for on drawings.)
   4. Concrete decks. (No reinforcing unless called for on drawings.)
   5. Concrete in breezeways between buildings, including roofed-over breezeways. (No reinforcing unless called for on drawings.)
   6. Footings for exterior masonry on concrete block walls.
   7. Concrete poured stairs.
   8. Redwood headers located in work listed above.
   9. Fine grading work required.
   10. Reflecting pool slab and footing.
   11. Footings for ornamental iron pieces.
   Excluded:
   1. Flatwork off site.
   2. Membrane.
   3. Concrete for exterior stair wells connected to building, exterior footings for free-standing light standards, carport slabs, building slabs and footings.
   4. Footings for wood fencing and wire fencing.
   5. Medium-weight concrete on bridges or placed over structurally supported floor decking.

.09 Asphalt paving and base course
   Included
   1. All asphalt paving and seal coat work.
   2. All crusher-run base rock for asphaltic paving.
   3. All crusher-run base rock for concrete paving.
   4. Redwood headers adjacent to paving, where called for.
   5. Fine grading of subgrade.
   6. Barricades and safety devices.
   Excluded:
   1. Subgrade (to be by grading subcontractor).
   2. Redwood headers in lawn area.
   3. Off-site work

.10 Parking and traffic controls
   Included:
   1. Pavement standard markings for car stalls at noncovered areas.
   2. Directional pavement markings where shown on drawings.
   3. Precast concrete bumpers as shown on drawings.
   4. Painted stall designations.
   5. Crossmatch walkways and speed control bumps where shown.
   Excluded:
   1. Exterior planted-on signs.

.11 Irrigation sprinkler system (All materials excepting those excluded)
   Included:
   1. Sprinkler lines and heads for all lawn and planted areas designated for sprinkling on landscape drawings, or as directed by builder. Backflow valves, valve boxes, stakes.
   2. Submittal of material list and shop drawings showing complete layout of lines and depths, sprinkler control locations, exact plumbing stub-out locations, pipe sizes; pertinent data required to result in an operative system, as laid out by builder's drawings.
   3. Submittal of as-built drawings of all approved and completed construction.
   4. Trenching, backfilling, compaction.
   Excluded:
   1. Hose bibs and lines for same shown on drawings.
   2. Water supply stub-outs to ±5'0" at buildings.
   3. Fire control water systems.

.12 Landscaping
   Included:
   1. Fine grading.

Schedule 1-E (*concluded*)

      2. Seeding.
      3. Sodding.
      4. Mulching.
      5. Sprigging.
      6. Compaction or rolling of topsoils as required.
      7. Redwood planter retaining walls 18″ or less, and redwood headers in lawn areas, as shown.
      8. Plants, trees, staking, headers, large rocks, grading of mounds.
      9. Cutting, watering, pruning.
    10. Sixty (60)-day maintenance.

Excluded:
      1. Redwood headers at perimeter of pavement.
      2. Topsoil placement

.13 Wood fencing

Included:
      1. Wood fencing, gates, hinges, and latch devices.
      2. Patio perimeter fencing as shown on drawings.
      3. Site perimeter as shown on drawings.
      4. Post holes and concrete footings for ornamental metal fencing and gateposts.
      5. Post holes and concrete footings for wood fences.

Excluded:
      1. Decorative masonry posts and/or metal fencing if shown on drawings.
      2. Balcony and stair railings.

Schedule 1-F: Indirect Construction Cost Plan (rental housing)

Schedule 1-F
Job No. _____
Date:
By:

			On site	Off site
14400	Indirect Construction Costs			
14410	Salaries, wages and fees			
	14411	Superintendents	$_____	$_____
	14412	Assistants, helpers, laborers	$_____	$_____
	14413	Purchasing	$_____	$_____
	14414	Watchman, security patrol	$_____	$_____
	14415	Trash cleanup	$_____	$_____
	14416	Trash hauling	$_____	$_____
	14417	Snow and water removal	$_____	$_____
	14418	_____	$_____	$_____
			$_____	$_____
14420	Equipment expense			
	14421	Temporary toilets	$_____	$_____
	14422	Material hoisting	$_____	$_____
	14423	Scaffolding	$_____	$_____
	14424	Temporary fence	$_____	$_____
	14425	Miscellaneous tools and equipment	$_____	$_____
	14426	Automobile and truck expenses	$_____	$_____
	14427	Taxes and insurance on equipment	$_____	$_____
	14428	Depreciation on equipment and tools	$_____	$_____
	14429	_____	$_____	$_____
			$_____	$_____
14430	Utilities expense			
	14431	Temporary electricity, lighting	$_____	$_____
	14432	Water, hookup, and related utilities	$_____	$_____
	14433	Temporary heat	$_____	$_____
14440	Field office, warehouse, and storage shed		$_____	$_____
	14441	Cost attributed to structures	$_____	$_____

Schedule 1–F (*continued*)

			On site	*Off site*
	14442	Set up of office and shed(s)	$_____	$_____
	14443	Move office and shed(s)	$_____	$_____
	14444	Telephone	$_____	$_____
	14445	Miscellaneous office expense	$_____	$_____
	14446	Warehouse expense	$_____	$_____
	14447	Depreciation	$_____	$_____
	14448	Other	$_____	$_____
			$_____	$_____

14450 Bonding of construction $_____ $_____

14460 Warranty expense $_____ $_____

14470 Miscellaneous expense
- 14471 Job signs $_____ $_____
- 14472 Access roadwork $_____ $_____
- 14473 Vandalism and theft $_____ $_____
- 14474 Maintenance and repairs $_____ $_____
- 14475 Other $_____ $_____
    $_____ $_____

14480 Professional Services—Land development and construction
- 14481 Architectural and engineering services $_____ $_____
  - .01 Planning and architecture $_____ $_____
  - .02 Landscape architecture $_____ $_____
  - .03 Engineering—civil $_____ $_____
  - .04 Engineering—soil $_____ $_____
  - .05 Engineering—hydraulics $_____ $_____
  - .06 Engineering—structural $_____ $_____
  - .07 Engineering—mechanical $_____ $_____
  - .08 Engineering—electrical $_____ $_____
  - .09 Environmental impact report $_____ $_____
  - .10 Construction scheduling $_____ $_____
  - .11 Computer service $_____ $_____
  - .12 Construction management service $_____ $_____
  - .13 Architectural construction Supervision $_____ $_____
  - .14 Other $_____ $_____
- 14482 Reproduction and prints $_____ $_____
- 14483 Arts and graphics $_____ $_____

14490 Permits, bonds, fees, taxes, insurance
- .01 Bonding of construction $_____ $_____
- .02 Offsite improvements bond $_____ $_____
- .03 Variance fee $_____ $_____
- .04 Zoning fee $_____ $_____
- .05 Tentative parcel map fee $_____ $_____
- .06 Subdivision map fee $_____ $_____
- .07 Annexation fee $_____ $_____
- .08 P.D. permit fee $_____ $_____
- .09 Building permit fee $_____ $_____
- .10 Off site improvement inspection fee $_____ $_____
- .11 Plan check fee $_____ $_____
- .12 Area and hook-up fee—storm $_____ $_____
- .13 Area and hook-up fee—sanitary $_____ $_____
- .14 Architectural and site control fee $_____ $_____
- .15 Utility service fee—water $_____ $_____
- .16 Utility service fee—telephone $_____ $_____
- .17 Utility service fee—sewer $_____ $_____
- .18 Utility service fee—electrical $_____ $_____
- .19 Utility service fee—gas $_____ $_____
- .20 Real property taxes $_____ $_____
- .21 Workmen's compensation $_____ $_____

Schedule 1–F: (*concluded*)

		On site	Off site
.22	Insurance—builders' all-risk	$_____	$_____
.23	Insurance-earthquake	$_____	$_____
		$_____	$_____
	Total Indirect Construction Cost	$_____	$_____

Allocation of Indirect Construction Cost
A. Total Direct Construction Cost $_____
B. Total Indirect Construction Cost $_____
   % of indirect to direct (B ÷ A)   _____%

Note: The percentage shall be applied against the direct construction cost for each unit built, to allocate indirect construction cost per unit.

Approved by: _____
Date: _____

Schedule 1–G: Financing Expense Plan (rental housing)

Schedule 1–G
Job No. _____
Date:
By:

```
50000  FINANCING EXPENSE
       51000  Land Development Loans
              51100  Title insurance              $_____
              51200  Service charges              $_____
              51300  Inspection fees              $_____
              51400  Points                       $_____
              51500  Interest on land development loan  $_____
              51600  Escrow recording fees        $_____
              51900  Other                        $_____   $_____

       52000  Construction Loan Expense
              52100  Title insurance              $_____
              52200  Service charges              $_____
              52300  Inspection fees              $_____
              52400  Points                       $_____
              52500  Interest on construction loan $_____
              52600  Escrow recording fees        $_____
              52700  Other                        $_____   $_____

       53000  Permanent Mortgage—Points and Fees
              53100  Points                       $_____
              53200  Standby fees                 $_____   $_____

       54000  Fees and Appraisals
              54100  Brokerage fees               $_____
              54200  Legal fees                   $_____
              54300  Appraisal fees               $_____
              54400  Other                        $_____   $_____

       56000  Interest on Notes                                $_____

       59000  Other                                            $_____

              Total Financing Expense                          $_____
```

Approved by: _____
Date: _____

Schedule 1-H: Marketing and Management Expenses (rental housing)

Schedule 1-H
Job No. _____
Date:
By:

- 60000 MARKETING EXPENSE
  - 61000 Start-up Budget
    - 61100 Models' expense
      - 61110 Interior plants — $_____
      - 61115 Accessories — $_____
      - 61120 Furnishings — $_____
      - 61125 Excess construction expense — $_____
      - 61130 _____ — $_____
      - 61135 _____ — $_____
      - 61190 Recoverable costs — $(_____) $_____
    - 61200 Models' compound expense
      - 61210 Excess landscape costs — $_____
      - 61215 Excess construction expense — $_____
      - 61220 Miscellaneous and alarm system — $_____
      - 61225 Temporary parking lot — $_____
      - 61230 _____ — $_____
      - 61235 _____ — $_____
      - 61290 Recoverable costs — $(_____) $_____
    - 61300 Rental office expense
      - 61310 Trailer rental — $_____
      - 61315 Excess construction expense — $_____
      - 61320 Furnishings — $_____
      - 61325 Accessories — $_____
      - 61330 Rental displays — $_____
      - 61335 Special artwork — $_____
      - 61340 Office equipment — $_____
      - 61345 Miscellaneous supplies — $_____
      - 61350 _____ — $_____
      - 61390 Recoverable costs — $(_____) $_____
    - 61400 Advertising and public relations
      - 61410 Initial brochures and stationery — $_____
      - 61415 Newspaper — $_____
      - 61420 Direct mail — $_____
      - 61425 Magazine — $_____
      - 61430 Radio — $_____
      - 61435 Television — $_____
      - 61440 Signs prior to opening — $_____
      - 61445 Public relations — $_____
      - 61450 Agency commission — $_____
      - 61455 _____ — $_____
      - 61460 _____ — $_____
      - 61490 Recoverable advertising allowance — $(_____) $_____
    - 61500 Miscellaneous expense
      - 61510 Extra clean-up costs — $_____
      - 61515 Extra construction costs — $_____
      - 61520 VIP party — $_____
      - 61525 _____ — $_____
      - 61530 _____ — $_____
      - 61535 _____ — $_____ $_____

Total Start-up Budget — $_____
No. units _____
Start-up Budget/unit — $_____

Approved by: _____
Date: _____

Schedule 1–H (*continued*)

- 70000 OPERATING AND MANAGEMENT EXPENSES
  - 71000 Renting Expenses
    - 71100 Advertising and public relations
      - 71110 Billboard rent — $_____
      - 71115 Billboard repainting — $_____
      - 71120 Special signs and flags — $_____
      - 71125 Bootleg signs — $_____
      - 71130 Brochures and stationery — $_____
      - 71135 Newspaper — $_____
      - 71140 Direct mail — $_____
      - 71145 Radio — $_____
      - 71150 Magazine — $_____
      - 71155 Television — $_____
      - 71160 Public relations — $_____
      - 71165 Advertising agency fees — $_____
      - 71170 Advertising production cost — $_____
      - 71175 Special events — $_____
      - 71180 _____ — $_____
      - 71185 _____ — $_____
      - 71190 Recoverable advertising allowance — $(_____) $_____
    - 71200 Commissions
      - 71210 Commissions to outside brokers — $_____
      - 71215 Listing fees — $_____
      - 71220 Commissions to rental personnel — $_____ $_____
    - 71300 Credit reports — $_____
    - 71400 Rental personnel salaries — $_____
    - 71500 Other — $_____ $_____
  - 72000 Administrative Expenses
    - 72100 Administrative salaries — $_____
    - 72200 Property management fees — $_____
    - 72300 Office expenses — $_____
    - 72400 Telephone and telegraph — $_____
    - 72500 Bad debts — $_____
    - 72600 Collection costs — $_____
    - 72700 Data processing — $_____
    - 72800 Other — $_____ $_____
  - 73000 Professional Services
    - 73100 Legal — $_____
    - 73200 Accounting — $_____
    - 73300 Market research — $_____
    - 73400 Other — $_____ $_____
  - 74000 Operating Expenses
    - 74100 Utilities
      - 74110 Gas — $_____
      - 74120 Electricity — $_____
      - 74130 Fuel — $_____
      - 74140 Water and sewer — $_____
      - 74150 Other — $_____ $_____
    - 74200 Engineering — $_____
    - 74300 Janitorial
      - 74310 Janitorial payroll — $_____
      - 74320 Janitorial services — $_____
      - 74330 Janitorial supplies — $_____ $_____
    - 74400 Trash removal service — $_____
    - 74500 Exterminating — $_____

Schedule 1-H (concluded)

	74600	Snow removal		$__
	74700	Other contractural services		$__
	74800	Vehicle and equipment expenses		$__
	74900	Other		$__
75000	Maintenance and Repair Expenses			
	75100	Redecorating	$__	
	75200	Maintenance payroll	$__	
	75300	Maintenance and repair contracts	$__	
	75400	Ground maintenance and repairs	$__	
	75500	Vehicle and equipment maintenance, repairs	$__	
	75600	Recreational facility payroll	$__	
	75700	Recreational facility services	$__	
	75800	Recreational facility supplies	$__	
	75900	Other	$__	$__
76000	Taxes and Insurance			
	76100	Real property taxes	$__	
	76200	Personal property taxes	$__	
	76300	Franchise taxes	$__	
	76400	License fees	$__	$__
	76500	Payroll taxes and insurance		
		76510 FICA taxes	$__	
		76520 Workmen's compensation	$__	
		76530 Unemployment insurance	$__	
		76590 Other	$__	$__
	76600	Property damage and liability insurance	$__	
	76700	Multiple peril and hazards insurance	$__	
	76900	Other	$__	$__
77000	Financial Expense			
	77100	Interest on mortgage payable	$__	
	77200	Interest on long-term notes payable	$__	
	77300	Other interest	$__	
	77400	Mortgage insurance	$__	
	77900	Other	$__	$__
78000	Depreciation Expense			
	78100	Buildings and components	$__	
	78200	Maintenance equipment	$__	
	78300	Motor vehicles	$__	
	78400	Furniture and fixtures	$__	
	78500	Recreational facilities	$__	
	78600	Other		$__
79000	Other Management and Operating Expenses			
	79100	_____	$__	
	79200	_____	$__	
	79300	_____	$__	
	79400	_____	$__	$__

Total Marketing and Management Expense $__

No. of units _____

Expense per unit $__

Approved by: _____

Date: _____

Schedule 1-I: Management Reports Summary (rental housing)

Report	Frequency	Directed To	Information conveyed	Purpose
Preconstruction Phase				
Market Analysis				
Feasibility Analysis				
Updated Market Analysis				
Updated Feasibility Analysis				
Preliminary Budget				
Postconstruction Budget				
Project Progress Report				
Summary Budget Comparison				
Construction Phase				
Project Progress Report				
Detailed Construction Progress Report				
Summary Budget Comparison				
In-Process Construction Budget				
Construction Cash Flow Report				
Fill-Up Phase				
Updated Market Analysis				
Project Progress Report				
Rental Absorption, Vacancy Notice and Turnover Report				
Delinquency Report				
Fill-up Cash Flow Report				
Detail, Marketing and Management Expense Report				
Project Cash Flow Report				
Statement of Net Annual Income (loss)				
General Ledger/Financial Reporting				
Profit and Loss Statement				
Balance Sheet				
Trial Balance				
General Ledger				
Month-End Check Register				
Cash Receipts				
Distribution				
Administrative Overhead Budget				

Sample Report A: Indirect Construction Cost Analysis Report (rental housing)*

Approved by: _____ Report
Date: _____ Job No. _____
　　　　　　　　　　　　　Date:
　　　　　　　　　　　　　By:

14400	Indirect construction cost	(A) Budget	(B) Variable	(C) Current forecast	(D) Prior billing	(E) Prior payment	(F) Paid this period	(G) Paid to date	(H) Cost to complete	(I) Percent complete	(J) Percent billed
14410	Salaries, wages and fees										
14411	Superintendents										
14412	Assistants, helpers, laborers										
14413	Purchasing										
14414	Watchman, security patrol										
14415	Trash cleanup										
14416	Trash hauling										
14417	Snow and water removal										
14418											
14410	Subtotal										
14420	Equipment expense										
14421	Temporary toilets										
14422	Material hoisting										
14423	Scaffolding										
14424	Temporary fence										
14425	Miscellaneous tools and equipment										
14426	Auto and truck expense										
14427	Taxes and insurance on equipment										
14428	Depreciation on equipment and tools										
14429											
14420	Subtotal										

* Partial report to indicate format.

Sample Report B: Direct Construction Cost Analysis Report (rental housing)°

Approved by: _____   Report
                              Job No. _____
Date: _____   Date:
                              By:

		(A) Budget	(B) Variance	(C) Current forecast	(D) Prior billing	(E) Prior payment	(F) Paid this period	(G) Paid to date	(H) Cost to complete	(I) Percent complete	(J) Percent billed
14300	Direct construction costs										
14310	Sitework—on site										
.01	Site cleaning and grubbing										
.02	Demolition										
.03	On-site staking and layout										
.04	Earth work										
.05	Soil export										
.06	Soil import										
.07	Storm drainage										
.08	Concrete for exterior flatwork										
.09	Asphalt paving and base course										
.10	Parking and traffic controls										
.11	Irrigation and sprinkler system										
.12	Landscaping										
.13	Wood fencing										
.14											
14310	Subtotal										
14315	Concrete work										
.01	Concrete										
.02	Lightweight concrete										
.03	Medium-weight concrete										
14315	Subtotal										

° Partial report to indicate format.

Sample Report C: Income and Expense and Annual Cash Flow Analysis Report (rental housing)

Approved by: _____ Report:
Date: _____ Project: _____
　　　　　　　　　　 Date:
　　　　　　　　　　 By:

Income and expense	Current month			Year to date			Annual		
	Budget	Variance	Actual	Budget	Variance	Actual	Budget	Variance	Forecast
Income 　Annual gross rent 　Vacancies 　Net rental income 　Laundry income 　Nonrefundable cleaning deposits 　Miscellaneous other income									
Effective gross income									
Expense 　71000　Renting Expense 　72000　Administrative Expense 　73000　Professional Services 　74000　Operating Expenses 　75000　Maintenance and Repairs Expense 　76000　Taxes and Insurance 　79000　Other Expenses									
Total all expenses									
Net operating income Debt service Annual net cash flow									

21 / Budgets, projections, controls, and analysis　　337

Sample Report D: Off-Site Cost Analysis Report (rental housing)

Report:
Job No. _____
Date:
By:

14100	Off-site development	(A) Budget	(B) Variance	(C) Current forecast	(D) Prior billing	(E) Prior payment	(F) Paid this period	(G) Paid to date	(H) Cost to complete	(I) Percent complete	(J) Percent billed
14120	Direct construction cost										
.01	Grading										
.02	Retaining walls										
.03	Import, export soil										
.04	Street lighting										
.05	Street improvement										
.06	Sidewalk, curb and gutter										
.07	Landscaping										
.08	Storm drains and catch basins										
.09	Flood control structures										
.10	Water systems										
.11	Telephone										
.12	Gas										
.13	Electrical										
.14	Fire hydrants										
.15	Perimeter wall, fencing										
.16	Relocations										
.17	Sewer										
.18	Contingency										
19											
.24	Subtotal less refunds										
14120	Subtotal										
14130	Indirect construction costs										
14140	Financing and interest										
14150	Professional services										
14100	Total										

Rental housing cash flow

The following tables, Statement of Annual Net Income (Loss), Construction Cash Flow, 1975, and Fill-Up Cash Flow, 1976, are cash flow exhibits for a hypothetical rental housing project. Assume that the project will be retained by the builder for seven years after completion and then sold. The remaining assumptions are included in the backup schedules to the rental housing cash flow which follow these tables. (See also, Chapter 19.)

The assumption in the cash flows and schedules represent hypothetical expenses and incomes and do not represent operating results for a particular project in a particular market or economic cycle. In preparing a cash flow analysis, use expense and income figures appropriate to the specific situation being analyzed and consult an attorney and accountant on matters requiring accounting or legal advice.* (In presenting the hypothetical cash flow analysis, we are not attempting to give legal or accounting advice; on the contrary, we recommend that the reader secure such advice from the appropriate professionals before proceeding.

Statement of Annual Net Income (Loss)

	1975	1976	1977	1978	1979	1980	1981	1982
Net operating income before debt service	0	$161,236	$235,377	$235,377	$235,377	$235,377	$235,377	$235,377
Deductions								
Deductible construction expenses°	$139,550	–	–	–	–	–	–	–
Mortgage interest	–	$162,815	$161,709	$160,496	$159,166	$157,708	$156,108	$154,355
Depreciation	–	152,298	131,453	114,775	101,405	90,466	80,794	73,301
Total Deductions	139,550	315,113	293,162	275,271	260,571	248,174	236,902	227,656
Net income (loss)	($139,550)	($153,877)	($57,785)	($39,894)	($25,194)	($12,797)	($1,525)	$ 7,721
Estimated tax savings @ 50% tax rate	69,775	76,938	28,892	19,947	12,597	6,398	762	(3,860)
Net operating cash flow	0	35,117	61,102	61,102	61,102	61,102	61,102	61,102
Annual return before reversion	69,775	112,055	89,994	81,049	73,699	67,500	61,864	57,242
Reversion from hypothetical sale	–	–	–	–	–	–	–	91,355
Total Return including Reversion	$ 69,775	$112,055	$ 89,994	$ 81,049	$ 73,699	$ 67,500	$ 61,864	$148,597
Cumulative Return	69,775	181,830	271,824	352,873	426,572	494,072	555,936	704,533

° From 1976, onward consult your CPA or attorney regarding amortization of this expense–IRS code section 189.

Significant Ratios and Economic Tests

1. Break-even Point

   $$\frac{\text{Break-even rental income}}{\text{Scheduled rental income @ 100\%}} \quad \frac{\$338,500}{\$420,028} = 80.59\%$$

2. Payback Period

   Year when total return based on 50% tax rate pays back equity = 4th Year

3. Debt Service Coverage

   $$\frac{\text{Net operating income}}{\text{Debt service}} \quad \frac{\$235,377}{\$174,275} = 1.35 \text{ times}$$

4. Ratio of Economic Value to Total Cost

   $$\frac{\text{Economic value}}{\text{Total cost}} \quad \frac{\$2,353,770}{\$2,065,325} = 1.14 \text{ times}$$

5. Average Cash Return on Equity

   $$\frac{\text{Annual net cash flow}}{\text{Equity}} \quad \frac{\$ 61,102}{\$300,000} = 20.4\%$$

6. Average Annual Total Return on Equity, Excluding Reversion:

   $$\frac{\text{Average annual total return}}{\text{Equity}} \quad \frac{\$ 77,629}{\$300,000} = 25.9\%$$

7. Total Return on Equity

   $$\frac{\text{Total cash returned and net tax benefits}}{\text{Equity}} \quad \frac{\$704,533}{\$300,000} = 2.35 \text{ Times}$$

° The author expresses his thanks to Alfred Harris & Associates, Certified Public Accountants, for reviewing the cash flows and back up schedules prepared by the author for conformance to accounting practices and industry standards.

Construction Cash Flow, 1975

	Preconstruction	May	June	July	August	September	October	November	December	Total
RECEIPTS										
Interim loan°°	—	290,666	210,666	210,666	210,666	210,666	210,666	210,666	210,666	1,765,328
Investor funds	200,000	70,000								270,000
Total Receipts	200,000	360,666	210,666	210,666	210,666	210,666	210,666	210,666	210,666	2,035,328
DISBURSEMENTS°										
Land	—	192,000	—	—	—	—	—	—	—	192,000
Land development		30,000	10,200							40,200
Direct construction	—	110,090	179,890	185,000	185,000	185,000	185,000	185,000	168,540	1,383,520
Indirect construction	70,500	39,500	11,020	10,500	10,500	10,500	10,500	10,500	10,500	184,020
Financing expense	34,480	22,240	6,000	8,000	9,500	10,000	11,400	13,200	14,711	129,531
Marketing and management expense								4,500	3,500	8,000
Overhead allocation	50,000	4,000	4,000	4,000	4,000	4,000	4,000	4,000	2,000	80,000
Total disbursements	154,980	397,830	211,110	207,500	209,000	209,500	210,900	217,500	199,251	2,017,271
Cash flow	45,020	(37,164)	(444)	3,166	1,666	1,666	(234)	(6,534)	11,415	18,057
Cumulative cash flow	45,020	7,856	7,412	10,578	12,244	13,410	13,576	6,642	18,157	18,057†

° See backup Schedule D, Summary Budget, above for disbursement amounts and totals.
°° See Schedule F.
† Cash flow not available for distribution but carried forward to next year to cover negative fill-up cash flow.

Fill-up Cash Flow, 1976

	January	February	March	April	May	June	July	August	September	October	November	December	Total
Revenue													
Carry forward of 1975 cumulative cash flow	$18,157	—	—	—	—	—	—	—	—	—	—	—	$ 18,157
Effective gross income*	4,375	$ 8,750	$13,125	$17,501	$21,876	$26,251	$30,626	$33,251	$33,300	$33,300	$33,300	$33,300	288,955
Investor funds	10,000	10,000	10,000	—	—	—	—	—	—	—	—	—	30,000
Total revenue	$32,532	$18,750	$23,125	$17,501	$21,876	$26,251	$30,626	$33,251	$33,300	$33,300	$33,300	$33,300	$337,112
Expense													
Marketing and management expense†	$ 7,452	$ 7,152	$ 7,352	$ 7,552	$ 8,633	$ 8,056	$13,162†	$13,672	$13,672	$13,672	$13,672	$13,672	$127,719
Net operating cash flow before debt service	$25,080	$11,598	$15,773	$ 9,949	$13,243	$18,195	$17,464	$19,579	$19,628	$19,628	$19,628	$19,628	$209,393
Debt service	14,523	14,523	14,523	14,523	14,523	14,523	14,523	14,523	14,523	14,523	14,523	14,523	174,276
Net cash flow	10,557	(2,925)	1,250	(4,574)	(1,280)	3,672	2,941	5,056	5,105	5,105	5,105	5,105	35,117
Cumulative cash flow	10,557	7,632	8,882	4,308	3,028	6,700	9,641	14,697	19,802	24,907	30,012	35,117	

* Refer to backup Schedule C, Fill-up Projection, to obtain effective gross income figures.
† Refer to Schedule 1-H, Marketing and Management Expenses, in this chapter for format used in developing marketing and management expenses during fill-up period.

Backup schedules for rental housing cash flow

The backup schedules for the rental housing cash flow exhibit include the following:

Schedule A: Income and Expense Schedule and Annual Cash Flow
Schedule B: Projected Rental Schedule
Schedule C: Fill-up Projection
Schedule D: Summary, Budget
Schedule E: Summary, Direct Construction Cost Budget
Schedule F: Construction Loan Interest Projection
Schedule G: Mortgage Computation and Equity Requirement
Schedule H: Amoritization Schedule
Schedule I: Depreciation Schedule
Schedule J: Basis Adjustments and Excess Depreciation
Schedule K: Hypothetical Sale after 7 Years' Operation

Schedule A: Income and Expense Schedule and Annual Cash Flow (rental housing)

INCOME

Source	Amount	Percent
Annual gross rent	$408,528	100.00%
Vacancies	20,426	5.00
Net rental income	388,102	95.00
Laundry income	4,500	1.10
Nonrefundable cleaning deposits	5,000	1.22
Miscellaneous other income	2,000	.49
Effective gross income	$399,602	97.81

EXPENSE

		Amount	Percent
70000	Operating and management expense		
71000	Renting expense	$ 8,170	2.0%
72000	Administrative expense	22,469	5.5
73000	Professional services	4,085	1.0
74000	Operating expenses	30,638	7.5
75000	Maintenance and repairs expense	24,512	6.0
76000	Taxes and insurance	69,449	17.0
79000	Other expenses	4,902	1.2
	Total all expenses	$164,225	40.2

Net operating income $235,377
Debt service $174,275
Annual net cash flow .... $ 61,102

Schedule B: Projected Rental Schedule (rental housing)

No. units		Type	Sq. ft. size	Monthly rental	Rent sq. ft.	Month gross	Annual gross
20	A	Studio	425	$157.25	$.37	$3,145	$37,740
25	B	Jr. 1	540	183.60	.34	4,590	55,080
38	C	1–1 bath	650	208.00	.32	7,904	94,848
30	D	1–1 bath	690	220.80	.32	6,624	79,488
32	E	2–1 bath	810	243.00	.30	7,776	93,312
15	F	2–1.5 baths	890	267.00	.30	4,005	48,060
160			106,670				

Annual gross rent: $408,528

Schedule C: Fill-up Projection (rental housing)
Fill-up Projection at 20 per Month
Average Rent, $218.76 per Month°

Period	Units rented	Gross	Cumulative gross
January 76	20	$ 4,375	$ 4,375
February	40	8,750	13,125
March	60	13,125	26,250
April	80	17,501	43,751
May	100	21,876	65,627
June	120	26,251	91,878
July	140	30,626	122,504
August	152	33,251	155,755

° Average rent for fill-up projection includes: apartment rent, laundry income, cleaning deposits, and miscellaneous other income prorated to each unit.

Schedule D: Summary Budget (rental housing)

Cost		Per unit	Total
13200	Land cost	$ 1,200.00	$ 192,000.00
14100	Land development costs	251.25	40,200.00
14300	Direct construction costs	8,647.00	1,383,520.00
14400	Indirect construction costs	1,150.12	184,020.00
50000	FINANCING EXPENSES	809.57	129,531.00
6000–7000	MARKETING EXPENSE	350.34	56,054.00
80000	GENERAL AND ADMINISTRATIVE EXPENSE	500.00	80,000.00
	Total costs	$12,908.28	$2,065,325.00

Note: Summaries are from the detail budget plans included in this chapter. For simplicity detail budget formats are shown to indicate how summary budget figures are arrived at, but detail budget figures are not given in the detail budget formats which are included.

Schedule E: Summary, Direct Construction Cost Budget (rental housing)

14300	Direct construction costs	Total	Per unit
14310	Site work	$ 103,000	$ 643.75
14315	Concrete work	88,000	550.00
14320	Masonry work	1,500	9.37
14325	Metal work	3,030	18.94
14330	Rough carpentry	177,000	1,106.25
14335	Finished carpentry	98,000	612.50
14340	Miscellaneous carpentry	115,000	718.75
14345	Moisture protection	43,000	268.75
14350	Doors, windows, glass, and mirrors	86,500	540.62
14355	Finishes	156,300	976.87
14360	Specialties	48,900	305.62
14365	Appliances	78,390	489.94
14370	Plumbing	132,400	827.50
14375	Electrical	108,000	675.00
14380	Heating, ventilating, air conditioning	83,000	518.75
14385	Amenities budget, common area	5,500	34.37
14390	Furnishings and equipment	18,000	112.50
14395	Contingencies	38,000	237.50
	Total Direct Construction Costs	$1,383,520	$8,647.00

Note: Refer to Direct Construction Cost Plan, Schedule 1-D, in this chapter for format used in developing detail direct construction costs which are summarized in this schedule.

Schedule F: Construction Loan Interest Projection (rental housing)
$1,765,328 @ $9\frac{1}{4}$/$1\frac{1}{2}$ points

Period	Draws	Cumulative	Monthly interest	Cumulative interest
May	$290,666	$ 290,666	$ 2,240	$ 2,240
June	210,666	501,332	3,864	6,104
July	210,666	711,998	5,488	11,592
August	210,666	922,664	7,112	18,704
September	210,666	1,133,330	8,736	27,440
October	210,666	1,343,996	10,360	37,800
November	210,666	1,554,662	11,984	49,784
December	210,666	1,765,328	13,609	63,393

Interest	$ 63,393
$1\frac{1}{2}$ points	26,480
Interest and points	$ 89,873
Other financing expenses°	$ 39,658
	$129,531

° Refer to the Financing Expense Plan, Schedule 1-G, in this chapter for the format of how the detailed financing expenses are developed.

Schedule G: Mortgage Computation (rental housing)

Net cash flow before debt service	$ 235,377
Capitalization rate	10%
Economic value	$2,353,770
Probable loan commitment	75%
Estimate of mortgage	$1,765,328

Equity Requirement

Total project cost	$2,065,325
Estimate of mortgage	$1,765,328
Equity (rounded)	$ 300,000

Loan Terms, Assumptions

Interest	9.25%	
Period	30 years	
Points	1½ = $	26,480
Yearly payments	$	174,275
Monthly payments	$	14,523

Schedule H: Amortization Schedule (rental housing)

Period	Interest	Principle	Balance
76	$162,815.07	$11,459.97	$1,753,868.03
77	161,708.89	12,566.15	1,741,301.88
78	160,495.97	13,779.07	1,727,522.81
79	159,165.96	15,109.08	1,712,413.73
80	157,707.57	16,567.47	1,695,846.26
81	156,108.40	18,166.64	1,677,679.62
82	154,354.89	19,920.15	1,657,759.47

Schedule I: Depreciation Schedule (rental housing)

Depreciable costs	
Building	$1,680,514
Nondepreciable capital items	
Land	192,000
Start-up costs	53,261
EXPENSES	
Interest and loan fees	127,050
Taxes and insurance	12,500
Total Costs	$2,065,325

Components	Cost	Life expectancy
Shell	$1,153,774	33⅓
Plumbing–Electrical	335,800	20
Carpets–drapes	94,550	7
Appliances	78,390	10
Furniture	18,000	5
Total	$1,680,516	

Depreciation method (shell) DDB _____
Depreciation method (others) DDB _____
First user? Yes _____ No _____

Schedule I (*continued*)

Year	Shell	Plumbing, electrical	Carpets, drapes	Appliances	Furniture	Total annual depreciation	Cumulative depreciation
1976	$69,226	$33,580	$27,014	$15,678	$7,200	$152,298	$152,698
1977	65,073	30,222	19,296	12,542	4,320	131,453	284,751
1978	61,168	27,199	13,782	10,034	2,592	114,775	398,926
1979	57,498	24,480	9,845	8,027	1,555	101,405	500,331
1980	54,048	22,031	7,032	6,422	933	90,466	590,794
1981	50,805	19,829	5,023	5,137	–	80,794	671,588
1982	47,757	17,846	3,588	4,110	–	73,301	744,889
Total	405,575	175,187	85,580	61,950	16,597	744,889	

Schedule J: Basis Adjustments and Excess Depreciation, Tax preference item (rental housing)

Year	Accelerated cumulative depreciation	Basis	Straight-line cumulative	Excess depreciation
1975		$1,680,514		
1976	$152,698	$1,527,816	$ 76,347	$ 76,351
1977	284,151	1,396,363	152,694	131,457
1978	398,926	1,281,588	229,041	169,885
1979	500,331	1,180,183	305,388	194,943
1980	590,794	1,089,720	381,735	209,059
1981	671,588	1,008,926	454,482	217.106
1982	744,889	935,625	527,229	217,660

STRAIGHT-LINE DEPRECIATION

Year	Shell	Plumbing, electrical	Carpets, drapes	Appliances	Furniture	Annual depreciation	Cumulative depreciation
1976	$34,611	$16,790	$13,507	$7,839	$3,600	$76,347	$ 76,347
1977	34,611	16,790	13,507	7,839	3,600	76,347	152,694
1978	34,611	16,790	13,507	7,839	3,600	76,347	229,041
1979	34,611	16,790	13,507	7,839	3,600	76,347	305,388
1980	34,611	16,790	13,507	7,839	3,600	76,347	381,735
1981	34,611	16,790	13,507	7,839	–	72,747	454,482
1982	34,611	16,790	13,507	7,839	–	72,747	527,229
Total	242,277	117,530	94,549	54,873	18,000	527,229	

Schedule K: Hypothetical Sale after 7 Years Operation (rental housing)†

Description	Personal Property	Real Property	Land	Total	Ordinary gains	Capital gains
Book value at time of sale						
Cost	18,000	1,662,514	192,000	1,872,514		
Accumulated depreciation	16,597	728,292	0	744,889		
Basis at time of sale	1,403	934,222	192,000	1,127,625		
Sale price (net of selling expenses)	3,000	1,800,000	397,000	2,200,000		
Gross profit	1,597	865,778	205,000	1,072,375		
Personal property gain	1,597				1,597	
Real property gain						
100% of post 1975 excess depreciation°		219,063			219,063	
Balance is capital gain	None	646,715	205,000			851,715
Total Gains					220,660	851,715

° Depreciation on personal property eliminated (see Schedule I and J). Schedule I ($746,889 − $16,597) − Schedule J ($527,229 − $18,000) = $219,063. Appliances, carpets, etc. are assumed to be real property for this purpose.
° Analysis between ordinary and capital gain on sale

Computation of tax on Sale and after Tax Proceeds Federal Income Tax (assuming no other income)

Tax on ordinary income		$ 125,442
25% of first $50,000 of long term gain		12,500
Tax on ordinary income plus capital gain deduction		
($220,660 + (50% of $851,715) = 646,517	Tax $423,541	
Less tax on ordinary income plus $25,000		
($220,660 + $25,000) = $245,660	Tax $142,942	280,599
		418,541
Minimum tax		
Tax preference item (50% of $851,715)	Tax $425,855	
Less 50% of regular tax (50% of $418,541)	Tax $209,270	
	$216,587	
Tax at 15%		32,488
Total Federal Taxes°		$ 451,029
	State tax†	
After-tax sales proceeds		
Sales price (net of selling expense)		$2,200,000
Less mortgage balance		1,657,616
		542,386
Less total federal taxes	$451,029	
Less total state taxes†		
		451,029
After-tax sales proceeds°		$ 91,355

° Federal tax impact can be lessened by income averaging, installment sale or other means.
† State taxes are not included in the calculation. Reader should figure the state taxes according to applicable state tax law.

22

Planning, organizing, and implementing a profit improvement program

A meaningful profit improvement program is a serious business which requires the continuous support of management at all levels. A profit improvement program is not a crash program but a sustained effort supported by policy, procedure, and resources on an ongoing basis. Crash programs can produce as much harm as good in the long run. A simple command from above to cut costs provides no leadership or direction to the line executive.

Profit improvement requires planning; the success of the program will be directly affected by the quality of the planning. The profit improvement program is as much a corporate planning activity as the profit plan. Both should receive equal status, and they should be carried out concurrently. The profit improvement plan is as much required in times of rising profits as when profits are declining.

Profits taken for granted are like friends taken for granted—they are seen less often.

A THREE-PHASE PROGRAM The three phases of the profit improvement program are: (1) appreciation, (2) education, and (3) application.

1. Appreciation In the appreciation phase the entire organization becomes aware of what the profit improvement program is and what it is not. They learn of their involvement in the program as individuals and their eventual participation as members of specific project groups. The organizational benefits and personal benefits to be derived from the profit improvement program are fully outlined to stimulate participants' interest, involvement, and enthusiasm. The appreciation phase is the initial phase in profit improvement, but later it becomes the key to the continuation of the program by completing the circuit of communication, by rewarding achievements, and by adding new information, direction, and scope.

Once a decision is made by top management to introduce a profit improvement program into the organization, all personnel should be told about the program at the same time. The grapevine system can twist facts till they are unrecognizable. Without fail, people mistrust what they do not understand.

Education   If a profit improvement program is to be carried out throughout an entire organization, everyone in it must be aware of the need for profit improvement and the benefits to be derived. Education is needed to orient everyone at all levels so that each understands the objective within the scope of his or her particular ability and responsibility.

In the education phase, the philosophy, policies, tools, and procedures for application are developed internally by small groups. The atmosphere created is one of research, innovation, and experimentation. The assignments and objectives assigned to the small groups are oriented to the ability and responsibility of those comprising each group.

Application   It is the application phase which achieves the end results that show up on the balance sheet. In this phase the policies, tools, and procedures developed in the education phase are applied to operations at every level of the organization.

CHARACTERISTS OF THE PROGRAM   A profit improvement program begins at the top of the organization when the yes-or-no man wants more information on such a program and takes specific action to get it. He must become interested, at least to the extent that he wants to learn more about the potential of an ongoing profit improvement program and how to go about organizing and implementing it. This is the first step in appreciation.

If it is to be effective, the program must be long term and not a shot in the arm or a crash program. The total program will consist of subprograms, some of which may be already in effect and going by various names: cost reduction program, work simplification, value engineering, sales incentive program, efficiency program, waste reduction program, zero defects program, quality control, and so on.

The effective profit improvement program must also extend to all levels of the organization and involve all personnel in an atmosphere of friendliness. It should be a philosophy of improvement through teamwork and understanding, in which the personal development of the individual is emphasized, as well as organizational profit objectives. Each individual should be given an opportunity to participate to the extent of her or his ability—workers as well as managers.

The fact that all individuals in an organization are given the opportunity to participate in such an important program, and the fact that management has considered their contributions important, has a markedly positive effect on employee's attitudes and feelings toward the company. The atmosphere of improvement mindedness and the team approach inspire those who previously may not have felt part of the team to aspire to greater productivity.

Involving all personnel in the profit improvement program requires planning an organizational and reporting structure for profit improvement activities. A pilot group is formed by key operating executives to plan and organize the activity, with the assistance of a profit improvement expert. Then a blue-ribbon steering committee is formed to provide policy direction, lend prestige, and supervise the progress of the program. In addition, a profit improvement coordinator is appointed, with the responsibility of coordinating the overall program and reporting results to the steering committee.

The pilot group and the steering committee establish a second management group (in addition to the top-level group) to take on profit improvement projects. Third and fourth management groups are subsequently established and assisted by the other management groups. The management groups in turn establish worker groups to take on profit improvement projects at their immediate level of involvement.

The structure, policies, and procedures of implementing a profit improvement program vary with each organization, to reflect specific organization needs and unique characteristics. One organization may desire or require a very formalized program, while another prefers an informal one. All programs, however, should have the essential element of continuity and a plan for maintaining it.

Recognizing that a profit improvement program may be as varied as the organization it is intended to serve, we will discuss the structure of a typical profit improvement program. It is assumed that the organization possesses several levels of management, including top-level, middle-level, and first-line management.

STARTING WITH A PILOT PROGRAM

A profit improvement pilot program is limited and is entered into to establish the feasibility of implementing an ongoing, organizationwide program. The success of the pilot program and its effect on the organization's attitudes, policies, and procedures is measured to determine the feasibility and desirability of a permanent, ongoing program.

The top executive group should participate in preliminary review and evaluation of the program and should have an opportunity to influence the yes-or-no man's decision. Because the group should become as well informed as possible about profit improvement programs, a conference meeting with a specialist in the field is usually called for. The subject matter usually consists of the philosophy, organization and planning requirements, general procedures of implementation, tools and techniques available, and a summary of the three phases of the profit improvement program. The final part of this meeting is utilized for problem solving and determining how the program can be implemented within the organization, and its advisability, desirability, and feasibility.

When initial feasibility has been determined, the larger companies generally start out with a pilot program, but smaller companies may launch immediately into a comprehensive profit improvement program, bypassing the pilot program. We will, however, assume a pilot program approach is undertaken, and a pilot group is set up to implement the profit improvement program through its three stages with pilot projects. These pilot projects will enable management to evaluate the program in relation to the specific needs of the organization. Appreciation sessions for the organization as a whole are also discussed in the meeting of the pilot group.

THE PILOT GROUP

The pilot group should consist of the operating leader of the critical operations within the organization, plus one or two top-management representatives. This group reviews in detail all educational material which other groups may use in subsequent sessions. They outline policy for other groups and experiment with procedures, tools, and techniques which may be introduced to other groups for further refinement. The principal responsibility of the pilot group is to analyze all materials presented by the profit improvement expert critically, to determine how they can be redesigned or modified to fit specific organizational needs. The group also needs to interface existing profit improvement programs with the new program so that new programs can build upon the old, where appropriate.

Each member of the pilot group is requested to select six or more operations or activities within his realm of accountability which need improvement or are suitable for experimentation or innovation. Each member is then requested to select one of these operations as a target for profit improvement. In this manner the pilot-group member becomes involved in the actual profit improvement process, while learning about it.

Pilot-group education

The pertinent facts with respect to his project are collected by each member and presented to the group. Techniques, tools, and procedures already introduced and discussed by the expert are used in this process. The group member also uses materials already available within the organization to build on, or he revises existing materials and procedures where appropriate.

In a group of nine, after each member has made his presentation of his project, three of the projects presented are chosen for further study by three-man teams. Actual situations are utilized in discussing the application of new procedures, tools, and techniques. The human relations aspects are also analyzed. Projects not immediately chosen for study become a backlog for further study.

The three-man teams meet independently of the overall pilot group, and each team works on its project. When the entire pilot group meets, a portion of the meeting is devoted to progress reports. Creative suggestions are offered by the group for each project.

As results from efforts filter in, policy and procedure become dominant topics of the meeting. These topics consider how to solve problems involved in the application phase. Committees are formed within the pilot group to organize material for presentation to succeeding groups, schedule progress, and review meetings.

Pilot-group application

Project teams are developed within the pilot group to apply the policy and procedures thus far developed in the educational phase. The project teams are developed by personal preference of the members; a suggested member of a project team, for example, may not be accountable for the activity that the project team seeks to improve. The project teams meet independently and schedule their own meetings, and the minutes of each meeting are directed to each member of the pilot group. At regular intervals the group as a whole meets to review progress, exchange new ideas, and provide creative input to help solve problems the individual teams may be having.

THE STEERING COMMITTEE

The steering committee of the profit improvement program is composed of members of the top executive group. Preferably the yes-or-no man is a member, along with several members of the pilot group. Members of the steering committee should be chosen according to their potential contribution and enthusiasm for the program.

The steering committee meets regularly to review progress of the program, evaluate effectiveness, clarify policies and procedures, and coordinate all efforts with long- and short-range plans. In the early stages of the profit improvement program the committee may meet frequently, but as the program matures the committee may meet quarterly, semiannually, or as requested by the program coordinator.

The steering committee is a blue-ribbon panel of key executives and policy makers. They back the program with authority and prestige and supply the recognition which contributes to appreciation of the program. Feedback is received through this committee, on the basis of which the committee acts to supply top-level counsel and arbitrate interdepartmental conflicts.

THE PROGRAM COORDINATOR

In larger organizations the coordinator has as his full-time responsibility the detailed operation and coordination of the profit improvement program. The coordinator will need special training in his role, which can be gained from seminars, universities, or experts in the field.

In the initial stages of the program, professional assistance by an expert in profit improvement is generally required. In general, this expert must educate the coordinator and the pilot group in profit improvement before it is advisable for the coordinator to attempt to lead the program. The coordinator is a member of the steering committee and usually a member of the pilot group.

PROJECT TEAMS

The ideal project team is one whose members are participating in the improvement process to the extent of their abilities. The team is made up of the individual who is accountable for the work being analyzed, his assistant, outside (outside of the immediate area of responsibility, but within the company) assistance provided by staff or related line functions, and a representative who actually does the work. The lead man in the team, who is accountable for the work being analyzed, can be anyone from the president all the way to a production worker. The reason for outside assistance being injected into the team is to provide an outside view—a fresh perspective. Having a representative on the team who actually does the work provides insights from the point of action and promotes more enthusiastic acceptance by workers.

The larger and more important the scope of the project, the higher is the level of help within the organization which is required. However, it is not always possible to have an ideal team. There may be more important activities on which key individuals must spend their time, though ideally they are a necessary part of the problem-solving processes of a project team. This situation leads to a policy whereby more and more decision making is delegated down the line as the project teams improve in ability through education and experience and warrant more confidence from above. The trend is to get decision making, within the bounds of policy, closer to the point of action where the job is performed (see Chapter 25)

MANAGEMENT TEAMS

The pilot group, upon completing the initial application phase of its pilot projects, forms new management teams to spread the profit improvement activities throughout the management organization. The management group which follows the pilot group usually consists of the right-hand man of each member of the pilot group. The new group goes through the education and application phases (they have already completed the initial appreciation phase).

In the education phase the new group studies and analyzes the objectives and the policies, procedures, and tools refined by the pilot group. This group adds more detailed analysis and insights to the material they have inherited from the pilot group. Each succeeding new group breaks the material into finer levels of detail, to reflect the increased detail involvement at each succeeding lower level of management.

Each new group also increases the emphasis on the human relations aspects of the program at its level of accountability. Each group has the opportunity to edit, refine, and expand upon the material as it passes through its review and analysis. This gives each group an opportunity to participate in policy and procedural formulation, a highly worthwhile effort which provides an opportunity for the group to participate in the development of the program to the extent of its member's abilities.

The members of each new group are requested to select six or more projects which appear to require improvement. Then each member chooses one project from his own list and contributes that project to the group for study and analysis by teams to be formed within the group. (This is a repeat of the process described in the pilot group.) The remaining project suggestions form a backlog for later study and analysis.

Each project team has the advantage of counsel from members of the project teams in prior groups. This liaison is encouraged because it initiates cooperative, as opposed to independent, action and smoothes the way for transition in the application phase.

Each new group determines how it can merge its activities with what has already been accomplished by previous teams. The basic activities and bounds of lower-level groups are prescribed by previous higher-level teams, so major changes do not generally originate at lower levels. Their activities involve changes in emphasis, human relations considerations, refinements, and innovations in procedures. Should there be a major innovation with potential introduced by a lower-level group, the innovation is brought to the attention of the steering committee at a meeting set up for that specific purpose. This recognition can provide significant team spirit and enthusiasm for team members who have participated in the innovation.

As each of the new groups progresses from the education phase to the application phase, new opportunities for reorganization to achieve optimum performance become apparent. With each new group relating to the previous group through a chain of command, a vertically integrated chain of project teams exists within the organization which enables management to delegate decision down to the point where the action associated with the decision takes place. New lines of communication are opened, and old lines are freed up for more effective use.

REPORTS AND COORDINATION

The need for reports and coordination between the groups increases as more people are brought in to participate in the profit improvement program. Everyone should be advised of progress in all projects carried on by all groups. Upper-level executives can set policy with respect to the comparative importance of the programs and place emphasis on the more critical ones. Others outside the group can pass along critical information and ideas which will affect the program being studied. Progress reports on the project provide a line of communication through which information can be contributed across boundaries of accountability and lines of communication.

FEEDBACK, RECOGNITION, AND REINFORCEMENT

In all successful profit improvement programs, top management realizes that the communication loop must be completed and successful achievement must be recognized and rewarded to stimulate new activity, which is vital to sustain improvement. Regular reports of accomplishment in such things as dollar savings, increased market penetration, improved quality, better customer relations, and productivity increases reinforce top management's appreciation of the benefits of the program. Resources are then made available to reward performance and sustain appreciation at all operating levels.

Personal recognition, in addition to monetary reward, is possibly the most important factor reinforcing appreciation in the profit improvement program. Recognition can be conferred in several ways. One way is to schedule regular dinner meetings, perhaps monthly, to be attended by the executive accountable for each critical activity or department. These individuals essentially comprise the original pilot group. All members of the top executive group are also invited, along with those completing project assignments, including workers.

The schedule at such meetings includes an introduction of those present for the first time, and top executives present make a brief address to reinforce interest. Results of completed projects are reported by those participating in them. This is followed by open discussion to bring out new ideas and new projects. A summary of progress for the year to date is given, with credit to the departments or groups responsible.

There are many other approaches which can be taken to grant recognition and reinforce involvement and enthusiasm. If top management feels that formal meetings involve too much fanfare, the feedback and recognition needs can be partially met with regular companywide distribution of performance reports highlighting the groups and individuals responsible for achievement.

EXAMINATION OF OBJECTIVES

Basic formats of objectives

Objectives are expressed in three basic formats: (1) subconscious, (2) verbal, and (3) graphic. Subconscious objectives tend to be spontaneous, emotional, and based on stored memories and experience, and they can often be vague and contradictory. For this reason subconscious objectives do not provide a reliable program for achieving specific results. The more tangible and clearly expressed the objective is, the more reliable it becomes in the achievement of specific results. Therefore, verbal objectives are more reliable than subconscious objectives, and graphic objectives, not requiring verbal translation, are even more reliable than verbal objectives.

The more specific and better understood the objective is, the more specific and appropriate the action is to achieve it. The more specific and appropriate the action to achieve an objective, the greater the probability it will be achieved. This is the essence of economy. The effectiveness of an objective is measured by the degree to which it elicits prompt, specific, and appropriate action (see Chapters 1 and 2).

Objectives categorized by importance and specificity

No day's work should be entered into by an organization which is not part of a monthly, quarterly, annual, and long-range plan. Appropriate economic action requires an integration of long-term and short-term plans and objectives. Long-term plans look far ahead to ultimate objectives; short-term plans prescribe what must be done in the immediate future. The difference between long-term and short-term plans is related to the timing and immediacy of objectives.

Objectives can also be categorized by importance and specificity into (1) primary objectives, (2) critical objectives, and (3) specific objectives. The primary objective states the principal results that the organization seeks to accomplish. Once the primary objective is stated, the critical areas of performance most vital to the accomplishment of their objective are identified. The statement of results required in the vital performance areas to achieve the primary objective dictates the critical objectives of the organization. The underlying principle of "critical objectives" is that 25 percent of the work produces 85 percent of the contribution toward achieving the primary objectives. Therefore resources are maximized when concentrated on the 25 percent of work which produces 85 percent of the results.

Spend after your genius, and by system. Nature goes by rule, not by sallies and salutations.

Ralph Waldo Emerson

To arrive at specific objectives, the needs, opportunities, and obstacles that stand in the way of accomplishing critical objectives are analyzed. Specific objectives focus in on immediate problems and circumstances. Needs and deficiencies of the organization in reaching the critical objectives are analyzed and recorded. Once needs and deficiencies are identified, specific objectives are drafted to satisfy them. The specific objectives contain performance standards to measure accomplishment and variance for control purposes. Success in attaining the specific objectives rests largely with the reasonableness of the objectives and the effectiveness of the control (see Chapter 28).

PROGRAMMING OF SPECIFIC OBJECTIVES

Specific objectives form the steps in an action plan which must be programmed to accomplish the critical objectives with economy. The profit center manager should develop his own program from the top down, but when specific objectives are delegated to subordinates, they should also develop their own programs from the bottom up. Each specific objective should have a program which coordinates with the master program or project program. If an organization does not vigilantly maintain a comprehensive program for controlling the accomplishment of specific objectives, it is not operating in the most economic manner and possesses much latitude for profit improvement, even though management may be generally content with present performance (see Chapter 29).

When contentment enters through the door, improvement goes out the window.

EXAMINATION OF POLICIES AND PROCEDURES

Policies and procedures should be carefully analyzed as to their effects on first-level management, where they all finally impact. Problems should be analyzed in terms of what will be helpful to the first level in producing better results, rather than what will be beneficial to upper-level management in maintaining control. The former is supportive of first-level performance; the latter generally places added burdens on the first level, at the expense of performance (see Chapter 20).

Purpose of policy

The purpose of policy is to advise people of managements' intent. To clarify this intent, the purpose of each policy statement should be given. This provides a feel for the importance of a policy, to help people determine how far they should go in adhering to it.

Policies should give broad direction to encourage employees in the desired direction and prevent wide deviations which waste resources. They should be minimal in number, as required for control, but should not leave a large margin of uncertainty. Inadequately defined policy which does not specify direction, intent, and purpose stops action. Small organizations often take pride in the fact that they have few policies, unaware that even very capable, self-starter executives need the direction of policy to make decisions which will assure the greatest economy in reaching overall objectives. Policy is particularly needed where there is a necessity for consistency or continuity and where the work of one function unduly affects the work of another (see Chapter 24).

Developing policy and procedure

The upper levels of management should decide policy but not necessarily develop it. Policy should ideally be developed by the people who will be most affected. Procedures are a limitation on authority to act. For this reason they should be broad enough to allow the affected people to solve their own problems. Accountability should always be firmly placed at the point where action takes place. When an employee feels fully accountable he is more insistent on providing feedback when policy and procedures interfere and stifle accomplishment rather than supporting it.

Emphasis on the most vital work

Management must continually evaluate policies to ensure that resources are being expended in the accomplishment of the most important work. The spontaneous tendency is to direct resources to the least important work. When a manager is required to perform both management work and technical work at the same time, he will tend to give priority to the technical work, which he perceives to be more pressing. The manager also tends to derive more satisfaction from accomplishing a more tangible, measurable technical function in which he is skilled than a less tangible management function where the results are not readily or immediately apparent. As a result, many managers will tend to place more emphasis on less important technical work than true managerial work, which is more important in accomplishing organizational objectives.

In a like manner, organizations often tend to expend resources on "correcting" symptoms rather than on discovering and correcting the root causes which produce the symptoms. The manner in which resources are consumed in the present largely determines the potential range of alternatives in the future. An overemphasis on solving immediate problems as they occur as opposed to planning the execution of objectives will greatly diminish future alternatives and the scope of potential objectives (see Chapter 25).

Cultivated labor drives out brute labor.
Ralph Waldo Emerson

IDENTIFICATION OF LEAKS IN COST CONTROL AND PROFIT EROSION

The establishment of an effective cost-control system designed to highlight deficiencies is often put off by management of small organizations as an unnecessary expense and a cumbersome task. The ability of the executive to put his finger on almost all operations and to view work and personnel directly causes him to have a false sense of security and to be reluctant to allocate resources to a management information system or profit improvement program. Only after severe difficulty in the marketplace has been experienced are such programs launched, and programs launched too late are often early casualties in the company's inevitable battle for its life.

The biggest problem in the world could have been solved when it was small.
Witter Bynner

Companies without adequate profit improvement programs are often unaware of their vulnerability until they try to expand to new levels of volume, new geographic areas, new products outside their immediate area of expertise, or an expanded personnel base. Meanwhile, the growing sophistication of competitors in the use of information systems provides them with a better base of knowledge on which to base decisions. Companies with better information will generally make better decisions than those that rely on seat-of-the-pants decisions.

Most companies fail due to insufficient planning (not having information to plan with), overexpenditure (failure to control costs), unrealistic pricing (due to failure to control costs), and insufficient sales (poor value offered in relation to the price). The potential for flexibility and a quick response, is realized only when management is operating on reliable information. Managers of small businesses often rely on their intuitive sense or feel for how things are going in general, and as a result they usually are handicapped by a chronic lack of specific information on which to act. Both small and large companies will ultimately owe their success or failure to the quality of management and the quality of information available to it.

Broad-scope projects for identifying leaks in cost control and profit erosion may involve analysis of administrative costs, direct construction costs, indirect construction costs, marketing costs, financing costs, technology and tools of implementation (including schedules, reports, budgets, standards, chart of accounts, controls) organizational structure, and so on.

DEVELOPING A DECISION-MAKING SYSTEM

One goal of the profit improvement system is to develop adequate warning systems to keep management on guard against sluggish organizational reaction to dynamic and cyclical change. Much can be said for spontaneity in decision making, intuitive hunch, or entrepreneurial audacity. However, rational, deliberate, planned decision making is necessary to balance the spontaneous, intuitive entrepreneurial drives management often exhibits. Spontaneous decisions can deteriorate into lazy decisions because they are based on previous conditioning, similar-type situations, or previously successful modes of operations. There is the danger with spontaneous decisions that they may be based on inappropriate comparisons or experience, or, worse, the decision maker may not really understand what the problem is, in which case most any decision is inappropriate. Adherence to a rational, planned decision-making process within an organization will safeguard it from the ravages of dynamic and cyclical change, better than spontaneous, shoot-from-the-hip decision making will.

It requires a great deal of boldness and a great deal of caution, to make a great fortune, and when you have got it, it requires ten times as much wit to keep it.

Ralph Waldo Emerson

Decision making begins with problem definition

Problems are rarely what they first appear to be from a superficial analysis. Superficial analysis generally uncovers symptoms rather than the problems which are the underlaying causes. A problem is a cause which interferes with the accomplishment of an objective — a cause, and not an effect. Management must dig down to the cause and not be deceived and sidetracked by the effects realized in the process.

A beginning point in problem analysis is to state the problem as it appears. From this point the circumstances surrounding the apparent problem are examined. This examination should focus on the most critical information, as too much information will confuse rather than clarify.

Information gathering

A fact is an elusive commodity because the same "facts" will be interpreted and represented differently by different people, depending on their point of view, personality, involvement, and intellect. A true fact in one location and time period is not a true fact in another. Adjustments in the facts will be required to compensate for differences in time and place, so that comparable situations are presented in a format appropriate to the problem at hand. One can compensate for differing points of view by seeking facts from persons with opposing points of view. Inappropriateness of facts due to locational and time differences can be compensated by adjustments which make the facts more nearly comparable to the problem at hand. For example, historic costs must be adjusted to reflect current costs.

One of the most critical facts to uncover is why the apparent problem exists; How did the problem develop? What other symptoms can be identified and associated with the apparent problem? Why does the problem occur in one situation and not in another? Causes for the symptoms should be sought from people who are directed involved, within the parameters of the apparent problem. This type of fact finding will lead to the identification of the real problem.

Identification of the real problem

Defining the organization's real problem is the most important aspect of decision making and the critical element in keeping management vigilant in the battle against sluggishness and obsolescence. As previously mentioned, a problem is a cause which interferes with the accomplishment of an objective. The manager must define with precision the objective which is blocked as a result of the problem. The objective should be stated in quantitative, measurable results which, when accomplished, will eliminate the cause of the problem. How to eliminate the cause is not considered at this point. The conditions which should exist when the objective is accomplished are determined before embarking on solutions to remedy causes of the problem.

Once the objectives are clearly defined, the solution of the problem rests in accomplishing the clearly defined objective. When the objective is established, standards must also be established to confirm when and how well the objective has been achieved. Once an objective has been clearly defined, timing is important because the objective will change with time. That is, the problem will take on different dimensions as time passes. Once the scope of the problem and objectives is identified as it relates to time, both long term and short term, objectives can be developed which will require long-term and short-term solutions.

Further information gathering and development of alternatives

Once the real problem has been defined, the manager should guard against making a decision too soon, before the alternatives are analyzed, or making the decision too late. If the decision is prolonged too long, a decision has really been made to do nothing.

Decisions made too early tend to be spontaneous applications of old solutions to new problems. The manager should seek to improve what has been done well in the past and not merely repeat old solutions. Each decision should represent an advancement of past technology and accomplishment. This is the essence of profit improvement; it requires constant upgrading of objectives. For management to increase the "value added" by the organization, management must make better decisions, since the output will not exceed the input.

Brainstorming has proved a valuable technique for developing alternatives. In brainstorming, alternatives should be advanced in an atmosphere of permissiveness. Audacity should prevail at this step in the decision making process; cool judgment comes in the selection process. Even fat-out, "preposterous" alternatives have their place, for what appears preposterous superficially may, upon further analysis, provide the key to the solution or provide the yeast which gives rise to new perceptions and innovations. It is important that there be no critical comment or analysis in the initial brainstorming process, for this will diminish audacity in favor of cool judgment and eliminate opportunities for the introduction of new ideas.

The brainstorming session should include those who will be affected by the outcome and who will implement the new decision. The greater the emotional involvement of subordinates in the decision-making process, and the greater their "ownership" in the design of the decision, the more enthusiastic they will be in achieving the objectives. This becomes an element in the choice of objectives which the manager must make. He should consider which alternative will be most enthusiastically accepted by those who are responsible for achieving the objective.

Selecting the most appropriate alternatives

The alternatives selected may encompass both short-term and long-term alternatives if the problem has been defined with long-term and short-term objectives. The problem at this stage has been greatly simplified because the manager can evaluate alternatives in relation to their ability in accomplishing the stated objectives. The alternative offering the greatest potential for success in accomplishing the objective is the best solution. This does not mean that the solution will be enthusiastically accepted by all those affected; there will always be dissatisfaction. The more important the decision, the greater the potential for dissatisfaction, even though the decision is the best one for the greatest number.

Implementing new objectives, policies, procedures

Management must expect resistance to the change which usually results from decisions. Change in perceived as a threat to most people, even when it is obviously required for the betterment of the greatest number. Those who are directly benefited, as well as those whose interests are diminished, may resist the change resulting from the management decision. Management must realize that this inertia to change is a fact of life; it can be minimized through skillful and sensitive management techniques but not extinguished (see Chapters 7 and 25).

To assure that change is successfully implemented, the management decision which introduces the change should also include a plan of action and standards for implementation and control. The plan should include alternate strategies which can be implemented to reflect a change of conditions in the future. If alternatives are not developed in advance, those proposed at a later date, in an emergency situation, are likely to be developed spontaneously and directed towards symptoms rather than causes. The plan should include policy, procedure, schedules, budgets, and standards (see Chapter 21).

VALUE ENGINEERING AS APPLIED TO A FORMAL PROFIT IMPROVEMENT PROGRAM

Value engineering seeks to obtain optimum value for every dollar spent through a creative effort in the analysis of functions. Alternate solutions are proposed for functions to omit costs attributable to a function which do not adequately produce its requirements.

Functions can be classified as primary and secondary. If a design or procedure is being value engineered, the functions of the design or procedure must be analyzed to determine which are primary and which are secondary functions. Primary and secondary functions are the performance characteristics which a design or procedure possesses. The primary function is basic to the purpose of the design or procedure and must remain to accomplish the objective. Theoretically, all other functions could be eliminated, but the primary function must remain. Secondary functions only aid in the implementation and are not absolutely required in achieving the basic purpose. If the design or procedure can be modified, the requirements for secondary functions can also be modified or even eliminated, along with their cost.

Functions must then be related to both value and cost to determine a cost/value ratio. If the cost exceeds the value, then there is an indication that expenditures may be utilized in less than an optimum fashion.

The value of a function can be determined in two ways. The first is to determine the lowest possible cost required to perform the primary function in the simplest manner feasible within the state of the art, with due consideration to asthetics and compatibility with the system. Normally there is no value assigned to secondary functions. This lowest cost, then, represents the value of the function.

The second way to determine value of the function is to determine the value which the function adds to the total system or the furtherance of the overall objectives. If a function possesses a value many times its cost, and the value proportionately increases as cost increases, it may be advisable to allocate a larger share of dollars to the high-yield function. On the other hand, an increase or decrease in cost will not increase or decrease the value of many features. These are called low-yield or low-sensitivity features. Value engineering reduces unit cost of low-yield features in order that part of the saving can be redirected to high-yield features, to increase return on investment.

The underlying principle of value engineering

The underlying principle of value engineering, is that it is easier to increase profits by reducing costs or increasing value than by increasing sales. Value engineering needs no elaborate organization and involves little expenditure. The dollars spent on a well-conceived value engineering effort will show astronomical returns as compared to the opportunity rate of capital for the organization as a whole. An aggressive, common-sense, value engineering program (including research, observation, investigation, imagination and audacity) can reap the same profit improvement, with minor expenditures, as an aggressive organizational expansion, such as the creation of a new division, which involves much more major expenditures (see Chapter 13).

The value engineering process

The steps in value engineering can be summarized as follows:

1. Select the target or subject of the value engineering analysis.
2. Determine purpose and function. Distinguish primary function from secondary functions.
3. Determine value of the function and cost currently required to perform it.
4. Determine the value sensitivity of the function. How is value affected as the function is modified, reduced or increased in cost, or omitted entirely?
5. Develop alternatives for achieving the required function and cost/value ratio.
6. Evaluate the alternatives and their cost/value effectiveness in relation to the total system and not just to the subsystem of which the function is a part.
7. Narrow in on the most attractive alternative and refine it.
8. Overcome obstacles by proving that the selected and refined alternative does not jeopardize the primary function and actually reduces cost or improves value.

9. Monitor results to compare expected results with actual results in order to determine the validity of value engineering change.

Direction and support from the highest level

Value engineering requires direction from the highest level of management to assure that all activities are coordinated to reflect overall policy as established in the profit plan. Often each discipline or division generates reviews and modifies its own requirements as the divisional or departmental executives perceive their importance or function in accomplishing the overall objective. Because they do not always perceive their own position correctly, their decisions do not always lead to optimum implementations of the objectives. The decisions that are made reflect the singular objectives of a particular discipline or division, often with provision for the maximum safety factors or contingencies it considers necessary. System performance is often unintentionally sacrificed in maximizing subsystem performance.

WORK SIMPLIFICATION TO CONTROL OF ADMINISTRATIVE COSTS

Increasing productivity does not necessarily mean speeding up, or making everyone work harder or faster. In a speedup, personnel are required to produce more without a corresponding change in techniques. Work simplification is a common-sense method for eliminating waste of time, energy, and materials in order to develop the one best way of doing the work. The result, increased productivity, is attained by the use of improved methods and not by speedup of the employee.

A work simplification program is considered effective within an organization when:

1. Quality is maintained or raised and costs are lowered as a result of coordinated efforts at all levels of the organization.
2. Personnel within the organization begin to develop personally faster, as a result of the improvement process in which they are participating.
3. Enthusiasm is high, and personnel eagerly seek out areas for increased work simplification. They realize that increased productivity adds to personal and economic satisfactions for the greatest number.

The methods of motivating people to comprehend and develop a positive, enthusiastic attitude toward a work simplification program and to participate to the extent of their ability is by far the most important yet most difficult aspect of such a program. Successful motivation will result in friendliness through teamwork and understanding, and an environment which encourages the personal development of the individual. An underlying premise of work simplification is that the greatest thinking comes from those with the greatest intellect, but the greatest power comes from the entire organization, working together as a cohesive, coordinated team.

CUTTING OVERHEAD BY UTILIZING GREATER OUTSIDE SUPPORT

The heightened cyclical movements of the economy and reductions in profit margins have acted as a restraint in the growth of staff service departments within real estate development organizations and in business in general. The trend for the seventies is to utilize outside service companies to cut down on the need to maintain staff services within companies. There is also a related trend to increase the use of management consulting firms which specialize in a specific functional expertise to analyze and reduce operating and production costs. Management consultants are also being used more widely to assist management in meeting the challenges of technology and complexity in today's world.

Temporary help agencies likewise are being utilized to a greater extent by management to reduce the high paper-work and fringe-benefits costs associated with hiring permanent employees. Temporary help can often provide the same skills to the organization as long-term staff employees can, at a reduced cost.

23

Loan submission

HOW AND WHERE TO GET THE FUNDS

Success in securing financing depends on a professional approach to and credibility with lenders. Knowledge of the types of loans a lender is interested in and his guidelines and underwriting pattern is essential. The most effective loan packages are tailored to the specific requirements of the lender. Lenders set a pattern in their preferences for certain types of loans, for large or small loans, for single-family or multifamily housing loans, for nonresidential loans, and so on.

Lenders can be further qualified as aggressive or conservative in their lending policies: High-rate lenders are aggressive, and low-rate lenders are conservative. High-rate lenders deal in higher risk properties, such as furnished apartments, motels, nursing homes, strip stores, and small communities, in secondary locations, and with builders who have acceptable but marginal financial statements. The higher risk is compensated for with higher interest rates. Conservative, low-rate lenders prefer lower ratio loans, premium locations, strong leases, builders and developers with strong financial statements and good track records, and generally superior real estate. There may be a spread between the percentage rates of aggressive and conservative lenders of 0.75 to 1.25 percent.

Savings and loan associations furnish more than 50 percent of single-family housing loans and more than 30 percent of multifamily housing loans. Larger multifamily loans are often funded by life insurance companies, which fund more than 20 percent of these loans. In single-family loans, however, life insurance companies normally fund only 1 percent. Commercial banks fund more than 25 percent of single-family loans but less than 10 percent of multifamily loans. Mutual savings banks fund less than 5 percent of single-family loans and less than 10 percent of multifamily loans. Private, noninsured pension funds and state and local retirement funds combined provide a nominal 1 percent of multifamily mortgage funds and less than 1 percent of single-family mortgage funds.

Savings and loan associations

A very substantial majority of savings and loan associations make both construction and takeout loans. Savings and loans have been substantial purchasers of FHA and VA loans originated by mortgage bankers. The service corporations of savings and loans have been active in land and development loans. The local nature of savings and loans and their knowledge of the area and its business conditions make them an important source of mortgage loans. Larger multifamily loans may be beyond their scope. Savings and loan are a cyclical source of mortgage funds, due to disintermediation, which is when funds of savers flow out of savings and loan associations during times of high interest rates because the saver can get a better return from treasury notes, commercial paper, bonds, and so forth. For this reason it is prudent for the developer to also maintain national in addition to local lending sources.

Commercial banks

Commercial banks are primarily involved in construction lending, with emphasis on apartment and commercial buildings. Large banks sometimes become rigid on loan procedures and may give preferential treatment to builders maintaining high average balances. Though it is advantageous to maintain a good ongoing relationship with a specific bank as the primary source of construction funds, it is dangerous to rely exclusively on one source. Relationships with several sources of funds should be maintained.

Life insurance companies

For the most part, insurance companies do not make construction loans, though some will do so. Most often construction lending by life companies consists of a combination construction and takeout loan. Insurance companies are generally interested in larger projects beyond the means of the local savings and loans. Percentage fees are generally higher, and participation-equity arrangements have been sought by the insurance companies. Insurance companies have been a continuous source of funds for larger projects, representing a more constant, though costlier, source of funds than savings and loans do.

Mutual savings banks

Combination construction and takeout loans or takeout loans are preferred by mutual savings banks.

Private noninsured pension funds

Private pension funds are primarily interested in takeout financing in the nonresidential and multifamily markets. They have not been interested in construction financing. Most investments are in negotiable securities.

Real estate investment trusts

Real estate investment trusts (REITs) have been aggressive lenders in the past in construction and development loans. They have also been active in placing takeout financing for multifamily and nonresidential construction, second mortgages, and purchase leasebacks. Most were severely crippled in the recession and have curtailed lending activities. Some are reentering the market with caution.

UTILIZING MORTGAGE BANKERS AND BROKERS

Mortgage bankers and brokers are the intermediaries between the builder and the lender. The builder does not generally have the time or the resources to keep up to date with trends within the lender community, preferences of individual lenders, and sources of funds and optimum terms at a given moment. Mortgage banker and brokers will develop or assist the builder in developing a loan package to fit the requirements of the particular type of investor attracted to the investment opportunity.

The builder or developer should shop to find the banker or broker who can provide him with the best service. There is a wide fluxuation in professionalism and capabilities within this industry. A competent banker-broker can generally quote, within a narrow range, the type of loan he can match up with a specific investment opportunity.

At the point in shopping when the builder feels that he has found a banker-broker who can really deliver a loan he can accept, he generally should enter into a written agreement with the banker-broker based on specific rate, fee, and term conditions and requiring a commitment to be delivered within a certain period of time, generally 60 days. With a written agreement, the banker-broker is guaranteed a fee if he delivers the commitment specified in the agreement, and he will work harder on such deals. The investor also will generally give more attention to a deal which is committed than to one which is open, because he knows if he makes a commitment the builder is also committed.

Mortgage bankers and brokers provide a valuable service by bringing their expertise and their contacts in a national mortgage market to bear in a local market. The medium and smaller life insurance companies receive the great majority of their loan business from these correspondents. Some of the larger life insurance companies have eliminated correspondents and have developed a nationwide system of service offices. Other large companies have both correspondent and national service office systems.

When the scale of the development opportunity limits the lending activity to the local market, bankers and brokers become a much smaller factor in loan origination. On a local basis, the builder can deal direct more readily, and generally does. Savings and loans generally receive less than 20 percent of their originations from bankers and brokers, and commercial banks receive an extremely small share. REITs, being nationally oriented, receive from 25 to 50 percent of their business from bankers and brokers.

Savings and loans and commercial banks have typically dealt directly with the borrower. There is a definite trend for the insurance companies and REITs to become more involved with direct lending. Nonetheless, the professional banker-broker is still a valuable contributor to the development process, paid only on performance delivered.

DEVELOPING THE LOAN PACKAGE

A portion of the fee the mortgage banker-broker is paid covers the cost of loan package preparation. The banker-broker is generally knowledgeable about the specific submission requirements of individual lenders and is responsible for submitting an appropriate and effective loan package to the lender. The quality of the loan package prepared can vary dramatically, depending on who prepares it.

It is advisable for the borrower to be intimately involved in the preparation of the loan package to see that all materials are included in a professional manner, which improves his credibility. Since the borrower has more at stake in the successful funding of the loan than does the banker-broker, he should devote optimum effort to the development of an effective loan package. The borrower may perform for himself some of the duties he pays his banker-broker to perform, but this extra effort will pay dividends in enhanced effectiveness in the mortgage marketplace.

The presentation will require varying levels of depth and comprehensiveness, depending on the relationship between the borrower, the lender, and the mortgage banker-broker. Where there is an ongoing relationship, less comprehensive detail is required than if there has been no previous contact between the borrower and the lender. Comprehensiveness will also depend on whether the anticipated lender is national or local. A national lender will benefit more from in-depth demographic, sociological, and local economic detail than a local lender who is already familiar with the area's economics and trends.

Both local and national lenders will benefit equally and will find it easier to reach a decision when the real estate improvement (the product) is well documented analytically and graphically. The presentation should establish the full development concept and explain why it will be effective in absorbing from the target market segments and how it will enjoy a superior market position over the competition.

Equally important are the methodology, insight, and rationale utilized in identifying market demand. When the loan package can identify and provide data supporting market demand and can deliver an economically sound product to fill that demand, firm lender interest will be aroused. Those loan packages that are easiest for the lender to process will be funded first.

The Feasibility Outline given as Exhibit 18–1 in Chapter 18 provides a comprehensive guide in preparation of the loan package. The loan package need not be as comprehensive as the feasibility outline, and the developer may be wise not to transfer all of the information included in the feasibility outline to his financial sources. The depth and comprehensiveness of the loan package material will depend on the merits of each situation.

24

Benefiting from standardization

One of the important concepts in relation to standardization is that standards are rarely standard. The moment standards become regarded as the one unwavering standard, stagnation sets in. Rather, standards are benchmarks for subsequent performance. They indicate what has been successful in the past, and no more. To be effective, they should be in a continuous state of evolution.

ADVANTAGES AND USES OF STANDARDS

Standards provide an economy by recording solutions to problems, so that the same problem does not have to be solved time and again for every project. Effectively used, standards are an extremely useful tool in the creative process rather than an obstacle, as some think. They alleviate the drudgery of routine decisions and allow more time for creative problem solving and innovation.

Provide restraint in change

Standards also act as a restraint to scattershot changes which keep design and policy in a state of flux. Some creative souls seem to feel that repetition is an unworthy effort, and to be worth their salt they must devise a different way of doing things which is distinctly their own. The pivot word is "different." A standard should be changed not merely for the sake of difference but when a better solution is found. There is no particular economic justification for being different for difference's sake. Change because a better solution has been found produces a cumulative benefit, and progress is directed to the accomplishment of objectives.

Of course, there is a merchandising justification for being different. This is a separate consideration, but in many instances merchandising is not pertinent to the setting of standards. There is a great deal of latitude in standards which makes it possible to create differences through the use of various details and components. Their selection and interrelationships make changes possible without changing the standards themselves.

Standards act as a feedback mechanism by which new ideas can be continually compared to existing ideas and evaluated to determine if they are merely different, or if they are better. If ideas are different but have a merchandising advantage they can be used to create an additional standard, without redesigning or omitting a current one. If the ideas are merely different and do not yield any particular advantage other than their difference, they should be rejected. If new ideas are better than current ideas, the current standard should be modified or omitted to make way for the improvement.

Aid creativity and innovation

Those who do not retrieve the benefits of their output over a period of time are neglecting one of their most precious assets—their experience and on-the-job track record. Organizations that do not record their experience with some type of organized information retrieval system, such as a standardization program, will fail to keep pace with the state of the art. They will be mired down in old problems rather than moving forward with innovations (see Chapter 7).

Standardization does not bolt the door to innovation. Rather, it provides an opportunity for it by freeing managers from the tedium of resolving the same problems time and again. When the need to rework the 80 percent of the work which is repetitious project after project is lessened by the application of standards, the manager can devote himself to the 20 percent of the work which is creative in solving specific problems.

Allow wide design variations

Standards should be used as a feedback mechanism to recapture information from the field by recording cumulative construction experience with details. For example, we worked out what we thought was a good plumbing wall detail for apartments but found through experience that the plumber was causing problems with the concrete subcontractor when he blocked out the concrete footing trenches before the concrete was poured. The block-outs were designed to allow the plumbing to pass through the footings where required, but the plumber consistently shoved the reinforcing bars out of position in inserting the styrofoam block-outs.

Feedback from the field alerted us to the problem, which we solved by moving the foundation slightly so that plumbing could pass by the foundation rather than extending through it. Later we found a better way. By designing a wide foundation that was in effect a reinforced, thickened slab we could meet structural requirements without having to have a foundation in at the time the rough plumbing is installed. Later we found a way to do the framing without the necessity of any type of foundation in the vicinity of the plumbing wall.

Standard details reflected all of the information coming in from the field which was related to a better way to handle the construction. As new details replace old ones, the latter are retained as a historical record.

Thus the organization's progress is "canned," and new people can quickly benefit from the organization's track record. And when an employee leaves, much of what he has learned stays with the organization, rather than going out the door with him.

Aid communication

Another use of standard details is to anticipate and thus reduce construction problems and unsatisfactory workmanship which may occur in the field. For example, field inspections and field reports alert the organization to common mistakes subcontractors are prone to make. Particularly when the drawings are not well detailed and subs have to make decisions on their own, unsatisfactory workmanship may result. When the organization knows where the sub is most likely to go wrong, that area should be thoroughly detailed to make the performance requirements perfectly clear.

When drawings are not adequately detailed and requirements are unclear, the builder is in a weak position to demand that unsatisfactory work be redone. For example, we have noted repeated field problems in getting good work on fences and railings. On a balcony railing that has vertical wood supports at, say 6 inches on center, the sub will start out from one end of the balcony and nail on wood vertical members at 6 inches on center. When he gets to a corner, one rail is 2 inches from the corner and the other is 4 inches, and this is unsightly. Or he may start out the verticals 6 or 3 inches from the building when to look right, the design requires the vertical to be flush against the building. If the details do not show how it should be, the sub can only guess (see Chapter 26).

Standard details should take the guesswork out and eliminate conditions in the field which jeopardize the design and create construction delays. Typically, a railing detail will consist of a section through the railing, but more information is needed to skirt construction problems in the field. With a standardization program the detail need be worked out only once and then repeated thereafter, thus allowing more initial design time. This does not mean that the same railing detail will be used throughout a project or number of projects. Railing design can be varied by selecting from among a number of standard details.

STANDARDIZING FLOOR PLANS AND BUILDINGS

The more times a floor plan is repeated, the more exhaustive can the design effort be which goes into its ultimate creation. The repetition of a floor plan from one development to the next allows for refinements to be designed in, as a result of experience with the plan.

Standard floor plans can be accommodated in standard-type buildings. A particular floor plan may be accommodated in several different building configurations, depending upon mix in the building, number of units, and layouts. The various arrangements allow environmental diversity with the same basic floor plan.

Standard-type buildings also allow for a good margin of diversity through selection of the standard details and through the addition or ommission of standard amenity treatments, such as roof towers, wing walls, chimneys, outriggers, trim, materials, or colors. Standard building foundation plans, floor plans, sections, and elevations can be modified by selection of details, materials, and amenities.

Standardization of the basic elements will allow the organization to devote more time to innovation and creative problem solving related to adopting the concept to the site, the marketing opportunity, and the building code and construction pecularities of the area. An organization that must approach every problem from scratch, due to lack of standardization, will have fewer resources to devote to cost reduction, creative land planning, and design innovations to suit the uniqueness of the market and the site.

POLICY STANDARDIZATION

Policy standardization is necessary for effective communication within the organization. A policy informs subordinates of management's desires, objectives, and intentions in a given circumstance. Standardization in this area eliminates time wasted in resolving the same problems time and again and provides a basis for predictable decision making and action.

A standard policy should only be standard until a better policy is found. The standard should then be revised to reflect the improvement. Effective policy originates not solely from above but at all levels of management and operation. The measurement of a policy's appropriateness is its effectiveness in achieving objectives, and not its source. Policy standardization documents the successful practices, techniques, and concepts of the organization. Because the organization and the environment in which it must operate are constantly evolving and changing as they expand and contract, the policies must also evolve and change. Otherwise they become an anchor holding back progress rather than a compass pointing the way to desired objectives (see Chapter 28).

Policy standardization enables the chief executive to extend his effectiveness. If there is no set policy, the executive may be required to give directions on repetitive-type decisions constantly, because subordinates must act without a sufficient understanding of policy and procedures. Standardization enables the chief executive and his subordinates to plan and manage, to work on causes rather than effects. Thus they are in a position to anticipate many problems and eliminate them in advance.

PROCEDURAL STANDARDIZATION

Whereas policy standardization provides guidelines in decision making and planning, procedural standardization provides them for the implementation of decisions and plans. Many of the functions in the real estate development process are routine and repetitive in nature, varying minimally from project to project. By devoting energies to determining the optimum method of performing the routine functions, an organization can realize large productivity gains and increase predictability.

Procedural standardization results in better coordination between departments and reduces value washouts. When each department knows what it is expected to do and the procedure to be used in accomplishing the goal, and when the procedures for the various departments are coordinated and complementary, organizational drag is minimized. (see Chapter 22).

STANDARDIZED BUDGETS, COST CONTROLS

Standardized budget and cost-control formats will simplify the management process and greatly aid in preparing current budgets and projections. Standardized formats should suit the particular type of operation for which they are intended, such as land development, single-family housing, or multifamily housing. All projects within a development should be controlled by use of the standard format for that development type.

Standardized budget formats enable management to compare all projects within a development type on the same basis. By providing a historical record of costs and operating ratios, they are a help in making projections for current projects and forward planning. The ability to compare similar projects through a standardized format also helps to minimize errors and omissions and to identify potential overruns. Chapter 21, on budgets and controls, gives standard budgets and control formats for for-sale and rental housing.

STANDARDIZED SCHEDULES

If all projects are scheduled in a standardized schedule format, the field organization and subcontractors will become familiar with the schedule and the time performance standards. The format also makes it possible for management to compare performance on similar projects easily. Historical performance data from recent standardized schedules provide a valuable input for current scheduling activities. Problem areas can be identified in recent schedules, and measures can be taken in advance to preclude them from continuing into current work.

Standardized schedules are an excellent communication tool between the builder and his subcontractors. Particularly once the subcontractors become familiar with the schedule through use, they can work out production problems in the schedule with the builder before construction, rather than on the job. The schedule should be continuously updated to reflect optimum construction performance. It is an invaluable record of performance and expectations to guide superintendents, both seasoned veterans and recruits (see Chapter 29).

STANDARDIZED DOCUMENTS

Standardized documents, such as contracts, order forms, specifications, general conditions, construction procedures, checklists, work forms, and warranties, are an effective means of communicating standard policy and procedures within the organization. They also help make the organization's position clear to subcontractors, suppliers, building contractors, and customers. (See Chapters 26 and 27 for the standards forms mentioned above.)

To assure that the standard documentation correctly reflects policy and procedures and actual operating conditions, it should be reviewed and updated on a regular basis. In addition to regular reviews, a formalized system of feedback from operations is necessary. Without such feedback as to the effectiveness of documents, the review process will represent a mere formality.

FEEDBACK TO KEEP STANDARDS CURRENT

A standardization program must receive regular feedback from operations if standards are to remain current. If they do not remain current, they are better discarded. We use the Standardized Policy for Budgeting presented in Chapter 21 as a feedback tool. The Budget Plan and architectural specifications for for-sale housing follows the same format as the Chart of Accounts, for example. Additionally, the bidding and contract letting are broken down into the same subcontract or separate contract groupings. The budget outline forms a backbone for the total development and construction operation, and thus it is a valuable feedback tool.

A feedback file contains folders for each major item in the budget as shown on the budget recapitulation sheet for the project. Whenever there is an ongoing budgetary problem requiring analysis, or a problem in contract letting or construction, information relative to the problem is put into the appropriate file folder. This simplifies communication and coordination because contracts and construction responsibilities follow the same format as the budget and specifications.

A coordinator should be in charge of feedback operations, and all personnel should be encouraged to forward suggestions for operations and standards improvement. The coordinator then places them in the appropriate file folders. On a regular basis all the folders should be reviewed, and, when appropriate, standards and operational procedures should be revised.

As an example, if a standardized architectural framing detail is causing problems on the job, information relative to the problem should be put into the rough carpentry file folder (Accounts No. 14330). At the time of review, the architect may be required to modify the standard detail to alleviate the field problem. This does not mean that remedial action must await a review; immediate problems require action. But too often, the action focuses on the immediate problem, which may be an effect of some other problem. Unless the other problem, in this instance an ineffective standard detail, is also solved, it will continue to be the cause of reoccurring construction problems. Remedial action must be addressed to root causes and must not stop at merely remedying the effect. The regular review process is a means of identifying root causes through feedback and remedying problems at the source (see Chapters 22 and 25).

Another feedback example involves a reoccurring overrun in the rough carpentry budget due to material cost overruns. Through reviewing the information in the rough carpentry feedback file, and further investigation in the field, the source of the problem is found. The framing subcontractors have been wasting lumber supplied by the developer because there was no lumber-waste clause in the specifications or the contract. Inordinate waste made it necessary for the developer to purchase additional lumber in order to complete the projects. The problem is solved by including a lumber-waste clause in the specification which states that the subcontractor is allowed 10 percent waste. Any waste in excess of that figure must be paid for by the subcontractor.

A formalized review process is necessary to keep standards current. In the day-to-day pressures of business, standards are not ordinarily updated. When problems occur, due to ineffective standards, the crisis atmosphere generally allows time to deal only with effects and not with the causes of problems. The review process is a management approach designed to get at the source and thus eliminate reoccurring problems.

The review process utilizes the concept of management by exception. The standards are only reviewed in those areas where feedback has indicated there is a problem. In this manner, the review process is simplified in that management only reviews exceptions and can then devote the review time to solving specific problems which have arisen. Reviewing the entire standard rather than exceptions only is nonproductive and would soon bring an end to the review procedure. Reviewing exceptions only allows management to get to the cause of a problem to provide solutions at the source rather than working on effects, which is fire fighting.

25

Management capability: The key to profit growth

In an age of rapid change a question management must ask often is, "What business are we really in?" Change in the environment calls for corresponding change in the organization and its objectives.

People can be the most flexible of all assets, and knowledge is the one thing which can give insight into change and its consequences. For an organization, the key assets are people and knowledge. To succeed, the organization must attract and motivate people who are as flexible as the times they are living in and who are not locked into fixed positions, static assumptions, or some present conclusion.

Planning in a time of cyclical change requires somewhat different management procedures than those that are adequate in a more stable economic environment. How does one cope? Does forward planning make any sense at all? The answer is yes. Forward planning can be done in the present business environment. However, the planning must be flexible enough to be adjustable to the conditions of the moment, and not those that existed when the planning was initiated (see Chapter 9).

DEVELOPING BOTH PEOPLE AND TECHNOLOGIES

An effective organization must excel in two critical areas: development and management of people, and development and management of technology (the tools and information with which the people must work). To some extent, a company can compensate for bad technology with great leadership, and for poor leadership with superb technology. But peak performance can never be achieved without quality in both domains—the human and the technological.

Middle managers can often make do with the tools they are given, however inadequate, but upper levels of management should not be misled by such heroic efforts. In effect, they have condemned their organizations to suboptimal performance—which usually means at higher costs than need be. Competitors who can achieve peaks in both the human and technological domains can set the pace for less enlightened rivals.

In too many cases, management fails to appreciate that it can make significant improvements to profits only if it can provide the tools the organization requires to change and improve its methods. Management must do the hard thinking about the basic nature of the activity and how it should be carried on. Managers unwilling to shoulder these really tough challenges may seek to counter competitive pressures and heightened productivity demands in other ways. One of the most attractive, but dangerous, is constant structural reorganization. However, reorganization is no substitute for the tough job of managerial thinking on the key factors involved in any important activity.

If significant improvement to profits is to be achieved, operating executives must focus on solving specific marketing and production problems and developing tools capable of the task. To put the emphasis on reorganizing current activities is merely to reorganize all of the organization's terrible inefficiencies. The tendency to meet new situations or to resolve difficulties by reorganizing is widespread, and it can be a wonderful method for creating the illusion of progress while producing confusion, inefficiency, and demoralization.

The successful developer starts out in the business of building buildings, but soon finds he is really in the business of building a company that builds buildings (see Chapter 28).

MANAGEMENT'S ROLE IN INNOVATION

The size of an organization has an effect on its productivity and competitive strength in the marketplace. Generally, all things being equal, a good, big fighter is likely to win over a good, little fighter.

The race does not always go to the swift nor the battle to the strong, but that's the horse to bet on.

Damon Runyon

Effects of size

All things are not equal, however. Though big business has the advantage of monopoly control, professional management, and access to lower-cost financing in the current economic environment, big business's advantages are often insufficient to offset its inflexibility. In a number of industries, the largest producers do not have the most versatile and efficient organizations. While large companies can usually carry out existing programs efficiently, they are often unable to innovate. There are two big problems: internally, the management controls which permit efficient operation also inhibit innovation, and, externally, the firm's image of an autocracy discourages more innovative personnel and executives.

It is always the minorities that hold the key of progress; it is always through those who are unafraid to be different that advance comes to human society.

Raymond B. Fosdick

Organizational structure and attitudes have a profound effect on innovation, efficiency, and productivity. In larger companies, inhibited innovation often waters down entrepreneurial spirit. Most top business executives, for example, would prefer to have middle and first-line managers who adhere rather strictly to company policies and procedures. They would like their managers to be generally resourceful, but they discourage genuine originality. An efficient business usually gets that way by training its managers to react to operating problems in a rather uniform way.

> *It is not enough that you form, and even follow the most excellent rules for conducting yourself in the world; you must, also, know when to deviate from them, and where lies the exception.*
>
> Greville

Entrepreneurs and managers Large organizations tend to be run by managers, not entrepreneurs. The assets of both the manager and the entrepreneur are required to keep the organization vital, however. Without the entrepreneur, there would be deadening routine, lack of audacity, and no new direction. Entrepreneurs create, managers execute. The manager wants the existing system to run as smoothly as possible, whereas the entrepreneur wants to change the system through creative destruction of the old order and its replacement with a more fitting new order. Those who hold on too long to the old order soon find they have little to hold on to. If a company's own management does not obsolete the present order of things, another's will (see Chapter 7).

Innovations may threaten the security of those who oversee the present order. There will be resistance to ideas which might obsolete the current operating procedures to which employees owe their organizational stature. Therefore, it is important that those to whom top management looks for innovation should have no personal ties or interest in the perpetuation of the present order of things. The innovator also should not report to anyone other than top management, particularly not to the department that may be affected by the innovation. This puts the department head in the unfair position of having to make an objective decision on a matter whose very mention he may view, rightly or wrongly, as a threat or an expression of lack of confidence in the department. This gives neither the plan nor the manager a fair chance.

An atmosphere of permissiveness which is tolerant of mistakes is most conducive to innovation. The more innovative the idea, the less possible it will be to offer substantiating proof of performance prior to the fact. On a truly innovative idea, conventional market research may be misleading because input may be based on inappropriate experience or inapplicable comparisons if comparables are nonexistent. Management must come to grips with the fact that no amount of simulation and testing prior to the fact can provide a reliable outcome; actual experience is required (see Chapter 12).

> *The man who makes no mistakes does not usually make anything.*
>
> Edward J. Phelps

Strategy and operating tactics

Strategy and operating tactics are best handled by separate individuals. Strategy requires comprehensive, integrated planning of abstracts and intangibles, and the formulation of complete networks and systems. Operational tactics are more tangible, limited in scope, and concerned with near-term results.

Since the here-and-now is more pressing than the future, tactics will dominate over longer-term strategies if handled by the same individual. Pressing current problems which demand immediate tactical solutions will try the patience and endurance of the line manager, thus leading to quickie, patchwork solutions. That is the reason there is so much fire fighting going on within organizations.

The value of expertness

Management must appreciate the value and use of expertness, which is more than the application of formal techniques and statistical analysis. In its essence, expertness is imaginative audacity. It calls for the ability to assimilate and interpret events in order to synthesize them and determine the inevitable outcomes and, from that point, to create action-oriented policies for management to follow.

One machine can do the work of fifty ordinary men. No machine can do the work of one extraordinary man.

Elbert Hubbard

Expertness has a license: It does not have to verify everything it says. One who could produce plans that can be statistically verified would be a technician who follows proven paths, and not an expert. Unless the expert has the right to stand on his opinion, he gets no benefit from his expertise, and management does not benefit from his opinions. The special skill of the expert is that he can cut through mountainous drudgery to see trends that cannot be adequately defined by the statistics or logically and systematically inferred from the facts. The trick is to become the master of techniques and data, not their slave.

The manager who implements an innovation must be able to endure the censure of his peers, since innovations incur a good deal of organizational resistance. They threaten prized positions which may be altered or eliminated, and other organization members may feel the innovator will be more easily recognized and thus promoted faster. People responsible for innovation must overcome a lot of inertia to get their jobs done.

"Can any good come out of Nazareth?" This is always the question of the wiseacres and knowing ones. But the good, the new, comes from exactly that quarter whence it is not looked for, and is always something different from what is expected. Everything new is received with contempt, for it begins in obscurity. It becomes a power unobserved.

Feuerbach

Accountability of staff as well as line managers

Marketing and merchandising analysis, when handled internally, is often accomplished by staff rather than line personnel, and a division is made between the two. In essence, this implies that line people are responsible for what happens to the company, and staff people are not. Staff also must have a sense of responsibility, or sterility will develop in their intellectual and imaginative skills, and the enthusiasm which provides bursts of creativity and intuitive inspiration will die.

Management can make staff members responsible for their data by requiring staff to utilize their data to interpolate positive suggestions of how the organization should react to internal and external changes. However, responsibility without authority does not get the job done. The research staff should also be represented in top management.

When staff personnel are brought into the highest policy-making levels of an organization, they can no longer hand over voluminous data to line managers and then decry their inability to do anything about the findings. Staff personnel must also have the spontaneity, audacity, and imagination necessary to develop ways to assimilate their own data, assess what it means to the future, and develop action plans to assure that the organization thereby benefits.

THE ENVIRONMENT OF SUCCESSFUL COMPANIES

Companies that are leaders in their field have achieved their prominence and retained it because of a certain positive climate or environment which is actively maintained within the organization. Successful companies have in common such essential elements of the environment as follows:

1. They characteristically have organized programs to seek out new products, markets, and business opportunities.

2. They are self-critical of their products and ever seeking ways to improve the present order. They are not satisfied with current success.

3. They set challenging goals for themselves, systematically develop strategies and action plans to achieve these goals, and implement tight controls to correct direction when results do not meet up to expectations. They demand superior performance and do not just hope to keep up with others.

4. Their top management is energetic, audacious, entrepreneurial. Managers are enthusiastic about their company's potential and spare no effort to develop new and better ways for the company to operate. They do not look back in fear of losing what they know they must discard along the way.

5. Management sets ambitious, no-compromise goals but plans for failure to achieve them should the unforeseen materialize.

6. Management creates an enthusiastic environment of exciting growth and plans opportunities for the enrichment and advancement of its personnel. The environment is results oriented but permissive, since management realizes that significant gains also require audacity and ventures into the new and untried.

7. Successful companies shape their future rather than letting it be molded by random patterns and events. They shape their future by daring to set high goals and assume the risks that leadership entails. They did not sit around to see whether everyone else will confirm that they are on the right path.

LEADING AN ORGANIZATION FROM PROSPERITY TO BUST

All major industries were once growth industries. Many ceased to have this distinction not because of market saturation or the burdens of sheer size, but because of a failure of management. Management tends to think in terms of a company's internal conditions and to lose perspective on external conditions which determine where change and the consumer are going. Industries that stop growing are product and operations oriented rather than marketing and customer oriented.

Hollywood thought of itself as being in the movie business rather than the entertainment business, and it was nearly devastated by television. The railroads thought of themselves as being in the railroad business rather than transportation, and they have been squeezed by trucking, air, and marine transport. Had these industries been customer rather than product oriented, they would still be growing. They declined because their executives defined their objectives improperly (see Chapter 2).

Such industries generally decline because the companies that comprise them lack the will to survive. Surviving requires inventiveness, audacity, and courage to reach out to the new and untried. Change requires the courage to abandon outdated operating procedures and products and to embrace those that are new and emerging.

Every great advance in science has issued from a new audacity of imagination.

John Dewey

Factors which can lead an organization from prosperity to bust include the following:

1. The belief that there is no competitive substitute for the product, and no competition which can match the organization's present performance.
2. The idea that growth is assured by an expanding and increasingly prosperous population, demographic changes in family size, age composition, or favorable legislation.
3. Relying too heavily on mass production and declining unit costs as a means of holding onto a market. This leads to rigidity and a focus on internal conditions rather than the external needs of the market.
4. Overreliance on methods and products that have proved successful in the past. In a dynamic marketplace, yesterday's success can be obsoleted by today's innovation.

5. Planning based on conditions that existed yesterday or now exist, rather than on probable conditions of the future.
6. A compelling desire to produce all an organization can with the resources available, which puts emphasis on production rather than marketing. Whenever money is available, builders will build; when lenders are flush with funds, they will find a way to get them out.
7. When output is prodigious, emphasis is placed on sales, or getting rid of the product, rather than on marketing. Then the product is generally not customer oriented and must be written down to reduce inventory. When what is offered for sale is determined by the seller and not the buyer, the product is generally not filling a true need in the marketplace.
8. Investigating customers' needs by looking into the range of products supplied in the past and offering what has proven successful. This preoccupation with the tried and true blocks out the sensitivity needed to capitalize on opportunities created by changing and emerging consumer needs.
9. Talking up marketing but not following through in deed. Operational implementation of marketing concepts rarely occurs, because it might require some discomfort, possible write-offs, obsolescence of current practices, or personnel adjustments.
10. When a plan does not work out, automatically laying the blame on the plan when the wrong people are put in the position of doing a job, failure can lie in the people and not in the plan.
11. Static assumptions—failing to see how innovations can change the environment in which the company does business. When a company introduces something new into a market, the market changes, as well as the company. For example, the introduction of recreation-oriented, empty-nester housing into a market which did not have that form of housing previously can create a market for it. It is no accident that antique stores and automobile agencies cluster in neighborhoods rather than locating at random; proximity creates the market traffic that was not there before.
12. A pathological fear of innovation by management of large companies, though the larger the company, the better its capacity is to succeed with an innovation. They feel there is too much to lose, and they are often judged by their judiciousness and sobriety rather than their audacity.
13. Larger companies have screening networks through which ideas must pass until they get to the top. This strangles all but the most obvious or most easily proven ideas, and what cannot be proven through severely critical feasibility studies is discarded. In such an environment only that which has already been done and proven can survive, and these are never true or total innovations. In smaller companies, more novel ideas make it to the top; as management becomes accustomed to innovative concepts, its receptivity grows.

14. The idea that proposed plans should make sense in the context of a manager's own direct experience and neatly fit into the established method of doing things. All other plans are viewed with skepticism. However, very few good plans are so obviously superior that they receive immediate acceptance and approval; most need a strong advocate to push them through. Companies which do not possess a permissive atmosphere which allows for going across the grain will suffer from mediocrity.

INCREASING MANAGEMENT PRODUCTIVITY

Peak performance requires superb management of both the human and technological aspects of the business. Technology is no better than the people who must use it to implement the goals set by management. Value engineering, industrialization, and economic theory can provide the means to get the most out of the material and money resources, but some of the biggest savings and productivity increases will result from the improved management of people (see Chapter 22).

Sowing initiative to harvest results

Initiative should be delegated to subordinates and kept there. If there is a construction problem, for example, top management should look to construction management to solve it. When construction management tries to transfer a problem to top management, construction management no longer has a problem, and those who do not have problems are not going to come up with solutions.

Once a manager assumes responsibility for a subordinate's problem and takes back the initiative, the roles have been reversed; the manager is accountable to the subordinate rather than vice versa. The first rule in achieving performance is to transfer initiative to the one who is to perform and keep it there. When authority is properly delegated and initiative firmly established, management gains leverage to plan and steer rather than fight fires.

Increasing productivity by increasing expectations

A high level of achievement should be demanded and supported with a step-by-step program which builds on a base of successively attainable objectives. Mediocre performance is often the result of management's failure to demand higher levels of performance. The manager must formulate attainable performance standards and have the courage to demand them. Too often, he bargains himself down to comfortable expectation levels, fearing to try for peak performance. His fears of rejection, antagonism, resistance from subordinates, or failure tremendously inhibit performance expectations. The struggle to attain peak performance exerts pressure on the insecure manager, spotlights him, and can expose his inefficiencies, uncertainties, and weaknesses.

We judge ourselves by what we feel capable of doing, others judge us by what we have done.

Henry W. Longfellow

Those companies outpacing their competitors are usually doing so because management is courageous enough to set challenging goals. Competitors may be living up their self-imposed goals, but too often these are mediocre goals which at best yield mediocre achievements. To stay competitive, management must aim high and have the courage to assume the same risk and have the same high level of expectations required from its subordinates, subcontractors, and consultants.

The hand can never execute anything higher than the heart can inspire.

Ralph Waldo Emerson

Small advances add up to large gains

To reach high levels of achievement, immediate goals should not be defined too broadly or ambitiously. A graduated program, built on successive achievements, will create a more results-oriented, positive environment for both manager and subordinate. If specific, attainable goals are set, the successful achievement of these goals can be used to establish belief in the attainability of a graduated series of goals which expand the initial success. Achievements are won a step at a time.

He who waits to do a great deal of good at once, will never do anything.

Samuel Johnson

Accountability and initiative must not be too disseminated throughout the organization. They should always go to a specific individual, although the contributions of many may be required. Whenever accountability and initiative are not clearly defined, subordinates tend to delegate responsibility to the boss, especially if he tries to play a helpful role. Energy should be focused on one or two sharply defined goals, preferably in writing.

The more subordinates participate in determining goals, the better. As part of the team they are more apt to share the belief that performance can be bettered. Once they recognize the need to improve performance, they will be encouraged to make positive suggestions as to how this can be achieved. This keeps the initiative with the subordinate.

Conveying goals positively

Goals should be conveyed in a positive, "must do", manner; the "like to do" approach is not likely to succeed. It is important to make clear that goals and the timetable for their achievement are reasonable expectations that *must* be achieved. At no time should the manager infer that these goals are negotiable or that he is seeking subordinates' acquiescence to or approval of the goals, once they have been established. He must not leave doors open such as, "Even though you may fail, your efforts are nonetheless appreciated" or "It's understandable that you fell short because the goals were too ambitious to begin with." Goals should be ambitious but realistic and achievable (see Chapter 29).

Meeting initial goals is an all-important part of ongoing improvement in productivity. Once success has been achieved on an initial set of demands, belief begins to take hold in the minds of subordinates. Successive achievement expands belief and faith. It removes fear, one of the major barriers to continued improvement. A step-by-step improvement strategy, clearly conveyed and with nonnegotiable goals, will overcome fears, uncertainties, and hostilities which impede progress.

> *For they conquer who believe they can.*
> Virgil

There exists a state in human work relationships which can be felt by all but which is difficult to define. We will call this tension. Phrases like "a slack operation" or "a taut ship" describe the degree of tension in the organizational condition.

There is a relationship between effectiveness and tension. Maximum effectiveness calls for people in an organization to feel some positive, complex sense of pressure, obligation, responsibility, accountability, or pride—all of which produce tension. If enough tension does not exist, the organization will be slack, and so will its effectiveness. If tension is increased beyond the optimum, however, effectiveness will again decline. Inept managers produce wild fluctuations in the tension state of the organization, constantly missing the optimum state by sharp reversals in emphasis. The only commands they know are hard right and hard left.

Enlightened managers achieve a high level of productivity by maintaining the optimum level of tension within the organization. If the right amount of tension exists, it must be directed toward the accomplishment of productive work. The key word is "productive." Many of the activities carried on in any enterprise are essentially nonproductive in the sense that they would be unnecessary if the work were properly analyzed, planned, and performed correctly in the first place. We will refer to this category of work as a washout (that is, it washes out previous nonacceptable work).

Not only can nonproductive work be washed out by better analysis and planning, but highly repetitive, tedious work can be washed out by standardization. Dramatic increases in productivity can be achieved by elimination of washes in the work flow (see Chapter 24).

> *Anyone can do any amount of work provided it isn't the work he is supposed to be doing at that moment.*
> Robert Benchley

Successful managers will be forceful in demanding the attainment of objectives and creating in subordinates a respect for objectives and a command of the means to achieve them. Without forceful management, there is a tendency for the means to take precedence and the objectives to be forgotten. People are more comfortable with the familiar and tend to place greater value on what they do, as opposed to what others do. In an organization, this can create an atmosphere in which each specialist department pursues its work as an end and a good in itself, without reference to overall organizational objectives. Such an organization, working at cross-purposes, will soon pull itself apart. It is management's job to keep departments pulling in the same direction toward agreed-upon objectives. Otherwise, economics will not allow an organization to prosper (see Chapter 26).

THE MANAGEMENT PROCESS

The management process consists of five primary functions: planning, organization, staffing, direction, and control. Each function is important to management success. Overemphasis on one function to the exclusion of others will not adequately compensate for misplaced emphasis in the long run.

Planning

Planning involves conceptual thinking, statement of problems, gathering of facts, objective analysis, and subjective evaluation to determine alternate solutions for arriving at a predetermined objective (see Chapter 1). Planning activities include:

1. Setting objectives and identifying constraints.
2. Forecasting where the present course and alternate courses will lead.
3. Developing strategies required to achieve objectives and action plans to implement the strategies.
4. Programming and scheduling to establish priority, sequence, and timing of strategies and action plans.
5. Budgeting and allocation of resources.
6. Establishment of procedures and standardization of methods.
7. Policy formulation to direct decision making in important recurring matters.

Organization

Organization is an administrative process involving the management of details in implementing objectives. It involves arranging and segmenting the total work load into manageable increments and developing the people requirements necessary for implementation of plans (see Chapter 28). Organization activities include:

1. Structuring the organization for the accomplishment of objectives. Organizational structures are graphically illustrated by organization charts.
2. Relationships and reporting and communication procedures are developed to relate people to activities, to functions, and to one another.
3. Job and position descriptions are developed to define the scope of relationships, functions and activities, and to specify objectives or the performance requirements of the position.
4. Qualifications for the positions are established as a guide in staffing.

Staffing Staffing is people oriented; leadership and communication are required to get things done through other people. Staffing matches people up to the position created in the organization (see Chapter 28) and includes:

1. Recruiting and selecting qualified people.
2. Orienting and familiarizing people with their new position and its context within the organization.
3. Training people to become proficient in their positions.
4. Developing people to improve attitudes, knowledge, and skills to assure continuity of management and guard against obsolescence.

Direction Direction is also people oriented, requiring leadership and communication to assure that objectives, plans, policies, and positions are understood and accepted. Direction is used to influence and enlighten people on the methods of achieving desired objectives. Direction (see Chapters 7 and 22) includes the following activities:

1. Delegation of responsibility and accountability of people for achieving specific results.
2. Motivating people to achieve the desired results.
3. Coordinating efforts to receive the optimum results with minimum conflict, expense, and effort.
4. Innovating to create a positive climate for independent thought for creativity and for managing conflict.

Control Another people-oriented function is control, which involves leadership communication and understanding in monitoring activities to assure that strategies and plans are being properly executed by people to arrive at predetermined objectives (see Chapters 20, 21, 22, and 29). Control activities include:

1. Developing a reporting system which provides management information in sufficient time to allow correction when activities do not progress according to plan.
2. Development of performance standards against which to measure accomplishment.
3. Measurement of results to determine the degree of deviation from performance standards.
4. Initiation of corrective action by adjusting standards or plans, staffing and directing people in a more effective manner, and implementing corrective action in the process.
5. Rewarding or disciplining people according to their performance as measured by performance standards.

26

Production and field management

There are many variables affecting an organization's potential for fast-paced construction, which varies in different parts of the country. Factors affecting construction speed include: quality and availability of labor, union regulations, quality of management, capabilities of the architect, ability of the development organization to support field operations, quality of field personnel, site conditions, type of construction, and climatic conditions.

Despite these many variables, it is possible to utilize a rule of thumb in establishing completion goals for construction. An aggressive, well-managed, and highly motivated organization can build in two thirds to three quarters the average construction time usual in its geographic area, wherever that may be. If the organization is not geared for this type of performance, management cannot expect to achieve its goal overnight.

Someone asked Woodrow Wilson how long he would prepare for a ten-minute speech. He said, "Two weeks." "How long for an hour speech?" "One week." "How long for a two-hour speech?" "I am ready now."

WHY BUILD SO FAST? Why should a developer try so hard to build one third faster than his competition? What is the advantage of pushing so hard? In a word, profit! The failure of income to keep pace with costs has reduced development profits. To the developer, this means increased risk to achieve smaller returns. He needs every advantage possible to keep profit and risk within tolerable limits, and building quickly reduces both cost and risk. Job-site overhead can be reduced for both the developer and his subcontractors, and so can the office expenses applicable to each job. Less construction time naturally means lower construction financing costs, and faster funding and payments make a better cash flow for all concerned.

Speed is a very tangible measure of performance, and a good track record builds confidence within the organization and outside it. The best subcontractors will gravitate to a developer who can build quickly, because everyone makes money faster in a clean, swift operation. When things get rough and shortages of labor, materials, or funds develop, the builder with the best track record will have a priority for the goods and services in short supply.

Building quickly also reduces the financial risk resulting from the holdback provisions that may be in the takeout loan. Cutting two months out of the construction schedule adds that much more time to achieve fill-up and meet holdback provisions. (The holdback is that portion of the permanent financing which the lender holds back until the developer has accomplished a predetermined occupancy or income level.) In soft markets, this could be the edge that allows funding of the holdback when the company has a close call. If there are a number of concurrent starts in the market area, the reduced construction time will put the new units on the market two to three months ahead of the competition. That would mean two to three months' less construction financing or fill-up expense, which can make or break some projects or mean the difference between whether or not to bring in another equity partner.

ORGANIZATION FOR PRODUCTIVITY AND EFFICIENCY

Both small and large builders can utilize productivity concepts. However, a goal of building quickly may require some changes within the organization, most notably more emphasis on planning, motivation of personnel, and development of production techniques.

In determining objectives, the organization must know the possible and to be courageous enough to set challenging goals. Setting the goal involves a commitment to perform at a high level of productivity. This could put a strain on some personnel and require a greater commitment from others. Thus the commitment to high levels of productivity also involves a commitment to motivate the staff and to support them in their efforts to achieve (see Chapter 25).

They can conquer who believe they can.
Virgil

When an employee is properly motivated and is aware of organizational goals, there is hardly such a thing as downtime. A motivated employee who has a slack period will generally take advantage of it by working on operations research, methods improvement, or whatever label the organization may attach to innovation and problem solving.

There is another side of the coin, however. When management sets tough goals for the organization, it must furnish the people in the organization with the backup they require so they can meet the high level of expectations. A construction field organization, for example, cannot provide superior performance without substantial technical backup in the areas of accounting, estimating, scheduling, contract documentation, and architectural input. A high level of productivity in the field is dependent upon excellence in the help provided by the organization.

Peak performance in the organization requires a close analysis of people and technology, as we have noted. However, many companies do not fully comprehend their total work flow and can neither anticipate nor program it adequately. The first step in improving performance is a thorough understanding of all operations comprising the total work flow and the interdependence of the operations (see Chapter 28).

Skilled employees must be supplied the technological tools required to operate at peak performance. One of the most valuable assets a developer has is the information gained from successful operating experience, but many let this slip through their fingers (see Chapter 24).

Operating experience, performance, and cost information must be retrieved, sorted, stored, and then fed back into the work flow and day-to-day decision-making process. The cumulative experience of an organization must be "canned," so that personnel coming into the organization will rapidly grasp how all operations relate to the total work flow. This type of systemization and control provides a stable basis against which subsequent performance can be measured, and it is a catalyst for internal growth.

Shortly after the entry of the United States into World War 1, General John J. Pershing was equally praised and criticized by those who thought they knew as much about running the army as he did. As is the case with most public figures, he had a hard time pleasing everyone. One of his chief critics called him to task for spending so much time on small details. Pershing replied: "I am doing this now, while I have the time, in order that those under me will know how my mind works when I have not the time to spend on minor details."

The Public Speakers Treasure Chest

NEED FOR AN INTEGRATED ACCOUNTING AND CONTROL SYSTEM

Rapid-paced construction requires an accurate and efficient estimating, accounting, and cost-control system which can service the needs of the construction operation. (See Chapters 20 and 21.) Unpaid bills or inadequate cost controls stall a construction program quickly. Fast, dependable payments are about the best recommendation a builder can have. Inadequate estimating and cost controls slow up a job because unexpected costs can necessitate design changes during construction and can even stop a job.

A construction scheduling system, linked with a detailed estimating system, gives the builder a guideline for forecasting his cash requirements. An integrated accounting and reporting system allows for the timely preparation of cash receipts and disbursements. Such a system makes no attempt to portray the flow of accounts receivable, accounts payable, or depreciation, but the cash flow statement allows management to determine the cash needs of the organization in sufficient time to plan borrowing needs. Nothing halts production faster than unpaid subcontractors or employees!

Cost reports should be prepared on a periodic basis, for they are the tool which enables management to locate and correct trouble spots on the job quickly. Cost reports compare actual costs with estimates and disbursement budgets. They are the feedback mechanism which keeps project status current and alerts management to problem areas.

Linking accounting with estimating, budgeting, scheduling, and cost control provides the basis for a comprehensive management information system, which is a prerequisite for speed of operations and profit. With such an information system, construction cost and schedule irregularities are so obvious they can be spotted before troubles get out of hand. Corrections or adjustments can be made immediately.

Such a system will not solve all of the developer's or builder's problems, but it will help identify those that require solutions. It may appear to be lengthy and time-consuming if the organization is not currently utilizing this type of information, but it is the shortest and most accurate method known for getting the job done reliably (see Chapter 20).

THE LAND AND THE ARCHITECTURE: TOPOGRAPHY, DESIGN, WORKING DRAWINGS

The capability of building quickly starts with the land. Use of relatively flat land will minimize structural, grading, and drainage complications and allow a high degree of structural repetition throughout each structure. In the architecture, structural and engineering simplicity is the key to design. For example, when it is necessary that a load-bearing wall also be a plumbing wall, foundations should be offset so plumbing stacks can bypass them. Many problems occur in the field when plumbing is designed to go through foundations.

Roof breaks, irregularities in exterior wall treatments, and close tolerances should be minimized. For example, conditions where a prefabricated vanity or cabinet must fit between two walls should be avoided. Rough framing can vary enough from unit to unit to cause difficulties in proper installation and fitting where both end conditions are fixed. When interior design allows, ceiling headers should be dropped rather than flush. Flush ceiling headers require more cutting and fitting of joists, better quality workmanship, and closer tolerances than dropped headers where the joist can run over the top of the headers. Reliance on preassembled and prefinished components such as cabinets, prehung doors, or appliances with pigtails attached, aids construction speed in the finishing stages. All around, construction speed is enhanced by having a simpler product to build (see Chapter 13).

Closer coordination between the field and the design staff is required. The field staff must keep the design staff advised of the work processes of subcontractors. Detail by the architect should reflect the particular subcontractor's techniques, to make field implementation of the desired effects as simple as possible.

Tough, nitty-gritty problems should not be left for solution in the field. Problems should be worked out in the design stage, with sufficient detailing so that field personnel do not have to make architectural decisions. This allows the superintendent and the subcontractors' foremen in the field to direct all their energies to construction (for which they are well suited) and frees them from having to make interpretive architectural and design decisions (for which they generally are not suited).

It is very important that the architect understand field conditions. Those who are unfamiliar with actual construction techniques may leave their drawings open for the man in the field to decide how things should be done. This is not good for numerous reasons, one of which is that incomplete drawings have a negative effect on construction speed and cost.

Architectural decisions should be made by the architect. If the architect is not competent and the field organization has to make the architect's decisions, a new one should be found.

METHODS IMPROVEMENT TO ACHIEVE COST BENEFITS

Because subcontractors assume the work is going to be done in the usual way—the wasteful way—architectural drawings must make clear what is not there, as well as what is there. For example, if a baseboard or headers over nonbearing openings and bridging have been omitted, the drawings must indicate it clearly. Otherwise the subcontractor, through habit, will assume the work is part of his cost of doing the job. When materials assemblies, such as a better design for common plumbing walls, reduce labor and materials requirements and eliminate trade conflicts, the advantage needs to show up in the drawings, or the subs will not give the builder any credit for methods improvement.

We have designed plumbing distribution systems where there is minimal need to cut framing members and have virtually eliminated conditions where plumbing must pass through a foundation when a plumbing wall is also a load-bearing wall. This reduces work, the interdependence of subs, and the friction when one sub damages the work of another. To be effective, such improvement techniques have to be effectively communicated to superintendents and subcontractors. This calls for both good quality drawings and coordination meetings to explain the advantages and cost benefits. These benefits will not come automatically just because they are designed in the drawings. Personal communication is also required to break down static assumptions: "Once you've seen one plumbing wall, you've seen them all." Improvement requires nothing less than retraining all concerned to discard costly methodology and adopt the improved methods. This retraining begins with the instructions to bidders; the subcontractors' estimators must be aware of the savings which can be realized through the improved methods (see Chapter 27).

Materials waste can be reduced by preplanning. If management is not concerned enough about materials waste to preplan for economy, subcontractors and workers will reflect this lack of concern and make decisions based on economy of labor at the expense of materials economy. Since a subcontractor's labor cost is already a fixed cost to the builder, the subcontractors "economy" can work to the disadvantage of a builder who is providing the materials.

Preplanning starts with the design by the use of modular dimensioning, whereby building dimensions closely reflect materials dimensions to reduce cutting and waste. Sheathing often can be stopped at windows and doors and scrap used over and under them, to save the waste due to cutting out openings. Construction practices in the past have been wasteful of materials because there has been no concern for economy. Subcontractors have adopted wasteful construction techniques which management must discourage. Value engineering or preplanning of materials use require more and better detailed drawings and schedules than most builders have been used to.

Techniques of methods improvement

Methods improvement consists of finding the best way to do things. This includes:

1. Designing simpler assemblies to be constructed.
2. Reducing the number of pieces to be assembled in the field through prefabrication techniques.
3. Implementation of labor-saving devices.
4. Simplification of work methods.
5. Reducing the number of subcontractors, or their interdependence.
6. Eliminating unnecessary operations and combining operations.
7. Identifying common trouble spots and implementing improved design and methods.
8. Eliminating practices which require needless rework.
9. Reducing materials handling by more efficient delivery, storage, and equipment.
10. Pinpointing schedule-related problems, working out problems with interested parties, and rescheduling to eliminate problems in the future.
11. Implementing all changes and pickup items immediately. A simple fault, not quickly remedied, can compound itself quickly and grow to such proportions that it cannot be corrected economically.
12. Checking actual performance against schedules, identifying conflicts, and getting feedback into the schedule to remedy such conflicts in the future.
13. Checking architectural detailing against efficient field procedures. Difficulties arising from architectural detailing should be fed back in order to eliminate reoccurrence of the same problems. Management can spend a disproportionate amount of time re-solving the same problems because it fails to eliminate them at the source.

REDUCING FIELD WORK THROUGH INDUSTRIALIZATION

Good scheduling (see Chapter 29) and controls can maximize the productivity of labor and materials and result in reduced construction financing costs. Design and planning contribute to construction economics if they result in a product that is simpler to construct. To go a step further, a product with larger but fewer pieces can be built more quickly than one with thousands of smaller pieces.

Reducing the number of building pieces to be assembled in the field has led to industralization of the production of mobiles, modulars, sectionals, components, panelization, and utility cores. This attempt to solve field-related problems has fostered new difficulties. For many companies, the cure has been worse than the illness. The industralization process has been beset with problems related to transportation, weather delays, peak-and-valley production, plant amortization, and higher costs than conventional construction. The most serious of these have been plant amortization and inventory carrying costs in an industry noted for cyclical peaks and valleys.

The plant amortization problem

Industrialized producers are finding the plant amortization problem equal to or greater than the problems of on site-construction costs which industralization was to cure. One way to deal with the plant amortization costs is to eliminate the plant. An industrialized housing organization does not automatically require a plant, with its attendant startup costs and the amortization millstone.

There are subcontractor shops, lumber yards, cabinet makers, and truss manufacturers hungry for added business. By utilizing the existing capacity of these facilities, the developer can subcontract panelization and prefabrication. By utilizing no more than 25 percent of a subcontractor's manufacturing capacity, a developer remains merely a good customer to the subcontractor. A manufacturing operation should not depend on one developer for survival, since every developer must at times cut back production.

By spreading work between manufacturing shops, the developers need for plant startup and amortization is eliminated, yet the advantage of factory labor is retained. Spreading the work load also spreads the credit load. Construction financing cost can be minimized by obtaining 30- to 45-day invoicing from the manufacturer, tightly scheduling field execution, and coordinating the manufacturing and erection operations with sales and take-out financing. Arranging with erection crews for payment by the unit, and as each one is completed, further reduces construction financing cost.

This procedure can eliminate direct plant amortization and operating cost to the industrialized developer, and can also limit construction financing costs. The procedure does require a high degree of management capability at the top. To make the operation work requires expertise in materials handling, scheduling, organizational planning, quality control, and marketing savvy.

Success thus far in industrialized housing has been won by those with low first costs and amortization costs. Failure has inevitably resulted for those with ambitious production facilities and those giving heavy emphasis to the economics of scale in mass production.

Site shops in staging areas or relocatable shops in the field are a logical progression for the developer who finds it more economical to produce selected components himself.

TECHNIQUES FOR THE FIELD

Conducting weekly job meetings with all subcontractors is a very effective technique for maintaining productivity and job harmony. Attendance at meetings should be made a contract requirement. (Coffee and rolls served at the meeting can be an incentive for attendance and promote cordiality.)

At these meetings, the job superintendent should review the past week's performance, and problems should be discussed and resolved so that they do not continue into the coming week's work. Production for the coming week should then be discussed and coordinated. An experienced job superintendent will be aware of potential problems in the coming week's work. He can anticipate a particular coordination or scheduling problem and determine which points in specifications or construction drawings the subcontractor may misinterpret. He should go over these with the subs to forestall crises before they occur.

In other words, the superintendent should anticipate rather than react. He should study contract documents and iron out incongruities, and bring light to areas requiring interpretation rather than waiting for a subcontractor to do it the wrong way. Management must make it clear to the superintendent that it expects this type of diligence. Subcontractors' personnel often do not even use the drawings; they just go to it the way they always have. If there is anything of an unusual nature in the drawings, it should be pointed out to the subs. They may catch it at bidding time but forget it in the field.

Difficulties between the subs can be ironed out in the weekly meetings. One great advantage of this type of meeting is that subs cannot hide behind one another, passing the buck to the next guy, because the next guy is right there to pass it back until it finds its true resting place. Assembling all the related parties together is the quickest way to cut to the heart of an issue and establish accountability.

There are times when a hard-nosed attitude is required, to the point where it may jeopardize the superintendent's ability to maintain good relationships with subs. It may be more effective for one who is not required to maintain a day-to-day relationship with subs—the owner, vice president of construction, or construction manager—to convey this attitude. The person applying the pressure should be in a decision-making capacity regarding future contractual services or purchase orders.

If a subcontractor repeatedly fails to do pickup work or to get men on the job to perform a task critical to the schedule, the superintendent should arrange to have the work performed by other means. He can bring in men himself and backcharge the subcontractor in a particularly aggravating situation. If such situations continue to occur, however, the sub may have to be permanently replaced.

When a sub is replaced, he should be required to leave behind all materials that have been delivered to the job site. These are taken over by the builder and assigned to the new subcontractor. This is a protection for the builder against liens that may be posted on the property by suppliers who have failed to receive payment from the sub. If suppliers are requested to remove materials from job, they can become partially "lost" in transit back to the warehouse, and a lien may be placed against the job for the "loss."

To make it easier for subs to bring in materials, driveways and parking areas are often laid out and paved before building foundations are begun. Temporary rock roadbeds may be laid in courtyards between buildings to provide access for forklifts and trucks. This hard surfacing at the outset of the project allows access for all the trades in all kinds of weather. Urgency is placed on getting the building under roof so that interior construction will not be stopped by inclement weather.

To maintain the schedule, subs must work very closely behind one another. This requires timely support and expediting from the field organization. For large projects, the job superintendent should have an assistant. The superintendent is a field man and the assistant is an office man who handles telephone communications and paper work.

An effective job superintendent is tough and demanding, pressing at all times to keep the schedule on stream. Subs will move men off jobs where superintendents are not demanding and put them on others where more pressure is applied: The squeaking wheel gets the oil. The sub usually will keep his best men on a job that is on schedule, because he can get a maximum return on a job that runs smoothly and quickly.

Timely inspections are important, particularly at the beginning of the job, to catch misunderstandings, misinterpretations of drawings, and unacceptable shortcuts by subcontractors. Nipping unsatisfactory work in the bud can save many a headache later. A good early understanding of acceptable performance is mandatory.

Immediate decisions at the job site are necessary to maintain schedule and keep costs down. Each subcontractor's downtime must be kept to a minimum so each can keep costs in control. If the sub knows prompt, clear-cut decisions will be made by the developer, his bids will reflect the advantage.

None of the techniques discussed above is particularly new or revolutionary; all represent good common sense and business practice. They do, however, require an aggressive attitude within the organization. A slack organization will pass off many of the techniques as requiring paper work, administrative effort, and planning details, which eat up the work day and increase front-end costs. The "we'll handle our problems as they arise" type of entrepreneur can be substantially outperformed by utilizing these methods, however.

Construction do's and don'ts

1. Keep the job site clean and safe. Coordinate underground utility work. Do trenching early and backfill quickly. The superintendent should work with the design team so other operations are not interfered with.
2. Assign marshaling areas to subs requiring them. When subs choose their own marshaling areas, they tend to get in one another's way and interfere with the schedule.
3. Do not accept materials too early or order them too late. Materials delivered too early are pilfered or damaged; materials arriving too late, of course, hold up construction.
4. Do not coddle subs or entertain wishful thinking that things will get better. When necessary, replace subs or have work done by others and backcharge.
5. Make it clear that the schedule will be rigorously enforced. The schedule is not a hypothetical, idealized situation but a record of reasonable expectations designed to make a profit for everyone. Any sub who will not honor prior commitments to maintain his portion of the schedule is in breach of contract and should be dealt with strictly.
6. Allow no personal automobiles on the job site, to cut down on theft by subs and their workers. If a problem is severe, a guard should be assigned at the gate to check trucks as they depart from the job site. Fencing of the job site is a must for security.

THE ROLE OF THE SUPERINTENDENT

The superintendent's function can be stated as the accomplishment of a predetermined quantity of work at an acceptable quality standard as established by the job's drawings and specifications, and on a timely basis as established by the construction schedule. The superintendent's role in accomplishing these results consists primarily of operating in a managerial function to direct and control the work of subcontractors and suppliers (see Chapter 25).

The superintendent's responsibilities should be set out in a position guide. It is important that others within the organization, including the chief executive, understand the superintendent's responsibilities. Often the superintendent must suffer the consequences of everyone's procrastinations, and as a result he must engage in constant fire fighting. In such a situation he does not have enough time for his primary functions of direction and control.

Many of the problems which develop in the field can be traced to ineffective performance by personnel or consultants who are not in the field. Realizing better performance in the field must begin with better support from the organization so that the superintendent is free to do his own work rather than that of others. The superintendent should be allowed to use his time as a manager and to work on the source of problems, rather than the effects. Generally the superintendent's responsibilities do not allow him to get to the source of problems that do not originate in the field (see Chapter 28).

Use a standardized Deficiency Notice (see Exhibit 26-2) makes it possible for deficiencies to be recorded and for trends to be recognized. The deficiency form, filled out by the superintendent or inspector, should contain space for identification of the cause of the problem and for recommendations of preventive action in the future. This makes it possible for the superintendent to get feedback to management so that remedial action can be taken and the field organization will receive adequate support.

> *It is not the burden but the overburden that kills the beast.*
> Spanish proverb

INSPECTION AND CONTROL OF WORK

Inspection and control of field work involves three basic steps:

1. Inspection to compare actual results with predetermined standards, including remedial measures when actual results fall short of standards.
2. Development or utilization of information and reporting procedures to get information to management so that the source of problems can be remedied, rather than just the effects.
3. Reduction or elimination of problems at their source by utilization of information received and by the application of management expertise and problem-solving skills.

An inspection procedure is helpful in spotting problems after they have occurred, but by itself inspection does not necessarily reduce the number of problems that will occur. Meeting field-related problems at their source requires a strong sense of accountability in the entire field organization. For example, each subcontractor should be held accountable for inspecting and controlling his own work, the entire inspection responsibility should not be left to the job superintendent.

Inspection of work should be carried out according to a standardized procedures and utilizing a standard checklist (see Exhibit 26–1). Standardization provides uniformity and predictability and aids in communication and understanding. When inspection is provided on a random basis by different individuals with differing subjective standards, control is lost and misunderstanding develops.

The most effective inspection procedures from a cost benefit standpoint concentrate inspection activities on previously identified problem areas. These problem areas are identified through feedback received through deficiency notices, complaints from a customer relations department, and operating and management personnel. The most cost-effective control, then, is a less than 100 percent effort but is based to a degree on the theory of management by exception. Areas that produce few or no problems receive the least inspection time; those that have the greatest propensity to develop problems receive the bulk of the inspection time.

In addition to knowing what to inspect, the inspector must also know when to inspect in order to receive the greatest benefit from his time expenditure. Some construction operations are more critical than others and require prompt inspection at a specific time. Some of these operations include:

1. Structural and trench excavation.
2. Base course for concrete slabs.
3. Rough framing inspection before cover-up.
4. Rough plumbing and electrical inspection.
5. Inspection of roofs and plywood floors before cover-up.
6. Insulation inspection prior to cover-up.

For a detailed inspection list refer to the Job Inspection Checklist (Exhibit 26–1) and the construction punch list or Deficiency notice (Exhibit 26–2).

Inspection instructions

Inspection, by an inspector or the job superintendent, is generally confined to the inspection of materials and workmanship. The duties of the inspector are to report the compliance or noncompliance of work and materials to the contract documents. He has no authority to approve materials and workmanship or procedures not in accordance with the provisions of the contract documents, most specifically the plans and specifications.

A construction job and the consequent finished product are generally judged by appearance. It is the responsibility of the inspector to see that the appearance standards contemplated in the contract documents are not compromised by careless or poor-quality work and materials. To this end the inspector is generally more interested in results than methods. Nonetheless, the inspector must possess a thorough knowledge of methods, because results at times are a direct result of methods utilized.

The inspector must be knowledgeable of both the subcontractor's and the builder's points of view and use tact and judgment to maintain a friendly, cooperative relationship between them. Arbitrary, careless, or dictatorial types of inspection create friction and hard feelings and may be counterproductive. Inspections must be fair, reasonable, and based on an understanding of the subcontractor's problems, construction principles, and industry standards. The inspector should maintain a daily diary in a book which he signs daily. The diary should include notes on significant conversations, unusual weather, controversial circumstances, or any other happenings which may affect work scheduling or quality. The data should be sufficient to permit other personnel to provide required reports, and the notes should be sufficient to provide ample documentation in the event of litigation.

Guidelines for inspectors

1. Try to be friendly with those on the job but develop familiarity with none. Familiarity dulls objectivity and authority.
2. Do not get involved in disputes on the job, but inform superiors of them for disposition. Until the dispute is clarified by a superior, use your own best judgment.
3. Never criticize superiors or the contract documents in the presence of job personnel.
4. Attempt to keep ahead of the work and anticipate problems before they occur. Often a timely reminder in advance can save much time and materials expense that will otherwise be required for rework.
5. Retain a neutral stance by refusing gratuities or gifts from job personnel or their companies.
6. Be firm and consistent. Good inspection requires firmness of purpose, adherence to predetermined standards, and consistency in application. Lack of consistency or firmness will be interpreted as a weakness by job personnel and will undermine your authority. The quality of the inspection will have a marked effect upon the ultimate outcome of the product.
7. Aid subcontractors whenever possible to do so without compromising the quality of the work. At times tradeoffs may be appropriate, whereby less-than-satisfactory work may be accepted in exchange for performance by the subcontractor of other work not in the contract.
8. Do not waste the time of job personnel by carrying on needless conversations.
9. Command respect through fairness, understanding of construction principles and standards, and force of personality.

Exhibit 26–1
Job inspection checklist

I. SITE WORK

   A. Earthwork
      1. Check that any overexcavation is backfilled with approved materials and/or that fill materials are suitable for compaction.
      2. Check that compaction is carried out as specified by the soils or civil engineer.
      3. Check that stockpiled topsoil is being stored in the location and manner specified.
      4. Check that rough grading provides for contouring and/or earth stockpiling, as required by landscaping drawings.

   B. Storm Drainage
      1. Check site for adequate storm drainage and water flow to drainage system.

Exhibit 26–1 (*continued*)

    2. Check field layout of storm drainage system against drawings.
    3. Check elevations of drains to see that water will actually drain into them.
    4. Check to see that trenches are properly backfilled and compacted, particularly under paved areas.

C. Concrete for Exterior Flatwork
    1. Check for adequate compaction.
    2. Check for base course as specified.
    3. Check concrete mix and required strength.
    4. Check for construction and expansion joints as specified.
    5. Check for reinforcing steel as required.
    6. Check surface finish against specification and/or sample.
    7. Check thickness of concrete, slopes, grades, or swales as required.

D. Ashpalt Paving and Base Course
    1. Check for adequate composition of pad. Double check compaction of trench excavations under paving.
    2. Check material and thickness of base course against specifications.
    3. Check fine grading for adequate storm drainage.

E. Irrigation Sprinkler System
    1. Check that system is laid out according to the drawings.
    2. Check that materials are as specified.
    3. Observe test of system.
    4. Check that backfilling and compaction are as specified.

F. Wood Fencing
    1. Check concrete foundations against drawings for location, depth, and spacing.
    2. Check design, workmanship, and materials against drawings and specifications.

G. Landscaping
    1. Check landscaping materials as delivered for conformance to drawings and specifications. Specifically check size and health of plants.
    2. Check fine grading for conformance to drawings and adequacy of storm drainage.
    3. Check that mulching is as according to specification. Particularly check quantities.
    4. Check that header boards are installed as required and that boulders and pole timbers, etc., are provided as required.
    5. Check that plants are installed and fertilized as per drawings and specifications.
    6. Check that plants are properly maintained and protected during construction period.

Exhibit 26-1 (*continued*)

II. CONCRETE WORK

    A. Structural and Trench Excavation
1. Check location, elevation, and dimensions.
2. Check depth of trenches and bearing qualities of soil at bottom.
3. Check size and location of structural steel.
4. Inspect to see that backfill is properly compacted.

    B. Concrete Slabs
1. Inspect that base course and waterproof membranes and wire mesh are as specified.
2. Check compaction of subgrade.
3. Check underslab rough plumbing and electrical.
4. Check that swales and/or drainage flows are provided in concrete as required.

    C. Concrete Walls
1. Check for straight and plumb wall forms, reinforcing steel.
2. Check for quality of concrete, continuous pour, and removal of air pockets.
3. Check for adequate curing time before removal of forms.
4. Check waterproof membranes where required.

III. MASONRY
1. Check masonry materials and workmanship against samples.
2. Check that joists are correct and watertight.
3. Check for placement of anchor bolts and their depth.
4. Check parging and waterproof membranes where required.
5. Check for proper openings, size, location, squareness.
6. Check for proper reinforcing steel, tying.
7. Check that sheathing paper is used between brick and wood.
8. Check for adequate masonry supporting ledges.
9. Check for required tier to tie masonry to framework.

IV. METAL WORK

    A. Structural Steel and Miscellaneous Metal Work
1. Check all steel for required size and wall thickness.
2. Check connectors for proper size gauge, and so on.
3. Check bolting and fittings for proper installation according to drawings and specifications.
4. Check that columns are vertical and beams level.

    B. Ornamental Metal Work
1. Check materials against samples.
2. Check design and workmanship against approved shop drawings.

Exhibit 26-1 (*continued*)

V. CARPENTRY

    A. Rough Carpentry and Miscellaneous Finish Carpentry Work
1. Check lumber for grading, physical defects, and moisture content.
2. Check for proper layout, straightness of walls, and spacing of studs.
3. Check required nailing, ties, straps, bracing, bolts, etc.
4. Check for proper wood bearing at masonry walls.
5. Check proper nailing of sheer diaphrams and for required blocking.
6. Check sill bolts, cord splices, straps against drawings and specification.
7. Check that nails are driven into joists, and they do not split out joists.
8. Check dimensions of openings.
9. Check that cantilevered joists extend the required distance back into building and that they are properly nailed.
10. Check that framers are not utilizing more lumber than required by drawings. Are they utilizing all the materials-saving techniques utilized in the drawings?
11. Check that framer is not creating excess wastage of materials through poor work practices.
12. Check that nailing is not damaging exposed siding, surfaces. Hammer marks should not mar the surface.
13. Check that joints are staggered on plywood subfloors.
14. Check for required wood preservatives.
15. Check trusses for material dimensions, conformance to approved drawings.
16. Check for proper tie of trusses to structure, proper bracing, bearing.
17. Check for proper nailing of roof and floor diaphragms, check for edge clips where required.
18. Check that structural integrity has not been compromised by heating, ventilating, and air conditioning; plumbing; or electrical cutting.
19. Check that carpenter keeps his area of work clean and safe.

    B. Finish Carpentry
1. Check materials and workmanship against the plans and specifications.
2. Check cabinets, vanities, doors, etc., against samples.
3. Check cabinet doors for warpage of doors and binding of hardware.
4. Check that cabinets are securely fastened.
5. Check for mars, scratches, and defects.
6. Check shelving for warpage, roughness, neatness.
7. Check joints for trueness of fit.
8. Check cased openings for proper workmanship.

Exhibit 26-1 (*continued*)

      9. Check that all trim has been installed where required.
     10. Check that required caulking is provided and that the workmanship is acceptable.
     11. Check that specified adhesive is used for installation of Marlite and other wall panelings.
     12. Check wall panelings against samples. Check neatness and trueness of workmanship.

  C. Insulation
     1. Check that required ceiling, wall, and floor insulation is properly installed in the required thickness.
     2. Check that cracks and openings have been filled and that insulation batts have not been unduly compressed by plumbing, etc.
     3. Check that vapor barriers have been installed where required.

  D. Gypsum Wallboard Work
     1. Check for specified thickness.
     2. Check that adequate blocking is provided.
     3. Check for bulges due to irregular subsurface.
     4. Check that taping and sealing of depressions, joints, corners is neatly performed.
     5. Check that walls are not textured in areas to receive wall covering.
     6. Check that gypboard fits snugly against rough framing before installing trim to prevent drafts.
     7. Check that waterproof gypboard is utilized where required.

VI. MOISTURE PROTECTION

  A. Roofing
     1. Check all materials against specification and samples.
     2. Check roof surfaces before cover-up. The deck should be completely dry, smooth, and clean of all debris.
     3. All materials should be applied in strict conformance with manufacturers' specifications.
     4. Bituminous roofing should not be applied when temperature is below 40 degrees F.
     5. Check for proper installation of all flashing.
     6. Check asphalt-impregnated felt for proper overlap and tightness.
     7. Check that adequate bituminous material has been mopped on.
     8. Take sample check of bituminous roof for thickness.

  B. Sheet Metal
     1. Check material against drawings and specifications, particularly gauge of material.
     2. Check that all roof penetrations are flashed.
     3. Check expansion joints and soldering of seams.
     4. Check that visible flashing is not dinted, irregular, or mashed, causing an unattractive appearance.

Exhibit 26-1 (*continued*)

    C. Dampproofing and Waterproofing
1. Check that waterproofing membranes and dampproofing emulsions are provided as required.
2. Check that the surfaces are dry, clean, and free of holes or rough areas.
3. Check that materials have been applied at the required thickness and that no pinholes exist.
4. Check that felt lays flat against the walls, with no wrinkles or buckles.
5. Check for material required to protect waterproofing during backfilling.

VII. DOORS, WINDOWS, GLASS AND MIRRORS
1. Check for weatherstripping of doors and windows as required.
2. Check caulking as required.
3. Check all materials and workmanship for conformance to drawings and specifications.
4. Check for proper clearance, ease of operation of doors and windows.
5. Check that sliding or bifold doors operate easily.
6. Check that aluminum sliding doors and windows operate easily.
7. Check mirrors for distortion, clarity, chips, polished edges, size, location, etc.
8. Check garage doors for ease of operation.

VIII. FINISHES

    A. Painting, Staining, Bleaching, Decorating
1. Check that siding and trim have been treated with water-repellent preservative as required.
2. Check that surfaces are properly prepared to receive paint or stain.
3. Check paint for conformance with specifications and color schedule.
4. Have sample wall section painted and approved for correct color effect before proceeding with painting of entire building.
5. Check that painter is correctly interpreting and following color schedule.
6. Check that wall covering is installed in the correct locations and that the pattern matches.
7. Check wall coverings against specifications and approved samples.

    B. Stucco, Plaster
1. Check that plaster stops are installed as required.
2. Check that corners are reinforced.
3. Check that plaster or stucco is smooth, with no bulges or indentations. Eliminate any waviness.

Exhibit 26–1 (*continued*)

       4. Check finish against sample finish; monitor quality of finish texture.
       5. Check thickness of application.

   C. Tile Work
       1. Check materials against approved samples.
       2. Check for loose tiles, caulking, neat grouting.
       3. Check that mortar joints are complete.
       4. Check that surface is clear and unblemished.

   D. Resilient Flooring
       1. Check materials against approved samples and specifications.
       2. Check subsurface to see that all high spots, holes, and rough areas have been eliminated.
       3. Check that flooring adheres properly and the correct pattern is being followed.
       4. Protect installed flooring.

   E. Carpeting
       1. Check carpet and underlayment against specification and approved samples.
       2. Check seam match and for minimum number of seams.
       3. Check that carpet is tight and appears continuous in room areas.
       4. Protect installed carpet.

IX. SPECIALTIES

   A. Clean Up
       1. Check all surfaces for dust, including floors, shelves, counter tops, windowsills, etc.
       2. Check for smudges, fingerprints, paint droppings, etc., on all surfaces.
       3. Check all windows and mirrors for cleanliness.
       4. Check for debris in buildings and on site.
       5. Check that all hard-surfaced floors are washed.
       6. Check that exterior flatwork areas are clean.
       7. Check that driveways and parking areas are clean and washed down to remove accumulated dirt, dust, etc.

   B. Draperies
       1. Check materials against specifications and approved samples.
       2. Check fit of draperies; correct fit at window and length.
       3. Check that drapery hardware operates easily.

   C. Finish Hardware
       1. Check hardware against specifications and approved samples.
       2. Check for proper installation and ease of operation.

   D. Counter Tops
       1. Check against shop drawings, specifications, and approved samples.

Exhibit 26-1 (*concluded*)

      2. Check for correct installation and fit.
      3. Check for blemishes, imperfections.

X. MECHANICAL
    A. Plumbing
      1. Check that all water lines are isolated from supporting members with vibration pads.
      2. Check that pipe is wrapped and insulated as required.
      3. Inspect or be present for testing of the plumbing system, and record results.
      4. Check that there is adequate fall in the horizontal runs.
      5. Check that floor drains are located and at the elevation where they will accommodate drainage requirements.
      6. Check all plumbing fixtures for correct installation and operation.
      7. Check garbage disposal and water heater for correct installation and operation.

    B. Heating, Ventilating, and Air Conditioning
      1. Check that installation is per approved drawings and specifications.
      2. Check duct insulation as required.
      3. Check ducts for gauge of metal, spacing of supports, bracing, vibration, etc.
      4. Check the system for proper operation.

XI. ELECTRICAL
      1. Check that load centers, transformers, outlets, etc., are located as indicated in the drawings.
      2. Check that rough-outs for lighting fixtures are located as shown on drawings. Are fixtures roughed out on center where required, at proper height?
      3. Is ceiling fixture in dining room properly roughed out to be above dining room table?
      4. Check that landscape and area lighting is roughed in according to plans.
      5. Check television and telephone locations, vertical and horizontal location on the wall.
      6. Check entrance box size, panel size, and service cable.
      7. Check electric range and oven, exhaust fans, intercom and alarm system, all switches and outlets.

EXHIBIT 26-2
Deficiency Notice

No. _____
Notice _____

Project _____ No. _____ Date _____
Subcontractor _____ Foreman _____
Superintendent _____ Other _____
Location _____ Workmanship _____ Material _____
Description _____
_____
Required correction _____
_____
Date correction completed _____ Work hours _____
Delay in job _____ Cost paid by _____
Are backcharges involved? _____
Who should pay backcharges? _____
Cause of problem _____
Preventive action for future _____
_____

Attitude: Uncooperative _____ Average _____
            Very cooperative _____

                                        Incidental _____ $0– $50 _____
                                        Important _____ $50–$100 _____
                                        Major   _____ $100–$200 _____
Superintendent _____   Critical   _____ $200 +   _____

27

Purchasing, contract letting, and progress payments

Purchasing and contract letting are among the most vital functions in the construction process. The majority of homebuilders reserve this function for the principal or owner. But whether the function is performed by the principal, or a purchasing agent, a purchasing and contracting system will simplify the detail and boost performance.

The details of purchasing and contract letting are routine, highly repetitive, and open to standardization. The decision-making and bargaining aspects of purchasing and contract functions require skill; shrewdness; a current, active knowledge of the market; and access to credit and performance ratings of suppliers and subcontractors. Most other details, however, such as entering into purchasing and subcontract agreements, developing materials and performance specifications, setting general conditions to the agreement, determining payment methods, establishing insurance and bonding requirements, giving delivery instructions, and schedule coordination, are subject to a high degree of standardization (see Chapter 24).

KEEPING ABREAST OF THE MARKET

A knowledge of local markets and products available is essential in the purchasing and contract-letting functions. Local manufacturers may duplicate a product of a national manufacturer and undercut the price, due to their lower overhead and promotional costs. For example, a local job shop may be able to manufacture light fixtures similar to the fixtures of a national manufacturer and sell them at an attractive discount. The purchasing agent needs to keep abreast of local job shop sources as well as national producers.

Flexibility in specifications is needed to take advantage of an unusual buying opportunity. For example, a freight car of aluminum sliding windows may be available at a substantial discount because the supplier had to repossess them from a delinquent builder. The windows may not be the exact size called for on the drawings, but if they can be incorporated into the building without an adverse effect on the design, they should be considered. In like manner, a discontinued line of carpeting may represent a substantial bargain, though the carpet is not as specified. If the carpet quality is within a satisfactory quality range, the purchasing agent should pursue the feasibility of the bargain purchase.

At other times, finished materials may be substituted when a less expensive material performs the same function and fits the design requirements. The purchasing agent needs to exercise great care, however, in changing materials and applications that present a particular visual impact. What may appear to be a minor visual change to a purchasing agent may be a very material change in the eyes of the designer and the marketing and merchandising divisions.

Purchasing the most suitable materials and applications at the optimum price implies a knowledge of materials, applications, availability, price, and source. Keeping abreast of the market is an ongoing function requiring an organized system of information filing. An effective system is to file materials and applications under the same format as used in the Chart of Accounts and direct construction cost plan (see Chapter 21). Information on subcontractors can be filed in the same format. For example, information on framing subcontractors is filed under rough carpentry (Chart of Accounts No. 14330), plumbing subcontractors under plumbing (No. 121370), and so on.

LOCATING SUBCONTRACTORS

The time spent locating and qualifying good subcontractors can be the most productive time spent in the construction process. Finding out a subcontractor weaknesses before the contract letting can save considerable time and money as opposed to finding out the subcontractors qualifications after he is on the job.

The financial health and performance of subcontractors must be monitored very closely. The ease of entry into some contracting trades has contributed to a high turnover rate, usually due to lack of management expertise and capitalization. A subcontractor's current status can be monitored through construction trade publications, other subcontractors and contractors, suppliers, and banks. Credit agencies can give information on subcontractor performance in paying bills.

The better subcontractors are usually busy. An investigation of competitors' projects now under construction will yield information as to which subcontractors are busy, and a visual inspection can be made of their work on the spot. The superintendent will probably discuss subcontractor performance, but some of what he reports should be discounted; he may want to keep the real value of his best subcontractors to himself. Inspectors also are a good source of leads to quality subcontractors.

In evaluating a subcontractor it is important to consider his record of prompt service, reputation for maintaining construction schedules, general responsibility, financial soundness, and willingness to do call-back and repair work. The subcontractor's quality of supervision should also be investigated: Does he work on the job himself? Does he protect the work of other subs, keep his job clean, and clean up afterwards? Can the subcontractor guarantee sufficient workmen to maintain the construction schedule? (See Exhibit 27–2.)

CONTRACT NEGOTIATION

It is typical in the building and development industry to negotiate subcontract prices and terms after the initial bids are received. The work should not necessarily go to the lowest bidder but to the one who will perform the required work in the optimum manner. Effective contract negotiation is a process whereby tradeoffs are made, to the benefit of both negotiating parties. A builder who merely attempts to drive subcontractor bids down without offering compensating tradeoffs will develop a reputation as a bid shopper. When this occurs, subcontractors and suppliers/ submit padded bids so they can give up the pad in contract negotiation. Or they will cut work quality commensurate with the price reduction demanded by the builder.

A more effective method of contract negotiation is for the builder to show the subcontractor where his costs have been reduced due to value engineering, superior construction drawings, specifications, scheduling, or supervision (see Chapter 13). Drawings should be reviewed with subcontractors to show them where costs have been engineered out. Such as baseboards material may have been omitted and less framing material may be required by modular design. Perhaps labor costs can be reduced because of a simpler design, use of preassembled components, improved logistics, and materials handling efficiencies resulting from a clean, well-maintained construction site and superior supervision. The construction schedule should be reviewed with sub contractors to demonstrate how a well-drafted, professionally executed schedule will benefit all subcontractors and reduce labor, job-site, and supervision costs (see Chapter 29).

Because subcontractors are apt to base bids on their experience with the building community as a whole, bid costs usually reflect average conditions and standard construction details and procedures. Builders who achieve above-average performance make every one else's job in the construction process easier and less costly to perform. These builders must get their story across to the subcontractors if they are to benefit from their superior expertise. Over time a developer who is really superior will gain a track record which speaks for itself. However, even those builders with a superior record and good reputations with subcontractors must continue to maintain the practices and principles which have produced that record. A track record must be reinforced and maintained regularly.

EFFECTIVE BIDDING

In the bidding process, construction drawings should be thoroughly reviewed with the subs, continuously cutting costs where possible and incorporating labor-saving techniques to speed construction time. In cutting costs to increase profits, the aim is always to shave costs where they are not seen by the consumer, so that there is no commensurate reduction in value of the project. The builder, however, has to be aware that hidden savings are also often hard to detect by subcontractors.

What may be efficient for one sub is not necessarily so for another. Each has his own set of peculiarities, and the builder should be flexible enough to make changes to keep a particular sub's cost down. It is also necessary to understand how a particular sub bids the job to plan for construction economies. A sub's bidding procedure may not allow for credit to the builder, even through the sub's portion of the work has been simplified in the builder's design process.

For example, in certain job markets a masonry sub bids work according to the number of block he must lay. In certain areas, it is common to extend joists into the masonry wall for support and fire cut the ends of the joist. The mason then must fill in between the joists with block and mortar (see Illustration 27-2), and each joist should be metal strapped into the wall to secure it against lateral movement.

A time and motion study would view this as requiring much more work than just securing a wooden ledge to the masonry wall and using joist hangers to support the joist from the ledge beam (see Illustration 27-1). Nevertheless, the masonry sub often does not grant credit to the builder who omits the fire-cut joist detail in the design process. The framer, however, will certainly add a cost for the ledge beam, making its costs higher than the fire-cut joist design. This cost does not really reflect the true picture, on a time and motion basis, of what optimum costs for this detail should be.

With good communication, subs can be educated to undertake a more thorough analysis of actual costs. They need to be shown how their labor costs can be reduced by innovations in construction techniques. However, if the developer is not willing or is unequipped to communicate closely

Illustration 27-1

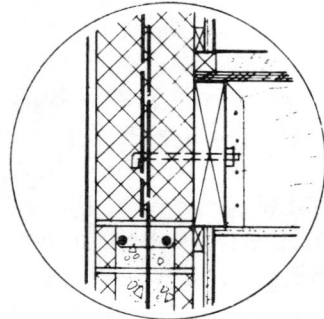

Illustration 27-2

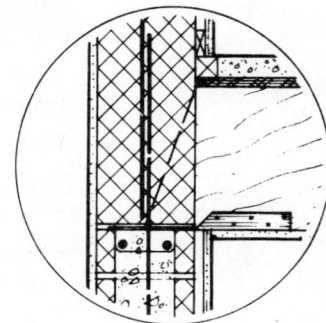

with his subs, it is best to stick with standards the sub is familiar with, even though they may not reflect optimum design.

We often work closely with the developer and his subs to implement construction innovations which produce a savings for everyone. At other times we find the best course of action is to utilize standard, accepted construction procedures, even though they may not represent the optimum we have found to work in other areas. The decision to innovate or stay with standards has to be made on the merits and disadvantages of each particular situation. The designer should dig deep enough to at least know the options available in each particular situation.

LETTING SUBCONTRACTS

For optimum performance work should be let in the same manner in which it is budgeted and specified. Chapter 21, on budgeting and controls, showed how all work can be budgeted and specified using the same format and breakdown of work units. The chart of accounts was developed in a format to reflect proven, successful subcontracting and purchasing procedures. Though procedures vary in different parts of the country, and from organization to organization, the format should fit most situations with minor modifications. For example, for rental housing, Account 14310, Site work—on site, is further broken down into at least 13 subaccounts, such as site clearing and grubbing, demolition, on-site staking and layout, earthwork, and soil export. Each subaccount is covered by a separate architectural specification section as outlined in Chapter 21, Schedule 1-E. Subcontractors wishing to bid on the site work may bid one subaccount (specification section) or any combination of them.

Matching subcontract accounts and budget accounts

An attempt should be made to keep accounts intact, that is not to split them off to different subcontractors. When a subcontractor bids on several subaccounts or specification sections, he should be requested to break down his bid price by each specification section which represents a specific subaccount in the Chart of Accounts. If it is not practical to do this, the aggregate subcontract amount should be recorded in the budget under the account which represents the primary work function. The other sections included in the aggregate bid would not receive any dollar figure in the budget but would have an explanation such as "included in Account 14310.04, Earthwork."

When work is not contracted for in the same format utilized for budgetary and control purposes, it becomes necessary to allocate costs. Cost allocation can become a very arbitrary and subjective process which results in loss of objectivity and control. An optimum system requires a very close interrelationship of budgets, costs, and controls.

Full documentation in contracts

The builder's policies and relationships with subcontractors should be established and finalized in detail for the contract letting. This will eliminate many problems that may otherwise arise on the job and provide orderly solutions for those that do occur. The contract documents should include the contract itself, drawings, specifications, special conditions, general conditions, construction schedule, and materials schedules as required.

Contracts must have enough specificity to establish the accountability of the contractual members and have enough teeth to be enforceable. Loose contracts lead to sloppy work, weak relationships, and poor habits. There must be enough guts in the contract to enable the builder to enforce the performance requirements or to get a poorly performing sub off the job. When a contract is written to the convenience of the subcontractor, the subcontractor is in the driver's seat, and, all too often, the job is run by the subcontractor. When each sub is trying to run the job to suit his convenience, no one makes money. The builder must run the job, and the contract must give him enough teeth to do so.

Construction schedules, comprehensive general conditions, and provisions for liquidated damages and backcharges should be incorporated into the contract documents. It is beneficial to incorporate materials schedules into specific subcontracts, such as for framing. If the schedules are not prepared in time for the contract letting, provisions can be made in the agreement for incorporation of the schedule at a later date, before any work is performed by the subcontractor. To finish the job on schedule, it is mandatory to incorporate the schedule into the contract.

Eliminating contingencies and reducing costs

A tough, inclusive contract should be written to cover the scope of the work. Yet, on the other hand, no attempt should be made to load the subcontractor up with contingencies for which he must provide allowances. Known contingencies are generally shouldered by the builder to eliminate subcontractor allowances, or a specific allowance is created within the contract itself to cover a contingency.

One of the best ways to eliminate contingencies at the job site is to provide thorough and complete working drawings, specifications, schedules, and construction supervision. When a subcontractor can rely on the builder's being thorough about providing these, contingencies will be minimized, and better bids will result.

Another way to minimize contingencies and reduce cost is to contract work with the sub who can handle the work best. This may sound so straightforward and logical that it is not even worth mentioning. However, often it is the obvious that escapes notice. We recently changed an exterior stair design from a tubular steel support with reinforced concrete steps to timber supports and timber steps notched into the support members on each side. We did this as an economy measure but were surprised to find that the carpenter was charging a premium for the wood stairs in figuring his bid, making them slightly more expensive than the steel and concrete stairway.

We went back over our estimating and found the problem was not in the estimating but in the bid. Though the framer was low bidder, he had an excessive figure for the stairs because he was unfamiliar with this type of work. As a result, we contracted out the stairs at the estimate figure, to another sub familiar with stair work. The remainder of the carpentry was awarded to the original low bidder, minus the stair cost.

For fast pace, construction contracts must have specificity and enough teeth to be enforceable, and they must award work to the sub who can perform it most efficiently. Even the low bidder may be coming in high on specific work within his overall bid.

MATERIALS MANAGEMENT AND PURCHASING

Efficient materials purchasing and management are essential to production speed and economy. It is often more economical and efficient for the builder to purchase materials than for the subcontractors to do so, especially for big-ticket items such as lumber, cabinets, windows, doors, carpets, and appliances. This, of course, depends on the builder and the subcontractor.

There are times when a good but relatively new subcontractor may not have the credit rating to have large material orders delivered to the job. Also, the builder may have more bargaining power than the sub in getting a competitive price. When the builder buys direct from the mill or factory, he need pay no markup from the subcontractor, the lumberyard, or the warehousing middleman.

Discounts given by suppliers for prompt payment range up to 5 percent for payment within ten days of invoice. The builder also can pick up a discount for direct mill shipment and advertising allowances for fixture purchases, which are a form of discount.

When the developer buys materials himself, he gets a better feel for the materials market—new products, availability, and price. This information, if properly fed back, assists decision making in the design process. For example, the joist sizes on one job were changed from 2×10 at 16 inches on center to 2×12 at 24 inches on center. Not only did this achieve a saving in board feet of lumber, but the decreased amount of board footage could be purchased at a better price because 2×10s were selling for a premium at the time.

Providing controls through materials and construction schedules

Materials schedules should be developed to itemize quantities required, and the construction schedule should be used as a guide for delivery dates. For example, a detailed lumber list broken down on a building-by-building basis is critical for both materials control and efficiency in the framing operation. When the framer knows exactly how much material he requires for each building, according to schedule, he will not keep running out and having to get more material, while his carpenters stand by. If he overstocks materials, there will be a greater percentage of materials waste. And if enough materials are delivered to a building, yet the framer comes up short, this is a good indication of excessive materials waste, and remedial action can be taken. Without the building materials schedule, the superintendent or framer cannot be aware of excess waste until the end of the job, when there are not enough materials left for completion. Of course, then remedial action is too late.

Purchase orders for materials should be posted by code number, as established in the chart of accounts. Purchase order costs can then be matched up against estimates which follow the same coding as the accounting system.

Follow-up and delivery of materials

Follow-up of purchase orders for materials is a necessary step to assure their on-time delivery. Particularly when the builder does not have alternate or backup sources, the follow-up should be a matter of routine.

In the event materials are shipped from other than a local source, the invoice may arrive before the materials do. The buyer should protect his discount for prompt payment by establishing the payment discount time from the date of delivery rather than the date of invoice. This will allow time to inspect and approve materials.

Materials should be checked at the time of delivery for conformance to purchase order conditions, specifically as to quantity and quality. The superintendent or his assistant is usually responsible for inspection and acceptance. He should have a copy of the purchase orders and a delivery schedule to check materials against. Any discrepancy should be brought to the attention of the purchasing or accounting department immediately.

A record should be kept of suppliers' performance in supplying materials. Notes of irregularities placed directly on the file copy of the purchase order provide a good historical record. On a periodic basis this information can be consolidated and included in the supplier's list. Such information will flag suppliers who are not performing acceptably.

BUILDER-SUBCONTRACTOR RELATIONS

It is typical for a builder to reuse the same subcontractor over and over again. In this case, the subcontractor bases his unit-price bidding on previous experience he has had with the builder.

Even after contract costs have been finalized, the builder can help subcontractors reduce costs throughout the construction process. Helping the subcontractor save money once the contract is let does not particularly benefit the builder on the current project but will put him in better light when subs are bidding on subsequent projects. Subs are more apt to comply with apparently tough demands of the builder if they can see that these demands will result in more profit for everyone.

When the builder is soliciting bids, the production capabilities of the subcontractor should be discussed to determine how many men he can supply to the job site and how many units he can rough in or finish per day. He should be informed that he will be required to deliver at the production pace agreed upon as a condition of the contract or be subject to liquidated damages or backcharges if the builder must step in to perform a critical function.

GENERAL CONDITIONS

The general conditions of the contract are not just a set of legal boilerplate to be referred to only in the event of a dispute on the job. Rather, they are a statement of construction policy and procedures designed to facilitate an optimal construction operation, and therefore they constitute operating instructions for all construction-related personnel. The general conditions should be reviewed regularly by the builder's construction personnel to make sure they are understood by all. These personnel should have the responsibility of seeing, in turn, that the subcontractors understand the general conditions.

The General Conditions set forth as Exhibit 27-15 define the builder's policy and procedures and form a record of standards. Standardized policy and procedures are communicated more effectively and are binding when they are part of the contract documentation. The same information in a standardized operations manual would be less effective.

In that the general conditions are a statement of policy and procedure, they vary from organization to organization to reflect differing policies, procedures, and conditions. Each organization should carefully evaluate its own. Geographic and climatic conditions also affect the general conditions. For example, the General Conditions in Exhibit 27-15 were developed for warm-weather climates and do not include a provision for snow removal.

SUBCONTRACTOR EXHIBITS

It should be noted that the exhibits in this chapter are for general reference only. We are not providing legal consultation or advice in this chapter, nor is the information presented intended to replace or augment such consultation or advice. The reader should consult an attorney before proceeding with activities requiring legal consultation or advice.

Exhibits in this chapter include the following:

Exhibit 27-1:	Subcontractor List
Exhibit 27-2:	Contractor's or Subcontractor's Statement of Qualifications
Exhibit 27-3:	Instructions to Subcontractors
Exhibit 27-4:	Subcontract Agreement Form
Exhibit 27-5:	Status of Bid Documents Form
Exhibit 27-6:	Application of Payment Form
Exhibit 27-7:	Conditions of Purchase Order Form
Exhibit 27-8:	Request for Quotation Form

Exhibit 27-9: Purchase Order Form
Exhibit 27-10: Field Order Form
Exhibit 27-11: Change Order Data Sheet
Exhibit 27-12: Exhibit Sheet: List of Items on Change Order No. ____
Exhibit 27-13: Change Order Authorization
Exhibit 27-14: Affidavit of Release of Liens
Exhibit 27-15: General Conditions of Contract

Exhibit 27-1
Subcontractor List

PROJECT _____ NO. _____
ADDRESS _____

Work section(s), no. (s)	Subcontractor	Address, phone	Representative

Exhibit 27-2
Contractor's or Subcontractor's Statement of Qualifications

Required in advance of award of contract at the discretion of the builder or owner. The undersigned, under oath, certifies the truth and validity of all answers provided in response to questions herein.

Organization _____ By _____
Address _____
Corporation ____ Individual ____ Partnership ____ Joint Venture ____ Other ____

1. How long in business? _____
2. How long under present business name? _____
3. Answer the following if a corporation:
   a. Date of incorporation _____
   b. State of incorporation _____
   c. President's name _____
   d. Vice president'(s) name(s) _____
   e. Treasurer's name _____
   f. Secretary or clerk's name _____
4. Answer the following if an individual or partnership:
   a. Date of organization _____
   b. All partners' names and addresses _____
5. If "other" describe organization and name principals:

6. Has organization ever failed to complete work awarded to it? If yes, note when, where, and why:

7. Who will supervise the work in the field? What is his capacity within the organization, his experience and time with the organization?

8. How many men will the organization be able to provide as required to maintain construction schedule? How many of the men are a part of the organization's own forces?

9. Has the organization or any of its principals been involved in a bankruptcy? If so, explain.

10. Has any partner or officer of the organization been a partner or officer of any other organization that has failed to complete work awarded to it? If so, explain.

Exhibit 27–2 (*continued*)

11. Provide names of prospects, architects, contractors, and owners, and size of projects on which your organization is currently working. Provide percentage completion for each project.

12. Provide major project names, sizes, architects, contractors, and owners on which the organization has worked for the past five years.

13. Is the organization or any of its officers a partner currently involved in litigation or arbitration? If so, explain.

14. Provide trade references.

15. List the construction experience of the key people within the organization:

16. List bank references:

17. Bonding company and name and address of agent:

18. Attach current financial statement. Provide name of firm preparing statement.

Name of organization _____
By _____ Title _____
Date _____

Exhibit 27-3
Instructions to Subcontractors Sheet

1. Changes in the Work
   a. Minor changes in the work will be accomplished by a field order issued by the builder or his agent. Neither the contract amount nor the construction schedule is affected by a field order.
   b. Other than minor changes which affect the construction schedule or contract amount will be carried out by means of a change order. Any requests by a subcontractor for a change in contract amount or a schedule change must be accompanied by a standard Change Order Data Sheet (Exhibit 27-11 below) available from the builder. Change orders must accompany monthly billing and must be identified separately from the regular contract billing in the invoice.
   c. A change order represents a change in the contract and as such becomes a part of the contract and subject to all the terms thereof.
   d. The value of any such extra work or change shall be determined in one or more of the following ways:
      (1) By estimate and acceptance in a lump sum. Estimate to include specific itemized breakdown of labor, material, etc., overhead and profit. Overhead and profit to be the same percentage of direct costs as stipulated in the contractor's form of proposal. No part of the executive or overhead expenses of the subcontract or salaries of persons employed exclusively in the main office shall be charged to the cost of the work.
      (2) By unit prices in the contract as subsequently agreed upon.

2. Purchase Orders

   In the event that special work is requested by the builder, the work to be accomplished and the lump sum amount or hourly rate must appear on a Purchase Order Form (Exhibit 27-9). At time of completing work, a separate invoice along with the purchase order number should be sent to the builder. If hourly work is involved, the invoice must contain signed tags from the superintendent approving hours or amount of work.

3. Invoicing Procedure
   a. All invoices must include the account number for the work performed. The account number(s) are marked on the specification section(s) specifying the work and on the subcontract document. Some contractors may have several numbers because they have several specification sections of work to perform. When there is more than one account number or section of work being performed by a subcontractor, the subcontractor shall break down his invoice according to the account numbers he is invoicing against.
   b. All invoices will be submitted on standardized invoice forms provided by the builder (see Application for Payment Form, Exhibit 27-6). The work must be broken down on a logical basis by building, apartment, or area, so that the field can approve the request in an objective manner. An example of the invoice procedure is shown below.

Exhibit 27-3 (*continued*)

Account description	Account no.	Breakdown description	Contract amount	Percent finish	Total bill to date	Less previous billings	Amount due
		Building A	$ 32,000	70	$22,400	$14,600	$ 7,800
		Building B	28,000	60	16,800	10,300	6,500
		Building C	35,000	45	12,250	9,000	3,250
		Building D	30,000	20	6,000	1,000	5,000
Total to date					$57,450	$34,900	$22,550
Less retention					5,745	3,490	2,255
Total payment			$125,000		$51,705	$31,410	$20,295

4. Shop Drawings, Design Drawings, and Calculations

   a. All shop drawings shall be submitted on dates sufficiently in advance of requirements to allow builder ample time (10 days minimum) for checking same, including time for correction, resubmission and recheck, and no claim for extension of the contract time shall be granted subcontractor or supplier by reason of his failure in this respect.

   b. All samples, material lists, and specifications must be sent to the builder as soon as possible, but no later than 21 days before the required order date. This will allow time to make changes and adjustments without delaying the job.

   c. All design drawings and calculations should be sent to builder for approval as soon as possible but no later than 21 days after entering into the contract.

5. Field Conferences

   Conferences will be held on the job site or nearby every Friday at 10:30 A.M. All subcontractor foremen are required to be present at the conference. Those subcontractors who are just starting work must appear at the Friday meeting prior to their starting date on the job. Scheduling and coordinating problems of the past and succeeding week will be discussed. These meetings keep the job running smoothly and profitably.

6. Scheduling

   a. The schedule is a contract document and, as such, binds subcontractor to perform accordingly. Subcontractor shall notify builder within five (5) days after receiving his copy of the schedule should he find any problem or have any doubts concerning the timing or scheduling for his work or other subcontractors' work preceding or following his work and which affect his work. Subcontractor shall in particular note if there is enough work assigned to keep his normal crew busy all day, as he will not be allowed to wait two (2) or three (3) days before starting work to have enough work to do for a full day, unless job is scheduled this way. If builder does not receive any written notification within five (5) days after subcontractor has received schedule, then the schedule shall be considered approved by and binding on the subcontractor.

   b. Subcontractor shall keep himself informed of the progress of the work at all times. Because of faster work by other subcontractors, schedule may be

Exhibit 27-3 (*continued*)

      ahead, in which case builder may notify subcontractor two (2) full days in advance to proceed with his work. Each subcontractor may work faster than the schedule provides providing it does not interfere with the work of other subcontractors and has the approval of the builder. A subcontractor may not slow down his work and use up time gained by another subcontractor without approval of builder.

   c. The builder reserves the right to slow or speed up the pace of the work or the sequence of the work at his option.

   d. All schedules will be posted at the job site and in the builder's office for review by all subcontractors. Additionally, each subcontractor will receive a schedule covering his portion of the work. He will not necessarily receive a complete schedule of the whole job, only his own and related work.

7. Deficiency Notices

When work is not performed in an acceptable manner and verbal instructions have not remedied the situation, the builder will issue a Deficiency Notice (see Exhibit 26-2, Chapter 26). No further payments will be made while a Deficiency Notice is outstanding. When the work is accomplished in an acceptable manner, the Deficiency Notice will be signed off by the job superintendent, and payments will proceed in the regular manner.

8. Insurance Requirements

Neither subcontractors nor their personnel are allowed on the job site until a certificate of insurance, in the amounts prescribed in the contract, is received in the builder's office.

9. Miscellaneous Provisions

   a. Monies received for the performance of work by subcontractor shall be used exclusively for labor and materials entering into the work under this contract and shall not be diverted to satisfy other obligations.

   b. The subcontractor agrees to accept full and exclusive liability for the payment of any and all contributions of unemployment insurance, taxes, and/or old-age retirement benefits, pensions, or annuities, now or at a later date imposed by the government, for remuneration paid to persons employed by the subcontractor on work performed under the terms of this contract.

   c. The subcontractor shall submit his application for payment for the month on or before the last day of the month for which the payment is requested. There will be a retention of _____ %. If the application is not received as specified above, the payment may be withheld for thirty (30) days additional.

   d. The subcontractor shall furnish, if requested by the contractor, sworn affidavits from time to time, in accordance with the form provided by the contractor, which shall state amounts due or to become due, amounts paid, and any other information clearly to indicate the financial condition of the

Exhibit 27-3 (*continued*)

subcontractor, insofar as it relates to labor and material furnished, and to be furnished under this subcontract, and the contractor may take such steps as he may deem necessary to protect himself against any claims. If at any time the contractor shall determine that the subcontractor's financial condition has become, in his opinion, unsatisfactory, the subcontractor shall furnish satisfactory security to the contractor within three days after written notice to his last known address, and in default of furnishing said security, the contractor shall have the option to cancel this contract. In case of such cancellation the rights of the contractor shall be the same as if the subcontractor had failed to perform this contract in whole or in part.

e. The subcontractor shall protect the owner and builder against all costs and claims for freight, transportation, and express for material, equipment, and men to be paid from the job and for all incidental expenses that may be incurred in the work and to prepay the transportation charges on all materials, etc., shipped.

f. The subcontractor shall pay the wage scale prescribed in the general contract or the scale prescribed by law.

g. If the subcontractor makes use of the builder's or contractor's hoisting facilities, he shall pay for the service unless specifically stated otherwise elsewhere in the agreement.

h. If the subcontractor deems that surfaces or work to which his work is to be applied or affixed are unsatisfactory or unsuitable, written notification of said condition shall be given to the contractor; otherwise, no consideration will be given to claims for extra compensation or nonresponsibility in connection therewith.

i. The subcontractor shall provide, at his own expense, whatever storage sheds, workshops, and offices are necessary for the performance of this subcontract and shall remove same and thoroughly clean the premises at the completion of the work.

j. The subcontractor shall clean up and remove from the site, as directed by the contractor, all rubbish and debris resulting from his work; also he shall clean up, to the satisfaction of the inspectors, all dirt, grease marks, etc., from walls, ceilings, floors, fixtures, etc., deposited or placed thereon as a result of the execution of this subcontract. If the subcontractor refuses or fails to perform this cleaning as directed by the contractor, the contractor shall have the right and power to proceed with said cleaning, and the subcontractor will on demand repay to the contractor the actual cost of said labor plus percentage of such cost to cover supervision, insurance, overhead, etc.

k. It is understood and agreed it has been the practice of the general contractor to carry builders' risk fire insurance in the amount of his estimate of full insurance to insurable value, including subcontracts. To the extent that such insurance is carried by the general contractor on the general contract, however, the provisions of this section do not make it mandatory upon the general contractor to carry any insurance whatsoever for the benefit of the subcontractor. Subcontractor agrees he will assume the responsibility to determine whether builders' risk insurance is in force.

Exhibit 27-3 (*concluded*)

In the event the general contractor should elect to carry builders' risk insurance, and only in such event, the subcontractor agrees to submit immediately, for the purpose of determining values under the insurance coverage, a complete breakdown of this contract price showing materials, labor, expendable tools, supplies or any other thing or article of value, the cost of which is included in the contract price stated in this agreement.

Exhibit 27-4
Subcontract Agreement Form

THIS CONTRACT, made this _____ day of _____ 19 _____ by and between _____ herein after called Contractor, and _____ hereinafter called Subcontractor, WITNESSETH:

The Subcontractor agrees that he will, at his own proper cost and expense, furnish all the materials, labor, tools, scaffolding, appliances, equipment permits and certificates necessary to complete in a diligent and workmanlike manner, the _____ located in _____, in accordance with the plans, specifications, general and special conditions, and addenda prepared by _____ and dated _____ and in accordance with all of the documents to the contract mentioned herein. Whether or not shown by the plans or mentioned in the specifications, the work includes the following:

- *a.* Any item of labor, service, and/or material reasonably inferred by the plans and/or specifications or customarily furnished by a subcontractor performing work in this line.
- *b.* Any item of labor, service, or material required to complete the work in compliance with any applicable law, ordinance or regulation, or necessary to obtain any inspection approvals being obtained by contractor.
- *c.* All work claimed by the Subcontractor's unions included in his contract.

SECTION 1. IN CONSIDERATION WHEREOF, the Contractor agrees to pay the Subcontractor for the full and faithful performance of his work the sum of _____ DOLLARS ($_____) in current funds, subject to additions and deductions for changes as may be agreed upon. Provided, that no payments are to be made unless the Subcontractor's rate of progress, work done, and material furnished are satisfactory to the Contractor and as herein agreed upon.

Payments to be made as follows: _____.

The Contractor employs the Subcontractor to do the work, as ordered, hereunder according to the terms and conditions contained in the contract documents identified herein.

The Subcontractor represents that he holds contractor's license No. _____ from the State of _____.

The parties hereto, before executing this contract, acknowledge that they have each read this entire contract and know the contents thereof, and fully understand each

Exhibit 27-4 (*continued*)

and every term of said contract and expressly agree that there are no oral agreements between the parties, and that the whole agreement between the parties is fully expressed within the contract documents, that this contract agreement is the whole and exclusive agreement between the said parties, and contains the entire contract between the parties hereto and the terms of this contract are contractual and not a mere recital. Time is of the essence hereof.

SECTION 2. The Subcontractor agrees: To keep himself thoroughly informed as to the progress of the job; to begin work within seven days after notification by the Contractor, to prosecute the work continuously and uninterruptedly with all possible speed; and to complete the entire work covered by this subcontract within _____ calendar days after the work covered hereby is commenced. The Subcontractor, however, shall not be held responsible for any delays caused by the neglect, delay, or default of the General Contractor, the Owner or any other Subcontractor.

In default of completion within the lapsed time herein specified, the Subcontractor shall pay to the Contractor, as liquidated damages, and not as a penalty, the sum of _____ dollars per day for each calendar day's delay in completion of the subcontract, it being agreed between the parties hereto that it would be impracticable or extremely difficult to fix the actual damage.

SECTION 3. DOCUMENTS OF THE CONTRACT

Contractor and Subcontractor shall sign the contract documents.

The documents constituting this contract consist of:
a. This agreement.
b. The drawings and specifications.
c. General Conditions and Special Conditions.
d. Any written addendum or amendment to any of the contract documents executed by both the owner and the subcontractor.
e. Subcontractor Instructions and Procedures.
f. Construction schedule.

SECTION 4. DUTIES AND OBLIGATIONS OF SUBCONTRACTOR

a. All workmen employed on this project must be members, in good standing, of the applicable trade union having jurisdiction of the type of work being performed. Subcontractor agrees, if his tradesmen are out on strike, to sign an agreement with the union that he will retroactively pay any additional wages and fringe agreement between the applicable union and the Contractors Agent(s).
b. Minimum insurance limits shall be as follows:
  1. Statutory workmen's compensation: As prescribed by state in which project is located.
  2. Employer's liability: $100,000.00.
  3. Comprehensive liability—general and automobile: Subcontractor further agrees to take out and keep in force during the term of the contract, at Subcontractor's sole expense, public liability insurance in companies and through brokers approved by Contractor to protect against any liability to

Exhibit 27–4 (*concluded*)

the public incident to the use of or resulting from any occurrence in or about said premises in the minimum amount of five hundred thousand dollars ($500,000.00) to indemnify against claims for bodily injury or property damage arising out of said occurrence in whatever combination or combinations said claims are made. Subcontractor further agrees to deliver to contractor a certificate confirming said insurance executed by an authorized representative of the insurance carrier, said certificate to contain an outline of the coverages afforded, and in accordance with paragraph 26 of General Conditions, and to contain an agreement that the insurance carrier will give builder written notice thirty (30) days prior to any discontinuance, reduction, restriction, or cancellation of such insurance.

c. Each Subcontractor shall examine the schedule and check it for timing, accuracy and compatability with his work and shall coordinate his work with the master schedule.

d. Subcontractor shall assist builder in coordination and scheduling of all work pertinent to his installation. Subcontractor, upon being familiar with construction schedule, shall inform builder of his requirements sufficiently to result in a well-coordinated job.

e. Subcontractor shall procure and pay for all necessary permits, authorizations, and licenses required by the state, county, city, or other authority having jurisdiction and any and all parts of the site and to pay any local, city, county, and/or state sales and excise taxes required.

IN WITNESS WHEREOF, the parties hereto have executed this agreement for themselves, their heirs, executors, successors, administrators, and assigns, on the day and year first above written.

Subcontractor

_____
_____
       Subcontractors' license no.

By: _____
                        President

By: _____
                        Secretary

Date: _____

Contractor

_____

By: _____
                        President

By: _____
                        Secretary

Date: _____

Exhibit 27-5
Status of Bid Documents Form

Project _____ No. _____
Address _____
Bidding date _____ Date bids due _____

Bidder, Phone, Address		Drawings		Specifications		Deposits		Addenda dates
		Issue	Return	Issue	Return	Receive	Return	
	No.							
	Date							
	No.							
	Date							
	No.							
	Date							
	No.							
	Date							
	No.							
	Date							
	No.							
	Date							
	No.							
	Date							
	No.							
	Date							
	No.							
	Date							
	No.							
	Date							

Exhibit 27-6
Application for Payment Form

Project _____ No. _____
Address _____
Application date _____ Period from _____ To _____
Subcontractor _____ By _____
Application No. _____ Code _____

Account description	Account no.	Breakdown description	Contract amount	Percent finish	Total bill to date	− Previous billings	Amount due
Total to date							
Less retention							
Total payment							

Exhibit 27-7
Conditions of Purchase Order Form

1. Supplier shall at his expense prepare and submit for approval all sketches, layouts, detail drawings, shop fabrication drawings, shop detail drawings, erection diagrams, setting drawings, catalog cuts, schedules, etc., and any other drawings as may be required by the specifications or as may be required in amplification of contract drawings.

2. Supplier shall, prior to submission, thoroughly check all shop drawings, detail drawings, etc., for complete dimensional accuracy, and to insure that work contiguous with and having a bearing on the work shown on the shop drawings is accurately and clearly shown, and that all work complies with the contract. If the supplier's drawings show variations from the contract requirements, supplier shall make specific mention of such variations in his letter of transmittal.

3. Supplier shall submit three (3) copies, until final approval is obtained, of manufacturers' catalog sheets, showing illustrated cuts of the item to be furnished, scale details, sizes, dimensions, performance characteristics, capacities, wiring diagrams and controls, and all other pertinent information. Catalog cuts or manufacturers' literature shall be marked, if necessary, to show the particular characteristics of the product to be approved. One (1) copy will be returned to subcontractor.

Exhibit 27-7 (*continued*)

4. Supplier shall submit samples with such promptness as to cause no delay in the work. Builder shall check and approve such samples with reasonable promptness. Supplier shall furnish only materials equal in every respect to approved samples. Samples shall be submitted in duplicate in adequate size, showing quality, type, color range, finish, texture; such samples shall be labeled with material name, quality, date, project name, supplier's name and other pertinent data.

5. Supplier shall submit name of proposed manufacturers, materialsmen, and dealers who are to furnish materials, fixtures, appliances, or other fittings for approval at earliest possible date to afford proper investigation, checking. No manufacturer will be approved for any materials to be furnished under contract unless he is of good reputation, has ample plant capacity, and has successfully produced similar products.

6. All materials are subject to inspection after delivery unless otherwise agreed upon in writing. If materials are found to be unacceptable they shall be held for disposition at supplier's risk and expense.

7. Whether discovered at first inspection or at a later date, defective materials will be charged to the supplier and will be either returned or held awaiting instructions from the supplier. Supplier shall pay expense of transportation both ways and shall not replace defective materials and goods except on replacement purchase order by buyer.

8. Supplier shall pay highway fees for damages to sidewalks, streets, or other public property or to any public utility caused by supplier. Should property of the buyer be damaged by the supplier in the process of delivery or otherwise, the supplier shall pay or satisfy all damage, including reasonable attorney's fees as set by the court in the event legal action is necessary for collection.

9. Materials and work shall be unconditionally guaranteed against premature wear (not occasioned by abuse) or failure due to inherent defects in material or improper installation for a period of at least one (1) year from date of final payment.

10. Supplier agrees to correct all defects within ten (10) days from the date notice is received of defect. Should supplier not correct defects within the prescribed time, buyer reserves the right to correct same, and supplier agrees to pay buyer all costs, attorney's fees in connection therewith, and expenses arising from or connected with defects.

11. Supplies shall only be delivered during regular business hours. Material dumping or unloading requires specific authorization from the builder's superintendent as to the timing of the delivery and the location(s) of the delivery at job site.

12. Builder and owner reserve the right to temporary or trial usage of any mechanical device, machinery, equipment, or any work or material supplied under the contract before final completion and written acceptance of same. Builder shall have the privilege of such temporary and trial usage for such reasonable length of time required for making a complete and thorough test of same; and no claim for damage shall be made by supplier for the injury to or breaking of any parts of such work which may be caused by weakness or

Exhibit 27–7 (*concluded*)

inaccuracies of structural parts or by defective materials or workmanship. If the supplier so wishes, he may, at his expense, place a competent person or persons satisfactory to builder to make such trial usage. The trial shall be under the supervision of the builder.

13. When submitting bid quotes, a "base bid" shall be submitted using only the materials of the specific manufacturer(s) or quality specified. If supplier desires to use "equals" or materials other than those specified, he may submit an alternate bid in addition to the base bid. He shall supply the name of the manufacturer and the specific brand and number of each product he offers as a substitute and shall state the amount to be added to or deducted for such substitution.

Exhibit 27–8
Request for Quotation Form

Seller _____ By _____
Buyer _____ By _____
Project _____ No. _____
Address _____
Shipping instructions _____
Date _____ Bids close _____ Date required _____

THIS IS NOT AN ORDER

Please provide itemized prices for material, goods and/or work in accordance with terms and conditions of plans and/or specifications and conditions of purchase contract.

Account no.	Quantity	Unit	Description	Price	Total

Special Instructions:

Transportation	
Taxes	
Total	

Seller _____ By _____ Date _____
Quote accepted _____ By _____ Date _____

27 / Purchasing, contract letting, and progress payments

Exhibit 27-9
Purchase Order Form

Purchase Order No. _____
Seller _____ Date of order _____
Buyer _____ By _____
Project _____ No. _____
Ship to _____ Via: _____
Date required _____

NOTE

This order is expressly subject to conditions of purchase, contract, plans and specifications. The purchase order number must appear on all invoices, packages, and correspondence.

Account no.	Quantity	Unit	Description	Price	Total

Special instructions:

Subtotal		
Transportation		
Taxes		
Total		

Exhibit 27-10
Field Order Form

Project _____ No. _____
Address _____
Subcontractor _____ Account No. _____
Field order by _____ Date _____
Field order No. _____ Delivered to _____

The above subcontractor is hereby directed to promptly execute this field order, which interprets the contract documents or orders minor changes in the work without change in the contract time or sum.

If the subcontractor considers that a change in the contract time or sum is in order, please submit the proposal on the Change Order Data Sheet which will be supplied by the superintendent on request. This should be done immediately and before proceeding with the work. If the proposal is found to be satisfactory, this field order will be superseded by a change order authorization.

DESCRIPTION AND ATTACHMENTS: (description of the interpretation or change and listing of attached documents which support description).

Exhibit 27-11
Change Order Data Sheet

You are hereby requested to submit the change in the contract cost for the work in question, whether it be an addition or subtraction from the contract. (An Exhibit Sheet for itemized descriptions is enclosed). Fill out a separate Change Order Data Sheet for each subcontractor involved or each itemized description.

Date: _____   Sheet _____ of _____
Change Order No. _____ Item: _____ Requested by: _____
Job Title: _____ Description: _____

(Complete details of field change must be submitted below)
Direct material costs (detail below) $_____
Direct equipment costs (attach detail sheet) $_____
Other (attach detail sheet) $_____
    Subtotal: $_____
Direct labor cost $_____
Overhead _____% $_____
Profit   _____% $_____
Bond   _____% $_____
    Subtotal: $_____
    Total Costs: $_____

  Detail of Additional Material Costs   Detail of Additional Direct Labor

Description   Quantity   Unit Price   Costs   Hours   Rate   Cost

Total Material Costs: $_____   Total Direct Labor Costs: $_____

Signed _____ Date _____
Completion of this summary sheet does not authorize this work to be done. Builder will issue a change order if work is to be accomplished.

Exhibit 27-12
Exhibit Sheet: List of Items on Change Order No. _____

Item	Account no.	Description	Effect on Construction schedule	Add	Deduct

Exhibit 27-13
Change Order Authorization

To: _____   Change Order No. _____
_____   Date issued _____
_____   Job title: _____
Account No. _____   Description _____

This change notice is issued to authorize the above Company to furnish the necessary labor, materials, et cetera, to make the building and process changes described below. This change notice shall in no way be construed to be an authorization to extend the previously agreed-upon final completion date, or cost of this project, except as noted below:

1. Description of change _____
2. Reason for change: _____
3. Effect on construction schedule: _____
4. Contract cost before change: _____
5. Total cost of change order: (deduct−add) _____
6. Total contract figure now reads: _____
7. Comment: _____

Contractor   *Architect*   *Owner*
By: _____   By: _____   By: _____
Date: _____   Date: _____   Date: _____

Exhibit 27–14
Affidavit of Release of Liens

Project _____ No. _____
Address _____
Application date _____ Period from _____ To _____
Subcontractor _____ By _____
Application No. _____ Code _____

The above signed, pursuant to Articles 23 and 33 of the General Conditions of the contract, certifies that to the best of his knowledge and belief (except as listed below under exceptions), the Lien Releaser to waivers attached to this document includes all subcontractors, all suppliers of materials and equipment, and all performers of work, labor or services who have or may have liens against any property of the owner arising in any manner out of the performance of the contract dated _____ for _____.

EXCEPTIONS: If there are no exceptions write "none." When required by owner the subcontractor shall furnish bond, satisfactory to the owner, for each exception.

Exhibit 27-15
General Conditions

TABLE OF CONTENTS

Section

01. DEFINITIONS, 1
02. EXECUTION, CORRELATION AND INTENT OF DOCUMENTS, 2
03. INTERPRETATION, INSTRUCTIONS AND SCHEDULES, 3
04. SHOP DRAWINGS, 3
05. OWNERSHIP OF DRAWINGS, 5
06. SAMPLES, MATERIAL SUPPLIERS AND EMPLOYEES, 5
07. ROYALTIES AND PATENTS, 5
08. PERMITS, LAWS, TAXES AND REGULATION, 6
09. LOCATIONS, LEVELS, 6
10. PROTECTION OF WORK AND PROPERTY, 7
11. INSPECTION, 7
12. SUPERINTENDENCE—SUPERVISION, 8
13. CHANGES IN THE WORK, 8
14. CLAIMS FOR EXTRA WORK, 9
15. DEDUCTIONS FOR UNCORRECTED WORK, 9
16. SCHEDULE AND COORDINATION, 9
17. COMMENCEMENT AND COMPLETION OF WORK, 10
18. CORRECTION OF WORK BEFORE FINAL PAYMENT, 11
19. CORRECTION OF WORK AFTER FINAL PAYMENT, 11
20. BUILDER'S RIGHT TO DO WORK, 12
21. BUILDER'S RIGHT TO TERMINATE CONTRACT, 12
22. SUBCONTRACTOR'S RIGHT TO STOP WORK OR TERMINATE CONTRACT, 14
23. PROGRESS PAYMENTS, 14
24. CERTIFICATES FOR PAYMENT, 15
25. PAYMENTS WITHHELD, 15
26. SUBCONTRACTORS' AND SUB-SUBCONTRACTORS' INSURANCE, 16
27. INSURANCE LIMITS, 16
28. INSURANCE APPROVALS AND CANCELLATIONS, 17
29. INDEMNIFICATION, 18

Section

30. OWNER'S INSURANCE, 18
31. BONDS, 20
32. DAMAGES, 20
33. LIENS AND FINAL PAYMENT, 20
34. ASSIGNMENT OF CONTRACT, 21
35. MUTUAL RESPONSIBILITY OF CONTRACTORS, 22
36. ACCEPTANCE OF WORK, 22
37. SUB-SUBCONTRACTS, 22
38. RELATIONS OF BUILDER AND SUBCONTRACTOR, 22
39. BUILDER'S CONTROL OF WORK, 23
40. ARCHITECT'S STATUS, 24
41. ARBITRATION, 24
42. CASH ALLOWANCES, 24
43. USE OF PREMISES, 25
44. CUTTING, PATCHING AND EXCAVATION, 25
45. CLEANING UP, 26
46. SPECIFICATION EXPLANATION, 26
47. SCOPE OF WORK REQUIRED, 26
48. BORING AND OTHER SITE CONDITION DATA, 27
49. MANUFACTURER'S NAME—SUBSTITUTIONS, 28
50. MANUFACTURER'S DIRECTIONS, 29
51. USE AND OCCUPANCY, 29
52. TEMPORARY AND TRIAL USAGE, 29
53. BUILDER'S REPRESENTATIVE AND JOB MEETINGS, 29
54. MATERIAL STORAGE, 30
55. TEMPORARY TOILETS, 30
56. TEMPORARY WATER SUPPLY, 30
57. TEMPORARY POWER AND LIGHT, 30
58. SCAFFOLDING AND SHORING, 31
59. GUARANTEES, 31
60. RECORD DRAWINGS, 32
61. MAINTENANCE INSTRUCTIONS, 32
62. ANTI-DISCRIMINATION LAW, 32
63. TITLE TO THE WORK, 32
64. NOTICES, 33

Exhibit 27–15 (*continued*)

GENERAL CONDITIONS

01. DEFINITIONS

- *a.* **Builder.** Owner's representative with full power to act for Owner excepting for any specifically stated limitations included in agreement between Builder and Owner.
- *b.* **Contractor.** A duly licensed person contracted by Builder.
- *c.* **Architect.** A duly licensed person contracted by Builder.
- *d.* **Owner.** One mentioned in agreement between Builder and Owner.
- *e.* **Subcontractor.** As employed herein, includes only those having a direct contract with Builder and includes one who furnishes material worked to a special design according to the plans and specifications of this work, but does not include one who merely furnishes material not so worked.
- *f.* **Sub-subcontractor.** As employed herein, includes all Contractors performing any portion of the work covered by this contract who do not have a direct contract with Builder, and includes one who furnishes material worked to a special design according to the plans or specifications of this work but does not include one who merely furnishes material not so worked.
- *g.* **Supplier.** One who provides materials not worked to a special design.
- *h.* **Engineer.** Builder's authorized engineering and consulting representatives.
- *i.* **Written notice** shall be deemed to have been duly served if delivered in person to the individual or to a member of the firm, or to an officer of the corporation for whom it is intended, or sent by mail, postage prepaid, to the last business address known to him who gives the notice.
- *j.* **Work** includes labor, materials, personal service, tools, equipment, special skills and transportation, all as may be required to carry out the contract agreement.
- *k.* **Provide** or **provided**, in connection with any item specified means, unless otherwise noted, that such item shall be furnished, installed, connected and rendered operable.
- *l.* **Words in the singular** shall include the plural wherever the context so indicates.
- *m.* **Approved** or **approval** means written approval by Builder's representative or his designee.
- *n.* **Or other approved, equal to, proper, acceptable,** or other general qualifying terms shall be understood to have reference to the written ruling and judgment of Builder.
- *o.* **Contract documents** shall be as defined in the agreement.
- *p.* **Completion—substantial and final.** The date of "substantial completion" of a structure or building is the date when the construction is

1

Exhibit 27–15 (*continued*)

sufficiently completed in accordance with the plans and specifications, as modified by any change orders agreed to by the parties, so that Owner can occupy the building for the use for which it was intended. The date of "final completion" of a structure or building is the date when any and all corrective work ordered by Builder, after a semi-final inspection, has been consummated to Builder's satisfaction and he feels warranted in issuing his Certificate of Final Completion, and all governmental entities having jurisdiction over the structure or building have likewise certified final completion and issued permits. Both dates shall be declared by Builder.

    q. **Certificate of final completion.** Document issued by Builder upon completion of any and all corrective work ordered and after final inspection has been made. It fixes Date of Final Completion, and must be issued prior to final payment by Builder.

02. EXECUTION, CORRELATION AND INTENT OF DOCUMENTS

    a. The Contract Documents are complementary and what is called for by any one shall be as binding as if called for by all. The intention of the documents is to include all labor and materials, equipment and transportation necessary for the proper execution of the work. Materials or work described in words which, so applied, have a well-known technical or trade meaning shall be held to refer to such recognized standards.

    b. Execute work per Contract Documents. Make no change therefrom without having first received written permission from Builder. Where detailed information is lacking, before proceeding with work, refer matter to Builder for information.

    c. Nothing in the Contract Documents is to be construed to permit work not conforming to all applicable municipal codes, rules, regulations and ordinances. In case of any conflict between the foregoing, the stricter or better-class workmanship, materials or methods, shall govern.

    d. Workmanship by Subcontractor shall be executed in the most thorough, substantial, neat, skillful, artistic and workmanlike manner known to the several trades, and should anything not in accordance with this be done, it shall be made satisfactory to Builder at Subcontractor's expense.

    e. If work is required in such a manner as to make it impossible to produce first-class work, or should discrepancies appear among Contract Documents, request interpretation from Builder before proceeding with work. If Subcontractor fails to make such request, no excuse thereafter will be entertained for failure to carry out work in a satisfactory manner. Should conflict occur in or between Drawings and Specifications, Subcontractor is deemed to have estimated on the more expensive of the various ways shown for doing the work unless he shall have asked for and obtained written decision from Builder before submission of Proposal as to which method or materials will be required.

Exhibit 27-15 (*continued*)

    f. The Drawings indicate arrangements and results to be accomplished. Subcontractor shall provide all such fastenings and accessories necessary therefor.

    g. "General Conditions" and "Supplementary General Conditions" apply with equal force to Subcontractors' work, extra work, change orders, and the like that may be specified herein or performed in or about building or site under this Contract.

    h. For convenience of reference and to facilitate letting of subcontracts, the specifications are separated into sections. Where sections overlap and may call for the same work, Builder shall make final determination as to which section the work will fall under and shall receive a credit from the other Suncontractor(s).

    i. Subcontractor shall include in his bid sufficient money to do all work called for in his contract according to all codes and ordinances, and shall not make claim against Builder for extra money to do his work according to such codes and ordinances. He shall notify Builder as soon as he discovers any discrepancy in the plans with codes and ordinances, so Builder can make necessary adjustments as required.

03. INTERPRETATION, INSTRUCTIONS AND SCHEDULES

    a. Builder shall interpret and furnish with reasonable promptness additional instructions by means of drawings or otherwise, necessary for the proper execution of the work. All such drawings and instructions shall be consistent with the contract documents, true developments thereof, and reasonably inferable therefrom.

    b. The work shall be executed in conformity therewith and Subcontractor shall do no work without proper drawings and instructions.

    c. Contractor shall submit the following schedules to Owner for approval within the days indicated below before award of contract:

        (1). *Contemplated Payment Schedule.* Indicate contemplated costs for this contract on a monthly basis. Submit within 10 days.

        (2). *Shop Drawing Schedule.* List all required shop drawings with reference to applicable Trade Section numbers. Submit within 30 days. Include submission and required return dates.

04. SHOP DRAWINGS

    a. Subcontractor or Supplier shall, at his expense, prepare and submit to Builder for approval all sketches, layouts, detail drawings, shop fabricating drawings, shop detail drawings, erection diagrams, setting drawings, catalog cuts, schedules, etc., and any other drawings of any kind as may be required by the specifications, or as may be required in amplification of the contract drawings.

    b. No fabrication, erection or construction shall be commenced by Subcontractor or Supplier until Builder shall have approved in writing the

Exhibit 27–15 (*continued*)

      shop drawings, detail drawings, erection diagrams, setting drawings, catalog cuts, schedules, etc., covering such work.

- c. All shop drawings shall be submitted on dates sufficiently in advance of requirements to afford Builder ample time (10 days minimum) for checking same, including time for correction, re-submission and recheck, and no claim for extension of the contract time will be granted Subcontractor or Supplier by reason of his failure in this respect.

- d. Subcontractor shall, prior to submission to Builder, thoroughly check all shop drawings, detail drawings, etc., for complete dimensional accuracy, and to insure that work contiguous with and having bearing on the work shown on the shop drawings is accurately and clearly shown, and that all work complies with the contract. If Subcontractor's drawings show variations from the contract requirements, Subcontractor shall make specific mention of such variations in his letter of transmittal.

- e. For standard manufactured items, Subcontractor shall submit three (3) copies until final approval is obtained of manufacturer's catalog sheets, showing illustrated cuts of the items to be furnished, scale details, sizes, dimensions, performance characteristics, capacities, wiring diagrams and controls, and all other pertinent information. Catalog cuts or manufacturer's literature shall be marked, if necessary to show the particular characteristics of the product to be approved. One (1) copy will be returned to Subcontractor.

- f. In submitting shop drawings for approval, all associated drawings relating to a complete assembly shall be submitted at one and the same time so that each may be checked in relation to the entire proposed assembly.

- g. Approval is for design only. Subcontractor is responsible for dimensions, quantities and coordination with other trades. Approval does not authorize changes to contract requirements unless stated in separate letter or change order. Corrected "Approved as Noted" drawings must be furnished to Builder for record of conformance to corrections.

- h. If Subcontractor shall alter any information on previously submitted shop drawings besides the notations called for by Builder, he must circle this new information to bring it to Builder's attention.

- i. Builder shall check and approve, with reasonable promptness, such shop drawings only for conformance with the design concept of the project and compliance with the information given in the Contract Documents. Builder's approval of such shop drawings shall not relieve Subcontractor of responsibility for accuracy of such shop drawings, nor for proper fitting, construction of work, furnishing of materials or work required by contract and not indicated on shop drawings. Shop drawing approval shall not be construed as approving departures from contract requirements.

4

Exhibit 27-15 (*continued*)

05. OWNERSHIP OF DRAWINGS

    a. All drawings, specifications and copies thereof are the property of Builder. They are not to be used on other work and, with the exception of the signed contract set, are to be returned to Builder upon request, at the completion of the work.

06. SAMPLES, MATERIAL SUPPLIERS AND EMPLOYEES

    a. *Samples:* Submit with such promptness as to cause no delay in his own work, or in that of any other Contractor, samples as specified or required. Do not order materials until receipt of written approval from Builder. Builder shall check and approve such samples, with reasonable promptness, only for conformance with the design concept of the project and for compliance with the information given in the Contract Documents. Furnish only materials equal in every respect to approved samples. Submit Samples in duplicate of adequate size, showing quality, type, color range, finish, texture; label such samples with material name, quality, Subcontractor's name, date, project name and other pertinent data.

    b. Submit name of proposed manufacturers, materialmen, dealers who are to furnish materials, fixtures, appliances, or other fittings for approval as early as possible, to afford proper investigation, checking. No manufacturer will be approved for any materials to be furnished under contract unless he is of good reputation, has ample plant capacity, has successfully produced similar products.

    c. In asking for material prices, provide manufacturer or dealer with complete information from specifications and drawings. Inform manufacturer or dealer of pertinent contract requirements.

    d. All workmanship and materials shall be of the best quality. Materials shall be new and the best of their respective kinds, and furnished in sufficient quantity to facilitate proper and timely execution of the work. Subcontractor shall furnish satisfactory evidence, if required, as to the kind and quality of materials.

    e. Subcontractor shall at all times enforce strict discipline and good order among his employees and shall not employ on the work any unfit person or anyone who, in the opinion of Builder, is not skilled in the work assigned to him.

07. ROYALTIES AND PATENTS

    a. Subcontractor shall pay all royalties and license fees. We shall defend all suits or claims for infringement of any patent rights and shall hold Builder and Owner harmless from loss on account thereof.

Exhibit 27–15 (*continued*)

08. PERMITS, LAWS, TAXES AND REGULATIONS

a. Subcontractor shall obtain and pay for all permits, licenses, certificates, inspections and other legal fees necessary for the commencement, prosecution and approval of his work, unless specifically excluded in the scope of the work for his particular section.

b. Subcontractor shall give all notices and comply with all Federal, State, County and Municipal laws, ordinances, rules and regulations (including the rules and regulations of The National Fire Protection Association) bearing on the conduct of the work as drawn and specified. If the Subcontractor observes that the drawings and specifications are at variance therewith, he shall promptly notify Builder in writing, and necessary changes shall be made as provided for in Sections 16 and 17. If Subcontractor performs any work contrary to such laws, ordinances, rules and regulations, and without such notice to Builder, he shall bear all costs arising therefrom, and shall hold Builder harmless from loss on account thereof.

c. Wherever the law of the place of building requires a sales, consumer, use, or other similar tax, Subcontractor shall pay such tax.

d. Subcontractor or materials Supplier shall pay highway fees for damages to sidewalks, streets or other public property, or to any public utility caused by Subcontractor or Supplier.

e. Subcontractor will file the application for his specific building permit as required. Subcontractor shall obtain the permit and pay the fees for same.

09. LOCATIONS, LEVELS

a. Builder shall locate building corners, establish bench marks, and verify boundary lines.

b. Subcontractor shall exercise care to keep within lot, property lines. Subcontractor shall not encroach on rights or property of surrounding owners. Subcontractor shall rebuild in approved manner any portion of building, wall or fence which he may have constructed over property line at no additional cost to Owner or Builder.

c. The responsible Subcontractors shall lay out building per drawings with respect to corner markers and elevations in relation to grade stakes, and shall establish, maintain grades, lines, levels, locations required for work, and shall be responsible for accuracy of same. Verify grades, lines, levels, locations, dimensions and all field measurements as indicated; report any errors or inconsistencies in above before commencing work.

d. Subcontractor shall provide, maintain well-built batter boards at corners, safeguard bench marks. Give exact levels of various floors and lay out on rough floor exact location of partitions as guide to trades.

Exhibit 27–15 (*continued*)

10. PROTECTION OF WORK AND PROPERTY

  a. Subcontractor shall continuously maintain adequate protection of all his work from damage, and shall protect Owner's property from injury or loss arising in connection with the contract. He shall make good any such damage, injury or loss. He shall adequately protect adjacent property as provided by law and the Contract Documents, and shall hold Owner harmless from any claims of injury from any surrounding property.

  b. Subcontractor shall take all necessary precautions for safety of employees, agents and licensees on the work; comply with all applicable provisions of Federal, State and Municipal safety laws and building codes to prevent accidents or injury to persons on, about or adjacent to the premises where the work is being performed. Subcontractor shall erect and properly maintain at all times, as required by the conditions and progress of the work, all necessary safeguards for the protection of workmen and the public.

  c. In an emergency affecting the safety of life or of the work or adjoining property, Subcontractor, without special instruction or authorization from Builder, is hereby permitted to act, at his discretion, to prevent such threatened loss or injury, and he shall so act, without appeal, if so instructed or authorized. Any compensation claimed by Subcontractor on account of emergency work shall be deemed by agreement or arbitration.

  d. Subcontractor shall always protect excavations, trenches, building, site from damage from rain water, spring water, ground water, backing up of drains or sewers, other water; provide pumps, equipment, enclosures, to provide this protection; provide constant protection against rain, windstorm, frost or heat so as to maintain work, materials, apparatus, fixtures, free from injury or damage. At end of day's work, Subcontractor shall cover work likely to be damaged. All work of any kind found to be damaged by the above elements shall be removed and replaced by Subcontractor, without cost to Builder.

11. INSPECTION

  a. Builder's representative, including Owner, shall at all times have access to the work wherever it is in preparation or progress.

  b. If the specifications, Builder's instructions, laws, ordinances, or any public authority require any work to be specially tested or approved, Subcontractor shall give Builder timely notice of its readiness for observation by Builder or inspection by another authority; and if inspection is by another authority, required certificates of inspection shall be secured by the Subcontractor. If any work shall be covered up without the approval or consent of Builder, it must, if required by Builder, be uncovered for examination at Subcontractor's expense.

Exhibit 27-15 (continued)

    c. Re-examination of questioned work may be ordered by the Builder and, if so ordered, the work must be uncovered by Subcontractor. If such work be found in accordance with the Contract Documents, Builder shall pay the cost of re-examination and replacement. If such work be found not in accordance with the Contract Documents, Subcontractor shall pay such cost.

12. SUPERINTENDENCE—SUPERVISION

    a. Subcontractor shall keep on his work, during its progress, a competent superintendent or foreman, and any necessary assistants, all satisfactory to Builder. The superintendent or foreman shall not be changed, except with the consent of Builder, unless such personnel proves to be unsatisfactory to Subcontractor and ceases to be in his employ. The superintendent or foreman shall represent the Subcontractor in his absence, and all directions given to him shall be as binding as if given to Subcontractor. Important directions shall be confirmed in writing to Subcontractor. Other directions shall be so confirmed on written request in each case. Builder shall not be responsible for the acts or omissions of Subcontractor's superintendent or foreman, or his assistants.

    b. Subcontractor shall give efficient supervision to the work, using his best skill and attention. He shall carefully study and compare all drawings, specifications and other instructions, and shall at once report to Builder any error, omission or inconsistency which he may discover, but he shall not be held responsible for their existence or discovery, except for violations of codes and ordinances for his work.

13. CHANGES IN THE WORK

    a. Builder, without invalidating the contract, may order extra work or make changes by altering, adding or deducting from the work, the contract sum being adjusted accordingly. All such work shall be executed under the conditions of the original contract, except that any claim for extension of time caused thereby shall be adjusted at the time of ordering such change and shall be approved by Builder.

    b. In giving instructions, Builder shall have authority to make minor changes in the work, not involving extra cost and not inconsistent with the purposes of the building, but otherwise, except in an emergency endangering life or property, no extra work or change shall be made unless in pursuance of a written order from Builder, and no claim for an addition to the contract sum shall be valid unless so ordered.

    c. All clauses of this contract shall apply to any changes or extra in like manner, and to the same extent as though said changes or extras were incorporated herein. Waiver of any breach, alleged breach, clause, covenant or condition of this contract by Builder shall not be construed as a waiver of any other clause of this contract, nor shall such waiver serve as estoppel of any other right Builder may have hereunder.

Exhibit 27–15 (*continued*)

14. CLAIMS FOR EXTRA WORK

a. If Subcontractor claims that any instructions by drawings other than the contract set or otherwise involve extra cost under this contract, he shall give Builder written notice thereof within a reasonable time but, in no event, more than ten (10) days, after the receipt of such instructions, and in any event, before proceeding to execute the work, except in emergency endangering life or property, and the procedure shall then be as provided for changes in the work. No such claims shall be valid unless so made.

b. Subcontractor's itemized estimate for changes or credits for additions to or deductions from work required by contract shall always be available for inspection by Builder.

15. DEDUCTIONS FOR UNCORRECTED WORK

a. If Builder deems it inexpedient to correct work injured or not done in accordance with the contract, an equitable deduction from the contract price shall be made therefor.

16. SCHEDULE AND COORDINATION

a. *Schedule:* Each Subcontractor shall examine the schedule and check it for timing, accuracy and compatibility with his work and shall coordinate his work with the master schedule.

   (1). Not all items of work or material are included in the schedule, but only those major items which are required to assist Builder's representative in directing the work.

   (2). The schedule is a Contract Document and, as such, binds Subcontractor to perform accordingly. Subcontractor shall notify Builder within five (5) days after receiving his copy of the schedule should he find any problems or have any doubts concerning the timing or scheduling for his work or other Subcontractors' work preceding or following his work and which affect his work. Subcontractor shall, in particular, note if there is enough work assigned to keep his normal crew busy all day, as he will not be allowed to wait two or three days before starting work to have enough work to do for a full day, unless job is scheduled this way. If Builder does not receive any written notification within five (5) days after Subcontractor has received schedule, then the schedule shall be considered approved by and binding upon Subcontractor.

   (3). If Builder and Subcontractor or Supplier fail to reach agreement on the schedule, Builder has the sole option of cancelling the contract without penalty, or going to arbitration as provided for in the Contract Documents. Subcontractor shall have recourse to arbitration should he notify Builder that he does not approve the schedule, after having entered into the contract, but not later than the time stated above after having received the schedule.

Exhibit 27-15 (*continued*)

    (4). Builder does not guarantee that the work will keep up with the schedule, but may, at his sole discretion, allow the work to proceed at a slower pace.

    (5). Subcontractor shall keep himself informed of the progress of the work at all times. Because of faster work by other Subcontractors, schedule may be ahead, in which case Builder may notify Subcontractor two (2) full days in advance to proceed with his work. Each Subcontractor is expected to perform not less than a unit of work each day, and to prosecute his work as soon as directed by Builder. A unit of work is defined by the schedule. Subcontractor shall order his material anticipating that the job may be ahead of schedule six (6) work days. Each Subcontractor may work faster than the schedule provides, providing it does not interfere with other Subcontractors and has the approval of Builder. A Subcontractor may not slow down his work and use up time gained by another Subcontractor without approval of Builder.

    (6). The schedule may be reissued from time to time to correct deficiencies or change the order of work because of weather or other unforeseen causes, all at Builder's sole discretion. Subcontractor shall review the schedule as per (a.) above.

  b. Coordination: Subcontractor shall assist Builder in coordination and scheduling of all work pertinent to his installation. Subcontractor shall make himself familiar with the construction schedule and inform Builder of his requirements sufficiently to result in a well-coordinated job.

    (1). Subcontractor shall coordinate his work and materials storage in order that he does not interfere with or make more difficult the work of others. Subcontractor shall be guided by and shall comply with directives of Builder in any disputes arising out of work coordination. This includes location and placement of work both in time and place; coordination with others shall be performed at no additional cost to Builder, even though such reasonable coordination may result in a cost to Subcontractor.

17. COMMENCEMENT AND COMPLETION OF WORK

  a. The work shall be commenced at the time stated in the agreement, and shall meet all completion dates called out in construction schedule. It is hereby further understood and mutually agreed by and between Subcontractor and Builder that the date of commencement, rate of progress, and time for completion of the work hereunder are essential conditions of the contract.

  b. It is expressly understood and agreed by and between Subcontractor and Builder that the time for completion of the work of this project is per the schedule, and in the absence of such schedule, a reasonable time for completion of same, taking into consideration the average climatic-range and usual labor conditions prevailing in this locality.

Exhibit 27-15 (*continued*)

    c. Subcontractor shall pay particular attention to the following: Where actual damages for any delay in completion are difficult to determine by reason of Builder's election not to terminate the right of Subcontractor to proceed, Subcontractor and his sureties shall be liable for and shall pay to Builder the sum stated in the agreement for liquidated damages for each calendar day of such delay until the work is brought up to schedule, is completed or accepted. However, Builder may accept the work if there has been such a degree of completion as will, in Builder's opinion, make the project reasonably safe, fit and convenient for the use and accommodation for which it was intended. In such case, Subcontractor shall not be charged with liquidated damages, but Builder may assess the actual damage caused by such delay.

    d. If Subcontractor be delayed at any time in the progress of the work by any act or neglect of Builder, or of any employee of Builder, or by any separate Subcontractor employed by Builder, or by changes ordered in the work, or by strikes, lockouts, fire, unusual delay in transportation, unavoidable casualties, or any causes beyond Subcontractor's control, or by delay authorized by Builder pending arbitration, or by any cause which Builder shall decide to justify the delay, then the time of completion shall be extended for such reasonable time as Builder may decide, provided Subcontractor shall have notified Builder in writing within one (1) day of the cause of the delay.

    e. No such extension shall be made for delay occurring more than one (1) day before claim therefor is made in writing to Builder. In the case of a continuing cause of delay, only one claim is necessary.

18. CORRECTION OF WORK BEFORE FINAL PAYMENT

    a. Subcontractor shall promptly remove from the premises all work condemned by Builder as failing to conform to the contract, whether incorporated or not, and Subcontractor shall replace and re-execute his own work in accordance with the contract and without expense to Builder, and shall bear the expense of making good all work of other Subcontractors destroyed or damaged by such removal or replacement.

    b. If Subcontractor does not remove such condemned work within a reasonable time, fixed by written notice, Builder may remove it and may store the material at the expense of Subcontractor. If Subcontractor does not pay the expenses of such removal within ten (10) days' time thereafter, Builder may, upon ten (10) days' written notice, sell such material at auction or at private sale and shall account for the net proceeds thereof, after deducting all costs and expenses that should have been borne by Subcontractor.

19. CORRECTION OF WORK AFTER FINAL PAYMENT

    a. Subcontractor shall remedy any defects due to faulty materials or workmanship and pay for any damage to other work resulting therefrom,

Exhibit 27–15 (*continued*)

which shall appear within a period of one (1) year from the date of final payment and in accordance with the terms of any special guarantees provided in the contract. Builder shall give notice of observed defects with reasonable promptness. All questions arising under this subparagraph (a.) shall be decided by Builder subject to arbitration, notwithstanding final payment.

20. BUILDER'S RIGHT TO DO WORK

a. If Subcontractor should neglect to prosecute the work properly or fail to perform any provision of the contract, Builder, after three (3) days' written notice to Subcontractor, may, without prejudice to any other remedy he may have, make good such deficiencies and may deduct the cost thereof from the payment then or thereafter due Subcontractor.

b. Subcontractor further agrees that, should he not be prosecuting the work defined herein diligently to completion by not keeping sufficient workmen, supplies and materials, tools and equipment, on the job to complete the job on or before the time provided herein for completion, Builder may, after giving Subcontractor one (1) day written notice, such notice to include telegraphic communications, of his breach, proceed to have the work done in the manner most expedient to Builder and charge the cost (including any incidental expenses) thereof to Subcontractor, and Builder shall be entitled to take possession of and use any materials, tools, equipment, plans, permits and diagrams on the jobsite or intended for the work, and use the same for the performance of the work. Subcontractor waives any claim, demand or cause of action against Builder for the loss, use, misuse, abuse or conversion of the tools, materials, equipment, plans, permits or diagrams taken or used by Builder in accordance with this agreement. In the event Builder is required to complete the work of Subcontractor in accordance with this agreement, Subcontractor agrees to reimburse Builder for all of his costs and expenses, plus an additional 15% of his cost and expenses as overhead, in addition to the sum allowed in other sections of these conditions and the Contract Documents.

21. BUILDER'S RIGHT TO TERMINATE CONTRACT

a. If Subcontractor should be adjudged a bankrupt, or if he should make a general assignment for the benefit of his creditors, or if a receiver should be appointed on account of his insolvency, or if he should refuse or should fail to supply enough properly skilled workmen or proper materials, or for any reason repeatedly delay the work, or if he should fail to make prompt payment to his employees or their union or for material or labor, or persistently disregard laws, ordinances, or the instructions of Builder, or otherwise be guilty of a substantial violation of any pro-

Exhibit 27-15 (*continued*)

vision of the contract, then Builder, without prejudice to any other right or remedy and after giving Subcontractor and his surety, if any, three (3) days' written notice, may terminate the employment of Subcontractor and take possession of all materials, tools and appliances thereon and finish the work by whatever method he may deem expedient. In such case, Subcontractor shall not be entitled to receive any further payment until the work is finished. If the unpaid balance of the contract price shall exceed the expense of finishing the work, including compensation for additional architectural, managerial and administrative services, such excess shall be paid to Subcontractor. If such expense shall exceed such unpaid balance, Subcontractor shall pay to Builder the difference, including all costs of collection and attorneys' fees. The expense incurred by Builder as herein provided, and the damage incurred through Subcontractor's default, shall be verified by Builder.

b. Builder may sell materials, tools and appliances of which he has taken possession, and use the proceeds toward payment of any excess cost due to Subcontractor's failure; but if such excess cost were paid by Subcontractor, the materials, tools and equipment would revert to his ownership.

c. If the work should be stopped under an order of any court or public authority, then Builder may, upon three (3) days' written notice to Subcontractor, terminate the contract. Any loss, damage and profit to which Subcontractor may be entitled shall not exceed that which shall have been sustained or accrued up to the time when the work shall have been so stopped.

d. If Subcontractor shall refuse or fail to prosecute the work or any part thereof with such diligence as will insure its completion within the period specified by Builder's schedule (or any duly authorized extension thereof), or shall fail to complete the work within the said period, or in accordance with his schedule of progress, then this shall also constitute a cause for terminating the contract in accordance with the provisions of this section.

e. Neither an extension of time for any reason beyond that fixed herein for the completion of the work, nor the doing or excepting of any part of the work called for by this contract, shall be deemed to be a waiver by Builder of the right to abrogate this contract for abandonment or delay in the manner provided for herein.

f. Builder may, at any time during the term of the contract, demand an acceptable surety bond up to the amount of the contract price, if Builder has doubts as to Subcontractor's financial responsibility or ability to prosecute the work on time or in an acceptable manner. If such bond is not produced within three (3) days after demand, Builder may cancel the contract. Builder will pay the usual bond charges, but any premium charges required on such bond must be borne by Subcontractor.

Exhibit 27–15 (*continued*)

22. SUBCONTRACTOR'S RIGHT TO STOP WORK OR TERMINATE CONTRACT

    a. If the work should be stopped under an order of any court or other public authority for a period of ninety (90) days, through no act or fault of Subcontractor or of anyone employed by him, then Subcontractor may, upon thirty (30) days' written notice to Builder, terminate the contract and recover from Builder payment for all work executed.

    b. Should Builder fail to issue any certificate for payment, through no fault of Subcontractor, within fourteen (14) days after the Subcontractor's formal request for payment, or if Builder should fail to pay to Subcontractor within twenty-one (21) days of its maturity and presentation any sum certified by Builder or awarded by arbitrators, then Subcontractor may, upon thirty (30) days' written notice to Builder, stop the work or terminate the contract as set out in the preceding paragraph.

23. PROGRESS PAYMENTS

    a. Within fifteen (15) days of receipt by Builder of the progress billing, Subcontractor shall be entitled to ninety per cent (90%) of the portion of the contract sum properly allocable to labor, materials and equipment incorporated in the work during the preceding month, less the aggregate of previous payments in each case and less credits and retentions to this contract. Builder shall not make more than one (1) progress payment in any 30-day period. Builder shall specify dates for submitting of progress billings by Subcontractor.

    b. When Subcontractor is required to pay for performance bond, the premium may be set up as an item by itself. All other "overhead" charges shall be distributed equitably over the balance of the items.

    c. Subcontractor agrees to furnish, as required by Builder, payroll affidavits, receipts, vouchers, releases of claims of labor, materialmen and subcontractors performing work of furnishing materials under the contract, all in a form satisfactory to Builder, and it is agreed no payment hereunder shall be made, except at Builder's option, until and unless such releases are furnished.

    d. Should Subcontractor neglect or refuse generally to take care of bills for work and materials hereunder promptly when they become due or as provided herein, Builder shall have the right to pay bills for work or materials or subcontracts hereunder directly to the persons performing the work or furnishing materials, and credit the same (plus five per cent (5%) to cover Builder's cost of handling) against amounts due to Subcontractor. Subcontractor agrees not to assign any monies due or to become due him under the terms of the contract, and any obligations so assigned are void and will not be honored unless Builder agrees in writing to the contrary.

    e. Payments will not be made for materials not incorporated in the work.

Exhibit 27-15 (*continued*)

 f. In applying for payments, Subcontractor shall submit a statement based upon the breakdown of contract price. Refer to contract instructions and procedures for proper method of submitting billings.

24. CERTIFICATES FOR PAYMENT

 a. No certificate issued, nor payment made to Subcontractor, nor partial or entire use or occupancy of the work by Builder, shall be an acceptance of any work or materials not in accordance with the contract.

 b. The making and acceptance of the final payment shall constitute a waiver of all claims by Subcontractor, except those previously made and still unsettled.

25. PAYMENTS WITHHELD

 a. Builder may withhold or, on account of subsequently discovered evidence, nullify the whole or a part of any payment to such extent as may be necessary to protect Builder from loss on account of:
  1. Defective work not remedied;
  2. Claims filed or reasonable evidence indicating probable filing of claims;
  3. Failure of Subcontractor to make payments properly to Sub-subcontractors or for materials or labor or union benefits or taxes or Internal Revenue Service;
  4. A reasonable doubt that the contract can be completed for the balance then unpaid;
  5. Damage to another Subcontractor's work or equipment;
  6. Failure to adhere to progress schedule.

 b. When the above grounds are removed, payment shall be made for amounts withheld because of them. Additionally, Builder may use as a setoff against subsequent billings any payment made on prior billings which should be nullified as a result of the subsequently discovered offsets or deductions from any of the foregoing.

 c. In any event, ten per cent (10%) of the amount of each payment or certificate shall be withheld until completion of Subcontractor's work hereunder and its final acceptance by Builder. After all the work to be performed by Builder hereunder has been finally completed and said completed work has been accepted by Owner as satisfactory, and Owner has issued to Builder the Certificate of Final Completion, and Owner has been furnished satisfactory evidence that all bills for labor, materials, and equipment and supplies, and all claims payable by Subcontractor hereunder have been paid or settled (such evidence to include any affidavits, certificates, releases or statements, as required under applicable laws relating to mechanics' liens or otherwise), final settlement will be made and Subcontractor will be paid all remaining amounts owed to him, except as provided under paragraph a. above.

Exhibit 27–15 (*continued*)

    d. Builder also reserves the right to withhold in excess of ten per cent (10%) if, in his opinion, a larger retention is warranted in order to insure the correction of faulty work, to settle claims for the account of Subcontractor, or for other valid reason. Builder will not pay interest on delayed payments.

    e. The terms of the subcontract between Subcontractor and his Sub-subcontractor shall provide for similar conditions of payment as specified in paragraphs c. and d. above, unless modified by Builder for earlier payments to Subcontractor.

26. SUBCONTRACTORS' AND SUB-SUBCONTRACTORS' INSURANCE

    a. Policy Requirements: Before starting any work and for the duration of the contract, Subcontractor shall maintain and have his Sub-subcontractors maintain, the following policy coverage:

      (1). *Statutory Compensation and Employers Liability Insurance:* Each and every Subcontractor shall take out and maintain during the life of the contract the statutory Workmen's Compensation and Employer's Liability insurance for all of his employees to be engaged in work on the project under the contract and, in case any such work is sublet, Subcontractor shall require Sub-subcontractor to provide Workmen's Compensation and Employer's Liability Insurance for all of the latter's employees to be engaged in such work.

      (2). *Automobile Liability Insurance:* Subcontractor shall provide and maintain bodily injury and property damage liability insurance on all owned, hired and non-owned motor vehicles engaged in the work and the limits of such insurance shall not be less than stated herein.

      (3). *Bodily Injury and Property Damage Liability Insurance:* Subcontractor shall secure, provide and maintain during the life of the contract such bodily injury, liability and property damage liability insurance as shall protect himself from claims for bodily injury and property damage which may arise from operations under the contract, whether such operations be by Subcontractor or by any Sub-subcontractor, or by anyone directly or indirectly employed by either of them, and the amounts of such insurance shall not be less than limits stated herein.

27. INSURANCE LIMITS

    a. Minimum limits shall be as follows:

      (1). Statutory Workmen's Compensation: As prescribed by state in which project is located.

      (2). Employer's Liability: $100,000.00.

Exhibit 27-15 (*continued*)

    (3). Comprehensive Liability—General and Automobile: Subcontractor further agrees to take out and keep in force during the term of the contract, at Subcontractor's sole expense, public liability insurance in companies and through brokers approved by Builder to protect against any liability to the public incident to the use of or resulting from any occurrence in or about said premises in the minimum amount of five hundred thousand dollars ($500,000.00) to indemnify against claims for bodily injury or property damage arising out of said occurrence in whatever combination or combinations said claims are made. Subcontractor further agrees to deliver to Builder a certificate confirming said insurance executed by an authorized representative of the insurance carrier, said certificate to contain an outline of the coverages afforded, and in accordance with paragraph 26, of General Conditions, and to contain an agreement that the insurance carrier will give Builder written notice thirty (30) days prior to any discontinuance, reduction, restriction or cancellation of such insurance.

28. INSURANCE APPROVALS AND CANCELLATIONS

  a. Subcontractor shall not commence work at the site until he has obtained all required insurance and until such insurance has been approved by Builder. Subcontractor shall not allow any Sub-subcontractor to commence work until all insurance required has been approved and obtained. Approval of the insurance by Builder shall not relieve or decrease the liability of Subcontractor hereunder. Certificates of insurance shall be filed with Builder prior to commencing work.

  b. The required insurance shall be written by companies licensed to do business in the state in which the work is located at the time the policies are issued. In addition, the companies shall be acceptable to Builder.

  c. Subcontractor shall not cause any insurance to be cancelled nor permit any insurance to lapse. All insurance policies shall include a clause to the effect that the policy shall not be cancelled or reduced, restricted or limited until thirty (30) days after Builder has received written notice, as evidenced by return receipt of registered or certified letter. Certificates of insurance shall contain transcripts from the proper office of the insurer, evidencing in particular those insured, the extent of the insurance, the location and the operations to which the insurance applies, the expiration date, and the above-mentioned notice of cancellation clause.

  d. Approval or review by Builder or by his representatives of any equipment or material or work of installation shall in no manner act to release Subcontractor, his sureties or insurers from any liability or indemnity as provided in these General Conditions related to such equipment, material or installation work, or to its performance.

Exhibit 27-15 (*continued*)

    e. Subcontractor or any Sub-subcontractors agree to keep all vehicles owned by their employees off of the construction site, and if any of their employees does enter upon the property with a privately-owned vehicle of any type, then Subcontractor or Sub-subcontractors will be personally responsible for any bodily injury or property damage to the limits set forth in Section 27.b. of these General Conditions.

29. INDEMNIFICATION

    a. Hold Harmless Indemnification: Subcontractor shall hold Builder, Owner and their elective and appointive boards, officers, agents and employees harmless from any liability for claims, for personal injury or property damage, including Builder's property, which may arise from operations under this agreement, whether such operation be by Subcontractor or by any Sub-subcontractor(s), or by any one or more persons directly or indirectly employed by, or acting as agent for, Subcontractor or Sub-subcontractors.

    b. Subcontractor shall defend Builder and Owner and their elective and appointive boards, officers, agents and employees from any suits or actions at law or in equity for damages caused, or alleged to have been caused, by reason of any of the aforesaid operations, provided as follows:

        (1). That neither Builder nor Architect waives any rights against Subcontractor which they may have by reason of the aforesaid hold harmless agreement, because of the acceptance by Builder or Owner, or the depositing with either of them by Subcontractor of any insurance policies described herein.

        (2). That the aforesaid hold harmless agreement by Subcontractor shall apply to all damages and claims for damages of every kind suffered or alleged to have been suffered by reason of any of the aforesaid operations, regardless of whether or not insurance policies shall have been determined to be applicable to any of such damages or claims for damages.

30. OWNER'S INSURANCE

    a. Property Fire Insurance: Unless otherwise provided, Owner shall purchase and maintain property insurance upon the entire work at the site to the full insurable value thereof. This insurance shall include the interests of Owner, Builder, Subcontractors and Sub-subcontractors in the work, and shall insure against the perils of fire, extended coverage, vandalism and malicious mischief.

    b. Coverage shall include items of labor and material connected therewith, whether in or adjacent to the structure insured, materials in place or to be used as part of the permanent construction, including surplus materials, shanties, protective fences, bridges, or temporary structures, miscellaneous materials and supplies incidental to the work, and such

Exhibit 27-15 (*continued*)

scaffolding stagings, towers, forms and equipment as are not owned or rented by Builder or Subcontractors, the cost of which is included in the cost of the work. *EXCLUSIONS:* This coverage does not cover any tools owned by mechanics, any tools, equipment scaffoldings, stagings, towers and forms rented by Builder or Subcontractors, the capital value of which is not included in the cost of the work. The loss, if any, is to be made adjustable with and payable to Owner as trustee for the insureds as their interests may appear, except in such cases as may require payment of all or a proportion of said loss to a mortgagee as his interests may appear.

c. Builder shall be named or designated in such capacity as insured jointly with Owner, and a certificate of such coverage shall be filed with Builder. If Owner fails to effect or maintain coverage as above and so notifies Builder, Builder may insure his own interest (and that of Subcontractors), and charge the cost thereof to Owner. If Builder is damaged by failure of Owner to maintain such coverage, or to so notify Builder, then Builder may recover damages from Owner.

d. If required in writing by any party in interest, Owner as trustee shall, upon the occurrence of loss, give bond for the proper performance of his duties. He shall deposit any money received from insurance in an amount separate from all his other funds and he shall distribute it in accordance with such agreement as the parties in interest may reach, or under an award of arbitrators appointed, one by Owner, another by joint action of the parties in interest, all other procedure being as provided elsewhere in the contract for arbitration. If, after loss, no special agreement is made, replacement of injured work shall be ordered and executed as provided for changes in the work.

e. Trustee shall have power to adjust and settle any loss with the insurers, unless Builder or one of the Subcontractors interested shall object in writing within three (3) working days of the occurrence of loss, and thereupon arbitrators shall be chosen as above. Trustee shall, in that case, make settlement with the insurers in accordance with the directions of such arbitrators, who shall also, if distribution by arbitration is required, direct such distribution.

f. Should all or any part of the work or construction covered by this agreement be damaged or destroyed by any of the perils covered by standard form fire insurance policy with vandalism and malicious mischief coverage endorsement, or by any other peril in fact insured against, or by war or acts of foreign aggression, fire storm, lightening, flood, earthquake, mob violence, or other casualty before final completion of said work, Subcontractor, upon written instructions from Builder, shall proceed to replace and repair and complete said work, in accordance with original plans and specifications to the extent said work is covered by the proceeds of a police with a fire insurance company. In this event, the provisions of this agreement shall remain in full force and effect, except that the compensation mentioned in the agreement shall be increased by the

Exhibit 27–15 (*continued*)

total cost of removing and replacing all of the damaged and destroyed work; and Subcontractor's compensation shall be increased as indicated above.

g. Builder, however, at its option, in the event of damage or destruction to the work by any of the aforementioned causes, may give written notice to Subcontractor declaring its desire to cancel the agreement and contract and, after paying or adjusting all of the accounts charged to the work in accordance with this agreement, this agreement may be cancelled or terminated.

31. BONDS

a. At option of Builder, the successful bidder may be required to deliver to Builder an executed Performance and Labor and Material Bond up to the full amount of the contract as security for the faithful performance and completion of the contract and the payment by Subcontractor of all persons or corporations for work done or materials or equipment furnished to Sub-contractor or any Sub-contractor in connection with the work of the contract; otherwise, the contract shall be null and void. Said bond shall be obtained as directed by Builder, in the form approved by Builder. Usual bond premium will be paid by the Builder; however, any premium charges over and above usual bond premium must be borne by Subcontractor.

32. DAMAGES

a. Should either party to the contract suffer damages because of any wrongful act or neglect or omission of the other party or of anyone employed by him, claim shall be made in writing to the party liable within a reasonable time of the first observance of such damage, and not later than the final payment, except as expressly stipulated otherwise in the case of faulty work or materials, and shall be adjusted by agreement or arbitration.

b. If an action at law or in equity is instituted on, in connection with or arising out of the contract by Builder or Owner against any Subcontractor and/or a third party or third parties, or against Owner or Builder by any Subcontractor and as a part of any such action, Owner or Builder shall be entitled to receive his cost and expenses in connection with such action or actions, attorneys' fees, in a reasonable amount shall be included in any judgment in favor of Owner or Builder.

33. LIENS AND FINAL PAYMENT

a. Subcontractor shall indemnify and save harmless Builder and Owner from any and all claims, demands, causes of action or suits of whatever

Exhibit 27–15 (*continued*)

nature arising out of the services, labor, equipment or materials furnished by Subcontractor in the performance of the work, and from all laborers', mechanics' and materialmen's liens upon the property upon which the work is performed and arising out of the services, labor, equipment or materials furnished by Subcontractor, and the Subcontractor shall keep all materials, tools, equipment or machinery used in connection with any of the work, free and clear of all liens, claims and encumbrances of any nature whatsoever arising from the performance of the work by Subcontractor or any of his Sub-subcontractors.

b. Neither the final payment nor any part of the retained percentage shall become due until Subcontractor shall deliver an affidavit that, so far as he has knowledge or information, the releases and receipts include all the labor and material for which a lien could be filed; but Subcontractor may, if any Sub-subcontractor refuses to furnish release or receipt in full, furnish a bond satisfactory to Builder to indemnify him against any lien. If any lien remains unsatisfied after all payments are made, Subcontractor shall refund to Builder all monies that the latter may be compelled to pay in discharging such a lien, including all costs and a reasonable attorney's fee.

c. Subcontractor, as a condition precedent to payment, shall submit with the final billing, waiver of lien rights and lien releases from all Sub-subcontractors, suppliers of materials, and/or labor either to Subcontractor ot to Sub-subcontractor and individual releases or waivers from all laborers, whether employed by Sub-subcontractors of Subcontractor or Subcontractor. Such releases shall be of such forms as to release any and all lien rights provided by the laws of the political entities having jurisdiction over the site, and shall cover all work performed to the date of the billing. Additionally, Subcontractor, as a condition precedent to payment, shall submit a statement executed by Subcontractor stating that the lien releases and waivers are valid and binding, duly executed and cover all laborers who have performed work at the site, regardless of whether they supplied material to Subcontractor or his Sub-subcontractors. Additionally, said statement shall set forth that Subcontractor warrants that he has paid for all labor and material supplied to the site up to the date of billing. Said statement shall conclude with a statement by Subcontractor that he understands that the representations made in the statement will be relied upon by Builder in making payment and that, but for the statements, Builder would not make the payment requested.

34. ASSIGNMENT OF CONTRACT

a. No Subcontractor shall assign the contract nor sublet it as a whole without the written consent of Builder, nor shall Subcontractor assign any monies due or to become due to him hereunder without the previous written consent of Builder.

Exhibit 27–15 (continued)

35. MUTUAL RESPONSIBILITY OF CONTRACTORS

a. Should Subcontractor cause damage to any other Subcontractor on the work, Subcontractor agrees, upon due notice, to settle with such Subcontractor by agreement or arbitration.

36. ACCEPTANCE OF WORK

a. If any part of Subcontractor's work depends for proper execution or results upon the work of any other Subcontractor, Subcontractor shall inspect and promptly report to Builder any defects in such work that render it unsuitable for such proper execution and results. His failure to so inspect and report shall constitute an acceptance of the other Subcontractor's work as fit and proper for the reception of his work, except as to defects which may develop in the other Subcontractor's work after the execution of his work.

b. To insure the proper execution of his subsequent work, Subcontractor shall measure work already in place and shall at once report to Builder any discrepancy between the executed work and the drawings.

37. SUB-SUBCONTRACTS

a. Subcontractor shall, as soon as practicable after the execution of the contract and before awarding any sub-subcontracts, notify Builder in writing of the names of Sub-subcontractors proposed for the principal parts of the work and for such other parts as Builder may direct, and shall not employ any that Builder may, within a reasonable time, object to as incompetent or unfit or for other reasonable objections.

b. Subcontractor agrees that he is fully responsible to Builder for the acts and omissions of his Sub-subcontractors and of persons either directly or indirectly employed by them, as he is for the acts and omissions of persons directly employed by him.

c. Nothing contained in the Contract Documents shall create any contractual relation between any Subcontractor and Owner.

38. RELATIONS OF BUILDER AND SUBCONTRACTOR

a. Builder agrees to bind every Subcontractor, and every Subcontractor and his Sub-subcontractors agree to be bound by the terms of the Contract Documents as far as applicable to his work, including the following provisions of this section, unless specifically noted to the contrary in a subcontract approved in writing by Builder.

b. Subcontractor agrees:
(1). To be bound to Builder by the Contract Documents and by all the provisions thereof.
(2). To submit to Builder applications for payment in such reasonable

Exhibit 27-15 (*continued*)

      time as to enable Builder to apply for payment under the section on "Applications for Payment" of these General Conditions.

    (3). To make all claims for extensions of time to Builder in the manner provided in these General Conditions.

  c. Builder agrees:

    (1). To be bound to Subcontractor by the Contract Documents and by all the provisions thereof.

    (2). To pay Subcontractor, upon the payment of certificates, if issued according to the provisions of the General Conditions, the amount allowed to Builder on account of Subcontractor's interest therein.

    (3). To pay Subcontractor to such extent as may be provided by the Contract Documents or the subcontract.

    (4). To pay Subcontractor on demand for his work or materials as far as executed and fixed in place, less the retained percentage, at the time the certificate should be issued, even though Owner fails to issue it for any cause not the fault of Subcontractor.

    (5). To pay Subcontractor a just share of any fire insurance money received by him, Builder, under General Conditions section on fire insurance.

    (6). To give Subcontractor an opportunity to be present and to submit evidence in any arbitration involving his rights.

    (7). To name as arbitrator under arbitration proceedings as provided in the General Conditions the person nominated by Subcontractor, if sole cause of dispute is the work, materials, rights or responsibilities of Subcontractor; or, if Subcontractor and any other Subcontractor jointly, to name as such arbitrator the person upon whom they agree.

  d. Builder and Subcontractor agree that:

    (1). In the matter of arbitration, their rights and obligations and all procedure shall be analagous to those set forth in the contract.

  e. Nothing in this section shall create any obligation on the part of Owner to pay or to see to the payment of any sums to any Subcontractor.

39. BUILDER'S CONTROL OF WORK

  a. Builder shall have full control of the work in all its phases, excepting for any conditions to the contrary in the agreement between Builder and Owner. Builder may authorize additional work, cancel work previously authorized, or make any other changes in either the scope or character thereof, subject to the terms of the Contract Documents.

  b. Builder will designate his representative, who will act for Builder on all work in the contract. He shall certify to Builder when payments under the contract are due and the amounts to be paid in accordance with the terms of the agreement. He shall make decisions on all claims of Subcontractors and, in the event that Subcontractor takes exception to any such decision, it shall be subject to arbitration.

Exhibit 27-15 (*continued*)

40. ARCHITECT'S STATUS

a. Architect shall act as the agent of Builder only insofar as Builder may so designate. He will perform the following specific services during the execution of the contract:
  (1). Check shop drawings, samples and equipment data for conformance to Contract Documents in accordance with these General Conditions.
  (2). Issue such additional drawings, instructions and data as may be required to interpret properly the drawings and specifications.

41. ARBITRATION

a. All disputes, claims or questions subject to arbitration under the contract shall be submitted to arbitration in accordance with the provisions then obtaining of the Standard Form of Arbitration procedure of the American Institute of Architects, and this agreement shall be specifically enforceable under the prevailing arbitration law, and judgment upon the award rendered may be entered in the court of the forum, state or federal, having jurisdiction.

b. Subcontractor shall not cause a delay of the work during any arbitration proceedings except by agreement with Builder.

c. Notice of the demand for arbitration of a dispute shall be filed in writing with the other party to the contract. The demand for arbitration shall be made within a reasonable time after the dispute has arisen; in no case, however, shall the demand be made later than the time of final payment, except as otherwise expressly stipulated in the contract.

d. The arbitrators, if they deem that the case requires it, are authorized to award to the party whose contention is sustained, such sums as they or a majority of them shall deem proper to compensate him for the time and expense incident to the proceedings and, if the arbitration was demanded without reasonable cause, they may also award damages for delay. The arbitrators shall fix their own compensation, unless otherwise provided by agreement, and shall assess the costs and charges of the proceedings upon either or both parties.

42. CASH ALLOWANCES

a. Subcontractor shall include in the contract sum all allowances names in the Contract Documents and shall cause the work to be done for such sums as Builder may direct, the contract sum being adjusted in conformity therewith. Subcontractor declares that the contract sum includes such sums for expenses and profits on account of cash allowances as he deems proper. If allowance is specified for purchase of material only, then only actual cost as charged by the seller shall be charged to the allowance, and it shall be understood that Subcontractor's profit, installa-

Exhibit 27-15 (*continued*)

tion cost, warehouse and storage costs, etc. are included in the overall bid or contract price, and shall not be charged to the allowance. No demand for delivery costs, expenses or profit other than those included in the contract sum shall be allowed.

43. USE OF PREMISES

a. Subcontractor shall confine his apparatus, the storage of materials and the operations of his workmen to limits indicated by law, ordinances, permits or directions of Builder, and shall not unreasonably encumber the premises with his materials.

b. Subcontractor shall not load or permit any part of the structure to be loaded with a weight that will endanger its safety.

c. In addition to the requirements of this section, the portion of Owner's property that may be used by Subcontractor shall be agreed upon with Builder and clearly designated, and trespass and encroachment on reserved space shall not be made. Any damage to space allowed for use shall be made good by Subcontractor on release of the space.

44. CUTTING, PATCHING AND EXCAVATION

a. All trades shall perform and time their work so as not to require unnecessary cutting. Subcontractor shall perform his work in accordance with information obtained from plans and specifications, detail drawings or instructions from the various trades so as to avoid, where possible, the necessity of cutting.

b. Promptly pre-set conduits, outlets, piping sleeves, boxes, inserts, anchors, equipment, etc., into walls, floors and other construction to meet requirements of construction progress of all other trades. All Subcontractors and trades shall cooperate freely under the coordinating direction of Builder, to the end that all parts of the work may proceed advantageously and in complete harmony. The mechanical and electrical trades shall be wholly responsible for the pre-placement of inserts in concrete and masonry, but Builder shall be at pains to see that such are given due advance notice and the devices are not carelessly displaced or damaged by others' operations. If any cutting is later necessary, it and the resulting corrective patching shall be done at the expense of the trade requiring it. Any cost caused by defective or ill-timed work shall be borne by the party responsible therefor, and not by Builder in any event. No cutting, patching or repairs shall be done until Builder has been consulted, given directions and arranged for observation. Subcontractors requiring insets in their work by other trades shall give Builder adequate notice, in order that Builder may inform other trades involved and give said trades reasonable time to act.

c. Subcontractor shall not endanger any work by cutting, excavating or otherwise altering the work, and shall not cut or alter the work of any other Subcontractor, save with the consent of Builder.

Exhibit 27–15 (*continued*)

45. CLEANING UP

a. Subcontractor shall at all times keep the premises free from accumulation of waste material or rubbish caused by his employees or work, and shall leave his work clean and ready for work by other trades or for occupancy by Owner. In case of dispute, Builder may remove the rubbish and charge the cost to Subcontractor.

b. At the end of each working day, Subcontractor shall gather and stockpile all waste material and rubbish, both in the building and on the site, in a location as directed by Builder.

c. Stockpiled rubbish shall be removed from the site at frequent intervals, or as directed by Builder.

46. SPECIFICATION EXPLANATION

a. The General Conditions and Specifications are of the abbreviated type or "streamlined" type, and include incomplete sentences. Omissions of words or phrases such as "the Subcontractor shall," "in conformity therewith," "shall be," "as noted on the drawings," "according to the plans," "a," "an," "the," and "all" are intentional. Omitted words and phrases shall be supplied by inference in the same manner as they are when a "note" occurs on the drawings. Words "shall be" or "shall" will be supplied by inference where a colon (:) is used within sentences or phrases.

b. Subcontractor shall provide all items, articles, materials, operations or methods listed, mentioned or scheduled on the drawings and/or herein, including all labor, materials, equipment and incidentals necessary and required for their completion.

c. References to known standard specifications shall mean and intend latest edition, unless otherwise noted, of such specifications adopted and published at date of invitation to submit proposals. In the case of codes and similar guidelines, the reference is always to the edition adopted by the governing bodies having jurisdiction over the work.

47. SCOPE OF WORK REQUIRED

a. The general extent and scope of work to be performed by Subcontractor under the contract is described by the Contract Documents. It is intended to include all work, even though not specifically shown or noted, but which is required to obtain a complete and operating project, as indicated by the Contract Documents, and as interpreted by Builder and his authorized Architect and engineer.

b. Subcontractor shall provide all labor, materials, equipment, appliances and services necessary to execute and complete all work of the contract as required by the drawings and described in the specifications, and perform all the work necessary to the complete satisfaction of Builder.

Exhibit 27-15 (continued)

c. It shall also be understood that, where details are given for any particular section, similar parts, not fully detailed, shall correspond with or be equivalent to those that have been detailed.

d. Subcontractor is cautioned that, in all specification sections, the included item is general for his convenience, and is not to be construed as all inclusive or limiting the work which must be performed under his contract. Subcontractor must do all work required to carry out the intent of the Contract Documents.

e. Where items are shown on drawings but are not specified, and where specified items are not shown on drawings, it is definitely assumed that Subcontractor has included such items in his base bid.

f. The intent of the drawings and specifications is to be all inclusive for any and all work necessary to completely construct this project; this shall include items that may not be shown or specified, but that good practice dictates.

g. Subcontractor shall provide any item of labor, service or material required to make the work comply with any local ordinance regulations and practices, or to meet site characteristics.

h. Subcontractor shall provide drawings, permits and fees required by law, regulations, ordinances or building codes.

i. Subcontractor shall provide all scaffolding, tools and equipment necessary or required for the performance of the work.

j. Subcontractor shall provide, at his own cost, adequate and efficient machinery, plant equipment, tools, equipment, sundries and supplies required for the work.

k. Subcontractor agrees to save and hold harmless Owner and Builder from public liability, property damage, infringement of patent or patent rights, workmen's compensation liability, or any other liability or loss made, suffered, caused or permitted by Subcontractor.

48. BORING AND OTHER SITE CONDITION DATA

a. Results of borings made upon site and other site condition data are issued with contract drawings for examination by Subcontractors, but are not part of contract drawings.

b. Subcontractor, however, is responsible for any conclusion to be drawn from boring data and other site condition data; if he prefers not to assume such risk, he is under obligation to employ his own experts to analyze available information; be responsible for any consequences of acting or conclusions obtained.

c. Neither Builder nor Owner guarantees continuity of conditions indicated at boring locations and by other site conditions tests and surveys.

d. Should Subcontractor suspect unusual sub-surface soil conditions not determined by borings and other site tests, he shall provide alternate

Exhibit 27–15 (*continued*)

unit costs to deal with said conditions. After contract is let, Builder shall not allow any increase in contract price for sub-surface conditions, except as specifically provided for in alternates, and encountered.

49. MANUFACTURER'S NAME – SUBSTITUTIONS

a. When submitting bid quotes, a "base bid" shall be submitted using only the materials of the specific manufacturer(s) or quality specified. If Subcontractor or supplier desires to use "equals" or materials other than those specified, he may submit an alternate bid in addition to the "base bid." He shall supply the name of the manufacturer and the specific brand and number of each product he offers as a substitute; and shall state the amount to be added or deducted for such substitution. Subcontractor will be notified within ten (10) days after the aware of the contract to him if such substitution or "equal" is accepted. If not so notified, Subcontractor shall follow the specifications in accordance with the "base bid." All approved substitutions shall be incorporated in the contract by change order.

b. The intention is not to exclude other manufacturers of like products believed by Subcontractor to be of the same merit as and functionally equivalent to the item specified, but the burden of proof of equivalency is upon Subcontractor, and Builder shall be the final judge. If Subcontractor elects to attempt to prove such equality and to substitute, he must request Builder's approval in writing to substitute for the specified item, stating his reasons for the substitution, the credit, if any, involved, and provide supporting data. Such supporting data shall include the basic specifications of the specified item(s), the specifications, characteristics and other information concerning the proposed substitution demonstrating its equality to the specified item(s), and the effect of the substitution on the progress schedule, if any. In the event that a substitution is approved by Builder, Subcontractor shall assume all risks and costs for redesign and adjustment of all work affected by the substitution, check-of its effect on adjoining work, and any delays occasioned by its use, all subject to the Builder's written approval. All materials, methods or equipment shall be as specified and/or shown, unless a substitute or change is approved in writing by Builder.

c. If restrictions of any government authority prohibit the purchase or use of certain items that are required by the drawings, or the specifications, substitutions for such items shall be determined by Builder. Subcontractor shall base his bid on furnishing all items exactly as shown and specified. Subcontractor is not authorized to make any substitutions on his own initiative, but in every instance must obtain a properly authorized change order before installing any work varying from contract requirements.

Exhibit 27-15 (*continued*)

50. MANUFACTURER'S DIRECTIONS

    a. Subcontractor shall apply, install, connect, erect, use, clean and condition manufactured articles, materials, fixtures and equipment per manufacturer's printed directions, unless specified to contrary.

51. USE AND OCCUPANCY

    a. Owner reserves the right of full or partial and/or temporary or permanent occupancy, even if Subcontractor may not have reached substantial completion.

    b. Builder reserves the right at all times to deliver, place and install furnishings, etc., as the work progresses, as long as it does not prevent Subcontractor from working.

    c. Such preliminary occupancy shall not be construed as acceptance of such occupied portions of the building, nor shall it prejudice Builder's right to reject unsatisfactory work or to withhold acceptance until directed corrective work is completed.

    d. Subcontractor shall cooperate with all persons or trades working for Builder furnishing or installing equipment, and shall ascertain from representatives of the same as to space requirements, access and details of equipment and installation.

52. TEMPORARY AND TRIAL USAGE

    a. Builder and Owner reserve the right of temporary or trial usage of any mechanical device, machinery, equipment or any work or material supplied under the contract before final completion and written acceptance of same. Builder shall have the privilege of such temporary and trial usage for such reasonable length of time required for making a complete and thorough test of same; and no claim for damage shall be made by Subcontractor for the injury to or breaking of any parts of such work which may be caused by weakness or inaccuracy of structural parts or by defective materials or workmanship. If Subcontractor so elects, he may, at his own expense, place a competent person or persons satisfactory to Builder to make such trial usage. The trial shall be under the supervision of Builder.

53. BUILDER'S REPRESENTATIVE AND JOB MEETINGS

    a. Builder's representatives will meet at regularly scheduled intervals with Subcontractors' representatives for purposes of expediting and coordinating the work. Attendance at these meetings is mandatory; failure to attend meetings is a violation of the contract.

Exhibit 27–15 (continued)

54. MATERIAL STORAGE

  a. Subcontractor shall provide ample protection for his building materials requiring shelter from the weather and shall locate same where approved by Builder.

  b. Material being stored outdoors on the property shall be located where directed or approved by Builder. Materials may be stored indoors only with special approval of Builder.

55. TEMPORARY TOILETS

  a. Builder shall provide proper and adequate temporary toilet accommodations for all persons employed on the project, in accordance with authorities having jurisdiction. The toilet facilities of the new building or any of Owner's other buildings shall not be used by any person employed on this project at any time during the duration of the contract.

56. TEMPORARY WATER SUPPLY

  a. Builder shall provide temporary water within the site when a water supply is immediately available to site. Should a water supply not be immediately available, Subcontractors shall supply their own water. At such time as water is available, Builder shall connect to and supply water to at least one distribution point on site. Builder shall not provide pressure or volume in excess of the immediately available supply to the site. The location, pressure and volume shall be at the sole discretion of Builder.

  b. Subcontractor is responsible for secondary distribution from Builder's distribution point. Should Subcontractor require an increased supply of water over and above that supplied by Builder, then Subcontractor shall provide such increase of water from his own source and at his own expense. In any case, Subcontractor shall verify water supply with Builder before entering into contract, and voice any objections or seek any conditions contrary to the above before entering into contract, and include such conditions in contract.

57. TEMPORARY POWER AND LIGHT

  a. Builder shall provide temporary electrical power within the site when electrical power is immediately available to the site. Should electrical power lines not be immediately available to the site, Subcontractor shall supply his own power by portable generators or other means. At such time as power lines are available, Builder shall connect to and supply the power to various points on the site. The location amperage and voltage shall be at the sole discretion of Builder.

  b. Subcontractor is responsible for secondary distribution from Builder's distribution points. Should Subcontractor require an increased or

Exhibit 27–15 (*continued*)

different voltage and/or amperage than that supplied by Builder, then Subcontractor shall provide such power requirements from his own source and at his own expense. In any case, Subcontractor shall verify power supply with Builder before entering into contract, and voice any objections or seek any conditions contrary to the above before entering into contract, and include such conditions in contract.

58. SCAFFOLDING AND SHORING

a. Subcontractor shall furnish, erect, maintain and remove all scaffolding necessary for his work, including ladders, stairs, ramps, runways, derricks, protection, hoists, elevators, rubbish chutes, and other temporary structures or equipment for the construction of the work.

b. Subcontractor shall furnish, erect, maintain and remove all necessary shoring for his work and be responsible for safety and strength of same.

c. Subcontractor shall make specific arrangements with Builder before signing his contract, if he does not intend to supply the above or any part thereof.

59. GUARANTEES

a. All work performed under the contract shall be unconditionally guaranteed against premature wear (not occasioned by abuse) or failure due to inherent defects in material or improper installation, for a period of one (1) year from date of final payment (unless a longer period is specified in particular cases).

b. This guarantee period does not deprive Builder or Owner of the right to prosecute any claim for breach of performance concerning which the laws and cases of the State provide and permit a longer period of time in which to prosecute. Builder and Owner reserve the right to prosecute any claim for breach of performance with full rights under limitation periods provided by State laws and cases.

c. Subcontractor will be served with a notice, his surety, if any, with a copy, and if he fails to respond within seven (7) days, Builder may proceed to effect necessary replacement or repairs and charge the cost thereof to Subcontractor, or to his surety, if that particular Subcontractor is no longer in business or in a responsible financial status.

d. The manufacturer of a product may be specifically mentioned as a party to a guarantee. Then it shall be Subcontractor's obligation to produce the required guarantee of the manufacturer and submit it to Builder for examination and approval prior to securing his release.

e. The cost of making good any work deteriorated or defective shall include any additional Architect's or other professional fees, if such work is unusual or extensive, and all contingent damages, such as damages to other work, whether installed by the particular Subcontractor or another, and to other property of Owner.

Exhibit 27–15 (*continued*)

60. **RECORD DRAWINGS**

    a. During the course of construction, the plumbing, heating, ventilating and air conditioning, and electrical Subcontractors shall keep an accurate record of all deviations in work as shown on drawings and indicate actual installation on a set of transparency drawings and forward the same to Builder.

    b. As work proceeds, Subcontractor shall be responsible that he or his Sub-subcontractors indicate all changes and revisions of piping, equipment and ductwork, and electrical work, etc., with particular attention to outside underground utility lines as to location, elevations, size, etc., in a neat and accurate manner satisfactory to Builder, and forward same to Builder.
    1. Title drawings, "Record Drawings of Work—As Built."
    2. Include cost of preparing record drawings in bid. When revisions are completed, deliver corrected drawings to Builder. Final payment for completed work will not be made until Builder receives and approves drawings.

61. **MAINTENANCE INSTRUCTIONS**

    a. Subcontractor shall, at the completion of the contract, deliver to Builder three (3) copies of manufacturer's manual presenting for Owner's guidance full details for the care and maintenance of all visible surfaces and equipment included in the contract.

    b. Subcontractor shall furnish all literature of the manufacturer, relating to equipment, including motors or other manufactured equipment; also cuts, wiring diagrams, instruction sheets and all other information pertaining to same that would be useful to Owner in the operation and maintenance of same.

62. **ANTIDISCRIMINATION LAW**

    a. In the hiring of employees for the performance of work under contract or under subcontract hereunder, neither Subcontractor nor any Sub-subcontractor shall, by reason of race or color, discriminate against any resident of the state who is qualified and available to perform the work to which the employment relates, nor shall Subcontractor or any Sub-subcontractors discriminate in any manner against or intimidate any employee hired for performance of work under the contract on account of race or color.

63. **TITLE TO THE WORK**

    a. The title to all the work completed in the course of construction and to all materials affixed to the builder under the terms of this agreement shall be in the Owner. The title to all materials and equipment delivered to the jobsite but not affixed to the building shall remain in Builder or Subcon-

Exhibit 27-15 (*concluded*)

tractor, and shall not be the property of Owner. Owner and Builder shall not be responsible for, except as specifically called out in the insurance section(s) of these General Conditions, and Subcontractor agrees to protect, his work, materials, tools, and equipment against loss or damage by fire, theft or accident and not make any claim or demand upon Owner or Builder for injury, loss or damage to Subcontractor, his agents or any third person or persons; but Subcontractor's right shall be limited, so far as Owner and Builder are concerned, solely and exclusively to receipt by Subcontractor of the contract price, subject to such additions, deductions and setoffs as herein provided, upon the terms and conditions herein contained.

64. NOTICES

    a. Any notice which Builder is required to give to Subcontractor may be delivered to Subcontractor personally or may be mailed to Subcontractor at the address set forth in the contract, or at such other address as may be designated in writing by Subcontractor to Builder; and such notice shall be deemed served when deposited in the United States mail so addressed and postage thereupon prepaid; the time of performance by Subcontractor of any act based on such notice, or the time for the exercise by Builder of any right based on such notice, shall be extended for twenty-four (24) hours, in the event such notice is served by mail.

    b. Builder shall file, upon completion of the improvements described in this agreement, a Certificate of Completion in the proper form and within the proper time limit as is provided by the lien laws of the State having jurisdiction over the site.

    c. Subcontractor agrees to file any and all notices permitted by the jurisdiction governing the site which would lessen, eliminate or terminate any and all lien rights which any and all Subcontractors, materialmen and laborers, or Subcontractor might otherwise be entitled to under the laws of the governing bodies having jurisdiction over the site.

28

Organizational development: Building the best team

The first step in organizational development is to define the company's business and enumerate all of the functions carried on in it. It is important that functions rather than responsibilities be identified in this step. Identification of functions is objective, whereas identification of responsibility is more subjective and has emotional overtones.

COMMUNICATION PROBLEMS

It is often difficult for the top executive—the president or head of the board of directors to get a thorough understanding of the organization. Upward communications to this executive are often poor, incomplete, or inaccurate. Information provided is also subjective and otherwise invalid or not useful for the following reasons:

1. Because those from whom the executives receive information may be rivals for power and recognition, they may provide inaccurate information, perhaps intentionally.
2. Since no subordinate wishes his superior to think poorly of him, he often provides only that information which he supposes the superior wants to hear. He screens out information which may discredit him and build up information which gives him credit.
3. When valid information is provided to the top executive, he may not be able to assess it properly because it is inconsistent with his own outlook, personality traits, and convictions, and it may threaten his personal security.
4. Because subordinates want to impress the executive with their own importance within the organization, they build up contributions from their department and downgrade those from other departments. This can give a misleading picture of the actual operations.

Problems in communication may cause the top executive to err in the following ways:

1. He will not have a true picture of what is actually happening in the day-to-day operations of the business.
2. He will institute and perpetuate inappropriate policies and practices, based on his inaccurate picture of his business.
3. He will lose his perspective on conditions in the marketplace and the company's role in filling its true needs.
4. He will fail to institute and implement effective controls because he will not have a good understanding of the business he is attempting to control.

Resistance to change   Adding to the executive's communications problems is the tendency for established management and department personnel to want to maintain the status quo. The top executive can assist himself in the communications battle by recognizing such dangers, particularly his own tendency to see only what he wants to see within his organization. The executive must be aware of the inherent problems in both upward and downward communication in an organization, recognizing that most levels of supervision comprise communication barriers rather than communication centers. He should also recognize the inadequacy of most personnel appraisal programs.

Appraising human resources   The top executive must be able to evaluate personnel in order to match them up with the functions to be performed. There are two very basic strategies for evaluating personnel: One is to have personnel evaluate themselves, and another is to have the personnel evaluated by others. The most effective result will be realized when both strategies are utilized. The first strategy has the benefit of involving personnel in planning and decision making which affects their working relationships and their livelihood. The benefit of the second approach is that the objectivity and perspective it provides can curb the dangers associated with ingrown management.

It is important for an organization to have an accurate, timely knowledge of its personnel assets (as much as its financial assets). Three methods of appraising the human resources of a business are: supervisory or a management appraisals, employee polls, and interviews with natural leaders.

Natural leaders are those who in effect get the work done and influence subordinates regardless of formal lines of authority as shown on an organization chart. To understand the organization, the top executive must have an intimate knowledge of its informal organization: What are the principal channels of informal communication within the organization? What are the capabilities of current management? Who is promotable, and who is not? What specialty departments can be eliminated by giving broader authority to other departments?

PRIVATE AND PUBLIC CORPORATIONS

In real estate development and construction, privately owned companies represent more than 97 percent of the firms doing business and more than 85 percent of all sales. In manufacturing, privately owned companies represent more than 93 percent of firms but less than 33 percent of sales. In all industries private firms represent the vast majority of all those within a particular industry. For organizational development purposes, it is appropriate to distinguish between the objectives of private and the public firms (see Chapter 2).

In private industry, growth can be limited by the preference of management, whereas in a public corporation management does not have the authority to limit the growth of the enterprise. In the private company, management generally represents ownership, whereas in the public company ownership is represented by stockholders. Those engaged in management of public companies generally have a minimal share of ownership. Public corporations stress earnings growth; private corporations may have any number of objectives which the ownership places above earnings growth. For these reasons, the management decisions in private corporations tend to be more subjective than those in public corporations, which of necessity are more objective.

Differing objectives within firms will create large differences in organizational attitudes and structures. Continuity is presumed in public corporations, but private corporations may not desire or provide for it. The question of whether the company will have continuity after the retirement or death of the founder will have profound implications on its management structure. Private companies often do not have any management audit; that is, the manager-owner is reportable only to himself. Public corporations have management audits in that the president of the company reports to the board of directors, which represents the shareholders. In privately held companies, owner-managers generally do not have to justify their actions, but in public companies they must do so.

The need to justify actions to absentee owners creates a different type of decision process in public companies than may exist in the private areas. Private companies have strong ties to family ownership, and this frequently shows up in management. Management structure in such firms is directly affected by family ownership and politics.

Management staffing in the private corporation is a much more subjective process than in the public corporation. Shares of private firms cannot readily be traded, as can the shares of public firms. In fact, a minority interest in a private corporation may have little or no value. Private corporations generally are in business not to produce reportable earnings but to break even. Private corporations have no pressure to report compounded earnings growth to shareholders; whenever possible, they prefer to break even rather than to show large taxable gain. Creative accounting practices enable private companies to control taxable income in this manner.

Because private companies do not have to submit to review by outside owners, owner-managers are often secretive, guarding information from those outside the organization and often even from nonownership management within it. One of the problems of continuity facing the private organization is that the owner-manager does not want to disclose information, even to his supporting management. Without information, responsibility cannot be delegated, and the owner-manager builds himself into a position in which he is the only one who can run the business. When private management is ill informed, loyalty and tenure are the criteria for advancement, not competence. For these and other reasons, private business do not have the continuity on which those that are publicly owned can rely. The keys to the business are locked up in the owner's head. Such businesses have little market value once the owner dies, unless he has consciously planned for continuity in much the same manner as the public corporation.

Thus the structure of the privately owned company will generally be shaped around the traits and subjective attitudes of the owner-manager, who is his own judge and critic. Most private businesses which have survived past their founder's time have generally done so through sale to a conglomerate or professionally managed public company which has infused new life into the company and redirected its management for continuity. Often all that remains to recall the founder is the name of the company.

SMALL COMPANIES AND LARGE COMPANIES

It is characteristic of small companies to economize on management development and minimize the delegation of authority. The importance of management leadership is overlooked, because the owner is intimately identified with the operation and knows how to survive in small markets.

Planning is more difficult in small companies. The environment is so unstable that setting overall goals is difficult. Any planning that is done is often problem oriented rather than opportunity oriented (see Chapter 1).

The No. 1 problem of most small companies is sales rather than management of people. In large companies, this is often reversed. A project failure in a small company may mean company failure. Therefore, small companies are more comfortable with product evolution or borrowed innovation rather than total innovation (see Chapter 7).

Small companies require generalists who can handle numerous responsibilities and large amounts of detail. Large companies tend to utilize specialists with more narrowly defined job descriptions and responsibilities.

Small companies cannot cope with growth as well as large companies can. Because management is typically spread thin in small companies, those that do succeed in dramatic volume increases usually are strangled by their growth because they lose control. In small companies top management is often also first-line management. When top management has to remove itself from first-line management due to the demands of increased volume, deterioration in first-line operations may destroy the company before adequate controls and first-line and middle managers can be developed (see Chapter 20).

Small companies require a higher entrepreneurial input than larger companies do. A larger company with a well-established market and product can be run by a manager with an entrepreneurial outlook. Small companies not blessed with a well-established market and product require leadership from an entrepreneur with a management outlook.

Organizational objectives, policies, and procedures in a small company are shaped closer to the unique characteristics of key management than is the case in larger, more institutionalized companies. Since the management resource is more limited in smaller companies, organization, policies, and procedures need to be more closely fitted to the strengths and weaknesses of the key management people.

Smaller companies generally cannot make decisions as rationally as large companies can through ROI analysis or IRR comparisons (see Chapter 19). Subjective considerations, constraints, limited opportunities, and resources, and personal prejudice may have more bearing on the decision than objective analysis. Small companies are often forced to do what it appears necessary to do for survival at the moment. Large companies generally have more latitude to do whatever is necessary to accomplish long-term objectives and are not so constrained in decision making by immediate problems. They can direct the bulk of their top-management resources to work on opportunities, whereas most small companies devote them to working on problems.

DEVELOPMENT CYCLE OF A PRIVATE BUSINESS

There are five basic time spans in the development of a privately held business.

1. Initial organization and capitalization.
2. Struggle-and-strife period.
3. Survival-and-growth period.
4. Success: The payoff period.
5. Redirection—continuity, or obsolescence and disvesture.

Initial organization and capitalization

Most private businesses have been formed out of a need of the owner to provide a living for himself and his family. The founders of businesses, for the most part, initially lack both the capitalization and the management expertise required to run the business. This is one of the reasons why private businesses have generally not been able to perpetuate themselves.

The problem is in the very roots of the business, its initial organization and capitalization. When the business is organized, the founder utilizes whatever personnel he can muster to perform the required functions. The chief qualification is willingness to work long hours with little or no remuneration. Family or willing friends without the needed technical or management skills often are recruited to perform required functions. This works because initially the functions are very simple. The new-born business has a minimum of complexity.

When times get rough these employees or family members may contribute capital in addition to labor to the business, thus becoming equity contributers as well as labor contributors in the initial stages. The growth curve in this original stage is relatively slow, with maximum emphasis being put on staying alive and maximum energy going into brute labor rather than planning, organization, and development. Employees, friends, and family members who participate in the early growth stages of the business buy tenure for sweat. In later years, as the business develops, these are the people who have the tenure for management positions.

Struggle-and-strife period

The business survives not because of keen management and enlightened decisions but because of maximum energy input. At this point more decisions prove faulty than prove good, but the owner-manager is able to cut his losses early and maximize those decisions that have proved correct. What matters at this time is: Are the decisions right for the moment, even though they may prove wrong for the long run?

During this stage the owner-manager becomes more secretive and tends to set his own business personality. All other functions and activities in the business radiate out from him like spokes in a wheel; he is in the hub, giving information to some people and not to others. Some people know parts of the picture but nobody knows the whole.

During this period the owner-manager locks himself into a central position where the business is unique to his particular capabilities, knowledge, and characteristics. The business is not inherently a unique type of business; he has made it so. Owner-managers, in this phase of their business development, are too busy doing and working to have time to spend on management processes which appear at the time philosophical and textbook-theory substitutes for muscle and action.

If you have knowledge, let others light their candles by it.
Margaret Fuller

Survival-and-growth period

During the third period, business growth is advancing rapidly and survival for the present is assured. The owner-manager begins to look for help but often he is looking for the help that is most available, pliable, and inexpensive. He is still calling all the key shots, and his idea of help is for others to lend a hand with what he has already decided to do. The help that he does retain is often inadequate. These helpers, being pliable, do not rock the boat or get in the way of the owner-manager's ego. They assist him in remedying the effects of his problems without going to the source to remedy the problems themselves (see Chapter 22).

At this point the owner-manager assumes many of his problems are the necessary, inevitable problems of business which must be tackled each time they occur. He does not see them as needless conflicts which would have never occurred in the first place with good planning, organization, and control. He continues to reinvent the wheel each time.

Success: The payoff period

During the payoff period, the business reaches a plateau where the owner-manager is content with current success and income and wants to cut down on his working hours to enjoy some of the benefits of his labors. He also is more interested in the status quo than in growth, and he becomes reluctant to risk his retirement capital for future growth. He does not trust his managers to carry on the business of the company unless he himself overlooks every detail; he has not trained them to do so.

The owner-manager does not realize that his skills are becoming obsolescent in the much more complex and technological business environment in which he is currently engaged. He does not see the rewards of growth as sufficient to justify the risk of his capital, as it did in the good old days.

Redirection: Continuity or obsolescence

Following the payoff period there is a redirection of the business, because it cannot stay on a plateau indefinitely. A direction will soon develop, up or down. If the owner-manager has planned for continuity of his business and has trained management to take over responsibility, the redirection will be toward renewed growth, spurred on by new blood. If the owner-manager has not planned for continuity, the business will become obsolete and most likely disvesture will be the end result (see Chapter 7).

Public companies do not have these same cycles, because they do not experience the same obstacles to continuity. They are capitalized and organized in a different fashion. Though private companies constitute the vast majority of construction and development companies, we will emphasize organizational development principles as they apply to public companies. The reason is that the more successful private companies plan for continuity, and thus they utilize the same management and organizational principles public companies do.

It is important that managers be aware of the inherent differences between private and public companies. These differences will effect the manner in which organizational and management practices are implemented. The development cycle outlined for the private company can be experienced to some degree in a public company, particularly those with close owner management control or those that do not receive an objective management audit from their boards of directors.

ENTRE-PRENEURIAL ILLUSIONS

As an entrepreneur and his business prosper, he usually begins to foster illusions about himself, his business, and how his business got where it did. Because the entrepreneur is very often a loner, is not subject to management audit, and does not have to sell his ideas to absentee owners, he is apt to become insular in his thinking and to suffer from tunnel vision, allusions, and rationalizations. The work and management practices which enable the entrepreneur to succeed often become constraints once the business has reached a successful plateau (see Chapter 12).

The entrepreneur fights off any idea which might suggest that the type of individual required to build a company is not necessarily the same type required to run the company best. The entrepreneur often sees himself as both a corporate builder and an operations and management man—in essence, a renaissance man. The corporation is his life; he has built it from scratch and is hesitant to turn over the reins to anyone else. To convince himself of his invincibility and indispensability to the company, he develops a number of illusions.

A fool flatters himself, the wise man flatters the fool.
Bulwer

Illusion 1: My business is unique

The entrepreneur sees his business as unique and requiring the skills, talents, and experience that only he can provide. He cannot visualize managers within his organization or outside it being able to take over the reins. It is no illusion that the business is unique: the entrepreneur has made it so. The illusion arises in identifying the reason why the business is unique.

The business is unique because it has been developed around the unique capabilities of a single individual rather than an organization. There has been a deficiency in management from the top. The entrepreneur has been so busy building and doing things that he has failed to plan, organize, staff, direct, and control. He has not provided for continuity by training management to run the various aspects of the business (see Chapter 25).

In an effective management process, the business would be staffed to operate successfully once the founding genius has departed. The entrepreneur is indispensable, not because of his genius but because of his failure to plan for continuity.

Illusion 2: It's my money; I'll do what I want

The entrepreneur has the illusion that he has done everything himself and he alone is responsible for his success. However, this generally is not the case. He has been often assisted with the financial support and energies of family, friends, and business associates who have a financial and personal interest in the business. His business associates and managers want to see the business grow and prosper. Investors, family, and friends also want to see the business prosper.

A conflict develops in the later stages of the entrepreneur's career, when he wants to coast on past achievements and in effect slowly liquidate the business by holding the purse strings and refusing to reinvest for continued growth. More than the entrepreneur's interests are at stake here. The entrepreneur has an obligation to those who stood by him during the period of struggle and strife.

Distrust, unrest, and fear will develop in the organization when the entrepreneur does not make provisions for continuity. Bright, aggressive managers will not be attracted to the business, and current managers will lose incentive and initiative after finding their ideas turned down time and again by the top executive. The entrepreneur who wants to slowly milk the business, while keeping it going to give him something to do up to and through retirement, may be rudely alerted to the fact that the business is not entirely his to do with as he pleases.

When planning and enthusiasm for growth stop, businesses do not generally coast for long before they come to a stop. When a business reaches the point of liquidation, the entrepreneur may find that his money and his business are worth very little, robbed of the vitality which propelled it to success. A business, like an airplane, cannot cut off its engines and coast in midflight for long. Both must either keep up speed and momentum, or descend.

Illusion 3: No one else can make my decisions because no one else has my experience

Success can leave the entrepreneur with the illusion that he is doing everything right. He is slow to give up the tried and proven for innovative or untested methods. He sees his many years of success as qualifying him to do things however he wants. His track record, he points out, verifies that his methods are the correct methods. What he often fails to realize is that, while he has been busy building his business, the world has changed dramatically, and his methods may no longer be appropriate. He maintains the illusion that he is doing things right, but in reality he may be doing things the only way he knows how.

> *If a little knowledge is dangerous, where is the man who has so much as to be out of danger?*
>
> Thomas Henry Huxley

As the business has grown, the world has changed. The environment has become much more complex, as technology has grown at an exponential rate over time. Competence must be measured in terms of both time and complexity. The entrepreneur's tenure of time in running his business is not an adequate measure of his competence in managing it in the present environment. As complexity increases, past experience becomes less relevant.

The present worth of past experience can be measured by using the same reasoning as in present-value theory (see Chapter 19). According to present-value theory, the further off a cash flow return is in the future, the less valuable it is at present. The reciprocal of this applied to experience would be that the older the experience is in years from the present date, the less is its present value.

All people become less flexible in time and at a certain time will strive to maintain status quo rather than to innovate and change the order of things. The entrepreneur who has let his innovative spirit burn out or dwindle may be repeating the experience of his earlier years in business over and over again, using the same methods at present as were used in the initial building of the company. Using the reciprocal of present-value theory, these methods would have little present value in assuring the continuance of the company.

It is usual to associate age with years only because so many man and women somewhere along in what is called middle age stop trying.

Henry Ford

Age will not be defined.

Francis Bacon

PIERCING ILLUSIONS WITH MANAGEMENT AUDIT

There comes a time in the life span of a private business when the owner-manager assumes his position of leadership on the basis of power and not current merit. This is a dangerous time for the business, a time when the entrepreneur most needs a management audit and a plan for continuity. The entrepreneur who does not open his company up to such an audit and who does not plan for continuity is like the fisherman who eats his bait. He will be full today, but his fishing career will be over.

The entrepreneur needs a management audit and advisors to keep him abreast of the world as it is today. The owner-manager who has arrived at a plateau tends to view the "good old days" as being the norm and the currently bewildering period of technology, complexity, and rapid change as a phase of his business that he hopes will subside so that conditions can return to the "norm." He needs the perspective of others, possibly younger men and women, to expand his vision. He must see that today's environment will be viewed as the "good old days" of tomorrow.

Accelerating complexity requires a venturesome, continuing adaptability. The entrepreneur must heed the advice and counsel of others and undertake the management role of keeping ahead of obsolescence. Technology is developing at a rapid rate in all industries; the education the average scientist receives in college is obsolete within a decade after graduation. A management audit will break down the insular tunnel vision which inevitably develops when an attempt is made to manage today's technology with yesterday's experience and tools.

Fools need advice most, but wise men only are the better for it.

Benjamin Franklin

The business arrives at a plateau because the owner-manager has reduced his options, through default in instituting an effective management process to plan for tomorrow with today's technologies. The management audit brings accountability to the owner-manager's decisions, replacing rationalization with objectivity. This is necessary if the business is to regenerate itself to begin a new business development cycle. A management audit, therefore, is essential for continuity.

Management audits can be implemented in several ways. One is by setting up an outside board of directors; another is by delegation of responsibilities within the organization. In the latter managers are given a free hand to set policy, plan, and organize, and an open forum is created in which policies are reviewed throughout the company and communication travels up and down the hierarchy, rather than just descending from above.

The entrepreneur should pick a successor with whom he will share all management problems and concerns. He should allow the successor to benefit from his expertise and judgment and train her or him to take over the reins.

The entrepreneur should also set up a council of advisors consisting of consultants and professional people with whom he deals in his business. It could include the company's attorney, accountant, banker, insurance man, broker, architect, contractor, marketing consultant, and other special experts as required.

The best possible people should be selected for the council of advisors, and their cumulative expertise should be applied in working out problems. The most benefits can be derived by bringing them together to solve problems, so that all can benefit from the aggregate experience of the group. With their cumulative experience, they can surround the problem and between them come up with solutions that would not have been possible had each person been working independently.

Entrepreneurial illusions are pierced by analyzing and formalizing the business operation to reflect the business, not as it existed in its formative stages but as it exists today and as it must become tomorrow to compete in the business environment. The process of analysis and formalization includes the development of an up-to-date organization chart and an informative accounting system designed as a management information tool rather than an elaborate manipulation to avoid taxes (see Chapter 20). Its components are an exacting identification of the total business process, a segmentation of its operations, a definition of relationships, position descriptions, and the establishment of position qualifications to ensure the proper staffing, training, and development of people. This can be a very enlightening process and also quite traumatic, when tenure is evaluated against merit.

Management audit requires the development of a reporting system, performance standards, and means of measurement to identify achievement, reward accomplishment, and discipline ineffectiveness. Such a control procedure, objectively and formally established within the business, provides criteria for measuring plans and people and providing corrective action when circumstances deviate from projected goals. Formalized controls provide an excellent management audit (see Chapter 21).

He who is always his own counsellor will often have a fool for his client.
Hunter

THE ORGANIZATIONAL DEVELOPMENT PROCESS

The organizational development process requires a reevaluation of the organization's objectives and strategies to make them reflect organizational capabilities and constraints, more accurately. The goal of organizational development is to increase the organization's effectiveness in accomplishing stated objectives. The organizational development process is generally implemented with the use of tools such as the organization chart and includes the definition of functions to be performed, positions, relationships, qualifications, performance standards, and measurements.

Organizational development requires both a systems approach and a behavioral approach: the systems approach because of the complex interrelationships of ideas and things, and the behavioral approach because objectives must be accomplished through people. Organizational development is a continuing process and not a one-time activity which occurs only during the initial formation of an organization. It enables an organization to respond to change and to provide continuous balance between the people and technology resources associated with accomplishment of its objectives.

Most literature on organizational development shows management what needs to be done to improve operations but stops short of implementing the organizational development process. In addition to direction, managers need effective tools for accomplishing the desired results. Knowing the direction is one thing; having the resources and capabilities to get there is quite another.

Managers need more than an organization chart and a list of position descriptions to carry out effective organizational development. The organization chart shows the basic divisions of work in an organization and the reporting structure, but it does not show the detailed functions and responsibility relationships which indicate how the organization actually works. These tools tend to isolate functions and management positions so that they appear to have total independence from other functions and positions, thus suggesting unilateral rather than cooperative action. They are often developed by managers at the highest levels and conveyed downward to lower levels of management. The process generally encourages independent action rather than group participation.

Without group participation and feedback, management will not know what behavioral problems are going to develop out of the management structure and may experience some rude surprises. Unless there is involvement of the work group which is to perform within the organizational structure, it is difficult to interrelate functions to achieve optimum effectiveness. The systems and behavioral approaches prevent the organizational development process from being a chance activity with a high probability of bringing about conflict and disorder.

What is the best government? That which teaches us to govern ourselves.
Johann Wolfgang Goethe

When the work group is involved and behavioral and systems approaches are utilized, operating management can solve its own problems internally. A systems-behavioral format is required for effective implementation of the organizational development process. The format should allow for group participation, reflect how the organization actually works as opposed to how it theoretically works, and recognize the need to interface functions with organizational and human relationships.

The systems approach recognizes that nothing in an organization exists as an independent entity. Everything is part of a whole, and a change in one element will produce changes in the whole and in other elements which comprise it. The systems-behavioral format is required to interrelate objectives, the organization, functions, positions, and responsibility relationships to one another for optimum accomplishment of objectives within operational and resource constraints. The organizational and control matrix is a format for management to use in managing the organizational development process.

THE ORGANIZATIONAL AND CONTROL MATRIX

An organizational and control matrix is a systematic approach to organizational development which considers behavioral attributes. It is a tool for management audit which helps management solve its problems, fills the requirements for the format specified above by fostering group participation, providing a mechanism for working out conflicts, identifying functions and objectives, establishing relationships and organizational configurations, and improving communication and interpersonal and intergroup relationships. It also facilitates the development of an organizational chart which reflects the actual effective relationships among specialists, departments, or divisions of the organization. It improves the ability of the organization to respond to change effectively and enhances management's understanding of the total picture and ability to see panoramas rather than independent close-up shots. It eliminates duplication of effort, overlapping responsibility, or responsibility gaps, and it sets performance and control standards.

How the organizational and control matrix works

The Organizational and Control Matrix included as Exhibit 28–1 in this chapter is a sample matrix form with work functions already filled in. The functions are those required for the development of a for-sale housing project; the matrix is project oriented and not specifically oriented to the administration of the business itself. Similar charts can be drawn up for the administration of the business, as opposed to project administration.

The chart is function rather than objective oriented because it deals with specific functions of implementation rather than broader based objectives related to the business in general. Though the functions have already been filled in the sample matrix, the identification of functions will be included in the methodology. The manner in which the matrix is used is as important to its success as is the utility of the tool itself.

Correct sequential implementation: A prerequisite for success

In building an organization, as in building any structure, the correct sequential implementation is a prerequisite for success. There are five basic steps in developing an organizational and control matrix.

Step 1: Identifying major work areas. In the first step, the total activity is broken down into basic work groups or classifications such as legal and financial, general and project administration, executive committee approvals, marketing, planning and design, and so on. The functions are identified by the people within each work group; for example, the people in the marketing department are requested to identify all of the marketing functions. Major functions are first identified, and then minor functions required in the implementation of each major function are grouped below. The functions are listed in a sequential order as they occur in the work process.

As noted above, the functions have been filled in in Exhibit 28–1. The major work areas or functions have been identified at the top of the forms as legal and financial, governmental interface approvals, engineering, and so on, and the subfunctions for each of the major functions have been listed down the left-hand side.

Objectivity is required in this first phase, and for this reason there is no attempt to identify relationships or positions. Positions and relationships can become very emotional issues, which would cloud the objectivity required for the functional analysis.

Step 2: Identifying positions. The second step in working with the matrix is identifying the positions. When an audit is made of an existing management organization, the positions will already be in existence and staffed. In setting up a new organization or reorganizing an existing operation, it will be necessary to establish new position descriptions.

Since development organizations usually work with a small nucleus of versatile managers and employees, they may round out their personnel requirements with outside consultants and service organizations. When these outside sources are regularly relied upon to perform functions for the organization, they should be included in the organizational structure because they form an integral part of the organizational structure on a separate contract basis.

All positions, whether filled by employees or by contracted-for service and consulting organizations, are listed on a positions schedule. The title of the position and the name of the person or contractor filling the position are listed.

Step 3: Developing responsibility relationships and resolving conflicts. In the third step, responsibility relationships are solicited. Each individual filling a position that might have a responsibility relationship to the functions within a work group is given a matrix sheet containing all of the functions for his particular work group, and is asked to identify that position's relationship to the function. The five relationships shown in Exhibit 28-1 are: operating responsibility, specific responsibility, must be consulted, must be notified, must approve. If an individual indicates that his responsibility or relationship should be an operating responsibility for a particular function, he is asked to indicate what he feels should be the responsibility of all the other individuals who he thinks are related to that particular function. Additionally, in this step he is asked to review the wording of each function and to modify it as he sees fit.

The matrix forms are collected from all individuals and the results are recorded in a master copy for each group. After reviewing the master copy for each group to identify overlaps and conflicts, a determination must be made as to how to resolve the conflicts.

At this stage, the individuals involved have taken a position, and a knowledge of the individuals involved is necessary to determine how to reconcile conflicting positions and points of view. Two basic approaches are to work the conflicts out within the group, or to work conflicts out on an individual basis. In all probability, the resolution of conflicts will involve both approaches to some degree.

The same approach used to resolve conflicts arising between individuals in a group can be used in resolving conflicts between groups. Individuals within one group review the matrix forms of another group and indicate what they feel their relationships should be to the functions within the other group.

Step 4: Solidifying functions and relationships. In the fourth step the functions and relationships are solidified. Once the conflicts have been resolved as best they can be, the functions and relationships are established and recorded. The organization chart should then be updated to reflect changes which may have come about as a result of the management audit. In this manner the organization chart will reflect how the organization actually works as opposed to how it theoretically functions.

Step 5: Solidifying performance standards and updating position descriptions. In the fifth step, performance standards are solicited, in the same manner as relationships were solicited, from those individuals who have a position relationship with the function. The performance standards consist of time standards and quality standards. Time standards are used for scheduling purposes, and quality standards are used to set the objectives which are recorded in the position descriptions. The individuals who have position relationships to a function are then asked to specify their own performance standards. The performance standards are discussed, conflicts resolved, and the standards are coordinated and finalized.

Position descriptions are then updated, as necessary, to reflect objectives and measurement standards for the individual positions. The individuals within each position are thus motivated to perform according to the objectives and measurement standards which they were instrumental in establishing. The time scheduling of performance measurements are incorporated into the project schedule (see Chapter 29).

Advantages of the matrix   The organizational and control matrix format enables an organization to apply its time, energies, and resources to effective planning, organization, direction, and control of its business, instead of fire fighting and working on symptoms rather than causes. Though the approach appears to be time-consuming, it actually saves time, energy, and resources, because the introduction of a better order of things is more productive than vast amounts of brute labor.

The greater the volume a developer has, the greater is his need for the type of organizational development process reviewed above. The developer who builds a project at a time and has a very small staff can keep most of the organizational development format in his head. The developer who has continuity of the organization as an objective, however, should use the process.

The scale and objectives of the organization and its financial restraints will determine the amount of control suitable. The level of control best for a specific organization may vary from maximum to minimum formalized control. Some organizations will desire and need formalized control for all functions; others will need it only for their major functions.

Control of all functions can be said to be 100 percent control. It is valuable to have software available for 100 percent control, even though economics may allow control of only major elements. The 100 percent control format not only provides a model for the better administration of major-element control, it allows the executive to read between the control points, spot deviations, and correct them before data on the major elements indicate the necessity. The 100 percent control format also serves as a valuable tool for training and developing personnel by allowing a panoramic view of the entire process, even though only the major elements will be controlled in a formalized procedure.

Exhibit 28-1
Organizational and Control Matrix

Page No. ___ Of ___	Ref.: Date: Approval: *Organizational and Control Matrix*	Legal and Financial Functions	*Operating responsibility*	*Specific responsibility*	*Must be consulted*	*Must be notified*	*Must approve*
	Prepare site purchase offer Open escrow Order preliminary title report Analyze and prepare financial feasibility Evaluate financial sources						
	Review cost estimates, budgets Prepare financial and legal budget Prepare cash flow Arrange seed capital Gather financial package input						
	Finalize and submit financial package File fees as required Review and update marketing and cash flow Select financial partner Prepare partnership papers						
	File and record partnership papers Obtain partner liability insurance Obtain and record land and development loan Pay plan check fees Obtain construction insurance						
	Obtain bonds Review and approve sales prices Obtain model loan Obtain construction loan, record Obtain takeout loan Close escrow Monitor cash flow						

28 / Organizational development: Building the best team

Exhibit 28–1 (*continued*)

Page No. ____ Of ____	Ref.: Date: Approval: *Organizational and Control Matrix*	General and Project Administration	Operating responsibility	Specific responsibility	Must be consulted	Must be notified	Must approve
	Retain marketing expertise Retain civil engineer Review market studies Review engineers studies Review title report						
	Prepare developmental feasibility Retain soil and geological engineer Review engineers' reports Retain land planner–architect Prepare development concept						
	Review and approve preliminary designs Select standard plans for reuse Approve specs and features Prepare input for financial package Receive, approve, and submit environmental impact report						
	Receive preliminary cost estimate Receive marketing budgets Review tentative map Prepare development budget Prepare detailed development concept						
	Review, update cost estimate Obtain off-site easements and agreements Submit engineering plans for plan check Review and approve designs prior to working drawings Review and approve all updated budgets.						
	Submit working drawings for plan check Monitor schedules and budgets						

Exhibit 28-1 (*continued*)

Page No. ____ Of ____	Ref.: Date: Approval: Executive Committee Approvals	Operating responsibility	Specific responsibility	Must be consulted	Must be notified	Must approve
	Organizational and Control Matrix					
	Approve land purchase Approve terms Approve feasibility Approve concept and cost estimate Approve tentative map					
	Approve preliminary drawing Approve spec and features list Approve finalized concept and estimates Review and finalize marketing concept Update sales prices					
	Go or no-go development decision Approve design features prior to working drawings Approve partnership, financing Go or no-go grading decision Close escrow					

Exhibit 28-1 (*continued*)

Page No. ___ Of ___	Ref.: Date: Approval:	Marketing					
	Organizational and Control Matrix		*Operating responsibility*	*Specific responsibility*	*Must be consulted*	*Must be notified*	*Must approve*
	Perform market studies Establish objectives Identify market opportunity Establish developmental concept Product recommendations						
	Establish features criteria Establish price range Obtain approvals Prepare marketing budget Prepare monthly site budget						
	Prepare model and sales office budget Select model site Select advertising expertise Review ad campaign layouts Review ad campaign						
	Obtain display proposals Select model elevations Update market report Obtain decorator proposals, let contract Approve decorator designs						
	Develop brochure Select renderer Prepare renderings, site plan, elevations Select sales agent, force Train sales force						
	Approve sales office design Order sales office furnishing						

Exhibit 28-1 (*continued*)

Page No. ____ Of ____	Ref.: Date: Approval: Marketing (Continued) Organizational and Control Matrix	Operating responsibility	Specific responsibility	Must be consulted	Must be notified	Must approve
	Order sales trailer Construct sales displays Finalize marketing, site, and sales office budgets Determine lot premiums Finalize brochures Obtain approvals Review landscape design Landscape approval Prepare sales bulletins Order model-area and trailer furniture Order on-site signs Erect on-site signs Set up and furnish sales trailer Printed materials delivered to sales trailer Order printed materials for sales office Develop bootleg sign program Erect off-site signs Prepare grand opening ads Prepare special promotions Obtain printed materials for sales office Install sales office displays Install sales offce and model decorating Inspect models with decorator Set up and train color selection coordinator Select and train customer relations representative Clean up VIP party, grand opening					

Exhibit 28-1 (*continued*)

Page No. ___ Of ___	Ref.: Date: Approval: Planning and Design *Organizational and Control Matrix*	*Operating responsibility*	*Specific responsibility*	*Must be consulted*	*Must be notified*	*Must approve*
	Formulate criteria Coordinate with engineering on land plan Prepare preliminary land use, get approval Prepare preliminary floor plans, approval Prepare landscape schematics, approval Prepare land plan, approval Prepare preliminary elevations, approval Prepare architectural loan package input Layout model compound, approval Design sales office, approval Design recreation center, approval Prepare preliminary landscape drawings Design model landscaping Prepare model working drawings Prepare recreation center working drawings Prepare unit working drawings Revise working drawings as per feedback Prepare overall landscape drawings Obtain exterior colors					

Exhibit 28-1 (*continued*)

Page No. ___ Of ___	Ref.: Date: Approval: Governmental Interface Approvals					
	Organizational and Control Matrix	*Operating responsibility*	*Specific responsibility*	*Must be consulted*	*Must be notified*	*Must approve*
	Governmental schedule review Obtain city and county requirements Zoning and EIR prefiling interview File zone change Submit EIR report					
	Submit tentative map Tentative map review 1st planning commission meeting, agenda lead time 1st subdivision committee meeting 2d planning commission hearing, obtain zoning recommendation					
	Obtain tentative map approval, agenda lead time 1st zoning hearing, agenda lead time 2d zoning hearing Obtain building permit for models, plan check time Zoning effective at end of appeal period					
	Submit for preliminary public report Obtain preliminary public report Obtain approval of final map, agenda lead time Record final map Obtain building permit, plan check time					
	Process white report Receive white report					

Exhibit 28-1 (*continued*)

Page No. ___ Of ___	Ref.: Date: Approval: Engineering *Organizational and Control Matrix*	*Operating responsibility*	*Specific responsibility*	*Must be consulted*	*Must be notified*	*Must approve*
	Obtain city and county requirements Prepare engineering feasibility Review title reports Coordinate with planning and design on land plan Prepare soils report					
	Prepare geology report Prepare civil engineer's report Request for amendments to title report Prepare engineering budget Submit reports and budget for approval					
	Prepare boundary and easement survey Prepare topo. Prefiling interview Prepare tentative map Prepare EIR, obtain approval					
	Approve title report Revise engineering budget Prepare plot plan Prepare final tract map, submit Design final rough-grading plan					
	Design final grade plan, submit Make corrections to final tract map Design street plan, submit Prepare quantity takeoffs Design storm, sewer, and water plans, submit					
	Coordinate with utility company drawings Receive utility company drawings Make corrections to final tract map Make corrections to engineering drawings Obtain approvals on engineering drawings					

Exhibit 28-1 (*concluded*)

Page No. ___ Of ___	Ref.: Date: Approval: Operations *Organizational and Control Matrix*	*Operating responsibility*	*Specific responsibility*	*Must be consulted*	*Must be notified*	*Must approve*
	Prepare preliminary cost estimates Update cost estimates Update cost estimate for land and development loan Bid improvement plans Develop improvement costs					
	Prepare construction loan estimate Bid construction Develop construction costs Award improvement contracts Break ground					
	Award model contracts Award construction contracts Install utilities Construct models Construct recreation facilities, sales office					
	Install model and recreation landscaping Begin production housing Construct streets					

29

Scheduling for profit improvement

Some developers think they do not need a schedule to run their business because they have it all in their head. They say scheduling would be a waste of time, but the real reason is generally that they do not know enough about their business to schedule the work. They have never taken the time to identify and classify all the functions involved in the development or construction process and cannot schedule functions because they are not sure what they are. For each project they must rediscover the necessary functions as they go, and often their action is reaction to a crisis, a signal that a function must be performed right away. These developers work from crisis to crisis rather than by plan. Because they are controlled by the work rather than controllers of the work, they are not managers (see Chapter 28).

Thinking is the hardest work there is, which is the probable reason why so few engage in it.

Henry Ford

EFFECTIVENESS OF IMPLEMENTATION DETERMINES THE VALUE OF PLANS

The value of any plan, including objectives and strategies, no matter how brilliantly conceived, is ultimately measured by the effectiveness of its implementation. Since effective implementation requires a system of review, measurement, analysis, and timely corrective action, scheduling and controls must be an integral part of the plan. The plan and its controls are both part of a continuous management process and are inseparable in practice. To expect a plan to be executed without proper schedules and controls is to trust to chance, and chance implementation is certain to stray from objectives.

When an adequate control procedure is built as part of the plan, the execution of the plan can be consistently measured in terms of its effectiveness in achieving objectives. The orderly and consistent feedback provided by an organized control procedure improves the day-to-day implementation of the plan by management and allows for timely corrective action when results fail to achieve objectives.

If objectives are stated precisely and are properly qualified, it is easier to work them into a control program. They should have beginning and ending points so that in-process progress evaluations can be made, and control is greatly simplified if objectives are stated as step-by-step specifics. Since the control program largely determines the outcome of an objective or strategy, it is an important criterion for success of the plan. *To evaluate the feasibility and practicality of a plan, management must also evaluate its control program (see Chapter 20).*

Merely to plan and schedule activities does not guarantee results, however, the schedule does no work but is a tool to be used by people, and as such it has a limited function. The schedule proposed for the plan must become a method of management, involving controls and performance measurements to equate performance with objectives. The schedule must in turn propose corrective action, because all plans will stray at times or be confronted with unanticipated obstacles. The corrective action must be farsighted enough to allow sufficient time to change course before collision.

Corrective action, therefore, requires a procedure whereby management can review progress in a timely manner and make decisions to improve performance. Progress reports that merely give management a postaudit type of review but do not allow management time to act to improve performance serve a limited function. Scheduling is 30 percent planning and 70 percent control.

Schedules must be understood by all involved, which requires personal communication by management. It must be clear to all that the schedule is not an idealized situation that management would "like" to achieve but a reasonable expectation of what "must" be accomplished.

Scheduling is one of the most important tools the builder utilizes to achieve orderly development and rapid-paced construction. However, it is the team that produces the results, not the schedule. The schedule merely documents the capabilities of the organization, the subcontractors, and the expectations of management (see Chapter 25).

THE OVERALL PROJECT SCHEDULE

The listing of project functions included in the Organizational and Control Matrix (Exhibit 28–1 in Chapter 28) provides the basis for an overall project schedule. The control matrix includes the major functions to be accomplished in the for-sale housing development process and lists them in a generalized chronological order. It is these functions that the overall project schedule (see Exhibit 29–1) is intended to control.

A critical-path type of format is suited to the overall project schedule because it makes work-flow interfaces readily observable in the graphic presentation of the critical-path flow. But while critical-path scheduling is a productive tool at the overall project management level, it is less effective for residential field construction. Many field personnel and subcontractors cannot readily understand critical-path charts, and their value as a management tool in the field is reduced. Bar-type charts based on critical-path methodology provide a better management tool for field personnel.

The project schedule serves as an overall master schedule for the entire project and merges the various backup schedules. The backup schedules are summarized in the project schedule to one degree or another. The construction schedule, for example, is summarized a great deal before inclusion in the project schedule. Other backup schedules may include an architectural and engineering schedule, a public hearing and zoning schedule, a marketing schedule, and an absorption schedule.

Developers who build a project at a time may be able to keep the schedule of project-related functions in their heads. However, those who are involved in a number of projects simultaneously must utilize a project-related schedule to exercise control. Even the small builder will benefit by having the total project functions organized into a schedule format. Even though the format may not be formally programmed for a specific project, it will nonetheless serve as a mental model for the developer.

THE CONSTRUCTION SCHEDULE

It is recommended that three schedules be utilized for the construction of an apartment complex: (1) site-work schedule (Exhibit 29–3), (2) rough-work schedule (Exhibit 29–4), and (3) finish-work schedule (Exhibit 29–5). The three schedules have the same format. In the exhibit, the construction functions are listed down the left margin of the schedule, and the construction work days are listed across the top. Exhibit 29–2, a hypothetical Project Plan, identifies the parts of the project referred to by letters in Exhibits 29–4 and 29–5.

Construction work days are not calendar days. A construction work day is a day in which construction crews work on the job. Holidays and weekends are not counted as work days, even though certain subcontractors may have men working on those days. Days when the job is shut down due to weather conditions or strikes also are not considered work days.

Calendar days are marked in above the work day each day to identify work days with calendar days. The reason for using the work day rather than the calendar day is that the schedule does not have to be revised for slippages due to weather and strikes requiring less administration time in maintaining the schedule.

Developing and implementing the construction schedule

If construction schedules are to work, they must be very detailed in terms of work function to be performed, where work is to take place, and at what time. Percentage completion figures that do not adequately document a specific work function, location, and time do not establish adequate accountability. The steps in developing a construction schedule are as follows:

Step 1. Identifying construction functions. Identify the construction functions, including required inspections, which must be performed. Not every construction function need be listed, but a substantial number of the functions do need to be identified and controlled, in order to effectively control construction progress on a daily basis. Once the construction functions for a typical apartment complex have been identified, they will be much the same for all other apartment projects of the same basic type. Help from field personnel and subcontractors should be solicited, as they are the ones closest to the operation.

Step 2. Separating functions into work groups. Separate the construction functions into three basic work groups: site work, rough work, and finish work. Once functions for the three work groups are identified, they should be listed in sequential order on the left-hand margin of their separate schedule sheets. Field personnel and subcontractors should be brought into the process to assure that the sequencing accurately reflects actual field conditions. They review, modify, and approve the final sequencing of work functions for the three work groups.

Step 3. Establishing a sequence of operations. For a garden apartment complex comprised of numerous buildings, select the first building to begin work on and each subsequent building in the construction sequence. Building sequencing will require consultation with other work groups, including marketing, property management, and construction trades. Considerations in building sequencing include:

1. Which buildings marketing and property management want to make available first (see Chapter 31).
2. Which buildings are important from a curb appeal and marketing standpoint. Will constructing these buildings first reduce fill-up costs?
3. What constraints on-site and off-site utilities distribution and availability could place on building sequencing.
4. How building sequencing will affect access of building trades to the work area. Costs will increase if sequencing creates access problems. Buildings which will interfere with access to other buildings in progress should not be constructed first.
5. Location and convenience of stockpiling and marshalling areas, to avoid logistics problems.
6. Weather considerations. Some buildings may be more difficult to reach in inclement weather than others. If they could be constructed while weather conditions are good, downtime could be reduced.
7. Sequencing of buildings should be in close proximity to one another, to aid supervision and reduce travel time of trades between buildings.
8. Sequencing identical or similar buildings together to allow trades time-saving benefits in layout and coordination.
9. Landscaping and amenities. If the buildings fronting on the main amenity area are completed first, the landscaping and amenities can go in earlier, and this will benefit absorption.

10. Marketing and property management's wishes for a good cross section of the unit mix to be completed early must be considered in both land planning and scheduling.

Step. 4. Establishing time constraints. Establish time constraints to the construction scheduling. These constraints include material and equipment availability, capacity and quality of subcontractors, weather conditions, complexity of design, difficulty of terrain, management ability of builder, quality of drawings and specifications, effectiveness of superintendent, and ability to meet cash flow and pay bills in a timely manner.

Generally there are one or two lead subcontractors whose volume capability constitutes the primary construction time constraint. In California, for example, the pace is set by the framing contractor, because framing constitutes the most labor-intensive trade. Whatever schedule the framing subcontractor can accomplish, the other trades can generally meet. The other trades must keep up with the framer and man their crews accordingly. Because so many apartments are in process at one time, there are few problems of trades interfering with one another within the same work area.

Step 5. Scheduling individual work functions. Having determined the overall construction pace, schedule each work function to accomplish the completion goal. The more important trades are consulted in setting up the schedule to work out time requirements and resolve conflicts. All trades are required to meet the pace of the constraining trade. In Exhibit 29-4, the framer is required to complete an average of 12 units per day for each work function listed. The blocks of apartment units to be completed per day are assigned for each work function in the construction schedule. For example, if building A consists of 20 units, the work function "frame second floor" would be assigned two days for building A because it is a rough-in work function scheduled to progress at approximately 12 units per day.

CONSTRUCTION SCHEDULING: A TEAM EFFORT

Construction management, field superintendents, and principal subcontractors should all be involved with the preliminary schedule. The tentative schedule is then further reviewed with the subcontractors to work out the best compromise for all concerned. The key is that the schedule is worked out with the subs from its very inception. Coordination difficulties that subs may have experienced on previous jobs are brainstormed and scheduled out.

The subcontractors, having thus agreed that they can perform under the terms of the construction schedule, should sign a contract by which they agree to perform under the construction schedule or pay liquidated damages or backcharges. Liquidated damages should be negotiated for each subcontractor depending on the amount of the subcontract and the subcontract's effect on the overall construction schedule. A $450 per day liquidated-damages agreement is sufficient for most subs.

A SCHEDULE IS NO BETTER THAN ITS FOLLOW-THROUGH

The construction schedule should be updated daily by the superintendent on the job, who calls in his report to construction management. At the end of each workday construction management is then aware of who is performing well under the contract and who is not. If a subcontractor is not performing according to his contract and normal communication has not remedied the problem, a telegram sent to the subcontractor informing him he is in breach of contract can be effective. Between the day-to-day monitoring of the schedule and weekly coordination meetings, a tight control can be exercised on all construction programs.

A reporting system that merely fulfills the function of a postaudit lets management know how much trouble it is in and does little in achieving productivity goals. Finding out a week later that a schedule is behind is like closing the gate after the horse has bolted. Days lost cannot usually be regained; schedule days must be accounted for one at a time.

Go, sir, gallop, and don't forget that the world was made in six days. You can ask me for anything you like, except time.

Napoleon Bonaparte

When a subcontractor is behind schedule in his work, he should be presented with, or requested to submit, a program of how he will bring his work back on schedule. Should he not be able to develop a satisfactory program, alternatives are available, such as the following:

1. Liquidated damages may be charged to the subcontractor to give him additional encouragement to perform according to his contract.
2. The builder may assume the work of the subcontractor, have it done by others, and bill the costs back to the subcontractor.
3. Should all of these procedures fail, the subcontractor is replaced. The builder must have a backup sub to pull in, just the way a producer must have stand-ins for the performers in a dramatic production company.

Four and one half work days represent a work week for the schedule. At the top of the schedule each work week is given an identifying color. When a day's work function is completed, the schedule is updated by filling in the square with the color of the work week in which the day's work function was completed. Thus it can be seen at a glance whether a work function has been completed ahead of schedule, on schedule, or behind schedule. If the work function was behind schedule one week, when it is completed the box is colored in with the color of the work week previous to the current work week. If on schedule, the box is colored in with the color of the current work week. If ahead of schedule one week, the box is filled in with the color of the work week ahead of the current week.

Schedules must be included in the contract (see Chapter 27) and enforced with liquidated damages. Construction management must anticipate, keep in front of the schedule, and respond immediately with corrective action as problems arise. Procrastination alerts subs that management is not really serious about performance requirements.

Maintaining a tough schedule requires cooperation from all parties. Earning this cooperation calls for a fair and equitable attitude on the part of management. All take and no give destroys team effort. Management too, must go the extra mile.

THE SCHEDULE AS A MANAGEMENT TOOL, NOT A CLUB

In anticipating construction problems and fine tuning procedures, the schedule must exhibit understanding of the interdependence of subs. A schedule which sets down a blistering pace but does not document in detail how subs are to perform as a team to accomplish the work will fail. An effective schedule will serve as a tool for the subcontractor. Ineffective schedules are usually those which burden rather than assist the subcontractor in expediting his work.

Subs usually find that they can make more money on jobs that are successfully scheduled. Management should not be afraid to set down a blistering schedule which has the backup to be realistic. An aggressive, well-thought-out schedule will earn the respect of good subs and will keep problem subs off the job.

The builder not the subs, must run the job

Most activities in a real estate development organization come to a head at the time of construction. If the activities leading up to the construction process were carried out in a thorough, professional manner, with speed and economy of construction in mind, the job can move ahead at a rapid rate.

If the job superintendent is on the receiving end of everyone else's procrastination and inefficiency, he cannot single-handedly reverse the process in the field. However, he can provide feedback to those who may not be aware of the effects their actions have on the construction process.

Effective scheduling and coordination demands good architectural drawings. Incomplete drawings almost guarantee unscheduled surprises. A developer who works with incomplete drawings which merely outline the work generally operates in a loose manner in other areas, including contracts. When both the drawings and the contracts only outline the work, it is up to the sub to decide how things should be done. When the subs run the job, the builder is at their mercy and has lost control of his investment.

When the subs are running the job, the superintendent is delegated to a position of fire fighting. Since he does not have the proper tools, he will not be able to keep all of the fires under control. Problems must be worked out in the design stage, and the developer must see that his architect provides sufficient detailing so that field personnel do not have to make architectural decisions. The product is not going to be any better than the planning, the detailed analysis, and the documentation which guide its construction (see Chapter 26).

Another popular game which developers play with subs is called "Don't build it the way the drawings show, but the way I tell you." If the developer must work with an inadequate set of drawings, he tries to improvise in the field as he goes. This adds confusion to inadequacy and is proof to the subcontractor that the developer is lost and he, the sub, is in a better position to run the job. The developer may find himself rudderless and at the mercy of external forces over which he has lost control. If he must engage in constant fire fighting, he will have to neglect his more important duties of providing direction and leadership. In an environment which requires increasing professionalism merely to survive, he will perish.

HOW CONSTRUCTION SPECIALIZATION AIDS PRODUCTIVITY

Since labor accounts for a substantial portion of construction cost, scheduling and efficient utilization of personnel are necessary to ensure not only speed but economy of construction. Specialization is critical in the efficient utilization of personnel.

Specialization, which developed out of a shortage of good all-around tradesmen, has enabled relatively unskilled workers to produce a limited job function to a degree of efficiency far surpassing that of the all-around tradesman. For example, a joister can set far more joists than an all-around carpenter. Scheduling should take maximum advantage of specialization and continuity, moving specific construction operations from one building to the next without changes in the work pattern or job function. In California, construction specialization and continuity are rather commonplace, but in less intensive, less volume-oriented housing markets, construction procedures tend to revert back to the building-by-building type of construction, in which a carpenter will work from plate line to roof, nailing with stops and starts, waiting for other subs to complete their work. By educating the subs in such an area to the economics of specialization and continuity in scheduling, great strides can be made in reducing construction time and expense.

A wall framing crew, after completing the first floor walls in building A, for example, should move into buildings B and C, and so on, doing exactly the same thing building after building, rather than performing the next framing operation in building A, laying second-floor joists. Other crews should follow the wall framing crew to lay the floor joists, to stack and nail the subfloor, and so on. The flooring crew is not brought on until the other trades have completed their required work, but when it is brought on, it should not have to wait for anyone or be constantly pulled on and off the job.

THE NEED TO THINK AHEAD OF SCHEDULE

In an apartment building, most everything done by the major trades is critical. Once a major sub gets behind schedule it is tough to get him back up to schedule again, because there is so little noncritical work; most of his men are probably already performing a critical work function. When a major sub falls behind one day, the entire project generally falls behind one day.

Very close reporting is required with a tough schedule because once the job gets behind, it is extremely difficult to pick it up again. Minor slippage can be picked up by increasing the efficiency of existing crews or adding a helper, or through a temporary increase in productivity. But where slack is major to the point that added crews are required, this requirement is passed onto all subsequent crews, to bring the job back onto schedule. Somewhere along the line, one of the subs is going to be unwilling or unable to put on an added crew. In this case, the weakest link breaks the chain and precludes the slack from being taken up through all operations.

We do not put emphasis on completing the first unit with great rapidity, but schedule to complete all construction substantially within the shortest time. The schedule of a 286-unit project, designed by Michael Halpin, which was substantially completed in 95 working days, went as follows: Five days were required from groundbreaking to complete site preparation and building layout for the entire project. After building layout, it took 11 days to compact pad, excavate footing, pour footing, install conduit and plumbing, backfill rock, sand visqueen, mesh, pour, and finish the first slab. After the finish slab, it took 18 days to dry in the first building. After the first building was dried in, it took 22 days to wire, insulate, sheetrock, trim, finish electrical and mechanical, paint, and carpet.

From groundbreaking to the day the first unit was substantially completed took 56 days. It then took 30 days from the day the first unit was complete to the day the last unit was complete. That is 86 days from groundbreaking until the last unit was substantially completed. After the last unit was completed, another nine days were required to finish landscaping and site work, a construction time overall of 95 working days. Completion was scheduled for 85 working days, but some slippage was incurred, mostly attributable to slower than anticipated electrical inspections. The apartment managers moved into their apartment in the fifth building 75 working days after groundbreaking.

PROJECT SCHEDULE WORK SHEETS

The Project Schedule Work Sheets given in Exhibit 29–1 list functions which occur in the real estate development process of a specific project. The functions are not all-inclusive but represent a complete enough listing to serve as a guide and checklist for the project planner. The functions listed, for a for-sale housing project, have been grouped by departments such as planning and design, marketing, legal and financial, and so on (see Chapter 28).

Each department can utilize the work sheets as a checklist and planning tool for charting its activities. The work sheets list only functions and do not indicate interrelationships of functions from department to department or the critical path of the work flow.

Case Study I, the project management network prepared by John Gildea and Associates which follows, graphically illustrates the interrelationships of the functions and their timing for a typical project. It also serves as a network guide for the planning of specific projects.

The project management network in the case study does not exactly depict the functions listed in the Project Schedule Work Sheets in Exhibit 29–1 but is included to illustrate how the timing of interrelationships and the critical path of work flow are depicted. As functions change and interrelationships vary between functions and departments, the project management network will also vary, to reflect the operations for a particular organization and project.

CASE STUDY I: THE PROJECT MANAGEMENT NETWORK

Projects will go faster and will be more profitable if planned on paper. Correct solutions to problems and decisions regarding construction costs, schedules, and performance usually can be made if the necessary information has been forecast. Sometimes correct solutions will occur if the needed information is at least current, but rarely will this happen if the information is one or two months old.

With a written plan one can forecast precisely, pinpoint the status of a project, and determine when it will be completed. While there are countless unknowns in the construction business, a charted plan can reduce their number and save money.

The most important method of expressing a planning system is to use a bar chart. (Illustration 29–1). The various activities of the project are plotted

Illustration 29–1
Bar chart

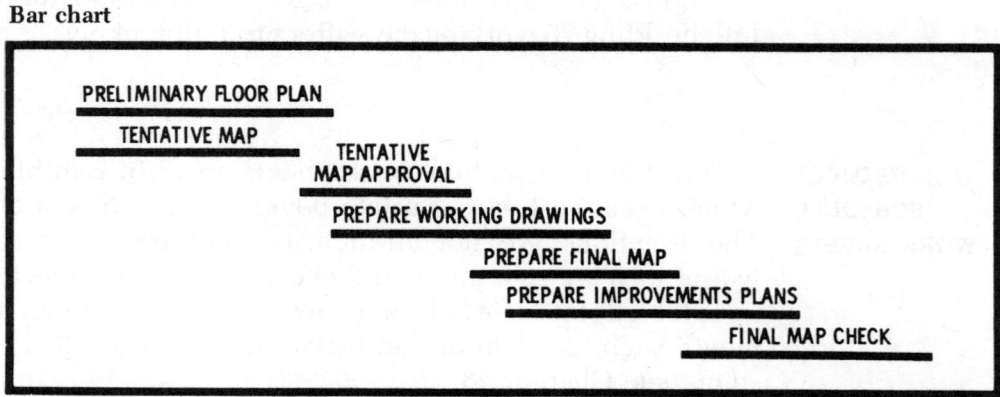

A bar chart is the most simple form of network planning. It shows activities and their relationships in time.

in the form of bars which represent the length of time the activity will take. They also are plotted against a calendar which shows their relationship in time. This method, although workable and a good start for project planning, will show neither the interrelationships of the activities nor the most critical activities.

Expressing the same activities in the form of a simple network chart (Illustration 29-2) will provide all the information of a bar chart. It also will reflect the interrelationships of each of the activities and their dependency upon each other. A more elaborate plan can be portrayed in this manner. All the detail included in project activity listings can be shown. Furthermore, the individual or department responsible for each activity is indicated. When completed, the chart will allow determination of those activities lying on the critical path.

An even more inclusive method is the definitive network chart (Illustration 29-3), which goes into extensive detail in listing each subactivity within a major activity. The definitive network chart is similar to the simple network chart, but complex activities are clearly spelled out in detailed fashion.

To supplement either of the planning networks described, many of the preconstruction activities may need a supplementary checklist. These lists act as reminders for activities too detailed to express entirely on the charts.

After a planning method has been determined and agreed upon by staff members and outside consultants, management can superimpose control points and reviews it wishes to make as the project proceeds. The plan should then be followed through on a weekly basis, preferably by making the network the focal point of the staff meetings.

In implementing any of these planning methods, a professional con-

Illustration 29-2
Simple network

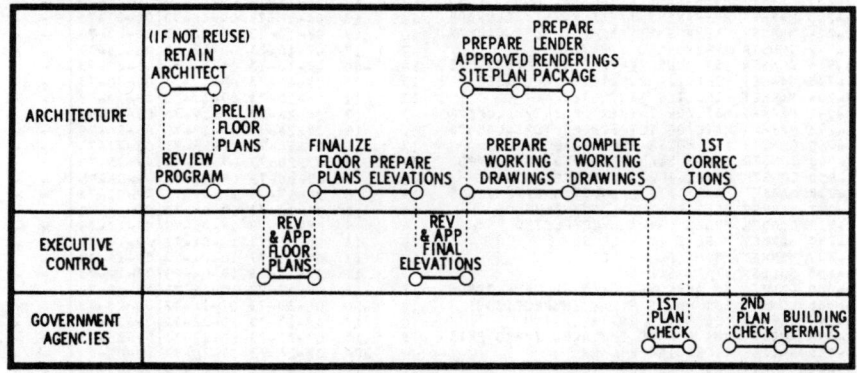

A simple network shows activities and their timing, and their interrelationships and dependencies. It also determines whether or not activities are critical.

Reprinted with permission of John Gildea and Associates.

29 / Scheduling for profit improvement

sulting firm can be of great assistance, not only in training the staff in improved scheduling methods and charts but also in forcing the scheduling effort itself to be completed on time and accurately.

Computer reports   The project management network developed by John Gildea and Associates is run on specific projects by use of a computer. The same computer generates reports designed to provide the builder with progress reports which measure progress against the standard and flag deficiencies. Illustrations 29-4, 29-5, and 29-6 give examples of these reports.

CONSTRUCTION SCHEDULES, MANUAL METHOD   Exhibits 29-2 through 29-5 illustrate how a 256-unit multifamily rental project is scheduled by Michael C. Halpin Consultants, using a manual method. (For the methodology in developing the manual schedule, refer to pages 503-5.)

Illustration 29-4
Case Study I: Expected completion report

MAY 10, 1973   PAGE   2

EXPECTED COMPLETION REPORT---ALL PROJECTS   JOHN GILDEA

ACTIVITY P=S	DEPT	ACTIVITY DESCRIPTION	ORIG DAYS	AH/BE	EXP START	COMPLETION DATES ORIG,SCH	EXPECT	ACTUAL	P C	REMAIN DAYS	PROJECT NAME
948-950	CONSTR	MODEL FRAMING INSPECTION	1	-23	07-10-73	06-06-73	07-10-73	- -		1	THE VILLAGE
855-869	GOVT	FHA ISSUE COMMITTMENTS	10	54	07-02-73	10-01-73	07-16-73	- -		10	GREEN WOODS
950-952	CONSTR	MODEL DRYWALL COMPLETED	4	-23	07-11-73	06-12-73	07-16-73	- -		4	THE VILLAGE
223-224	MARKET	PLOT DISPLAY	15	11	06-28-73	08-03-73	07-19-73	- -		15	GREEN WOODS
886-888	GOVT	CO APPROVAL OFFSITE DEVELOPMEN	5	-14	07-17-73	07-02-73	07-23-73	- -		5	THE VILLAGE
830-831	GOVT	P.C. PROCESS OFFSITE SIGN PERMT	20	22	06-27-73	08-24-73	07-25-73	- -		20	GREEN WOODS
922-924	CONSTR	AWARD ONSITE CONTRACTS	15	-17	07-05-73	06-29-73	07-25-73	- -		15	GREEN WOODS
892-894	GOVT	FHA APPRVL IMPLACED IMPROVEMTS	5	-14	07-24-73	07-10-73	07-30-73	- -		5	THE VILLAGE
296-281	MARKET	MODEL LANDSCAPING	15	-19	07-17-73	07-10-73	08-06-73	- -		15	THE VILLAGE
882-884	GOVT	PROCESS OFFSITE SIGN PERMIT	10	22	07-26-73	09-10-73	08-08-73	- -		10	GREEN WOODS
936-938	CONSTR	INSTALL CURB + GUTTER	10	-17	07-26-73	07-16-73	08-08-73	- -		10	GREEN WOODS
226-227	MARKET	PREPARE PREL.MKTG PLAN,GRAPHIC	15	11	07-20-73	08-24-73	08-09-73	- -		15	GREEN WOODS
960-962	CONSTR	1ST HOUSE FRAMING + INSPECTION	24	-50	07-09-73	05-29-73	08-09-73	- -		24	THE VILLAGE
952-956	CONSTR	FINISH HOUSE COMPLETE	19	-23	07-17-73	07-10-73	08-10-73	- -		19	THE VILLAGE
938-940	CONSTR	INSTALL UNDERGROUND ELECTRIC	5	-17	08-09-73	07-23-73	08-15-73	- -		5	GREEN WOODS
231-232	MARKET	OBTAIN SIGN PERMIT	5	16	08-10-73	09-10-73	08-16-73	- -		5	GREEN WOODS
410-412	SALES	MODEL GRAND OPENING	4	-23	08-13-73	07-16-73	08-16-73	- -		4	THE VILLAGE
219-239	MARKET	FABRICATE & PROCESS MODEL FURN	42	18	06-22-73	09-17-73	08-21-73	- -		42	GREEN WOODS
289-290	MARKET	PREPARE INT/EXT PAINT/WALLPAPR	10	13	08-10-73	09-12-73	08-23-73	- -		10	GREEN WOODS
292-294	MARKET	PREPARE INT SCHEME TOPS-CABNTS	10	13	08-10-73	09-12-73	08-23-73	- -		10	GREEN WOODS
940-942	CONSTR	APPLY BASE + PAVING	7	17	08-10-73	09-19-73	08-24-73	- -		7	GREEN WOODS
962-964	CONSTR	1ST HOUSE DRYWALL TAPE/TEXTURE	14	-50	08-10-73	06-19-73	08-29-73	- -		14	THE VILLAGE
228-233	MARKET	FINALIZE PUBLICITY RELEASES	15	11	08-10-73	09-17-73	08-30-73	- -		15	GREEN WOODS
229-234	MARKET	FINALIZE BROCHURES	15	11	08-10-73	09-17-73	08-30-73	- -		15	GREEN WOODS
290-291	MARKET	MAIL/DE INT/EXT PAINT/WALLPAPR	5	13	08-24-73	09-19-73	08-30-73	- -		5	GREEN WOODS
294-295	MARKET	MAIL/DE INT SCHEME TOPS-CABNTS	5	13	08-24-73	09-19-73	08-30-73	- -		5	GREEN WOODS
958-960	CONSTR	1ST HOUSE POUR SLAB	12	-17	08-16-73	08-08-73	08-31-73	- -		12	GREEN WOODS
946-948	CONSTR	MODEL SLAB +FRAMING COMPLETED	29	9	07-26-73	09-18-73	09-05-73	- -		29	GREEN WOODS
948-950	CONSTR	MODEL FRAMING INSPECTION	1	9	09-06-73	09-19-73	09-06-73	- -		1	GREEN WOODS
232-238	MARKET	FABRICATE & ERECT ONSITE SIGNS	15	16	08-17-73	10-01-73	09-07-73	- -		15	GREEN WOODS
239-297	MARKET	DELIVER MODEL FURNISHINGS	15	18	08-22-73	10-10-73	09-12-73	- -		15	GREEN WOODS
950-952	CONSTR	MODEL DRYWALL COMPLETED	4	9	09-07-73	09-25-73	09-12-73	- -		4	GREEN WOODS
233-236	MARKET	PUBLICITY RELEASES	10	11	08-31-73	10-01-73	09-14-73	- -		10	GREEN WOODS
234-237	MARKET	PRINT BROCHURES	10	11	08-31-73	10-01-73	09-14-73	- -		10	GREEN WOODS
406-408	SALES	START SALES	3	11	09-17-73	10-04-73	09-19-73	- -		3	GREEN WOODS
886-888	GOVT	CO APPROVAL OFFSITE DEVELOPMEN	5	18	09-13-73	10-15-73	09-19-73	- -		5	GREEN WOODS
964-966	CONSTR	1ST HOUSE FINAL INSPECTION	18	-50	08-30-73	07-16-73	09-25-73	- -		18	THE VILLAGE
298-299	MARKET	DECORATER INSTALLATION	10	18	09-13-73	10-22-73	09-26-73	- -		10	GREEN WOODS
892-894	GOVT	FHA APPRVL IMPLACED IMPROVEMTS	5	18	09-20-73	10-22-73	09-26-73	- -		5	GREEN WOODS
414-416	SALES	CLOSE 1ST ESCROW	4	-50	09-20-73	07-20-73	10-01-73	- -		4	THE VILLAGE
296-281	MARKET	MODEL LANDSCAPING	12	11	09-20-73	10-22-73	10-05-73	- -		12	GREEN WOODS
960-962	CONSTR	1ST HOUSE FRAMING + INSPECTION	24	-17	09-04-73	09-12-73	10-05-73	- -		24	GREEN WOODS
952-956	CONSTR	FINISH HOUSE COMPLETE	19	9	09-13-73	10-22-73	10-09-73	- -		19	GREEN WOODS
410-412	SALES	MODEL GRAND OPENING	4	9	10-10-73	10-26-73	10-15-73	- -		4	GREEN WOODS
962-964	CONSTR	1ST HOUSE DRYWALL TAPE/TEXTURE	14	-17	10-08-73	10-02-73	10-25-73	- -		14	GREEN WOODS
964-966	CONSTR	1ST HOUSE FINAL INSPECTION	18	-17	10-26-73	10-26-73	11-20-73	- -		18	GREEN WOODS
414-416	SALES	CLOSE 1ST ESCROW	4	-17	11-21-73	11-01-73	11-27-73	- -		4	GREEN WOODS

Illus
Case

0

1

2

3

4

5

6

7

8

9

Illustration 29-5
Case Study I: Department report

MAY 10, 1973 PAGE 2

DEPARTMENT REPORT--ALL PROJECTS   JOHN GILDEA

ACTIVITY P-S	DEPT	ACTIVITY DESCRIPTION	ORIG DAYS	AH/BE	EXP START	COMPLETION DATES ORIG,SCH	EXPECT	ACTUAL	P C	REMAIN DAYS	PROJECT NAME
916-920	CONSTR	AWARD IMPROVEMENT CONTRACTS	3	11	05-14-73	06-01-73	05-16-73	- -	1	2	GREEN WOODS
930-932	CONSTR	GRADING	16	2	05-14-73	06-01-73	05-29-73	- -	1	12	GREEN WOODS
932-934	CONSTR	INSTALL SEWER + WATER (START)	10	2	05-31-73	06-15-73	06-13-73	- -		10	GREEN WOODS
910-912	CONSTR	BID ONSITE PLANS	12	-17	06-06-73	05-28-73	06-21-73	- -		12	GREEN WOODS
914-916	CONSTR	BID OFFSITE DRAWINGS	12	-17	06-06-73	05-28-73	06-21-73	- -		12	GREEN WOODS
934-936	CONSTR	INSTALL SEWER + WATER (COMPL)	10	2	06-14-73	06-29-73	06-27-73	- -		10	GREEN WOODS
944-946	CONSTR	COMPL MODEL UNDRGRD CURBS ETC.	10	28	06-14-73	08-07-73	06-27-73	- -		10	GREEN WOODS
922-924	CONSTR	AWARD ONSITE CONTRACTS	15	-17	07-05-73	06-29-73	07-25-73	- -		15	GREEN WOODS
936-938	CONSTR	INSTALL CURB + GUTTER	10	-17	07-26-73	07-16-73	08-08-73	- -		10	GREEN WOODS
938-940	CONSTR	INSTALL UNDERGROUND ELECTRIC	5	-17	08-09-73	07-23-73	08-15-73	- -		5	GREEN WOODS
940-942	CONSTR	APPLY BASE + PAVING	7	17	08-16-73	09-19-73	08-24-73	- -		7	GREEN WOODS
958-960	CONSTR	1ST HOUSE POUR SLAB	12	-17	08-16-73	08-08-73	08-31-73	- -		12	GREEN WOODS
946-948	CONSTR	MODEL SLAB +FRAMING COMPLETED	29	9	07-26-73	09-18-73	09-05-73	- -		29	GREEN WOODS
948-950	CONSTR	MODEL FRAMING INSPECTION	1	9	09-06-73	09-19-73	09-06-73	- -		1	GREEN WOODS
950-952	CONSTR	MODEL DRYWALL COMPLETED	4	9	09-07-73	09-25-73	09-12-73	- -		4	GREEN WOODS
960-962	CONSTR	1ST HOUSE FRAMING + INSPECTION	24	-17	09-04-73	09-12-73	10-05-73	- -		24	GREEN WOODS
952-956	CONSTR	FINISH HOUSE COMPLETE	19	9	09-13-73	10-22-73	10-09-73	- -		19	GREEN WOODS
962-964	CONSTR	1ST HOUSE DRYWALL TAPE/TEXTURE	14	-17	10-08-73	10-02-73	10-25-73	- -		14	GREEN WOODS
964-966	CONSTR	1ST HOUSE FINAL INSPECTION	18	-17	10-26-73	10-26-73	11-20-73	- -		18	GREEN WOODS
918-920	CONSTR	AWARD IMPROVEMENT CONTRACTS	3	-41	05-11-73	03-15-73	05-11-73	- -	3	1	THE VILLAGE
922-924	CONSTR	AWARD ONSITE CONTRACTS	20	-50	05-11-73	03-15-73	05-24-73	- -	2	10	THE VILLAGE
944-946	CONSTR	COMPL MODEL UNDRGRD CURBS ETC.	10	-23	05-14-73	04-24-73	05-25-73	- -		10	THE VILLAGE
936-938	CONSTR	INSTALL CURB + GUTTER	10	-50	05-25-73	03-29-73	06-08-73	- -		10	THE VILLAGE
938-940	CONSTR	INSTALL UNDERGROUND ELECTRIC	5	-50	06-11-73	04-05-73	06-15-73	- -		5	THE VILLAGE
940-942	CONSTR	APPLY BASE + PAVING	10	-17	06-18-73	06-06-73	06-29-73	- -		10	THE VILLAGE
958-960	CONSTR	1ST HOUSE POUR SLAB	14	-50	06-18-73	04-25-73	07-06-73	- -		14	THE VILLAGE
946-948	CONSTR	MODEL SLAB +FRAMING COMPLETED	29	-23	05-28-73	06-05-73	07-09-73	- -		29	THE VILLAGE
948-950	CONSTR	MODEL FRAMING INSPECTION	1	-23	07-10-73	06-06-73	07-10-73	- -		1	THE VILLAGE
950-952	CONSTR	MODEL DRYWALL COMPLETED	4	-23	07-11-73	06-12-73	07-16-73	- -		4	THE VILLAGE
960-962	CONSTR	1ST HOUSE FRAMING + INSPECTION	24	-50	07-09-73	05-29-73	08-09-73	- -		24	THE VILLAGE
952-956	CONSTR	FINISH HOUSE COMPLETE	19	-23	07-17-73	07-10-73	08-10-73	- -		19	THE VILLAGE
962-964	CONSTR	1ST HOUSE DRYWALL TAPE/TEXTURE	14	-50	08-10-73	06-19-73	08-29-73	- -		14	THE VILLAGE
964-966	CONSTR	1ST HOUSE FINAL INSPECTION	18	-50	08-30-73	07-16-73	09-25-73	- -		18	THE VILLAGE

Illustration 29-6
Case Study I: Critical path report

```
                                                                              MAY 10, 1973  PAGE   1
                      GREEN WOODS                                             05-10-73                048012
MOST CRITICAL PATH REPORT---ALL PROJECT         JOHN GILDEA

    ACTIVITY                              ORIG              EXP    COMPLETION DATES              P  REMAIN
  P-S    DEPT    ACTIVITY DESCRIPTION     DAYS AH/BE        START ORIG.SCH  EXPECT   ACTUAL      C   DAYS    COMMENTS

524-526 ARCHIT  PREPARE WORKING DRAWINGS    20  -17         05-11-73 04-24-73 05-17-73   - -     3     5
838-840 GOVIT   WORKING DRAWING PLAN CHECK  12  -17         05-18-73 05-10-73 06-05-73   - -          12
910-912 CONSTR  BID ONSITE PLANS            12  -17         06-06-73 05-28-73 06-21-73   - -          12
914-916 CONSTR  BID OFFSITE DRAWINGS        12  -17         06-06-73 05-28-73 06-21-73   - -          12
221-222 MARKET  PREPARE FINAL JOB PLAN INPUT 4  -17         06-22-73 06-04-73 06-27-73   - -           4
320-322 FINANC  PREPARE FINAL JOB INPUT      4  -17         06-22-73 06-04-73 06-27-73   - -           4
648-650 DIVMGR  PREPARE FINAL JOB PLAN       4  -17         06-22-73 06-04-73 06-27-73   - -           4
150-182 REGMGR  APPROVE SALES PRICE          1  -17         06-28-73 06-05-73 06-28-73   - -           1
068-070 OPERAT  REV & APPRV FINAL JOB PLAN   3  -17         06-29-73 06-08-73 07-03-73   - -           3
922-924 CONSTR  AWARD ONSITE CONTRACTS      15  -17         07-05-73 06-29-73 07-25-73   - -          15
936-938 CONSTR  INSTALL CURB + GUTTER       10  -17         07-26-73 07-16-73 08-08-73   - -          10
938-940 CONSTR  INSTALL UNDERGROUND ELECTRIC 5  -17         08-09-73 07-23-73 08-15-73   - -           5
958-960 CONSTR  1ST HOUSE POUR SLAB         12  -17         08-16-73 08-08-73 08-31-73   - -          12
960-962 CONSTR  1ST HOUSE FRAMING + INSPECTION 24 -17       09-04-73 09-12-73 10-05-73   - -          24
962-964 CONSTR  1ST HOUSE DRYWALL TAPE/TEXTURE 14 -17       10-03-73 10-02-73 10-25-73   - -          14
964-966 CONSTR  1ST HOUSE FINAL INSPECTION  18  -17         10-26-73 10-26-73 11-20-73   - -          18
414-416 SALES   CLOSE 1ST ESCROW             4  -17         11-21-73 11-01-73 11-27-73   - -           4
860-861 GOVIT   ISSUE BUILDING PERMITS       1  -15         06-29-73 06-08-73 06-29-73   - -           1
841-864 GOVIT   ASP 9 FHA ACCEPTANCE W/CONDIT. 1   2        05-11-73 05-15-73 05-11-73   - -           1
930-932 CONSTR  GRADING                     16    2         05-14-73 06-01-73 05-29-73   - -    1     12
932-934 CONSTR  INSTALL SEWER + WATER (START) 10  2         05-31-73 06-15-73 06-13-73   - -          10
934-936 CONSTR  INSTALL SEWER + WATER (COMPL) 10  2         06-14-73 06-29-73 06-27-73   - -          10
946-948 CONSTR  MODEL SLAB +FRAMING COMPLETED 29  9         07-26-73 09-18-73 09-05-73   - -          29
948-950 CONSTR  MODEL FRAMING INSPECTION     1   9          09-06-73 09-19-73 09-06-73   - -           1
950-952 CONSTR  MODEL DRYWALL COMPLETED      4   9          09-07-73 09-25-73 09-12-73   - -           4
952-956 CONSTR  MODEL FINISH HOUSE COMPLETE 19   9          09-13-73 10-22-73 10-09-73   - -          19
410-412 SALES   MODEL GRAND OPENING          4   9          10-10-73 10-26-73 10-15-73   - -           4
530-532 ARCHIT  WORKING DWG 1ST PLAN CHK CORR. 6 11         06-06-73 06-28-73 06-13-73   - -           6
849-850 GOVIT   2ND CHECK WORKING DRAWINGS   5  11          06-14-73 07-06-73 06-20-73   - -           5
536-538 ARCHIT  WORKING DWG FINAL PLAN CHK CORR 5 11        06-21-73 07-13-73 06-27-73   - -           5
223-224 MARKET  PLOT DISPLAY                15  11          06-28-73 08-03-73 07-19-73   - -          15
226-227 MARKET  PREPARE PREL.MKTG PLAN,GRAPHIC 15 11        07-20-73 08-24-73 08-09-73   - -          15
228-233 MARKET  FINALIZE PUBLICITY RELEASES 15  11          08-10-73 09-17-73 08-30-73   - -          15
229-234 MARKET  FINALIZE BROCHURES          15  11          08-10-73 09-17-73 08-30-73   - -          15
233-236 MARKET  PUBLICITY RELEASES          10  11          08-31-73 10-01-73 09-14-73   - -          10
234-237 MARKET  PRINT BROCHURES             10  11          08-31-73 10-01-73 09-14-73   - -          10
406-408 SALES   START SALES                  3  11          09-17-73 10-04-73 09-19-73   - -           3
296-261 MARKET  MODEL LANDSCAPING           12  11          09-20-73 10-22-73 10-05-73   - -          12
918-920 CONSTR  AWARD IMPROVEMENT CONTRACTS  3  11          05-14-73 06-01-73 05-16-73   - -    1      2
289-290 MARKET  PREPARE INT/EXT PAINT/WALLPAPR 10 13        08-10-73 09-12-73 08-23-73   - -          10
292-294 MARKET  PREPARE INT SCHEME TOPS-CABNTS 10 13        08-10-73 09-12-73 08-23-73   - -          10
290-291 MARKET  MAIL/DE INT/EXT PAINT/WALLPAPR  5 13        08-24-73 09-19-73 08-30-73   - -           5
294-295 MARKET  MAIL/DE INT SCHEME TOPS-CABNTS  5 13        08-24-73 09-19-73 08-30-73   - -           5
231-232 MARKET  OBTAIN SIGN PERMIT           5  16          08-10-73 09-10-73 08-16-73   - -           5
232-238 MARKET  FABRICATE & ERECT ONSITE SIGNS 15 16        08-17-73 10-01-73 09-07-73   - -          15
940-942 CONSTR  APPLY BASE + PAVING          7  17          08-16-73 09-19-73 08-24-73   - -           7
214-218 MARKET  PREPARE RENDERINGS          24  18          05-18-73 07-18-73 06-21-73   - -          24
```

Exhibit 29-1
Project Schedule Work Sheets

	Original		Revised	
	Start	Finish	Start	Finish
LEGAL AND FINANCIAL FUNCTIONS				
Prepare site purchase offer				
Open escrow				
Order preliminary title report				
Analyze and prepare financial feasibility				
Evaluate financial sources				
Review cost estimates, budgets				
Prepare financial and legal budget				
Prepare cash flow				
Arrange seed capital				
Gather financial package input				
Finalize and submit financial package				
File fees as required				
Review and update marketing and cash flow				
Select financial partner				
Prepare partnership papers				

Exhibit 29-1 (*continued*)

	Original		Revised	
	Start	*Finish*	*Start*	*Finish*
File and record partnership papers				
Obtain partner liability insurance				
Obtain and record land and development loan				
Pay plan check fees				
Obtain construction insurance				
Obtain bonds				
Review and approve sales prices				
Obtain model loan				
Obtain construction loan, record				
Obtain takeout loan				
Close escrow				
Monitor cash flow				

GENERAL AND PROJECT ADMINISTRATION

Retain marketing expertise				
Retain civil engineer				
Review market studies				
Review engineers studies				
Review title report				
Prepare developmental feasibility				
Retain soil and geological engineer				
Review engineers' reports				
Retain land planner—architect				
Prepare development concept				
Review and approve preliminary designs				
Select standard plans for reuse				
Approve specs and features				
Prepare input for financial package				
Receive, approve and submit environmental impact report (EIR)				
Receive preliminary cost estimate				
Receive marketing budgets				
Review tentative map				
Prepare development budget				
Prepare detailed development concept				
Review, update cost estimate				
Obtain off-site easements and agreements				
Submit engineering plans for plan check				
Review and approve designs prior to working drawings				
Review and approve all updated budgets				
Submit working drawings for plan check				
Monitor schedules and budgets				

EXECUTIVE, COMMITTEE APPROVALS

Approve land purchase				
Approve terms				
Approve feasibility				
Approve concept and cost estimate				
Approve tentative map				
Approve preliminary drawing				
Approve spec and features list				
Approve finalized concept and estimates				

Exhibit 29-1 (*continued*)

	Original		Revised	
	Start	*Finish*	*Start*	*Finish*
Review and finalize marketing concept				
Update sales prices				
Go or no-go development decision				
Approve design features prior to working drawings				
Approve partnership, financing				
Go or no-go grading decision				
Close escrow				

MARKETING

Perform market studies				
Establish objectives				
Identify market opportunity				
Establish developmental concept				
Product recommendations				
Establish features criteria				
Establish price range				
Obtain approvals				
Prepare marketing budget				
Prepare monthly site budget				
Prepare model and sales office budget				
Select model site				
Select advertising expertise				
Review ad campaign layouts				
Review ad campaign				
Obtain display proposals				
Select model elevations				
Update market report				
Obtain decorator proposals, let contract				
Approve decorator designs				
Develop brochure				
Select renderer				
Prepare renderings, site plan, elevations				
Select sales agent, force				
Train sales force				
Approve sales office design				
Order sales office furnishing				
Order sales trailer				
Construct sales displays				
Finalize marketing, site and sales office budgets				
Determine lot premiums				
Finalize brochures				
Obtain approvals				
Review landscape design				
Landscape approval				
Prepare sales bulletins				
Order model area and trailer furniture				
Order on-site signs				
Erect on-site signs				
Set up and furnish sales trailer				
Printed materials delivered to sales trailer				
Order printed materials for sales office				
Develop bootleg sign program				
Erect off-site signs				

Exhibit 29-1 (*continued*)

	Original		Revised	
	Start	Finish	Start	Finish

Prepare grand opening ads
Prepare special promotions
Obtain printed materials for sales office

Install sales office displays
Install sales office and model decorating
Inspect models with decorator
Set up train color selection coordinator
Select and train customer relations representative

Clean up
VIP party, grand opening

PLANNING AND DESIGN

Formulate criteria
Coordinate with engineering on land plan
Prepare preliminary land use, get approval
Prepare preliminary floor plans, approval
Prepare landscape schematics, approval

Prepare land plan, approval
Prepare preliminary elevations, approval
Prepare architectural loan package input
Layout model compound, approval
Design sales office, approval

Design recreation center, approval
Prepare preliminary landscape drawings
Design model landscaping
Prepare model working drawings
Prepare recreation center working drawings

Prepare unit working drawings
Revise working drawings as per feedback
Prepare overall landscape drawings
Obtain exterior colors

GOVERNMENTAL INTERFACE APPROVALS

Governmental schedule review
Obtain city and county requirements
Zoning and EIR prefiling interview
File zone change
Submit EIR report

Submit tentative map
Tentative map review
1st planning commission meeting, agenda lead time
1st subdivision committee meeting
2nd planning commission hearing, obtain zoning recommendation

Obtain tentative map approval, agenda lead time
1st zoning hearing, agenda lead time
2nd zoning hearing
Obtain building permit for models, plan check time
Zoning effective at end of appeal period

Submit for preliminary public report
Obtain preliminary public report

Exhibit 29–1 (*continued*)

	Original		Revised	
	Start	*Finish*	*Start*	*Finish*
Obtain approval of final map, agenda lead time				
Record final map				
Obtain building permit, plan check time				
Process white report				
Receive white report				

ENGINEERING

Obtain city and county requirements				
Prepare engineering feasibility				
Review title reports				
Coordinate with planning and design on land plan				
Prepare soils report				
Prepare geology report				
Prepare civil engineers report				
Request for amendments to title report				
Prepare engineering budget				
Submit reports and budget for approval				
Prepare boundary and easement survey				
Prepare topo.				
Prefiling interview				
Prepare tentative map				
Prepare EIR, obtain approval				
Approve title report				
Revise engineering budget				
Prepare plot plan				
Prepare final tract map, submit				
Design final rough grading plan				
Design final grade plan, submit				
Make corrections to final tract map				
Design street plan, submit				
Prepare quantity takeoffs				
Design storm, sewer, and water plans, submit				
Coordinate with utility company drawings				
Receive utility company drawings				
Make corrections to final tract map				
Make corrections to engineering drawings				
Obtain approvals on engineering drawings				

OPERATIONS

Prepare preliminary cost estimates				
Update cost estimates				
Update cost estimate for land and development loan				
Bid improvement plans				
Develop improvement costs				
Prepare construction loan estimate				
Bid construction				
Develop construction costs				
Award improvement contracts				
Break ground				
Award model contracts				
Award construction contracts				
Install utilities				

Exhibit 29–1 (*concluded*)

	Original		Revised	
	Start	Finish	Start	Finish
Construct models	___	___	___	___
Construct recreation facilities, sales office	___	___	___	___
Install model and recreation landscaping	___	___	___	___
Begin production housing	___	___	___	___
Construct streets	___	___	___	___

Exhibit 29–2
Hypothetical Project Plan

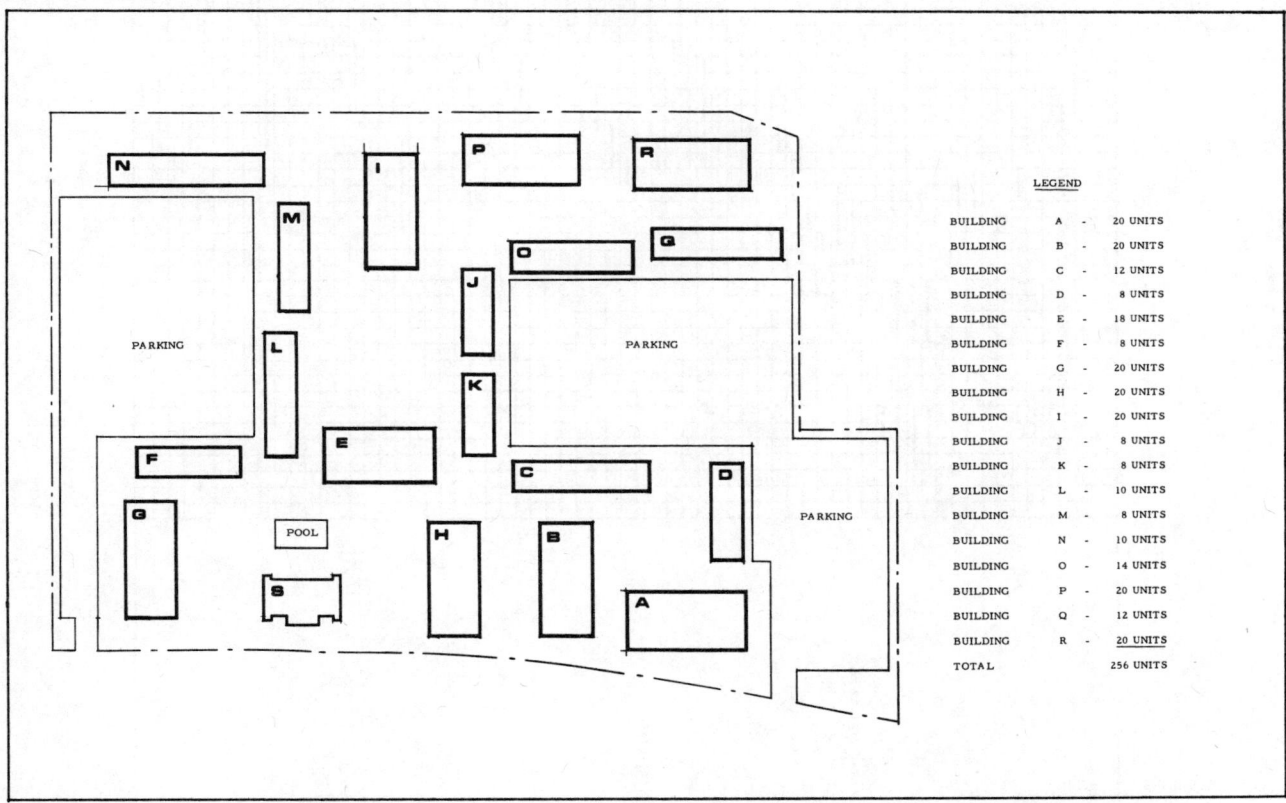

LEGEND

BUILDING	A	–	20 UNITS
BUILDING	B	–	20 UNITS
BUILDING	C	–	12 UNITS
BUILDING	D	–	8 UNITS
BUILDING	E	–	18 UNITS
BUILDING	F	–	8 UNITS
BUILDING	G	–	20 UNITS
BUILDING	H	–	20 UNITS
BUILDING	I	–	20 UNITS
BUILDING	J	–	8 UNITS
BUILDING	K	–	8 UNITS
BUILDING	L	–	10 UNITS
BUILDING	M	–	8 UNITS
BUILDING	N	–	10 UNITS
BUILDING	O	–	14 UNITS
BUILDING	P	–	20 UNITS
BUILDING	Q	–	12 UNITS
BUILDING	R	–	20 UNITS
TOTAL			256 UNITS

29 / Scheduling for profit improvement 519

Exhibit 29-3
Site-Work Schedule

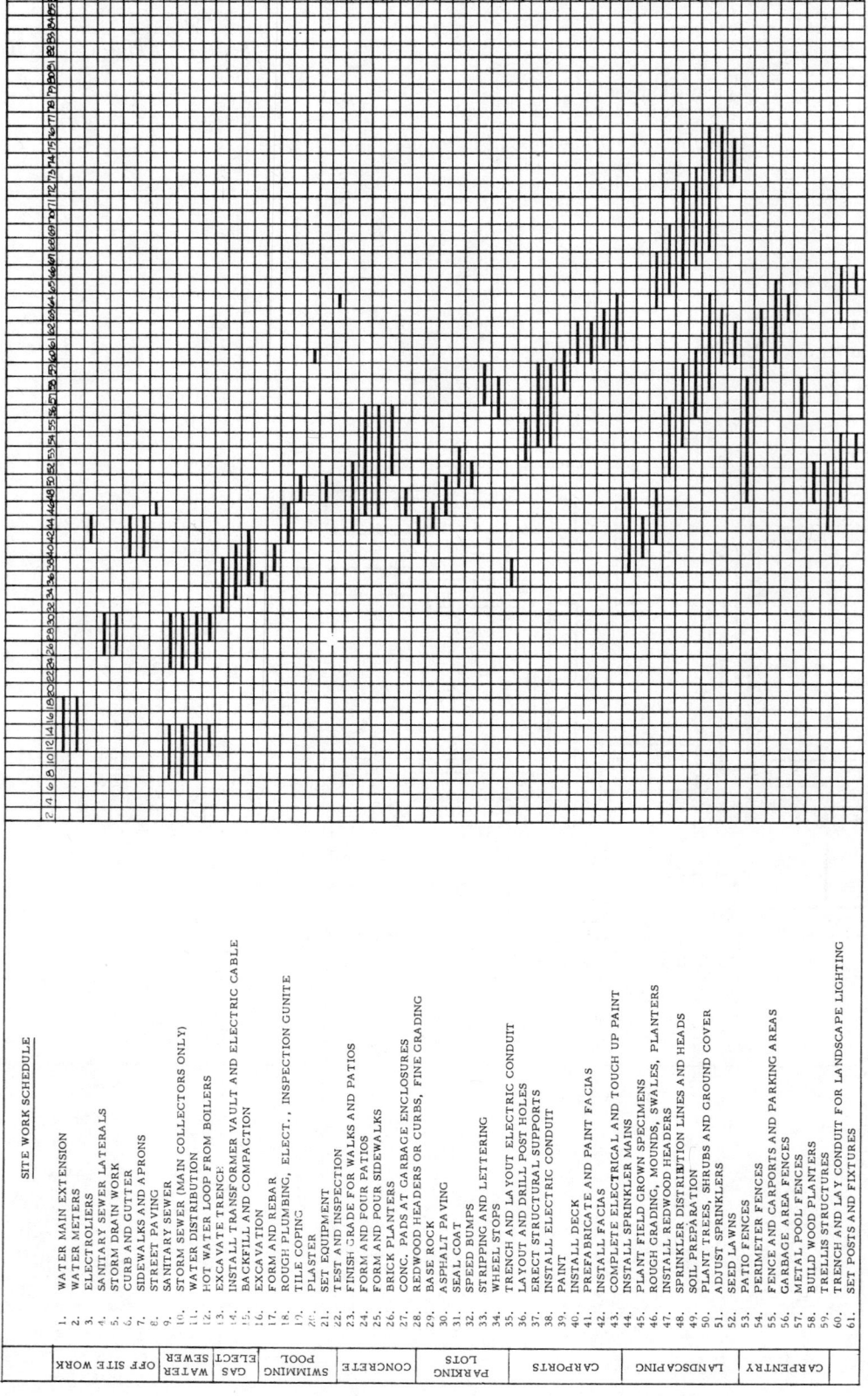

Exhibit 29-4
Rough-Work Schedule

ROUGH SCHEDULE

1. LAYOUT AND TRENCH FTGS AND PLUMB. TRENCH
2. FORM AND REBAR AT FOOTINGS
3. ELECT. INSTALLATION - GROUND WIRE
4. CITY AND ARCH. INSPECTION
5. POOR FOOTINGS
6. INSTALL PLUMBING WASTE LINES
7. INSTALL TEL. AND PG. AND E CONDUIT
8. INSPECTION AND BACKFILL OR WASTE LINES,
9. UNDERSLAB ROCK W. P. MEMBRANE AND MESH
10. INSPECTION
11. POUR SLAB
12. LAYOUT SILLS STRIP CONC. FORMS
13. FRAME WALLS AT FIRST FLOOR
14. FORM METER ENCLOSURES AND STAIR LANDINGS
15. POUR MTR ENCLO. AND STAIR LANDINGS
16. PLUMB WALLS AT FIRST FL. -INSTALL PLUMB. STACK 2ND FLOOR
17. FRAME SECOND FLOOR JOIST'S AND DECKS
18. INSTALL MAIN WATER LINES
19. LOAD AND DISTRIBUTE PLYWOOD FOR DECK AND SUB FLOORS
20. NAIL OFF PLYWOOD DECK AND SUB FLOOR
21. FRAMER PULL BRACES AND PICK UP WORK AT FIRST FLOOR
22. INSTALL SASH, SLIDING DOOR FRAMES AND EXT. DOOR - 1ST FLOOR
23. PLYWOOD SIDING AT FIRST FLOOR
24. FRAMER LAYOUT SECOND FLOOR
25. INSTALL BRANCH WATER LINES AND GAS AT FIRST FLOOR
26. FRAME SECOND FLOOR
27. ELECT BORE AND INSTALL BOXES AT FIRST FLOOR
28. LOAD TRUSSES
29. PLUMB WALLS SECOND FLOOR
30. INSTALL TEMP. STAIRS AND DECK RAILINGS
31. DELIVER SHEET MTL "2" BAR, PORCH FLASHING, EAVES, VENTS, ETC.
32. FRAME ROOF
33. LOAD AND DISTRIBUTE ROOF PLYWOOD
34. INSTALL PLUMBING STACK THROUGH ROOF
35. NAIL OFF ROOF PLYWOOD
36. FRAMER PULL BRACES AND PICK UP WORK AT SECOND FLOOR
37. INSTALL SASH, SLIDING DOOR FRAMES AND EXT. DOOR AT 2ND FLOOR
38. FRAME ABOVE ROOF - INSTALL FACIA AND CANT STRIP
39. INSTALL SHEET METAL FLUES
40. ROOF INSPECTION
41. ELECT.BORE AND INSTALL BOXES AT SECOND FLOOR
42. INSTALL BRANCH WATER LINES AT SECOND FLOOR
43. PLYWOOD SIDING AT SECOND FLOOR
44. INSTALL EXHAUST FAN DUCTS AT FIRST FLOOR
45. INSTALL EXHAUST FAN DUCTS AT SECOND FLOOR
46. DRY-IN ROOF
47. CLEAN UP SECOND FLOOR FOR LIGHT WEIGHT CONCRETE
48. POUR LIGHT WEIGHT CONCRETE
49. COMPLETE ROOF AND ROCK
50. ELECTRIC PULL WIRE AT FIRST FLOOR
51. ELECTRIC PULL WIRE AT SECOND FLOOR
52. TV AND TELEPHONE RUF-IN
53. FIXED GLASS AT SPA
54. INSTALL DOWNSPOUT AND LOUVERS
55. ELECTRICAL INSPECTION
56. SET BATH TUBS
57. PLUMBING INSPECTION
58. INSTALL WALL INSULATION
59. STOCK SHEETROCK FIRST FLOOR
60. STOCK SHEETROCK SECOND FLOOR

Exhibit 29-5
Finish-Work Schedule

FINISH SCHEDULE

1. INSTALL SHEETROCK
2. FIREWALL INSPECTION
3. FINISH FIREWALL
4. TAPE SHEETROCK
5. APPLY TOPPING AT SHEETROCK
6. SKIM COAT AT SHEETROCK
7. COMPLETE SHEETROCK PREPARATION AND PATCHING
8. SPRAY TEXTURE WALLS AND ACOUSTIC CEILING
9. PUNCHLIST - GYPSUM WALL BOARD
10. INSTALL EXTERIOR STAIRS
11. INSTALL BALCONY RAILING AND SIDING
12. PAINT EXTERIOR
13. SET ELECTRIC PANEL BOARDS AND METER BASES
14. INSTALL MASTER TV AMPLIFIERS
15. BLOW CEILING INSULATION
16. INSTALL INTERIOR WOOD TRIM AND DOORS
17. DRYWALL CLEAN UP AND SCRAPE FLOORS
18. PAINT INTERIOR WALLS AND FIRST COAT ENAMEL
19. PAINT SECOND COAT ENAMEL
20. HANG WALLPAPER
21. PUNCHLIST - PAINTER
22. INSTALL WARDROBE DOORS
23. INSTALL FINISH HARDWARE
24. INSTALL MAIL BOXES
25. INSTALL HOT WATER BOILERS AND STORAGE TANKS
26. CONNECT BOILER TO FLUE
27. HOOK-UP BOILERS AND TEST
28. INSTALL FIRE EXTINGUISHERS
29. RECEIVE AND STOCK CABINETS AND VANITIES
30. INSTALL CABINETS AND VANITIES
31. PUNCHLIST - CARPENTRY
32. INSTALL LAMINATED PLASTIC TOPS
33. INSTALL MIRRORS
34. CLEAN APARTMENTS FOR RESILIANT FLOORING
35. INSTALL RESILIANT FLOORING
36. PUNCHLIST - RESILIANT FLOORING
37. SET TOILETS - SINKS LAVS.
38. SET GARBAGE DISPOSERS, DISHWASHERS AND TOILET ACCESSORIES
39. PUNCHLIST - PLUMBER
40. INSTALL STOVES, HOODS
41. INSTALL EXHAUST FANS, HEATERS, INTERIOR LIGHT FIXTURES
42. INSTALL EXTERIOR BUILDING MOUNTED LIGHT FIXTURES
43. PUNCHLIST - ELECTRICAL
44. CLEAN APARTMENTS FOR CARPET
45. INSTALL TACK STRIP AND PAD
46. INSTALL CARPET
47. PUNCHLIST - CARPETING
48. INSTALL REFRIGERATOR
49. CLEAN WINDOWS
50. TEST TV ANTENNA SYSTEM
51. INSTALL DRAPES
52. FINAL CLEAN UP (MIRRORS PLG FIXTURES, RESILIANT FLOOR)
53. CITY INSPECTION
54. OWNERS FINAL INSPECTION AND ACCEPTANCE
55. INSTALL ELECTRIC METERS
56. INSTALL LAUNDRY EQUIPMENT

30
Merchandising nonincome properties

Effective merchandising is a means by which a developer can substantially outperform his competition. If the competition is weak in merchandising, it is vulnerable and will lose a portion of its market to the developer who can effectively merchandise (see Chapter 7).

MERCHANDISING: AN EXTENSION OF MARKETING

Marketing is a process of establishing and meeting objectives. Stating the precise goals to be reached is beneficial, but sales success depends on the marketing objectives being implemented through a merchandising strategy. This strategy determines the nature and direction of the broad approach to be used in the achievement of the marketing objective. An overall strategy prevents the merchandising organization from engaging in scattershot activities in all directions. Until a specific strategy is defined to achieve marketing objectives, a meaningful plan of action cannot be detailed (see Chapters 1, 2, 15, and 18).

TAPPING EMOTIONS TO DEVELOP PROJECT PERSONALITY

Once the marketing program has identified the objectives, it is up to the merchandising program to "sell the sizzle," stimulating emotion and excitement about the product. The merchandising program must develop a total project personality, a complete image to help the buyer identify with the community. If the buyer can emotionally identify with the lifestyle the project affords, a strong sales impetus has been created.

Creating excitement and strong emotional appeal usually means doing something different. This can mean bringing in new ideas or doing a substantially better job of presenting tested and proven ideas to create a more favorable effect. In any event, merchandising should sell the uniqueness of the project, the qualities which make it stand apart from the competition. This could consist of a well-integrated community theme relating to the history of the property or the atmosphere of the location. The design and planning of the product, as it relates to the lifestyle of the potential buyer, could be the unique feature. Even in overbuilt markets, there will always be a handful of builders doing quite well because of their merchandising and product excellence (see Chapter 11).

ZEROING IN ON THE CENTRAL THEME

A developer who has a unique image or something special to offer must promote his product in a special way. This requires a thorough understanding of the market objective and merchandising strategy. An understanding of the consumer for whom the project is designed is critical, so that every possible appeal can be directed to the type of consumer which the market research has identified as having needs the project can meet (see Chapter 8).

When a developer is delivering a new innovation to a market or breaking into the market for the first time, advertising should set the tone by concentrating on image before getting into the specifics of the product. A strong advertising commitment is needed to break through the market and establish a high profile. The whole story should not be told in one advertisement, only the principal concept to whet appetites and tease curiosity. A cohesive, well-executed theme can save many advertising dollars by repetition, and gradually zeroing in on a theme, thus providing for easy recall.

ALLOCATING ADVERTISING AND PROMOTION DOLLARS

In establishing advertising budgets it should be remembered that the more put into advertising, the less is received for each additional dollar. Doubling the advertising budget does not double traffic flow, because there are diminishing returns. Advertising expenditures can be reduced by creativity, imagination, and attention-getting advices. A small creative ad will draw better than a large unimaginative one.

For a developer, advertising is only a substitute for a good self-advertising site. If a site generates adequate traffic flow, media costs can be minimized. An important source of traffic is word-of-mouth mention. A project that presents a good image will spontaneously create word-of-mouth advertising from those who have experienced the environment. They will send their friends to enjoy the same experience.

No more than 5 to 10 percent of the advertising budget should be committed until the project is ready. Presales have an enormous attrition rate; the further ahead the presales, the greater the loss of sales before move-in. Presales require continuous, strong follow-up, a campaign budget to hold onto sales, and an incentive program for presales which are not lost.

Advertising dollars should be spread over a number of media types. Real estate sections of newspapers and home builders' type magazines are the No. 1 draw, and billboards are second. Billboards are a good means of establishing communications with potential buyers because they can build up interest over a period of time whereas a newspaper ad must work on a same-day basis. Billboards also serve to establish project identity and lead the buyer to the site. For presales, 25 percent of the billboards should be up; 30 percent more 40 days before the grand opening; and all should be up by the grand opening date.

Public relations generally costs less than advertising. The developer can plan events that make news to get editorial coverage in the real estate sections of newspapers, such as parties for buyers and friends. Referables should comprise more than 40 percent of business. The model complex and recreational buildings can be turned over to key charities and leading social groups for fund-raising projects. These people are the influence leaders and trend setters. Furnishing food and beverages and letting the charities charge to go through the model complex creates strong word-of-mouth advertising, and the word is particularly good because it is coming from the influence leaders in the community.

Newspaper ads in sections other than real estate can give the developer better identity with a smaller ad. The women's section, the sports section, or the financial pages could be tried, depending on the potential buyer.

Radio advertising can be effective in reaching a precise age or income group or demographic breakdown. However, it cannot buy the geographic audience as well as print can. In order to get good recall from radio, a saturation through repeats is needed, and this is expensive.

SELECTIVITY IN A DIRECT MAIL CAMPAIGN

A direct mail program can be very successful if the right mailing list is matched up with the right promotional copy. For example, if there are many renters in an area of a lower- to moderate-cost condominium project, 40 percent or more of the buyers should come out of nearby apartment projects. A direct mail campaign to these residents can be very effective. Random direct mailings invite failure; people often will not even bother to open an envelope when it is recognized as being a sales promotion.

Everybody reads postcards, however. A postcard with a clever photo and copy can be an effective advertisement. The photo need not even be of the project; for example, an enticing mountain scene could have copy such as "If you lived in Woodlake you would have more time to enjoy your other favorite places."

In follow-up mail to a prospect who has visited the sales office, the card could be directed to a child in the family: "Dear Ronney: Come see us again at Woodlake. Three families with children about your age moved in by the lake. You'd have a great time with them in our playground. Bring Mommy with you, but don't tell her we told you; it can be our secret." It does no harm to be clever and poke fun.

Brochures are an effective selling tool. A well-designed brochure which conveys the essence of the community and its lifestyle can aid a potential buyer emotionally relive his visit to the project. All other factors being approximately equal, the emotional appeal of a project will be decisive, and a brochure which can assist in this recall will be a strong sales tool. Give brochures to industrial employers who may distribute them to their employees and may use them to attract employees to their company by showing the superior housing available in the area. How much should brochures cost? For quantities of 8,000, $4,000 is considered low and $10,000 high.

There should be a unified theme in all advertising, promotion and signs, and the way-of-living concept should also be projected by the model complex. Theme and identity are all-important in achieving identity and recall; the buying situation, it should be recalled, is not so much logical as emotional. The successful promotion of an emotional experience will lead to sales success and enthusiastic word-of-mouth referrals from those who have experienced the "romance" of a visit to the project.

SELLING WITH THE MODEL COMPLEX

The model complex is an invaluable tool for not only generating sales but holding presales. Often presales drop out because the actual project is not up to the expectations that have been created in the advertising and promotional program. The model complex must reinforce and enhance the expectations built up in the presales program. If the community has been oversold and the model complex does not deliver up to expectations, both presales and new sales will suffer.

The first step in designing the model complex is to relate the merchandising strategy to dollars, in order to establish a budget. The budget can be heavily influenced by the sales price of the units, demographics and size of project, and competition in the marketplace. Decorating budgets are difficult to generalize because they are dependent on the specific situation. However, the developer can generally get back 50 to 75 percent of his upfront investment in interior design by selling the furnished models intact.

With landscaping, 100 percent of the up-front costs can generally be recovered, because landscaping appreciates as it grows and is highly valued by home buyers. The extra value attributable to landscaping will also be reflected in the appraisal of the property. Landscaping adds greatly to sales appeal by setting the environment and giving an established look. Landscaping softens the visual impact and can be used effectively to screen problem areas and to compensate for detail which the structure may lack. Trees should be deciduous in the model compound, and seasonal color should be maintained at all times by rotating annuals and the proper selection of perennials.

The decor of the model area must match the lifestyle of the potential buyer so that the prospect can see himself living in the house. Models should have a lived-in look and should be designed slightly above the means of the buyer, in order to satisfy the striving for achievement. They should be made memorable through clever utilization of space, application of an encompassing theme, and effective utilization of color. No two models should have the same color scheme. A strong color theme aids recall.

The cost between doing a mediocre job and an outstanding job is not great. The difference in marketing impact will make the difference between being part of the crowd or standing out in it. The edge the project has on the competition is what turns on prospects and gets them excited, talking, buying (see Chapter 6).

SELLING THE COMMUNITY AND ESTABLISHING A THEME

Money should be spent not on unrelated eye-catchers but on those items that will give the entire project a coordinated look, a personality, a theme. The repetitive use of coordinated graphics is a good way to set the image and develop strong recall.

Once advertising, promotion, and curb appeal have pulled the potential buyer in, the sales office is where the first impression is registered and personal, eye-to-eye contact is made. To establish the buying mood, the sales office must be the epitome of the lifestyle image of the potential buyer. The way of life offered should be immediately recognizable in the sales office, to reinforce and hold the ownership desires aroused by the lifestyle appeal. There should be a strong continuity of theme between the sales office and models so the buyer is not let down at the most important moment, the closing.

The sales office should be planned for both traffic control and visual control. Salespeople should be able to monitor the models and prospective buyers from the office, send an expansive view of the model area from the sales office also attracts buyers. It is very helpful if the recreational facilities are also within easy view of the sales office, because as another display they reinforce the lifestyle concept. Salespeople can use the setting as a subconscious motivater while working up to the closing.

Plants in the office and model area add to charm, soften the visual effect, and can be used to screen out problem areas. A rental service for plants ensures that they will look good and be properly maintained.

MAINTAINING THE MOOD

Maintenance is extremely important to the image of the model complex. A poorly maintained model complex can destroy much of the image building which was the justification for the model expense.

When models are initially set up, detailed pictures should be taken of every room. Then every 60 to 90 days, photos should be compared to the room, and items that are missing replaced. If units have been downgraded since the opening, remedial action should be taken. On a day-to-day basis it is often difficult to see how much the models have deteriorated, and comparison with the pictures makes the faults evident.

Salespeople must walk through the models every morning and evening to check models and list pick-up items. All deficiencies should be listed and appropriate action taken immediately.

EXPLAINING THE MERCHANDISING STRATEGY

A salesperson who thoroughly understands the product, the planning that went into it, and the marketing concepts has self-confidence, is excited about the project, and motivated to sell. Salespeople should know the benefits of each model and the marketing advantages over competitors. A salesperson who goes out and does his own research of the competition will remember it better, and the marketing differences will be more vivid in his mind.

Regular meetings on a weekly basis are important to maintain recall over the sales period. However, care should be taken that the salesperson does not become so knowledgeable he talks right past the close.

31
Merchandising income properties

COORDINATING CONSTRUCTION AND MARKETING SCHEDULES

Proper coordination between the construction and marketing phases of a project can substantially reduce fill-up expense. The marketing organization should get in at the earliest possible date and fill up the apartments as they become available. In garden-type apartments, preplanning for the earliest possible introduction of the marketing organization can have a marked effect on fill-up costs.

Marketing timing should be taken into consideration in the initial site planning and layout of the complex. The buildings along the front of the development, which provide the marketing window for the development, should be constructed first. The early construction of these buildings will enable the developer to establish an image at the earliest possible date and make possible the earliest possible move-in. The recreation building and amenity features also should be constructed early and coordinated with the construction of the first units.

The next construction scheduling priority from a marketing standpoint is to finish the buildings around the central court area, where the recreation building and the swimming pool are located. This makes it possible to finish off the environment in the court area and add to merchandising appeal. There may be a certain amount of objection to this from the construction organization because it disrupts their normal construction schedule somewhat. For example, to finish off the central court area before the rest of the development it is necessary to bring the landscape contractor in earlier than usual (see Chapter 29).

The landscape contractor generally will not want to come in at the earlier date required by the marketing program, because he cannot get maximum utilization out of his work force in this manner. However, the goal is so important from the marketing and fill-up expense standpoint that the developer must see that marketing interests are reflected in the construction schedule. In a larger project the difference can mean as much as a month or two in fill-up expenses. Developers who do not so plan and coordinate their marketing with their construction end up with a significantly greater fill-up expense.

As a development reaches substantial completion, most of the construction work has been completed, and what remains is landscaping, clean-up, and satisfactory completion of punch-list items. This phase of the work tends to drag out more than any other in the development. Yet it is this final clean-up and landscaping stage that must be completed before the marketing can really become effective.

In planning our projects, we often put our recreation building and swimming pool courtyard areas up at the front of the project. This is done not only to establish curb appeal but to locate the facilities in an area that can be finished off at the earliest possible date, to get the rents moving and keep fill-up expense down.

PRECOMPLETION RENTS

When marketing units at a precompletion stage, the offering of precompletion rents or other incentives is helpful in achieving the initial strong absorption which holds down fill-up expense. However, caution is in order if there is any hint of possible rent controls. Developers who have been caught in their rent-up program at precompletion rents have been severely hurt when rent controls were clamped onto their projects. In the feasibility stages, the projects were not designed to operate economically with precompletion rents, and developers have lost otherwise sound projects through being caught in this critical period by rent controls.

Ideally, the marketing organization should attempt to rent the units prior to completion so that there is a waiting list as the units are released by the construction organization. In order to do this, marketing must have reliable information when the units can be made available, and this requires credibility in the construction schedule. If a unit is promised to a resident by a specific date and then not delivered, serious inconvenience to the resident may cause the lease to be terminated and promote ill will.

SETTING AND REVISING RENTAL SCHEDULES

Rental rates will have a significant effect on the rate of absorption. If a particular type of unit is renting significantly more rapidly than other units, this may indicate that the rent on the fast-moving unit is too low or the other rents are too high. Absorption of the various unit types can be artificially controlled by shifts in the rental rate structure.

Rates should also adequately reflect the locational benefits associated with the units. If the primary initial demand is for units of a particular location in the project, and these units are being absorbed at an unusually rapid rate, that will generally be an indication that adequate locational premiums are not being charged for these units. Management should set the premiums at such a level so that only those residents who strongly desire the premium location and are willing to pay for it will select and rent units there. In this manner the project will fill up in a homogeneous manner, and premium units will be saved for those willing to pay for premium locations (see Chapter 11).

Should management find that a mistake has been made in the mix of units provided, so that there is a much stronger demand for one particular unit over another, a restructure of the rental program may compensate. For example, the slow-moving units can be offered at a rate lower than was anticipated in the original projections, while the fast-moving units, which management did not provide enough of, could be rented for premium rents. The attempt would be to average out at near the aggregate rent structure which was anticipated in the feasibility study. That is, the developer can use his strong positive features to offset, wherever possible, those units that are not producing as expected.

In setting rental premiums, care should be taken that the premiums are not put beyond what the market will bear. If unrealistic premiums are charged on the more desirable units, and if, even though several units are rented for these premiums the developer finds that he is not experiencing significant enough absorption with the remaining ones, he could reduce the premium. In this event, tenants who rented the first units at the very high premium will become disgruntled tenants, however, if the developer does not reduce their rents accordingly. This may be painful, but it will create tenant goodwill rather than "bad mouthing" from disgruntled tenants.

EFFECTS OF AMENITIES ON RENTAL SCHEDULES AND ABSORPTION

Another danger management must be aware of is that a developer who sees that a substantial premium can be charged for an amenity feature, such as a fireplace, is apt to want to put fireplaces in all the units. On paper, significantly greater return is possible with fireplaces in all of the units, as opposed to only having fireplaces in 25 percent of the units. But what works on paper does not necessarily work in the marketplace.

The danger is that, when all of the units have a design feature such as a fireplace, then all must be charged for the cost, and this in effect raises the base price on all the units. The fireplace becomes a standard rather than a premium item. What the developer has done is not to create more premium units but to eliminate them all by making them standard. Therefore he has to raise the rental base and must attract a higher income market in order to rent his units (see Chapter 17).

Developers have destroyed their chances for market success by adding items which they thought were premiums but which, in reality, turned out to be standard items. The items were added to all units, thus eliminating the concept of premium units and raising the base rents beyond the ability of the market to pay. In this instance, the developer is in essence dictating to the market: "You will pay extra for these particular features which I have chosen that you must have or else you can't live in my apartment complex." This serves to narrow down the market absorption potential rather than add to it.

The developer must provide amenities only for those who are willing to pay for them, and bread-and-butter units for those who are in the market for such units. Not every tenant has the same appreciation of a lake view or convenience of location to the clubhouse facilities. Some are willing to pay, others are not. The developer must provide a mix to serve both those who are very sensitive to convenience amenities and environmental features and bread and butter units for those who are not. In this manner the broadest possible market can be served, and the maximum number of premium dollars can be squeezed out of the percentage which is willing and eager to pay the required rental premiums (see Chapter 8).

ATTRACTING PROSPECTS THROUGH CURB APPEAL AND LAND PLANNING

Rental experience in many market areas around the country indicates that the highest percentage of traffic into the rental office results from people driving by the project. This indicates the significance of the self-advertising qualities of the site and curb appeal. The property should radiate a strong future promise to motorists passing by the project.

Not only must the project look interesting and inviting to the passing motorists, it must have enough punch to stop them and get them to park their cars and cross the curb to see what is inside. For this reason, it is advantageous to locate the amenity features where they can be seen off site. This creates the environmental way-of-living impact to pull the passing motorist into the project to see what's inside, either because of an immediate need for rental housing or merely to satisfy curiosity. Because the decision to rent an apartment is emotional rather than logical, as we have frequently noted, the potential resident must be reinforced at all times to foster a high level of initial satisfaction (see Chapter 13).

In most instances it is advantageous to locate the recreation building so that prospects enter through the recreation building (with the leasing office inside), where their impression is reinforced by the impact of the decorater-designed interiors and furnishings. When the rear wall of the recreation building is more than 70 percent, glass, the strong positive environmental impact of the interior of the recreation building is supplemented by the courtyard, swimming pool, and the many amenity features planned in close proximity.

The intent in merchandising income properties is to sell potential residents on the total community and on the planning and social concept before they ever see the apartment. The close can be partially made in advance, and prospects should feel that if the apartment is anywhere near satisfactory, this is the place they want to live. The trip between the rental office and the model unit, which should be located in the immediate vicinity of the amenity package, should be highly controlled. The most desirable portions of the development should be shown.

In many instances, the reverse happens; potential residents are taken across parking lots and past the backs of buildings, so that they experience the least desirable areas in the project. By the time they reach the unit, they have already decided that this is not the type of project they want to live in. Therefore the trip from the rental office to the unit should be designed with great care.

SHOWING THE APARTMENTS

Once prospects reach the unit, they should be emotionally, reinforced by a bright, cheerful, pleasantly designed living environment—interior decor, wall coverings, and furnishings. Care should be taken to furnish the model unit with furniture that is appropriate for the income levels of prospective tenants, so they can picture themselves living there. If the unit is overdesigned and beyond their tenants means, they cannot identify and may attribute the attractiveness of the unit to decorations which are not included.

One of the more successful approaches is to furnish the model units with rental furniture which is available within the complex. This adds credibility to the environment being offered in the show model, and furniture specifically selected for the unit design and offered by the developer gives him a strong marketing advantage over competitors who do not offer a furnished package with their units. Since the developer is in the business of renting apartments and makes his money off the apartments, he can afford to offer the furniture package at a lower cost than a commercial furniture rental organization. The developer also does not have the furniture moving costs associated with a commercial furniture-leasing organization, since the furniture generally always remains in the apartment. The developer thus has lower overhead costs in maintaining a furniture rental program than a commercial furniture leasing organization would have.

Lenders prefer apartments which are unfurnished because they have much lower turnover rates. Yet, even though furnished apartments may experience greater turnover, properly furnished and merchandised units can in many instances enjoy higher occupancy rates than unfurnished units, due to the marketing edge gained by the tasteful furnishing. The cost of turnover can be offset through proper utilization of clean-up and security deposits.

In renting to the young married and singles market, apartments provided with gay and attractive wall coverings with patterns do well. The total interior should be color coordinated to be very bright, cheerful, and attractive. Young marrieds and singles typically do not have much in the way of furnishings and accessory items to brighten and liven up their units. They can see by the way the model unit is decorated that their own units will be livable and gay, though their furnishings are scanty.

For more sedate markets patterns are not provided in wall coverings because they could conflict with the accessory items and furnishings already owned by the prospective tenants. Incompatability with current accessories and furnishings will dissuade some from renting.

Small details are important. There should be complete place settings for the dinner table, a floral centerpiece, and plants throughout the apartment. The drapes should be open to show the view, and plants on balconies or patio areas add to the environment. Lights should be on in the apartment at all times so it is bright and cheerful. A radio should be playing, and magazines should be on the tables.

If the radio is placed on the kitchen counter, the apartment takes on the air of someone living there. There should be canned goods in the kitchen cabinets and decorative trim on shelf fronts to give a pleasant surprise as people open doors. Shelves in closets should be trimmed, and striking color on the clothes pole and some decorated novelty hangers hanging on it give a good impression of closet space.

In the bathrooms, colorful toilet accessories should be matched with towels and shower curtain. The bathroom area should be made vibrant and lively through color coordination and rich accessory items.

Messages in the drawers for those curious enough to open them are a nice touch. Linens in the linen cabinet could bear such a message as: "You'll love to live here because the management is so thoughtful in looking after your every need."

This type of care for extras indicates a thoughtful management. Not only do they show the unit well, but they give an indication of the concern of management in pleasing and accommodating residents.

THE RENTAL OFFICE

The rental office serves two purposes. It is a place to do business, and a place to reinforce the sales presentation concept established by the entire development. The environmental quality of the rental office should not be neglected because it's "just a utilitarian business office." This is where the prospect may be making his final determination of to rent or not to rent, and it should be a strong reinforcement of the lifestyle concept established in the overall development. If it is warm and lively, it says something about the management as well as the environmental quality of the complex.

Project graphics should reinforce the overall theme and tie the project together. This includes building identification, directional maps, the overall project identification, parking area identification and direction, identification of individual apartments, and decorative graphics used strictly for environmental impact. All should tie together to reinforce a central theme that is memorable and arresting.

THE OPENING

The manager must leave sufficient time prior to the opening for preparation of the project brochure. The brochure is designed to aid recall of the prospective tenant after he sees the project and returns to his home to consider it among a number of alternatives.

The brochure should convey the central theme of the project and reinforce the most marketable benefits associated with it. The brochure should be tastefully done. A hurriedly prepared brochure which does little more than convey rudimentary facts will emphasize management's lack of sensitivity, warmth, and caring. It should depict the lifestyle and the benefits to be derived from the location, amenities, planning, social activities, floor plans, and general character of the complex. Most importantly, the brochure should reflect the pride of management in the housing offered.

The brochures need not be overelaborate, for in the final analysis it is the housing environment and lifestyle and location which will be the deciding factor. The brochure serves as a reminder of the benefits to be gained from living in the project; it is not a benefit in itself. An excellent brochure will do little for a project that is mediocre.

The public relations and advertising campaign should precede the grand opening to pave the way with an image-building campaign to establish lifestyle concept to be marketed. Best results can be gained from a balanced program, which may include newspaper advertising, radio spots, and billboards.

DIRECT CONTACT

Direct personal contact is also an important ingredient in establishing traffic to the site. The manager can create traffic by calling on personnel directors of the leading business organizations in the immediate vicinity. Personnel directors who have new personnel coming from out of town are anxious to direct them to quality housing projects in the vicinity.

Additionally, a business organization may lease a block of rental units to house personnel brought in from other regions at regular intervals for training or reorientation purposes. Many organizations have found it less costly to house these people in apartment buildings rather than in hotels or motels. It has become a rather common practice for an organization to rent as many as 10 or 15 apartments in a project to house visiting personnel. These units are generally rented furnished including linens, kitchen utensils and dishes. A housekeeping type of service is also required in this type of arrangement. In addition to providing income for 10 or 15 units, the association between the apartment management and the business organization provides good word of mouth for those employees currently living in the area, who are interested in rental housing, or who may refer friends to rental housing projects

GENERATING TRAFFIC

Traffic can be generated to the project by offering meeting rooms to social organizations such as ski clubs, boating and hiking clubs, and lecture organizations. This creates identity in the community and provides word of mouth advertising.

At first the advertising and public relations campaign should optimize traffic, not necessarily qualify prospects. When a building is first put on the market, it is important to generate traffic and to create a feeling of acceptance, success, and recognition.

The more people are attracted to the project and see other people there, the more they are assured that their judgment is right in coming to the project. It is obviously a success judging by the traffic it has been able to create. Thus people tend to convince one another about the project.

This builds enthusiasm not only for potential residents but for management as well. Initial enthusiasm is important to success because it contributes so heavily to the quality of life the community will enjoy.

A QUALITY RENTAL STAFF EQUALS QUALITY RESIDENTS

Care should be taken in selecting and recruiting the rental staff, because its members will tend to rent to people like themselves. The first people into the project will tend to establish the tenor of the development and the quality of the typical resident. If the project starts off on a bad foot with mediocre residents, it will most probably continue in that direction, because the trend will tend to reinforce itself. On the other hand, if the initial residents are of good quality and are good neighbors, others of a like nature will be attracted, and the trend will tend to reinforce itself.

Projects have been damaged because of a bad image created as a result of the type of tenant initially attracted to the building complex. The complex from that time thereafter is handicapped by a negative image which tends to be self-fulfilling until the situation becomes unmanageable. In a number of instances, it has been necessary to replace the management, and the new management, in turn, has had to replace many of the current tenants in order to reverse the image. Alert, clean-cut, youthful managers will attract the same type of residents. Sloathful, indifferent managers will attract like residents, to the detriment of the rental project.

Training the rental staff

The rental staff should be thoroughly knowledgeable of the project, how it compares to others in the area, and able to compare features and amenities in addition to rents. The sales staff should know facts about the neighborhood: distance to shopping, churches, transportation, expressways, parks, recreation areas, employment centers, and so on. Prospective residents, faced with having to make a decision to lease, will often look for reasons why they should not do so in order to postpone the decision. A well-informed and well-trained staff can handle objections, reinforce with positive input, and show the prospect why he should lease and why the particular complex offers the best value in the neighborhood. This requires additional training of the staff and a constant follow-up (see Chapters 6 and 14).

EVALUATING THE TRAFFIC TO PROVIDE FEEDBACK

Feedback is important to evaluate the performance of any operation. The advertising and public relations operations need feedback to determine effectiveness. This can best be accomplished by evaluating the traffic. The first step in evaluating the traffic is to qualify visitors to see if they are prospective residents. Find out also how they heard of the project and what influenced them to come into the rental office. The rental staff should keep an accurate record of the number of prospects each day. From this information a ratio can be developed between the number of people visiting the project and the number of leases rented, and the ratio can be used as a measure of the performance of the rental staff, validity of the rent schedule, and the appropriateness of the total marketing effort.

32

Applying profit planning and controls to commercial development: A case study approach

Most of the profit planning and control concepts and techniques presented in the previous chapters are applicable to commercial as well as residential development with some adjustments made in the application.

The following cast study of a commercial garden office park development is included to illustrate the transferability of the marketing, value engineering, and management concepts and techniques presented. Frequent cross references will be included in the cast study to direct the reader to the particular chapter in the book which has a bearing on the cast study. Keep in mind that some modification is necessary in applying the referenced concepts and techniques to commercial development. Nonetheless the compatability of the material to commercial office development can be readily seen by referring back to preceeding chapters. Many of the forms, work sheets, budgets, charts, and reference materials in the book can be tailored for use in commercial development, while others can be utilized with little or no modification.

GARDEN OFFICE CASE STUDY

How does a garden office park command rents 15 percent per square foot above the majority of the competition in a market area experiencing a 45 percent vacancy factor in new speculative office space? How does one reach 100 percent occupancy in such a market area by absorbing roughly 30 percent of the new speculative office space within the immediate market area and operate at a 79 percent break-even point in a market experiencing numerous failures? The answer, of course, is that you have to do everything right from market identification, concept and product development, construction, merchandizing, maintenance, and everything in between down to the smallest detail (see Chapters 1 and 2). At the time that the subject office park on the west coast which we researched, planned, and designed was financed, real estate companies, insurance firms, and a few savings and loans were completely out of the speculative realty market. Yet the developer was able to obtain favorable financing for the subject office park (see Chapter 18 and 23).

Learning from the competition

Naturally in a market area with such a high vacancy factor in speculative office space one can find some noteworthy lessons in what not to do (see Chapters 6 and 14). The comparable properties experiencing the highest vacancy factors were buildings with deep office spaces extending from corridors to exterior walls. Normally, this type of design allows for a high efficiency factor in an office building yet, interestingly, a number of these buildings possess a lower efficiency factor than the subject office complex. The deep spaces were not attractive to the smaller space users—those in the average 1,000- to 3,000-square-foot range—which predominates the office market in the subject market area.

The larger users of space and institutional type users congregate in the downtown core area, typically in high-rise office space. The median rent in the more expensive to construct, high-rise office space in the downtown core area was interestingly less than the median rent which the subject office complex was able to command.

The projects experiencing the high rate of vacancy were predictably not as well planned, designed, maintained, or merchandized as the subject office complex, though their median construction costs equaled or exceeded sometimes substantially, the costs of the subject complex.

Defining the market

The primary market for the subject development was the small space user with an average space need of approximately 1,000 to 3,000 square feet. These small users need space to grow and therefore represent an incubator market. This market is of great value to the developer who manages his properties in a professional manner, because he can then control his current tenants and provide for their future space needs in new construction phases (see Chapters 8 and 12). Each new building in the subject office complex consisting of four buildings received a range of 15 percent to 20 percent of its tenants from existing space users within the same complex who had requirements for larger space.

The target market for the office complex was prestige oriented, interested in planning with a high degree of environmental character. The prestige market is interested in planning and design concepts and willing to pay for a superior, well-maintained environment. The typical tenant for the subject property was a concept-oriented tenant as opposed to an economic-necessity oriented tenant. It is important to understand which broad tenant group an office complex is oriented towards (see Chapter 15). Absorption can be achieved by possessing the marketing edge of being able to deliver the best price in the market or the best concept and environment. The middle ground between these two marketing strategies, concept or economic necessity, can be dangerous from a marketing standpoint. A project in this middle category may have no distinguishing attributes of significant enough consequence to provide a marketing edge over its competition (see Chapter 11).

In such a situation, if the developer makes a half hearted effort to appeal to the concept market without truly producing the environmental quality and detail sought by that market, he will not capture the concept market and, due to cost, will also limit his ability to attract the economic necessity market. A developer in such a predicament has limited his attractiveness to the two basic market groupings which his potential tenants fall into, and ends up in a middle group of mediocrity slugging it out with other owners who find themselves in the same predicament. That is, the owners of the mediocre projects have produced no significant distinguishable marketing attributes and possess a fuzzy perception of who their potential tenants really are and how to reach them (see Chapter 12).

Accumulated versus ongoing demand

At the top of the concept market are those individuals and firms willing to pay rental premiums, sometimes substantial, for that space which ideally suits their image and environmental preferences, both corporate and personal. The cream at the top of the concept market for office space may not represent a very large percentage of the total demand for speculative office space. This relatively small percentage of tenants may be housed in space that does not adequately measure up to their environmental preferences. Those owners who have captured the top of the market in a specific market area may be doing so partially by default, due to lack of sophisticated competitive product to serve this market segment. There can be a fairly sizeable accumulated demand for premium-quality office space, though the ongoing demand represents a fairly small percentage of total demand for new speculative office space (see Chapter 11).

If a firm hand can be kept on cost, through value engineering, while delivering a superior environment, the developer can then enjoy an additional marketing edge of being able to deliver top quality office space at the best price to the concept market. Those few competitors who are delivering a similar quality of space to that market will suffer a competitive disadvantage if they must offer their space at a higher rent to achieve the same return (see Chapter 13).

When a developer can properly identify an accumulated demand for premium office space and identify the weaknesses of the competitors who attempt to supply a premium product for this demand, the developer can produce a marketing monopoly. When a developer truly understands the need, and can draw upon the expertise and professionalism to deliver a product that can obsolete his competitors products, he can create a market monopoly (see Chapter 7).

Irrational versus rational market behavior

When a marketing monopoly is accomplished, the developer adds a large subjective element to the feasibility process (see Chapter 18). That is, an appraisal of the market area done for feasibility purposes may indicate that there is not sufficient depth to the market to justify construction of new premium-quality office facilities. Appraisal, however, implies average conditions and rational behavior in the market place. The subjective element referred to is that a skilled developer, utilizing marketing and value-engineering expertise, can produce a result in the market place far from what average conditions indicate and can create "irrational behavior" in the market place through skillful merchandizing.

Appraisal theory utilizes a concept of "rational behavior"; however, the subjective element of marketing value engineering and merchandizing can produce results in a market place that could be termed "irrational" in the context of traditional appraisal practices (see Chapter 19). The essence of skillful marketing, value engineering, and merchandizing is to enlarge preceved value while holding a firm line on costs to induce market action not available to less sophisticated entrepreneurs.

Effect of accumulated demand on absorption forecasting

When the above formula is successfully accomplished the successful project may command a very large share of the target concept market, sometimes exceeding 30 percent of a combination of both the accumulated and ongoing market demand and accounting for rapid absorption even in soft markets (see Chapter 11).

A development success such as this may then give off a false market signal to other developers. Other developers seeing the rapid absorption of the subject development at premium rents, may conclude that the subject development is an indication that a strong market exists for similar types of construction (see Chapter 10). What they do not understand, however, is that the major absorption for the subject property was taken out of accumulated demand, possibly a large percentage of accumulated demand, and that the owner of the subject development, if he has continuing development plans, may control a good portion of the ongoing demand in the market place, as well as having already absorbed the bulk of the accumulated demand (see Chapter 9).

Marketing monopolies are best accomplished with smaller to medium size projects. Large projects cannot generally benefit sufficiently from accumulated demand alone, but must also be supported by strong ongoing demand. In markets that are experiencing worrysome vacancy rates, a large project will be difficult to pencil out. However, smaller projects that can capture pockets of accumulated demand can receive sufficient absorption from that demand to thrive despite the prevailing market condition. Larger projects, which will be fewer in the foreseeable future, depend on strong ongoing demand. Without the combination of strong ongoing as well as accumulated demand larger projects can experience troublesome and financially threatening fill-up and carrying costs.

Location

The subject office park is located on a busy commercial/residential street within walking distance of 2,000 apartment units, 6 restaurants and 1 shopping center. Freeway access is one block away with the complex being visible from the freeway. Driving time to airport and downtown is ten minutes. (See Chapters 3 and 10.) The land was assembled from several residential lot purchases. The site and landscape plan takes maximum advantage of the site's self-advertising aspects.

Matching the concept and product to market need

Identifying the market need is critical but being able to fill the market need with the correct product is where the profit is. The closer the concept and the actual product reflect the needs of the subject market segment, the greater will be the chances of success and of achieving a market monopoly. Some of the concept and product features which relate to the market need will be described briefly (see Chapters 15 and 16).

Garden setting. The landscaping is very important to the success of a garden office complex. The landscaping design should be an integral part of the developmental concept and implemented with great care. The view from the individual offices to the landscaped areas should create a prestigious, relaxed, and comfortable environment for the space user.

Window area. Particularly when there is a pleasant landscaped view, the square footage of windows area available adds to marketability and prestige of space. Increased window area, however, also adds to HVAC operating costs. To gain the prestige without undue sacrifice in operating costs, the building glass areas in the subject development were handled in the following manner.

The corridors of the building run in a reference east-west direction. The offices off of the corridors have a northern exposure on the front side of the building and a southern exposure on the rear of the building. The building is set back further from the street than required by the zoning code (average 32 feet of landscaping between building and sidewalk) in order to create an attractive landscaped area in front of the building.

The offices along the front of the building, facing the premium landscaped area, have larger windows than the offices at the rear of the building, to take advantage of the landscape view. In that these larger windows are on the North side of the building, a sun control problem does not exist and operating costs are not unduly penalized. The units on the front of the building can justify a rental premium over the offices at the rear of the building.

Through the glass area for the offices at the rear of the building is less than on the front of the building the size of the window is none the less generous, being four feet by five feet. These windows are shielded from the southern sun by a four-foot overhand at the roof, also the second floor cantilevers over the first floor by four feet. Vertical columns which project out beyond the second floor wall provide a vertical sun shade to the windows in addition to the horizontal sun protection offered by the roof overhang and the second floor cantilever.

At the ends of the building, sliding glass doors provide access to balconies on the second floor and enclosed patio areas on the first floor. These offices at both ends of the building can then be marketed at premium rents as patio garden offices.

Square footage of window space, in and of itself, does not justify a rental premium. As an example, a competitor building has 100 percent glass (wall to wall and floor to ceiling) for the first floor offices. The owner of the competitor building was attempting with little success to get a rental premium for those offices over the offices on the floors above, which have less window area. However, the first floor offices do not have a view. For the most part they look onto the unattractive parking lot separated from the glass by four feet of unimaginative landscaping. Though the owner was asking less per square feet for the offices on the floors above, they would be a better value than the first floor offices if both spaces were offered at the same price, because the offices above do have some view as contrasted to the 100 percent glass walled offices on the first floor which have no view.

Office depth. Three different office depth alternatives were offered within the typical office building in the subject office park. At the first floor level the office depths are the same 28 feet on both sides of the corridor. Because the rear of the building is cantilevered out four feet at the second floor for sun protection a second office depth of 32 feet is introduced. The office depth at the ends of the building is 36 feet. (The hall does not run through to the end of the building).

What all of this means is that the various office depths from corridor to building exterior allow a great deal of flexibility in laying out the internal office space efficiently to reflect the needs of small space users, which are the primary market. Buildings possessing less flexibility in internal office layout are not able to meet the very specific needs of the individual small space user as well as can be accomplished in the subject building.

As an example, there was a new office building of approximately 34,000 square feet by a competitor in the market area which had been leasing for more than three years yet was only 50 percent occupied. The building is of generally attractive design with an average to better-than-average location within the market area. The feature which created the strongest contrast with the subject office park is that there is only one office depth offered, and it is a 60-foot depth. Such an office depth assumes a large or institutional user and closes the door to the smaller space user, who constitutes the primary market for the space (see Chapter 14).

Average size of tenant spaces. A standard building design had been developed by us for the subject office complex with three standard office depths from hallway to exterior wall. However, the interior tenant space requirements vary in average size for each building, with the first building possessing the smallest average tenant space and each succeeding building possessing a larger average tenant space and fewer tenants per building.

The first building possesses an average tenant space of approximately 1,000 square feet and the fourth building possesses an average tenant space of 3,000 square feet or about a third as many tenants per building.

There are two primary reasons for increasingly larger tenant spaces as the office park matures. The first is that, for the owner to control his earlier "incubator tenants," he must have larger spaces readily available for them to move into. This he can accomplish by providing later buildings with increasingly larger tenant spaces. The second reason is to increase the breadth of the concept market which the office park can accommodate. The wide range in average size of tenant spaces in the various buildings offers the owner flexibility in retaining his "incubator tenants," and flexibility in being able to accommodate a broad range of the concept market tenant size requirements.

Tenant improvements. Eighty percent of the tenant improvements were constructed in the prime construction contract at the same time as the building shell was constructed. That is, tenant improvements for pre-leased tenants were designed and constructed, but in addition, tenant improvements for unleased space were also designed and constructed at the time the shell was constructed, even though leases had not been obtained. By knowing the needs of the target market, it was possible to prebuild the tenant improvements prior to leasing.

By constructing the tenant improvements within the prime building contract at the same time as the shell, the owner was able to gain a substantial reduction in tenant improvement costs (see Chapter 27). Additionally, the predesigned and constructed tenant space provided the owner with a marketing advantage in leasing to those tenants who have an urgent need for space, or have a difficult time visualizing what the finished space will look like when they are viewing the competitor's shell building with unfinished interior spaces. For the owner who has the advantage of knowing his market well, preconstructing tenant improvements can yield impressive cost and marketing advantages over the competition.

Common facilities and leasing inducements. Each building possesses a prestigiously decorated conference room for the common use of the building tenants. A Xerox machine was provided in a separate Xerox room for the common use of the building tenants. This eliminated the necessity for the tenants to buy or rent their own copying equipment. Each tenant has a plug-in key/copy counter. Each month the tenants are billed by the owner for their portion of the copying costs. Tenants are charged 9 cents per copy. This allows the owner to make a profit on the copy machine. The owner thus gets a double benefit from the common copy machine, in that it both assists in attracting and retaining tenants, and produces additional income to the owner.

A small lunch room is provided in each building with a sink area and counter top, refrigerator, and vending machines. Though the room is not large enough to eat in, the convenience it offers is valued by the tenants. Additionally, the vending machines provide a source of income.

The lobby area is warm, inviting, providing a comfortable and relaxing residential character to the building as opposed to an institutional or impersonal character. The lobby contains a fireplace with flooring of paver tiles and a beamed ceiling. Accessory items in the lobby include handsome and distinctive wall-mounted lighting fixtures and paintings. The paintings are not limited to the lobby area but are included in the corridor areas as well. The lobby area is furnished with comfortable couches, lounging chairs, coffee tables and distinctive antiques, such as grandfather clocks and bookcases. Large indoor plants in attractive containers are utilized generously to provide the finishing touch (see Chapter 17).

All finishes in the public areas are of the highest quality including carpeting and under layment, accoustic ceiling tiles, vinal wall coverings, and trim. Costs that we value-engineered out in the basic shell of the building were partially invested back into the building in the finishes, where they add greatly to the prestige and marketability of the space. This carried through to details such as hand-carved wood exit signs, prestigious and costly looking occupant identification signs in the corridors, and project graphics such as project signing and miscellaneous directional and identification signing.

Financing the complex

The mortgage banker reports that the primary reasons he was able to arrange the loans for the subject project at a time when most lenders were out of the market are:

1. The developer was more effective in leasing and management of office space than the competitors (see Chapter 31).
2. The product represents a superior value in the marketplace even at above market rents.
3. The project is well located to serve the target market (see Chapter 3 and 4).

The economic value (see Chapter 19) is based on higher-than-market rents because the developer's previous buildings are all experiencing higher than market rents and are 100 percent occupied. Also, the effective operating expenses used to compute the economic value are 35 percent or 3 percent below the market operating expenses for the area.

The developer has been able to successfully demonstrate to the lender (see Chapter 23) that his actual operating expenses are less than market and is given credit for this in the calculation of economic value. The bulk of the savings is attributable to reduced utility expense. There is no preleasing requirement in the loan and the holdback is funded at break even which is 79 percent occupancy.

Marketing the complex

The developer is the leasing agent for the office park. Leasing and management are handled on a day-to-day basis by a full-time girl who is both leasing agent and building manager. The girls selected for the responsibility are attractive, courteous, personable, attentive, and prompt in giving attention to tenant needs. Ninety percent of all leases are handled by the developer. Ten percent of the leases are through realtors who receive a full commission.

The mortgage banker reports that by keeping all leasing and property management in house, the developer has been successful in offering personal and customized service to tenants and potential space users. The personal service offered provides a marketing advantage which most complexes utilizing impersonal contract property management companies cannot provide.

Direct mail has been utilized very successfully. A reverse phone directory is used to establish a mailing list of the tenants in competing office developments within the market area. Direct mail materials include a brochure with rendering and site plan of the office park. Also postal cards are utilized with a color rendering on the front.

Advertising has been utilized to advantage in local newspapers financial section and the *Wall Street Journal*. Public relations efforts include a periodical, all day, bay cruise on the developer's yacht for tenant executives. The leases are minimum two years and maximum five years.

The initial tenants in the newly constructed office space are generated from the following sources and in the percentages indicated below:

Tenants moving to new construction from existing subject office space 15 percent.

Tenants generated from direct mail and advertising, 20 percent.

Tenants derived from self-advertising aspects of site and drive-by traffic, 25 percent.

Tenants from public relations and word of mouth referrals, 30 percent.

Tenants resulting from outside realtors, 10 percent.

Index

A

Absorption forecasting, 125–36
  accumulated demand, effect of, 542
  form innovation, 127–28
Absorption rate, 26, 119
  amenities economics, 219–20
  competitive position and, 126–27
  effects of amenities on, 531–32
  future, 133–34
  income characteristics, effects of, 130
  innovation and, 127
  location, effects of, 133
  optimized, 176, 178
  population characteristics, effects of, 129–30
  projection of, 121
  rental rates, 133–34, 530
  sales rates, 133–34
  supply, effects of, 130–33
  value, effects of, 133
Absorption stratification, 126
Acceptance of materials, 420
Accessibility, 27
Accounting for Profit Recognition on Sales of Real Estate, 87
Accounting standards board rulings, 112–13
Accounting System for All Builders, 264, 281
Accounting systems, reports and requirements; *see* Automated accounting system *and* Budgets
Accumulated demand, 132, 542
Action plans, 8–9
  define, 9
  feasibility considerations for, 16–17
Active retired persons, 97
Activity
  defined, 261
  effect on budget, 261
Administrative costs, work simplification to control, 365
Advertising, as land source, 24
Advertising dollars
  income property merchandising, 535

Advertising dollars—*Cont.*
  nonincome property merchandising, 524–25
After-tax cash flow stream, 253
After-tax return for a single year, 246
After-tax yield, 243
Age distribution in population, 129
Aggregate market, 95
Amenities, 194, 198, 203–4, 207–9
  absorption, 219–20
  addition profitably without increasing rents, 221
  addition to reduce equity requirements, 220–21
  asset or liability?, 215–23
  consumer willing and able to pay for, 215–17
  cost/benefit ratios of, 222–23
  design, 153
  effects of, 531–32
  emotional impact, continuity of, 220
  encouragement of amenity/resident interaction, 221–22
  functional and attractive, 220
  income, 219–20
  increase through reductions elsewhere, 217
  landscaping, 217–19
  mistakes in planning, 223
  nonuniform provision of, 216
  recreation facilities, 215–17
  tenant retention, 219–20
American Plywood Association, 188
Analysis and formalization of business operation, 485–86
Analytical information, use of, 7
Antiques, appeal of, 91
Apartment models, showing of, 533–34
Apartment property; *see* Income property merchandising
Apartments, 99
  occupancy rates, 123
  showing of, 533–34
Appraisal
  defined, 225
  objective nature of, 225

Appraising human resources, 476
Appreciation in value
  factors causing, 21–22
  greatest potential for, 25
  rate of, 47
Architectural decisions, 394
Architectural drawings, 507
Attributes of property, 243
Automated accounting system, 264–77
  benefits of, 265–66
  cash disbursements–accounts payable subsystem, 275–77
    accounts payable, division–vendor, 275
    check register, 275
    machine checks and remittance advices, 275
    reports generated, 275
    retentions payable, 275
    system features, 275
  design objective, 265
  general ledger–financial reporting subsystem, 267–72
    administrative overhead budget register report, 272
    balance sheet, 267
    cash deposits, 270–71
    distribution, 271
    general ledger, 269
    month-end check register, 269–70
    overhead budget variance, 267–68
    profit and loss statement, 267
    reports generated, 267–72
    system features, 267
    trial balance, 268–69
  project cost subsystem, 272–74
    customer options/deposits, 274
    job cost summary, 272
    plan monitor, 272
    project cost detail, 272–74
    reports generated, 272–73
    system features, 272
  remote job entry environment, 265–66
Average annual return, 248

549

B

Back-to-back design, 153–55, 209–10
Backcharges, provision for, 418, 505
Backup schedules, 503
Band-of-investment method, 250–51
Bargain sites, 22
Base data, 117–24
    sources, 119–20
Base prices, 71–72
Before-tax yield, 243
Behavioral approach, 486–87
Bidding process, 416–17
    reflecting value engineering in, 180–81
Billboards in nonincome property merchandising, 524–25
Blue sky, 240
Brainstorming, 362
Break-even point, 244, 251
Broad market defined, 96
Brochures
    income property merchandising, 534–35
    nonincome property merchandising, 525–26
Budget accounts, matching with subcontract accounts, 417
Budget plans, 9
Budgeting; *see also* Budgets
    defined, 258
    objectives, 258
Budgets; *see also* Budgeting
    activity, effect on, 261–62
    capacity, effect of, 261–62
    cash, 261
    chart of accounts in relation to, 259, 281–82; *see also* Chart of Accounts
    construction-in-process forecasts, 281
    establishment of, 259–60
    firm contract, 281
    fixed, 260–61
    flexible, 260–61
    for-sale housing plan; *see* For-sale housing budget plan
    functions performed in development of, 259
    level of detail desired, 259–60
    objectives of, 261
    organization chart, 259
    policy, 279–80
    postcontract, 281
    preliminary cost estimate, 280–81
    procedure, 280–81
    purpose, 279
    rental housing; *see* Rental housing budget plan
    reporting against standard of, 256
    standardized, 375
    types required for each project, 279–80
Builder-subcontractor relations, 420–21
Builders as land source, 24

Building activity, 119
Building elevations, 150
Buildings
    and construction, 112
    standardization in, 374
Business cycles; *see* Market cycles
Business expansion/recession cycle, 108–9
Business risk, 249
Buy and sell prices, 42–43
Buyers; *see also* Market segments
    apartments, 99
    cluster housing, 98
    duplex, 99
    economic necessity, 98–99
    enticed by a concept, 98
    fourplex, 99
    investment aspects, 98
    luxury income, 99
    middle-class comfort, 99
    moving up or down within community, 98
    moving within market area, 134–35
    needs of, 7
    newly formed households, 98, 134–35
    out of town, 98
    particular location desired, 98
    patio homes, 99
    renters turned, 98
    second or third homes, 98
    single-family attached, 99
    single-family detached, 98
    sources of, 134
    speculation, 98
    starter home, 99
    town houses, 99
    zero-lot-line housing, 99
Buying potential, 134

C

Calendar days, 503
Capabilities, 14–16
    development of people and technology, 379–80
    increasing management productivity, 386–89
    innovation, role in, 380–83
    leading organization from prosperity to bust, 384–86
    management process, 389–90; *see also* Management process
    profit growth key, 379–90
    successful companies, environment of, 383–84
Capacity
    defined, 261
    levels of, 261–62
Capital dollars, allocation of, 145
Capitalization, overall rate of, 247
Capitalization approach to market value, 242
Carport costs, 150
Cash budgets, 261

Cash on cash return, 245–46
    average, 245
    one-year basis, 245
Cash flow, 249
    rental housing; *see* Rental housing cash flow
Cash flow analysis, 252–53
    economic panorama, 253
    evolutionary process, 253
Cash flow calculation, 46, 49–50
Cash flow projections, 253
Cash-out period, 43
Census information breakdown, 121
Change, 102
    management's fear of, 139–40
Chart of Accounts, 259, 282–92, 414, 417
    balance sheet accounts, 282–87
    budget relationship to, 281–82
    categories, 282
    control of costs, 282–83
    defined, 282
    income statement and expense accounts, 282, 287–92
    long form, 283–92
    unit costs, 282–83
Chart of Accounts, Policy and Procedure for Budgeting and Accounting Report, 282
Checklists
    existing financing, 52
    job inspection, 403–10
    negotiation, 51
    site selection, 33–38
    title, liens restrictions, 51
Clean Air Act (1970), 55
Close-in development patterns, 110–11
Cluster housing, 98, 191–92
Coastal Zone Management Act (1972), 56–57
Commercial banks, 367–68
Commercial development
    accumulated demand effect on absorption forecasting, 542
    accumulated versus ongoing demand, 541
    application of profit planning and control to, 539–46
    common facilities, 545
    defining the market, 540–41
    financing of, 545–46
    garden office park, 539–46
    irrational versus rational market behavior, 541–42
    landscaping, 543
    learning from competition, 540
    leasing inducements, 545
    location land cost, 542
    marketing of, 546
    matching concept and product to market need, 542
    office depth, 543–44
    tenant improvements, 544–45
    tenant spaces, average size of, 544
    window area, 543

Commission on Housing and Community Development, 60
Commitment to perform, 392
Committee on Accounting for Real Estate Transactions, 113
Communication, standards as aid to, 373
Communication problems, 475–76
Community analysis, 25–26
Community facilities, 123–24
Company size, effects of, 87–88
Comparable projects and their prices, 71, 74–75
Comparative sales approach to market value, 233, 239–41
Compatibility between site, development concept and market opportunity, 29–30
Compatibility with sponsor objectives, 226–28
Competition
  innovation to outperform, 86
  mistakes made by, 65–66
  research of, 64–67
  researching as means to leading, 67–68
  site selection factor, 26
  source of technical information, 187–88
  weaknesses of, 63–64, 192–93
Competitive evaluation, 63–84; see also Competition
Competitive position and absorption, 126–27
Competitive pressures, 379–80
Comprehensive loan package, Feasibility Outline, guide for, 228–31
Comprehensive overview, importance of, 175–77
Concept market, 96–98
Condominium market, 29–30, 95–96, 113
  concept market for, 96–97
  cycles in, 105–7
  economic necessity, 96–97
  occupancy rates, 122
  persons interested in, 97
  public companies' emphasis on, 12
  segments of, 15
  submarkets of, 96
  value washout, 179–80
Constraints, 9
  availability of equity, 14
  competition, 26
  establishment of, 11–19
  legal, political and environmental, 53–62
  overcoming, 30–33
  regional growth, 25
  zoning, 27
Construction
  do's and don'ts, 400
  speed of, 391–92
  variables affecting speed of, 391
Construction Cost Data Components, 18

Construction drawings, 418
  inadequacy of, 508
  review of, 415–16
Construction of new units, 122
Construction-in-process forecasts, 281
Construction schedules, 418–20, 503–5
  coordination with marketing schedules, 529–30
  development of, 503–5
  establishing sequence of operations, 504–5
  establishing time constraints, 505
  follow-through, 506–7
  hypothetical project plan, 519
  identifying construction functions, 504
  implementation of, 503–5
  individual work functions, 505
  manual method, 512, 519–22
  review of, 415
  separating functions into work groups, 504
  system of, 393
  team effort, 505–7
  updating of, 506
Construction specifications, 418
Construction work days defined, 503
Constructive obsolescence, 140
Consumer confidence, 134
Consumer dissatisfaction, 7, 87
Consumer research, 186–87
  benefits of, 186–87
  limitations, 186
Consumer satisfactions, 7–8, 10
Contingencies, elimination of, 418–19
Contract documents, 418
Contract letting, 413–73
  general conditions, 421
  knowledge of local markets and products available, necessity for, 413
  reflecting value engineering in, 180–81
  routine aspects of, 413
  standardized functions of, 413
Contract negotiation process, 415
Contract period versus down payment, 43, 45
Control, 262–64
  activities involved in, 263, 390
  application to commercial development, 539–46
  defined, 258, 262, 390
  delegation of authority, facilitation of, 262–64
  manager, necessary for, 262
  subordinate, necessary for, 262
Control of field work, 401
  most-cost effective, 401–2
Controller's functions, 262
Corrective action, 502
Cost accounting, 257–58
  construction of system of, 258
  defined, 257
  functions in, 257
  functions assisted by, 257

Cost/benefit ratios of amenities, 222–23
Cost-conscious construction, tips for, 156–58
Cost control, 211–13
  identification of leaks in, 359–60
  importance of, 177
  standardized, 375
  work simplification program, 365
Cost data sources, 260
Cost of mortgage funds, 244
Cost-of-sales plan for for-sale housing; see For-sale housing cost-of-sales plan
Cost reduction, 144, 418–19
  planning decision for, 150–52
Cost reports, preparation of, 393–94
Cost saving benefit, 174–75
  contract incorporation of, 180–81
Cost savings tips, 156–58
Cost/value ratio, 363
Council on Environmental Quality, 55
Counteroffer to seller, enhancement of, 46
Critical-path flow, 502
Critical-path scheduling, 502
Critical-path type of format, 502
Curb appeal of developments, 153
  attracting prospects through, 532
  poor, 65
Current market value, 234
Customer-orientation, 384
Customer's preferences, 92
Cyclical nature of business; see Market cycles

D

Data Collection Sheets, 78, 80, 82
Debt coverage ratio, 251
Decision making
  alternatives, selection of, 362
  brainstorming, 362
  clearly defined objectives, 361
  development of system of, 360–62
  immediate, at job site, 399
  implementing new objectives, policies and procedures, 363
  information gathering, 361–62
  planned, 360
  policy standardization guidelines in, 374
  problem definition, 360–62
  or rationalization, 139
  spontaneous, 360
Deferred yield, 246
Deficiencies, 263–64
  corrective action for, 264
Deficiency form, 401, 411
Delegation of authority, facilitation of, 262–64
Delivery of materials, 420
Demand Estimates by Income Distribution Chart, 134, 136
Demand Estimates by Population Increase Chart, 135–36

Demand for housing, 118–19; see also Housing demand and Market demand
Demographics, 70, 117–24, 126
Density without sacrificing marketability, 191–92, 194
Department of Housing and Urban Development (HUD), 188
  insulation standards for new construction, 59
  noise regulations, 57
Depreciation write-offs, 252–53
Design factors, identification of, 163–72
Development Comparables Relationship Chart, 71, 84
Development concept, establishment of, 189–200
Development programs, 9
Developmental trends, 124
Dilution of the product, 97
Direct capitalization rate, 247
Direct construction cost plan, 414
Direct mail campaign in nonincome property merchandising, 525–26
Direct personal contact in income property merchandising, 535
Direction
  activities involved in, 390
  defined, 390
Discardable commodity, energy waste/conservation cycle, 110
Discretionary dollars
  defined, 146
  plowed-back, 146
Discriminating market, 193–94
Distribution of jobs, 120–21
Diversification, 114–15
Documents, standardization of, 375–76
Downside risk, computation of, 46–47
Downtime, 392
Downward communication, 476
Driving through territory as land source, 24
Duplex, 99

E

Economic ability to pay, need for, 199
Economic approach to market value, 239, 242–43
Economic environment, 103
Economic feasibility, 226–27
Economic necessity, 96–99
  fourplex units, 106
Economic needs, 117–19
Economic obsolescence, 248
Economic rent increases, 118
Efficiency, organization for, 392–93
Eleventh-hour profit analysis, 160–63
Emotional appeal, 523–24
Emotional impact, continuity of, 220
Emotional needs, 92
Employment/housing trends, 119
Employment trends, 120
Empty nesters, 15, 29, 97, 191–92, 194
End purpose for land, 23

End-user economics, 21–22
Energy crisis, 53, 110–11
Energy legislation, 59–60
Entertainment facilities, 123
Entrepreneural illusions, 482–84
  piercing with management audit, 484–86
Environmental controls, 53–54
Environmental constraints, 53–62
Environmental factors, 28
Environmental impact report (EIR), 27
Environmental problems, 65
Environmental Protection Agency (EPA), 55
Environmental quality, 90
Environmentally-oriented housing, 193–95, 197–98
Equity buildup, 246
Equity capitalization, 247, 249
  variables which affect, 249–50
Equity return, 244–45
Errors, 5, 88
Errors of commission, 88
Errors of omission, 88
Evaluation of personnel, 476
  strategies of, 476
Exceptions, reporting by, 256
Excess-tax shelter, need for, 246
Exclusionary zoning, 110
Existing financing checklist, 52
Existing housing inventory, 122
Expectations, increase in, 386–87
Experience, 234
Experimentation, 88; see also Innovation
Expertness, value of, 382
External economic data, reporting of, 257
Eyewash, 17

F

Failure, factors causing, 360, 384–86
Families, 97
  with children, 190–91, 194
Family market, 15
Feasibility, 110
  considerations of, 15–16
  defined, 225
  determination of, 17
  establishment of, 225–31
  key indication of, 252
  operating ratios as yardsticks for, 17–19
  product and marketing innovation to achieve, 194–95, 197–98
  requirements for, 15
  retention of, 194
  subjective nature of, 225
Feasibility analysis, 9
  backup analysis, 253
  components of, 226–28
  guide for, 228–31
  identifying problem and objectives, 226
  optimization through, 225
  purpose of, 225

Feasibility analysis—Cont.
  standardized formats, 226
  systematic simplification, need for, 225–26
Feasibility Outline, 228–31, 370
Feasibility process, 225–26
Feasibility research, 103
Feasibility study, 149, 206
Federal Disaster Relief Program, 55
Federal Energy Administration, 59
Federal Flood Insurance Program, 56
Federal legislation; see National legislation or specific name of law
Federal Water Pollution Control Act (1972), 55
Feedback, 6, 9, 68, 353, 358, 372, 376–77, 394, 401, 486, 501
  coordinator of, 376
  income property merchandising, 536–37
Feedback file, 376
Field management, 398–400
Field work reduction through industrialization, 397–98
Financial accounting, 257
Financial analysis, 233–53; see also specific topics
  band-of-investment method, 250–51
  cash flow analysis, 252–53
  investment value, 243–45
  market value, 239–43
  methods for measuring return, 245–49
  payback period, 251–52
  present-value theory, 235–39
  ratios, 251
  risk analysis, 249
  sensitivity analysis, 249–50
  value classifications, 233–34
  whole picture, 235
Financial objectives, 12–13
  private companies, 12
  public companies, 12
  risk, 13
  yield, 12
Financial risk, 249
Financial statements required; see Automated accounting system and Budgets
Financing acceptability, 176–77
Financing commercial development, 545–46
Financing sources, 367–70
Finding the land, 24
Finish work, 504
Finish work schedule, 522
Firm contract budget, 281
First-class errors, 5
First-level management, 255–56, 358
Fixed budgets, 260–61
Flexibility in specifications, 413–14
Flexible budgets, 260–61
Flood Disaster Protection Act (1973), 55–56
Floor plans, standardization in, 373
Follow-the-leader, 64–65

Follow-up of purchase orders, 420
For-sale housing, 134
For-sale housing budget plan, 292–98
    balance sheet statement, 295, 297–99
    cash flow statement, 295, 297
    control-information flow diagram, 292
    gross profit plan, 292, 294
        analysis of, 295–96
    gross profit plan per unit, 295
    planning-information flow diagram, 292–93
    profit plan, 295–96
    sales plan, 292–93
    summary, cost-of-sales plan, 292, 294
    summary, operating expense plan, 295
For-sale housing cost-of-sales plan, 299–307
    direct construction cost plan, 299, 303–5
    finished-lot cost plan, 299, 302
    indirect construction cost plan, 299, 306–7
    land cost plan, 299, 301
    land development cost plan, 299, 301–2
    summary, cost plan, 299–300
For-sale housing management reports, 311–14
    need for, 311
    operating expense analysis report, 311, 314
    profit plan analysis report, 311, 313
    review of need for, 311
    summary, 312
For-sale housing operating expense plan, 307–11
    financing expense plan, 307–8
    general and administrative expense plan, 307, 311
    marketing expense plan, 307, 311
For-sale markets, 122, 129
Formalized reviews, 210–11
Formalizing business operation, 485–86
Fourplex, 99
    boom in, 106–7
Functional obsolescence, 248
Functional reporting, 256
Functions
    classified, 363
    defined, 363
    value of, 363–64
Funds, how and where to get, 367–70
Future needs, 102–3
Future overruns, 18

G

Garden court areas, 153
General accounting, 257
Generalized data, misleading nature of, 95–96
Generative benefits, 234–35

Geographic market defined, 95
Go-or-no-go decision, 70, 215
Goals; see Objectives
Good planning, 30–33
Grapevine system, 350
Gross income multiplier, 241–42
Group participation, 486
Growth, in new jobs, 120
Growth corridors, 25
Growth markets, 114
Gym facilities, 222–23

H

High-pressure areas for development, 25
High-yield features, 364
Historic development patterns, 25
Historical performance data, 375
Historical perspective, 68
Historical ratios, 18
Holding period, 43
Hole in market, 132, 196, 206, 211
Homebuilders' problems, 103
Homogenization of markets, 86
Hot market areas, 114
Hot market/overkill cycle, 107–8
Hotspots, 24
House-cost ratio, 18
Household formation, 121
Household size, 129
Housing demand, 129
    earnings range, 130
    percentage, 130
Housing inventory, 122
Housing needs, 117–19
Housing obsolescence, 122, 125, 132
    replacement of, 131
Housing occupancy rates, 122–23

I

Identifiable submarkets versus statistical generalizations, 190
Identification of growth trends, 25
Improved management of people, 386–89
In-house consultants, 139
Income and amenities economics, 219–20
Income approach to market value, 239, 242–43
Income characteristics, absorption effects on, 130
Income distribution
    absorption stratification by, 126
    by census tract, 25
Income-producing housing project, 149
Income property merchandising, 529–37
    absorption, effects of amenities on, 531–32
    advertising, 535
    amenities, effects of, 531–32
    attracting prospects through curb appeal and land planning, 532
    brochure explaining, 534–35

Income property merchandising—Cont.
    coordinating construction and marketing schedules, 529–30
    direct personal contact, 535
    evaluation of traffic to provide feedback, 536–37
    generating traffic, 535–36
    intent in, 532
    opening preparations, 534–35
    precompletion rents, 530
    public relations, 535
    record of prospects, 536–37
    rental office environment, 534
    rental schedules, effects of amenities on, 531–32
    rental schedules, setting and revising of, 530–31
    rental staff, quality and training of, 536
    showing the apartments, 533–34
Income residential properties
    basic value to measure, 39
    value of, 233–34
Income trends, 121
Industrial activity, 123
Industrialization, reducing field work through, 397–98
Inflation, 103, 111, 262
Information filing system, 414
Information sources, 119–20, 122
Initiative, 386–87
Innovation
    absorption and, 127
    absorption forecasting for, 127–28
    borrowing of, 88
    catalyst to new growth, 125
    caution, exercise of, 93
    consumer's preferences, 92
    defined, 69, 183
    emotional needs of people, 92
    entrepreneurs, importance of, 381
    evaluation of feasibility of, 186
    expertness, value of, 382
    feasibility achieved by, 194–95, 197–98
    goal of, 91, 183
    internal economic needs and market needs meshed through, 192–94
    key to profits, 85–93
    latent markets, opening of, 104
    line personnel, accountability of, 383
    management's role in, 380–83
    managers, role of, 381
    methods, 89–90
    multiuse planning, 22
    objective evaluation of, 91
    obsolescence of existing housing, 125
    operating tactics, 382
    opportunities for, 91–93
    product research required for, 183
    program of, 6
    researching result, 69
    risk element in, 86–87

Index   553

Innovation—Cont.
   size of organization, effect of, 380–81
   smaller company size, 87–88
   social clues for, 90
   staff personnel, accountability of, 383
   standards as aid to, 372
   strategy tactics, 382
   submarkets, 92
   undervaluation of importance of, 86
   vacancy rate increase, 125
Inspection of field work, 401–10
   checklist, 403–10
   guidelines for inspectors, 403
   instructions for, 402–3
   operations requiring promptness in, 402
   standardization of procedure, 401
Inspections, 399, 504
   materials, 420
Inspector
   duties, 402
   guidelines for, 403
   qualifications, 402
Institute of Real Estate Management, 188
Institutional romance/fallout cycle, 113
Insufficient mortgage funds, 103
Insufficient planning, 360
Insufficient sales, 360
Intangible benefits, 234, 239
Integrated accounting and control system, need for, 393–94
Integrated reporting, 256
Interactions of specialists, overseeing of, 144–45
Interest rate versus contract period, 43, 45
Interest rate versus down payment, 43, 45
Interest rate versus price, 43–45
Internal economic needs versus market needs, 189–92
   innovation, 192–94
   sensitivity, 192–94
Internal rate of return (IRR), 46, 49–50, 253
   analysis of, 236–38
   defined, 237
International Conference of Building Officials, 188
Inventory of Unsold New Homes, 122
Investment, subjective nature of, 244
Investment decisions
   ability to retain tenants, 176, 178
   financing acceptability, 176–77
   optimized absorption rate, 176, 178
   optimized loan value, 176
   proper assessment of, 176–77
   risk reduction, 177
   salability, 176–77
   self-advertising value, 176–77
   transferability, 176–77
Investment planning and analysis tool, value engineering as, 147–48

Investment value, 39, 233–34, 243–45
   attributes of property, 243
   basis of, 242–43
   defined, 244
   measure of, 244–45
   variability in, 245
Irrational behavior, 541–42

J

Jacuzzi pools, 198, 222
Job/housing ratio, 118–19
Job inspection checklist, 403–10
Job superintendent
   meetings with subcontractors, 398
   responsibilities, 400–401
   role of, 400–401
   traits of, 399
Judgment, 234–35, 239
Justified price, 39–41
   defined, 234
   location analysis, 40
   off-site improvements, 40
   site evaluation, 40
   time of sale, 40
   zoning, 41

L

Land/building ratios, 247
Land Comparables Adjustment Sheet, 40–41, 47
Land Comparables Ranking Sheet, 41, 47
Land Comparables Relationship Chart, 41, 48
Land development, 112–13
Land packaging, preparation and development, 112
Land planning, attracting prospects through, 532
Land-residual method of value, 248–49
Land selection; see Selecting land
Land type for speedy construction, 394
Land use
   dormant stage, 22–23
   growth stage, 22–23
   maturity stage, 22–23
   stages in, 22–23
Land-use policies, 53–54, 57–59
   local and municipal, 58–59
   national, 57
   state, 57–58
Land-value trend line, 22–23
Landscape sprinkler cost, 150
Landscaping, 543
   cost, 140
   importance of, 217–19
Large companies
   line and staff functions, 262
   organizational development, 478–79
   vulnerability of, 88
Leading developers, research of, 68–69
Leasing inducements, 545
Legal constraints, 53–62
Legal feasibility, 226–27

Legislation; *see also* National legislation
   keeping abreast of, 60
Legislative-induced cycles, 112–13
Lender oversteering, 212–13
Lenders, 367–70
Leventhal, Kenneth, and Company's packaged computer information system, 264–77; *see also* Automated accounting system
Leverage, 14, 22, 42, 244–45, 252
   creation of, 146–47
Life insurance companies, 367–68
Line functions, 262
Line manager, 88–89
   accountability of, 383
Liquidated damages provisions, 418, 505–6
Living, planning for, 153
Loan coverage ratio, 244
Loan package, development of, 228–31, 370
Loan submission, 367–70
Loan value, 234
   optimized, 176
Loan/value ratio, 242, 245, 250
Local brokers as land source, 24
Local growth trends, 123
Local market conditions, national influences on, 103
Location analysis, 21–38; *see also* Selecting land
   price adjustment factor, 40
Location land cost, 542
Location of land, effects on absorption of, 133
Long-term objectives, 6, 9, 12, 15
Long-term trend, 101
Lot-cost ratio, 18–19
Low-end condominiums, 105
Low-priced condominiums, 127
Low-sensitivity features, 364
Low-yield features, 364
Lower-level managers, 89
Luck versus skill, 86
Luxury buyers, 99

M

Management actions to correct deficiencies, 264
Management audits, 484–86
Management capability; *see* Capabilities
Management information systems (MIS), 255–77
   advantages of, 359
   automated versus manual, 264; *see also* Automated accounting system
   basis for comprehensive, 394
   budgeting, 258; *see also* Budgeting and Budgets
   computer, 264; *see also* Automated accounting system
   control, 258, 262–64
   cost accounting, 257–58

Management information systems—*Cont.*
  essential characteristics of, 256–57
  first-level management, 255–56
  general accounting, 257
  integrated reporting, 256
  reporting by exception, 256
  reporting external economic data and marketing data, 257
  reporting performance ratios, 257
  reporting by responsibility or function, 256
  reporting against a standard, 256
  upper-level management, 255–56
  zero-base reporting, 256
Management and maintenance sins, 65–66
Management process, 389–90
  control, 390
  direction, 390
  organization, 389
  planning, 389
  staffing, 390
Management reports for for-sale housing; *see* For-sale housing management reports
Management styles, 114
Management teams, 354–55
Manager
  control necessary for, 262
  freedom from excessive detail, 263
Market in transition, 131
Market analysis, 67–68
  defined, 9
Market approach to market value, 233, 239–41
Market cycles, 6–7, 101–15
  analysis of, 192–93
  awareness of, 113
  business expansion/recession, 108–9
  discardable commodity, energy waste/conservation, 110
  hot market/overkill, 107–8
  how to utilize an understanding of, 113–15
  importance of understanding, 103–4
  innovation, effect of, 104
  institutional romance/fallout, 113
  legislative-induced, 112–13
  mortgage money boom/bust, 111–12
  new concept/market overkill, 105–7
  shaping the future, 102–3
  shorter duration of, 102
  urban sprawl/retreat, 110–11
Market demand, 125–26
  households moving within market area, 134–35
  new household formation, 134–35
  population increase, 134–35
Market growth, 118–19
Market need, 134
  matching concept and product to, 542
Market planning for optimum results, 5–11
  consumer satisfactions, 7–8

Market planning for optimum results—*Cont.*
  defined, 5, 7–8
  implementation of, 8–9
  need for, 5–6, 117
Market research, 103
  decision making or rationalization, 139
  fear of change, 139–40
  flight from risk to conformity, 138
  imaginative audacity, lack of, 137
  irresponsibility about findings, 137
  limitations of, 137–39
  management's need for, 139–40
  mediocrities in reports of, 137
  objective analysis, need for, 140–42
  refuge in statistics of, 138
  unintentional cover-up of data, 137
  utilizing to optimum advantage, 137–42
  verification of facts, 137
Market segments, 95–99; *see also* Buyers
  absorption stratification by, 126
  buying capabilities of buyers, 99
  consideration of, 15
  economic necessity, 99
  fitting to organizational objectives, 99
  identification of, 97–99
  importance of understanding, 96–97
  what buyers buy, 98–99
  where buyers come from, 98
  why buyers buy, 98
Market value, 39, 233, 239–43
  approaches to, 239–43
    correlation of, 239, 243
  basis of, 239–40
  constancy of, 245
  defined, 243
  determination of, 239
  legislative effects, 239
  objective nature of, 244
Marketing
  commercial developments, 546
  defined, 18, 139, 523
  merchandising as extension of, 523
  selling distinguished, 7
  undervaluation of importance of, 86
Marketing data, reporting of, 257
Marketing expertise, need for, 211
Marketing schedules, coordination with construction schedules, 529–30
Marketing studies, 206
Matching correct product with marketing need, 189–200
Materials management and purchasing, 419–20
Materials-scarce economy, 110
Materials schedules, 419–20
Materials shortage, 110
Maximizing natural amenities and site potentials, 201–3
Memoribilia, appeal of, 91, 104

Merchandising
  defined, 523
  improvements in, 173–74
  income properties, 529–37; *see also* Income property merchandising
  nonincome properties, 523–28; *see also* Nonincome property merchandising
  planning for, 153
  strategy of, 523
Methods improvement
  cost benefits achieved by, 395–96
  techniques of, 396
Middle-class buyers, 99
Mistakes in matching concepts to market opportunities, 199–200
Mixed-use developer, 90
Model complex in nonincome property merchandising, 526–27
Mom-and-pop organizations, 92
Monopoly, creation of, 69–70, 91, 93
Mortgage Bankers Association, 60
Mortgage bankers and brokers, 369–70
Mortgage loans in commercial development, 545–46
Mortgage money boom/bust cycle, 111–12
Motivation, 365, 392
Move-up market, 131
Multifamily construction, 111
Multifamily rental buildings, 150
Multifamily-zoned area, 189–92
Multifamily zoning, 41
Multimarket builders' strategy, 14
Multimarket consultant, risk reduction through services of, 87
Multimarket developers, 64
Municipal officials as land source, 24
Mutual savings banks, 367–68

N

National Association of Home Builders, 60, 188
National development corporations, 86
National Emergency Program Project Independence, 59
National Environmental Policy Act (1969), 55
National legislation
  conflicting, 53–54
  specific listing of, 55–57; *see also specific names of laws*
National Lumber Manufacturers Association, 188
National Oceanic and Atmospheric Administration, 56
National policies, 53
National political trends, 103
Natural and inherent appreciation during holding period, 42–43
Negotiation checklist, 51
Negotiation options, 43–45
New concept/market overkill cycle, 105–7
New family formations, 129
Newly formed households, 98, 134–35

Newspaper advertising in nonincome property merchandising, 525
No-growth market, 125
No-growth policy, 53, 58
No-leverage purchase, 42
Noise Pollution and Control Act (1972), 57
Nonfinancial objectives, 13
Nonincome property merchandising, 523–28
  allocating advertising and promotion dollars to, 524–25
  direct mail campaign, 525–26
  establishing a theme, 527
  explaining the strategy of, 527–28
  maintaining the mood, 527
  model complex, 526–27
  sales office, 527
  selling the community, 527
  tapping emotions to develop project personality, 523–24
  zeroing in on central theme, 524
Nonincome residential properties
  basic value to measure, 39
  value of, 233
Normal capacity, 261–62
Nostalgia, appeal of, 91, 104
Nuisance rent increases, 118
The numbers, 17

O

Objective analysis, need for, 140–42
Objective value, 244
Objectives, 6–9
  attainment of, 387–89
  determination of, 392
  dimensions of, 11
  effectiveness of plan in achieving, 501–2
  establishment of, 11–19
  feasibility as related to, 16–17
  financial, 12–13
  fitting market segments and product types to, 99
  formulation of, 16
  grouping, 15
  implementation of, 8
  nonfinancial, 13
  positive means of conveying, 387–89
  profit improvement program, 356–57
  reevaluation of, 70
  types, 12
  unrealistic, 16
Obsolescence; see Housing obsolescence
Obsolescence of company, 86
Obstacles, 28–29
  early recognition of, 33
  overcoming, 30–33
Occupancy, 118
Occupancy rates, 122–23
Off-site factors, 28
Off-site improvements as price adjustment factor, 40
Office depth, 543–44
On-site factors, 28
Ongoing demand, 132

Operating actions to correct deficiencies, 264
Operating expense plan for for-sale housing; see For-sale housing operating expense plan
Operating ratios, 17–19
Operating tactics, 382
Opportunities, 28–29
  early recognition of, 33
  evaluation of, 16
  for innovation, 91–93
  key to, 63–64
  maintaining perspective to spot, 64
  mistakes in matching concepts to, 199–200
  optimization of, 189–200
Opportunity value of capital, 43
Optimum terms, negotiation of, 43–44
Organization
  activities involved in, 389
  defined, 389
  efficiency, 392–93
  productivity, 392–93
Organization chart, 259
Organization of Petroleum Exporting Countries (OPEC), oil embargo by, 60
Organizational and control matrix, 487–99
  advantages of, 490
  basis for overall project schedule, 502
  chart, 491–99
  correct sequential implementation, 488–90
  developing responsibility relationships, 489
  identifying major work areas, 488
  identifying positions, 488–89
  nature of, 487–88
  resolving conflicts, 489
  solidifying functions and relationships, 489
  solidifying performance standard, 489–90
  updating position descriptions, 489–90
Organizational development, 475–99
  appraising human resources, 476
  behavioral approach, 486–87
  communication problems, 475–76
  entrepreneural illusions, 482–84
    piercing with management audit, 484–86
  evaluation of personnel, 476
  first step in, 475
  identification of functions, 475
  identification of responsibility, 475
  large companies, 478–79
  private corporations, 477–78
    time spans in, 479–81
  process of, 486–87
  public corporations, 477–78
  resistance to change, 476
  small companies, 478–79
  systems approach, 486–87

Organizational objectives; see Objectives
Out of town buyers, 98
Outside service consultant, 139–40
  cutting overhead through greater use of, 366
Overall capitalization rate, 247
Overall interest rate on property, 250–51
Overall project schedule, 502–3
Overbuilding, 86, 92, 95
Overexpenditure, 360
Overkill, 105–8
Overleveraging, 14–15
Oversupply of housing, 117
Owner value, 39, 233

P

Parking areas, 153
Parking courts, 150
Patio homes, 99
Payback period, 251–52
  cash flow used in figuring, 252
  measurement of, 251–52
Peak performance, requirements for, 386–89, 393
Pedestrian circulation, 153
People, development and management of, 379–80
Percentage cash flow return, 245
Percentage yield, 246–47
Performance feasibility, 226–28
Performance ratios, reporting of, 257
Performance standards
  development of, 263
  measurement of performance against, 263
Physical factors, 28
Physical fitness, 90
Pilot group, 351–53
Pilot program, 351–52
Planned Developments Form, 76
Planned unit development (PUD)
  marketing–value engineering review for, 189–92
  zoning matters affecting, 27–28
Planning, 379
  activities involved in, 389
  defined, 389
  implementation of, 501–2
Planning agencies, proliferation of, 54
Planning decisions
  back-to-back design, 153–55
  cost reduction, 150–52
  individual buildings for profit, 153–55
  living, 153
  merchandising, 153
  value engineering to shape, 149–55
Planning for profit improvement program, 349, 351
Plant amortization problem, 397–98
Pocket growth areas, 25
Policy defined, 374
Policy standardization, 374
Political constraints, 53–62

Political feasibility, 226–27
Poor curb appeal, 65
Poor location, 65
Population characteristics, effects on absorption of, 129–30
Population demographics, 121–22
Population growth, 120–21, 134–35
Population trends, 121–22
Postcards in nonincome property merchandising, 525
Postcontract budget, 281
Potential residents, 153
Practical capacity, 261
Precompletion rents, 530
Preconstruction sales, 128–29
Preliminary concept, formation of, 70
Preliminary cost estimate, 280–81
Preplanning of materials, 396
Presales, 128–29, 524
Present value
  defined, 236
  measure of, 236
  principle of, 236
  steps in estimating, 236
Present-value analysis, 236–37
Present-value indexing, limitations of, 238–39
Present-value theory, 235–39, 245
Present worth of yield, 243
Previous year's performance, reporting against, 256
Price
  defined, 234
  flexibility, 211–12
  information sources, 260
Price Adjustment Format Sheets, 71, 77, 79, 81
Price versus contract period, 43, 45
Price versus down payment, 43, 45
Price indicators, 71
Pride of ownership, 11, 13, 243
Primary courtyards, 150–52
Primary functions, 363
Priorities, establishing system of, 145–46
Private companies or corporations
  advantages of, 87
  capitalization, 479–80
  continuity, 481
  financial objectives, 12
  initial organization, 479–80
  obsolescence, 481
  organizational development, 477–78
  public companies distinguished, 477–78, 481
  redirection, 481
  struggle-and-strife period, 480
  success: the payoff period, 481
  survival-and-growth period, 480–81
  time spans in development of, 479–81
  yield, timing and method of, 12
Private noninsured pension funds, 367–68
Problem defined, 360–61
Problem solving, 238–39

Procedural standardization, 374–75
Product-cost approach to market value, 239–40
Product design, 201–13
  control through formalized reviews, 210–11
  cost control, 211–13
  end result, 210
  feasibility study, 206
  marketing expertise, need for, 211
  marketing study, 206
  maximizing natural amenities and site potentials, 201–3
  review of first phase, 204–6
  right product for right market, 204–10
  standards as aid to variations in, 372–73
  strategy, 206–10
  value engineering expertise, need for, 211
Product-orientation, 384
  lopsidedness of, 86
Product research, 183–88
  benefits of, 185–86
  consumer research, 186–87
  format for, 184–85
  how to conduct, 184–85
  product types subject to, 184
  steps in, 184–85
  structuring the activity, 183–85
  successful versus unsuccessful projects, 183
  technical research, 187–88
Product standardization, 14
Product types, fitting to organizational objectives, 99
Productivity
  maximization of, 397
  organization for, 392–93
  specialization as aid to, 508
Productivity, increase in, 145, 386–89
  conveying goals positively, 387–89
  expectations, increase in, 386–87
  small advances add up to large gains, 387
  sowing initiative to harvest results, 386
Professionals as land source, 24
Profit
  capability as key to growth of, 379–90
  innovation as key to, 85–93
  opportunities for, 15–16
  total picture, 180–81
Profit analysis, eleventh-hour, 160–63
Profit concept, deviations from, 158–60
Profit erosion, 175–76
  identification of leaks in, 359–60
Profit formula, 144
Profit improvement program, 145, 349–66
  application phase, 349–50, 353, 355
  appreciation phase, 349–50
  characteristics of, 350–51
  coordination, need for, 355–57

Profit improvement program—Cont.
  coordinator, 353–54
  cost control, identification of leaks in, 359–60
  crash program, 349–50
  critical objectives, 357
  decision-making system, 360–62; see also Decision making
  education phase, 349–50, 352–55
  effective, 350–51
  feedback, 356
  goal, 360
  long-term, 349–50
  management teams, 354–55
  nature of, 349
  objectives, examination of, 356–57
    basic formats, 356–57
    categorization of, 357
  outside support, greater utilization of, 366
  personnel involvement in, 350–51
  phases of, 349–50
  pilot group, 351–53
    application, 353
    education, 352–53
  pilot program, 351–52
  planning required for, 349, 351
  policy
    development of, 358
    emphasis on most vital work, 359
    evaluation of, 359
    need for, 358
    purpose of, 358
  primary objectives, 357
  procedures, examination of, 358–59
  profit erosion, identification of leaks in, 359–60
  project teams, 354
  recognition and reinforcement, 356
  reports, need for, 355–56
  specific objectives, 357
    programming of, 357–58
  steering committee, 351, 353
  subprograms, 350
  value engineering as applied to, 363–65; see also Value engineering
  work simplification program, 365
Profit planning application to commercial development, 539–46
Profit sensitivity, 43
Profitability computation, 45–46
Profitability factors, 42–43
Program coordinator, 353–54
Progress reports, 502
Project graphics in rental office, 534
Projective management network, 510–12
  bar chart, 510
  computer reports, 512
  critical path report, 514
  development report, 513
  expected completion report, 512
  simple network, 511
Project schedule, 502–3

Project schedule work sheets, 509–10, 514–19
Project teams, 354
Promotion; *see* Merchandising
Public companies or corporations
    accounting requirements, disadvantages of, 87
    condominium market, emphasis on, 12
    financial objectives, 12
    organizational development, 477–78
    private companies distinguished, 477–78, 481
    rental market, abandonment of, 12
    yield, timing and method of, 12
Public-private partnership, need for, 60–62
Public relations
    income property merchandising, 535
    nonincome property merchandising, 525
Purchase criteria, 23
Purchase don'ts, 23
Purchase orders for materials
    follow-up, 420
    posting of, 420
Purchasing, 413–73
    changes in details, care in making, 414
    flexibility in specifications, 413–14
    keeping abreast of the market required for, 413–14
    knowledge of local markets and products available, necessity for, 413
    materials management and, 419–20
    routine aspects of, 413
    standardized functions of, 413

Q

Qualitative analysis, 238, 249
Quality property, 22
Quality restaurants, 123
Quantitative analysis, 238–39, 249

R

Radio advertising in nonincome property merchandising, 525
Ranking of companies, 41, 47
Ranking of investments, 246
Rational behavior, 541–42
Real estate evaluation questions to be answered, 120–24
Real estate investment trusts (REITs), 368–69
Recession, 108–9
Record of materials, 420
Recreational facilities, 123, 153, 215–17, 223
Recreational housing, 125
Redirection of expenses, 156–58
Regional analysis, 25
Regional growth trends, 123
Regulatory influences, 27–28
Rent/income ratio, 134
Rent increases, 118

Rental housing, 125
Rental housing budget plan, 315–47
    backup schedules, 315
    direct construction cost analysis report, 281, 315, 336
    direct construction cost plan, 315, 318–23
        detail backup to, 315, 323–28
    income and expense and annual cash flow analysis report, 315, 337
    indirect construction cost analysis report, 281, 315, 335
    indirect construction cost plan, 315, 328–30
    financing expense plan, 315, 330
    land cost plan, 315–16
    land development cost plan, off-site development, 315, 317
    management reports summary, 315, 334
    marketing and management expenses plan, 315, 331–33
    off-site cost analysis report, 281, 315, 338
    summary, budget plan, 315
    summary, direct construction cost plan, 315, 318
Rental housing cash flow, 338–47
    amortization schedule, 340, 342
    basis adjustments and excess depreciation, 340, 343
    computation of tax on sale and after-tax proceeds federal income tax, 344
    construction cash flow, 1975, 338, 345
    construction loan interest projection, 339, 341
    depreciation schedule, 340, 342–43
    fill-up cash flow, 1976, 338, 346
    fill-up projection, 339–40
    hypothetical sale after 7 years' operation, 340, 344
    income and expense schedule and annual cash flow, 339
    mortgage computation and equity requirement, 340, 342
    projected rental schedule, 339–40
    significant ratios and economic tests, 347
    statement of annual net income (loss), 338, 347
    summary, budget, 339–40
    summary, direct construction cost budget, 339, 341
Rental market, 122, 129–30
    public companies' abandonment of, 12
Rental office
    environmental quality of, 534
    project graphics, 534
    purposes of, 534
    traffic into, 532
        evaluation of, 536–37
        generation of, 535–36

Rental premiums, 531
Rental property; *see* Income property merchandising
Rental rates, 133–34
    absorption rate affected by, 530
Rental schedules
    effects of amenities on, 531–32
    setting and revising of, 530–31
Rental staff
    quality of, 536
    record of prospects, 536–37
    training of, 536
Renters
    interest in condominiums, 105
    sources of, 134
    turned buyers, 98
Replacement approach to market value, 239–40
Replacement cost, 233, 239–40
    duplication, 239–40
    substitution, 239–40
Reports required; *see* Automated accounting system *and* Budgets
Research; *see also specific types*
    competition, 64–67
    innovation as result of, 69
    leading developers, 68–69
Research information, use of, 7
Residential income-producing property
    basic values to measure, 39
    value of, 233–34
Residential nonincome-producing property
    basic values to measure, 39
    value of, 233
Residual land value technique, 248–49
Resistance to change, 476
Resources, 14–15
Responsibility, reporting by, 256
Retail activity, 123
Retired persons, 97
Retirement housing, 125
Return
    components of, 245–46
    methods of measuring, 245–49
Return on equity, 247, 252
Return on investment (ROI), 244, 252–53
Return on investment (ROI) analysis, 234, 249
    limitations of, 234
Rezoning, 22–23, 27, 41, 43
Right product for right market, 204–10
Risk, 13
    downside, 46–47
    identification of factors, 163–72
    increase in, 244
    innovation, element in, 86–87
    minimization of, 87
    reduction of, 13, 177, 245
Risk analysis, 238, 249
Rough work, 504
Rough work schedule, 521
Routine functions, standardization of, 374–75

S

Saleability, 176–77
Sales activity, rate of, 119
Sales office in nonincome property merchandising, 527
Sales rates, 133–34
Savings and loan associations, 367–68
Scarcity of housing, 117
Scarcity, times of, 262
Scheduling, 501–22; see also specific types of schedules
   construction schedule, 503–5
   corrective action proposed by, 502
   economy of construction through, 508
   getting behind, 506, 508–9
   importance of, 501–2
   management tool, 507–8
   need to think ahead of, 508–9
   overall project schedule, 502–3
   specialization as aid to productivity, 508
   standardization in, 375
Screening of undesirable service functions, 150, 153
Second-class errors, 5
Secondary courtyards, 150–52
Secondary functions, 363
Segmented industry, opportunities for innovation in, 88; see also Market segments
Selecting land
   absorption rate, 26
   checklist, 33–38
   community analysis, 25–26
   competition factor, 26
   guidelines for, 24–27
   regional analysis, 25
   site identification, 26–27
Selection procedure, 149
Self-advertising site, 26–27
   accessibility, 27
   traffic count, 27
Self-advertising value, 176–79
Seller, needs of, 7
Selling
   defined, 7, 139
   marketing distinguished, 7
Sensitivity analysis, 41–42, 71, 249–50
   computer models, 250
   defined, 42
Sensitivity to market cycles, 92
Shopping centers, 90, 123
Short-term objectives, 6, 9, 12
Single family attached, 99
Single family detached, 98
Single family home, cost breakdown of, 17–18
Single-market developer, 64
Single persons, 97, 191–92, 194
Site analysis, 149
Site evaluation, 21–38
   price adjustment factor, 40
Site identification, 26–27
Site selection; see Selecting land

Site selection checklist, 33–38
Site work, 504
Site work schedule, 520
Skill versus luck, 86
Slow-moving rental units, 531
Small companies
   line and staff functions, 262
   organizational development, 478–79
Smaller company size, 87
   advantages of, 87
   innovation efforts of, 87–88
Smaller household size, 129
   trend toward, 121
Social clues for innovation, 90
Social involvement, need for, 90
Social trends, 103
Soft market, 132
Sources of land, 24
Specialization as aid to productivity, 508
Speculative activity, 88
Speculative market pressures, 234
Speed in construction, 391–92
   integrated accounting and control system needed for, 393–94
   reasons for, 391–92
   variables affecting, 391
Spendable dollars, 236
Square footage, 71
Stabilized value, 234
Staff functions, 262
Staff personnel, accountability of, 383
Staffing
   activities involved in, 390
   defined, 390
Standard boiler-plate provisions, 421
Standard house plans, value engineering with, 173–75
Standard prices, 71
Standard selling price, 72
Standardization; see also Standards
   benefiting from, 371–77
   budgets, 375
   buildings, 374
   contract letting, 413
   cost controls, 375
   documents, 375–76
   feedback from program of, 376–77
   floor plans, 373
   inspection of field work procedure, 401
   policy, 374
   procedural, 374–75
   purchasing function, 413
   schedules, 375
Standardized Deficiency Notice, 401, 411
Standardized Policy for Budgeting, 279, 376; see also Budgets
Standards; see also Standardization
   advantages of, 371–73
   communication aided by, 373
   creativity aided by, 372
   defined, 371
   design variations allowed by, 372–73
   feedback mechanism, 372

Standards—Cont.
   innovation aided by, 372
   restraint to change, 371–72
   review process, 377
   uses of, 371–73
Starter home, 99
Static assumptions, guarding against, 104
Static market areas, 92
Steering committee, 351, 353
Strategy, 206–10, 382
   basic, 13–14
   defined, 8
   environment of rapid change, 140
   formulation, 9
   multimarket builders, 14
   negotiation of, 44–45
   reevaluation, 70
Subcontract accounts, matching with budget accounts, 417
Subcontract letting, 417–19
   eliminating contingencies and reducing costs, 418–19
   full documentation in contracts, 418
   matching subcontract accounts and budget accounts, 417
Subcontractor exhibits, 421–73
   affidavit of release of liens, 422, 439
   application of payment for, 421, 433
   change order authorization, 422, 438
   change order data sheet, 422, 437
   conditions of purchase contract sheet, 421, 433–35
   exhibit sheet: list of items on change order, 422, 438
   field order form, 422, 437
   general conditions, 421–22, 440–73
   instructions to subcontractors, 421, 425–29
   purchase order form, 422, 436
   request for quotation form, 421, 435
   statement of qualifications, 421, 423–24
   status of bid documents form, 421, 432
   subcontract agreement form, 421, 429–31
   subcontractor list, 421–22
Subcontractors
   behind schedule, 506
   bidding process, 415–17
   builder's relations with, 420–21
   construction schedule efforts, 505
   economy of, 395–96
   evaluation of, 414–15
   filing information on, 414
   locating, 414–15
   maintenance of schedule by, 399
   meetings with, 398
   qualifying, 414–15
   scheduling as tool for, 507–8
   source of grass-roots construction expertise, 187
   standardized schedules for, 375
   utilization of capacity of, 397
Subjective value, 244

Submarkets, 92, 95–96, 127
  analysis of, 192–93
  identification of, 190
  planning designed to meet needs of, 192
Subordinates
  accountability of, 263
  control necessary for, 262
  participation in determining goals, 387
Success
  key to, 15–16
  means of achieving, 85
  preoccupation with, 86
  private corporations, 481
  sensitivity required for, 113
  shaping the future, 102–3
Successful companies, environment of, 383–84
Successful profit formula, 211
Suitability of property, 23
Superintendent; see Job superintendent
Supply
  defined, 130
  effects on absorption, 130–33
  houses included in, 130–31
Supply/demand pressures, 234
Supply/demand relationship, 118–19
Sustaining benefits, 234–35
Swinger apartments, 106
  negative image of, 106
Systems approach, 486–87
Systems-behavioral format, 487

T

Tangible benefits, 234, 239
Technical decisions, primary investment values guiding, 177–78
Technical expertise, need for, 211
Technical needs, 117–19
Technical research, 187–88
  application of, 188
  need for, 187
  sources of, 187–88
Techniques for the field, 398–400
Technology, development and management of, 379–80
Temporary help agencies, use of, 366
Tenant improvements, 544–45
Tenant spaces, average size of, 544
Tenants
  ability to retain, 176, 178, 219–20
  sources of, 153
  traffic passing as source of, 153
  word-of-mouth recommendations of, 153
Theoretical capacity, 261
Time and motion study, 416
Time of sale as price adjustment factor, 40
Time value of money
  internal rate of return analysis, 236–38
  present-value analysis, 236–37
  two methods for computing, 236

Timing of resale, 242
Title, liens, restrictions checklist, 51
Total return before tax savings, 246
Townhouses, 99, 191–92
Trading on the equity, 242, 244
Traffic count, 27
Traffic into rental office; see Rental office
Transferability, 176–77
Transportation system, 124
  analysis of, factors in, 124
Trend analysis, need for, 16
Trend line, 72, 101
Trends, 72, 101, 118, 243, 401
  in cycles, 101–2
  information sources, 260
Two-bedroom unit, redesign of, 164–68
  building structure and systems, 168–72
Two-tier condition, 130

U

Ultimate leverage, 42
Underground work, 150–51
Unemployment level, 120
Upper-level management, 255–56, 358
Upward communication, 475–76
Urban Land Institute, 188
Urban sprawl/retreat cycle, 110–11
Utilities moratoriums, 54

V

Vacancies, 118
Vacancy rates, significance of, 96
Value
  classifications, 233–34
  components, 240–41
  defined, 143, 234
  effects on absorption, 133
Value added during holding period, 42–43
Value engineering, 133, 143–81, 396
  bidding process, reflection in, 180–81
  capital dollars, allocation of, 145
  comprehensive overview, importance of, 175–77
  contract-letting process, reflection in, 180–81
  cost reduction, 144
  cost saving benefit from, 174–75
  defined, 143–48
  deviations from profit concept, 158–60
  direction and support from highest level of management, 365
  eleventh-hour profit analysis, 160–63
  function of, 143
  fundamentals, emphasis on, 177
  identification of design and marketing risk factors, 163–72
  investment decisions, proper assessment of, 176–77

Value engineering—Cont.
  investment planning and analysis tool, 147–48
  leverage, creation of, 146–47
  need for, 211
  objective of, 363
  overseeing interactions of specialists, 144–45
  planning decisions shaped by, 149–55; see also Planning decisions
  planning function, extenuation of, 144–45
  priorities, establishing system of, 145–46
  productivity increase, 145
  profit improvement program, application to, 145, 363–65
  redirection of expenses, 156–58
  standard house plans, 173–75
  steps in process of, 364–65
  technical decisions guided by primary investment values, 177–78
  total profit picture, 180–81
  underlying principle of, 364
  value enhancement, 144
  values sought in, 143–44
  washing out site, 178–79
    poor planning, 179–80
  waste, minimization of, 146
Value engineering study, 10
Value relationship analysis, 71–72, 241
  defined, 71
  procedure for, 72–73
Value wash, 146
  offsetting resulting in erosion of profit, 175–76
Value washout, 8, 178–79, 388
  poor planning, 179–80
Variances, 263–64

W

Washing out site; see Value washout
Washout; see Value washout
Waste, minimization of, 146
Way-of-living concept, 153, 526
Widows, 97, 192
Window area, 543
Work-flow interfaces, 502
Work simplification program, 365

Y

Yes-or-no-man, 351
Yield, 12
  defined, 237
Young couples, 97
Young families, 191–92

Z

Zero-base reporting, 256
Zero-lot-line housing, 99, 190–92, 194–96
Zoning, 27–28, 87
  exclusionary, 110
  multifamily, 41
  price adjustment factor, 41